ADVANCE PRAISE

'This book is extremely useful to all who are interested in understanding and measuring human behaviour in organisations. It is a compilation of nearly 70 instruments which can be used by students, researchers, academicians, trainers, consultants and practitioners. I constantly refer to this book and recommend it to others who are looking for reliable and valid instruments to measure facets of behaviour.'

Rupande Padaki, *Founder Director, The P&P Group, Bengaluru*

Training Instruments in HRD and OD is the culmination of half a century of research and continuous learning by the trailblazer of the HRD movement in India—Dr Udai Pareek—and revised and enhanced by Dr Surabhi Purohit.

This book covers extensive topics which will greatly enable corporate HR professionals and OD specialists to use these simple, self-administered and non-threatening tools to make their teaching and training more effective. It is a valuable resource and asset for any HR professional which I strongly recommend.'

Fr. E. Abraham S. J., *Director, Xavier School of Management (XLRI), Jamshedpur*

'The first edition by Udai Pareek, a distinguished scholar in organisational behaviour, is a classic now. The book has served as a huge aid to professionals to use research-based instruments to develop human processes in both formal and informal organisations. The updated edition by Surabhi will be immensely valuable to the community of HR/OD practitioners, trainers and academicians. This timeless book is a must for every practitioner of human processes.'

Anil K. Khandelwal, *Author and Former Chairman and Managing Director of Bank of Baroda and Dena Bank, India*

'Being an Original 100 Change Agent and Global Colleague of Dr Pareek since 1963, I authoritatively say this republished masterpiece with daughter, Surbahi Purohit, without question is the most relevant, practical tool book ever to exist in the Asian HR/OD world. I doubt something better will ever replace. Purchase without hesitation. For any serious practitioner, a must-have!'

Roland Sullivan, *CEO and Founder, Sullivan Transformation Agents, USA*

'I have had the opportunity to use the book *Training Instruments in HRD and OD* written by Dr Udai Pareek and Dr Surabhi Purohit multiple times, over last two decades, in my various roles in Industry, consulting at TVRLS and academics; at XIMB, Essae-TAPMI, IIM Bangalore (as student and visiting faculty) and here, at IIM Indore, too. The instruments in various sections were widely used by me for individual-, team- and organisation-level, including extensive use of role efficacy in consulting. These instruments are simple to use and powerful tools too.

To me, this book is a very valuable resource for the academicians and practitioners in management, in general, and OB/HRD professionals, in particular. I strongly recommend this as a text-cum-reference book for OB/psychometric and HRD field.'

Gopal P. Mahapatra, *Professor of Practice, OB and HRM Area, IIM Indore*

'No profession, including HR, is worth being called a specialised function unless it has a body of knowledge and tools of its own. This book by Dr Udai Pareek has truly given HR a distinctive status as a profession. Training and OD instruments designed by him significantly reduce our dependence on western literature. This book is not just a compilation of instruments already developed but it builds capability on how to design new ones. This integrated thinking always made Udai and his work so distinctive.'

Santrupt Misra, *CEO, Carbon Black Business; Director, Group HR, Aditya Birla Group*

'The instruments from the book can be applied in real time by an OD and learning manager for assessing and developing employees. The knowledge dissemination by Late Dr Pareek serves as an institution in itself for lifetime. A must-have for all HR professionals!'

Nidhi Vashishth, *Head-MDP, Training and Consultancy,*
Area Chair-OB and HR, Jaipuria Institute

'This book is Udai Pareek's magnum opus. Meaningful learning and behavioural change for effectiveness cannot be done by reading and lectures only. Process-based experiential learning is essential for that. It provides the widest coverage of instruments for diagnosis and feedback along with insightful text for intrapersonal, interpersonal, team and organisational levels. It is invaluable compendium for all working in the fields of OB, HRM, L&D and OD. For me it is the "Bible" of Applied Behavioural Science.'

Abad Ahmad, *Former Dean, Faculty of Management Studies and*
Former Pro-Vice Chancellor, University of Delhi

'Dr Udai Pareek was a doyen of human resources movement in India and his book *Training Instruments in HRD and OD* was a valuable guide on which we relied substantially during our early career. It contains well-researched instruments relevant to Indian industry and context.

The collection of instruments covers a wide array of topics with varied application. The reliability of such instruments is particularly noteworthy. Professionals today are highly dependant and influenced by instruments and tools applicable to different culture and there is a misconception that the same is applicable as reliably in India. This book breaks that myth by providing insights into Indian mind in a reliable manner. Dr Surabhi Purohit's effort to reprint this long lost work deserves appreciation as it will once again connect HR professionals today with work of Dr Udai Pareek, a great thinker and an outstanding professional. I would also recommend this book to line managers interested in human resources as it will provide them greater insight.'

Aquil Busrai, *CEO, Aquil Busrai Consulting; Former Director HR,*
Shell Malaysia, Kuala Lumpur

Training Instruments in

HRD and OD

4e

Training Instruments in
HRD and OD

4e

Udai Pareek
Surabhi Purohit

SAGE | Response Business Books

Los Angeles | London | New Delhi
Singapore | Washington DC | Melbourne

First published in 2018 by

SAGE Publications India Pvt Ltd
B1/I-1 Mohan Cooperative Industrial Area
Mathura Road, New Delhi 110 044, India
www.sagepub.in

SAGE Publications Inc
2455 Teller Road
Thousand Oaks, California 91320, USA

SAGE Publications Ltd
1 Oliver's Yard, 55 City Road
London EC1Y 1SP, United Kingdom

SAGE Publications Asia-Pacific Pte Ltd
3 Church Street
#10-04 Samsung Hub
Singapore 049483

Published by Vivek Mehra for SAGE Publications India Pvt Ltd, typeset in 11/14 pts Garamond by Fidus Design Pvt. Ltd., Chandigarh and printed at Chaman Enterprises, New Delhi.

Library of Congress Cataloging-in-Publication Data
Names: Pareek, Udai, author. | Purohit, Surabhi, author.
Title: Training instruments in HRD and OD / Udai Pareek and Surabhi Purohit.
Description: New Delhi, India ; Thousand Oaks, California : SAGE Publications India, 2018. | Includes index.
Identifiers: LCCN 2018009030 (print) | LCCN 2018013017 (ebook) | ISBN 9789352806911 (E pub 2.0) | ISBN 9789352806904 (pbk) |
    ISBN 9789352806928 (web pdf)
Subjects: LCSH: Employees—Training of—India. | Personnel management—India. | Organizational change—India.
Classification: LCC HF5549.5.T7 (ebook) | LCC HF5549.5.T7 P28155 2018 (print) | DDC 658.3/1240954—dc23
LC record available at https://lccn.loc.gov/2018009030

ISBN: 978-93-528-0690-4 (PB)

SAGE Team: Manisha Mathews, Sandhya Gola, Kumar Indra Mishra and Nishant Dhawan

I dedicate this book to my father and Guru, Late Professor Udai Pareek, who motivated and inspired me to connect with people. The best human to have ever lived, whose humility, illustrious career, opulent knowledge, immense commitment and contribution in the field of human resource, organisational psychology, behaviour and development transformed many organisations, inspired and empowered numerous individuals to believe in themselves to bring change.

Thank you for choosing a SAGE product!
If you have any comment, observation or feedback,
I would like to personally hear from you.

Please write to me at **contactceo@sagepub.in**

Vivek Mehra, Managing Director and CEO, SAGE India.

Bulk Sales

SAGE India offers special discounts
for purchase of books in bulk.
We also make available special imprints
and excerpts from our books on demand.

For orders and enquiries, write to us at

Marketing Department
SAGE Publications India Pvt Ltd
B1/I-1, Mohan Cooperative Industrial Area
Mathura Road, Post Bag 7
New Delhi 110044, India

E-mail us at **marketing@sagepub.in**

Get to know more about SAGE

Be invited to SAGE events, get on our mailing list.
Write today to **marketing@sagepub.in**

This book is also available as an e-book.

CONTENTS

PART III: Personal and Interpersonal Styles

LIST OF ILLUSTRATIONS

TABLES

FIGURES

FOREWORD

Many psychologists, starting with the Harvard Psychologist Henry Murray (1893–1988), who started the need-press theory and founded the most famous test, that is, Thematic Apperception Test (TAT); Abraham Maslow (1908–70), founder of the theory of hierarchy of needs; B. F. Skinner (1904–90), founder of operant conditioning, who also laid foundation for programmed learning and educational technology; David McClelland (1917–98), the promoter of achievement, power and affiliation motives for entrepreneurship and institution-building; Saul Rosenzweig (1907–2004), founder of a new methodology to measure reactions to frustration; and Eric Berne (1910–70), who created a theory of transaction analysis, to mention a few, have made outstanding contributions to our understanding of human behaviour, its measurement, control and development. Based on the early contributions of Sigmund Freud (1836–1939), Alfred Adler (1870–1937) and Cal Jung (1875–1961), many behavioural scientists have developed psychometric tools, called 'instruments', to measure and gain deeper insights into human behaviour.

The work of British Behavioural Psychologist H. J. Eysenck (1916–97) to measure extraversion–introversion, activity level and neuroticism the MBTI of the mother daughter pair (Katherine Briggs and Isabel Myers) to measure the personality typology of individuals; social learning theorist Julian Rotter's (1916–2014) work that laid foundations for measuring the locus of control and interpersonal trust; McClelland's achievement motivation and psychosocial maturity; and, in recent years, measurement of emotional intelligence by Daniel Goleman (1946–), empathy by Robert Rosenthal (1933–), and Martin Seligman (1942–) on learnt optimism are all noteworthy as they have influenced our understanding of human behaviour and development of talent using these measurement tools based on sound theories and research.

Many psychologist and behavioural scientists contributed to measurement techniques. Significant among them is Rensis Likert (1903–81) who has given the five-point scale framework and also established through the Social Research Centre, Michigan, methods of measuring organisational climate and management effectiveness. Robert Blake (1918–2004) and Jane Mouton (1930–87) provided grid methodology and Douglas McGregor (1906–64) provided theory X and Y and laid foundations for measuring leadership styles and beliefs. These are just a few additions to the projective and semi-projective techniques popularised by Murray, McClelland and Rosenzweig.

India had one of the most famous behavioural scientists, who falls very much in the league of the psychologist and behavioural scientists of the world mentioned here. His contributions are original and also built on the contributions of most of the scholars mentioned. In motivational theory, Udai Pareek's Extension Motivation as a motive influencing development of people and society is widely acknowledged across the world. His use of TAT and other tools to measure and manage motivation, his work on role efficacy and related scales measuring and managing effectiveness in performing various roles, MAO-B and such other scales that use transactional analysis as a base to apply them to managerial class, and application of picture frustration test methodology to measure various behavioural patterns are just a few to mention. This book finds place for most of these tools and measuring tools with detailed instructions to use.

The tools included in this book are tools devised by or built on the contributions of most of the behavioural scientists mentioned here. Udai Pareek's contributions are in developing his own model of integrated HRD. Integrated HRD involves understanding the person as a person or individual, as a role holder performing various roles and exhibiting his or her own style of influencing others (interpersonal competence), and working and influencing the teams and contributing to the organisation. This book is not a mere compilation; rather, it is based on sound theory of the understanding of human behaviour, measuring it and helping individuals, teams and organisation to manage the same. The tools provide insights for self and avenues for enhancing the talent and potential of teams and collectives.

This kind of work was possible only for an individual or a scholar who has deep insights into people and their behaviour in different settings. Udai Pareek, in his life, worked in different settings, such as, rural India, corporate India, educational institutions, etc., and with a variety of role holders, such as, farmers, teachers, students, health workers, doctors, civil servants, institution builders, managers, supervisors, workers, CEOs, board members, administrators, small-scale entrepreneurs, etc. Using his life's experiences with various categories and with an intention to provide insights into their own behaviour as individuals, dyads, teams and an organisation, Udai has put together various instruments and made available the same in this book. First published about 20 years ago, this book has been received well and has been found useful to many trainers, policymakers, managers, teachers, behavioural scientists and change agents from all professions. Later on, Surabhi Purohit added years of research and her own work with different groups in the last decade or so and enriched the tools and instruments originally published by Udai Pareek. By joining Udai Pareek's contributions and extending it to others, Surabhi Purohit has done a marvellous job. She too has developed a number of instruments for various groups. She deserves to be complimented for her efforts to make such a great contribution that excels the contributions of any single psychologist and behavioural scientist across the world. SAGE deserves special compliment for making this book available to the public once again with renewed effort and in a new format.

T. V. Rao
Chairman, TVRLS, and Former Professor and Board member, IIMA

PREFACE TO THE FOURTH EDITION

The third edition of the book has had innumerable reprints, indicating its wide use by the concerned readers. Several readers of the book sent us the data they collected by using the instruments. They also sent us some suggestions to improve the scoring of a few instruments. As we received more data, norms of several instruments were revised in light of the new information received. We are grateful to them for helping us to update the norms. We hope to receive more data, as well as critical comments and suggestions, from the users of the instruments so that these can be used in the next revision of the book. I am grateful to the SAGE team for their encouragement, keen interest and effort in this venture. I shall appreciate receiving feedback on the new edition, as also additional data from the users, to help us revise some aspects for a possible future edition.

Surabhi Purohit
Jaipur, November 2017

PREFACE TO THE THIRD EDITION

The second edition of the book has had 13 reprints, indicating its wide use by the concerned readers. Several persons using the book sent us the data they collected by using the instruments. They also sent us some suggestions to improve the scoring of a few instruments. In the meantime, some new instruments were also developed. Surabhi Purohit conducted a number of workshops on the use and development of the instruments. Some of those instruments that she has developed have been included in this book. As we received more data, norms of several instruments were revised in light of the new information received. We are grateful to them for helping us in updating the norms. In order to facilitate the scoring of most of the instruments, Shri Naga Siddharth Seetharaman (Siddhu), who had attended a workshop on instruments, offered to help in developing auto scoring of the instruments. Auto scoring was then developed under his guidance. We are happy to include a CD containing the auto-scoring versions of a large number of instruments. This will help in the online use of the instruments. We are grateful to Siddhu for his valuable help.

Udai Pareek
Surabhi Purohit

PREFACE TO THE SECOND EDITION

The first edition of the book received a very enthusiastic positive response. The instruments were widely used for both research and organisational development. In the meantime, working with some other groups helped me to develop a few more instruments. Many of my colleagues too developed instruments using the concepts discussed in the first edition. All these have been included in the first edition.

Moreover, some new source material on instruments has also been added to make the referral system more comprehensive.

A major change has been made in this edition by merging the last part, that is, Part VI (Non-corporate Sector), into the four main parts devoted to personal orientation and behaviour, personal and interpersonal styles, the role, and the organisation.

In several instruments, reliability and validity information have been added, based on new researches done on those instruments. Norms have also been revised wherever necessary.

Two new indices—another index and title index—have been added to help search and locate instruments.

Software for several instruments has been developed and is made available for detailed analysis, interpretation and suggestions for the use of the concerned instruments for raising individual or organisational effectiveness.

Several persons have contributed in the revision of the book. I am grateful to them all. I am grateful to my secretary, K. Binil, for his creative commitment and competence which contributed a great deal to the high quality of production of the book.

Udai Pareek
Jaipur, March 2001

PREFACE TO THE FIRST EDITION

It has been almost 50 years, since my interest in the measurement of human behaviour was first aroused. I had prepared a clerical aptitude test as part of my postgraduate work which led me to get involved in studies of similar nature. With some training in the clinical aspects, followed by my involvement in cross cultural research in Italy and later using the Rosenzweig P-F Study for my doctoral work, my interest shifted to projective techniques. Work relating to education, health and rural change resulted in focusing my interest on social behaviour. A two-year stint at the Indian Agricultural Research Institute, about 30 years ago, was very enriching, and along with some brilliant and committed doctoral students (later my colleagues), I started working on the measurement of social behaviour very intensively.

Since I was involved with bringing about change and also developing groups and organisations, I was very fascinated with the idea of the use of instruments as a developmental intervention. In designing and using instruments, my bias shifted from psychometry to group dynamics. So much so, that until today, I continue to integrate my training in psychometry with clinical psychology and group dynamics. Readers will find this aspect reflected in several instruments. For instance, Role Pics, an instrument for measuring coping styles with stress, has clear evidence of the influence of the Rosenzweig P-F Study, which I had adopted for India. This instrument has become quite popular in several Indian universities.

As the interest of trainers and HRD professionals grew in this area, the demand for instruments too increased. But, what was also palpable was the lack of consistency in the availability of data. There were doctoral dissertations with a lot of information—more than was required—and there were instruments with too less information. There were a number of requests and queries from colleagues working on various issues, doctoral students and also companies for a compendium of instruments covering a vast spectrum of topics. Therefore, this book came into being, a repertoire of all the instruments with which I have been involved during my professional life for almost half a century.

Many of these instruments have been used by institutions and organisations based in Indonesia, Malaysia, the Philippines, Ireland, Canada and the United States of America. The experiences from these countries have broadened the application potential of these instruments. This compilation would be of immense use in these countries and with adaptation, in other cultural surroundings, too.

The first part of the book presents clear lines of direction to the reader on how to use the instruments. Importantly, it contains guidelines for preparing new instruments which are specific to the needs of different groups, organisations, etc. The first part is followed by three more parts. There is an introduction to each part with discussions on the relevant theories behind the instruments. Proper understanding of the theory, as we know, is the key to further development of the instruments.

Several individuals in the groups have contributed to the publication of this book. I am grateful to several managers, consultants, teachers and students whose tremendous enthusiasm in procuring and using the instruments made me seriously consider compiling and publishing them. I appreciate the support given to me by the Jaipur HRD Research Foundation to complete the work on the book. I am indebted to my colleagues who have contributed ideas and suggestions and more importantly, used some of the instruments to give me feedback. I wish to thank Dr Neelu Jain who helped me in the hectic work of compiling, organising and checking the material, Professor V. N. Shrivastav for his help in checking the proofs, and my secretary, Ms Lizy Thomas, for her assistance in many ways.

Udai Pareek

PART

I

INSTRUMENTS FOR HRD

Introduction

Several well-known instruments are currently being used by HRD facilitators, consultants and teachers for organisational development and training. These have mostly been borrowed from Western countries and, though well designed, tested and standardised, they largely remain untested in India—a fact that may lead to several problems. Even though more relevant instruments are now increasingly being developed in India, there still remains a dearth of good instruments for human resource development. This book is an attempt to fill this gap.

Instruments are needed for various HRD units. These comprise individuals, such as, persons, roles, small groups or teams, and the total organisation. The most important HRD unit is the person. Each individual working in a system (organisation) should have an opportunity to know his basic orientations, ways of working, behaviour (both functional and dysfunctional), stresses experienced, and ways of coping with stress.

Chapters 2 and 3 in Part I of this book provide minimum information about the use and development of instruments. The users of instruments should, in due course of time, develop their own simple instruments. They should be familiar with statistics that are also given in these chapters. The users of the volume may benefit more by attending a short programme on the development and use of instruments for HRD.

In this volume, Parts II and III deal with various aspects of instruments. Part IV focuses on organisational roles—behaviour, stress and ways of coping with stress. The organisational role links a person with the system. If roles are properly designed, they can, on one hand, create high motivation among individuals and, on the other hand, create an enabling climate in the organisation.

Part V focuses on the total organisation—key functions, leadership, empowerment and organisational effectiveness by properly blending openness with perceptiveness at various levels. Two important emerging topics of interest are organisational learning and organisational culture. Organisational culture is a complex field, requiring more detailed analysis. Part V has several instruments to help look at organisational learning and various related aspects of organisational culture. It also contains instruments for the use of hospitals and entrepreneurs.

In all, 69 instruments are included in this volume—26 on personal and interpersonal orientation, 19 on styles, 10 on role and 14 on the organisation. There are some instruments for non-corporate groups—hospitals, nurses and general. Each instrument is briefly introduced with relevant instructions for its administration, its reliability, validity, norms and correlates.

Instruments as aids to training and organisational development help to generate data on an individual's orientation, attitude, style or behaviour; interaction between an individual (employee) and a collectivity (organisation); interaction amongst collectivities; and the dynamics of a collectivity. Since individuals (employees) and collectivities (organisations) are involved, the instruments are embedded in psychological and sociological theories.

Psychological theories are older than sociological theories, and the latest are the organisational theories. Human behaviour involves interaction between a person and the environment. Psychological theories have been divided on the primacy of the person (psychodynamics) or the environment (conditioning) in shaping individual's behaviour, values, attitudes, etc. Later, with the development of the technology of psychological measurement, some psychologists used an eclectic approach, developing theories from the results of analysis of human responses (psychometry). Thus, we have what can be called first order theories—psychodynamic theories (Freud, Jung), conditioning theories (Pavlov, Skinner) and psychometric theories (Guilford, Cattell, Eysenck). Similarly, we have first order sociological theories (Weber, Merton, Kluckholm).

Different concepts from the primary theories stimulated later theorists to develop new conceptual frameworks important for instruments. Some of these are as follows:

1. **Psychodynamic Theories**
   a. *Maturation* (psycho-sexual), leading to
      i. 8-stage maturity theory (Erickson, 1993).
      ii. 4-stage theory of psycho-social maturity (Stewart, who has developed an instrument, adapted in India by T. V. Rao).
   b. *Ego*, leading to
      i. Transactional analysis (Berne & Harris, 1969) (A few instruments are included in this volume.)
      ii. Frustration coping (Rosenzweig [1978], with an instrument) (An instrument is included in this volume.)
   c. *Instinct*, leading to work on motivation. A few instruments are included in the volume.
   d. *Transference*, leading to the theories of helping and counselling (Rogers, 1951).
2. **Conditioning Theories**
   Contingency, leading to theories of learning (of special interest are Rotter's concept of locus of control, modification by Levenson [1976]). Some instruments are included in this volume.

3. **Psychometric Theories**

    Personality theories with instruments (Guilford, 1988; Eysenck & Eysenck, 1969; Catell, 1965; etc.).

4. **Sociological Theories**

    a. *Values* (Kluckholm, 1951; McClelland, 1984; Hofstede, 2001). An instrument is included in this volume.

    b. *Group* (Blake, 1968; Sherif, 1968). An instrument is included in this volume.

    c. *Role* (Merton, 1936). Several instruments are included in this volume.

    d. *Bureaucracy*, leading to organisational theories (Weber, 1969; Parsons, 1995).

With new researches, including participative and action research, some areas, with different theories, emerged. These are most relevant for instruments to be used in organisations. These are as follows (names of some contributors to the theories and instruments are mentioned in parentheses):

1. Personality

    a. Self-actualisation (Maslow, 1954).

    b. Self-efficacy (Bandura, 1977). An instrument on personal efficacy is included in this volume.

    c. Self-disclosure and openness (Luft, 1991). An instrument is included in this volume.

    d. Typology (Myers, 1974 ; Stewart, 1975).

    e. Locus of control (Rotter, 1966; Levenson, 1976; Pareek, 1982; Rao, Unpublished). An instrument is included in this volume.

    f. Attribution (Pareek, 1982; Weiner, 1972). An instrument is included in this volume.

    g. Interpersonal trust (Rotter, 1971). An instrument is included in this volume.

    h. Creativity (Khandwalla, 1984a). An instrument is included in this volume.

2. Motivation

    a. Hierarchy of motives (Maslow, 1954).

    b. Two-factor theory (Herzberg, 1966).

    c. Achievement motive (McClelland, 1975).

    d. Power motive (McClelland, 1975).

    e. Approach avoidance in motives (Birney, 1969; Heckhausen, 1967a; Pareek, 1976). Instruments are included in this volume.

    f. Contingency theory (Lawler & Porter, 1981).

    g. Interpersonal underworld (Schutz, 1958). An instrument is included in this volume.

    h. Work–life balance (Gallop). An instrument is included in this volume.

3. Role and Style
   a. Role efficacy (Pareek, 1987). Instruments are included in this volume.
   b. Role stress (Katz & Kahn, 1966; Pareek, 1983a). Instruments are included in this volume.
   c. Coping with role stress (Lazarus, 1988; Pareek, 1983a). An instrument is included in this volume.
   d. Lifestyles of executives (Marrow). An instrument is included in this volume.
   e. Interpersonal styles (Pareek, 1986a). An instrument in this volume.
   f. Assertiveness (Wolpe, 1958). An instrument is included in this volume.
   g. Decision-making (Scott and Bruce, 1995). An instrument is included in this volume.
4. Leadership
   a. Leadership continuum (Tannenbaum & Schmidt, 1958).
   b. Managerial grid (Blake & Mouton, 1970).
   c. Contingency theory (Fiedler, 1967).
   d. Situational theory (Hersey & Blanchard, 19). A few instruments are included in this volume.
   e. Nurturant task leader (Sinha, 1980).
   f. Transformational leader (Burns, 1978; Bass, 1997; Bennis, 1989). An instrument is included in this volume.
   g. Leadership substitutes (Kerr, 1977). An instrument is included in this volume.
   h. Direct and indirect influence (Flanders, 1960a). An instrument is included in this volume.
5. Change
   a. Process of change (Lippitt, Watson & Westley, 1958).
   b. Organisational learning (Argyris, 1990). An instrument is included in this volume.
   c. Learning organisation (Senge, 1990). An instrument is included in this volume.
   d. Adoption of innovation (Rogers, 1995). An instrument is included in this volume.
   e. Diffusion of innovation (Rogers, 1986). An instrument is included in this volume.
6. Counselling
   a. Helping relationship (Rogers, 1961).
   b. Contact counselling (Sperry & Hess, 1976).
   c. Performance counselling (Pareek & Rao, 1992).
7. Environment and Culture
   a. External environments (Khandwalla, 1984b).
   b. Environment of an organisation (Jaques, 1989).
   c. Environment-technology interface (Lawrence & Lorsch, 1969).
   d. Participative organisations (Likert, 1961).
   e. Organisational culture (Schein, 1985). An instrument is included in this volume.
   f. Organisational climate (Litwin & Stringer, 1968). An instrument is included in this volume.

The use of an instrument requires the understanding of related theories. Scores cannot be interpreted without familiarity with relevant concepts. The first part of each chapter is therefore devoted to discussion of the relevant concepts. In some cases, such discussions are more exhaustive than other cases, depending on how much a user of these instruments needs to know. Conceptual inputs are discussed with the instruments. It is strongly recommended that the user reads the relevant conceptual section before using an instrument.

Some instruments have been standardised and relevant information about their reliability, validity and norms are provided. However, in some cases, the instruments have not been standardised. Since these instruments are to be used for HRD, standardising is not strictly required.

The instruments are printed in such a way that these can be directly photocopied from the book for the purpose of administration. In most cases, answer sheets are provided separately to help participants score fast. While photocopying, care should be taken to photocopy answer sheets on a separate page. Self-scoring helps respondents get better insights into the instrument and its interpretation.

The formatting of the instruments ensures that while the actual scoring key is not shared with the participants, the results are. The instruments also include an advisory. With the advent of e-mail for transactions in companies, the instruments can also be used in applications such as a culture survey.

All the instruments contained in this volume are behaviour-oriented. This enables an individual, a small group or a team to plan changes and monitor these at a later stage. For example, instead of suggesting a person to increase his perceptiveness, it may be more correct to suggest to the person to listen for a few minutes before interrupting and providing his own input. The person can later try out this new behaviour (waiting and listening) and see how much it contributes to the desired outcome. The volume follows SAFI (self-awareness through feedback on instruments) approach (see Pareek, 1995, pp. 269–72).

In SAFI, the participant takes the major initiative, and actively uses results of the instrument for planning his/her effectiveness. The following nine steps are involved in SAFI:

1. *Responding to instrument*: The participant responds to any instrument standardised by experts for the purpose. (Later we shall briefly discuss the procedure of developing and standardising an instrument.)

2. *Conceptual input*: The participant reads the theory and the related concepts about the instrument responded. This helps him/her to become familiar with both the conceptual framework of the instrument and the meaning of the various aspects. If a facilitator is available, he/she explains the conceptual aspects to the individual or the group of participants.

3. *Prediction*: Based on the understanding of the theory and meaning of the categories used in the instrument, the participant predicts his/her own score to reflect self-perception and understanding of own style/behaviour.

4. *Scoring*: The participant then scores the completed instrument according to the procedure explained by the author of the instrument.

5. *Interpretation*: The participant, preferably, writes down the detailed interpretation and implication of his/her scores. Software, if available, can be used for this purpose.

6. *Feedback*: The participant checks with some other significant person(s) whom he/she trusts, some factual evidence to confirm or question the interpretation and implications of his/her scores.

7. *Action planning*: Deciding to improve some aspects of style/behaviour, the participant prepares a plan to behave differently, experiments with a new style, etc. The software provides specific suggestions for the use of the participants.

8. *Experimentation*: The participant implements the action plan, keeping detailed notes of various satisfactory and frustrating experiences. If available, the facilitator is used for guidance.

9. *Follow-up*: The participant again responds to the instrument to see if there is any significant change in the scores and receives feedback, from people he/she trusts, on the change observed.

When a facilitator is available, he monitors these steps with individuals, even when they work in a group. The advantage of working in a group is to have an opportunity of giving feedback to one another and to reinforce mutual learning.

Norms are useful for better interpretation of scores. Some norms are given. We need to build norms based on larger samples and collected from diverse groups. The authors will appreciate receiving data collected using the instruments given in the book by the readers. These will be kept strictly confidential and will be used only to add to the growing database. Those who send data will in turn get the latest comparative norms on the concerned instruments. Feedbacks on this book will also be appreciated. Throughout this book, the masculine pronouns (he/his/him) will be used generically for convenience only; it refers to both men and women.

Using Instruments for HRD

2.1 INSTRUMENTS FOR HRD

Instruments are devices used for collecting data on behavioural aspects to help derive some tentative generalisations. Like other instruments, an HRD instrument has a referent (what is to be measured or diagnosed), consisting of units that have some internal consistency and uses an index of some kind to express the results of the analysis/diagnosis.

The simplest HRD instrument may be a question raised with respondent about three main areas needing improvement in an organisation. We may then have a few more questions. Interviews for purposes of selection are another familiar form of instrument. However, when we discuss HRD instruments, we usually mean well-prepared devices. These can be in any form. Some of the more familiar forms are questionnaires, interviews and check lists. Another better-known device is rating scale. Lesser-known forms are semantic differential (rating on bipolar continua) and projective devices (e.g., stories, cartoon like pictures, dreams, etc.). The devices in which respondents are required to answer questions, rate items or write something are called paper-and-pencil instruments. Instruments can be in other media also, for example, audios, pictures or other materials. Normally, however, paper-and-pencil instruments are used for HRD.

2.2 THE USES OF INSTRUMENTS

Instruments are widely used. Following are some of the purposes for which instruments are employed:

Selection: Instruments are used widely for selection and recruitment. After some criteria have been decided upon, appropriate instruments are researched or developed for use with candidates. Cut-off points can be fixed for selection. All admission or selection tests contain appropriate instruments, for example, to measure basic ability (intelligence), aptitude, knowledge, personality, etc.

Research: Instruments are used to collect data and then to draw conclusions to test or validate a set of hypotheses or a theory. For example, if we want to test the relationship between the achievement motive and managerial effectiveness, we need two instruments—one to measure achievement motivation and the other for managerial effectiveness. We administer them to a large sample of managers and then find out the correlation between these two variables. This is research. Research can be very simple (involving two variables) or very complex (involving more than two variables).

Potential appraisal: Instruments are used for career planning, mainly for potential appraisal. A well-known device called assessment centre uses a large number of instruments to measure various critical attributes such as visioning, decision-making, strategic-thinking, coping ability, etc. Different types of instruments are administered to managers attending the assessment centre and the results are used for potential appraisal as an input for career planning, placement, advancement and counselling.

Individual growth: An instrument can be used to help individuals prepare action plans for their own growth. SAFI is useful for individuals to examine their scores on different instruments, reflect on these and prepare plans for improvement.

Training: Instrumented training is becoming increasingly popular. Instruments used for analysing individual responses or developing team/group profiles generate useful data which a trainer/facilitator can use as a part of training. Concrete data may help to make abstract concepts more understandable.

Organisation development: In organisation development (OD), the initial stage is that of diagnosis. At this stage, instruments are very useful for collecting data and developing an understanding based on the data. Survey feedback, a well-known OD intervention, involves the use of an instrument, for example, in understanding the ethos, or the climate or culture, of an organisation. Instruments are also used for follow-up and evaluation.

2.3 OPTIMISING THE USE OF INSTRUMENTS

Instruments can be useful in generating data for training. They have the potential to make training more effective by basing training on data generated by the participants, which helps to make them more involved. The instruments also reduce psychological threat as the pooled data does not attribute opinions to specific individuals. Data related to individuals is also less threatening as these are generated by the individuals themselves, and they examine, analyse and interpret the data for their own use only. If the instruments contain behaviour-related items, action planning to improve behaviour becomes easier. Instruments can help not only in planning action, but also in assessing if the action led to any desirable change; the same instrument (or its parallel form) can be used later for collecting data again.

There are some potential limitations of instruments. Sometimes instruments can be misused, or at least may not be used properly. For example, if confidentiality of data is not ensured, it can cause problems. If the data generated by instruments is not 'processed' enough, full use cannot be made of the instrument. Sometimes, there is a tendency to use all types of instruments, resulting in data overload, causing participants to feel overwhelmed. Sometimes the facilitator may unwittingly 'brand' individual respondents into types or categories. At other times, instruments may become alternatives to confronting problems within or by a group. There could be a difficulty to understand the scores and their interpretation, thereby increasing dependency on the facilitator as an 'expert' like this.

In order to optimise the use of instruments for training, potential limitations should be kept in mind so that usual pitfalls can be avoided. For example, it should be explained that the scores are not 'fixed' or 'permanent' and are only pointers to consider their implications and then to prepare strategies for change, if such change is seen to be desirable by the concerned participants. The scores need to be explained and processed in details, helping demystify the instruments. Enough group work can be done with generated data. As far as possible, the focus should be on the behaviour of individuals or groups so that plans can be developed to change this. The suggestions provided here will help in the proper use of instruments for training:

Selection of instruments: The first step is the selection of the instrument to be used. Selection is guided by the purpose, the group/individuals with whom the instrument will be used and the confidence of the facilitator (familiarity with the instrument and its conceptual framework). The most important element in selection is the facilitator's familiarity, or rather his mastery of the instrument and its theory. The facilitator should first try out the instrument. If it is a person-focused instrument, he should use it on himself and be quite clear about its various aspects and the interpretation of scores. As a rule, no instrument should be used unless it has been tested by the facilitator on himself or his group/organisation.

For selecting an instrument, Pfeiffer and Ballew (1988, pp. 38–40) have listed 25 'technical' considerations: validity, reliability, objectivity, theoretical base, behavioural orientation, observability, special training, language, sophistication, complexity, supplementation, adaptability, transparency, fakeability, norms, availability, copyright restrictions, time required, expense, special materials, noxiousness, scoring complexity, data reduction, handouts and familiarity.

Out of the technical aspects, reliability, validity and objectivity are the most important. The instrument should have high reliability and validity. However, instruments for HRD may have face validity, as the purpose is that of development, not taking decisions of recruitment, promotion, etc.

The theoretical base of the instrument should be sound; otherwise, it may become only a list of items. Special attention should be given to this aspect. Another aspect deserving attention is behavioural orientation of the instrument. Since the purpose of an instrument is to improve behaviour, instruments having behavioural items may be more appropriate to help participants prepare action plans for improvement, follow-up and monitoring.

Administration of the instrument: As far as possible, instruments should be adminis-
tered on the first day or early in the training programme so that what is being discussed later does not affect responses. In a particular module or session, no theoretical explanation should be given before the instrument is completed by the participants. The broad purpose may be stated, although, in some cases, even this may influence responses. For example, if Least Preferred Coworker (LPC) Scale, developed by Fiedler, is used, any mention of its purpose as measuring leadership style may affect responses.

An instrument should preferably be administered in a group. Respondents can be allowed to read the items; in some cases, the facilitator may read aloud the instruc-
tions so that participants can understand them clearly. A few minutes can be spent on clarifying doubts. If the instrument contains special instructions, such as, ranking the items (i.e., MAO-C in Chapter 64 or organisation culture in Chapters 67 and 68), this can be brought to the notice of the respondents. In many cases, without special attention to such instructions as in the example cited, participants are likely to rate, rather than rank, the items.

If the instrument is to be completed by any individual alone, the instructions should be clarified before they are given the instrument as a take home assignment.

Since the scores are confidential, some instruments may not require respondents to write their names. In other cases, they can write an identity symbol or a number that is known only to the facilitator.

Scoring: As far as possible, the instrument's answer sheet should help participants to do the scoring themselves. This would save time and scoring will become simple. For example, for most of the instruments contained in this volume, the answer sheets require participants to add the ratings given across the rows, thus making scoring simpler. Similarly, a special answer sheet is designed for the instrument for leadership style (Chapters 30–32) so that the scoring of the dominant/backup styles as well as the calculation of effectiveness are much easier as compared to the scoring of LEAD by Hersey and Blanchard (1982).

Scoring should preferably be done by the participants themselves. This will help them to gain an insight into the instrument. If scoring is to be done in a group, the facilitator must help the participants to score and calculate indices, etc., step by step. Explanations regarding the rationale of scoring should be postponed. After scoring, if the group has enough openness, each respondent can exchange his answer sheet with another respondent to check the scoring and ensure that the responses have been properly scored.

If time is a constraint, the responses can be scored by the facilitator or another outsider or software in advance, and the scores can be brought to the classroom. In other cases, depending on the availability of computer facilities, the group's scores can be fed into the computer, and the analysis, including norms, high/low scores, etc., can be printed out and distributed at the time of interpretation.

Interpretation of scores: Interpretation and processing of data with the group is the most important part of using instruments in HRD. The user should be familiar with some basic statistics (given in a later section). After the scores are available, the facilitator needs to explain the conceptual framework and the relevant theoretical aspects. For interpreting scores, both the relevant theory and the norms are important. Available national, regional or industry-wide norms, or those based on the analysis of responses from other groups, may be used. An obvious question in interpreting the scores is whether a particular score is high, low or average. The answer can be given only by examining the norms. Norms can also be developed for a specific group. If the group is large (30 or more people), mean and standard deviation (SD) can be used. However, in smaller groups, median and quartile deviation can be used.

If norms are not available, a simple way is to divide the scores (ascending order) into four quartiles, with 25% scores in each quartile. The lowest score of the fourth quartile (highest 25%) can be used as the cut-off point for high scores—any score equal to or above that score may be regarded as high. Similarly, the upper-most score in the first quartile (the lowest 25%) may be the cut-off point for 'low' scores—any score equal to or lower than that will be regarded as 'low' scores.

After the facilitator's explanation, it may be useful to form small groups to understand the interpretation and raise questions for further understanding. Sometimes it is useful to ask the members of small groups (say, triads) to guess the scores of other members, based on the explanation. Showing them the scores then may raise interesting issues such as transparency (Are the scores reflected in the behaviour?), perceptiveness of the person guessing the scores, contradiction in scores and behaviour, etc.

Before interpreting scores and explaining the relevant theory, it may be mentioned that the scores are not to be taken too seriously—the responses could have been influenced by misunderstanding of the item or some other factors—and that nothing is good or bad. The participants should certainly become aware of the implications of the scores, and examine these for any action they may want to take.

Action planning: The last step in using an instrument is to generate ideas for action. Participants should work in small groups. Groups can be formed on the basis of 'low' scores (for example, all having low scores on openness may form one group, or a group may be formed for 3–4 'weak' areas of organisational ethos), on the basis of natural groups (same roles, institutions or departments), or on the basis of closeness (for personal scores, respondents may like to sit with those with whom they feel more at home, and who can help them by providing feedback on those aspects).

The groups may focus on a specific action which can be monitored later. In developing action plans, several points should be kept in mind: specific action steps, dates when these will be taken, difficulties envisaged, resources or help needed to carry out action, indicators of the successful effect of the action, evaluation plan, follow-up and monitoring plan. It may be useful to prepare a written action plan. In case of individual scores, action ideas may be sufficient. However, help and follow-up and monitoring could certainly be discussed in detail and, if possible, arrangements to review progress after specific time periods could be worked out.

In case of organisational or role-related instruments, it may be useful to invite the top or senior managers and brief them on the scores. Action plans can be presented, suggesting the support needed from them. Such a dialogue at the end may be useful in developing better understanding and mutuality.

Instruments can be very useful in contributing to the development of individuals, roles, teams and the total organisation. If properly selected, used and processed, instruments are a powerful HRD tool.

2.4 BASIC STATISTICS

Users of instruments should be familiar with a few basic statistical terms and measures for better interpretation of the scores.

2.4.1 Definitions

- *Measurement* is assigning numbers or symbols to characteristics of object according to rules.
- A *constant* is a symbol for a specific unchanging number. Usually constants are denoted by italic lower case letters (e.g., *n* stands for the number of respondents to a test, a constant).
- A *variable* is a symbol which can have a variety of numerical values. Usually variables are denoted by capital italic letters (e.g., *X* may denote achievement motive score).
- Variables can be discrete or continuous. A *discrete variable* can take only selected values, whereas a *continuous variable* can take any of an infinite number of values. A *dichotomous variable* is one which has only two values.
- A *population* is a specific (usually large) group of respondents or items.
- A *sample* is a subset of respondents or items chosen from the population.
- A *parameter* is a characteristic of a population.
- A *statistic* is a characteristic of a sample.
- *Statistics* are used to estimate parameters.
- *Descriptive statistics* describes a distribution.

- *Inferential statistics* helps to infer properties of the entire population from a sample of scores from the population.
- *Parametric statistics* make assumptions (such as normality) about the population values (called parameters).
- *Nonparametric statistics* make no or very few assumptions about the parameters or the shape or nature of the population. These are also called distribution-free statistics.

2.4.2 Symbols

Generally, Greek letters are used to denote parameters, while lower case Roman letters are used for sample statistics. Greek letters (lower case) are used for several statistical measures. Some common ones are given here.

α: significance level (type I error)
$|a|$:   absolute value of a
β: probability of a Type II error
CI: confidence interval
d: difference between paired data
d: denotes item discrimination index
df: degrees of freedom
e: constant, approximately equal to 2.718
E: denotes error score
f: denotes frequency
HT: hypothesis test
H_o: null hypothesis
H_1 or H_a: alternative hypothesis
i: (subscript) denotes the ith value of a variable
IQR: interquartile range
M: median
n: sample size
n: denotes numbers
N: population size
ND: normal distribution
ρ: correlation coefficient for a population
Pk: kth percentile. For example, P90 = 90th percentile
Q1:   first quartile
Q3:   third quartile
r: denotes sample correlation
σ: standard deviation
t: t-score

X: denotes a score
$\overline{x}$:   (called x bar) denotes mean of the scores
z: score denotes standard score
>:   denotes greater than
<:   denotes smaller than

2.4.3 Greek Letters in Statistics

Letter	Name	Statistical Reference
α	Alpha (lower case)	Significance, i.e., the probability of a Type I error Confidence is $(1 - \alpha).100\%$
β	Beta (lower case)	Consumer's risk, i.e., the probability of a Type II error
μ	Mu (lower case)	Population mean
σ	Sigma (lower case)	Population standard deviation
Σ	Sigma (upper case)	Tells the reader to sum what follows it in a formula
ρ	Rho (lower case)	Population correlation coefficient
θ	Theta (lowercase)	Population proportion (in some texts)
χ^2	Lower case chi-squared (Greek letter squared)	A type of probability distribution used in testing hypotheses involving more than two possible outcomes

2.4.4 Describing Data

Data can be described statistically in various ways, some of which are given here.

1. *Frequency distribution*: Distribution of the scores in same categories.
2. *Measures of central tendency*: Indices of the central value or location of a frequency distribution. If the sample is not large or when scores are not normally distributed, median or mode may be better measures than mean.
   a. The *mean* is the average (test scores divided by numbers of respondents, or $\Sigma x/n$).
   b. The *median* is the middle ranking score, so that 50% of the scores are equal to or above, and 50% equal to or below. This measure is less influenced by outlying values than the average or mean and is therefore used widely in smaller groups as a measure of central tendency.
   c. The *mode* is that value which appears most frequently in a given set of data. This is not always a central value and indeed, in some sets of data, there can be more than one modal value where data is clustered around a centre. It can be useful to show which value(s) occurs most frequently.
3. *The normal curve*: It is a symmetrical bell-shaped curve showing the distribution of a variable. When the sample is large and scores are normally distributed, mean and SDs are used. Mean is the average (total divided by n). Most commonly used statistical

FIGURE 2.1   Area Under Normal Curve

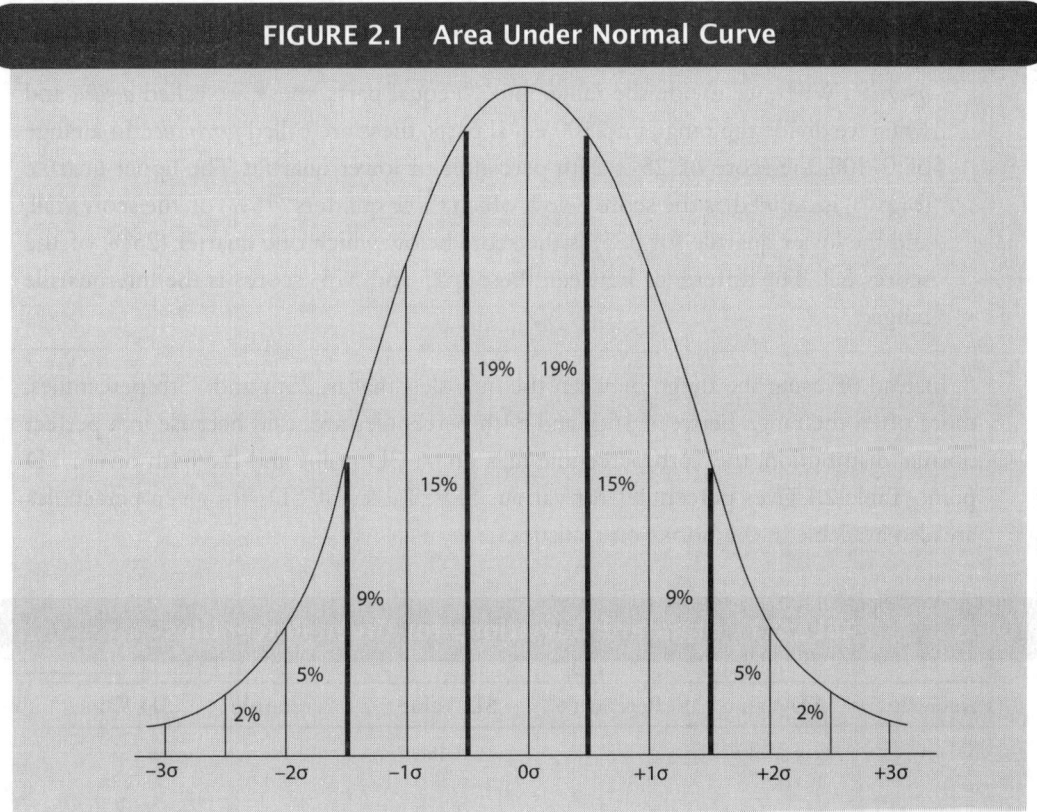

methods and computer programs are based on the assumption that data is normally distributed. Individual items are evenly distributed above and below the average (mean), and they cluster around the mean. In very few cases are data 'normally' distributed, but are close enough to make no real difference. An example would be the height of children at a given age; most would cluster round the average with a few extremes. The distribution of large data when plotted assumes a bell-shaped curve called normal distribution. This is shown in Figure 2.1.

Let us move from left to right on the line showing mean and SDs (s). The ordinate at –2 SD cuts off about 2% of the area, the ordinate at –1 SD cuts off 16% (2% + 5% + 9%), and so on.

There are two main characteristics of normal distribution. First, the curve is symmetrical around the mean of the distribution; the numbers in ranges on the left are equal to those on the right. Second, the scores concentrate closely around the mean and taper off equally on either side, as illustrated in Figure 2.1.

4. *Measures of variability*: Variability is an indication of how scores are scattered or dispersed.

a.   Range is the difference between the highest and the lowest score.
b.   If we divide the range or spread of scores into four equal parts, these are called *quartiles*. When we divide the range into 10 equal parts, these are called *deciles*, and when we divide the range into 100 equal parts, these are called *percentiles*. In a range of 0–100, the score of 25 is 25th percentile or lower quartile. The upper quartile (or p75) is defined as the score below which three quarters (75%) of the scores fall, and the lower quartile (or p25) is the score below which one quarter (25%) of the scores fall. The difference between these (p25 and p75) scores is the interquartile range.

Instead of using the range between the quartiles, that is, 25th and 75th percentiles, more often the range between 16th and 84th percentiles are used because in a perfect normal distribution, the 16th percentile falls on –1 SD point and the 84th on +1 SD point. Table 2.1 gives percentiles for various SDs. Tables of SDs for given percentiles are also available in the books on statistics.

TABLE 2.1   Standard Deviations for Given Percentiles

Percentile	SD Value	Percentile	SD Value	Percentile	SD Value
.1	−3.090	32	−0.468	71	+0.553
.2	−2.878	33	−0.440	72	+0.583
.3	−2.748	34	−0.412	73	+0.613
.4	−2.652	35	−0.385	74	+0.643
.5	−2.576	36	−0.358	75	+0.675
.6	−2.512	37	−0.332	76	+0.706
.7	−2.457	38	−0.305	77	+0.739
.8	−2.409	39	−0.279	78	+0.772
.9	−2.366	40	−0.253	79	+0.806
1	−2.326	41	−0.228	80	+0.842
2	−2.054	42	−0.202	81	+0.878
3	−1.881	43	−0.176	82	+0.915
4	−1.751	44	−0.151	83	+0.954
5	−1.645	45	−0.126	84	+0.995
6	−1.555	46	−0.100	85	+1.036
7	−1.476	47	−0.075	86	+1.080
8	−1.405	48	−0.050	87	+1.126
9	−1.341	49	−0.25	88	+1.175
10	−1.282	50	−0.000	89	+1.227
11	−1.227	51	+0.025	90	+1.282
12	−1.175	52	+0.050	91	+1.341
13	−1.126	53	+0.075	92	+1.405
14	−1.080	54	+0.100	93	+1.476

Percentile	SD Value	Percentile	SD Value	Percentile	SD Value
15	−1.036	55	+0.126	94	+1.555
16	−0.995	56	+0.151	95	+1.645
17	−0.954	57	+0.176	96	+1.751
18	−0.915	58	+0.202	97	+1.881
19	−0.878	59	+0.228	98	+2.054
20	−0.842	60	+0.253	99	+2.326
21	−0.806	61	+0.279	99.1	+2.366
22	−0.772	62	+0.305	99.2	+2.409
23	−0.739	63	+0.332	99.3	+2.457
24	−0.706	64	+0.358	99.4	+2.512
25	−0.675	65	+0.385	99.5	+2.576
26	−0.643	66	+0.412	99.6	+2.652
27	−0.613	67	+0.440	99.7	+2.748
28	−0.583	68	+0.468	99.8	+2.878
29	−0.553	69	+0.496	99.9	+3.090
30	−0.524	70	+0.524		
31	−0.496	71	+0.524		

Source: Garrett (1966, p. 165).

When calculating quartiles and other measures, it should be ensured that the sample is sufficiently large to support the results. In broad terms, it is usually accepted that for a measure to have any validity, there should be at least three scores in each part in which the sample of data is divided, but preferably more. For example, medians should not be defined on less than six observations and even this can be misleading if the data included in the sample is in any way unrepresentative.

There are various formulae for calculating quartiles. The following are the most commonly used. If there are n observations, and these are ranked in descending order, then

$$\text{Median} = (n + 1)/2 \text{ observations from the top}$$

(If there are 20 values, this gives 10.5, i.e. the average of the 10th and 11th observations.)

$$\text{Upper quartile} = (n + 3)/4 \text{ observations from the top}$$

c. *Average deviation* (AD) = $|x - \bar{x}/n$ (from the mean)
d. *Variance* (s^2) is the mean of the squares of the differences between the scores in a distribution and their mean.
e. *SAD* (s) (σ is the SD of the population) is the square root of the average squared deviations around the mean.

SD is of great importance in many branches of statistics and is widely used especially in instrumentation training. It requires a relatively complex calculation, although it is available on statistical packages.

$$\sigma = \sqrt{\dfrac{\sum (x - \mu)^2}{N}}$$

Where x represents each value in the population, μ is the mean value of the population, Σ is the summation (or total) and N is the number of values in the population.

f.   *Skewness* indicates the nature and extent to which symmetry is absent. Scores can be skewed positively or negatively.
g.   *Kurtosis* indicates steepness of a distribution in the centre.

2.4.5 Correlations

Several methods are used to find out the association between two variables.

1. *Pearson correlation coefficient* (r) is the most common method of calculating association between two variables which are continuous and reach an interval or ratio level of measurement.
2. *Phi coefficient* (φ) is used as an index of the strength of association between two dichotomous variables.
3. *Tetrachoric correlation coefficient* (rtet) is used to correlate two artificially dichotomised variables that have a bivariate normal distribution.
4. *Biserial correlation* is used to correlate an artificially dichotomised, normally distributed variable with a continuous one.
5. *Point-biserial correlation coefficient* (rpbis) is used as an index of the association between a dichotomous variable and a continuous or multistep variable.
6. *Spearman rank-order correlation coefficient* is used to correlate two multistep or continuous variables measured at the ordinal level (e.g., rank-ordered).
7. *Kendall's tau* (t) is also used for ordinal-level data.

Correlation measures how closely two variables are related. Correlation coefficients vary from +1 to –1 and typically assume a straight line relationship. A value close to +1 indicates that a high value in one variable will be reflected by a high value in other. A value close to –1 indicates that high value in one variable will the reflected in a low value in the other, and near 0 indicates that there is no correlation and so a high value in one variable can reflect any value in the other.

Level of significance: A correlation can be accepted if we are sure that the relationship is not by chance. We also define the limits of such acceptance. Generally, we accept the correlation if it may occur by chance in less than 5% cases, or its chance occurring is not more than 5%. Five per cent can also be expressed as 0.05; this is called the *level of significance*. Generally, 0.05, 0.01, and 0.001 levels of significance are seen. The lower the value, the higher is the confidence with which we can accept the relationship represented by the coefficient of correlation. A level of significance of 0.001 means that the relationship can occur by chance in only 1 case out of 1000. Level of significance depends both on the value of correlation and on the total number of respondents (n). Statistical tables are available to know the levels of significance. Table 2.2 can be used to find the significance of correlation at two levels—the 0.05 and 0.01 levels.

TABLE 2.2   Correlation Coefficients at the 5% and 1% Levels of Significance

Example: When n is 52 and df is 50, r must be 0.273 to be significant at 0.05 level, and 0.354 to be significant at 0.01 level.

Degrees of Freedom $(n-2)$	0.05	0.01	Degrees of Freedom $(n-2)$	0.05	0.01
1	0.997	1.000	24	0.388	0.496
2	0.950	0.990	25	0.381	0.487
3	0.878	0.959	26	0.374	0.478
4	0.811	0.917	27	0.367	0.470
5	0.754	0.874	28	0.361	0.463
6	0.707	0.834	29	0.355	0.456
7	0.666	0.798	30	0.349	0.449
8	0.632	0.765	35	0.325	0.418
9	0.602	0.735	40	0.304	0.393
10	0.576	0.708	45	0.288	0.372
11	0.553	0.684	50	0.273	0.354
12	0.532	0.661	60	0.250	0.325
13	0.514	0.641	70	0.232	0.302
14	0.497	0.623	80	0.217	0.283
15	0.482	0.606	90	0.205	0.267
16	0.468	0.590	100	0.195	0.254
17	0.456	0.575	125	0.174	0.228
18	0.444	0.561	150	0.159	0.208
19	0.433	0.549	200	0.138	0.181
20	0.423	0.537	300	0.113	0.148
21	0.413	0.526	400	0.098	0.128
22	0.404	0.515	500	0.088	0.115
23	0.396	0.505	1000	0.062	0.081

2.4.6 Regression

Correlation coefficient shows the strength of the relationship between two variables (x and y); it also reflects the accuracy of a linear prediction. Linear regression helps to determine the equation for the best prediction line, the regression line. It helps to predict scores on y variable from scores on x variable.

We use linear regression when we want to predict an unknown y score from a known x score. For example, the HRD department may want to predict the future performance of a candidate from some scores on a selection test in order to decide whether to select him or not. We need to have scores on the test and actual performance scores from a representative sample of employees. Then, we use means, SDs and correlation coefficient of the test scores and performance score to obtain the regression equation. *Multiple regression* helps in determining the weights for the predictors to obtain the most linear prediction of a criterion from several predictors. The weights are called *beta values* (b).

2.4.7 Factor Analysis

Factor analysis is a technique to identify dimensions underlying a set of measurements (or to find internal structure of the items or variables measured). The following steps are involved in factor analysis:

1. Select some variables, items or instruments.
2. Prepare inter-correlation matrix by calculating correlations amongst these measures (say, items of an instrument). As already stated variance (squared value of a correlation), also called the *coefficient of determination*, indicates how much the two variables have in common.
3. Factor the inter-correlation matrix. There are various methods of factoring, easily carried out with the help of SPSS package. *Principal components analysis* is a popular and widely used method. After factoring, we get a matrix, with factor loadings of each factor on each variable. This is like correlation between a variable and the factor.
4. Rotate the factors obtained. Several methods are used, the most popular being *varimax rotation*. SPSS package has a program for rotation. All the aspects are printed out. The rotated factor matrix improves the analysis and sharpens the factors explaining the underlying common dimensions.
5. Calculate *eigenvalue* of each factor. It indicates the relative strength of each factor. This is generated by the software. We generally accept factors with a minimum eigenvalue of 1.00.
6. Calculate *total variance* in percentage, accounted by the factor. This is done by dividing the eigenvalue by the number of variables and multiplying the result by 100. This is also generated by the software.

7. Calculate *communality* (also printed by the software) for each variable. It is found out by adding the squared factor loadings of the variable (it ranges from 0 to 1.00).

2.4.8 Making Scores Comparable

With different lengths of instruments, their varying ranges and different rating scales, the comparison of scores becomes difficult. One way to increase comparability is to use a converted score, making the range from 0 to 100. This is done by converting raw scores with a formula to neutralise the scale values and the length of the instrument. For example, we convert raw scores of MAO-C (see Chapter 70). The range of scores in MAO-C is 12–72. First, we change the range by subtracting 12, so the range becomes 0–60. Then, we convert the range from the original 0–60, to one from 0–100 by multiplying the score by 5/3. Or, we can say converted score = (raw score − 12) × 100/60.

The same approach has been used to prepare operating effectiveness quotient (OEQ) in MAO-B (see Chapter 28), and TSI instruments, etc. There, the ratio is converted into an index ranging from 0 to 100. This is done by subtracting the lowest point of the range in the approach score, that is, the number of items in the scale—3 in case of the TSI-M, 4 in the case of TSI-T and 5 in the case of MAO-B—then dividing it by approach + avoidance − 6, 8 or 10 respectively, and finally multiplying it by 100.

Standard scores: Raw scores can also be converted into standard scores by the formula (Raw Score − mean/SD). The scores thus obtained will be comparable with standard scores similarly calculated for another variable. In such scores, the mean is 0 and SD is 1; such scores will be in small fractions. These can be changed with any mean and SD value. For example, we can express them with a mean value of 50 and SD value of 10 by the following formula:

$$\frac{\{(\text{Raw Score} - \text{Mean}) \times 10\} + 50}{\text{SD}}$$

In order to improve comparability of scores, they are converted into normalised standard scores, generally called '*T* scores'. The scores are converted into a distribution with a mean of 50 and SD of 10. The *T* scale begins at −5 SD and ends at +5 SD. The following steps are involved in converting raw scores into *T* scores:

- Arrange items in the increasing order of scores.
- Prepare a table as shown in Table 2.3. In column 2 are the frequencies for each score (number of respondents giving the score).
- Enter cumulative frequencies in column 3.
- In column 4, enter the number of respondents who fall below each score plus half of those who have the score. These can be calculated from columns 2 and 3.

- Convert the entries in column 4 into percentages of N (total number of respondents) and enter these in column 5.
- Write T scores in column 6 for the entries in column 5 by referring to Table 2.4.

TABLE 2.3 To Illustrate the Calculation of T Scores

(1) Test Score	(2) f	(3) Cum. f	(4) Cum. f Below Score + 1/2 of Given Score	(5) Col. (4) in %	(6) T Scores
10	1	62	61.5	99.2	74
9	4	61	59	95.2	67
8	6	57	54	87.1	61
7	10	51	46	74.2	56
6	8	41	37	59.7	52
5	13	33	26.5	42.7	48
4	18	20	11	17.7	41
3	2	2	1	1.6	29
	$N = 62$				

Source: Garrett (1966, p. 316).

TABLE 2.4 To Facilitate the Calculation of T Scores

The percentage refers to the percentage of the total frequency below a given score +1/2 of the frequency on that score. T scores are read directly from the given percentages.*

%	T Score	%	T Score	%	T Score
0.0032	10	9.68	37	91.92	64
0.0048	11	11.51	38	93.32	65
0.007	12	13.57	39	94.52	66
0.011	13	15.87	40	95.54	67
0.016	14	18.41	41	96.41	68
0.023	15	21.19	42	97.13	69
0.034	16	24.20	43	97.72	70
0.048	17	27.43	44	98.21	71
0.069	18	30.85	45	98.61	72
0.097	19	34.46	46	98.93	73
0.13	20	38.21	47	99.18	74
0.19	21	42.07	48	99.38	75
0.26	22	46.02	49	99.53	76
0.35	23	50.00	50	99.65	77

%	*T* Score	%	*T* Score	%	*T* Score
0.47	24	53.98	51	99.74	78
0.62	25	57.93	52	99.81	79
0.82	26	61.79	53	99.865	80
1.07	27	65.54	53	99.903	81
1.39	28	69.15	55	99.931	82
1.79	29	72.57	56	99.952	83
2.28	30	75.80	57	99.966	84
2.87	31	78.81	58	99.977	85
3.59	32	81.59	59	99.984	86
4.46	33	84.13	60	99.9890	87
5.48	34	86.43	61	99.9928	88
6.68	35	88.49	62	99.9952	89
8.08	36	90.32	63	99.9968	90

Source: Garrett (1966, p. 467).

Note: *T scores fewer than 10 or above 90 differs so slightly that they cannot be read as different two-place numbers.

2.5 NON-PARAMETRIC METHODS

Parametric statistics (using mean, SD, test, correlations, regression, etc.) assume a large sample and normal distribution of data. When these cannot be used, chi-square is an oft-used non-parametric test. An excellent book for non-parametric tests is written by Siegel (1956).

In most non-parametric tests, median is used in place of mean. When data is small, non-parametric tests are more appropriate. One popular non-parametric test is chi-square. It is described further in a little detail. Some non-parametric tests can be used without the help of a computer. Some can be simplified, so that these can be easily used by trainers/HRD facilitators and no computations are involved. Two such tests—sign test and Mann-Whitney U test—are discussed in the chapter. Both the tests are self-explanatory.

2.5.1 Chi-square Test

Chi-square test is a statistical test used to examine differences with categorical variables, such as sexual orientation, religious affiliation, political preference, etc. The chi-square test is used for

1. estimating how closely an observed distribution matches an expected distribution—we'll refer to this as the *goodness-of-fit test*, and
2. estimating whether two random variables are independent.

The other primary use of the chi-square test is to examine whether two variables are independent or are related.

2.5.1.1 The Goodness-of-Fit Test

The following steps are used in calculating a goodness-of-fit test with chi-square:

1. *Establish hypotheses*—The null hypothesis is that the two variables are independent or, in this particular case, that the likelihood of being punctual is the same for boys and girls.
2. Calculate chi-square statistic on the basis of
   - The number of observations
   - Expected values
   - Observed values

As with the goodness-of-fit example described earlier, the key idea of the chi-square test for independence is a comparison of observed and expected values. How many of something was expected and how many were observed in some process? Rather, in this use of the chi-square test, expected values are calculated based on the row and column totals from the table. The expected value for each cell of the table can be calculated using the following formula:

$$\frac{\text{Row total} \times \text{Column total}}{\text{Total } n \text{ for table}}$$

3. Assess significance level.

$$\text{Chi-square} = \text{Sum of } \frac{(\text{observed frequency} - \text{expected frequency})^2}{(\text{expected frequency})}$$

4. Finally, decide whether to accept or reject the null hypothesis.
   Lastly, to determine the significance level, we need to know the 'degrees of freedom'. In case of the chi-square test of independence, the number of degrees of freedom is equal to the number of columns in the table minus one multiplied by the number of rows in the table minus one.

2.5.2 Sign Test

Use: This can be used when a variable under consideration has a continuous distribution, but quantitative measurement is not available, and two members of each pair can be ranked or rated. For example, subjects rated before and after training, or a subject who attended a programme paired with his colleague who did not attend, can be rated on an attribute.

Steps:

1. Prepare all pairs to be studied.
2. Note down the direction of difference (positive '+', negative '–' or no difference '0').
3. Ignore no difference ('0'). Consider the remaining pairs. N is the total number of pairs in which there is a positive or negative difference. X is the smaller number of pairs with a difference. For example, if out of 10 pairs, 7 pairs show positive difference (+) and 3 negative (–), $N = 10$, $X = 3$.
4. Consult Table 2.5 to find the level of significance of the difference. Usually, the minimum acceptable level is 05 (any level higher, e.g. 0.02, 0.01, 0.001 is better). X beyond 8 is not given, as the level of significance for X of 8 to 25 (and beyond) is more than 0.10.

2.5.3 Mann–Whitney U Test

Use: This is one of the most powerful tests to test significance of differences between two groups (say experimental and control groups), especially when there are small numbers.

Steps:

1. Combine scores from both groups, and rank them in order of increasing size. N_1 is the smaller, and N_2 the larger of the two groups.
2. Count the number of N_1 cases that precede each score in the N_2 group. Add all these. This is U value.

   For example, experimental (E) Group N_1 (4 persons) has scores of 5, 8, 10 and 13; Control (C) Group N_2 (5 persons) has scores of 3, 4, 6, 9 and 12.

   The scores can then be rearranged as shown:

3	4	5	6	8	9	10	12	13
C	C	E	C	E	C	E	C	E

   For C scores 3 and 4, there are no scores proceeding. For C score 6, 1 E score precedes; for 9, 2 precedes; for 12, 3 precedes.

   $$U = 1 + 2 + 3 = 6$$

3. Consult Table 2.6 to see what value of U is significant at 0.05 level, using N_1 and N_2. In the given example with $N_1 = 4$ and $N_2 = 5$, we should have a minimum value of 2 of U for significance of difference at 0.05 level. The value in this case is 6, so the difference is clearly significant.

TABLE 2.5 Level of Significance in Sign Test*

X \ N	5	6	7	8	9	10	11	12	13	14	15	16	17	18	19	20	21	22	23	24	25
0	031	016	008	004	002	001	001														
1	188	109	062	035	020	011	006	003	002	001											
2	500	344	227	145	090	055	033	019	011	006	004	002	001								
3	812	656	500	363	254	172	113	073	046	029	018	011	006	004	002	001					
4	969	891	773	637	500	377	274	194	133	090	059	038	025	015	010	006	004	002	001	001	
5		984	938	855	746	623	500	387	291	212	151	105	072	048	032	021	013	008	005	003	002
6			992	965	910	828	726	613	500	395	304	227	166	119	084	058	039	026	017	011	007
7				996	980	945	887	806	709	605	500	402	315	240	180	132	095	067	047	032	022
8					998	989	967	927	867	788	696	598	500	407	324	252	192	143	105	076	054

Note: *Decimal points have been omitted.

TABLE 2.6 Level of Significance in U Test*

X \ N	5	6	7	8	9	10	11	12	13	14	15	16	17	18	19	20	21	22	23	24	25
0	031	016	008	004	002	001	001														
1	188	109	062	035	020	011	006	003	002	001											
2	500	344	227	145	090	055	033	019	011	006	004	002	001								
3	812	656	500	363	254	172	113	073	046	029	018	011	006	004	002	001					
4	969	891	773	637	500	377	274	194	133	090	059	038	025	015	010	006	004	002	001	001	
5		984	938	855	746	623	500	387	291	212	151	105	072	048	032	021	013	008	005	003	002
6			992	965	910	828	726	613	500	395	304	227	166	119	084	058	039	026	017	011	007
7				996	980	945	887	806	709	605	500	402	315	240	180	132	095	067	047	032	022
8					998	989	967	927	867	788	696	598	500	407	324	252	192	143	105	076	054

Note: *Decimal points have been omitted.

Developing Instruments for HRD

S ometimes, standardised instruments are not readily available and HRD facilitators may like to develop their own instruments. In some cases, the available instruments may have been developed and standardised either in another culture or on a sample unrelated to the population with which the HRD facilitator is dealing. For example, leadership styles or conflict management styles assessed from the responses to a set of industrial situations may not be relevant for an NGO or a public health system. In such a case, standard instruments can be tested and, if found applicable, adapted to a particular situation. There may be a third reason for developing an instrument. Evaluation of training programmes/inputs may require the use of special and quickly developed instruments.

There is a fairly standard procedure for preparing an instrument, which can be found in any textbook of psychometry. Although the process is simple, the creativity of the person who prepares instruments is important. Creativity lies in choosing appropriate conceptual models, innovating in the design of the instruments and making them practical and usable by practicing managers.

3.1 STEPS INVOLVED IN PREPARING INSTRUMENTS

3.1.1 Identifying Variables to Be Measured

Among the variables that are relevant to a particular phenomenon related to individuals, groups or organisation, the one that is critical and central is selected. For example, in participative style of management, locus of control, empathy, assertiveness, leadership style, decision-making style (for individuals) cohesion, productivity (for groups), or climate, culture, delegation, organisational health (for organisations) may be relevant variables for preparing instruments.

3.1.2 Seeking an Appropriate Theory

The variable selected can be explained by using some conceptual framework. A conceptual framework that is most relevant, capable of generating meaningful data and with potential for practical implications may be selected. For example, in measuring managerial style, the transactional analysis framework, both popular and having application potential, was selected in developing an instrument for managerial styles—TSI-M (Chapter 35). Details and frameworks are also given in the chapter.

3.1.3 Collecting Items

Items are collected by observing and interviewing practitioners. For example, for the instrument just cited, managers involved in counselling and helping interactions were observed. 'Effective' and 'less effective' managers were then interviewed on how they behaved in situations requiring, for example, parental role (establishing norms and nurturing), and the ways they found (based on their experiences at the receiving end) to be more effective in enabling them to deal with issues. All such experiences are converted into 'items' (statements, in this case, in behavioural terms). A long list of items is then ready. In the given example, about 60 items were prepared.

Since the main purpose of an HRD instrument is to help individuals, groups and/or organisations to use feedback data for change and improvement, it is useful to use behavioural statements; also, it is easier to modify one's behaviour than to change one's orientation, 'motivation' or 'attitude'. To take the example of TSI-M, the OK Parent (supportive style of a manager) would show the following behaviour:

1. Be available for help to subordinates, and assure them of his availability.
2. Help subordinates to know their own strengths.
3. Reassure subordinates of his continued help to them.

In contrast to this is the not-OK Parent's rescuing style which would show the following behaviour:

1. Give his subordinates the needed solutions to their problems almost always, thereby depriving them of an opportunity to develop their own capabilities to find solutions.
2. Guide subordinates in details, rather than giving broad guidelines and encouraging them to ask questions.
3. Encourage subordinates to come (almost always) for advice and help, thereby increasing their dependence.

While preparing items, such behavioural indices may be kept in mind. The exact item statement will depend on the format to be used. If a 3- or 5-point scale is used, the frequency from 'rarely' to 'always' can be used; if paired comparison is to be used, then the statement has to be much more exact.

3.1.4 Editing Items

The first editing is done by thoroughly examining the list, consulting some colleagues in this process and eliminating the obviously less relevant items. In the current example, about 10 items were eliminated, leaving a list of about 50. A response pattern (say 5-point scale) is used for scoring.

3.1.5 Item Analysis

Item analysis is done to decide whether an item should be included in an instrument or not. For item analysis, the draft instrument is administered to a large (above 50) representative sample of respondents. Then, item difficulty and item discrimination indices can be calculated. Item difficulty is the proportion of respondents answering an item correctly. The greater the proportion of respondents with correct answers, the less is the difficulty level of the item. The range of 0.3–0.7 is desirable.

Since most of the instruments we use do not have 'correct' answers, we can replace correct by 'positive'. We can term such an index as 'response index', showing how much varied the responses are. In a 5-point scale (the mostly used format), we can use three ways to calculate 'response index': (a) we can add the two extreme ends (1 + 2, and 4 + 5) and use these for calculation; (b) we can use the mean value of an item (The range of mean should be between 1.5 and 4.5, preferably between 2 and 4. Items outside this range need to be examined.); and (c) we can use SD(s) of items. If SD of an item is 1 or less, then we may re-examine that item because it shows low variability of the item.

The item discrimination index shows how much the item discriminates between high and low scorers on an instrument. There are two ways of finding item discrimination. High or low scorers are between top and bottom 25 and 33% in a large sample. To get item discrimination index (Di) we subtract the number of bottom low scorers on the total instrument (say 30%) who answered an item positively (Li) from the number of top scorers on the total instrument (say 30%) who answered the item positively (Ui), and then divide it by the total number of those who are the top upper (or lower) scorers ($\dot{m}$).

$$Di = Ui - Li/\dot{m}$$

The second method of calculating item discrimination is to find out the point-biserial correlation between an item and the total score of the instrument. Item discrimination index should always be positive.

3.1.6 Standardisation

The instrument thus prepared is administered to a large sample (say 500). Standardisation involves establishing reliability, validity and norms for the instruments.

Reliability: In everyday language, reliability means dependability or consistency. In psychometrics, reliability refers to the consistency in measurement. Reliability coefficient is the degree of reliability of an instrument. The following are the three common methods of testing reliability of an instrument.

1. *Test-retest reliability*: This is found out by correlating the scores of the respondents answering the same instrument twice. In order to avoid carry-over effect due to memory (if the interval between two administrations is very short) and change effect due to various factors (if the interval is too long), it is advisable to have the second administration between six weeks and three months after the first administration.

2. *Parallel-forms reliability*: This is calculated (also known as coefficient of equivalence) by correlating scores of a set of respondents on two parallel forms of the instrument.

3. *Internal-consistency reliability*: Internal-consistency reliability is a way to gauge how well a test or survey is actually measuring what you want it to measure. This is the most widely used method of reliability. It is calculated by using only one instrument. It is very convenient. Statistical packages such as SPSS have internal-consistency programs, and various coefficients can be generated from the instrument data. The most widely used is the split-half method. The instrument can be split in the middle, or into even and odd items, and the scores of the halves are correlated. A more sophisticated method (called the method of random subsets) involves the following steps:
   a. Calculation of item difficulty index (proportion of respondents with positive response)
   b. Biserial or point-biserial correlation between the item score and the total score
   c. Pairing items close on the graph plotted with these two statistics and forming two parallel forms of the instruments
   d. Correlating the two forms

If the halves of an instrument are parallel (equal mean and variance), Spearman–Brown formula (Spearman, 1910; Brown, 1910) is used. If the halves have unequal variance, Cronbach's coefficient alpha is used, giving the lower bound for the reliability (high value shows high reliability, but low value does not necessarily show low reliability). Kuder and Richardson (1937) had originally suggested the formula, and their 20th formula became popular (called KR-20), which was later modified by Cronbach. Spearman–Brown formula is used to predict the effects of changes in the length of the instrument on its reliability. The formula is also used to decide the length of an instrument.

Validity: An instrument is valid if it measures what it is meant to measure. There are three types of validity: content validity, criterion-related validity and construct validity.

1. *Content validity* is based on a subjective examination of the items. There are two types of content validity: face validity and logical validity. An instrument has face validity if an examination of the items leads to the conclusion that the items are measuring what they are supposed to measure. Logical validity is based on a careful comparison of the items to the definition of the domain being measured.
2. *Criterion-related validity* can be found by relating a test score to a criterion score. A predictor score (X) can be used to predict a criterion score (Y) using linear regression. When the criterion is dichotomous, a hit rate—the proportion of decisions that are correct—can be compared to base rates calculated from other classification procedures or to a base rate determined by the more frequently occurring outcome. Taylor–Russell tables (Nugent, 2013) allow the instrument user to estimate the number of correct decisions that a test score will produce, based on the test-validity coefficient, selection ratio (the proportion of applicants who are chosen) and the base rate (the proportion of applicants who would be successful). Use of the Taylor–Russell tables assumes that the predictor (test) scores and criterion scores have a bivariate normal distribution.
3. *Construct validity* involves the verification of predictions made about the test scores. Multitrait-multimethod validity is a type of construct validity that is based on examining the pattern of correlations among tests measuring a set of traits in different ways. Instruments measuring the same traits should correlate highly, converging on the trait. Instruments measuring different traits should correlate less highly, discriminating among the traits. There should be no method bias revealed in the correlations. Factor analysis is also used to establish construct validity by factor analysing the correlations of scores on an instrument and obtaining a predicted factor loading pattern.

Norms: These are the standards against which a score can be judged as low, normal or high. Generally, these are calculated from a large sample data (say 1,000) in terms of the mean and SD values. Generally, mean +1 SD is high and mean –1 SD is low. Sometimes, we also use .5 SD difference for the cut-off points of low and high. However, the score one obtains is more meaningful when it is compared with the group to which the participant belongs (e.g., Indian vs. American, middle managers vs. top managers, engineering industry vs. service industry, etc.). Norms can be developed for specific groups based on age, languages, gender, rural–urban, grades, etc.

3.1.7 Revision of the Instrument

The collected data and a person's experience in administering the instrument may help to suggest some changes. For example, for the instrument being cited, one additional aspect of the child ego state was pointed out by a colleague, leading to an addition of six more items. The revised version then had 36 items. Revision can also be made on the basis of factor analysis of the data. For example, factor analysis of data from eight role stresses suggested addition of two more variables. The instrument—organisational role stress—then had 10 stresses (see Pareek, 1993, Chapter 6).

3.2 FORMAT OF THE INSTRUMENT

Several formats can be used to get responses to items in an instrument. Some of the common formats are discussed in this section.

3.2.1 Checklist

A simple format requires respondents to check each item in a list to indicate 'yes' or 'no' response. This is a popular format as respondents find it much easier to answer as 'yes' or 'no', rather than to make finer discriminations in their responses.

3.2.2 Paired Comparison

Asking respondents to choose one item in a pair is the most convenient format. The items in a pair need to be equally 'socially desirable' and should represent two contrasting variables. For example, the following may be a suitable pair of proverbs to measure locus of control:

   a.   Man proposes, God disposes.
   b.   God helps those who help themselves.

The first statement (a) in the pair shows external locus of control while the second (b) shows internal locus of control. A series of such statements can be used to prepare a locus of control instrument.

Paired comparison can also be used with several variables. In such a case, each variable is paired with every other variable and the number of pairs will be $n(n-1)/2$. If there are six variables, there will be 15 pairs. While preparing such pairs, each variable needs to be half the time in the first place (a) and half the time in the second place (b) in a pair, and they should be put at the maximum distance of its recurrence in the instrument. Sophisticated scaling analysis can be done by paired comparison. Good references are available on this technique (see Edwards, 1957, Chapters 2, 3; Torgerson, 1958, Chapter 11).

An example of scaling preferences for five contraceptive methods by a group of 18 health administrators is used here. In paired comparison, the following steps are involved:

1. Prepare pairs of the items to be scaled. For example, to find out scale values of the preference of five contraceptive methods, pair each method with the other. We shall have $(n*n - 1)/2$ or, in this case, $5*4/2 = 10$. Make sure that each item appears about half the time as the first item and about half the time as the second item in the pairs, and that the pairs containing it are kept at maximum distance in the order.

2. Present the pairs (in the example, 10 pairs) to each respondent, asking him to check the one item he prefers in each pair over the other.

3. Prepare a frequency matrix (F matrix), giving the frequency with which the items in the column are preferred over the items in the row. Table 3.1 gives the F matrix prepared from individual responses.

4. By dividing each cell entry in F matrix by n (number of respondents) prepare P matrix (see Table 3.2).

5. Prepare Z matrix by consulting Table 3.3. For each P value in the P matrix (see Table 3.2), write the corresponding Z value from Table 3.3. The Z matrix thus prepared is shown in Table 3.4.

6. Add the columns in the Z matrix, find the mean values of each column and add the highest negative value to all the items. The item with the highest negative value will become zero (0). Round off the scale values. Now, we have the scale values of all the items. See Table 3.4, which gives scale values of the five contraceptive methods obtained from the group.

7. Internal consistency of the scale can be checked. This will show how well the observed preferred values agree with those to be expected in terms of the derived values. This is a reliability test. The following steps are involved:

    a. Prepare a matrix (theoretical normal deviates) with the obtained increasing scale values from Table 3.4, row 8, reproduced in both the first column and the first row of Table 3.5.

    b. Subtract in order the entries in the first column from the entries shown in the first row and complete the matrix below the diagonal. These are shown in Table 3.5.

    c. Prepare a matrix (theoretical proportions) from Table 3.3 by locating in each value the columns of Table 3.4 in the body and reading the corresponding P values given in the first column. Write these down in the new matrix (see Table 3.6).

    d. Prepare a discrepancy matrix (see Table 3.7) by subtracting entries in Table 3.6 from the corresponding entries in Table 3.2.

    e. Add the columns in discrepancy matrix (see Table 3.7). Add all the total discrepancy values given in the last row and divide it by the number of discrepancies (entries) in the matrix. This will give the mean discrepancy value. If the value is lower than 0.03, the internal consistency is of acceptable level. In this case, the value is 0.5. This falls short of the acceptable level of 0.03.

TABLE 3.1   Column Item is Preferred over Row Items

Contraceptive Methods	1	2	3	4	5
1. Oral pill	–	10	13	5	13
2. Condom (F)	8	–	10	12	10
3. Copper T	5	8	–	11	11
4. Sterilisation (M)	13	6	7	–	7
5. Sterilisation (F)	5	8	7	11	–

TABLE 3.2   P Matrix Proportion of Times Column Items are Preferred over Row Items

Contraceptive Methods	1	2	3	4	5
1. Oral pill	0.500	0.556	0.722	0.278	0.722
2. Condom	0.444	0.500	0.556	0.667	0.556
3. Copper T	0.278	0.444	0.500	0.611	0.611
4. Sterilisation (M)	0.722	0.333	0.389	0.500	0.389
5. Sterilisation (F)	0.278	0.444	0.389	0.611	0.500
Total	2.242	2.277	2.556	0.2667	0.2778

TABLE 3.3   Table of Normal Deviates Z Corresponding to Proportions P of a Dichotomised Unit Normal Distribution

P	0	1	2	3	4	5	6	7	8	9
0.99	2.326	2.366	2.409	2.457	2.512	2.576	2.652	2.748	2.878	3.090
0.98	2.054	2.075	2.097	2.120	2.144	2.170	2.197	2.226	2.257	2.290
0.97	1.881	1.896	1.911	1.927	1.943	1.960	1.977	1.995	2.014	2.034
0.96	1.751	1.762	1.774	1.787	1.799	1.812	1.825	1.838	1.852	1.866
0.95	1.645	1.655	1.655	1.675	1.685	1.695	1.706	1.717	1.728	1.739
0.94	1.555	1.563	1.572	1.580	1.589	1.598	1.607	1.616	1.626	1.635
0.93	1.476	1.483	1.491	1.499	1.506	1.514	1.522	1.530	1.538	1.546
0.92	1.405	1.412	1.419	1.426	1.433	1.440	1.447	1.454	1.461	1.468
0.91	1.341	1.347	1.353	1.359	1.366	1.372	1.379	1.385	1.392	1.398
0.90	1.282	1.287	1.293	1.299	1.305	1.311	1.317	1.323	1.329	1.335
0.89	1.227	1.232	1.237	1.243	1.248	1.254	1.259	1.265	1.270	1.276

P	0	1	2	3	4	5	6	7	8	9
0.88	1.175	1.180	1.185	1.190	1.195	1.200	1.206	1.211	1.216	1.221
0.87	1.126	1.131	1.136	1.141	1.146	1.150	1.155	1.160	1.165	1.170
0.86	1.080	1.085	1.089	1.094	1.098	1.103	1.108	1.112	1.117	1.122
0.85	1.036	1.041	1.045	1.049	1.054	1.058	1.063	1.067	1.071	1.076
0.84	0.994	0.999	1.003	1.007	1.001	1.015	1.019	1.024	1.028	1.032
0.83	0.954	0.958	0.962	0.966	0.970	0.974	0.978	0.982	0.986	0.990
0.82	0.915	0.919	0.923	0.927	0.931	0.935	0.938	0.942	0.946	0.950
0.81	0.878	0.882	0.885	0.889	0.893	0.896	0.900	0.904	0.908	0.912
0.80	0.842	0.845	0.849	0.852	0.856	0.860	0.863	0.867	0.871	0.874
0.79	0.806	0.810	0.813	0.817	0.820	0.824	0.827	0.831	0.834	0.838
0.78	0.772	0.776	0.779	0.782	0.786	0.789	0.793	0.796	0.800	0.803
0.77	0.739	0.742	0.745	0.740	0.752	0.755	0.769	0.762	0.765	0.769
0.76	0.706	0.710	0.713	0.716	0.719	0.722	0.726	0.729	0.732	0.736
0.75	0.674	0.678	0.681	0.684	0.687	0.690	0.693	0.697	0.700	0.703
0.74	0.643	0.646	0.650	0.653	0.656	0.659	0.662	0.665	0.668	0.671
0.73	0.613	0.616	0.619	0.622	0.625	0.628	0.631	0.634	0.637	0.640
0.72	0.583	0.586	0.589	0.592	0.595	0.598	0.601	0.604	0.607	0.610
0.71	0.553	0.556	0.559	0.562	0.565	0.568	0.571	0.574	0.577	0.580
0.70	0.524	0.527	0.530	0.533	0.536	0.539	0.542	0.545	0.548	0.550
0.69	0.496	0.499	0.502	0.504	0.507	0.510	0.513	0.516	0.519	0.522
0.68	0.468	0.470	0.473	0.476	0.479	0.482	0.485	0.487	0.490	0.493
0.67	0.440	0.443	0.445	0.448	0.451	0.454	0.457	0.459	0.462	0.465
0.66	0.412	0.415	0.418	0.421	0.423	0.426	0.429	0.432	0.434	0.437
0.65	0.385	0.388	0.391	0.393	0.396	0.399	0.402	0.404	0.407	0.410
0.64	0.358	0.361	0.364	0.366	0.369	0.372	0.375	0.377	0.380	0.383
0.63	0.332	0.335	0.337	0.340	0.342	0.345	0.348	0.350	0.353	0.356
0.62	0.305	0.308	0.311	0.313	0.316	0.319	0.321	0.324	0.327	0.329
0.61	0.279	0.282	0.285	0.287	0.290	0.292	0.295	0.298	0.300	0.303
0.60	0.253	0.256	0.259	0.261	0.264	0.266	0.269	0.272	0.274	0.277
0.59	0.228	0.230	0.233	0.235	0.238	0.240	0.243	0.246	0.248	0.251
0.58	0.202	0.204	0.207	0.210	0.212	0.215	0.217	0.220	0.222	0.225
0.57	0.176	0.179	0.181	0.184	0.187	0.189	0.192	0.194	0.197	0.199
0.56	0.151	0.154	0.156	0.159	0.161	0.164	0.166	0.169	0.171	0.174
0.55	0.126	0.128	0.131	0.133	0.136	0.138	0.141	0.143	0.146	0.148
0.54	0.100	0.103	0.105	0.108	0.111	0.113	0.116	0.118	0.121	0.123
0.53	0.075	0.078	0.080	0.083	0.085	0.088	0.090	0.093	0.095	0.098
0.52	0.050	0.053	0.055	0.058	0.060	0.063	0.065	0.068	0.070	0.073
0.51	0.025	0.028	0.030	0.033	0.035	0.038	0.040	0.043	0.045	0.048
0.50	0.000	0.003	0.005	0.008	0.010	0.013	0.015	0.018	0.020	0.023
0.49	−0.025	−0.023	−0.020	−0.018	−0.013	−0.010	−0.008	−0.005	−0.003	
0.48	−0.050	−0.048	−0.045	−0.043	−0.040	−0.038	−0.035	−0.033	−0.030	−0.028
0.47	−0.075	−0.073	−0.070	−0.068	−0.065	−0.063	−0.060	−0.058	−0.055	−0.053
0.46	−0.100	−0.098	−0.095	−0.093	−0.090	−0.088	−0.085	−0.083	−0.080	−0.078
0.45	−0.126	−0.126	−0.123	−0.121	−0.118	−0.116	−0.113	−0.111	−0.108	−0.105
0.44	−0.151	−0.148	−0.146	−0.143	−0.141	−0.138	−0.136	−0.133	−0.131	−0.128
0.43	−0.176	−0.174	−0.171	−0.169	−0.166	−0.164	−0.161	−0.159	−0.156	−0.154

(Table 3.3 Continued)

(Table 3.3 Continued)

P	0	1	2	3	4	5	6	7	8	9
0.42	−0.202	−0.199	−0.197	−0.194	−0.192	−0.189	−0.187	−0.184	−0.181	−0.179
0.41	−0.228	−0.225	−0.222	−0.220	−0.217	−0.215	−0.212	−0.210	−0.207	−0.204
0.40	−0.253	−0.251	−0.248	−0.246	−0.243	−0.240	−0.238	−0.235	−0.233	−0.230
0.39	−0.279	−0.277	−0.274	−0.272	−0.269	−0.266	−0.264	−0.261	−0.259	−0.256
0.38	−0.305	−0.303	−0.300	−0.298	−0.295	−0.292	−0.290	−0.287	−0.285	−0.282
0.37	−0.332	−0.329	−0.327	−0.324	−0.321	−0.319	−0.316	−0.313	−0.311	−0.308
0.36	−0.358	−0.356	−0.353	−0.350	−0.348	−0.345	−0.342	−0.340	−0.337	−0.335
0.35	−0.385	−0.383	−0.380	−0.377	−0.375	−0.372	−0.369	−0.366	−0.364	−0.361
0.34	−0.412	−0.410	−0.407	−0.404	−0.402	−0.399	−0.396	−0.393	−0.391	−0.388
0.33	−0.440	−0.437	−0.434	−0.432	−0.429	−0.426	−0.423	−0.421	−0.418	−0.415
0.32	−0.468	−0.465	−0.462	−0.459	−0.457	−0.454	−0.451	−0.448	−0.445	−0.443
0.31	−0.496	−0.493	−0.490	−0.487	−0.485	−0.482	−0.479	−0.476	−0.473	−0.470
0.30	−0.524	−0.522	−0.519	−0.516	−0.513	−0.510	−0.507	−0.504	−0.502	−0.499
0.29	−0.553	−0.550	−0.548	−0.545	−0.542	−0.539	−0.536	−0.533	−0.530	−0.527
0.28	−0.583	−0.580	−0.577	−0.574	−0.571	−0.568	−0.565	−0.569	−0.566	−0.552
0.27	−0.613	−0.610	−0.607	−0.604	−0.601	−0.598	−0.595	−0.592	−0.589	−0.586
0.26	−0.643	−0.640	−0.637	−0.634	−0.631	−0.628	−0.625	−0.622	−0.619	−0.616
0.25	−0.674	−0.671	−0.668	−0.665	−0.662	−0.659	−0.656	−0.653	−0.650	−0.646
0.24	−0.706	−0.703	−0.700	−0.697	−0.693	−0.690	−0.687	−0.684	−0.681	−0.678
0.23	−0.739	−0.736	−0.732	−0.729	−0.726	−0.722	−0.719	−0.713	−0.710	
0.22	−0.772	−0.769	−0.765	−0.762	−0.755	−0.752	.021	−0.806	−0.803	−0.800
0.21	−0.806	−0.803	−0.800	−0.796	−0.793	−0.789	0.786	−0.782	−0.779	−0.776
0.20	−0.842	−0.838	−0.834	−0.831	−0.827	−0.824	−0.820	−0.817	−0.813	−0.810
0.19	−0.878	−0.874	−0.871	−0.867	−0.863	−0.860	−0.856	−0.852	−0.849	−0.845
0.18	−0.915	−0.912	−0.908	−0.904	−0.900	−0.896	−0.893	−0.889	−0.885	−0.882
0.17	−0.954	−0.950	−0.946	−0.942	−0.938	−0.935	−0.931	−0.927	−0.923	−0.919
0.16	−0.994	−0.990	−0.986	−0.982	−0.978	−0.974	−0.970	−0.966	−0.962	−0.958
0.15	−1.036	−1.032	−1.028	−1.024	−1.019	−1.019	−1.015	−1.011	−.007	−1.003
0.14	−1.080	−1.076	−1.071	−1.067	−1.063	−1.058	−1.054	−1.049	−1.045	−1.041
0.13	−1.126	−1.122	−1.117	−1.112	−1.108	−1.103	−1.098	−1.094	−1.089	−1.085
0.12	−1.175	−1.170	−1.165	−1.160	−1.155	−1.150	−1.146	−1.141	−1.136	−1.131
0.11	−1.227	−1.221	−1.216	−1.211	−1.206	−1.200	−1.195	−1.190	−1.185	−1.180
0.10	−1.282	−1.276	−1.270	−1.265	−1.259	−1.254	−1.248	−1.243	−1.237	−1.232
0.09	−1.341	−1.335	−1.329	−1.323	−1.317	−1.311	−1.305	−1.299	−1.293	−1.287
0.08	−1.405	−1.398	−1.392	−1.385	−1.379	−1.372	−1.366	−1.359	−1.353	−1.347
0.07	−1.476	−1.468	−1.461	−1.454	−1.447	−1.440	−1.433	−1.426	−1.419	−1.412
0.06	−1.555	−1.546	−1.538	−1.530	−1.522	−1.514	−1.506	−1.499	−1.491	−1.483
0.05	−1.645	−1.635	−1.626	−1.616	−1.607	−1.598	−1.589	−1.580	−1.572	−1.563
0.04	−1.751	−1.739	−1.728	−1.717	−1.706	−1.695	−1.685	−1.675	−1.665	−1.655
0.03	−1.881	−1.866	−1.852	−1.838	−1.825	−1.812	−1.799	−1.787	−1.774	−1.762
0.02	−2.054	−2.034	−2.014	−1.995	−1.977	−1.960	−1.943	−1.927	−1.911	−1.896
0.01	−2.326	−2.290	−2.257	−2.226	−2.197	−2.170	−2.144	−2.120	−2.097	−2.075
0.00		−3.090	−2.878	−2.748	−2.652	−2.576	−2.512	−2.457	−2.409	−2.366

Source: Edwards (1957, pp. 246–47).

TABLE 3.4 Z Matrix Normal Deviants of P Values

Contraceptive Methods	1	2	3	4	5
1. Oral pill	0.000	0.141	0.589	−0.589	.589
2. Condom	−0.141	0.000	0.141	0.432	.141
3. Copper T	−0.589	−0.141	0.000	0.282	.282
4. Sterilisation (M)	0.589	−0.432	−0.282	0.000	.282
5. Sterilisation (F)	0.589	−0.141	−0.282	0.282	.000
Total	−0.730	−0.573	0.166	0.407	.730
Means	−0.146	−0.115	−0.033	−0.081	−.146
Means + 146	.000	0.031	0.179	0.227	0.292
Rounded (Scale Values)	000	3	18	23	29

TABLE 3.5 Theoretical Normal Deviates of Scale Distances

Contraceptive Methods	Scale Values	1 0.000	2 0.031	3 0.179	4 0.227	5 0.292
1. Oral pill	0.000					
2. Condom	0.031	−0.031				
3. Copper T	0.179	−0.179	−0.148			
4. Sterilisation (M)	0.227	−0.227	−0.196	−0.048		
5. Sterilisation (F)	0.292	−0.292	−0.261	−0.113	−0.065	

TABLE 3.6 Theoretical Proportion of Normal Deviates

Contraceptive Methods	1	2	3	4
1. Condom	0.488			
2. Copper T	0.429	0.441		
3. Sterilisation (M)	0.410	0.422	0.481	
4. Sterilisation (F)	0.385	0.397	0.455	0.474

TABLE 3.7   Discrepancy Table of Proportion (Tables 3.2 and 3.6)

Contraceptive Methods	1	2	3	4	5
1. Oral pill					
2. Condom	0.044				
3. Copper T	0.151	0.003			
4. Sterilisation (M)	0.312	−0.089	−0.092		
5. Sterilisation (F)	0.107	0.047	−0.066	0.137	
Total	0.010	−0.039	−0.158	0.137	= −0.50

8. Another test of consistency for individual responses is the number of circular triads present in the responses of a respondent. If a is preferred to b, b to c, and c to a, then it is called a circular triad, an evidence of inconsistency because, logically, a should be preferred to c. Zeta (index of consistency) can range from 0 to 1.00. The steps followed in calculating circular triads and Zeta can be found in any book of scaling (e.g., Edwards, 1957).

3.2.3 Summated Ratings

This format, Likert scale, popularly known by the person who introduced it, is widely used. Usually a 5-point scale is used—very high or almost always; high or frequently; sometimes; low or occasionally; and very low or rarely. In order to avoid people choosing a middle response, a 4-point scale can be used. A 3-point scale can be used with respondents who find it difficult to make a finer discrimination. Various aspects of reliability and validity in this technique have been discussed very well by Edwards (1957, Chapter 7).

3.2.4 Semantic Differential

Semantic differential, originally suggested and used by Osgood, uses a bipolar scale—two contrasting poles of a variable such as good and bad, strong and weak, fast and slow.

Sometimes, the space between the two poles is numbered from 1 to 7, and sometimes from −3 to +3. The first system gets rid of the minus sign while the second clearly indicates whether the rating is positive or negative. Osgood and his colleagues (1957) found three basic dimensions that accounted for various ways in which people understood or reacted to things. These are evaluation—whether the person likes it; potency—whether the person thinks it is powerful; and activity—whether the person thinks it is moving.

The person who develops semantic differential can add bipolar labels that fit his area of interest. For example, open–closed, risky–cautious, demanding–yielding. The social objects that are to be rated may be better limited by time and energy. For example, this organisation, this organisation 10 years from now, me, my ideal self, my role, etc. can be used for semantic differential.

3.2.5 Equal Appearing Interval Scale

This is popularly known as Thurstone scale (1927) (after the person who first proposed it). The following steps are involved:

1. Collect a large number of items on the subject from several sources.
2. Edit them (have a minimum of 50).
3. Write each item on a separate card or a slip of paper.
4. Select judges (at least 30, who know the subject very well).
5. Have each judge rate each item on an 11-point scale for the degree to which it represents the variable (subject)—from the 'most characteristic' (11) to the 'least characteristic' (1).
6. Collect data from all judges and tabulate it in a table (Table 3.8). F = frequency of judges; P = proportion (f divided by total number of judges); cp = cumulative proportion.
7. Calculate mdn (median) Q1 and Q3 values of each item by the following formulae and prepare a table like Table 3.9.

$$\text{Median } [(\text{mdn}) = L + [(0.50 - 3\text{epb})/\text{pw}]$$
$$Q1 = L + [(0.25 - \text{epb})/\text{pw}]$$
$$Q3 = L + [(0.75 - \text{epb})/\text{pw}]$$

Where L = the lower limit of the interval in which the mdn (0.50), Q1 (0.25) or Q3 (0.75) falls; epb = the sum of the proportions below the interval in which mdn, Q1 and Q3 fall; pw = the proportion within the interval in which mdn, Q1 and Q3 fall.

8. Renumber and tabulate the items in descending order of their scale values along with their Q values, as shown in Table 3.9.
9. Select items (about 10–11 or 20–21) showing equal intervals and low Q values.
10. Prepare the scale by putting items in random order. Use the scale requiring the respondent indicate his agreement with the items.
11. His score is the median scale value of the items checked by him—the score value of the middle item.

TABLE 3.8   Summary of Judgements

						Judgement Categories						
Items		1	2	3	4	5	6	7	8	9	10	11
1	f											
	p											
	cp											
2	p											
	cp											
...												
...												
...												
...												
...												
...												

TABLE 3.9   Item Analysis

Item	Median				Q1				Q3				Q & Scale Value	
	L	Epb	pw	Mdn	L	Epb	pw	Q1	L	Epb	pw	Q3	Q	Mdn Scale Value
1														
2														
3														
•														
•														
n														

3.2.6 Projective Instruments

Projective instruments are unstructured or semi-structured devices. Since they help respondents to project their mental states (thinking, attitudes, orientations, etc.), they are called projective techniques. The least structured projective instrument is the Rorschach test, which consists of some inkblots. After looking at an inkblot for a few seconds, a respondent is required to write whatever he sees in the pattern. Several personality aspects are scored from the responses. This is a very popular test. Another famous projective test is the Thematic Apperception Test (TAT), consisting of several pictures. A respondent looks at a picture and writes a story. The story is scored to analyse achievement and other motives (needs). McClelland popularised this test by using six selected pictures to measure achievement motivation (Atkinson, McClelland, Clark, 1958).

Several devices can be used to project orientations, attitudes, values, etc. Some of the devices used for HRD are as follows:

1. *Essays*: Essays on 'Who am I?' (see the instrument in Chapter 4) can be analysed for measuring personal efficacy. The same can be used to score sense of efficacy (Pfizer in the appendix in McClelland and Winter, 1969). Essays on 'My role' can be analysed to measure role efficacy (see Chapter 49).
2. *Adjectives*: Open-ended adjectives on a phenomenon, such as, role, also help a person to project his attitudes. These can then be analysed.
3. *Sentence completion*: Incomplete sentences can be given to stimulate imagery in a respondent, who is likely to project his attitude/values, etc., when completing them. Sentences such as, *My main goal in life is* …, *This organisation can be described as* …, etc. can be used to get a projected response.
4. *Guessing responses*: Some situations are briefly described, and the respondent is required to 'guess' how a person responded or would respond. In guessing the response, the respondent projects his own orientation. This has been employed for measuring fear of failure (see Chapter 22).
5. *Cartoon pictures*: A semi-structured device is an instrument in which several cartoon-like pictures are drawn, in which one character in the picture is shown saying something. The respondent is required to complete the blank box by guessing how the other person responded. This has been used in measuring attitudes to family planning, change-proneness, etc. A more complex phenomenon, such as, style of coping with stress, has also been measured by the use of such pictures (see Chapter 57).

In addition to paper-and-pencil instruments, instruments can be developed by using other sensory stimuli (auditory, olfactory, tactile, etc.). Situational tests have also been employed (e.g., a game). Unobtrusive measures (see Webb, Campbell, Schwartz, & Sechrest, 2000) and secondary source data can be imaginatively used to assess or measure phenomena. The field of measurement of orientation, values, behaviour, etc. is a creative field, and innovative devices can be developed by HRD managers, always ensuring their reliability and validity.

3.3 SCALES AND SCALING TECHNIQUES

There are four different levels or scales of measurement.

1. *Nominal scales*: A nominal level of measurement is simply a matter of distinguishing by name, for example, 1 = male, 2 = female. The binary category of 0 and 1 used for

computers is a nominal level of measurement. They are categories or classifications. Nominal measurement is like using categorical levels of variables, classification or sorting into exclusive and exhaustive sets, for example, gender.

2. *Ordinal scales*: Ordinal refers to order in measurement. An ordinal scale indicates direction in addition to providing nominal information. Low/medium/high or faster/slower are examples of ordinal levels of measurement. Many psychological scales or inventories are at the ordinal level of measurement. Ordinal scales can be produced by

   a. *Sorting techniques*. Q-sort requires respondents to distribute specified number of items into categories, usually conforming to the normal distribution curve. Each pile has a scale value. The value of an item is the mean of the 'pile scores' given by the respondents.

   b. *Paired comparison*. Discussed subsequently in this chapter (Section 3.2.2).

   c. *Rating scales*. Usually called method of summated ratings, popularly known as Likert scale. Use some points for scaling, usually 5 points.

3. *Interval scales*: Each unit is exactly equal to any other unit. Thurstone's scale (discussed in this chapter) is an example. Interval scales provide information about order and also possess equal intervals. An example of an interval scale is temperature, measured on either a Fahrenheit or a Celsius scale. A degree represents the same underlying amount of heat, regardless of where it occurs on the scale. Measured in Fahrenheit units, the difference between a temperature of 46 and 42 is the same as the difference between 72 and 68. Equal-interval scales of measurement can be devised for opinions and attitudes. Constructing them involves an understanding of mathematical and statistical principles beyond those covered in this course. But it is important to understand the different levels of measurement when using and interpreting scales.

4. *Ratio scales*: In addition to possessing the qualities of nominal, ordinal and interval scales, a ratio scale has an absolute zero—a point where none of the quality being measured exists. Using a ratio scale permits comparisons such as being twice as high or one-half as much.

PART

II

PERSONAL ORIENTATION AND BEHAVIOUR

Since the core of human resource development is the *self*, the final test of the effectiveness of HRD efforts is the changes that take place in a person. These changes include improved self-understanding and self-confidence, higher motivation (taking initiative, perseverance, meaningful relationships, etc.), impact making, optimising and belief that one can shape most of one's destiny. Part II of this book focuses on several aspects of personal and interpersonal orientation. The various chapters in this part briefly discuss conceptual models relevant to the instruments in this part.

1. Personal Efficacy and Effectiveness
   a. Personal Efficacy
   b. Personal Effectiveness
   c. Creativity
   d. Androgyny
   e. Interpersonal Trust

2. Locus of Control and Attribution
    a. Locus of Control
    b. Attribution
    c. Locus of Control and Health
    d. Optimism
    e. Rumination and Flow
3. Motivation
    a. Basic Psychological Needs
    b. Interpersonal Needs
    c. Intrinsic and Extrinsic Motivation
    d. Emotional Intelligence
    e. Work-Life Balance
4. Power
    a. Bases of Power
    b. Assertiveness
5. Values and Value Orientation
    a. Concept of Values
    b. Concept of Value Orientation

Personal Efficacy: Who Am I?

4.1 THE INSTRUMENT AND ITS ADMINISTRATION

This is a projective instrument. As discussed, a respondent is asked to write an essay on 'Who am I?' This helps him to project his self-concept and contains elements of personal efficacy. It is useful to have standardised instructions for this essay. If instructions differ, the essays written will reflect different dimensions and comparability will become difficult. The following is suggested:

Who Am I?
Think about yourself and write roughly two pages (about 400 words) about yourself. You may take about 30–40 minutes for this.

4.2 CONCEPTUAL FRAMEWORK

The self is at the centre of a person's competence. The term 'efficacy' has been used in the sense of potential effectiveness. Several related terms denoting efficacy need to be distinguished. Such distinctions have been discussed, for example, by Brockner (1988), and some of them are briefly defined here. *Self-esteem* is a 'trait reflecting an individual's characteristic, effective evaluation of the self (for example feelings of self-worth or self-liking)' (Gist & Mitchell, 1992). *Self-efficacy* 'refers to beliefs in one's capacities to mobilise the motivation, cognitive resources and courses of action to meet given situational demands' (Wood & Bandura, 1989).

Bandura (1982) proposed the concept of self-efficacy, and a lot of research has been done on this concept. Three aspects are important in self-efficacy. First, judgement of one's perceived capability to perform a specific task. Second, this judgement is not static and can change with new information. Third, it involves a mobilisation component, that is, differential performance.

Gist and Mitchell (1992) have proposed a three-dimensional model of efficacy determinants—locus of causality (external–internal), variability (over time and occasions) and controllability of the causal influence. Using two dimensions of the locus and variability of determinants, they have suggested that external determinants are task-related (attributes, complexity, number, sequencing) or environmental (interpersonal and task environments) and that ability–personality and performance strategy efforts are internal determinants. These determinants have implications for interventions to increase self-efficacy.

The concept of the sense of efficacy has been proposed by Pfizer (McClelland & Winter, 1969) in relation to goal (being vs. doing), locus of resources (internal vs. external resources or lack of resources), state (global vs. specific), action (initiative vs. compliance) and approach to problems (approach vs. avoidance).

Personal efficacy is the general sense of adequacy which is likely to contribute to a person's effectiveness in working for a task-related goal. It may be useful to consider what contributes to personal efficacy as this may help to devise the ways of measuring and analysing the variable. It is proposed here that four sets of factors contribute to personal efficacy—motivation, self-awareness, proactivity and action orientation.

4.2.1 Motivation

It is obvious that motivation is an important aspect of personal efficacy. An individual with high personal efficacy is a highly motivated individual.

Three motives (or needs) are fairly high in such a person—the need for efficiency or excellence (achievement motive); the need to influence others (power motive); and the need to pursue goals that are likely to help a large number of persons (extension motive).

Achievement motivation is reflected in the concern a person shows for competition either with others or with his own standards of performance, unique accomplishment or long-term involvement (McClelland, 1961). *Power motivation* is reflected in the urge to influence others or to change things etc. *Extension motivation* is reflected in the superordinate goal of an individual and the concern he shows for others. Super ordinate goal is one which transgresses the individual's personal needs. Sherif has used the concept in the sense of a goal being related to the needs of more than one individual or one group, and that which cannot be attained by the efforts of one individual or group alone (Sherif & Sherif, 1953). Concern for others would include concern for one's family, for other persons and for society at large.

4.2.2 Self-awareness

A person with high personal efficacy has higher awareness of both his strengths and his weaknesses. Such awareness helps him to use his strengths effectively and to manage his weaknesses by taking steps to remove them. He is also aware of his achievements. With such awareness, his concern for self-development—increasing his strength and dealing with his weaknesses—produces better results for him.

4.2.3 Proactivity

Personal efficacy is related to an individual's ability to take initiative. A person can either wait and react to situations or can take the initiative. The latter is called proactive behaviour. Proactivity (as contrasted with reactivity) includes at least three aspects. First, a proactive person feels that he can change things or, in general, determine a course of action. Such a person is said to have an internal locus of control. A person who believes that events depend on outside forces—fate, God, the governments, parents, boss, etc.—is said to have an external locus. Second, proactivity is reflected in the attitude towards a problem. A proactive person solves a problem instead of waiting for a solution from outside or avoiding it altogether. This can be called proactive orientation. Third, a proactive person looks for available resources and utilises them. The more resources a person sees around him, the more proactive he is.

4.2.4 Action Orientation

Personal efficacy results in action. In fact, action orientation is a part of efficacy. Action orientation may be shown in three ways. An action-oriented person shows some amount of self-discipline or what McClelland (1975) called 'activity inhibition'. For example, he works hard, denies himself opportunities for immediate gratification of some of his desires, sticks to schedules, spends long hours on the job and so on. Planning orientation is the second aspect of action orientation. The person plans detailed activity schedules to reach a goal. Not satisfied only with formulating a goal, he prepares functional linkages between the goal and his present state. Finally, such a person is also future oriented. Instead of living in the past or only confining himself to the present, he is obsessed by the future—what he wants to achieve; how he will act and so on.

Several methods are available for analysing or measuring personal efficacy. One well-known self-checking instrument is Personal Orientation Inventory (POI), which measures several dimensions of personal efficacy (Banet, 1976).

Another method is through the analysis of self-descriptive and reflective essays by individuals on 'who am I?' It is assumed that self-descriptions reveal significant aspects of an individual's psychic dynamics. 'Who am I?' combines reflective introspection (retrospection) with prospection of the future and self-presentation. The instructions given for writing 'who am I?' are crucial since these could stimulate one for more of these dimensions.

Two methods of analysing this essay are worth mentioning. One is Pfizer's method (McClelland and Winter, 1969) in which five aspects are analysed and scored. Each aspect can be scored as +1 or –1 for personal efficacy. These aspects are goal (activity vs. essence), locus of resources (internal vs. lack or external), global state (scored –1), initiative vs. compliance and problem-solving vs.

problem avoidance. Sarabhai (1978) has developed a modified version of Pfizer's system. Stewart (1975) developed a scheme of analysis of self-definition in terms of maturation stages (Rao, 1975).

4.3 SCORING

One dimension is scored only once. The same sentence(s) can be scored for more than one dimension. Check, or tick mark, each dimension if it is present in the essay. At the end, the total of all the checked dimensions (present in the essays) gives the total score of personal efficacy. The following dimensions are to be scored:

1. *Super ordinate goal orientation (SGO).* Statements indicating a person's concern for a larger goal or a goal beyond his own needs.
    Examples:
      I want to serve my country.
      I want to serve humanity.
      I am to fulfil the will of God.
2. *Concern for personal excellence (E).* Statements indicating the need and desire to achieve something unique, those having long-term involvement or standards of efficiency and excellence or those indicating competition with others.
    Examples:
      I want to become a doctor.
      I increased the profits of the company.
      I am worried about the low returns on my capital.
3. *Concern for influence (I).* Statements indicating the need or wish to change things, situations or people.
    Examples:
      I want to improve the educational system.
      I want to change the society.
      I am guiding people in my company.
      I was always captain of the first eleven in school.
4. *Concern for the family (EF).* Statements showing the need or desire to do something for parents, brothers, sisters and other members of the family. Even references to them showing concern are scored.
    Examples:
      I want to help my father in his old age.
      I am worried about my brother.
      I brought up my younger brothers after my father's death.
5. *Concern for others and society (ES).* Statements indicating concern for other people and society at large.

Examples:

I want to donate my eyes for the blind after my death.

Poverty pains me.

I am working on plans to provide better welfare services for my staff.

6. *Awareness of personal strength (SP)*. Statements indicating strength.

Examples:

I am a good student.

I am strong in mathematics.

I am known for my technical knowledge and insights.

7. *Awareness of personal weaknesses (BP)*. Statements indicating limitations or weaknesses.

Examples:

I am poor in health.

My English is weak.

I am short-tempered.

8. *Awareness of achievement (A)*. Statements indicating past achievements.

Examples:

I scored very high marks in the examination.

I developed the control system for the company.

I won several prizes.

9. *Concern for self-development (DP)*. Statements indicating the need and desire and plans to do something for further growth and development.

Examples:

I am planning to improve my English.

I want to gain experience through visits to other units.

I want to develop motivation.

10. *Internal locus of control (ILC)*: Statements showing that one can do something about a problem.

Examples:

With my hard work and determination, I hope to overcome this difficulty.

I am pretty sure I can turn the corner.

11. *Proactive orientation (PO)*: Statements indicating that one wants to solve problems and take the initiative in understanding and analysing a situation.

Examples:

I met each of the persons involved in the conflict to understand the course of the conflict.

When the raw material was not allowed to be imported, I toured the district to explore what else could be used.

12. *Resource utilisation (RU)*. Statements showing desire and tendency to make use of the facilities and resources one sees outside.

Examples:

I joined classes to improve my English.

I took a loan from the bank.

I consulted the extension officer to discuss my plans.

13. *Self-discipline (D)*. Statements showing that the person is working hard, shows self-discipline, spends long hours on work, postpones immediate gratification, etc.

Examples:

I work about 14 hours a day.

I postponed my marriage because I was busy in setting up the unit.

I work hard.

14. *Planning orientation (P)*. Statements showing involvement in some plans for which one is taking some steps.

Examples:

I am studying biology to become a doctor.

I am preparing to learn accountancy so that when my business grows I can manage it properly.

I am planning to expand my business twice its present size.

15. *Future orientation (F)*: Statements talking about the future or indicating future plans and concerns. Such statements use the future tense.

Examples:

I shall start a new business as soon as I am relieved of my present job.

I plan to start a new business.

I hope to expand the present facto.

To summarise, the following categories are to be scored by checking their presence:

1. Superordinate goal orientation (SGO)
2. Concern for personal excellence (E)
3. Concern for influence (I)
4. Concern for family (EF)
5. Concern for others and society (ES)
6. Awareness of personal strength (SP)
7. Awareness of personal weakness (BP)
8. Awareness of achievement (AP)
9. Concern for self-development (DP)
10. Internal locus of control (ILC)
11. Proactive orientation (PO)
12. Resource utilisation (RU)
13. Self-discipline (D)
14. Planning orientation (P)
15. Future orientation (F)

4.4 NORMS

Based on responses from 38 managers, the means and SD values are given in the following table.

	Dimension	Mean	SD
1.	SGO	0.39	0.50
2.	E	0	0
3.	I	0.08	0.27
4.	EF	0.31	0.47
5.	ES	0.46	0.51
6.	SP	0.35	0.49
7.	BP	0.50	0.51
8.	AP	0.77	0.43
9.	DP	0.27	0.45
10.	ILC	0.12	0.33
11.	PO	0.39	0.50
12.	RU	0.08	0.27
13.	D	0.08	0.27
14.	P	0	0
15.	F	0.04	0.20

4.5 USES

The data generated is useful for reflection. Participants may examine which aspects are missing and discuss in small groups how these could be developed. Group profiles can also be discussed and relevant HRD interventions could be planned to increase weak aspects.

Personal Effectiveness Scale—General (PE-G)

5.1 THE INSTRUMENT AND ITS ADMINISTRATION

Personal effectiveness (PE) scale is meant to be used for various groups such as managers, counsellors, consultants, students and teachers. The PE scale gives personal effectiveness types in terms of self-disclosure, feedback and perceptiveness. It contains 15 statements, five for each of the three aspects. A respondent checks each statement, indicating the extent to which it is true of him or her (on a 5-point scale). This instrument is self-administered. Details of its administration, conceptual framework, scoring and use for HRD are given.

5.2 CONCEPTUAL FRAMEWORK

One precondition for personal effectiveness is better self-awareness. But only understanding one's self does not make a person effective. One simple model for self-awareness, which is widely used, is the Johari Window, developed by Luft and Ingham (Luft, 1991). In this model, there are two main dimensions for understanding the self—the aspects of a person's behaviour and style that are known to him (self) and those that are known to people with whom he interacts (others). A combination of these two dimensions reveals four areas of knowledge about the self (Figure 5.1).

The upper left-hand square is the *arena* or the public self—a part of an individual's behaviour known both to himself and to others. The *arena* includes information such as name, age, physical appearance and familial or organisational affiliation.

The *blind* area contains the aspects of the person's behaviour and style that are known to others but the person himself does not know about. A person may have mannerisms of which he is unaware but which are perceived by others as funny, annoying or pleasing. For example, an individual might be surprised to hear that his method of asking questions annoys others who may interpret them as cross-examination rather than curiosity or a request for information.

FIGURE 5.1 Johari Window

	Known to self	Not known to self
Known to others	Arena (A)	Blind (B)
Not known to others	Closed (C)	Dark (D)

The *closed* area involves the behavioural traits known to the person but not revealed to others; things in this area are secret. For example, a subordinate may be annoyed if his supervisor does not ask him to sit down during a meeting, but he will remain standing without letting the supervisor know that he is annoyed. The supervisor may think that the subordinate does not mind standing and may accept his behaviour as part of their hierarchical relationship. Most of us have many such feelings in our closed areas that we are unwilling to reveal to the persons concerned.

The fourth area is the *dark area*, inaccessible to both the self and others. Some psychologists believe that this is a very large area indeed, and that certain circumstances (for example, an accident), a particular stage of one's life or special techniques such as psychoanalysis or psychodynamics may suddenly make a person realise some hidden aspects of himself. Because the *dark* area cannot be consciously controlled or changed, this discussion will be limited to the arena, the blind and the closed areas.

In the Johari Window model, the size of the arena or open space is critical for personal effectiveness. Arena increases in proportion to the decrease in the blind and the closed areas.

5.2.1 Openness

Openness, then, is critical for personal effectiveness. Openness has two aspects—self-disclosure (sharing with others what others do not seem to know about one's self) and the use of feedback (being open to what others say on aspects which one may not be aware of). In addition, perceptiveness or sensitivity to others' feelings and non-verbal cues are also important. Let us look at these three aspects.

The extent to which one shares ideas, feelings, experiences, impressions, perceptions and various other personal data with others shows the degree of openness which is an important quality and contributes a great deal to a person's effectiveness.

Openness in combination with perceptiveness and communication makes a person much more effective. But openness alone is often misunderstood as sharing everything with everyone. Pfeiffer and Jones (1972) have used the term *Carolesque openness* to describe openness without accompanying sensitivity to others in a situation. The word was coined from Carol's behaviour in the movie,

Bob & Carol & Ted & Alice. Carol, recently 'turned on' by a weekend growth centre experience, pours out her feelings in a way that embarrasses her dinner companions and confronts a waiter with feeling data. Although such behaviour may indicate that the person is 'in touch' with his own feelings, it also indicates that he is out of touch with the feelings of others.

Pfeiffer and Jones (1972) suggest that *destructive openness* can result from an inordinate value being placed upon 'telling it like it is, from insensitivity to the recipients of the communication, or from a desire to be punitive' (p. 197). They suggest what they call *strategic openness* as an alternative, that is, 'determining how much open data flow the system can stand and then giving it about a ten per cent boost'.

Openness can be characterised as effective, first, if the person sees that sharing what he wants to share is appropriate. Inappropriate sharing does not contribute to effective openness. For example, a typical task group is usually an inappropriate place for a person to share marital problems. Second, openness can be characterised as effective if the person is aware of what his openness is likely to do to others. Those who practise openness by calling others names or pouring out all their feelings are unlikely to be effective. For example, a supervisor who takes out his anger on a subordinate without taking into consideration that person's ability to process and use the data generated will not be effective. The supervisor would be better advised to listen to the subordinate and share his concerns in a manner that will help the subordinate use the data he receives.

5.2.2 Receiving Feedback

Feedback on those aspects of a person about which others are aware but the person himself is not may be positive or negative. Generally, there is no problem in positive feedbacks. Negative feedbacks, however, create dissonance with self-image and may be threatening to the ego. When one receives negative feedback, for example, if he criticised or blamed, he tends to be defensive and generally uses defensive behaviour to deal with the feedback. Table 5.1 summarises the various defensive (and the alternative, confronting) behaviours to deal with negative feedbacks.

Defensive behaviour to deal with threatening feedback is like using pain-killing drugs to deal with pain; they merely reduce the awareness of the pain. Defensive behaviour may create an illusion of having dealt with the situation; it does not change the situation or behaviour. For example, if a subordinate receives negative feedback from his superior officer saying that his motivation in the past year has been low, he may feel threatened. He may then reduce the threat by projecting his anger onto the superior officer and saying that the feedback is based on prejudice. This may satisfy him and he may not feel threatened anymore. However, this neither changes the situation (the superior officer will continue to feel that his subordinate has low motivation) nor the behaviour of the subordinate (who will continue to feel that his superior officer is prejudiced, and that, therefore, he need not change his behaviour). Defensive behaviour does not serve the purpose and although it may reduce anxiety, the conflict in the self is not resolved. Excessive use of defensive behaviour is likely to result in a *conflicted self*. On the other hand, if confronting

TABLE 5.1 Defensive and Confronting Behaviour in Dealing with Feedback	
Defensive Behaviour	**Confronting Behaviour**
Denial	Owning
Rationalisation	Self-analysis
Projection	Empathy
Displacement	Exploration
Quick acceptance	Data collection
Withdrawal	Expressing feelings
Aggression	Help seeking
Humour	Concern
Competition with authority	Listening
Cynicism	Positive critical attitude
Intellectualisation	Sharing concern
Generalisation	Experimenting
Pairing	Relating to group
Results in a conflicted self	Results in an integrated self

behaviour is used, the conflict is reduced. Continued use of such behaviour will result in an *integrated self.*

The intention is not to suggest here that defensive behaviour is bad in all situations. Nor is it suggested that no defensive behaviour should be used. In many situations, defensive behaviour may be functional. However, if the main purpose of feedback is to develop mutuality and if both the persons involved in giving and receiving feedback are interested in a relationship of trust and openness, the more defensive behaviour is used, the less effective it will be. The individual receiving feedback should examine his defensive behaviour and prepare a plan (preferably with the help of one or more persons) for reducing it and moving towards the corresponding confronting behaviour as indicated in Table 5.1.

5.2.3 Perceptiveness

The ability to pick up verbal and non-verbal cues from others indicates perceptiveness. However, like openness, this dimension must be combined with the other two dimensions for effectiveness. A person who is not open may receive many cues and much feedback from others at first, but soon he may be seen as being manipulative and generally unavailable. Perceptiveness and openness reinforce each other and, if used effectively, are likely to increase personal effectiveness. Like openness, perceptiveness can be used appropriately or inappropriately. If a person is too conscious of others' feelings, he may inhibit his interactions. Similarly, a person who is too conscious of his own limitations will tend not to take risks. Effective perceptiveness can be increased by checking others' reactions to what is said. A person who does not do this (in other words, if he is not open) may become over-concerned about the cues he receives. Two instruments, one for individuals (Chapter 5) and the other for a group or an organisation (Chapter 29), are based on this three-dimensional concept of personal effectiveness.

5.3 RELIABILITY

Alpha for a group of 68 managers was found to be 0.90.

5.4 NORMS

Mean and SD values based on responses of 68 managers are in the following table.

Variable	Mean	SD
Self-disclosure	10	3
Openness to feedback	14	3
Perceptiveness	13	3

5.5 USE FOR HRD

An exercise can be conducted by asking each group member to identify himself with one (or with the closest one) of the eight types mentioned in 'C' of the score sheet. Similarly, another exercise can be conducted, asking every member in the group to identify every other member with one (or the one closest to it) of the eight types. Data thus generated can be used in the process work in helping individuals take the necessary steps to increase their personal effectiveness by experimenting with openness and empathic functional feedback. Then the actual scores can be calculated and the discrepancies between self-perceived or group-perceived profile and the score profile can be discussed. Small groups (preferably triads) can work on helping each other to improve effectiveness by increasing scores in deficient areas.

Personal Effectiveness Scale
Score Sheet

A. Enter your responses below after reversing (*) marked ones.

	0	1	2	3	4
Original Responses	0	1	2	3	4
Reversed Responses	4	3	2	1	0

Item	Response	Item	Response	Item	Response
*1	…	2	…	*3	…
*4	…	*5	…	*6	…
7	…	8	…	9	…
*10	…	*11	…	*12	…
13	…	14	…	*15	…
	…		…		…
Total Category	Self-disclosure		Openness to feedback		Perceptiveness

1. Total the three columns.
2. Write L or H below each of the three total scores: If the total score is 11 or below, write L; if the score is above 11, write H.
3. Mark one category out of the eight given below, based on the combination of your three totals. This is your effectiveness type.
4. Look in A at items on which your response is 2 or below. Develop your own action plan to change your behaviour to become more effective.

	Category	Self-disclosure	Openness to Feedback	Perceptiveness
1.	Effective	High	High	High
2.	Insensitive	High	High	Low
3.	Egocentric	High	Low	Low
4.	Dogmatic	High	Low	High
5.	Secretive	Low	High	High
6.	Task-obsessed	Low	High	Low
7.	Lonely Empathic	Low	Low	High
8.	Ineffective	Low	Low	Low

Personal Effectiveness Scale (G)

Name: _____   Role: _____

Organisation: _____   Date: _____

This instrument is for your own use. So, be frank in your responses.

Read each statement given below and indicate on the left-hand blank space how much it is true of your behaviour by using the following guidelines:

Write 4   if it is the most characteristic of your, or if you always or most often behave or feel this way

Write 3   if it is fairly true of you, or you quite often behave or feel this way

Write 2   if it is somewhat true in your case

Write 1   if it is not true of you, or if you only occasionally feel or behave this way

Write 0   if it is not at all characteristic of your, or you seldom feel or behave this way

1. _____ I find it difficult to be frank with people unless I know them very well.
2. _____ I listen carefully to others' opinions about my behaviour.
3. _____ I tend to say things that turn out to be out of place.
4. _____ Generally, I hesitate to express my feelings to others.
5. _____ When someone directly tells me how he feels about my behaviour, I tend to close up and stop listening.
6. _____ On hindsight, I regret why I said something tactlessly.
7. _____ I express my opinions in a group or to a person without hesitation.
8. _____ I take steps to find out how my behaviour has been perceived by the person with whom I have been interacting.
9. _____ I deliberately observe how a person will take what I am going to tell him and communicate with him accordingly.
10. _____ When someone discusses his problems, I do not spontaneously share with him my experiences and personal problems of a similar nature.
11. _____ If someone criticises me, I hear him at that time but do not bother myself about it later.
12. _____ I fail to pick up cues about others' feelings and reactions when I am involved in an argument or a conversation.
13. _____ I enjoy talking with others about my personal concerns and matters.
14. _____ I value what people have to say about my style, behaviour, etc.
15. _____ I am often surprised to discover (or told) that people were put off, bored or annoyed when I thought they were enjoying interacting with me.

Creativity Assessment Inventory (CAI)

6.1 THE INSTRUMENT AND ITS ADMINISTRATION

Creativity Assessment Inventory (CAI) was developed to measure six dimensions—challenge, freedom, liveliness, openness, conflict and risk-taking. It contains 24 statements, four for each of the six aspects. A respondent checks each statement, indicating the extent to which it is true for him (on a 4-point scale). This instrument is self-administered.

6.2 CONCEPTUAL FRAMEWORK

Creativity and innovation are sometimes seen as synonymous. At a minimum, creativity can be defined as problem identification and idea generation while innovation can be defined as idea selection, development and commercialisation. Innovation often means that outside decision-makers have to get involved, as complete development and commercialisation commonly requires the competencies and knowledge of a team. Different competencies, structures, processes, resources and timescales are required. There are many different approaches to the study of creativity; some of them are discussed here.

Learning versus talent: Can creativity be learned and developed or is it a talent/special gift? Why is it that some people are just more creative? Nature–nurture arguments are notoriously inconclusive, and trait theories assume stability across situations and time. The best way to answer this question is to investigate whether creativity improves with practice. The experience curve, automisation, learning theories and the experiences of practitioners suggest that it does improve, but there are caveats.

Motivation: Motivation is arguably more important than nature/nurture or traits. Someone with natural ability or placed in the right environment may not take advantage of it unless motivated. There is intrinsic motivation, synergistic and non-synergistic extrinsic motivation. How can it be induced and measured? There are many elements—material reward, progress to the ideal self, self-determination, self-evaluation, feedback, enjoyment, competency expansion, recognition and feasibility.

Role of knowledge: What type and level of knowledge helps creativity the most? Can someone with limited knowledge of a field make a significant contribution to it? Does excess knowledge cause a blinkered vision? Intellectual cross-pollination fosters creativity, but how do we overcome competency traps and other negatives? How do we frame break, reduce path dependency and collaborate effectively?

Radical versus incremental creativity: Radical/transformational/disruptive creativity is very much glamourised. But, is this what is required most often? Is it wiser to target radical or incremental ideas? Is radical really radical or the result of incremental improvement? How is radical defined? If we want a radical idea as opposed to an incremental change, what are the implications? Incremental and radical creativity require vastly different structures, processes, skills and resources.

Process: Many people question the concept that creativity can be a process. Ask the practitioners what process they engage in, and they may well deny there is one. But if you examine the activities of the creative people, common patterns of behaviour emerge. This common process makes insight/eureka/the aha! experience more likely. The process includes identifying and intensely investigating the problem; forcing production of ideas using creative versus critical thinking and other techniques; seeking stimuli and allowing the unconscious mind to take over by engaging in rest and unrelated activities.

Valuation: How do we value an idea so as to decide how to invest resources? Even a painter who creates for pure pleasure has to decide which one of his ideas is the best; there is always a value system and (some argue) some sort of promotional instinct. There are decisions as to whether you are looking for applied creativity; who the consumer is; and how do they benefit? There is no sure fire way to evaluate perfectly because there is no sure fire route to commercial success. But we can benchmark against those types of ideas that have succeeded in the past: Firms must make a decision as to their strategic, competence and technical fit; there are comparisons against rivals and practical impediments; how do we make the go or kill decision and what are the trade-offs? A quantitative tool for measuring the value of ideas has been developed.

The relationship between creativity and intelligence has always been a central concern of psychology (Guilford, 1950). Parenthetically, it is interesting to note that a major impetus for Guilford's theory was his interest in creativity. The divergent production operation identifies a number of different types of creative abilities.

Much effort has been devoted towards the measurement of creative potential (e.g., Guilford, 1950; Torrance, 1979). A common framework for creative thinking processes is described by Torrance (1979). Each aspect is defined further along with ways to facilitate the respective aspect by using key words and application activities.

Fluency refers to the production of a great number of ideas or alternate solutions to a problem. It also implies understanding, and not just remembering information that is learned.

Flexibility refers to the production of ideas that show a variety of possibilities or realms of thought. It involves the ability to see things from different points of view to use many different approaches or strategies.

Elaboration is the process of enhancing ideas by providing more detail. Additional detail and clarity improves interest in and understanding of the topic.

Originality involves the production of ideas that are unique or unusual. It involves synthesis or putting information about a topic back together in a new way.

There have also been many attempts to increase creative behaviour (e.g., Osborn, 1993; Parnes, 1967). Taylor and Williams (1966) provide a survey of the relationship between creativity and instruction.

Osborn's Seven-Step Model for Creative Thinking:

1. *Orientation*—pointing up the problem
2. *Preparation*—gathering pertinent data
3. *Analysis*—breaking down the relevant material
4. *Ideation*—piling up alternatives by way of ideas
5. *Incubation*—letting it develop
6. *Synthesis*—putting the pieces together
7. *Evaluation*—judging the resulting ideas

While there are many views about the nature of creativity (see Finke, Ward & Smith, 1992; Sternberg, 1988), there is some agreement that the creative process involves the application of past experiences or ideas in novel ways.

Langley et al. (1987) have argued that creativity in the context of scientific discovery is a form of problem-solving. Specifically, they propose that finding problems and formulating them involves the same underlying cognitive processes of heuristic search and sub goal generation as any other kind of problem-solving behaviour.

The *creative problem-solving (CPS) model*, based upon the work of Osborn and Parnes, suggests that the creative process involves following five major steps:

1. Fact-finding
2. Problem-finding
3. Idea-finding
4. Solution-finding
5. Acceptance-finding

Certain cognitive skills seem to underlie creative behaviour such as

1. Fluency
2. Flexibility

3. Visualisation
4. Imagination
5. Expressiveness and
6. Openness (resistance to closure)

These skills may be personality characteristics, which may be learned or situational. There is also general acknowledgement that social processes play a major role in the recognition of creativity (Amabile, 1983).

In the current instrument, creativity has following dimensions:

1. *Challenge*—a creative person approaches challenges and difficulties energetically and with enjoyment.
2. *Freedom*—a creative person prefers to be independent and happy to take initiatives and voice his ideas.
3. *Liveliness*—a creative person is busy most of the time. He mostly remains excited and happy.
4. *Openness*—a creative person tends to be trusting and considers mistakes as something to learn from.
5. *Conflicts*—a creative person looks for helpful win-win compromises, which needs willingness to communicate with understanding and empathy.
6. *Risk-taking*—a creative person takes responsibilities readily and does not hesitate to act on new ideas.

6.3 RELIABILITY

Split-half reliability coefficient was found to be 0.22.

6.4 NORMS*

Based on the data collected from 596 students from various schools, the following norms are suggested. Norms can be developed for specific groups.

	Challenge	Freedom	Liveliness	Openness	Conflicts	Risk-taking
Mean	8	15	9	9	10	8
SD	2	2	2	2	5	2

Note: Developed by Rachita Sinha under the guidance of Surabhi Purohit.

---

　* Norms are provided by Bharti Aggarwal.

6.5 USE FOR HRD

Data generated can be used in the process work in helping individuals take the necessary steps to increase creativity by experimenting with openness and empathic functional feedback. The actual scores can then be calculated, and the discrepancies between self-perceived or group-perceived profile and the score profile can be discussed. Small groups (preferably triads) can work on helping each other to improve creativity by increasing scores in deficient areas.

6.6 SCORING

1. Transfer the ratings to the Response Sheet.
2. Make sure that starred items are reversed.
3. Total scores on each aspect at the end of the columns; these will range between 4 and 16.
4. Multiply the total by 6.25. The range will be 0–100.
5. Total all totals and deduct 24 × 1.39. This will range between 0 and 100.

Reverse the responses of the following statements (these have been starred in the Response Table—6, 7, 8, 14, 16, 18, 24, so that 1 becomes 4, 2 becomes 3, 3 becomes 2, and 4 becomes 1).

Response Table

Items	Items	Items	Items	Items	Items
1 ___	2 ___	3 ___	4 ___	5 ___	6* ___
7* ___	8* ___	9 ___	10 ___	11 ___	12 ___
13 ___	14* ___	15 ___	16* ___	17 ___	18* ___
19 ___	20 ___	21 ___	22 ___	23 ___	24* ___
Total ___	Total ___	Total ___	Total ___	Total ___	Total ___
_X_6.25___	X_6.25___	X_6.25___	X_6.25___	X_6.25___	X_6.25___
Challenge	Freedom	Liveliness	Openness	Conflict	Risk-taking

Creativity Assessment Inventory (CAI)

Name: _____   Designation: _____
Age: _____   Date: _____

Read each statement carefully and write down one of the following numbers in the space provided on the left side. (There are no wrong or right answers.)

Write 1   if you always feel or behave this way
Write 2   if you often feel or behave this way
Write 3   if you sometimes feel or behave this way
Write 4   if you never feel or behave this way

S. No.	Response	Item
1.	_____	If I come across a problem, I try and solve it immediately.
2.	_____	I like to be myself.
3.	_____	I get involved in a lively debate or discussion.
4.	_____	Every mistake is a learning experience for me.
5.	_____	I question a stated opinion/position.
6.	_____	I hesitate in taking initiative.
7.	_____	I feel threatened if I come across a problem.
8.	_____	I consult others before taking a decision.
9.	_____	I enjoy jokes/hobbies/movies.
10.	_____	I trust others easily.
11.	_____	My work atmosphere is relaxed.
12.	_____	I take responsibility readily.
13.	_____	I think of alternatives to accomplish difficult tasks.
14.	_____	I find it hard to take a decision.
15.	_____	I like enjoying with friends.
16.	_____	I get upset easily by mistakes.
17.	_____	I give ideas and suggestions to people when they need it.
18.	_____	I hesitate giving or acting on new ideas.
19.	_____	I make use of available resources to develop new ideas and solve problems.
20.	_____	I work well when there are no hard-line rules.
21.	_____	I am excited about new programmes and projects.
22.	_____	I like to work in groups.
23.	_____	In case of arguments, I keep calm and communicate with understanding and empathy.
24.	_____	People think that I am impractical.

Balanced Orientation: Androgyny Scale

7.1 THE INSTRUMENT AND ITS ADMINISTRATION

Androgyny Scale is meant to measure the respondent's level of androgynous orientation. It can also be used to measure stereotype of the two genders by the respondents.

The scale contains 20 pairs. The respondent is required to distribute 4 marks between two items of each pair. He is required to do it twice, once to indicate how the person actually feels (Actual) and the other how much he would like to have (Desired).

7.2 THE CONCEPTUAL FRAMEWORK

Andro is Greek word for male and *gyne* for female. As pointed by Tarcott Parson (1960) masculinity has been associated with an instrumental cognitive orientation focused on getting things done or a problem-solving approach and feminity with an expressive orientation, an effective concern for others' welfare and for group cohesiveness.

Traditionally different characteristics are attributed to the two genders. Men are attributed with toughness, competitiveness, aggression, perseverance and assertiveness. Women are seen as having qualities such as compassion, empathy, harmony, collaboration, nurturance, aesthetics and creativity. If a society emphasises the differences between the gender roles and allocates social roles according to such differences, it would expect men to work in areas of achievement and physical activities (work and defence) and women to work in areas requiring 'female characteristics' (nursing, house-keeping, etc.). This is a sexist orientation. In contrast, if there is less differentiation between gender roles, if social roles are not allocated according to the traditional views of the two genders and the qualities attributed to men and women are both valued and integrated, we have an androgynous culture. One symbolic image of androgyny found in India is the depiction of Shiva as *Ardhanarishwara* (half man and half woman). Both men and women need to develop the qualities which contribute to their effectiveness as members of the society and the organisation that they work in.

The word androgyny describes this sex-role model. The term suggests that it is possible for people to exhibit both masculine and feminine qualities and that such values, attitudes and behaviours reside in varying degrees in each of us.

Persons of either sex need both masculine and feminine characteristics to be flexible adults, and this fact has significant social consequences (Bemi, 1993; Spence & Helmureich, 1994).

Gender role orientation is found to be related to the expression of personality traits in adolescents. There are two widely accepted patterns of sex-role types, namely, the traditional that is based on the fundamental principle of masculine superiority and feminine inferiority, and the egalitarian that is based on the principle that differences between the sexes are smaller than was formerly believed.

Sandra Bem (1993) proposed the concept of psychological androgyny at an UCLA Symposium on Women in 1972. She said, 'Extreme feminity untempered by a sufficient concern for one's own needs as an individual may produce dependence and self-denial, just as extreme masculinity untempered by a sufficient concern for the needs of others may produce arrogance and exploitation.'

Spence and Helmreich (1994) have suggested four models: traditionally male (high masculine, low feminine), traditional female (high feminine, low masculine), undifferentiated (low masculine and feminine) and androgyny (high masculine and feminine).

Koteswairi and Ravi found that parents with a masculine and androgynous orientation expressed a more direct and active form of aggression than those with a feminine orientation. Sex roles are flexible and may be influenced by life situations and demands.

People with high masculinity are found to be more assertive, self-assured, independent, talk-ative, expressive and experimental while people with a low masculinity are more warm, submissive, sober, moralistic, practical and conservative (Kumar & Kukreja, 1995).

A new paradigm for sex-role identity sees masculinity and feminity as a continuum rather than as opposites, a dualistic concept rather than a bipolar model. In this new paradigm, a healthy adult will be androgynous if he possesses both masculine independence and feminine spontaneity and nurturance.

7.3 RELIABILITY

Coefficient of parallel forms was found to be 0.70, equal-length Spearman–Brown was 0.82 and unequal-length Brown coefficient was also 0.82. These show high internal consistency of the instrument.

7.4 NORMS

The following norms are based on a sample of students and teachers from different parts of India. Mean and SD values of different groups are shown below. The range is also shown for the total sample. Distribution within the range was even.

Groups	Desired Feminity			Actual Feminity	
	No	Mean	SD	Mean	SD
Girls	54	50	9	49	10
Boys	68	48	8	50	8
Total	122	49	8	50	8
Teachers	45	50	10	50	10

The following cut-off points can be used as norms

Below 36	High Masculine
36–46	Masculine
46–55	Androgynous
56–65	Feminine
Above 65	High Feminine

7.5 USING THE INSTRUMENT FOR TRAINING

This instrument has been prepared to help the respondents realise the value of developing qualities usually attributed to members of the other gender. It will also help them become aware of their gender-related stereotypes and their tendency to devalue their own sex-related strengths, and/or their deficiency in such qualities. The following suggestions are made in this regard:

1. The participants complete the instrument.
2. They may be involved in scoring their own responses, using the score sheet (appended).
3. The facilitator explains the relevant theory discussed in the conceptual framework.
4. The facilitator then explains the concept of scores on each dimension.
5. Each respondent examines his androgyny measure (ratio between totals of the two columns) and examines his score against the norms given.
6. The respondents may discuss in small groups if the ratio is related to their gender (women valuing women-related and men valuing men-related qualities).
7. Small groups may also discuss how the other qualities are important for effectiveness in life.

8. The participants also examine their scores on 'deficiency' and 'devaluation' of their own sex-related qualities and the reasons for this.

9. Those who are in 'extreme' groups, valuing only their own gender-related qualities, may discuss how other qualities are equally important for them, and how to develop these without reducing the importance of those qualities that they value. In fact, the more they see the importance of the 'other' qualities, the more effectively they will be able to use their own gender-related qualities.

10. The facilitator may sum up and discuss the importance of developing androgynous persons.

11. The participants may also discuss in small groups how to become androgynous in action, for example, men taking more responsibilities at home (helping in household chores, child rearing, etc.) and similarly women taking more responsibilities outside the home.

Androgyny Scale
Score Sheet

Name: _____ Sex: _____ Date: _____

1. Transfer to this sheet the scores from the completed instrument.
2. Total each column. These scores are for feminine attributes.
3. Multiply totals of Desired and Actual columns by 1.25. The range will be 0–100. These will also be the androgyny scores.
4. Total Column 3. The range will be between –80 and +80. Positive and negative scores indicate feminity deficiency and feminity devaluation respectively. Masculinity deficiency and masculinity devaluation scores will be the same with opposite signs (plus or minus). Individual items can be examined for detailed analysis.
5. Add 80 to the total of Column 3 and then multiply by 0.625. The range will be 0–100.
6. Any score below 50 indicates devaluation and above 50 deficiency of the feminine aspect, and deficiency and devaluation of the masculine aspect of androgyny.

	1 Desired	2 Actual	3 D – A
1a.	_____	_____	_____
2a.	_____	_____	_____
3a.	_____	_____	_____
4b.	_____	_____	_____
5b.	_____	_____	_____
6b.	_____	_____	_____
7a.	_____	_____	_____
8a.	_____	_____	_____
9b.	_____	_____	_____
10b.	_____	_____	_____
11a.	_____	_____	_____
12b.	_____	_____	_____
13a.	_____	_____	_____
14b.	_____	_____	_____
15a.	_____	_____	_____
16b.	_____	_____	_____
17a.	_____	_____	_____
18b.	_____	_____	_____
19a.	_____	_____	_____
20a. Total	_____	_____	_____
%	_____	_____	_____

Androgyny Scale*

Name: _____   Sex: _____   Date: _____
Organisation: _____   Role: _____

Given below are 20 pairs. There are two columns for your responses for each pair. Consider two items in each pair, and indicate in the first column (Desired) how important each one is for your effectiveness/ success. In the second column (Actual), indicate how much of each you actually have now. There are no right or wrong answers.

Distribute 4 marks between two items in each pair to indicate their importance for you (first column) and how much you actually have (second column). You may give all 4 marks to one item if you think this item is very important/you have it, and 0 to the other item which is not important/you do not have it at all. Or, you may give 3 to one (and 1 to the other), or 2 to each (if you think both are equally important for you/you have them in equal strength). Do not leave any pair unanswered.

		Desired	Actual
___ 1a.	Compassion	_____	_____
___ 1b.	Courage	_____	_____
___ 2a.	Caring	_____	_____
___ 2b.	Firmness	_____	_____
___ 3a.	Empathy	_____	_____
___ 3b.	Drive	_____	_____
___ 4a.	Assertiveness	_____	_____
___ 4b.	Helping	_____	_____
___ 5a.	Competition	_____	_____
___ 5b.	Nurturance	_____	_____
___ 6a.	Calculating	_____	_____
___ 6b.	Intuition	_____	_____
___ 7a.	Patience	_____	_____
___ 7b.	Bravery	_____	_____
___ 8a.	Success in career	_____	_____
___ 8b.	Working for a cause	_____	_____
___ 9a.	Result-orientation	_____	_____
___ 9b.	Emotional support	_____	_____
___ 10a.	Motivation for progress	_____	_____
___ 10b.	Concern for the weak	_____	_____
___ 11a.	Coping capability	_____	_____
___ 11b.	Goal-orientation	_____	_____
___ 12a.	Accountability	_____	_____
___ 12b.	Sensitivity to other's feelings	_____	_____
___ 13a.	Commitment	_____	_____
___ 13b.	Achievement	_____	_____
___ 14a.	Risk-taking	_____	_____
___ 14b.	Support	_____	_____
___ 15a.	Trust	_____	_____
___ 15b.	Power	_____	_____
___ 16a.	Winning	_____	_____

	Desired	Actual
__ 16b. Sharing		
__ 17a. Harmony		
__ 17b. Boldness		
__ 18a. Speaking		
__ 18b. Listening		
__ 19a. Collaboration		
__ 19b. Independence		
__ 20a. Tolerance		
__ 20b. Toughness		

Interpersonal Trust Scale 8

8.1 THE INSTRUMENT AND ITS ADMINISTRATION

This instrument will help in assessing the level of interpersonal trust in an organisation. Interpersonal Trust Scale (IPTS) can be administered in a group. The respondents should be told that the instrument is meant to help them get to know certain aspects of their own organisation. There is no right or wrong answer. The scores can be discussed to show the level of interpersonal trust.

8.2 CONCEPTUAL FRAMEWORK

IPTS measures trust in four aspects: communication, openness, professional support (concern) and competency.

Interpersonal trust is the perception you have that the other person will not intentionally or unintentionally do anything that harms your interests. It is the feeling that you can depend on that other person to meet your expectations when you are not able to control or monitor his behaviour. Interpersonal trust always involves one person making himself vulnerable to another person's behaviour. Usually, what you get from the expected behaviour is not as valuable as what you could lose if your trust is violated. Trust is violated when you don't get the behaviours you expected from the trusted person or you get unexpected behaviour.

People are not comfortable in low-trust relationships and often take steps to remove themselves from the relationship. People who have established a high level of trust have the cohesion with which to withstand considerable external challenges. High-trust relations are enduring because they are comfortable and satisfying to both parties.

8.2.1 Dimensions of Trustworthy Behaviour

Our trust in another individual can be grounded in our evaluation of his ability, integrity and benevolence. That is, our level of trust in a person is likely to grow we observe his characteristics more.

Ability refers to an assessment of the other's knowledge, skill or competency. This dimension recognises that trust requires some sense that the other is able to perform in a manner that meets our expectations.

Integrity is the degree to which the other person adheres to principles that are acceptable to you. This dimension leads to trust based on consistency of past actions, credibility of communication, commitment to standards of fairness and the congruence of the other's word and deed.

Benevolence is our assessment that the trusted individual is concerned enough about our welfare to either advance our interests or, at least, not impede them. The other's perceived intentions or motives of the trustee are most central. Honest and open communication, delegating decisions and sharing control indicate evidence of one's benevolence.

Although these three dimensions are likely to be linked with each other, each of them contributes separately to influence the level of trust in another within a relationship. However, ability and integrity are likely to be most influential early in a relationship as information on one's benevolence needs more time to emerge. The effect of benevolence increases as the relationship between the parties grows closer. The next section describes trust development in relationships in more detail.

8.2.2 Levels of Trust Development

Early theories of trust described it as a unidimensional phenomenon that simply increased or decreased in magnitude and strength within a relationship. However, more recent approaches to trust suggests that trust builds along a continuum of hierarchical and sequential stages such that as trust grows to 'higher' levels, it becomes stronger and more resilient and changes in character. This is the primary perspective we adopt in the remainder of these essays.

At early stages of a relationship, trust is at a *calculus-based* level. In other words, an individual will carefully calculate how the other party is likely to behave in a given situation depending on the rewards for being trustworthy and the deterrents against untrustworthy behaviour. In this manner, rewards and punishments form the basis of control that a person has in ensuring the other's behavioural consistency. Individuals deciding to trust the other mentally contemplate the benefits of staying in the relationship with the trustee versus the benefits of 'cheating' on the relationship, and the costs of staying in the relationship versus the costs of breaking up the relationship. Trust will only be extended to the other to the extent that this cost-benefit calculation indicates that the continued trust will yield a net positive benefit. Over time, calculus-based trust (CBT) can be built as individuals manage their reputation and assure the stability of their behaviour by behaving consistently, meeting agreed-to deadlines and fulfilling promises. CBT is largely cognitively driven trust phenomenon, grounded in the judgements of the other person's predictability and reliability.

However, as the parties come to a deeper understanding of each other through repeated interactions, they may become aware of shared values and goals. This allows trust to grow to a higher and qualitatively different level. When trust evolves to the highest level, it is said to function as *identification-based* trust (IBT). At this stage, trust has been built to the point that the parties have internalised each other's desires and intentions. They understand what the other party really cares about so completely that each party is able to act as an agent for the other. Trust at this advanced stage is also enhanced by a strong emotional bond between the parties, based on a sense of shared goals and values. So, in contrast to CBT, IBT is a more emotionally driven phenomenon, grounded in the perceptions of interpersonal care and concern and mutual need satisfaction.

8.3 SCORING

The instrument has 24 items; the 4 parameters have 6 items each. Each parameter has 3 positive and 3 negative items. All odd items are positive, and all even items are in the negative form. Items are randomly mixed in the instrument, as shown in the following table.

Communication	1	6*	9	18*	17	24*
Openness	3	8*	11	16*	19	14*
Professional Support	5	4*	13	12*	23	22*
Managerial Competence	7	2*	15	10*	21	20*

Take the following steps for scoring:

1. Reverse the responses on items marked with an asterisk: 2, 4, 6, 8, 10, 12, 14, 16, 18, 20, 22, 24 (0 becomes 3, 2 becomes 1, 1 becomes 2, and 3 becomes 0).
2. Add the 6 ratings (including the reversed ones) for each row to get the score for the aspect represented by the row (Communication, Openness, Professional Concern, and Managerial Competency).
3. Multiply the total of each row by 5.5 so that the scores range from 0 to 100.

8.4 RELIABILITY

The reliability coefficient is 0.91, which is significant at 0.001 level.

8.5 NORMS

The following mean and SD values from one group can be used as tentative norms. Norms for specific groups can be worked out.

	Mean	SD
Communication	50	10
Openness	50	10
Professional Support	45	11
Managerial Competence	45	11

8.6 USE FOR HRD

IPTS can be used for self/team and individual/team counselling. A respondent can examine his score and then plan to improve the behaviour on which he has a low score by examining the related items in the instrument and inferring the behavioural implications. The counsellor can help the individual to plan new behaviour.

In a diverse group, the participants can exchange feedback and then hold discussion in a small group.

Interpersonal Trust Scale

Name: _____ Date: _____

Organisation: _____ Role: _____

This instrument is for your own use, so be frank in your responses. Read each statement given below and indicate your frank response about your institute (in the space given on its left) by using the following guidelines:

Write 0   If you totally disagree
Write 1   If you somewhat disagree
Write 2   If you agree to a large extent
Write 3   If you totally agree

No.	Response	Items
1.	_____	When people deliver work to me, I draw attention of those who do not meet my expectations.
2.	_____	I experience partiality at workplace.
3.	_____	I ask for help when I can't handle a job myself.
4.	_____	I don't get cooperation from my peers and subordinates.
5.	_____	I encourage my people to work on the projects they initiate.
6.	_____	I keep reminding my people to complete the tasks given to them.
7.	_____	I have confidence in my seniors' leadership.
8.	_____	I feel that there is no major need to share internal information with my peers and others.
9.	_____	I share my presentations with my peers in other departments before the final presentation to the superiors.
10.	_____	I feel that not everyone is treated equally in the team.
11.	_____	I give straight answers to my colleagues.
12.	_____	I have to take decisions because my people are slow and reluctant to make decisions in their assigned areas.
13.	_____	My peers/subordinates ask for help when they can't do a job.
14.	_____	I rarely share my dissatisfaction with my subordinates and colleagues if a task has not been done as per my expectation.
15.	_____	My supervisor is competent to manage the team.
16.	_____	Given a choice, I would like to work alone, not sharing information with others.
17.	_____	I can easily communicate and share my feelings with people.
18.	_____	I prefer to be formal with my colleagues.
19.	_____	I don't hesitate in giving feedback, even if it is harsh.
20.	_____	I can't express my feelings on the various issues.
21.	_____	Actions of my superior/top management reflect strong leadership skills.
22.	_____	I ask people to move out of the team if they do not show results as per the average performance of the team.
23.	_____	I help and support underperformers.
24.	_____	I communicate with my peers and my people only through e-mails/written communication.

Locus of Control (LOCO) Inventory

9.1 THE INSTRUMENT AND ITS ADMINISTRATION

The LOCO inventory has 10 items each for internality, externality (others) and externality (luck). LOCO inventory has been developed for use in organisations. The locus of control orientations are reflected in the way people feel about what happens in the organisation: How much control they, other significant persons, or neither (being a matter of luck), have in important organisational matters. These matters relate to success or effectiveness, influence, acceptability, career advancement and rewards. The distribution of the 30 items in the inventory is shown in Table 9.1.

The inventory is self-administered. Respondents rate each statement on a 5-point scale, indicating how strongly they feel about the statement.

TABLE 9.1   Distribution of Items in Locus of Control Inventory

	Internality	Externality (Others)	Externality (Chance)
General	1,27	4,30	7,24
Success or effectiveness	3,1,0,16	6,1,9,22	9,1,3,21
Influence	28	17	26
Acceptability	25	29	18
Career	2	5	8
Advancement	23	11	14
Rewards	20	15	12

9.2 CONCEPTUAL FRAMEWORK

The concept of locus of control by Levenson (1972) was used to develop LOCO inventory (locus of control in organisations inventory). He distinguished between two types of external loci of control: significant others and luck or chance.

There are two contrasting attitudes regarding the way rewards and outcomes are determined. Some people believe that we can neither predict nor influence significant events whereas others believe that we can do both. Issues related to the prediction and causation of social and personal matters have intrigued philosophers, politicians, behavioural scientists and psychologists alike.

One of the most popular terms developed for discussing these issues is *locus of control*. This was suggested by Rotter (1954), which subsequently generated a great deal of research. The concept is based on the extent to which people perceive contingencies to affect outcomes. Individuals who have a high perception of such contingencies are said to have an internal locus of control; they believe that their own actions produce the outcomes. Persons with an external locus of control believe that outcomes are the result of chance rather than of their own actions. Internal and external loci of control are represented by the terms 'internality' and 'externality' respectively. Similarly, people with high internality are called *internals* while those with high externality are called *externals*.

Internality is related to effectiveness and adjustment. Compared to externals, internals have been reported to be more sensitive to new information, more observant, more likely to attend to cues that help resolve uncertainties (Lefcourt & Wine, 1969) and more prone to both intentional and incidental learning (Wolk & Ducette, 1984). It seems logical to associate internality with various aspects of learning such as curiosity, eagerness to obtain information, awareness of and desire to understand situations and their contexts, and the ability to process the available information. For example, in order to influence or control outcomes, an internal must acquire as much information as possible and then process it as quickly as possible. Evidence supports the assumption that an internal locus of control leads to academic achievement (Crandall, Katkovsky & Crandall, 1965; Harrison, 1968; Lessing, 1969).

Some studies have also shown a high and positive correlation between internality and perseverance. This is characterised by extra time spent on work (Franklin, 1963), continued involvement in difficult and complex tasks and willingness to defer gratification (Mischel, 1966). Lefcourt (1976) summarised the research on the relationship between internality and deferred gratification. Involvement in long-term goals requires deferment of gratification. Since persistence in effort requires undivided attention, this is not possible unless the temptation of immediate gratification is resisted. Because internals believe that their efforts lead to favourable outcomes, they can rely on their own understanding and predictability. In contrast, externals—perceiving a lack of personal predictability and fearing that unforeseen external factors will affect outcomes—may find it more attractive to seek immediate gratification than to try to achieve distant goals.

Internality was found to be an important characteristic of people with high achievement motivation (McClelland, 1961). It was further reported that internal locus of control generates moderate or calculated risk-taking. One study indicated that the correlation between achievement motivation and preference for moderate risk was significant and positive among internals but almost zero among externals (Wolk & DuCette, 1984).

Internality seems to be a cornerstone of the process of valuing, which includes awareness of one's own values, willingness to declare these values in public and adherence to them and the behaviour associated with them in spite of outside pressures. This process of developing ethical norms and using those norms even in period of crisis have also been called inner-directedness or the state of being directed by one's own, internalised standards rather than by merely conforming to outside expectations, norms or pressures.

Some studies have indicated a significant relationship between internality and morality. This leads to the resistance of temptation (Johnson, Ackerman, Frank & Fionda, 1968), helping others (Midlarsky, 1971) and low Machiavellianism (Miller & Minton, 1969). Apparently, internality is important in the development of standards for judging one's own behaviour. Both personal autonomy and responsibility are involved in the process of valuing, which is necessary for the development of a healthy and proactive society.

One study (Mitchell, Smyser & Wood, 1975) uncovered relationship between internality and certain organisational attitudes and behaviours. For example, internals experienced greater job satisfaction than externals. Internals also preferred a participatory management style, whereas externals preferred a directive style. Further, comparisons indicated that internals believed that working hard was more likely to lead to rewards and that they had more control over the ways they worked. Supervisors with an internal orientation believed that persuasive power was the most productive approach, whereas their external counterparts relied on coercive power. Furthermore, the use of rewards, respect and expertise was seen by internally focused supervisors as the most effective way to influence subordinates; those with an external orientation saw coercion and their formal positions as most effective.

To sum up, internality plays an important role in human development and meaningful living. Nevertheless, the internal pays a price. Those who perceive their own abilities and actions as being solely responsible for their failures are likely to experience stress and may become self-punitive. Attribution of failure or negative conditions to external factors can help people cope with adverse experiences more effectively to perceive social reality in the proper perspective, to fight justice and to rectify undesirable situations.

Rotter (1966) developed the first instrument to measure internality and externality. Although Rotter's instrument has been used extensively in research and training, his unitary concept of internality has been challenged. On the basis of factor analysis on the responses on Rotter's instrument, several studies found multidimensionality in the instrument, which seemed to contain items related to control ideology, personal control, system modifiability and race ideology (Gurin, Gurin, Lao & Beattie, 1969; Guttentag, 1972; McDonald & Tseng, 1971; Minton, 1972; Mirels, 1970). Valecha (1988) developed a scale to measure locus of control in organisations. Levenson (1972, 1973) questioned the putting together of three external factors: chance, fate and powerful others. He also proposed a new scale to measure both internality and externality simultaneously instead of viewing these elements along a continuum. Furthermore, he proposed two subscales for externality: one to measure perceived influence of chance (EC) and the other to measure perceived influence of powerful others (EO). Using Levenson's scale, Sinha, Singh and Shukla (1986) found mixed locus of control (both internal and external). Narayanan Venkatapathy and Govindaraju (1984) proposed the concept of probabilistic orientation—a balance perception of choice and bondage—as relevant to India.

Locus of control orientation is reflected in the way a person views what happens in an organisation, that is, how much control the person believes that he has in important organisational matters; how much control the person believes is held by certain others; and to what degree the person believes events are a matter of luck. The LOCO inventory links the locus of control to seven areas: general, success or effectiveness, influence, acceptability, career, advancement and rewards.

Proverbs widely used in a society can be a rich source to measure several orientations, including locus of control (Chapter 9). Another relevant concept in this context is the causal attribution of Weiner (1974), who has added another dimension to locus of control. This is concerned with the perception of causal attributions, whether a person attributes the outcome to internal or external 'causes'. Weiner has also suggested a stability-variability dimension. Both the internal and external causes can be either stable or variable, thus giving four categories of factors to which outcomes can be attributed. This is shown in Figure 9.1. Internal causes are either stable (those which do not change easily, e.g., ability) or variable (those that can vary or change, e.g., effort). Similarly, external causes are either stable (difficulty of a task) or variable (luck or chance). Weiner has further proposed that the interaction between locus of control and stability has a different significance for the attribution of positive outcomes (success) and negative outcomes (failures). Based on several investigations, Weiner has proposed that persistence in achievement activity will result if

1. *Success* is attributed to an internal variable factor (effort). If a person perceives that this effort (which he can vary) has resulted in the desired outcome, he will find more pleasure in further engaging in (increasing his effort for) the activity;

FIGURE 9.1   The Perceived Determinants of Outcomes

	Internality–Externality	
	Internal	External
Stable	Ability	Task difficulty
Variable	Effort	Luck

2.   *Failure* is attributed to variable factors (both internal, i.e., effort, and external, i.e., luck or chance). If a person perceives that his failure is due to factors which can change (e.g., luck) or which can be varied such as effort, he still has hope for improvement by putting in more effort. If a person attributes his failure to stable factors (ability or task difficulty), he is likely to give up his efforts because, on the one hand, his ability level cannot change so easily and, on the other, the level of the task difficulty remains a hindrance and there appears no sense in persisting in the activity. Weiner's concept has wider implications. Das (1989) has standardised an instrument (Bankers' Attribution Profile) for the use of bank managers.

9.2.1 Understanding Internality–Externality

Internality is the general orientation of a person that is based on the belief that he 'causes' most of the phenomena or at least can influence them. Such a belief can range from paranoid or maniac syndromes—exaggerated belief in one's capability to cause or influence all phenomena—to self-determination. In order to have a comprehensive understanding of internality, it may be useful to look at its different dimensions.

A person may perceive contingency as an individual, or several individuals may perceive it as a group. Both will form part of internality. These aspects are combined with the stability–variability dimension suggested by Weiner. One may thus have four dimensions of internality: personal stable, personal variable, group stable and group variable.

Similarly, externality can be seen in two dimensions: human and non-human. An outcome may be attributed to either human factors (social system and other people) or non-human factors (fate and luck). By combining these with the stability–variability dimensions, one has four externality dimensions: human stable, human variable, non-human stable and non-human variable. Table 9.2 gives these dimensions. This table shows four internality and four externality determinants of

TABLE 9.2   Internality–Externality Factors and Behavioural Modes

Locus of Control and Stability/Variability	Determinants	Resultant Mode
Internality		
Personal stable	Ability	Superman ship
Personal variable	Effort	Self-determination
Personal stable + variable	Personal strengths	Self-directedness
Group stable	Race/caste	Super-racism
Group variable	Group effort	Social-determination
Group stable + variable	Group strengths	Social-directedness

(Table 9.2 Continued)

(Table 9.2 Continued)

Locus of Control and Stability/Variability	Determinants	Resultant Mode
Externality		
Human stable	Social system	Role-taking
Human variable	Others	Cooperation
Human stable + variable	Significant others	Compliance
Non-human stable	Fate	Fatalism
Non-human variable	Luck/chance	Probabilism
Non-human stable + variable	External factors	Resignation

outcome and their resultant mode of behaviour. These are only speculative at this stage and need to be tested with research. The detailed implications of the various determinants, and the time perspective of locus of control have been discussed (Pareek, 1988a).

9.3 SCORING

A 5-point scale is used in scoring responses. Score Sheet (appended) can be used to get the scores on I, E-O and E-C. Scores on each of the three dimensions of locus of control (internality, externality–0, and externality–C) should be totalled; these will range from 0 to 40 for each. In order to convert them into a 100-point scale, the total can be multiplied by 2.5.

9.4 RELIABILITY

Split-half reliability coefficient for the instrument were 0.43, 0.45 and 0.55 respectively for I, E-O and E-C subscales, and even–odd reliability coefficients were 0.41, 0.48 and 0.54 respectively (similar to the results of Keshote, 1991).

9.5 VALIDITY

High correlation (0.89) between Levenson's instrument and LOCO inventory in a sample of 26 bankers indicates the validity of the inventory.

The three measures (I, EO and EL) were correlated with internality, both on Rotter's (1966) and Valecha's (1988) instruments. Three ratios were also used from LOCO inventory (I/E-O; I/E-L; and I/E-O + E-L). These give the 'pure' forms of internality. Table 9.3 shows the inter-correlations.

TABLE 9.3 Inter-correlations Among Locus of Control Variables

	I	EO	EO	I/ED	I/EL	I Total
1. LOCO inventory						
2. LOCO externality-others	−0.41					
3. LOCO externality-luck	−0.27	0.68**				
4. LOCO I/E-D	0.70**	−0.87**	−0.61**			
5. LOCO I/E-L	0.19	−0.32	−0.67**	0.21		
6. LOCO I/total E	0.60	−0.79**	−0.76**	0.93**	0.30	
7. Rotter internality	0.27	−0.63**	−0.78**	0.66*	0.33	0.78**
8. Valecha internality	0.15	−0.47*	−0.048*	0.36	0.28	0.41

Note: *Significant at 0.05 level;
**Significant at 0.01 level.

It may be seen from Table 9.3 that externality scores (both others and luck) are negatively correlated with internality scores on Rotter's and Valecha's instruments; the level of significance is higher on Rotter's scale. The ratio of internality/EO and internality/total E are significantly correlated with Rotter's internality, although the correlation with Valecha's internality is not significant. These data indicate acceptable validity of LOCO inventory, although further studies are desirable.

Factor analysis of data from 328 managers belonging to a large multilocational public sector steel company showed three factors. Table 9.4 shows the loadings of 30 items on the three factors. Principal components analysis was used with equamax rotation. The three factors explained about 49% variance.

Factors 1, 2 and 3 are externality-others, externality-luck and internality, respectively. Some items have significant loadings on more than one factors. Factor analysis shows the construct validity of the instrument.

9.6 NORMS

Mean and SD values of a group of managers are given as follows:

	Variable	Mean	SD
1.	Internality	28	5
2.	Externality (O)	24	5
3.	Externality (C)	15	5

TABLE 9.4   Three-factor Solution of LOCO Inventory (PCA with Equamax Rotation) Loading Below 0.3 Are Not Mentioned

Items	Factor 1	Factor 2	Factor 3
11	0.74		
5	0.72		
6	0.70		
19	0.64		
15	0.64		
29	0.63		
17	0.56	0.32	
30	0.51		
4	0.51		
22	0.43		
26		0.79	
13		0.77	
18		0.70	
21		0.75	
24		0.63	
8	0.50	0.58	
12	0.47	0.47	
7	0.52	0.41	
9	0.61	0.32	
14	0.53	0.26	
23			0.74
2			0.67
16			0.67
20			0.66
3			0.66
27		0.37	0.58
1			0.56
28	0.45		0.53
25	0.36		0.45
10			0.43

9.7 CORRELATES

In a study of 400 bankers, Sen (1982) found a high positive correlation (significant at 0.001) between internality and role efficacy (Chapter 49) and a negative correlation with E-D and E-C (both correlations significant at 0.01 level), using Levenson's instrument. Surti (1983) reported similar results with 320 professional women (significance levels being 0.05, 0.001 and 0.05, respectively). In other words, internals tend to have higher, and externals, lower role efficacy. Surti

(1983) reported a significant contribution of internality to the prediction of role efficacy in the regression analysis of data from 320 professional women.

There is some evidence to show that externals, especially those who believe things are controlled by powerful others, have higher role stress. Surti (1982) found positive correlation (all values significant at 0.01 level) between E-O (on Levenson instrument) and five role stresses (inter-role distance, role overload, result inadequacy, resource inadequacy, role inadequacy and total entrepreneurial role stress) in 40 women entrepreneurs (see Pareek, 1983b, for the concept of entrepreneurial role stress). There were significant positive correlations (at 0.01 level) between EC and inter-role distance and role overload. She also reported correlations (significant at 0.05 level) between E-C and avoidance (positive) and approach styles (negative) of coping with stress (see Chapter 57).

Using MAO-B (Chapter 25), Sen (1982) found positive correlations between internality and operational effectiveness of five motives (the levels of significance are shown in parenthesis): achievement (0.001), influence (0.003), extension (0.05), affiliation (0.01) and dependence (0.001). He also reported significant negative correlations (most of them significant at 0.001 level), both with EO and EC and operational effectiveness of all six motives. This shows that internals use the motivational behaviour more effectively in organisations than externals.

Using LOCO inventory with 212 managers in engineering firms, Keshote (1991) found negative correlations (significant at 0.05 level) between E-O, E-C and interpersonal trust measured by Rotter's scale (Rotter, 1967); externals seem to have low interpersonal trust.

Using an instrument to measure perception of and need for coercive and persuasive power (see Chapter 18) and LOCO inventory, Keshote found positive correlation (significant at 0.01 level) between 1 and value for persuasive power, between E-O and value for coercive power, and need for coercive and persuasive power. E-C scores had negative correlation (significant at 0.05 level) with value of persuasive power and positive correlation with need for coercive power (0.01 level). This means that internal managers use and value persuasive power; E-D managers use more coercive bases; E-C managers use less persuasive bases; and externals of both types want more coercive power.

Using an instrument to measure the styles of managing conflict (see Chapter 44) and LOCO inventory, Keshote found significant positive correlation between negotiation style and internality. Externals of both types showed preference for other styles. Regarding interpersonal styles (Chapter 43); E-O managers were found to have lower operating effectiveness on task orientation; and E-C managers had lower operating effectiveness on regulating function.

To summarise, internal managers tend to have higher role efficacy, experience less role stress, use the problem-solving approach for stress and conflict that they experience, use their motivational behaviour more effectively and use more persuasive bases of power in working with their employees. Externals seem to be the opposite and have lower interpersonal trust. They want more coercive power; E-Os use more coercive bases of power while working with their employees; and E-Cs use less persuasive bases.

Organisational environment and climate seem to influence the development of internality. Baumgartel, Rajan and Newman (1985) tested a group of 3,200 students (78% men and 22% women in a centre for postgraduate management education in India), using four indices of organisational environment, namely, freedom-growth, human relations, performance pressure and person benefit. They found clear evidence of the influence of organisational environments on the locus of control, as measured by Levenson's instrument; however, this effect was more striking for women than men postgraduate students. Regression analysis of data from 320 professional women, using role efficacy as a variable, showed that out of the 14 variables that finally emerged in the step-wise regression, organisational climate alone explained about 34% variance, showing a very large effect on role efficacy (Surti, 1982).

9.8 USE FOR HRD

LOCO inventory can be used for both research and training (in HRD, OD or training packages). In research, it may give more insight into the dynamics of internality and externality, including correlates of internality and both types of externality. One useful research would be in-depth case studies of the three types of managers—I, E-O and E-C. Research would generate more standardisation data for the instrument—norms, reliability and validity.

However, the instrument has been developed primarily for training and has been used in several groups. The following steps have been found to be useful:

1. Score the responses of the participants in advance and, preferably, calculate mean and SD values of the group on I, EO and ELC.
2. Explain the concept of internality and externality (both types).
3. Ask each participant to predict his level of the three dimensions—high, medium or low. In more open groups, form triads, each member of the triad estimating the levels of the other two members.
4. Distribute the scores and explain how to interpret them (mean + 1/2 SD being high and mean – 1/2 SD being low). Available norms can also be used. If the group is small, grouping all the scores in equal parts (quartiles) can be used as high, medium-high, medium-low and low for interpretation.

According to the norms shown earlier, respondents who get a total I score of 33 and above have very high internality, indicating that they have high self-confidence. However, they may be unrealistic sometimes in assessing the difficulties and problems in achieving their goals. On the other hand, respondents having a score of 17 or less on I have very little confidence in their efforts and will not utilise their potential.

A score from 29 to 32 shows high trust in one's ability and effort and is likely to lead to effective use of these. A score of 18–21 shows that the individual lacks such self-trust and needs to take steps to examine his strengths by using feedback from others.

Interpretation of scores on E-O and E-L can similarly be made. E-O shows reliance on significant others—boss, peers, subordinates—in achieving goals.

Very high scores (30–34) on E-O show rather dysfunctional dependence on significant others; scores of 21–29 show a realistic dependence; those between 17 and 20 show an independence orientation; and scores of 16 and below show an orientation of counter dependence.

On E-L, the lower the score the better. However, a score of 10 and below shows that the individual may have problems coping with frustration when unforeseen factors come in the way of achieving goals.

1. Interpretation of the scores can also be done in terms of ratios, I/E-O I/E-C and I/ total E. If the ratios are more than one, the respondent has more internality than externality of that type. Similarly, a ratio of less than one would indicate lower internality. Obviously, higher ratios are more desirable.
2. Form triads to discuss discrepancies between self-predicted and other-assessed levels and the levels revealed by the scores, mainly in terms of observed behaviour.
3. Present the implications of internality for managerial effectiveness (research data and results of correlates on internality).
4. Form triads to discuss how to increase internality and reduce externality as individuals, managers (in relation to the employees) and as an organisation person. Discuss what organisational practices promote I, E-O and E-C, and how to use and change them to increase internality amongst employees. Some ideas on how to increase internality are discussed elsewhere (Pareek, 1982).

Baumgartel et al. (1985) concluded that internality could be developed by creating educational and work environments characterised by freedom to set personal performance goals, opportunity for personal growth and opportunity to influence important events or conditions. Reichard (1975) demonstrated that a training workshop altered the locus of control in the direction of internality and that the perceived influence of powerful others decreased. However, the effect of training on perceived influence of chance, while generally supporting the research hypothesis, was inconclusive. The training was a 6-day programme that focused on internal control of things. The five modules were on discussion skills, self-awareness (task assignment, feedback, communication and motivation), managing time, management by objectives and motivation. Each module had a typed input posing questions on internality versus externality and exercises to help the participants decide and determine matters themselves.

The extensive experimental fieldwork done on high school students—in India by Mehta (1968) and in USA by De Charms (1972)—showed that the locus of control in children could be altered in the direction of internality through a series of action focused on changing the self-concept and altering the educational environment. The instrument can be used after feedback on diagnosis of the work environments. A number of interventions can be worked out by involving employees to modify HRD system such as appraisal, counselling, reward, role efficacy, etc.

LOCO Inventory
Score Sheet

Name: _____   Role: _____

Organisation: _____   Date: _____

The numbers below correspond to the item numbers in the LOCO inventory. Transfer the ratings you assigned by writing them in the appropriate blank spaces below. Then total the ratings that are transferred to each column.

Item	Rating	Item	Rating	Item	Rating
1	...	4	...	7	...
2	...	5	...	8	...
3	...	6	...	9	...
10	...	11	...	12	...
16	...	15	...	13	...
20	...	17	...	14	...
23	...	19	...	18	...
25	...	22	...	21	...
27	...	29	...	24	...
28	...	30	...	26	...
	...		...		...
Total	(I)		EO		EC

LOCO Inventory

Name: _____   Role: _____

Organisation: _____   Date: _____

Given below are some statements that show how people experience their organisations. There are no right or wrong answers. Read each statement and indicate the extent to which you feel that way, based on your experience in the organisation. Use the following key in indicating your rating. Mark it on the left-hand side of each statement.

Write 4   if you strongly feel this way
Write 3   if you generally feel this way
Write 2   if you somewhat feel this way (and somewhat not)
Write 1   if you slightly feel this way
Write 0   if you hardly or never feel this way

1. _____ I can largely determine what matters to me in the organisation.
2. _____ The course of my career largely depends on me.
3. _____ My success or failure depends mostly on the amount of effort I put in.
4. _____ The persons who are important control most matters here.
5. _____ To a large extent, my career depends on my seniors.
6. _____ My effectiveness in this organisation is mostly determined by senior people.
7. _____ The organisation one joins or the job one gets is to a large extent accidental happenings.
8. _____ One's career is to a great extent, a matter of chance.
9. _____ Success of a person depends on the breaks or chances he gets.
10. _____ Successful completion of assignments is mainly due to my detailed planning and hard work.
11. _____ Being liked by seniors or making a good impression usually influence promotion decisions.
12. _____ Getting rewards in the organisation is a matter of luck.
13. _____ Success of one's plans to a large extent is a matter of luck.
14. _____ Getting promotion largely depends on my being in the right place at the right time.
15. _____ Senior person's preference determines who would be rewarded in the organisation.
16. _____ My success, to a large extent, depends on my competence and hard work.
17. _____ How much I am liked in the organisation depends on my seniors.
18. _____ It is a matter of luck that people listen to you.
19. _____ If my seniors do not like me, I probably would not succeed in this organisation.
20. _____ Usually, I am responsible for getting, or not getting, rewards.
21. _____ My success or failure is mostly a matter of luck.
22. _____ My success or failure depends mostly on those who work with me.
23. _____ My promotion in the organisation depends mostly on my ability and effort.
24. _____ My experience is that most things in the organisation are beyond one's control.
25. _____ I can work hard enough to get my suggestions accepted in the organisation.
26. _____ I am acceptable to others in my organisation because I am lucky.
27. _____ Generally, I determine what happens to me in the organisation.
28. _____ My acceptability to others will depend on my behaviour with them.
29. _____ My ideas get accepted if I make them fit with the desires of my seniors.
30. _____ Pressure groups are more powerful (and control things) in the organisation than individual employees.

10

Locus of Control in Health (Lochi) Inventory

10.1 THE INSTRUMENT AND ITS ADMINISTRATION

The Locus of Control in Health Inventory (Lochi) Survey measures locus of control in relation to three aspects of health: cure (of illness), prevention of ill health and maintenance of good health. It measures two types of internality—personal (IP) and collective (IC); and four types of externality—luck (EL), fate (EF), God (EG) and doctor (ED). It contains 18 items, 1 for each category, as shown in Table 10.1. The inventory is easy to administer. The respondent records his degree of agreement (on a 5-point scale) for each of the 18 items.

TABLE 10.1 Distribution of Lochi Survey Items

Internality-Externality Factors and Behavioural Modes

Locus of Control and Stability/Variability

		Determinants			Resultant Mode	
Internality	Personal stable	Personal variable	Personal stable + variable	Group stable	Group variable	Group stable + variable
	Ability	Effort	Personal strengths	Race/caste	Group effort	Group strengths
	Supermanship	Self-determination	Self-directedness	Super-racism	Social-determination	Social-directedness
Externality	Human stable	Human variable	Human stable + variable	Non-human stable	Non-human stable	Non-human stable + variable

	Social system	Others	Significant others	Fate	Luck/chance	External factors
	Role-taking	Cooperation	Compliance	Fatalism	Probabilism	Resignation
Health Aspect	**IP**	**IC**	**EL**	**EF**	**EG**	**ED**
Cure of illness	15*	16*	3	14	17	18
Prevention of illness	3*	4*	1	2	5	6
Building good health	9*	10*	7	8	11	12

10.2 CONCEPTUAL FRAMEWORK

10.2.1 Locus of Control and Health

The focus on the patient is primarily to build his morale and will to cope with health problems. Patients who perceive their active role in the process of recovery (that they can and do contribute to this process) seem to recover faster (Wallston & Wallston, 1978). The intention to lose weight has been reported to be influenced by this variable (Saltzer, 1978).

To facilitate the study of the relationship of locus of control with health and illness, several instruments have been developed and used. Wallston and associates developed two scales: Health Locus of Control (HCL) Scale (Wallston, Wallston, Kaplan & Maides, 1976) and Multidimensional Health Locus of Control (MHCL) Scales (Wallston, Wallston & de Vellis, 1978). Both these scales focused on health behaviour (health maintenance and illness prevention). Coreil and Marshall (1982) reported an 11-item Locus of Illness Control Scale (LICS) containing items related to both health and illness behaviour, including illness cure. An instrument for children, Children Health Locus of Control Scale (Parcel & Meyer, 1978), and another specifically for weight control, Weight Locus of Control Scale (Saltzer, 1978), have been proposed.

In this connection, locus of control has two main dimensions, the context and the orientation itself. The context could be health or illness, or both. As already mentioned, Coreil and Marshall (1982) attempted a comprehensive approach by including illness (both prevention and cure) along with health (maintenance) in their scale. The orientation of locus of control could be internal or external. Levenson (1972b) suggested two aspects of externality: chance (or luck) and significant others. Factor analysis of data on an instrument developed in India (Pareek, 1990), however, showed four kinds of externality significant others (e.g., doctor or elders in the case of health and illness), luck (in the variable sense, i.e., chance), fate (stable) and supernatural power. In the literature on locus of control, internality has been treated as a single dimension.

Again, in the context of developing countries, most of which have a collectivistic orientation, internality also seems to have two aspects—individual (I) and collective (we). An individual may perceive some events being influenced by individual action and some by collective action. An orientation of collective internality may help a community organise some effective action to deal with both individual and community problems.

To summarise, for the concept of locus of control to be comprehensive, it should include both maintenance of health and prevention and cure of illness. It should also include both the individual and collective internality on the one hand and four kinds of externality—significant others (SO), luck (L), fate (F) and supernatural power (SP)—on the other.

10.3 SCORING

Reverse the starred items marked in the Score Sheet (Table 10.1; internality items): 4 becomes 1, 3 becomes 2, 2 becomes 3 and 1 becomes 4. The higher the score, the higher the external locus of control in health matters. To obtain a group profile, scores can be obtained for all eighteen cells.

10.4 RELIABILITY

Homogeneity was tested by item–total correlation for a group of 119. All items (except numbers 6 and 18) had high correlation with the total.

10.5 VALIDITY

Validity was tested by two methods. Theoretically, high externals recover slowly from illness, compared with the internals. Lochi scores were correlated with self-reported speed of recovery from illness on a 4-point scale—very soon, soon, after some time and after a long time—for a group of 35. The correlation of total Lochi scores (showing externality) had low but significant (at 0.05) level positive correlation with later recovery. Age had positive (significant at 0.01 level) correlation with externality.

The second way to test construct validity was to factor analyse the responses of 119 respondents, using principal component analysis with Varimax rotation. It gave four factors, explaining 61% variance. Factor analysis results are given in Table 10.2.

Factor I (explaining 32% variance) has five items of internality (all the three of I-P and two of I-C). It also contains one each from EC, EG and ED. This factor can be called an internality

TABLE 10.2   Factor Loading of Lochi

Items	Factor I	Factor II	Factor III	Factor IV
95	0.87			
3	0.74			
15	0.74			
10	0.77			
4	0.78			
1	0.61			
12	0.81			
5	0.70			
14		0.68		
2		0.64		
8		0.51		
13		0.78		
7		0.47		
16			−0.78	
17			0.50	
11			0.63	
18				0.69
6				0.66

factor; Item 12, relating to doctors, is also partly in internality item ('doctors helping us to be healthy' or 'not making us healthy').

Factor II has three items of fate and two of luck. In India, fate and luck usually have the same meaning. This factor can be called fatalism factor.

Factor III has two God-related items and one I-C item (on which there is negative loading). This can be called the faith in God factor.

Factor analysis has to a large extent validated the concept of locus of control used in this instrument. Internality (collective) has however not emerged as a separate factor.

▮ 10.6 USE FOR HRD

Suggestions given for LOC Inventory (Chapter 9) and ASUFA Inventory (Chapter 11) are relevant here.

Lochi Survey

Name: _____   Role: _____

Organisation: _____   Date: _____

The purpose of this instrument is to survey people's thinking about health and illness. There are no right or wrong answers. Please give your honest reactions. Read each statement and write down one of the following numbers in the space provided on the left-hand side.

Write 4   if you fully agree with the statement
Write 3   if you mostly agree with the statement
Write 2   if you disagree with the statement
Write 1   if you strongly disagree with the statement

1. _____   Illness is a matter of bad luck.
2. _____   If it is in your fate, you cannot avoid sickness.
3. _____   People can prevent sickness by taking enough precaution.
4. _____   People, together, can plan to prevent occurrence of some diseases.
5. _____   If God sends a disease, no one can prevent it.
6. _____   Doctors can help a lot in preventing the occurrence of some diseases.
7. _____   Keeping good health is a matter of good luck.
8. _____   If fate favours people, they keep healthy.
9. _____   One can maintain good health by paying attention to nutrition, exercise, etc.
10. _____   Members of a community can do a lot to ensure good health in the community.
11. _____   God helps us to keep healthy.
12. _____   Doctors and other specialists can help us keep healthy and fit.
13. _____   Cure from a disease is a matter of good luck.
14. _____   There is no use worrying about illness; it will be cured when the time comes.
15. _____   The patient himself can do a lot to fight and get over an illness.
16. _____   People can learn to help each other in dealing with many diseases.
17. _____   If God wills, a person can be cured of a disease.
18. _____   Good doctors can cure most illnesses.

Optimism: Attribution of Success and Failure Inventory— General (ASUFA-G)

11.1 THE INSTRUMENT AND ITS ADMINISTRATION

Attribution of Success and Failure (ASUFA) Inventory assesses the respondent's attributional thinking—to what they attribute success and failure to (internal or external, and the stable or variable factors). There have been several versions. In the latest version, the inventory has 32 items (pairs).

The inventory contains 16 items for success and 16 for failure. The respondents distribute four marks between the two items in each pair. Personal and non-personal factors in both, internality and externality, with the combination of stable and variable aspects have been paired for both success and lack of success.

ASUFA is designed to measure and enhance managers', students', teachers', health workers' and parents' level of optimism and related aspects.

11.2 CONCEPTUAL FRAMEWORK

One important variable for effectiveness in all aspects of life is optimism. Seligman (1991) has popularised the key role of optimism in several aspects of life, including health (see Chapter 17). He narrates the story of a paediatric nurse, Madelon Visintainer, who did pioneering experiments on rats in 1978. She experimented on three groups of rats: (a) mild escapable shock was given to the first group (optimist rats); (b) mild inescapable shock to the second group (pessimist rats); and (c) no shock was given to the third group (control group). A few days before the experiment, she planted a few cells of sarcoma on each rat's flank. The tumour is lethal if it grows and not rejected by the animal's immune defences. Visintainer had planted the right number of sarcoma so that 50% would reject the tumour and live. Within a month, 50% died in the 3rd group ('control'), 70% rejected it in the first group ('optimist') and only 27% rejected it in the second group ('pessimist') (Visintainer, Volpicell & Seligman, 1982). This proved the role of control and optimism in fighting cancer. Interestingly, a rat's childhood experience of mastery made the difference. Most of the rats who had been trained in mastery rejected the tumour, whereas the most helpless ones died (Seligman & Visintainer, 1985).

Optimism seems to be critical for health. George Valliant studied 200 men between 39 and 44 years and followed up their lives. Health at 60 years was strongly related to optimism at 25 years (Person, Seligman & Valliant, 1988).

How does optimism promote better health? Optimism seems to improve the functioning of the immune system by preventing helplessness. We have two types of cells in our immune system. T-cells recognise specific invaders, greatly multiply and kill the invaders (such as virus, bacteria, tumour). While natural killer (NK) cells kill anything foreign. The brain and the immune system are connected through hormones. When depressed, neurotransmitters, especially catechol-amines, become depleted and another chemical called endorphins go up. The immune system detects its presence and turns itself down. As a result, T-cells do not multiply rapidly when they come across specific invaders. NK cells from the spleen lose their ability to kill foreign invaders.

Optimism has been reported to help people cope with stress and reduce risk of illness (Horowitz, Adler & Kegeles, 1988; Scheier & Carver, 1985). Optimists used more problem-focused coping, sought social support and saw positive aspects of the situation (Scheier, Weintraub & Carver, 1986). Optimism was also found to be an important predictor of recovery from surgery in case of coronary artery bypass patients (Scheier et al., 1989). Optimism has been reported to be associated with faster recovery and better adjustment in the post-surgery period (Fitzgerald, Moroczek, Brignall, Silvestro & Voss, 1993).

Seligman (1991), building on the works of Rotter (locus of control) and Weiner (causal attribution), using the time and space dimension, suggested two types to stable factors (permanent and universal) and two types of variable factors (temporary and specific). He defined optimism in two ways: attributing success or good events to permanent and universal factors, and attributing failure or misfortunes to temporary or specific factors. He developed a 48-item (pairs) instrument for measuring optimism, pessimism and internal locus of control ways; attributing success or good events to permanent and universal factors; and attributing failure or misfortunes to temporary or specific factors. He developed a 48-item (pairs) instrument for measuring optimism, pessimism and internal locus of control.

Scheier and Carver (1985) developed a 12-item yes–no instrument (Life Orientation Test or LOT) to measure optimism. Four items are filler items, four items are positive and four negative, which are reversed to score optimism. LOT has been used in a large number of investigations.

ASUFA inventory measures several aspects of locus of control and optimism. It analyses to what the respondents attribute success and failures.

In one study, reported in Kaplan, Sallis and Patterson (1993, p. 43), women diagnosed with breast cancer were given LOT. They were interviewed the day before their surgery and then again 7 and 10 days and 3 months following surgery. At the time of the surgery, women who scored higher on optimism reviewed the situation in a positive light and accepted its reality. Women who scored higher on pessimism denied the reality of the situation and reported giving up or feeling that the surgery was hopeless. For women undergoing surgery, optimism was associated with a positive mood and the ability to maintain a sense of humour. Pessimism was associated with more reports of emotional distress, denial and disengagement. These studies also demonstrated that acceptance of the reality of the situation is important. Those who demonstrated acceptance prior to the surgery did not show serious distress after the surgery.

In other cases of surgery, optimists and pessimists differed from the beginning. Even before the surgery, the pessimists reported higher levels of hostility and depression than the optimists. After the surgery, pessimists reported to be less happy and less relieved than the optimists. The optimists seemed to be less focused on the negative experiences associated with surgery. After the surgery, the optimists sought information that would help them in the recovery process, got up and began walking around their rooms after surgery in contrast to the pessimists. Six months after surgery, optimists returned to vigorous exercise, better adaptation to the surgery and appeared to return to their normal lives at a more rapid pace.

Optimism seems to be an important variable in various aspects of life. Seligman (1991) has fascinatingly discussed how it is important in political leadership. Success in the presidential and senate elections in the United States of America was predicted on the basis of scores on pessimism and rumination. Rumination is defined as a tendency to recall miserable experiences and failure, mull over them and constantly think about them, including what caused them. Those who had high scores on 'pessrum' (combination of pessimism and rumination) failed to win the elections. Seligman (1991) has given enough evidence to show how optimism is important in sports, school achievement and in work.

A study of insurance agents showed that less optimistic agents were twice as likely to quit as more optimistic ones. The agents from the top half scores on optimism sold 20% more than the less optimistic ones (from bottom half); those from the top quarter sold 50% more than those from the bottom quarter (Seligman, 1991, p. 102). When a special force of high optimist agents was created, they outsold the pessimists in the regular force by 21% during the first year and by 57% in the second year (p. 104).

To sum up, the competent persons not only want to have control over the outcome but also to take personal responsibility for their success or failure. In other words, they attribute the outcome to themselves—their activities and effort (or lack of it). This is called internal locus of control or internality. Less competent persons attribute the outcome to external factors, called external locus of control or externality.

Weiner (1974) added a new dimension to the locus of control paradigm. He suggested that locus of control interacted with stability–variability. Internality can be perceived as related to either the stable (ability) or variable factor (effort). Similarly, externality can be perceived as related to the stable factor (task difficulty or opportunity) or the variable factor (luck or chance). Locus of control has been studied in the West only as a personal characteristic. Locus of control can also be collective, a group or a team having an orientation of controlling the situations or being controlled by them.

Seligman (1991) proposed optimism and pessimism as resulting from attribution of outcome to stable or variable factors. Based on the findings of Weiner and Seligman, and combining internality (personal and collective) and externality (personal and non-person) with stable and variable aspects, we can get the following measures of locus of control and optimism-pessimism:

1. *Self-directedness* is defined as high personal internality. A self-directed person will exercise his choices in most situations.
2. *Group-directedness* is defined as high collective internality. A group-directed person will follow group norms and work with his team to influence situations.
3. *Conformity* is defined as high personal externality. A conformist will be guided by the wishes of the significant persons.
4. *Fatalism* is defined as high non-person externality. A person with a high score will attribute most outcomes to external forces (government, fate, circumstances, etc.) and is not likely to exercise much effort to bring about change.
5. *Optimism* is defined as attributing failure and miseries to variable factors (both internal and external).
6. *Pessimism* is defined as attributing failures and miseries to stable factors (both internal and external).
7. *Hope* is defined as the ratio between attribution to variable and attribution to stable factors.
8. *Self-confidence* is defined as the ratio between internality and externality.

11.3 SCORING

Scoring of ASUFA inventory is complicated and thus preferably software available for scoring and interpretation should be used. Follow the steps given below to score your responses to ASUFA inventory:

1. Transfer your responses (scores) of 32 items of ASUFA inventory to Table 11.1.
2. Once you have transferred the responses, total them as indicated. For example, put the sum of 1a, 7b, 9b, 14a under Total (1) and so on.
3. You will see that all totals and totals of totals are printed bold. For example, the total of items no. 1 and 3 is 17. The total of no. 1 and 2 is 25; 37 is the total of no. 17, 19, 21 and 23. Similarly, 38 is the total of 18, 20, 22 and 24.
4. Read out your quotients of Self-directedness, Group-directedness, Compliance and Fatalism from Table 11.2 and note these down below in the respective places. All quotients range from 0 to 100.
5. Read out your quotient of Optimism and Pessimism from Table 11.3 and note it down below in the respective place.

TABLE 11.1 Score Sheet

Transfer below your ratings on the various items

		Stable				Total	Variable				Total	Total
Success	I(P)	1a___	7b___	9b___	14a___	___(1)	1b___	3b___	10a___	13a___	___(2)	___(25)
	I(C)	2a___	8a___	11b___	14b___	___(3)	5a___	8b___	10b___	16a___	___(4)	___(26)
					Total	___(17)				Total	___(18)	___(27)
	E(O)	2b___	4a___	12a___	13b___	___(5)	4b___	6a___	9a___	16b___	___(6)	___(28)
	E(NP)	5b___	7a___	12b___	15a___	___(7)	3a___	6b___	11a___	15b___	___(8)	___(29)
					Total	___(19)				Total	___(20)	___(30)
Lack of Success	I(P)	17a___	23b___	25b___	30a___	___(9)	17b___	19b___	26a___	29a___	___(10)	___(31)
	I(C)	18a___	24a___	27b___	30b___	___(11)	21a___	24b___	26b___	32a___	___(12)	___(32)
					Total	___(21)				Total	___(22)	___(33)
	E(O)	18b___	20a___	23a___	29b___	___(13)	20b___	22a___	25a___	32b___	___(14)	___(34)
	E(NP)	21b___	23a___	23b___	31a___	___(15)	19a___	22b___	27a___	31b___	___(16)	___(35)
					Total	___(23)				Total	___(24)	___(36)

Total of 17, 19, 21, 23 ___(37)

Total of 18, 20, 22, 24 ___(38)

6. Read out your quotients of Self-confidence and Hope from Table 11.4 and note them down below in the respective places.

ASUFA Dimensions	Quotient	Your Level	Norms Mean	SD
1. Self-directedness				
2. Group-directedness				
3. Compliance				
4. Fatalism				
5. Optimism				
6. Pessimism				
7. Hope				
8. Self-confidence				

1. *Self-directedness* is the orientation of taking personal responsibility for and influencing most matters significant to oneself (personal internal control).

2. *Group-directedness* is the orientation of attributing (giving credit or blaming for) results in most matters significant to oneself and to group to which one belongs (collective internal control).

3. *Compliance* is the orientation of attributing (holding responsible for) results in most matters significant to oneself, to significant persons in one's group and to accept their influence (personal external control).

4. *Fatalism* is the orientation of attributing (holding responsible for) results in most significant personal matters to external forces like fate, luck, work and other systems (non-personal control).

5. *Optimism* is attributing lack of success, miseries and bad experiences to variable (temporary or specific) factors.

6. *Pessimism* is attributing success and good experiences to variable (temporary or specific) factors and lack of success, miseries and bad experiences to stable (permanent or pervasive) factors.

7. *Self-confidence* is the ratio of internality to externality.

8. *Hope* is the ratio of attribution to variables to attribution to stable factors.

Five forms of ASUFA inventory are available—general, students, teachers, parents and health workers. The details provided are applicable to all ASUFA forms.

TABLE 11.2   Conversion of Raw Scores to Quotients of Self-directedness (25 + 31), Group-directedness (26 + 32), Compliance (28 + 34) and Fatalism (29 + 35) [Formula (X – 8) × 100/48]

Score	Quotient	Score	Quotient	Score	Quotient	Score	Quotient
8	0	20	25	32	50	44	75
9	2	21	27	33	52	45	77
10	4	22	29	34	54	46	79
11	6	23	31	35	56	47	81
12	8	24	33	36	58	48	83
13	10	25	35	37	60	49	85
14	12	26	37	38	62	50	87
15	15	27	40	39	64	51	89
16	17	28	42	40	67	52	92
17	19	29	44	41	69	53	94
18	21	30	46	42	71	54	96
19	23	31	48	43	73	55	98
						56	100

TABLE 11.3   Conversion of Raw Scores to Quotients of Optimism (22 + 24) and Pessimism (21 + 23) [Formula (X – 16) × 100/32]

Score	Quotient	Score	Quotient	Score	Quotient
16	0	27	34	38	69
17	3	28	38	39	72
18	6	29	41	40	75
19	9	30	44	41	78
20	13	31	47	42	81
21	16	32	50	43	84
22	19	33	53	44	88
23	22	34	56	45	91
24	25	35	59	46	94
25	28	36	63	47	97
26	31	37	66	48	100

TABLE 11.4 Conversion of Raw Scores to Quotients of Self-confidence (27 + 33) and Hope (38) [Formula (X − 32) × 100/64]

Score	Quotient	Score	Quotient	Score	Quotient	Score	Quotient
32	0	48	25	64	50	80	75
33	2	49	26	65	51	81	76
34	3	50	28	66	53	82	78
35	5	51	29	67	54	83	80
36	6	52	31	68	56	84	81
37	8	53	32	69	57	85	83
38	9	54	34	70	59	86	84
39	11	55	35	71	61	87	86
40	12	56	37	72	62	88	87
41	14	57	38	73	64	89	89
42	15	58	41	74	65	90	90
43	17	59	42	75	67	91	92
44	18	60	44	76	68	92	93
45	20	61	45	77	70	93	95
46	22	62	47	78	71	94	97
47	23	63	48	79	73	95	98
						96	100

11.4 NORMS

The mean and SD ranks of 109 respondents are given below:

	Mean	SD
Self-directedness	60	7
Group-directedness	51	6
Compliance	59	7
Fatalism	35	7
Optimism	68	9
Pessimism	53	5
Self-confidence	59	7
Hope	73	8

The following norms, based on the data of approximately 1,000 responses, can be used. However, specific norms can be developed for specific groups.

Attributes	Very Low	Low	Mean	SD	High	Very High
Self-directedness	Below 48	48–53	58	5	63–68	Above 68
Group-directedness	Below 38	38–41	44	3	47–50	Above 50
Conformity	Below 43	43–47	51	4	55–59	Above 59
Fatalism	Below 28	28–36	44	8	52–60	Above 60
Optimism	Below 45	45–49	53	4	57–61	Above 61
Pessimism	Below 44	44–48	52	4	56–60	Above 60
Hope	Below 45	45–49	53	4	57–61	Above 61
Self-confidence	Below 47	47–52	57	5	62–67	Above 67

11.5 RELIABILITY

Split-half reliability was found significant at 0.01 level (76).

11.6 VALIDITY

The following correlations were found between self-rating and rating by the supervisors of 30 persons in one organisation. All the correlations, except for self-directedness, were formed to be significant at 0.01 or higher level. In case of self-directedness, the correlation was significant at 0.05 level. Therefore, the validity of the instrument is established.

Self-directedness	0.34
Group-directedness	0.34
Conformity	0.69
Fatalism	0.71
Optimism	0.61
Pessimism	0.48
Self-confidence	0.47
Hope	0.61

Correlation of ASUFA inventory with rotter's SRI (1954) for a group of 164 managers indicated external locus of control. Except for the last eight dimensions, all other coefficients of correlation were significant at 0.001 level (except for luck in success, at 0.01 level, and task difficulty in failure, at 0.004 level). Thus, the construct validity of attribution to internal–external and stable–variable factors as independent constructs has been established.

I/E ratios, both for success and failure, had negative correlation with Rotter's scale (showing externality score) as well as with the internality factors in success and failure and with total internality. The correlations with all measures of externality were found to be positive. These findings establish the validity of the instrument.

11.7 USE FOR HRD

Divide the participants into small groups, with each participant discussing, in turn, his plans to deal with a problem. Other observer participants interrupt the narrator if he makes an external locus of control statement and may ask him to convert it into an internal statement. For example, if the narrator says 'The bank will help me', he may change it to 'I shall approach the bank for help'. Similarly, changes are suggested for statements showing attribution of failure to stable factors.

Small group can also be formed where each participant discusses his plans to overcome some of his deficiencies. Thus, effort as an attributional factor is reinforced.

11.8 CORRELATES

Two inventories were administered to 65 executive trainees in a Malaysian agricultural bank— What Do You Look for in a Job? (giving 'motivators' and 'hygiene' factors, see Chapter 15) and Work Preference Schedule (see Chapter 13)—measuring the four motives of achievement, power, affiliation and security. The former instrument was also administered to a group of 42 managers from the same bank; both the groups also responded to the ASUFA inventory (earlier version).

Motivators and hygiene did not correlate with any of the ASUFA variables in either group. Regarding the four motives, achievement correlated with stable failure, internal failure and total internality (positive at 0.01, 0.01 and 0.001 levels, respectively); power motive with attributional competence (variable/stable; positive at 0.01 level); security with stable failure (negative at 0.01 level); while correlations of affiliation were not significant with any ASUFA variable. These results show that people with high achievement motive take personal responsibility for failure and have high internality. Those with high power motive attribute results to variable factors. Those with low security need tend to attribute failure to stable factors, or, in other words, those who attribute failure to stable factors tend to have a lower security motive.

ASUFA Inventory

Name: _____   Role: _____

Organisation: _____   Date: _____

Many factors contribute to the success or lack of success of people. Some of these are given below in pairs. Please distribute four points between each of the two terms of each pair (4,0; 3,1; 2,2; 1,3; 0,4) to indicate how much you believe they contribute to success or lack of success. There are no right or wrong answers. We are interested in your personal opinion.

In your opinion, how much each of the two factors in each pair contributes towards success of a person?

__ 1a.	Talent		__ 9a.	Supportive boss
__ 1b.	Hard work		__ 9b.	Basic ability
__ 2a.	Family background		__ 10a.	Efficiency
__ 2b.	Competent guides		__ 10b.	Supportive team
__ 3a.	Market dynamics		__ 11a.	Social conditions
__ 3b.	Motivation		__ 11b.	Competent colleagues
__ 4a.	Competent colleagues		__ 12a.	Competent guide
__ 4b.	Supportive colleagues		__ 12b.	Fate
__ 5a.	Supportive family		__ 13a.	Hard work
__ 5b.	Fate		__ 13b.	Competent guide
__ 6a.	Supportive boss		__ 14a.	Talent
__ 6b.	Specific opportunity		__ 14b.	Affluent family
__ 7a.	Support system		__ 15a.	Fate
__ 7b.	General ability		__ 15b.	Resources
__ 8a.	Cultural background		__ 16a.	Supportive family
__ 8b.	Supportive family		__ 16b.	Supportive colleagues

A.   In your opinion how much each factor in each pair contributes more towards failure of a person?

__ 17a.	Lack of talent		__ 25a.	Bad boss
__ 17b.	Laziness		__ 25b.	Lack of ability
__ 18a.	Family background		__ 26a.	Inefficiency
__ 18b.	Incompetent guides		__ 26b.	Hostile team
__ 19a.	Bad market conditions		__ 27a.	Unfavourable conditions
__ 19b.	Lack of motivation		__ 27b.	Incompetent colleagues
__ 20a.	Incompetent colleagues		__ 28a.	Incompetent guide
__ 20b.	Hostile colleagues		__ 28b.	Fate
__ 21a.	Indifferent family		__ 29a.	Laziness
__ 21b.	Fate		__ 29b.	Incompetent guide
__ 22a.	Bad boss		__ 30a.	Lack of talent
__ 22b.	Lack of opportunity		__ 39b.	Poor family
__ 23a.	Bad organisation		__ 31a.	Fate
__ 23b.	Low ability		__ 31b.	Lack of resources
__ 24a.	Cultural background		__ 32a.	Unsupportive family
__ 24b.	Uncooperative family		__ 32b.	Unsupportive colleagues

Rumination: Dealing with Emotions

12.1 THE INSTRUMENT AND ITS ADMINISTRATION

Dealing with Emotions contains seven items. Three items are pairs; the respondent is required to choose one item in each pair. The others contain statements which the respondent is required to rate on a 5-point scale, indicating the frequency of occurrence. It is simple to administer.

12.2 THE CONCEPTUAL FRAMEWORK

When we sit alone or daydream and recall all our miseries, misfortunes, failures or bad experiences with people, it is called *rumination*. Sitting in groups and talking about past miseries or current disappointments is also rumination. We almost relive the same experiences and indulge in such recollections. On the other hand, when we recollect our good experiences, enjoy such recollection or are involved in a highly absorbing activity, it is called *flow*.

Worrying about matters is also rumination. It is dysfunctional and damaging. It makes the situation even worse, particularly when one is under pressure. Often it is better to put off thinking in order to do ourselves good. We can learn to control not only what we think but also when we think.

Women are twice more likely to suffer depression than men because they tend to think about problems in ways that amplify depression. Men tend to act rather than reflect, but women tend to contemplate their depression, mulling it over and over, trying to analyse it to determine its source.

When a woman gets fired from her job, she tries to figure out why, broods and relives the events over and over again. A man upon getting fired acts. He gets drunk, beats someone up or otherwise distracts himself from thinking about it.

Psychologists call this process of obsessive analysis *rumination*, the usual meaning of the word being 'chewing the cud'. Ruminant animals such as cattle, sheep and goats chew a cud which is regurgitated, partially digested food. It is not a very appealing image of what people who ruminate do with their thoughts, but an exceedingly apt one! Rumination combined with a pessimistic explanatory style leads to severe depression.

People who mull over bad events are called ruminators. A ruminator can be either an optimist or a pessimist. Optimist ruminators are action oriented. They have a pessimistic explanatory style, but they rarely talk to themselves and when they do, it is usually about what they plan to do, not about how bad things are. However, the belief structure of a pessimist ruminator is pessimistic and they repeatedly tell themselves how bad things are.

There is a positive relationship between pessimism and rumination, with both of them leading to depression. If a person believes that he is helpless in some situation and the cause of the situation is permanent, pervasive and personal, the consequences are depression.

The more a person ruminates, more the feeling of helplessness arises. And the more the feeling of helplessness, the more depressed the person is. Ruminators keep thinking about how bad things are.

People who do not ruminate tend to avoid depression even if they are pessimists. Similarly, optimists who ruminate also avoid depression. Changing either rumination or pessimism helps relieve depression. Changing both helps the most.

Susan Noalen Hocksama of Stanford University is the originator of the *rumination theory*. When asked to rate what they actually did when they were depressed, the majority of women subjects said that they tried to analyse their mood or the cause behind it, whereas most men said they did something they enjoyed.

The concept of flow is the opposite of rumination. Mihaly Csikszentmihalyi (1976) proposed the concept of 'flow' as deep involvement in positive activity and thought, the joy one gets in recollection of good and positive experiences or in activities demanding high involvement.

According to Mihaly, flow exists in the present, and it is possible to flow while engaged in any activity. In *Flow and Mindfulness: An Instructional Cassette*, Daniel Goleman (1976) suggests five steps in achieving flow; these are (a) fit difficulty to skill (even match between the difficulty of a challenge and a person's ability to meet it); (b) focus attention (focusing attention to allow the merging of awareness and activity); (c) forget time (the ability to focus on the moment, on here and now); (d) relax and wake up (alert mind and relaxed body); and (e) training for flow (e.g., dance, meditation, some eastern martial arts, music, etc.). Thus, flow means involvement in positive thinking, recalling pleasant experiences, pleasant daydreams and involvement in activities that one enjoys.

12.3 SCORING

1. The first three items are scored four for a 'yes' and zero for a 'no'.
2. Item number four to seven are scored as rated. Scale will be from zero to four for each.

3. Rumination score can be calculated by adding the following:

    1a + 2b + 3b + 4a + 4b + 4c + 5a + 5b + 6b + 6c + 7a + 7b + 7c + 7d + 7e.
    Multiply the total by 1.67.

4. Flow score can be calculated by adding the following:
    1b + 2a + 3a + 4d + 4e + 5c + 5d + 6a + 6d.
    Multiply the total by 2.78. The range will be 0–100.

5. Rumination Index can be calculated by using the following formula: (Rumination/
    Rumination + Flow) × 100. It ranges between 0 and 100.

12.4 RELIABILITY

For a group of 32 college teachers, Guttman split-half index was found to be 54, and equal-length
and unequal-length Spearman-Brown indices were 55. Guttman Lambda ranged from 44 to 74.

12.5 NORMS

Mean and SD of two groups (43 college students and 32 college teachers from all over India) are
given below:

	Teachers		Students	
	Mean	**SD**	**Mean**	**SD**
Rumination	52	10	53	12
Flow	60	13	59	16
Rumination Index	47	10	57	15

12.6 USE FOR HRD

The participants may discuss in small groups how rumination may affect their effectiveness and
therefore develop ways of reducing rumination. One group, for example, decided that they would
not criticise things in the organisation or the society, unless they do something about them.

There are two ways to deal with rumination. The first is simply to distract oneself when
pessimistic beliefs occur—try to think of something else. The second is to dispute them. This is
more effective in the long run because successfully disputed beliefs are less likely to recur when
the same situation presents itself again.

Pessimistic explanatory style and rumination can be changed and that, too, permanently.
Cognitive therapy by Aaron Beck and Albert Ellis uses five tactics to create explanatory style and

curtail rumination. The first step is to recognise the automatic thoughts hitting through your consciousness at the time you feel worst. Automatic thoughts are quick phrases or sentences, so well-practiced as to be almost unnoticed and unchallenged, for example, a mother screams at her children and later feels depressed about it. She says to herself that she is a terrible mother. She learns to become aware of these automatic thoughts and learns that they are her explanations which are permanent, pervasive and personal.

The second tactic is learning to dispute automatic thoughts by marshalling contrary evidence. The mother is helped to remember that when kids return from school, she plays with them, tutors them and listens to their problems. She learns to focus on this evidence and sees that it contradicts her automatic thought that she is a bad mother.

The third tactic is learning to make different explanations, called reattributions and use them to dispute automatic thoughts. The negative statements are replaced by saying, 'I'm fine with the kids in the evening and terrible in the morning'. This statement is less permanent and pervasive.

The fourth tactic is learning to distract oneself from depressing thoughts. The mother learns that having these negative thoughts now is not inevitable. It is better to put off thinking. One can learn to control not only what he thinks but also when to think.

The fifth tactic is learning to recognise and question the depression-sowing assumptions.

Dealing with Emotions

Name: _____   Date: _____

Institution: _____

We are studying how people deal with some happenings and feelings. There are no right or wrong ways. Please answer the following questions frankly.

A. For each of the three questions below pairs are given. Choose one item in each pair that you do more frequently than the other. Put a tick mark (4) on that item.

1. When bad mood strikes you, what do you generally do?
    __ a. Analyse your mood
    __ b. Do something to distract your attention

2. When you quarrel with your friend/partner, how do you react?
    __ a. Get away and take attention off one some other things and not be over-concerned with it.
    __ b. Express your emotions and be quite concerned about it.

3. What events do you generally recall and relive?
    __ a. Pleasant ones which you enjoyed.
    __ b. Unpleasant ones and the sufferings you have had.

B. Read each item given below and respond how often you do them. Use the following key to give your responses.

> Write 4 if this happens (or you do so) most frequently
> Write 3 if this happens (or you do so) often
> Write 2 if this happens (or you do so) sometimes
> Write 1 if this happens (or you do so) occasionally
> Write 0 if this happens (or you do so) almost never

1. When you are depressed for some reason, how often do you do the following?
    __ a. Think about the events causing depression.
    __ b. Recall details of the events.
    __ c. Analyse to determine the source of depression.
    __ d. Get involved in music, play or some other activity.
    __ e. Go to sleep.

2. When you are having some problem and you are sitting by yourself, how often the following thoughts come to your mind?
    __ a. Detailed analysis of the causes of the problem.
    __ b. Related emotions of anger/resentment/frustration.
    __ c. Alternative solutions to be attempted.
    __ d. Some other thoughts to turn the attention away from the problem.

3. If you sit and daydream (think or fantasise), which of the following are the main themes of your daydream?
    __ a. The good time you had with family and friends.
    __ b. Problems people created for you.
    __ c. The suffering you underwent.
    __ d. Work-related matters.

4. How often do you do the following?
    __ a. Recall the events when you failed to achieve what you wanted to achieve, think why you failed and what you should have done instead.
    __ b. Relive the quarrel you had to analyse who started it, what was the cause and whether your relations deteriorated with the person?
    __ c. Regret why you did what you did, what you should have done or wonder why the other person(s) did which hurt you.
    __ d. Rethink similar events which happened to you in the past and wonder why it happens to you.
    __ e. Talk about and lament amongst friends the deteriorating conditions/values in our country/society.

Psychological Needs: Work Preference Schedule

13.1 THE INSTRUMENT AND ITS ADMINISTRATION

The main purpose of the Work Preference Schedule is to get a profile of a respondent's four psychological needs as reflected in the choice of occupations.

13.2 CONCEPTUAL FRAMEWORK

A person's behaviour is the result of several factors or motives. A knowledge of the typical, primary motivators of behaviour in a work setting can help managers and consultants to deal more effectively with people.

Murray (1938) developed a long list of human motives or needs, and his work has inspired further studies, which have produced different lists of significant behavioural motives. McClelland, Atkinson, Clark and Lowell (1953) suggested three important motives—achievement, affiliation and power—and elaborate methods for measuring them. McClelland subsequently demonstrated the importance of the achievement motive for entrepreneurship and marketing (McClelland & Winter, 1969) and of power as a motivation in management (McClelland, 1975; McClelland & Burnham, 1976). Litwin and Stringer (1968) used the three motives of achievement, affiliation and power in their study of organisational climates and organisational behaviour.

Although McClelland's study of achievement and affiliation motives showed them to be rather simple variables, he found the power motive to be a complex one. According to him (McClelland, 1975), the desire for power contains three different elements that are as follows:

1. Need to control others (personalised power).
2. Need to make an impact on others.
3. Need to use power to do something for other people and groups, for instance, organisations (socialised power).

It is helpful to make clear distinctions between these three. Control seems to focus on keeping track of developments according to an agreed plan and on being informed about 'how things are going'. This seems to be an important need or motive in managerial behaviour. Mehta (1994) has proposed the concept of social achievement motive. The so-called socialised dimension of power, reflected in the use of power for the benefit of others, seems to be a separate need or motive. Pareek (1968a, 1968b) suggests that this need is important for social development and calls it the extension motive.

13.3 SCORING

Only the reasons are scored in this instrument. A total of 11 reasons are given (A to K). These relate to each of the four psychological needs—one reason being common to both achievement and power. The following steps are involved in scoring:

1. Give scores of 3, 2 and 1 for the first three choices respectively.
2. Write down the scores against the reasons from A to K.
3. Add the scores.
4. The following motives are to be scored:

Achievement	B, F, G	Affiliation	C, I, K
Power	E, F, H	Security	A, D, J

   Add the scores of B, F and G; this is the total score of achievement motivation. Likewise, find the total scores of the other three main motives. The maximum and minimum scores for each motive are 72 and 0 respectively. The higher the score, the higher is the motive.
5. Rank-order the motives according to the scores.

13.4 VALIDITY

Construct validity is provided by rank-order correlations amongst the four motives in a group of Malaysian managers—Ach-Power (0.25), Ach-Aff (–0.78), Ach-Security (–0.62) and Aff-Sec (0.52). These are all conceptually predictable.

13.5 NORMS

Values of mean, SD, median and mode of the four motives were calculated for a group of 65 executive trainees in a Malaysian agricultural bank. Based on these, the following norms are suggested. Norms (mean) for various groups need to be worked out.

Achievement	37	Affiliation	8
Power	24	Security	20

13.6 CORRELATES

Some correlations were calculated from the data of 65 executive trainees of an agricultural bank in Malaysia. The achievement motive had significant (0.001 level) negative correlation with the security motive and with hygiene factors and positive correlation, significant at 0.001 level, with attribution of failure to the internal stable factor, and with attribution to internal factors (significant at 0.01 level). The power motive had significant (0.01 level) positive correlation with attribution competence, that is, ratio between attribution to variable and stable factors. It also had negative correlation (significant at 0.001 level) with the security motive. Affiliation had significant correlation (at 0.001 level) with hygiene factors. The security motive had negative correlations with motivators, attribution to failure to stable factors, in addition to the achievement and power motives, as already stated.

13.7 USE FOR HRD

The higher the score, the more dominant is the need in the individual. Such a profile can help a person to become aware of his psychological needs.

It may be useful to get the profile of needs and then to divide the participants into small groups to discuss the implications of these for themselves and whether they would like to see a different profile of themselves. Motivation development programmes can then be planned.

The HRD facilitator can also develop a group profile of all the respondents (presuming them to be from the same group). The group may discuss if the profile is desirable and if not, what factors contribute to it and what can be done to change it. This can help in designing OD interventions.

Work Preference Schedule

Name: _____   Role: _____

Organisation: _____   Date: _____

Instructions

Below are given several pairs of vocations or work areas. Indicate, by a tick mark, which of the two you would prefer if you were given a choice. Also, give three reasons why you choose that vocation or work activity by writing the letters corresponding to your reasons (as given below). The three answers should be in order of their importance to you.

A. It will provide a more stable income.
B. It will give me quick returns in terms of profits.
C. It will help me to be with my family or friends.
D. It does not involve much risk.
E. It is highly prestigious in the society.
F. It will give me independence and freedom to work.
G. It is challenging.
H. It will help me to make larger impact in the society.
I. It will give me enough leisure to enjoy myself.
J. It provides good prospects for the family after retirement.
K. It provides opportunity to be with colleagues of my choice.

Choose one of the items in each pair and indicate three reasons for your choice by writing the appropriate letters (A, B, C, etc.), in order of importance, from the list given above.

		Reasons	
1.	a. University teaching	1st	...
	b. Business	2nd	...
		3rd	...
2.	a. Selling	1st	...
	b. Manufacturing	2nd	...
		3rd	...
3.	a. Wholesale trading	1st	...
	b. General supermarket	2nd	...
		3rd	...
4.	a. Operating one business	1st	...
	b. Operating many businesses	2nd	...
		3rd	...
5.	a. Agency of a fast selling product	1st	...
	b. Manufacturing the product	2nd	...
		3rd	...
6.	a. Heading an institution	1st	...
	b. Civic administration	2nd	...
	(Head of a city corporation)	3rd	...

	Reasons	
7. a. Film-making	1st	...
b. Religious work	2nd	...
	3rd	...
8. a. Teaching (university professor)	1st	...
b. Research	2nd	...
	3rd	...
9. a. Film-making	1st	...
b. Business	2nd	...
	3rd	...
10. a. Teaching (university professor)	1st	...
b. Selling	2nd	...
	3rd	...
11. a. Manufacturing	1st	...
b. Civic administration	2nd	...
(Head of a city corporation)	3rd	...
12. a. Political career (being a legislator)	1st	...
b. Civic administration	2nd	...
(Head of a city corporation)	3rd	...

14
Interpersonal Needs Inventory (IPNI)

14.1 THE INSTRUMENT AND ITS ADMINISTRATION

The Interpersonal Needs Inventory (IPNI) was developed to measure six interpersonal needs. Five items for each need are contained in it, and it is self-administered. Respondents rate 60 items on a 6-point scale: from never (or none) to usually (or most people). A separate answer sheet (appended) is used to facilitate scoring of the inventory.

14.2 CONCEPTUAL FRAMEWORK

Schutz (1958) drew attention to three basic interpersonal needs involved in interaction among people—inclusion, control and affection. His main contribution was suggestion of directionality in each of these three needs, what he termed as *expressed* (giving to others) and as *wanted* (receiving from others). He defined the three needs behaviourally as follows:

The interpersonal need for inclusion is defined behaviourally as the need to establish and maintain a satisfactory relationship with people with respect to interaction and association. 'Satisfactory relationship' includes (a) a psychologically comfortable relationship with people somewhere on a dimension ranging from originating or initiating interaction with all people to not initiating interaction with anyone, and (b) a psychologically comfortable relationship with people with respect to eliciting behaviour from them somewhere on a dimension ranging from always initiating interaction with the self to never initiating interaction with the self. On the level of feelings, the need for inclusion is defined as the need to establish and maintain a feeling of mutual interest with other people. This feeling includes (a) being able to take an interest in other people to a satisfactory degree, and (b) having others take interest in the self to a satisfactory degree. With regard to the concept of self, the need for inclusions is the need to feel that the self is significant and worthwhile.

The interpersonal need for control is defined behaviourally as the need to establish and maintain a satisfactory relationship with people with respect to control and power. 'Satisfactory relationship' includes (a) a psychologically comfortable relationship with people somewhere on a dimension ranging from controlling all the behaviour of other people to not controlling any behaviour of others, and (b) a psychologically comfortable relationship with people with respect to eliciting behaviour from them somewhere on a dimension ranging from always being con-trolled by them to never being controlled by them. With regard to feelings, the need for control is defined as the need to establish and maintain a feeling of mutual respect for the competence and responsibility of others. This feeling includes ability to respect others to a satisfactory degree. The need for control, defined at the level of perceiving the self, is the need to feel that one is a competent and responsible person.

The interpersonal need for affection is defined behaviourally as the need to establish and maintain a satisfactory relationship with others with respect to love and affection. Affection always refers to a two-person (dyadic) relationship. 'Satisfactory relationship' includes (a) a psychologically comfortable relationship with others, somewhere on a dimension ranging from initiating close, personal relation-ship with everyone to originating close, personal relationship with no one, and (b) a psychologically comfortable relationship with people with respect to eliciting behaviour from them on a dimension ranging from always originating close, personal relations toward the self, to never originating close, personal relationships towards the self. At the feeling level, the need affection is defined as the need to establish and maintain a feeling of mutual affection with others. This feeling includes (a) being able to love other people to a satisfactory degree, and (b) having others love the self to a satisfactory degree. The need for affection, defined at the level of the self-concept, is the need to feel that the self is lovable.

This type of formulation stresses the interpersonal nature of these needs. They require that the person establishes a kind of equilibrium in three different areas between the self and other people. In order to be anxiety free, a person must find a comfortable behavioural relationship with others with regard to the exchange of interactions, power and love. The need is not wholly satisfied by acting toward others in a particular fashion. A satisfactory balance must be established and maintained.

Schutz was eager to simplify the typology of interpersonal needs and argued that various needs suggested by other writers and researchers were included in these three needs. However, each of the three needs has some aspects which claim independent status as needs. Let us take the first need of inclusion. In addition to a mere social need of interaction and inclusion in a group, the individual has a basic need for recognition by other people and of giving recognition to others. This need is much more than and in some ways different from the inclusion need. The control need or the *power need* is much more complex. A distinction is necessary between two types of power needs—the need to control (to restrict and direct matters and behaviour of others) and to influence (make an impact on others). The distinction is a subtle one. The work of McClelland (1975) points towards such a distinction. Coercion and authority are part of control, whereas independence and expertise are part of influence.

What Schutz (1958) calls affection need is the well-known *affiliation need*. This is the need for close personal relationships. Schutz also includes in this the concern a person has for others— indicated by the need to be useful, to serve others, to sacrifice for others—although this is a distinctly different need. While affiliation is reflected in close personal relationships, it is the

	TABLE 14.1	**Behavioural Types of Interpersonal Needs**	
Needs	**High**	**Low**	**Medium**
BG	Over-social	Under-social	Social
BR	Interaction-avid	Interaction-shy	Socially responsive
AG	Over-personal	Reserved	Friendly
AR	Intimacy-avid	Intimacy-shy	Intimacy-responsive
EG	Over-considerate	Unconcerned	Caring
ER	Care-avid	Care-shy	Care-responsive
RG	Ingratiating	Unappreciative	Gracious
RR	Visibility-avid	Visibility-shy	Appreciative
CG	Autocrat	Abdicate	Democrat
CR	Dependent	Counter-dependent	Inter-dependent
IG	Influence-avid	Influence-shy	Influential
IR	Over-amenable	Unreceptive	Receptive

extension need that is reflected in concern for others, including a group or a society. Those who die for their country or for a cause show this need.

Thus, it may be necessary to expand the typology of the basic needs. It is proposed here that the following six basic needs may be used to develop a theory and instruments for interpersonal relationships:

1. *The need for interaction*: belonging, recognition
2. *The need for relationship*: affiliation, extension
3. *The need for power*: control, influence

The two aspects, called expressed and wanted, by Schutz are termed *giving* (G) and *receiving* (R) by us. As Schutz suggests, extreme scores (low and high) may show *under* or *over* status of the need. The 'behavioural types' of various needs are shown in Table 14.1.

14.3 SCORING AND SCORE SHEET

1. Transfer your ratings to the Score Sheet.
2. Add the five ratings in each row. The total will range from 5 to 30.
3. Subtract 5 from the total, then multiply it by 4. The range will now be 0–100. Scoring key is given in Table 14.2

IPNI Categories	Items and Responses					Total	%
____Give Belonging	1.____	13.____	25.____	37.____	49.____	____	____
____Receive Belonging	2.____	14.____	26.____	38.____	50.____	____	____
____Give Affiliation	3.____	15.____	27.____	39.____	51.____	____	____
____Receive Affiliation	4.____	16.____	28.____	40.____	52.____	____	____
____Give Extension	5.____	17.____	29.____	41.____	53.____	____	____
____Receive Extension	6.____	18.____	30.____	42.____	54.____	____	____
____Give Recognition	7.____	19.____	31.____	43.____	55.____	____	____
____Receive Recognition	8.____	20.____	32.____	44.____	56.____	____	____
____Give Control	9.____	21.____	33.____	45.____	57.____	____	____
____Receive Control	10.____	22.____	34.____	46.____	58.____	____	____
____Give Influence	11.____	23.____	35.____	47.____	59.____	____	____
____Receive Influence	12.____	24.____	36.____	48.____	60.____	____	____

TABLE 14.2   Scoring Key of IPNI

Category	Items
Give Belonging (BG)	1, 13, 25, 37, 49
Receive Belonging (BR)	2, 14, 26, 38, 50
Give Affiliation (AG)	3, 15, 27, 39, 51
Receive Affiliation (AR)	4, 16, 28, 40, 52
Give Extension (EG)	5, 17, 29, 41, 53
Receive Extension (ER)	6, 18, 30, 42, 54
Give Recognition (ER)	7, 19, 31, 43, 55
Receive Recognition (RR)	8, 20, 32, 44, 56
Give Control (CG)	9, 21, 33, 45, 57
Receive Control (CR)	10, 22, 34, 46, 58
Give Influence (IG)	11, 23, 35, 47, 59
Receive Influence (IR)	12, 24, 36, 48, 60

14.4 RELIABILITY

Cronbach Alpha for a group of 25 persons was found to be 0.97.

TABLE 14.3 IPNI Norms				
IPNI	Mean	SD	Low	High
BG	60	20	50	70
BR	60	20	50	70
AG	60	20	50	70
AR	60	20	50	70
EG	70	20	60	80
ER	60	20	50	70
RG	80	20	70	90
RR	50	20	40	60
CG	40	20	30	50
CR	40	20	30	50
IG	50	20	40	60
IR	70	20	60	80

14.5 NORMS

Based on responses from a large number of managers, the mean and SD values of different needs are given in Table 14.3, along with cut-off points for low (under) and high (over) scores.

14.6 USE FOR HRD

The instrument can be useful for participants to get some insight into their patterns of interpersonal behaviour. As suggested by Schutz (1958), the extreme scores indicate problem areas. An interpretation of the total profile may be helpful in understanding the dynamics of an individual's interpersonal style. The comments given in the chapter may be helpful for interpreting a profile.

IPNI

Name: _____   Role: _____
Organisation: _____   Date: _____

Different persons interact with others in different ways on various dimensions. Some statements are given below to indicate such ways of interaction. Read each statement and indicate to what extent the statement is true in your case by using the following key. Do not indicate what should be the response but how you tend to think or behave. There are no right or wrong answers. There are no good or bad ways to interact. Be honest and frank.

Use the following key for checking the statements:

Write 1   for never or none
Write 2   for rarely or for very few persons
Write 3   for sometimes or for a few persons
Write 4   for occasionally or for some people
Write 5   for often or for many people
Write 6   for usually or most people

IPNI

1. _____ I join groups and organisations when I get an opportunity.
2. _____ I like to be made a member of committees.
3. _____ I try to develop personal relations with others.
4. _____ I like people to be close to me.
5. _____ I tend to help people resolve their conflicts.
6. _____ I like people to empathise with me (try to feel as I do).
7. _____ I appreciate other people's accomplishments.
8. _____ I like people to appreciate my work.
9. _____ I tend to dominate the group I work with.
10. _____ I dislike taking independent decisions.
11. _____ I try to maintain my reputation in a group.
12. _____ I enjoy trying out something after reading about it.
13. _____ I do not like to join committees and other groups.
14. _____ I like people to include me in their groups.
15. _____ I tend to share emotions with people.
16. _____ I like people to express their emotions to me.
17. _____ I enjoy working for myself rather than for a group or a community.
18. _____ I do not like people to share my grief and distress.
19. _____ I like to compliment people for their experience and expertise.
20. _____ I like people to compliment me for my accomplishments.
21. _____ If people ignore my views in a group, I tend to keep quiet.
22. _____ I like my seniors to solve problems for me or guide me to find solutions.
23. _____ I try to influence other people.
24. _____ I like to get more ideas from books.
25. _____ I try to participate in group activities.
26. _____ I do not want people to invite me to parties.

27. _____ I like to be close to people.
28. _____ I like people to keep a distance from me.
29. _____ I tend to empathise with people (feel as they do).
30. _____ I like people to collaborate with me in achieving a goal.
31. _____ I pay attention to people.
32. _____ I do not care whether people give me credit for my contribution or not.
33. _____ I enjoy competing for power in a group or organisation.
34. _____ I do not like others to try to get me to do things their way.
35. _____ I enjoy seeing people accept my point of view, even though they do not openly express it.
36. _____ I do not like others giving me suggestions.
37. _____ I invite people for visits.
38. _____ I like people to consult me.
39. _____ I am cool and distant with people.
40. _____ I like people to share their emotions with me.
41. _____ I tend to tolerate discomfort for the sake of others.
42. _____ I like people to help me when I need some help.
43. _____ I am impatient with people when I am busy.
44. _____ I like people to use my skills and expertise.
45. _____ I like others to do things my way.
46. _____ I like it if others tell me what I am supposed to do.
47. _____ I try to leave an impression on people.
48. _____ I take a decision after consulting people.
49. _____ I like to do work with people.
50. _____ I like to be invited for visits.
51. _____ I enjoy having close relationships.
52. _____ I like people to be warm and personal to me.
53. _____ I tend to collaborate with others in achieving a goal.
54. _____ I like people to support me in crises.
55. _____ I applaud people for their achievements.
56. _____ I like people to quote me.
57. _____ I like to tell others what is to be done.
58. _____ I like others to guide me.
59. _____ It makes no difference to me if people agree with me or not.
60. _____ I like people to give new ideas and suggestions.

Intrinsic and Extrinsic Motivation: What Do You Look for in a Job?

15.1 THE INSTRUMENT AND ITS ADMINISTRATION

What do you look for in a job? It measures intrinsic and extrinsic motivation or what Herzberg called motivators and hygienes. The instrument contains 14 items, 7 related to intrinsic and 7 to extrinsic motivation.

It's administration is simple. It is self-administered, and respondents are asked to rank-order the 14 items depending on their importance to them—from 1 (highest rank) to 14 (lowest rank).

15.2 CONCEPTUAL FRAMEWORK

Maslow's (1954) famous theory of hierarchy of needs drew attention to different types of motivation. This theory distinguishes between self-actualisation, which is the need characterised by development and growth of the individual, and the other needs, which make up for some deficiency. This distinction was dramatically sharpened by Herzberg (1966a), whose theory of work motivation is most widely known, applied and discussed. His theory is also called the two-factor theory of motivation, as he discusses two main classes of the deficit and development needs.

Using the critical incident technique, Herzberg collected data about people's satisfaction and dissatisfaction in their jobs. The analysis of his data led him to two sets of factors: one set of needs that caused dissatisfaction if they were not met and another set which provided positive satisfaction to people. Using his background experience in the field of health, Herzberg proposed a two-factor theory. He classified the various needs into, what he called, the hygiene factors (those, which may prevent dissatisfaction) and motivators (factors which may provide satisfaction). These can also be called extrinsic and intrinsic motivation respectively because, according to Herzberg, the former needs are contextual (external or extrinsic) and the latter relate to the content of the job (internal or intrinsic). These are shown in Table 15.1.

TABLE 15.1   Herzberg's Two-factor Model of Work Motivation

Hygiene Factor	Motivators
Salary	Advancement
Working conditions	Development
Company policy	Responsibility
Supervision	Recognition
Work group	Work itself

Based on the review of several Indian studies using Herzberg's methodology, Roy and Raja (1977) tentatively concluded that the evidence regarding the two factor theory of job satisfaction and dissatisfaction, representing two different continual, found support in most studies.

Job satisfaction and dissatisfaction, representing two different continual, found support in most studies. On the other hand, the motivators and hygienes have generally been found to influence satisfaction and dissatisfaction in a mixed fashion. While intrinsic factors (e.g., job content, promotion and growth) contribute to dissatisfaction, the extrinsic factors (e.g., security, co-worker relations and friendliness of superior) contribute to satisfaction. They also concluded that criticism about the Herzbergian model being method-bound and artefactual seemed also to apply to the Indian context. It appears that the higher order needs of even the managers are thwarted by organisational practices. A study of a sample of Indian managers found them equally divided between lower and higher order needs; the order of needs was related directly with the level of management and inversely with age.

Lawler and Porter (Roy & Raja, 1977) found that higher levels of management assigned greater importance to intrinsic incentives such as interesting work and self-expression as determinants of job satisfaction. The lower level groups preferred pay, security and co-worker. Indian evidence along these lines is also available. Laxmi Narain (Roy & Menon, 1977) found that overall need satisfaction increased from lower to higher levels of management. Jaggi (1979) found higher-level managers reporting higher order needs than managers at the lower level. Haire et al. (Jaggi, 1979) found Indian managers reporting the lowest degree of fulfilment of esteem and autonomy needs, the second lowest fulfilment of actualisation needs in comparison with managers from other countries. However, Pareek and Keshote (1982) did not find any hierarchical differences in a group of Malaysian managers and executive trainees in a Malaysian agriculture bank.

Seven intrinsic motivational factors are advancement, interesting work, respect and recognition, responsibility and independence, achievement, a technically competent supervisor, and an equitable pay. The seven extrinsic motivational factors are security, adequate earnings, fringe benefits, comfortable working conditions, sound company policies and practices, a considerate and sympathetic supervisor, and restricted hours of work.

IPNI measures the six needs: inclusion (I), recognition (R), affiliation (A), extension (E), control (C) and influence (In) on two aspects of giving (G) and receiving (R).

15.3 SCORING

The ranks given are added for intrinsic motivation (item numbers 4, 6, 8, 9, 10, 12 and 14) and for extrinsic motivation (item numbers 1, 2, 3, 5, 7, 11 and 13). The lower the score, the higher is the value given to the concerned motivational factors.

15.4 RELIABILITY

Split-half reliability (N = 108) was found to be 0.88.

15.5 VALIDITY

Factor analysis (principal axis factoring with Varimax solution) of data from a Malaysian bank (N = 108), using a two-factor solution, is given in Table 15.2. Out of seven extrinsic aspects, six are included in Factor 1 (which explains 42% variance). Restricted hours of work have almost zero loading on both the factors. This aspect seems to be irrelevant to motivation. Equitable pay is a

TABLE 15.2 Factor Loadings*

	Aspects	Factor 1	Factor 2
1.	Security	0.75	
2.	Adequate earnings	0.63	
3.	Fringe benefits	0.93	
4.	Advancement	0.73	0.35
5.	Working conditions	0.88	
6.	Interesting work		0.40
7.	Company policy	0.31	
8.	Respect and recognition	0.75	0.54
9.	Responsibility/independence		0.53
10.	Achievement	0.37	0.65

	Aspects	Factor 1	Factor 2
11.	Considerate supervisor	0.76	0.57
12.	Competent supervisor		0.49
13.	Restricted work hours	—	
14.	Equitable pay	0.67	

Note: *Loading of 0.3 and above are given.

loading on Factor 1 but not on Factor 2, although this is included in intrinsic motivation. Three intrinsic aspects—advancement, recognition and achievement—also have significant loading on this factor. This is a general motivation factor.

Factor 2 (explaining 8% variance) is a pure intrinsic motivation factor, although 'considerate supervisor' also has high loading on it, and 'equitable pay' has very low loading.

The factor analysis has partially validated the two-factor classification. When intrinsic and extrinsic motivations were correlated, in one case ($N = 65$), the correlation was 0.87, and in the other ($n = 43$), it was 0.99. Further work is needed on the instrument.

15.6 NORMS

Mean values of all 14 items and extrinsic and intrinsic motivation for a group are given in Table 15.3.

TABLE 15.3 Mean and SD of Factors in Jobs

		Mean	SD
1.	Security	4.5	5.8
2.	Adequate earning	4.6	4.5
3.	Fringe benefits	7.4	7.3
4.	Advancement	4.7	5.2
5.	Comfortable working conditions	9.0	8.4
6.	Interesting work	3.6	2.9
7.	Sound company policies and practices	8.3	3.2
8.	Respect and recognition	9.5	9.4

(Table 15.3 Continued)

(Table 15.3 Continued)

		Mean	SD
9.	Responsibility and independence	7.1	3.6
10.	Achievement	7.0	4.3
11.	Considerate and sympathetic supervisor	11.6	10.5
12.	Technically competent supervisor	11.4	3.2
13.	Restricted hours of work	11.5	3.3
14.	Equitable pay	10.1	6.3

15.7 USE FOR HRD

This instrument can be used to help participants become aware of their motivational profile. Without intrinsic motivation, creative work cannot be done and growth does not occur. The participants can discuss in small groups what could be done in a department or organisation to develop intrinsic motivation amongst employees.

What Do You Look for in a Job?

Name: _____   Role: _____

Organisation: _____   Date: _____

Different persons look for different things while deciding to take up a job. This instrument is meant to collect information about such factors. There is no right or wrong answer. Rank the 14 factors given below in terms of their priority to you in a job. Put 1 against the item that is most important to you while deciding whether or not to take up a job; put 2 against the second most important item, and so on. Place 14 against the factor with lowest priority to you. Do not leave any item unanswered and use each number (1–14) only once.

1.	_____	Job security
2.	_____	Adequate salary
3.	_____	Fringe benefits (perks, etc.)
4.	_____	Opportunities for promotion
5.	_____	Comfortable working conditions
6.	_____	Interesting work
7.	_____	Sound company policies and practices
8.	_____	Respect and recognition
9.	_____	Responsibility and independence
10.	_____	Doing something worthwhile
11.	_____	Considerate and sympathetic supervisor
12.	_____	Technically competent supervisor
13.	_____	Restricted hours of work
14.	_____	Pay according to ability and competence

16

Emotional Intelligence (EI) Scale

16.1 THE INSTRUMENT AND ITS ADMINISTRATION

Emotional Intelligence (EI) Scale measures emotional intelligence. Respondents complete the instrument given here.

16.2 CONCEPTUAL FRAMEWORK

There has been an emphasis on exclusive intellectual achievement in terms of higher percentage marks in the examination, both by the schools and the parents. This trend still continues. While intellectual excellence is highly desirable, exclusive emphasis on it, at the cost of other important aspects, is both self-defeating (because in the long run, intellectual excellence requires emotional maturity) and dysfunctional (producing anxiety and depression in children). There is a need to bring about balance by recognising the importance of 'non-intellectual' or emotional aspects also.

Goleman (1995) has drawn attention to this neglected aspect. He calls it 'emotional intelligence'. Gardner (1983) proposed the expansion of the concept of intelligence, which was confined to two varieties of academic kind—verbal and mathematical–logical. His model of multiple intelligences included, in addition to the verbal–mathematico-logical abilities, spatial ability (seen in artists and architects), kinaesthetic ability (seen in sports), musical ability and two personal abilities (interpersonal and intrapersonal).

Salovey and Mayer (1990) was the first to use the term 'emotional intelligence'. He suggested five main domains of emotional intelligence—knowing one's emotions, managing emotions, motivating oneself, recognising emotions in others and handling relationships.

Emotional intelligence contains two major aspects—'emotions' and 'intelligence'. Emotions or feelings have both a physiological component and cognitive element that influence behaviour.

Intelligence is the capacity to understand the world, think rationally and use resources effectively when faced with challenges. Emotional intelligence refers to the ability that one requires for efficient living.

Traditional intelligence (symbolised by IQ, i.e., intelligence quotient) does not guarantee a well-balanced personality, emotional intelligence (also, emotional quotient) does. That is why some school and university toppers do not do quite so well in their professional lives. Goleman has referred to a study conducted on 95 Harvard students with high IQ. The students were followed up into their middle age. The study revealed that men with highest test scores in college were not particularly successful in productivity and status in their field. These students were found to be highly dissatisfied and they did not fare well in other spheres also.

Goleman's popular books (1995 and 1997) spell out four dimensions of emotional intelligence, although he mentions some others. One important element in emotional intelligence is optimism, so well researched by Seligman (1991). Optimism, according to Seligman, is an attitude that buffers people from failing into apathy and hopelessness. Optimism means having a strong expectation that in general things will turn out alright in life, despite setbacks and frustrations. People who are optimistic see failure as due to something that can be changed. Optimism has been found to be critical for success in various pursuits—academic work, business, health, politics, sports, religion, etc.

Goleman (1999, pp. 32–34) has suggested 25 competences—12 personal and 13 social competences for 5 dimensions of emotional intelligence. The competences are mentioned in parentheses after each dimension of emotional intelligence—self-awareness (emotional awareness, accurate self-assessment, self confidence), self-regulation (self-control, trustworthiness, conscientiousness, adaptability, innovation), motivation (achievement drive, commitment, initiative, optimism), empathy (understanding others, developing others, service orientation, leveraging diversity, political awareness), social skills (influence, communication, conflict management, leadership, change catalyst, building bonds, collaboration and cooperation, team capability).

Pareek (1999) has suggested androgyny framework for emotional intelligence that it balances 'attributes' traditionally attributed to men with those traditionally attributed to women.

Based on Salovey's concept, and including new researches reported by Seligman and others, the following aspects of emotional intelligence have been used in developing this instrument:

1. *Self-awareness.* It includes the ability to recognise and understand one's own moods, emotions and drives and accepting oneself with strengths and weaknesses.
2. *Self-management.* It includes the ability of a person to redirect and control disruptive impulses and moods, judging how others might feel before taking action, and postponing gratification of immediate needs for long-term goals.
3. *Internality and optimism.* These include an orientation of taking charge of the situations, seeing failures as temporary, high hope and intense involvement in experiences (flow) as contrasted with brooding over arid recollecting miseries (rumination).

4. *Motivation.* It involves a person's passion to work for reasons that go beyond money or status, resilience (i.e., ability to bounce back from disappointments) and pursuing goals with energy and persistence.

5. *Empathy.* It is the ability of a person to understand the emotional makeup of other people. It also involves skill in dealing with 'people according to their emotional reaction'. 'At the very least, empathy requires being able to read another's emotions; at a higher level, it entails sensing and responding to a person's unspoken concerns or feelings. At the highest levels, empathy is understanding the issues or concerns that lie behind another's feelings' (Goleman, 1999, p. 160).

6. *Social skills.* It refers to a person's proficiency in managing relationships and building networks. It is reflected in building and leading teams.

The instrument measures six aspects of emotional intelligence.

16.3 SCORING

Scoring is simple; follow the following steps:

1. Transfer the ratings (responses) from the instrument to the Score Sheet, making sure that the original responses of the starred items (*) are reversed (0 becomes 3, 1 becomes 2, 2 becomes 1, and 3 becomes 0).
2. Add each row.
3. Multiply each total by 4.17. It will range from 0 to 100.

Sum up all totals to get the score of emotional intelligence which will range from 0 to 144 and multiply by 0.7. The total score of emotional intelligence will then range from 0 to 100.

16.4 RELIABILITY

Alpha coefficient for a sample of 72 students was found to be 0.42.

16.5 NORMS*

The following mean and SD values from 270 women entrepreneurs can be used for norms. Norms for specific group can be developed:

---

* Developed by Surabhi Purohit. Norms have been provided by Ms Pragaya Dashora.

S. No.	Aspects	Mean	SD
1.	Self-awareness	80	10
2.	Self-management	65	10
3.	Internality	74	10
4.	Motivation	75	10
5.	Empathy	57	10
6.	Social skills	72	10
7.	Total EI	71	

16.6 USE FOR HRD

EI scale can be used for self-analysis and individual counselling. A respondent can examine his score and then plan to increase the behaviour on which he received a low score by examining the related items in the instrument and inferring the behavioural implications. The counsellor can help the individuals to plan new behaviour. The participants can also get feedback from other participants and then discuss in groups.

Score Sheet

Items								Total	% Score	Aspects
1 __	7* __	13 __	19* __	25 __	31 __	37* __	43 __	____× 4.17	____	Self-awareness
2* __	8 __	14 __	20* __	26 __	32 __	38* __	44 __	____× 4.17	____	Self-management
3* __	9* __	15 __	21* __	27 __	33* __	39* __	45 __	____× 4.17	____	Internality
4* __	10 __	16 __	22* __	28 __	34 __	40* __	46 __	____× 4.17	____	Motivation
5* __	11 __	17 __	23 __	29 __	35 __	41* __	47* __	____× 4.17	____	Empathy
6 __	12 __	18* __	24 __	30* __	36 __	42* __	48 __	____× 4.17	____	Social skills
	Total							____×.7	____	Emotional Intelligence

Emotional Intelligence Scale

Name: _____   Date: _____
Organisation: _____   Role: _____

Read each statement given below, and rate in the space at its left to indicate how much true it is about you. Use the following key for your ratings:

Write 0   if it is not true about you
Write 1   if it is a little true about you
Write 2   if it is fairly true about you
Write 3   if it is definitely true about you

No.	Response	Items
1.	_____	I can tell when I am getting upset and why.
2.	_____	I get angry when I am criticised by my peers.
3.	_____	I constantly worry about my weaknesses.
4.	_____	When faced with a problem, I tend to postpone working on it if I can.
5.	_____	I trust only myself to get things done.
6.	_____	People like me.
7.	_____	I often wish I was someone else.
8.	_____	I prefer not to stir up problems, if I can avoid doing so.
9.	_____	I have been continually frustrated in my life because of failures.
10.	_____	I know I can find solutions to difficult problems.
11.	_____	I can tell when my close friend is upset.
12.	_____	When I have a problem I know whom to go to or what to do to help solve it.
13.	_____	I accept myself even when I know that I am not perfect.
14.	_____	I do not hesitate in expressing my disagreement.
15.	_____	I can accomplish most of the things with my effort.
16.	_____	I see challenge as opportunity for learning.
17.	_____	I can put myself in someone else's shoes.
18.	_____	I find it difficult to establish contact with important persons.
19.	_____	I cannot accept compliments easily.
20.	_____	I find it difficult to accept others' opinions different from mine.
21.	_____	Circumstances are beyond my control.
22.	_____	I find it difficult to bounce back (come back to normal self) after feeling disappointed.
23.	_____	I appreciate my friends' positive qualities.
24.	_____	I can socialise well.
25.	_____	I like myself as I am.
26.	_____	I know how to say 'no' when I have to.
27.	_____	I greatly enjoy the activities I am involved in.
28.	_____	I enjoy taking responsibility.
29.	_____	I cannot know about people's pain and problems unless they talk about it.
30.	_____	I do not enjoy taking leadership roles.
31.	_____	I am aware of my feelings.
32.	_____	I think about what I want before I act.

No.	Response	Items
33	_____	I experience eating problems (loss of appetite, overeating, no time to eat).
34	_____	Studies are fun for me (I enjoy studies).
35	_____	I use different ways of expressing my emotions, depending on who I am interacting with.
36	_____	I have several friends I can count on, as when I need them.
37	_____	I am jealous of friends who score more than I do.
38	_____	I avoid confrontations (frank unpleasant discussions).
39	_____	I have trouble in concentrating.
40	_____	I find it difficult to work under pressure.
41	_____	I am not emotional and I am not moved by other persons' emotional experiences.
42	_____	I feel lonely and have very few good friends.
43	_____	I know what I want.
44	_____	I remain calm even in situations when others get angry.
45	_____	While sitting alone or daydreaming, I recollect pleasant events and happenings.
46	_____	I can accomplish what I need to, if I put my mind to it.
47	_____	I do not care how others might feel.
48	_____	I enjoy taking roles and responsibilities in groups.

17

Work–Life Balance Scale

17.1 THE INSTRUMENT AND ITS ADMINISTRATION

Work–life (W–L) Balance Scale is meant to diagnose the level and areas of W–L balance in an organisation, as perceived by its employees. It should be responded by the employees at various levels in different departments/sections.

17.2 CONCEPTUAL FRAMEWORK

While in the pastoral and agrarian societies work and life were integrated, the industrial revolution brought about divorce between the two. Each had its own requirements, often in conflict with each other. Then the demand to have some balance between the two was voiced, especially by women employees. During the 1960s and 1970s, employers considered W–L balance mainly an issue for working mothers who struggled with the demands of their jobs and raising children. During the 1980s, recognising the value and needs of their women contributors, pioneering organisations such as Merck, Deloitte & Touche and IBM began to change their internal workplace policies, procedures and benefits. The changes included maternity leave, employee assistance programmes (EAPs), flexitime, home-based work and childcare referral. During the 1980s, men also began voicing W–L concerns. By the end of the decade, W–L balance was seen as more than just a women's issue, affecting men, families, organisations and cultures. The 1990s solidified the recognition of W–L balance as a vital issue for everyone—women, men, parents and non-parents, singles and couples. This growing awareness of the central importance of the issue resulted in major growth in attempted W–L solutions during this decade.

W–L balance has been conceived in various ways. However, at the core of an effective W–L balance definition are two key everyday concepts that are relevant to all of us. They are achievement and enjoyment, ideas almost deceptive in their simplicity (Bird, 2006):

1. W–L balance is a person's control over the conditions in their workplace. It is accomplished when individuals feel dually satisfied about their personal life and their paid occupation. It mutually benefits the individual, business and society when a person's personal life is balanced with his own job.
2. Satisfaction and good functioning at work and at home with a minimum of role conflict (Clark, 2000).
3. W–L balance is about people having a measure of control over when, where and how they work. It is achieved when an individual's right to a fulfilled life inside and outside paid work is accepted and respected as the norm to the mutual benefit of the individual, business and society.

There are different views regarding relation between work and life. The following are the main models of W–L balance:

1. *Segmentation model.* This model hypothesises that work and life are two different aspects and they do not affect each other.
2. *Spillover model.* The model hypothesises that one world can influence the other in either a positive or negative way.
3. *Compensation model.* Compensation model proposes that what may be lacking in one sphere, in terms of demands or satisfactions, can be made up in the other. For example, work may be a routine and undemanding but this is compensated for by a major role in local community activities outside work.
4. *Instrumental model.* The model suggests that activities in one sphere facilitate success in the other.
5. *Conflict model.* This model suggests that with high levels of demand in all spheres of life, some difficult choices have to be made, resulting in some conflicts and possibly some significant overload on an individual.

Clark (2000) proposed border theory, which professes that every individual is a daily border-crosser as he moves daily from home to the workplace and vice versa. This led to further analysis of nature of borders, their permeability, the ease with which they can be managed or moved and so on. In terms of any analysis of W–L 'balance', the analysis of borders can help to illuminate how far individuals are in control of issues determining balance. It also allows for the analysis of physical and psychological controls. While a heavy emphasis in the recent literature suggests that technology and competition have resulted in more intensive and extensive work, any analysis needs to accommodate human agency. Border theory begins to permit this. In other words, it opens up scope for the social construction or cognitive distortion of boundaries to create a defensible subjective sense of balance.

The concept of boundary-less work culture, which was initiated by Arthur and Rousseau (1996) professed that there is no such distinction or boundary between work and non-work life.

Models of W–L balance can also be enriched by the psychology of individual differences. For example, psychological theory concerned with the aspects of personality can enhance our understanding of the perceptions of balance. For example, there has been some research on 'workaholics'—people characterised as those who choose to work long hours even when they may not need to do so. Furthermore, they tend to do so at the expense of other activities. In a review of some of the literature on workaholics, Peiperl and Jones (2000) note how it was initially viewed as a disease akin to alcoholism (Bailyn, 1977), but another research by Machlowitz (1980) suggested that it was more properly viewed as a form of extreme work involvement. More recently, Scott, Moore and Miceli (1997) have linked it to three relatively stable personality types— the achievement-oriented, the perfectionist and the compulsive-dependent. Peiperl and Jones distinguish workaholics, who choose to work long hours and perceive some rewards from doing so from 'over workers' who may also work long hours but have little choice in the matter and do not believe that the returns they receive justify the long hours. This stream of research needs considerable development, but it highlights the importance of taking into account individual differences in any attempt to establish what we mean by balance.

17.2.1 W–L Balance and Its Effect

W–L balance not only affects the individual but also the organisation. Therefore, today, solving W–L balance conflict is the concern for all growing organisations, and can be taken as a part of organisational development.

Following are the benefits to the organisation:

1. Increase in individual productivity, accountability and commitment
2. Better teamwork and communication
3. Improved morale
4. Less negative organisational stress

Benefits to the individual are as follows:

1. More value and balance in daily life
2. Better understanding of the best individual W–L balance
3. Increased productivity
4. Improved relationships both on and off the job
5. Reduced stress

W–L balance also results in the following:

1. Reduced absenteeism
2. Reduced turnover

3. Reduced overtime cost
4. Increased production
5. Client retention, and most of all
6. Satisfaction among the employees (monetary and non-monetary)

This would, in turn, help the organisation as well as individuals to grow and fulfil their needs. This would benefit in improving work culture and creating conducive work environment.

17.2.2 Variables in W–L Balance

One set of variables relate to the individual's satisfaction (subjective feelings), and the other with the individual's perception of the organisation. The former includes the following:

1. *Enjoyment at work.* Joy in work results in stress-free mind.
2. *Motivation at work.* Motivation at workplace includes giving the employees recognition, appreciation and also giving them new and challenging jobs.
3. *Achievement from work.* Achievement refers to success one achieves in his workplace or in his personal life. The feeling of achievement leads to better output in next task. Achievement leads to the motivation of employees due to the accomplishment of work. That can be in the form of promotions, awards and recognition and also in the form of social upliftment of the individual's status in the society.
4. *Social satisfaction.* If a person is unable to give time to social activities, such as, religious functions, family functions, etc., he is considered to be isolated, which is stressful.
5. *Mental satisfaction.* Mental satisfaction can be achieved through meditation, mental rest, feeling of existence (i.e., identity). The absence of mental satisfaction can lead to stress in workplace and in personal life which would result in unwanted work imbalance which further leads to unhappiness and anger harms his personal and social life and end up with W–L imbalance.
6. *Personal satisfaction.* Personal life consists of
   a. Caring of wife, children and parents (Adams, King & King, 1996; Allen, 2001)
   b. Giving time to enjoy with family members
   c. Fulfilling the household needs
   d. Keeping track of his bank account
   e. Going for outing with family
   f. Entertainment
7. *Emotional satisfaction.* Getting support from office colleagues, family members and society to fulfil emotional needs, which include
   a. Support from subordinates in work, in terms of respects, affection and follower
   b. Support in terms of appraisal and official counselling for teamwork, etc.

    c.   Support from family and home, in terms of love, affection, respect, etc.

    d.   Support from society, in terms of social recognition, respect as good citizen

The second set of perception-related variables include the following:

1.   Fulfilment of social needs
2.   Fulfilment of personal needs

This variable include activities such as exercise, investing time in planning for life insurance policies and other related financial matters which certainly play a vital role in the aspect of W–L balance, and enjoying the activities of interest include the arena of W–L balance.

1.   *Time management.* Time management is taken as one of the variables of W–L balance just because time affects human life in any situation: How an individual utilises his time and how he divides his time between work and life.

2.   *Teamwork at workplace.* As we have discussed, environment and work culture in workplace affects working style of the person. It has a direct effect on his emotional and social life. Employee should be in the state in which he can rely on his colleagues and thus feel satisfied at workplace. Not only for the kind of work he is doing, that is, the output he gives to the organisation, but also with the fact that how organisation treats him. Satisfying treatment in the workplace would bring in the satisfaction in the professional life of the individual leading to satisfaction in personal life as these two together would form the part of W–L balance.

3.   *Job type.* Type of job a person is involved into contributes towards the W–L balance, as his W–L schedule can be formulated on the basis of the nature of the job performed. Satisfaction, as discussed earlier, is the primary base for W–L balance. Therefore, how an individual takes and performs his job directly affect his nature and actions way back home.

4.   *Compensation and benefits.* Monetary satisfaction is an important factor contributing towards the W–L balance of the individual. Monetary satisfaction also includes the benefits and privileges offered by the organisation. Various other items as reimbursement and compensation for extra efforts lead to workplace satisfaction; therefore, we can conclude that compensation and benefits contribute to the W–L balance.

5.   *Capabilities to work under stress.* Stress is considered to be the part of professional life. But still, to maintain W–L balance, it is very important to manage stress. Therefore, for this, we need to consider the complexities of professional life and thus understand the necessity of stress management. Stress at workplace should not affect your personal life, thus it is important to understand how an individual cope up with the stress at workplace as well as at home. Is he really able to take charge of the stressful environment? This is the topic of concern that would affect the W–L composition.

6. *Sociability.* Sociability refers to enjoying relationships and association at work place. The instrument measures W–L balance in the areas of personal needs, social needs, time management, teamwork, compensation and work itself.

17.3 SCORING

Scoring is simple; follow the following steps:

1. Transfer the ratings (responses) from the instrument to the Score Sheet, making sure that the original responses of the starred items (*) are reversed (0 becomes 4, 4 becomes 0, 1 becomes 3, 3 becomes 1, and 2 remains 2).
2. Add each row.
3. Multiply each total by 4.17. It will range from 0 to 100. This is W–L Balance Index. Total all totals to get the overall W–L Balance Index, ranging from 0 to almost 100.

Score Sheet

Items						Total	W–L Balance Index	Aspects
1 __	7*__	13 __	19*__	25*__	31 __	__ × 4.17	__	Social Needs
2 __	8*__	14 __	20*__	26 __	32*__	__ × 4.17	__	Personal Needs
3*__	9 __	15*__	21 __	27*__	33 __	__ × 4.17	__	Time management
4 __	10*__	16 __	22*__	28 __	34*__	__ × 4.17	__	Teamwork
5 __	11*__	17 __	23 __	29*__	35*__	__ × 4.17	__	Compensation and Benefits
6*__	12 __	18*__	24 __	30*__	36 __	__ × 4.17	__	Work
					Total	__ *0.69	__	Overall

17.4 USE FOR HRD

The instrument can be used to diagnose and develop interventions for improving W–L balance. Based on the cumulative responses of employees in the department, weak aspects, as indicated by low scores, can be identified. Workshops can be organised to deal with the issues. If an organisation has a declared policy of achieving W–L balance on different aspects and if that aspect is found weak as reflected by employees' ratings, the organisation may explore the reason of the gap between the organisational policy and employee perceptions. The instrument can also be useful for comparative studies of different departments/sections in an organisation, or different organisations.

Work–Life Balance Scale

Name: _____ Date: _____

Organisation: _____ Role: _____

Read each and rate in the space at its left to indicate how much true it is in your experience. Use the following key for your ratings:

Write 0   if it is not true
Write 1   if it is a little true
Write 2   if it is somewhat
Write 3   if it is fairly true
Write 4   if it is definitely true

No.	Response	Items
1.	_____	I do not find it difficult to take leave at the time of social emergencies.
2.	_____	I do exercises and take care of my health.
3.	_____	I work for extra hours to get my work done.
4.	_____	I meet the expectations of my colleagues and workmates.
5.	_____	I comfortably fulfil the basic requirements of my family.
6.	_____	I feel pressure while working when given a deadline.
7.	_____	I do not find enough time to spend with my family and friends.
8.	_____	I get stuck in a meeting on the day of parent–teacher meet in my child's school.
9.	_____	I meet prescribed deadlines and schedules, without affecting my home life.
10.	_____	I experience work pressure while doing a group task.
11.	_____	I do not have access to Internet and telephone for my family emergencies.
12.	_____	I am left with good energy level at the end of the day.
13.	_____	I am able to participate in community activities and attend to religious commitments.
14.	_____	I help my children in preparing for their exams.
15.	_____	I often take additional work to home.
16.	_____	I share the work with my colleagues whenever needed.
17.	_____	I get opportunity to enjoy holidays with my family.
18.	_____	I cannot manage more than one project at a time.
19.	_____	I find difficult to attend and enjoy the parties.
20.	_____	I do not get time for my sick partner/child/parents.
21.	_____	I can adjust my working schedule to attend to my life priorities.
22.	_____	I enjoy doing my job alone rather than with my team.
23.	_____	I enjoy the privileges I am offered by the organisation.
24.	_____	I love to do the kind of work I do, without any stress.
25.	_____	I do not get time to invite my friends for a party at home.
26.	_____	I get time to attend to my financial obligations, such as, checking my bank account, insurance, income tax.
27.	_____	I am not comfortable with the traveling time to the organisation. I prefer doing all assigned jobs in a team.
28.	_____	I have difficulty in getting the expenses reimbursed.
29.	_____	I am not clear about the objectives of my job.
30.	_____	I put in efforts for social advancement of the poor and needy.

No.	Response	Items
31.	_____	I am not able to attend to my household requirements.
32.	_____	I do not do overtime to complete my work.
33.	_____	I have difficulty in meeting the expectations of my supervisor and seniors.
34.	_____	I do not get compensated for my extra efforts in the organisation.
35.	_____	I enjoy doing my job.

Power Bases: Coercive and Persuasive Power (CPP) Scale

18.1 THE INSTRUMENT AND ITS ADMINISTRATION

Coercive and Persuasive Power (CPP) Scale is based on the concept of bases of power. Although the scale is developed for managers, it can also be used with trainers and consultants for whom the concepts are very relevant. Originally, five coercive and five persuasive bases were included, but later 6 bases were included in each category.

The instrument has the following objectives:

1. To help respondents become aware of the different bases of power.
2. To help them examine their own value and need profiles (sufficiency–deficiency) of different power bases.
3. To help them to explore the consequences of their power profiles.
4. To survey power profile in a group/department/organisation for OD interventions.

The CPP scale is self-administered. A respondent reads each of the items related to a power base and indicates, in the first column, how important it is for role effectiveness (called power value) and, in the second column, how much more of it he wants for effectiveness (called power need in terms of sufficiency–deficiency).

18.2 CONCEPTUAL FRAMEWORK

Power has been defined in many ways. Kotter and Schlesinger (1979) seems to capture the spirit of most definitions when he defines power as 'a measure of a person's potential to get others to do what he or she wants them to do, as well as to avoid being forced to do what he or she does not what to do'. Kurt Lewin defined power as 'the possibility of inducing forces of a certain magnitude on another person' (Raven, 1993). Power as potential to influence (individuals and groups), as suggested by Rogers (1973) and Hersey and Blanchard (1982), may be an adequate concept to work with. Influence of people can be both covert (attitudes, values, thinking) or overt (behaviour and action).

One concern in studies of power relates to the sources of power. This question has engaged the attention of several researchers and organisation interventionists. French and Raven (1959) were amongst the first to propose six bases of power—reward, coercion, legitimacy, expertise, reference and information. Since then, many more bases have been proposed. Raven (1992, 1993) has reviewed three decades of developments in the work on bases of power and has been updating references on the subject.

18.3 BASES OF POWER

Ever since Machiavelli (1950), a couple of centuries ago, suggested fear and love as bases of power, some suggestions have been made to dichotomise power bases. Flanders (1970), in his seminal work on classroom strategies of influence by teachers, differentiated *direct* influence from *indirect* influence on the basis of how much freedom the influencing behaviour of the teacher gave to the student. Taking (lecturing) by the teacher, scolding, criticising, disapproval, etc. were classified as direct influence, because these *coerced* the students into accepting what the teacher wanted them to do or think. Influencing behaviour that gave freedom to the student to think and experiment—encouragement, compliments, open questions with alternative answers, sensing and voicing individual and group feelings, etc.—were put in the category of indirect influence. Flanders thus seemed to use a similar classification—coercion (fear) or persuasion (love).

Hersey and Blanchard (1982), in their work on situational leadership, proposed seven bases of power—coercive, legitimate, expert, reward, referent, information and connection—and accepted the dichotomy of *position power* and *personal power*, although they pointed out the limitations of dividing 'the pie always into two pieces'.

Berlew (1986) suggested two influence strategies—*push* and *pull*—the first being located in the system and the second being a part of the spirit of the individual that influences others. This suggestion is similar to position and personal power.

Pettigrew (1986) has suggested the dichotomy of overt and covert, the first being concerned with 'preferred outcome in conflict' and the second (which is unobtrusive) 'ensuing no conflict through use of symbols and myths to manage meaning'.

All the dichotomies suggested have a common thread, whether influence is used to force the other individual into accepting what the influencer wants him to think or do (fear power, direct influence, position power, push energy, overt influence) or to help the individual choose to think or do things (love power, indirect influence, personal power, pull energy, covert influence). The first has the element of coercion and the second that of persuasion. It seems to be useful to classify the bases of power into coercive and persuasive bases. CPP scale is based on this classification.

18.3.1 Coercive Bases

From the literature, it is clear that position, power and punishment are coercive bases. Power drawn from the organisational position (legitimate power in the role or power to allocate resources) coerces people to accept influences. Punishment deserves to be listed separately as coercive power.

Power derived from close affectionate bonds (relationship) often acts like coercion because the person accepting influence does so more out of emotional need rather than conscious choice. It has therefore been put into the category of coercive power. The main rationale has been that when people accept an act of influence because of emotion (fear, excessive love) they are being coerced, being manipulated. For the same reason, charisma is included in coercive power, because a charismatic leader arouses strong emotions and gets things done. The leader does not treat his followers as mature people who are competent to make their own choices. Referent power is different, as we shall see in the next section.

Another base included in coercive power is the power derived from a person with larger power bases. For example, the private secretary of the chief executive may use his association with the CEO as a source of influence. This is reflected power from another source and a kind of manipulation, and so is included in the group of coercive power.

Another type of manipulation is exercised by withholding or depriving a person of information or by delaying action. Some role occupants exercise power by delaying decisions and withholding critical information.

Thus six bases of power are included in the coercive power group—organisational position (legitimate power), punishment (coercive power), charisma (charismatic power), personal relation-ship (emotional power), closeness to a source of power (reflected power) and withholding information or resources (manipulative power).

18.3.2 Persuasive Bases

Personal power has been accepted as the opposite of coercion, that is, it can be put into the category of persuasive power. There are three main sources of personal power—expertise (special knowledge), competence (general effectiveness to produce results) and modelling (example set by behaviour). We accept the suggestion of a mechanic because he is an expert. A competent manager influences because he can get results. A person who 'lives' certain values (not smoking, encouraging others to speak, listening, giving credit for new ideas, etc.) influences others into behaving the same way or at least into attempting such behaviours, because they admire him. He does not make any covert appeal. He models a behaviour, which is more eloquent than the words used by somebody else. This is often called referent power. These three bases have been included in the category of persuasive power.

Reward has also been included here, because reward encourages people to experiment, gives them more autonomy, unless, of course, it is manipulated, as in the case of operant shaping.

Another base included is concern and caring for others and helping them to develop. Again, this helps in widening the autonomy of the individuals.

Raven suggested information as a base of power (French & Raven, 1959), but this was subsequently dropped because his co-author, French, did not agree (Raven, 1992). It was listed only as a form of influence in 1959 but was subsequently included as a base of power. Many people are influenced by given facts and by the logic behind information. This can be called logical power, as the basis is the rational aspect of information. This is also included as a persuasive base.

We thus have six bases of power in the category of persuasive power—reward (reinforcing power), expert power, competence power, referent power (being a role model), extension power (empathy, caring and helping others) and logical power (based on information and the rationale of the information). The bases and types of power are shown in Table 18.1.

18.3.3 Perceived Importance of Power Bases

Some studies have been reported on the relationship of compliance with different power bases. Based on a study of 40 production personnel, which used the five power bases of French and Raven (1959), Student (1968) reported legitimate, expert, reward, referent and coercive power (in this order) as stated reasons of compliance of employees with their foremen. Ivancevich and Donnelly (1970) found the rank order of power bases for the compliance of salesmen, belonging to a large firm, as expert, legitimate, reward, referent and coercive powers. Students rank ordered

TABLE 18.1   Bases and Types of Power

Coercive power		Persuasive power	
Base	**Type**	**Base**	**Type**
1. Organisational position	1. Status	1. Expertise	1. Expert
2. Closeness to power source	2. Reflected	2. Competence	2. Competence
3. Charisma	3. Charismatic	3. Role modelling	3. Referent
4. Punishing	4. Coercive	4. Rewarding	4. Reinforcing
5. Personal relationship	5. Emotional	5. Helping/caring	5. Extension
6. Withholding/depriving information	6. Manipulative	6. Information	6. Logical

power bases for their importance as high school students—legitimate, coercive, expert, reward and referent; graduates—expert, legitimate, reward, coercive and referent (Jamieson & Thomas, 1974).

One non-government service organisation in Indonesia (18 people) ranked 10 bases for compliance as—extension, competence, expert, referent, emotional, legitimate, reinforcing, manipulative, coercive and charismatic.

In the use of power bases, a person's perception of the power that he has and how much more he needs may be quite relevant. Perception of having and using power empowers a person while the need for power shows a sense of lacking power. This difference has been used in this instrument.

18.4 SCORING

The scale contains 6 coercive bases of power. According to the serial numbers in the scale, they are 1 (status), 2 (reflective), 4 (coercive), 7 (charismatic), 9 (manipulative) and 12 (emotional). The 6 persuasive bases in the scale are 3 (logical), 5 (expert), 6 (referent), 8 (reinforcement), 10 (extension) and 11 (competence). Ratings on each power base range from 1 to 5.

1. *Value for coercive power (VCP):* The total value for six coercive bases. VCP scores range from 6 to 30.

2. *Value for persuasive power (VPP):* The total value for six persuasive bases. VPP scores range from 6 to 30.

3. *NCP (need for coercive power):* The total need for six coercive bases. NCP scores range from 6 to 30. Scores from 6 to 12 show coercive power deficiency (CPD), and those from 17 to 30 show sufficiency coercive power (SCP).

4. *Need for persuasive power (NPP):* The total need for six persuasive bases. NPP scores range from 6 to 30. Scores from 6 to 12 show deficiency persuasive power (DPP), and those from 18 to 30 show sufficiency persuasive power (SPP). The higher the DPP, the more the need for self-development.

5. *Effectiveness of power value (EPV):* This is the ratio between VPP and VCP. It can be calculated by the following formula:

$$EPV = \frac{VPP - 6}{VPP + VCP - 12} \times 100.$$ EPV will range from 0 to 100.

The higher the value of EPV, the more effectively a person is using his profile of values for power bases.

6. *Effectiveness of power need (EPN):* It is the ratio between NPP and NCP, and can be calculated by the following formula:

$$EPN = \frac{NPP - 6}{NPP + NCP - 12} \times 100.$$ EPN will range from 0 to 100.

The higher the value of EPN, the more effectively a person is using his profile of need for power.

18.5 RELIABILITY

Internal consistency of the scale was tested for a sample of about 200 managers by Keshote (1991). He found split-half and even–odd correlations for four scales—coercive power value (VCP), persuasive power value (VPP), coercive power need (NCP) and persuasive power need (NPP). The coefficients ranged from 0.29 (split-half for NPP) to 0.72 (even–odd for NCP). Correlations of various items of the scales with the totals for the four scales—VC, VP, NC and NP—range from 0.63 to 0.82, showing that the scales have acceptable reliability.

18.6 VALIDITY

The responses of about 200 managers (Keshote, 1991) on 10 power bases were factor analysed (information, item 3 and manipulation, item 9 in the present scale were not included). Principal axis factoring with Varimax for a two-factor solution was used. All 20 items (5 items each of VCP, VPP, NCP and NPP) were factor analysed. The results are shown in Table 18.2. The two factors

TABLE 18.2   Rotated Factor Matrix of Power Variables

Items	Factor 1	Factor 2
N8	**0.86**	0.14
N9	**0.80**	0.16
N10	**0.78**	0.13
N5	**0.77**	0.23
N4	**0.70**	0.18
N7	**0.69**	0.19
N6	**0.67**	0.24
N3	**0.59**	0.23
N1	**0.54**	0.07
N2	**0.42**	0.10
V10	0.36	**0.56**
V6	0.31	**0.57**

(Table 18.2 Continued)

(Table 18.2 Continued)

Items	Factor 1	Factor 2
V8	0.30	**0.63**
V7	0.26	**0.73**
V9	0.25	**0.64**
V5	0.09	**0.63**
V4	0.07	**0.63**
V3	0.12	**0.53**
V1	0.11	**0.46**
V2	0.00	**0.36**

explained about 50% variance. As the table shows, Factor 1 is the value factor (first 10 items are VCP + VPP) and Factor 2 is the need factor (item 11 to 20 are NCP + NPP). These are two clean factors. Value for power and need for power were also factor analysed from the same data. The results are given in Tables 18.3 and 18.4.

It can be seen from both the tables that all the items related to persuasive power are in Factor 1, while 3 out of the 5 coercive items have high loadings in Factor 2. Factors 1 and 2 can be named persuasive power and coercive power factors respectively, for both power value and power need. Items 6 and 10 (charisma and emotional relationship) have high loadings in Factor 1. The construct validity index from these can be put at 0.80 (average of 100% for persuasive power and 60% for coercive power). This is a very high-validity index.

TABLE 18.3   Rotated Factor Matrix of Value for Power Factor Loadings

Items	Factor 1	Factor 2
8	**0.80**	0.11
9	**0.75**	0.16
7	**0.67**	0.37
4	**0.52**	0.31
5	**0.48**	0.39
6	**0.52**	0.32
10	**0.64**	0.21
3	0.27	**0.58**
1	0.21	**0.57**
2	0.08	**0.54**

TABLE 18.4   Rotated Factor Matrix of Need for Power Factor Loadings

Items	Factor 1	Factor 2
8	**0.85**	0.26
9	**0.82**	0.22
5	**0.76**	0.30
4	**0.66**	0.30
7	**0.58**	0.42
10	**0.77**	0.23
6	**0.66**	0.27
1	0.24	**0.76**
3	0.33	**0.73**
2	0.18	**0.61**

18.7 NORMS

Based on Keshote's (1991) data of about 200 managers, the following norms are proposed (using 1/2 standard deviation and mean values). The norms for larger and different types of population need to be worked out.

Variables	Mean	SD	High	Low
Value for coercive power (VCP)	18	2	20	16
Value for persuasive power (VPP)	21	2	23	19
Need for coercive power (NCP)	14	3	17	11
Need for persuasive power (NPP)	15	3	18	12
Effectiveness index of value	55	3	58	52
Effectiveness index of need	54	3	57	51

18.8 CORRELATES

Keshote's (1991) results from one multinational, one public sector and one private corporation showed that production managers had significantly higher value as well as NCP than 'service' managers who, in turn, had higher NPP than production managers, who had higher NCP than marketing managers. These differences were statistically significant at 0.05 level. Regarding organisational levels, value and need for both types of power were highest among junior, levels.

Using LOCO inventory (Chapter 9), Keshote (1991) found that internals had higher VPP and externals had higher value as well as NCP, and external (chance) lower VPP. He also reported significant positive correlation between VPP and negative correlation of NPP with an enlarging lifestyle (see Chapter 33). No significant correlation was found with coercive power.

18.9 USE FOR HRD

CPP scale can be used for various groups including managers, trainers, HRD professionals and consultants. Managers need to examine their bases of power and realise that the process of empowerment—use of persuasive bases to increase the power of others—is the most effective process for self-empowerment. Change agentry roles—HRD facilitators, OD specialists, consultants, trainers—can be effective only if the change agents expand their persuasive bases and do not use coercive bases.

CPP scale can also be used as a research tool for diagnosis and for designing interventions to expand power bases in an organisation. Such work should multiply power in an organisation at all levels.

CPP Scale

Name: _____ Role: _____

Organisation: _____ Date: _____

Below are given some items which may contribute to the effectiveness of your role in the organisation. Read each item and write in the first column how important it is, or would be, for your role effectiveness. Use the following key:

Write 1 if it is not important
Write 2 if it is a little important
Write 3 if it has some importance
Write 4 if it is quite important
Write 5 if it is very important or critical

Now read the items again and indicate in the second column how much more you need, or would need, each one to be more effective in your role.

Write 1 if you do not need it (what you have is sufficient).
Write 2 if you need a little more of it.
Write 3 if you need some more of it.
Write 4 if you need it much more.
Write 5 if you need it a great deal (you have very little of it now).

	Importance for Your Role	Your Need
1. Formal authority	_____	_____
2. Close contact with and/or direct access to the Chief Executive	_____	_____
3. Knowledge and information to explain the logic and convince others	_____	_____
4. Capacity to take action/punish	_____	_____
5. Functional and/or operational expertise	_____	_____
6. Modelling influence (convincing people through personal example and behaviour)	_____	_____
7. Charisma (ability to arouse emotions for action)	_____	_____
8. Capacity to reward people (all kinds of rewards, including recognition and positive feedback)	_____	_____
9. Capacity to hold back critical information, resources or decisions	_____	_____
10. Helping (providing care/help to others when needed)	_____	_____
11. Competence (achieving the goals you work for)	_____	_____
12. Close personal relationships to which you can appeal to get things done	_____	_____

19

Assertiveness Inventory

19.1 THE INSTRUMENT AND ITS ADMINISTRATION

Assertiveness inventory is a self-administered instrument and contains 48 items, 16 items for each type of behaviour. A 5-point scale has been used. It is designed to assess the level of assertiveness, submissiveness and aggressiveness in a person. Although the instrument is self-administered and self-scored, the facilitator also can collect the instruments and score it for them. If administered in a group to construct a group profile, respondents should be explained that the instrument is to help them understand their existing behaviour and plan to enhance their effectiveness by reducing dysfunctional and increasing functional aspects. Scoring key should not be distributed to the respondents until they complete the instrument.

19.2 CONCEPTUAL FRAMEWORK

Assertiveness has been of great interest to behavioural scientists for more than five decades. It caught their special attention in the early 1970s, when they were not only challenged but also concerned regarding the increasing number of non-assertive people. Since then, thousands of studies have been conducted to get to the root cause of non-assertive behaviour. Somewhere along the line, it has been confused with aggression. Generally, people assume that being assertive means, being pushy, demanding or asking for self-importance. Assertiveness does not mean being unpleasant to people, getting away with behaviour that upsets a team or dictating your terms. Assertiveness is respecting the self enough to become aware and state what one wants and, at the same time, being sensitive and respecting others' needs too. Assertiveness simply can be defined as, 'taking charge of your life'.

Dictionary meaning of 'to assert' is 'to state or affirm positively, plainly, assuredly or strongly', but behavioural scientists felt this explanation was not sufficient; it had to do something with interpersonal relationships that affected peoples' effectiveness. It is important to understand the genesis of our behaviour. Pavlov's classical experiments of conditioned reflex (Pavlov, 1960) explained how animals and human beings behave adaptively to changing conditions in the environment.

Since the era of Pavlov, various theories on assertiveness have been suggested, major among them being the works of Andrew Salter (1949), Joseph Wolpe (1969) and Arnold Lazarus (1968), who developed various concepts of assertiveness based on Pavlovian perspective directly or indirectly. Andrew Salter proposed that when excitatory forces dominate, people are action oriented, meet life on their own terms and are emotionally free, whereas excess of inhibitory forces cause people to be passive, unsure of themselves and low on self-sufficiency, who suffer from 'constipation of emotions'. According to Andrew Salter, there must be a proper balance of excitatory and inhibitory forces for normal psychological health. He also believed that this balance could be achieved by deliberate and conscious effort until a new spontaneous behaviour occurred, forming a natural part of the personality.

Joseph Wolpe (1969) defines assertive behaviour as 'the proper expression of any emotion, other than anxiety towards another person'. He proposed people behaved unassertively because of interpersonal fears. If these fears could be reduced, a new behaviour would emerge. He applied this knowledge in the clinical treatment of patients successfully. His 'reciprocal inhibition principle' has become one of the milestones of behaviour therapy. The principle states, 'If a response inhibitory of anxiety can be made to occur in the presence of anxiety-provoking stimuli, it will weaken the bond between the stimuli and the anxiety'. He taught his patients to respond to social situations with emotions such as anger or affection that inhibit or counter anxiety through role-playing until anxiety totally disappeared. Once the patients learnt, they carried this new behaviour to real life situations and became more assertive.

Arnold Lazarus (1968) defines emotional freedom as 'the recognition and appropriate expression of each and every effective state'. He proposed that assertive behaviour emerges as the aspect of emotional freedom that concerns 'standing up for your rights'. He further states, 'knowing what you feel is not enough. You must express it too, appropriately'. That involves knowing your rights, doing something about it and doing this within the framework of striving for emotional freedom. According to him, recognition of rights also involves a recognition of and respect for the rights of others.

James Allen (1950) offered the following formula on self-esteem:

$$\text{Self-esteem} = \text{Success/pretensions}$$

Self-esteem in simplistic terms means how you feel about yourself. It comes from a feeling of knowing what is good and having done it. Pretensions part concerns goals. He felt that people may possess many unrealistic and conflicting goals and success at one goal has to be at the cost of suppression of others. He proposed, 'Seeker of his truest, strongest, deepest self must review his list (of possible goals) and carefully pick up the ones on which to stake his salvation'. By this, James meant that one could fulfil himself only through accepting certain limitations and every success meant a rise in the degree of self-assertion.

People behave non-assertively due to social conditioning. Right from our childhood, we are taught by the society, parents and teachers to comply with the wishes of others. Children who obediently follow what others tell them to are rewarded, whereas children who speak for themselves or raise any questions are dealt with sternly. This type of training results in two types of behaviours:

1. Either people become submissive and let other people push them around and define their roles or
2. Rebel and become aggressive and dominate, humiliate or put down other people.

Both the behaviours are inappropriate and hinder proper assertion of our self. We adopt either of the two styles of behaviours, even when we grow up, take up jobs and perform various roles in life, for example, employee, employer, friend, spouse, parent, etc., and live throughout our life in the same manner. Non-assertiveness has sad and severe consequences such as disrupted relationships, lack of personal growth and development, migraines, fatigue and depression.

The submissive or timid souls do not recognise their own strengths. They feel and behave inferior. They are passive in all the situations. They give thousands of reasons for not acting, so that over a period of time, they become very skilled at creating an empty life. They become conditioned to certain fears such as rejection, criticism, failure, looking foolish and expression of emotions such as anger or tenderness. They tend to avoid situations where they might come across these fears. Out of fear, they do not set any goals and live a purposeless life. Goal setting is an important aspect of assertiveness because goals direct, motivate and reinforce self-esteem. They do not understand the difference between being liked and being respected. Their need to be liked is so great that they sacrifice their self-respect.

On the other hand, aggressive people feel that their desires are of utmost importance. Because of certain bitter experiences and hurts, their goal becomes to hurt and humiliate others. They have a notion that it is acceptable, even necessary, to step on others to get ahead. They look at the world as they would like it to be, not as it is. They feel and think that the world should revolve around them, which is not only unrealistic but also futile. They are compulsive complainers. They are like a wounded tiger which is always in the search of a prey to attack and attacks at the first opportunity available. Sometimes, their victims retaliate or, at other times, they run away and avoid them. In the bargain, they become frustrated, miserable, vindictive and manipulative. They burn with rage almost all the time and become increasingly aggressive.

Assertion is often confused with aggression. Aggressiveness is an act against others whereas assertiveness is appropriate standing up for one's own rights. Assertiveness primarily means self-mastery or taking charge of one's own life. Assertive behaviour is a direct, open, honest and appropriate expression of one's opinions, values, beliefs and feelings. Assertive communication demonstrates self-confidence and self-respect in addition to the awareness and respect for other's feelings, opinions and values. Mahatma Gandhi best exemplified assertive behaviour, who stood for India's independence and succeeded in his mission without any violence or aggression. He strongly believed that freedom was the fundamental right of every human being, and he had every right to demand it.

Assertiveness is based on the belief that you have a right to be listened to and taken seriously, to commit mistakes, to ask for favours and to refuse unreasonable requests without feeling guilty. At the same time, it is also important to understand that the other person has identical rights. Your relationships become much more genuine because you are communicating openly and honestly. When you ask for a favour and are refused, you may feel disappointed, which is a natural process, but you don't have to feel bad or hurt about it. When you communicate openly, directly and honestly, your relationships with people become much more genuine and at the same time, you earn their respect. Herbert Fensterheim (1975) gives a seemingly simple, yet a very powerful equation: assertion = self-esteem.

Some of the traits observed in an assertive personality are optimism, active orientation to life, taking personal responsibility for one's failures and successes, taking calculated risks, setting realistic goals, ability to take decisions, appropriate communication skills, etc. Assertive person acts out of inner strength. He knows exactly what he wants and makes things happen, rather than waiting passively for things to happen.

Based on various theories, research findings and observation of human behaviour, the three types of behaviour are summarised here.

Submissiveness: Submissive people do not recognise their own strengths. They behave inferior because they feel inferior. They live their lives by the rules and whims of others. They are low on self-sufficiency. They are passive in all the situations. They possess no control of their own lives. They do not know who they are, what they want, what they feel or what they think. They become increasingly unsure of themselves. Passive or non-assertive behaviour comes primarily from the obedient/adapted child or nurturing parent ego. Passive people adopt the life position 'I am not OK you are OK'. Passive behaviour is an avoidance mode of behaviour or an accommodation of others' wishes without standing for one's own right. It involves self-denial and sacrifices. A person who is unassertive or passive by reason of his interpersonal fears may not be able to complain about the poor service in a restaurant/hotel room, contradict a friend with whom he disagrees, get up and leave a social situation that has become boring or express affection, appreciation or praise. Such persons as employees learn early in their careers that if they speak up they are not likely to get a raise or promotion and may even lose their jobs. Passive people often have very poor self-esteem and are unhappy. The passivity is based on unknown fears—fear of failure, fear of rejection, fear of displeasing others, fear of retaliation, fear of hurting others and being hurt and fear of getting into trouble. Passivity of behaviour is not by birth, but it is because of what is learnt in early childhood.

Aggressiveness: Over-assertiveness is often aggression and is always inappropriate. When we behave aggressively and come on too strong, we may accomplish things temporarily, but, in most cases, it leads to disrupted communication with others, calls forth counter aggression from others and tends to make us even more aggressive. The purpose of aggressive behaviour is to dominate, humiliate or 'put the other person down'. Aggression is an act against others whereas assertion is proper standing up for ourselves. Aggressive behaviour comes primarily through critical parent or rebellious child. Aggressive people are demanding, rude and dominating. They want their own way and force to gain control. Aggressive people are very competitive and do not like to lose. For winning in any interpersonal conflict, they will not hesitate to cheat to gain control. They have a tendency to violate the rights of others to get their way. Non-verbal communication used by aggressive people includes cold response, speaking loudly, threatening gestures and belligerent postures, showing impatience, shaking fingers and making fists. People avoid contact with aggressive people and transaction is minimal. Aggressive people appear to be self-confident but the behaviour is more often the result of poor self-concept. Although they are in 'I am not OK' position, but they consistently try to prove that they are in 'OK' position by attacking and controlling others. Since they have inherent inferiority complex, they try hard to prove their worth by violating others' rights.

Assertiveness: Assertive behaviour is a direct, open, honest and appropriate expression of one's feelings, opinions, values and beliefs. Assertive communication demonstrates self-respect and self-confidence in addition to awareness and respect for others' feelings, opinions, values and belief. Assertive behaviour comes out of adult ego state with 'I am OK, you are OK' position. Assertive people express their feelings, emotions and thoughts without being aggressive. They express their ideas, feelings and thoughts firmly and emphatically without being rude and unreasonable and without offending others. These persons stand up to their rights without violating the rights of others. Non-verbal communication of an assertive person includes positive facial expression such as smiling, eye contact, pleasant voice, erect postures and firm gestures. The person with assertive behaviour is having positive self-concepts. They do not get threatened, and do not allow others to control their behaviour. They project positive image of themselves.

Assertiveness training aims at helping people to understand what is wrong with their lifestyle and what they could do to change it. Its other aims are to help people to understand the importance of interpersonal communication skills, to take charge of their life, to learn to recognise and express all emotions including anger. According to Fensterheim (1975), assertiveness training offers following two assumptions:

1. What you do serves as the basis of your self-concept.
2. Behaviours do not exist in isolation but interact with each other, that is, if you change one behaviour, you change a whole series of related behaviours.

19.3 SCORING

1. The following items correspond to the three types of behaviours:
   - Submissiveness: 1,4,7,10,13,16,19,22,25,28,31,34,37,40,43,46
   - Aggressiveness: 2,5,8,11,14,17,20,23,26,29,32,35,38,41,44,47
   - Assertiveness: 3,6,9,12,15,18,21,24,27,30,33,36,39,42,45,48
2. Add the rating for each type of behavior. Total will range from 0 to 64.
3. Multiply each total by 1.56. It will range from 0 to 100.
4. Calculate Assertiveness Effectiveness Quotients (AEQ) using the following formula:
   AEQ = Assertiveness/(Submissiveness + Aggressiveness) × 100
5. EAQ will range from 0 to 100. The higher the EAQ, the more effective the person is using his/her assertive behaviour in relation to submissiveness or aggressiveness.

19.4 RELIABILITY

Split-half reliability (N = 120) was found to be 0.58.

19.5 NORMS

Based on the responses of 80 undergraduates, tentative norms are proposed on the basis of mean and SD values given here. Specific norms can be developed for specific groups based on the mean and SD values.

Aspects	Mean	SD	Very low	Low	Average	High	Very high
Submissiveness	45.55	13.31	10 and below	19–32	33–59	60–72	73 and above
Aggressiveness	35.1	12.82	11 and below	10–23	24–48	49–61	62 and above
Assertiveness	48.57	13.92	19 and below	11–35	36–62	63–76	77 and above

Assertiveness Inventory

Name: _____   Date: _____

Organisation: _____   Role: _____

The purpose of this inventory is to help you to assess your assertive style. Answer as honestly as possible. Read each item carefully and write your answers in the space provided on its left hand side according to the following key.

Write 4   if you almost always behave this way
Write 3   if you often behave this way
Write 2   if you sometimes behave this way
Write 1   if you occasionally behave this way
Write 0   if you never or rarely behave this way

No.	Response	Items
1.	_____	I generally keep quiet and do not argue with others when they don't listen to me.
2.	_____	I feel very hurt and angry, if the other person refuses when I ask for a favour.
3.	_____	I am able to recognise and express my strengths.
4.	_____	I feel I am not as good as others.
5.	_____	I become resentful, angry and defensive, when criticised.
6.	_____	I try to reason out with others, when they don't listen to me.
7.	_____	I always check with others, if it is okay with them, what I plan to do.
8.	_____	I become physically or verbally abusive when angry.
9.	_____	I do not feel shy in asking for a favour or making a request.
10.	_____	I have the tendency to make self-deprecating remarks when I succeed or achieve something (e.g., 'Oh, I was just plain lucky!' or 'I can't believe I really did that!' or 'I am not really very good at that!').
11.	_____	I often have my share of fun at the expense of others.
12.	_____	If I cannot complete any given task by the deadline, I tell openly and honestly the reason for delay rather than making up excuses.
13.	_____	Though I feel people often take advantage of me, but I guess nothing can be done about such people.
14.	_____	If I am angry with a person of higher authority (e.g., parent, teacher or boss), I take out my anger on inanimate objects (e.g., throwing a book, banging the telephone, kicking a chair, etc.).
15.	_____	I can start and carry on a conversation comfortably, even with strangers.
16.	_____	I feel very embarrassed and don't know how to react when I receive compliments from others.
17.	_____	I tend to grumble about other people's behaviour (e.g., 'You never...' or 'You always...').
18.	_____	I speak clearly and directly, keeping my voice calm and controlled, even in a conflict.
19.	_____	I feel hurt and depressed when someone criticises me, but I don't say anything and just sulk.
20.	_____	If I do not like what the other person says, I ignore him and walk away.

No.	Response	Items
21.	_____	If others laugh at me, I too laugh with them or disagree in good humour.
22.	_____	I go out of way to help people, even at my own inconvenience and later on regret doing so.
23.	_____	I get angry and defensive, when others laugh at me.
24.	_____	I listen to the other person attentively, even when I might disagree with him.
25.	_____	In a discussion, if I feel I have nothing worthwhile to say, I just sit quietly and do not participate.
26.	_____	There is no harm in using people or manipulating things to succeed in life.
27.	_____	I have no problem in paying a compliment to anyone if I like something about him.
28.	_____	I control and suppress my anger, because I don't want to create a scene.
29.	_____	When I am angry with someone, I usually become silent and indifferent.
30.	_____	I can express very easlly my feelings of tenderness towards others.
31.	_____	I find it difficult to take initiative in discussion and wait for somebody else to take charge.
32.	_____	I do not bother when told that I am being unfair, and try to prove the other person wrong.
33.	_____	If I hear some rumour or gossip about me, I directly go to the person concerned and ask for clarification.
34.	_____	I pay compliments to people just to be comfortable with them.
35.	_____	I shout or snap back at others when they don't listen to me.
36.	_____	I can refuse a request without feeling guilty or over explaining.
37.	_____	I do not like to be compared with others.
38.	_____	In discussion, if I feel, the other person is talking something irrelevant, I tell him to shut up.
39.	_____	If I get irritated by someone's habit that drives me up the wall, I ask him to stop.
40.	_____	I find it very difficult to make eye contact while talking.
41.	_____	I feel my desires, needs and suggestions are very important, and others should go along with them.
42.	_____	I can take criticism without being defensive.
43.	_____	I find it very difficult to ask for a favour.
44.	_____	When I succeed, I make it a point to let everyone know that I outsmarted everybody else.
45.	_____	I do not avoid confrontation for the fear of spoiling relationships.
46.	_____	I feel bad if I have to refuse a request and try my best to explain it.
47.	_____	I do most of the talking in a conversation.
48.	_____	I take initiative in discussion and raise questions if I do not understand a point.

20 *Values: Opinion Survey**

20.1 THE INSTRUMENT AND ITS ADMINISTRATION

Opinion survey measures farmers' value orientation, consisting of four aspects—conservatism–liberalism (C–L), fatalism–scientism (F–S), authoritarianism–non-authoritarianism (A–N) and cosmopoliteness–localiteness (C–L). It contains 24 items, six for each aspect. A respondent is required to respond to each item on a 4-point scale of agreement. The items are in random order. After administration of the inventory, the scores obtained by an individual on the different items on each of the four scales are totalled.

Farmers are usually interviewed during their leisure time when they are willing to cooperate. If they can read and write, they may be administered the instrument in a group. After establishing a rapport with them for the interview, a respondent is asked to respond to a few statements by stating whether he agrees or disagrees with each statement. If he agrees, he is asked whether he simply agrees or strongly agrees; likewise, if he disagrees, whether he simply disagrees or strongly disagrees. The inventory is used in the local language; it was tried out in Hindi. Since most of the respondents were illiterate, group administration was not possible and each respondent was interviewed separately.

20.2 CONCEPTUAL FRAMEWORK

The term *value* varies with shifting connotations in different disciplines and social sciences. Even in a specialised field, there is lack of general consensus regarding its meaning. In psychology, confusion in the conception of the term may arise when it is considered as the nexus of all relationships between persons, groups, objects or events. Another source of confusion about

---

* This section has been written jointly and with substantial inputs from Somnath Chattopadhyay.

value is 'their relationships and differences from such other enduring dispositions as attitudes, interests and sentiments' (Kilby, 1961, p. 194).

Values may be conveniently viewed in the perspective of normative as against existential propositions. Thorndike (1936) has stated that values, positive or negative, statements, represent an expectation, that is, in effect, a prediction. Expected behaviour of some kind is implicit in all 'ought' statements. All *ought* statements can be received by at least one premise. That premise implies a *desideratum*.

The interrelationship between evaluative and the factual statements is further corroborated in the light of what Cantril, Ames, Hassorf and Ittelson (1949) stated. They observed that because man inevitably builds for himself an assumptive world in carrying out his purposeful activities, the world he is operating on and the world that is operating on him is the result of a transactional process in which man himself plays an active role. Man carries out his activities in the midst of concrete events which themselves delimit the significance he must deal with.

Kluckhohn (1951, p. 394) hold that 'existence and value are intimately related, interdependent, and yet—at least at the analytical level—conceptually distinct'. They state that there are three types of experiencing—existential, desire and the desirable. 'Values are manifested in ideas, expressional symbols, and in the moral and aesthetic norms evident in behavioural regularities. Whether the cognitive or the cathectic factors have primacy in the manifestation of a value at a particular time, both are always present'.

Dodd (1951) has defined values as 'desiderata, i.e., anything desired or chosen by someone sometime'.

Kluckhohn et al. (1951, p. 395) have forwarded a general definition. 'A value is a conception, explicit or implicit, distinctive of an individual or characteristic of a group, of the desirable which influences the selection from available modes, means, and ends of action.' In this definition, they emphasise the effective (desirable), cognitive (conception) and connective (selection) as essential elements in the concept of value.

In the psychological frame of reference, as pointed out earlier, the concept of value is blurred to some extent by the closely related concepts of attitudes, interests, sentiments, motivation and such other phenomena of human behaviour. As Kilby (1961, p. 194) points out, the fact is that all are of the same general class, being of enduring dispositions, share common features and overlap. Effort at sharp differentiation is pointless. The question is whether there is enough behavioural difference to warrant the separate categories. A value is motivational, as are the others. It sometimes involves interest or sentiment and often has the for-or-against quality of an attitude.

Whereas attitudes usually involve specificity, there are some guiding behavioural dispositions within individuals that cannot be properly covered by terms such as attitude and may conveniently be called values.

Kluckhohn et al. (1951, p. 425) have alternatively stated in psychological terms that 'value may be defined as that aspect of motivation which is referable to standards (personal or cultural) that do not arise solely out of immediate tensions or immediate situations'.

The form in which English and English (1958, p. 576) have put the term, value, may be recognised as a summary of the concept. First, value means 'the worth or excellence, or the degree of worth, ascribed to an object or activity or a class thereof'. They reside in the satisfaction or annoyance felt by animals, persons or deities. According to him, values are functions of preferences. So, in values, the conception of the nature of things is in relation to human interests.

Lepley (1943), while stating, among other things, that 'the whole gamut of events and relations can be referred to by both forms of statement' implies that the same thing may be thought at the same time about its value and about its existence.

Lundberg (1948) recognised the essential basic similarity of scientific and ethical statements. According to him, all *should* or *ought* statements as well as scientific state that though ascribed to the object value is a function of the valuing *transaction*, not of the object. 'Valence is a specific embodiment of a value in a particular concrete situation'. Second, value is 'an abstract concept, often merely implicit, that defines for an individual or for a social unit what ends or means to an end are desirable'. They have added that these abstract concepts of worth are usually not the result of the individual's own valuing; they are social products that have been imposed on him and only slowly internalised, that is, accepted and used as his own criteria of worth. Third, value may also be recognised as a 'goal object' which implies that instead of saying that a goal *has* a value, in this age, a goal *is* a value.

20.3 DEVELOPMENT OF THE INSTRUMENT

The quantitative measurement of the four dimensions of values—conservatism–liberalism, fatalism–scientism, authoritarianism–non-authoritarianism, cosmopoliteness–localiteness—required separate measuring scales for each. A modified form of Likert technique was used in developing the instrument.

20.3.1 Collection of Items

After formulating the working definition of the three aspects of value-orientation, items for each dimension were collected. The collection started with a number of post-graduate students in the division of agricultural extension that offered psychology, rural sociology or extension as major subjects of study. Each student was interviewed separately. The interviews were long and often in different sessions. The students were asked to state what they meant by each of the terms, in as many ways as they could. Each response was critically considered and probed further. They were asked to narrate the concept in meaningful verbal expressions. They were also asked to pick out individuals known to both them and the interviewer in relation to any particular value which the person embodied more distinctly (according to the interviewee). The students were asked why they identified the person depicting a particular value. They were asked to narrate the situations in which the unique behaviour of each of the persons influenced their conclusions. A number of responses were thus obtained. The interviews were quite informal, and the interviewees, in many cases, did not realise that they were being interviewed for a specific purpose. They were later told the specific purpose of the interview and were requested to add more items, if they wanted.

Several adults in different walks of life were also interviewed for the same purpose and the method of interview was the same.

It was felt that items collected from people in urban areas have an urban bias and might not be suitable for scales to be developed for measuring value orientation of rural people. So, 15 adult farmers were interviewed. The main difficulty in interviewing rural people for this purpose was that they were not sophisticated enough to conceptualise the different values. Therefore, the concepts of the different values were first explained to them. During conversation, as they got involved in the discussion, they started reacting, expressing their opinions and narrating experiences. This provided an opportunity to note their reactions and collect some items.

An important source of items was the available scales. But the main handicap in using these items was their incompatibility with the existing cultural pattern of the community to be studied. For that matter, most of the items were not found suitable. Some items were, however, included in the preliminary list. These, of course, needed some changes in their form, often drastic ones. The available scales consulted for this purpose were mainly Ferguson (1944), Adorno, Frenkel-Brunswik, Levinson and Sanford (1950), Eysenck (1960), Kamala (1960) and Rao (1962).

About 250 items thus collected were grouped into eight pools of conservatism, liberalism, fatalism, scientism, authoritarianism, non-authoritarianism, localiteness and cosmopoliteness on the basis of *prima facie* evidence of each item belongs to a particular group.

20.3.2 Item Selection

The next phase consisted in determining the relevance of a particular item to the particular value to be measured in reducing considerably the number of items to form a small but efficient scale and in maintaining the internal consistency of the scale.

The items were properly screened and edited. Those items which seemed to overlap were critically examined. Either the item conveying the idea most clearly was retained or the language of an item was changed to make it more suitable in its expression.

Several criteria were formulated for selection (and rejection) and editing of statements, especially those suggested by Edwards (1957, pp. 13–14). A total of 105 items were retained, maintaining a more or less equitable proportion from each of the six groups.

The list of 105 items was sent to 75 judges to determine the relevance of each item to a particular value dimension. The list of items can be seen in another source. The judges, all experts, were psychologists, sociologists and anthropologists in various universities and institutions in India.

After obtaining responses from judges, they were summarised for each item. Those items that did not receive any judgement were interpreted as not belonging to any of the six values. For each item, the number of responses in each of the six categories and the total responses from the six categories were calculated. The criterion of selection of items was that it should have received at least 80% unanimity as a threshold value out of the total responses it received.

In the final construction of the three scales—the C–L scale, the F–S scale and the A–N scale—six items for each of the scales were finally selected. The unanimity of judges about the items belonging to a scale was taken to be an indicator of the internal consistency of the scale. Later, the six items, properly searched and tested, were added for cosmopolite and localite dimensions. These were borrowed from a scale by S. N. Singh (1965).

20.4 SCORING

The responses are scored on a 4-point scale—strongly agree, agree, disagree and strongly disagree. A middle category of undecided was not kept to prevent a respondent from avoiding judging the item.

The scoring is unidirectional. High scores in the four scales indicated high degree of conservatism, fatalism, authoritarianism and localiteness, respectively. The following is the scoring key for the values. Items with an asterisk (*) are to be reversed to make the items unidirectional.

1. Conservatism: 2*, 5, 9, 14, 18, 21*
2. Fatalism: 1, 6, 10*, 13, 17*, 22
3. Authoritarianism: 4, 7, 11, 16, 20*, 23
4. Localiteness: 3, 8, 12, 15*, 19, 24*

Each of the four scales thus have the possible range of 6–24. Multiply each total by 5.5. Then the range will be 0–100 for each scale.

20.5 VALIDITY

No validational studies were done for the value scales. However, validity was built during the preparation of these scales. Some experts were used as judges for rating the statements for their relevance to various value dimensions. The criterion for the selection of the statements was the unanimity of judges (at least 80%). This ensured the validity of the items in indicating the status of an individual on the value dimension concerned. Since the scoring system was a priori determined (4, 3, 2, 1), the scales may be called absolute scales, in the sense that these are not affected by the distribution pattern of the scores in the group under study.

However, whenever the farmers have been designated as conservative, liberal, fatalist, etc., it is always meant to convey 'conservative as tested by the scale in the study' or 'liberal as tested by the scale in the study' and so on.

The distribution of the scores of 173 farmers in one north-Indian village showed that mean, median and mode values were almost the same.

20.6 NORMS

Based on data from 173 farmers from a north-Indian village and 54 farmers from another village, the following norms, based on mean ± 1 SD, are suggested:

Scale	Low	High
Conservatism	71	93
Fatalism	49	95
Authoritarianism	41	69
Localiteness	63	91

20.7 CORRELATES

Fatalism and conservatism had a negative correlation (significant at 0.01 level) with multiple adoption behaviour (–0.585 and –0.396 respectively) in a study of 173 farmers (Chattopadhyay & Pareek, 1982). A stepwise multiple regression analysis showed that fatalism and conservatism were the most powerful predictions of adoption behaviour, accounting for almost 49% variance.

Opinion Survey

Name: _____   Date: _____

Organisation: _____   Occupation: _____

Below are given 24 statements. We want your opinion about each. There are no right or wrong answers. Give your response by writing any number from 1 to 4 as indicated below:

Write 1   if you strongly disagree with the statement
Write 2   if you disagree with the statement
Write 3   if you agree with the statement
Write 4   if you strongly agree with the statement

1. _____   Mantras have far-reaching effects. If a person can chant and accurately recite the right mantra on the right occasion, he can produce miraculous effects.
2. _____   The present pattern of education is better than the earlier one.
3. _____   These days, when communication has advanced so much, a farmer should know more about life outside.
4. _____   If one believes that something is truly good, one is justified in ruthlessly imposing it on others.
5. _____   The good old days were golden.
6. _____   Every event in a man's life has already been settled and determined by his fate.
7. _____   Meetings, committees, corporate bodies, etc. are useless; members are usually involved in politics and no work gets done.
8. _____   A farmer can learn everything from experience in his own village.
9. _____   Caste system has more virtue than vice.
10. _____   There cannot be any real relationship between the constellation of stars (in a horoscope) and happenings in life.
11. _____   In any organisation, the decisions of the head should be final as too many cooks spoil the broth.
12. _____   He who does not consult others can act better.
13. _____   A basic human tragedy is that man proposes but God disposes.
14. _____   All relations of kin should be maintained as they have always been.
15. _____   A man can escape numerous troubles and worries, if he consults friends and neighbours.
16. _____   People should be forced to contribute to the National Defence Fund.
17. _____   It is better to disbelieve in what is not proved and tested; but when it is proved, it is to be relied on.
18. _____   To deny our past and break with it is to uproot people and make them surplus.
19. _____   A farmer can fulfil all his needs with the help of his village folk.
20. _____   The judgement of a tribunal of judges is better than that of a single judge.
21. _____   Marriage within one's own caste should not be strictly pursued; inter-caste marriage should be favoured.
22. _____   Those who say that they have seen ghosts either distort the truth or tell a lie.
23. _____   It is better to rule in hell than to serve in heaven.
24. _____   Many things that a farmer ought to know are not only confined in his village, but are alike in other villages.

21

Perseverance: Value Preference Survey and General Beliefs Inventory

21.1 THE INSTRUMENT AND ITS ADMINISTRATION

This instrument consists of two inventories. The objective of both is to help a respondent examine his score on orientation-to-perseverance (PO) and plan to raise his level of perseverance. The instrument is given separately as inventories to assess general beliefs and values. The values relate to the achievement motive, and the instrument is primarily used for entrepreneurs.

The two inventories are separately administered as independent instruments, preferably by administering other instruments between them.

21.2 THE CONCEPTUAL FRAMEWORK

It has been reported (e.g., Rao & Moulik, 1979) that one significant factor in the success of an entrepreneur is perseverance, that is, the tendency to persist with the effort in achieving a goal in spite of various difficulties. McClelland's concept of 'activity inhibition' is quite close to the concept of perseverance.

Perseverance is reflected in several ways at work: in a person's obsession with a goal, his not giving up the goal despite various problems, the large amount of time spent in the effort to reach the goal, hard work, focussing attention on the task until it is completed and so on. PO can be measured by taking these dimensions into account.

According to some theories, attitudes are a product of values and beliefs (value × belief = attitude). If either of them is zero, the result is zero. This approach has been utilised in developing these two instruments, which are to be used together to give a score on PO.

Perseverance has been broken down into seven aspects. A person will have a positive PO if he (a) believes that perseverance leads to some result (say, achievement of goals) and (b) has high value for this result. General beliefs inventory measures the perceived instrumentality, while value survey measures the value of the various outcomes (various aspects of achievement). To camouflage the perseverance items, five filler items have also been included.

21.3 SCORING

Only the relevant seven items are scored. The five filler items are ignored. The score sheet (appended, also to be used as scoring key) indicates which items are to be multiplied with which ones. After the multiplication of the pairs, the scores are added. These will range between 0 and 112. The higher the score, the stronger is the PO. Multiply the total by 0.89 to make the range 0–100.

21.4 RELIABILITY

Split-half reliability ($N = 20$) was found to be 0.43.

21.5 VALIDITY

Sarupriya (1983) reported a small amount of difference (statistically not significant) between successful and unsuccessful entrepreneurs. The trend can be taken as an indirect test of the instrument's validity.

21.6 NORMS

Sarupriya (1983) reported a mean score of 65 and a standard deviation of 9 for a small group of successful entrepreneurs. It can tentatively be said that a score of 74 and above shows a high PO, and a score of 56 and below suggests a low orientation. The norms for larger samples need to be worked out.

21.7 USE FOR HRD

The higher the score, the more positive is the person's attitude towards perseverance; and he is likely to persevere further in pursuing objectives. Norms can be developed for various groups. Respondents, both individually and in groups, can be helped to plan various steps to raise their PO.

General Beliefs Inventory

Name: _____   Role: _____

Organisation: _____   Date: _____

Read the statements given below and indicate your agreement or disagreement with each by using the following key:

    Write 0   if you completely disagree with it
    Write 1   if you disagree with it
    Write 2   if you are undecided
    Write 3   if you agree with it
    Write 4   if you strongly agree with it

1. _____ You can achieve your goal if you pursue it, and do not give it up despite many difficulties.
2. _____ You achieve real independence, if you try different ways of solving a problem, when the original way does not work.
3. _____ Doing something for society satisfies your conscience.
4. _____ The harder you work, the more profit you earn.
5. _____ You may be able to shape things according to your ideas if you work on a task until it is finished.
6. _____ Your progress in life is in proportion to your ability to impress people.
7. _____ Your achievement is largely related to your good behaviour with people.
8. _____ A challenge can be met if you work out the details of what you want to do, including how to go about doing it.
9. _____ The person who is bothered about incomplete tasks is likely to succeed in achieving them.
10. _____ People help a person to achieve his goals if he is helpful to them.
11. _____ Those who assert themselves in meetings are able to get tasks done by others.
12. _____ The person who has to do things by himself should spend a lot of time on the task at hand.

Value Preference Survey

Name: _____   Role: _____

Organisation: _____   Date: _____

The purpose of this survey is to find out the value preference of people. There are no right or wrong answers. Read each item given below and indicate, in the space given on its left-hand side, how much you value it. Use a number to indicate your preference, according to the following key:

     Write 0   if you do not have any value for it at all
     Write 1   if you value it a little
     Write 2   if you have some value for it
     Write 3   if you value it highly
     Write 4   if you value it very highly

No.	Score	Item
1.	_____	Earning profit.
2.	_____	Determining or shaping things according to one's ideas.
3.	_____	Progressing in life.
4.	_____	Achievement in life.
5.	_____	Achievement of a goal.
6.	_____	Meeting a challenge.
7.	_____	Satisfaction of the conscience.
8.	_____	Independence.
9.	_____	Getting other's help.
10.	_____	Accomplishing things through one's own efforts.
11.	_____	Getting tasks done by others.
12.	_____	Continuously thinking about a task.

VPS and GBI
Score Sheet

C.   Ignore items 3, 4, 7, 9, 11 in VPS
     Ignore items 3, 6, 7, 10, 11 in GBI

D.   Transfer the responses below and then multiply the following items:

VPS Items Score		GBI Items Score		Result of Multiplication
5 __	×	1 __	=	__
8 __	×	2 __	=	__
1 __	×	4 __	=	__
2 __	×	5 __	=	__
6 __	×	8 __	=	__
12 __	×	9 __	=	__
10 __	×	12 __	=	__

Total Score of PO

22

Fear of Failure: Guessing Test

22.1 THE INSTRUMENT AND ITS ADMINISTRATION

The Guessing Test instrument is intended to help respondents gain an insight into their level of fear of failure, which is a dimension of the achievement motive. This is to be used primarily as a training instrument. Its administration is simple. The instrument consists of 15 pairs of statements, and the respondent is required to choose one item from each pair.

22.2 CONCEPTUAL FRAMEWORK

The achievement motive has been found to be a critical factor in entrepreneurship and is reflected in a person's concern for excellence and success. Such concern may be generated either by hope of success (HS) or by fear of failure. The first (HS) is the approach dimension, and the other (fear of failure) is the avoidance dimension of achievement motivation. The first is concerned with approaching challenges and the second with avoiding hurdles and factors that may cause failure (for detailed discussion, see Birney & Burdick, 1969; Heckhausen, 1967b).

Based on a study of entrepreneurs, who had undergone entrepreneurial motivation development training in four countries, Varga (1977) found fear of failure to be an important intervening variable to explain who would translate the gains from training into setting up an enterprise. He found that fear of failure prevented people from going into entrepreneurial activities, even if they had a high achievement motive. Varga measured fear of failure from the stories written by the respondents, and he used Heckhausen's method of scoring (Heckhausen, 1967b).

The Guessing Test is based on the same concept. It has been developed as a semi-projective test, using Heckhausen's scoring method as the basis. Heckhausen (1967b) proposed some common categories for the HS and fear of failure—need, goal anticipation, instrumental activity, reaction of others (praise or blame) and feelings about the result. All these five categories have been used to prepare three forced-choice pairs for each category, making a total of 15 items. Care has been taken to equate the pairs on social desirability. In addition to the these dimensions, Heckhausen also proposed two dimensions—result (failure) and thema. These two dimension have not been used in this instrument.

22.3 SCORING

The following scoring key gives the alternatives that are to be scored for fear of failure. The total number of fear-of-failure items, checked by the respondent, gives his total score, which ranges from 0 to 15.

The following alternatives indicate fear of failure:

1.	b	9.	b
2.	a	10.	a
3.	b	11.	b
4.	a	12.	b
5.	b	13.	b
6.	a	14.	a
7.	b	15.	b
8.	a		

Count the number of items, given here, checked by a respondent. This is the score for fear of failure. Minimum and maximum scores are 0 and 15, respectively.

22.4 VALIDITY

Sarupriya (1983) reported the difference between the mean values of successful and unsuccessful entrepreneurs. Because of the small size of the sample and large SD, the difference was not statistically significant. However, the trend was in the predicted direction.

22.5 USE FOR HRD

The interpretation is simple. The total score is the index of an individual's fear of failure motive. However, the various items can also be examined to see on which dimension fear of failure is higher.

The facilitator may use the results to discuss how fear of failure prevents a person from being successful. Reinforcement of HS can be done through writing of stories with high HS, preparing plans with HS, and detailed planning of movement towards success. It may be useful to emphasise that small challenges that are successfully achieved develop an urge to achieve (take on more challenges). Gradually, challenging goals help to develop HS. Special emphasis may be given to realistic but challenging goal setting moderate risk.

Guessing Test

Name: _____ Role: _____

Organisation: _____ Date: _____

Some situations involving entrepreneurs are given below. We would like to see if you can correctly guess what is happening. In each situation, two answers are given. Choose one of the two to indicate your opinion of what happens.

1. An entrepreneur is showing a machine to his friend. What is he saying to him?
   __ a.   I want to improve this machine.
   __ b.   I hope this machine works; otherwise, I shall not be able to make much profit.
2. Some entrepreneurs are having a meeting after seeing government officials. What are they discussing?
   __ a.   How to defend the mistakes pointed out by the government officials.
   __ b.   How the various tasks can be completed on time.
3. An entrepreneur is talking with a friend. What is he telling him?
   __ a.   I am sure my factory will make huge profits.
   __ b.   If my factory is not profitable, I shall be ruined.
4. An entrepreneur has called his manager for a discussion. What does he think about his manager?
   __ a.   That he lacks drive and has not been able to promote product sales.
   __ b.   That he is an efficient person.
5. An entrepreneur is talking with his wife. What is he telling her?
   __ a.   I do a good job and I enjoy it.
   __ b.   I am upset that we could not get the contract.
6. An entrepreneur is talking about his plan with a friend. What is he saying?
   __ a.   I do not want to be left behind the others in these contracts.
   __ b.   I shall certainly finish the contract on time.
7. An entrepreneur has called an outside consultant. What is he discussing with him?
   __ a.   He is asking him to design a new system.
   __ b.   He is getting his plans checked by the consultant.
8. A group of entrepreneurs has a dinner party. Two of them are talking in a corner. What are they saying?
   __ a.   We shall not succeed if we cannot work together.
   __ b.   We have extremely good chances of success.
9. An entrepreneur is talking with his manager about their foreman. What is he saying?
   __ a.   If the foreman achieves the target we shall reward him.
   __ b.   The foreman will have to do better if he wants a raise in his salary.
10. An entrepreneur is leaving his desk late in the evening. What do you think is happening?
   __ a.   He says to himself, 'My God, I am stuck again. I will come back to it tomorrow'.
   __ b.   He has at last finalised his plan, and gives a sigh of relief.
11. An entrepreneur is working out the details of a plan. What does he want to do?
   __ a.   Try not to over-quote so that he can get the contract.
   __ b.   He does not want to lose the contract and is thinking what can be done.
12. An entrepreneur is sitting in a chair and thinking. What about?
   __ a.   How to increase his production.
   __ b.   He is wondering whether any mistakes were made in the plan of production.

13. An entrepreneur has called his manager to ask him about the proposed schedule of work. What does the manager think to himself?

    __ a.   He believes that the work will be done.

    __ b.   He is apprehensive that they have problems, but hesitates to tell his boss.

14. Two officers in a government department are discussing the case of an entrepreneur. What are they saying?

    __ a.   He should be given the contract depending on whether he will be able to complete this task or not.

    __ b.   He should be given the contract as he does his job very well.

15. An entrepreneur is standing before a machine he has designed. What is he thinking?

    __ a.   What a good machine we have been able to make!

    __ b.   Why on earth couldn't we find the nagging fault!

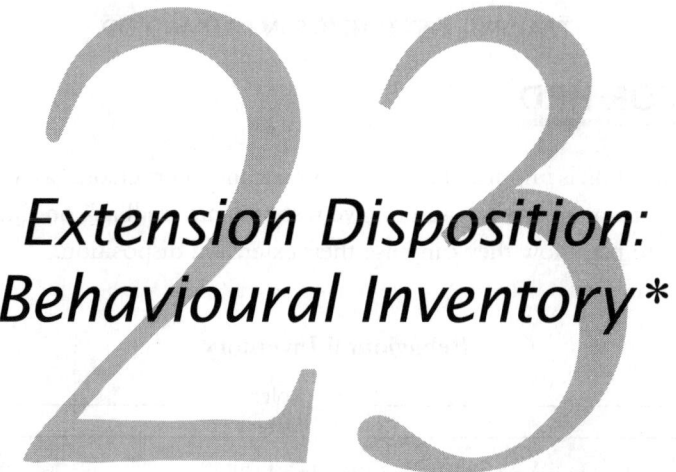

Extension Disposition: Behavioural Inventory*

23.1 THE INSTRUMENT AND ITS ADMINISTRATION

Behavioural Inventory is a self-checking instrument to measure extension disposition (D Ext), that is, a respondent's tendency to show extension behaviour. The respondent checks 10 items, which measure the frequency of his behaviour on a 5-point scale.

23.2 CONCEPTUAL FRAMEWORK

The concept of extension motivation is discussed in Section 4.2.

23.3 SCORING

Reverse scores on items 9 and 10 (1 = 5, 2 = 4, 3 = 3, 4 = 2, 5 = 1), then add all the scores. The total scores will range from 10 to 50.

23.4 VALIDITY

Pareek and Dixit (1976) found a significant correlation of 0.52 between D Extension and Cooperative Disposition (D Coop.) as measured in the game behaviour.

---

* Developed jointly with Narendra Dixit.

23.5 USE FOR HRD

Since extension motivation is important for development and interpersonal as well as organisational effectiveness, this instrument can be used to give respondents feedback on their behaviour. They can then be helped to plan how they can raise their extension disposition.

Behavioural Inventory

Name: _____   Role: _____

Organisation: _____   Date: _____

Check below each item by writing a number on its left hand side:

Write 1   if you rarely or never do so
Write 2   if you do so once in a while
Write 3   if you do so sometimes
Write 4   if you often do so
Write 5   if you very often or always do so

1. _____   Think how to help others with their problems.
2. _____   Care for others while working on a task so that they can successfully complete it.
3. _____   Share with others the solution of a problem when I have solved it.
4. _____   Want to know why a person is sad when I see a sad person.
5. _____   Think how useful my work can be for the organisation.
6. _____   Have concern whether what I do in the organisation contributes to the betterment of the society.
7. _____   Take an interest in the development of society.
8. _____   Undergo personal inconvenience to be of some help to others.
9. _____   Feel reluctant to give time to a person asking for my help, because this may interfere with my personal plans.
10. _____   Get engrossed in my own affairs, having hardly any time for others.

Extension Proneness: Guessing Responses*

24.1 THE INSTRUMENT AND ITS ADMINISTRATION

Guessing responses contains five competitive situations in which a person involved has three alternative responses. The respondent is required to guess which of the three responses the persons involved will choose.

24.2 CONCEPTUAL FRAMEWORK

Extension proneness (P Ext) can be defined as a person's intrinsic characteristic (of extension behaviour), which is likely to result in overt behaviour. Details may be seen in Chapter 23.

24.3 DEVELOPMENT OF THE INSTRUMENT

The instrument was originally developed for children (Pareek & Dixit, 1976). Before selecting situations for this instrument, judges rated items for their relevance to extension behaviour.

24.4 SCORING

The following scoring key can be used. The total scores will range from 0 to 10.

---

* Developed jointly with Narendra Dixit.

Scores for Alternative Responses

Situation	A	B	C
1	2	0	1
2	0	2	1
3	0	1	2
4	0	1	2
5	1	0	2

24.5 CORRELATES

Pareek and Dixit (1976) reported a significant (at 0.01 level) positive correlation of P Ext with classroom adjustment, total adjustment, dependency and cooperative disposition, and a significant negative correlation with competitive proneness.

24.6 USE FOR HRD

Respondents can be given feedback on their sources. They can work in small groups to think of organisational situations, and reflect on their usual behaviour. Role-plays can also be used.

Guessing Responses

Name: _____   Date: _____

Organisation: _____   Role: _____

Below are given some situations. In each situation, the person involved is to choose one of the three alternative responses. Read the situations and guess which response the person will choose. Tick mark or encircle the serial number of the response you choose. There are no right or wrong answers.

1. _____   In a competitive examination where several candidates appeared, Shyam was fumbling for or not finding his pen. Krishna had two pens. He saw Shyam with his problem. What will Krishna do?
   _____   a. He will give one pen to Shyam.
   _____   b. Shyam being his competitor, he will not give his pen to him.
   _____   c. If Shyam asks for a pen, he will give it to him.

2. _____   Three salesmen—Nazir, Utpal and Anand—were assigned an area for sales. Sales targets were fixed for the area. Utpal completed his targets, but Nazir was falling behind. The deadline was approaching. What will Utpal do?
   _____   a. He will ignore Nazir's problem because he would like to be seen as the best salesman.
   _____   b. He will help Nazir, as he himself has completed his target.
   _____   c. He will mention Nazir's difficulty to his friend Anand.

3. _____   Students were preparing for a tough competitive examination. A list of books was suggested for preparing an important aspect. Only Suresh had all those books. What will he do?
   _____   a. He will keep all the books so that he alone can read them thoroughly without allowing others access to them.
   _____   b. He will offer the books to others after he has read them.
   _____   c. He will share the books with others, so that everyone can prepare for the exam.

4. _____   The teacher distributed some wooden pieces among four students and asked them to prepare a pattern using the blocks. Ramesh discovered that the blocks he received made a meaningful pattern, while a few did not fit. The rule allowed blocks to be given, but no one could ask for them. Everyone could see the patterns kept in front of each other. What will Ramesh do?
   _____   a. He will be happy that he has a pattern, and will do nothing.
   _____   b. He will give his extra blocks to those who can use them to complete their pattern.
   _____   c. He will persuade all four to get together and make one pattern for the team.

5. _____   Raju got information from his father about some attractive work-cum-study fellowship in a foreign country. The information was not publicised in the town where Raju lived. What will Raju do?
   _____   a. He will share the information with his best friend so that both of them can apply and prepare for the test and interview.
   _____   b. He will not share the information with anyone and will quietly prepare and appear for the test and interview.
   _____   c. He will share it with his colleagues so that those who are interested can take advantage of it.

Motivational Analysis of Organisations—Behaviour (MAO-B)

25.1 THE INSTRUMENT AND ITS ADMINISTRATION

Motivational Analysis of Organisations—Behaviour (MAO-B) was developed to study manager or employee behaviour in an organisation. MAO-B contains 60 items, 5 for each dimension (approach and avoidance) of each of the 6 previously discussed motives—achievement, affiliation, extension, influence, control and dependency.

MAO-B can be administered in a group. The participants should be told that the instrument is meant to provide a profile of motivational aspects of role behaviour and that there are no right or wrong answers. If the instrument is used for HRD purposes, the results can be used to help individuals and the group plan for increased effectiveness in their respective roles.

If the instrument is used with students of management, they should be asked to respond as they would if they were in managerial positions in an organisation. The scores can then be discussed to show the motivational trends of the students.

25.2 CONCEPTUAL FRAMEWORK

One motive that is relevant for organisational behaviour is dependence. Although it has generally been regarded as a negative force, McGregor (1966) recognised the positive value of dependence in management, and Kotter and Schlesinger (1979) further drew attention to its importance. Levinson (1982) has also pointed out its importance in the development of managers. This need is acknowledged in the process of mentoring (Levinson, 1982), which has received considerable attention in recent management literature (e.g., Kraur, 1985).

Thus, six primary needs or motives, which are relevant for understanding the behaviour of people in organisations, have been identified. These are as follows:

1. *Achievement.* Characterised by concern for excellence, competition with the standards of excellence set by others or by oneself, the setting of challenging goals for oneself,

awareness of the hurdles in the way of achieving those goals, and persistence in trying alternative paths to reach one's goals.

2. *Affiliation.* Characterised by a concern for establishing and maintaining close, personal relationships, by value on friendship, and a tendency to express one's emotions.

3. *Influence.* Characterised by a concern to make an impact on others, a desire to make people do what one thinks is right, and an urge to change matters and (develop) people.

4. *Control.* Characterised by a concern for orderliness, a desire to remain informed, and an urge to monitor and take corrective action when needed.

5. *Extension.* Characterised by concern for others, interest in superordinate goals, and an urge to be relevant and useful to larger groups, including society.

6. *Dependence.* Characterised by a desire for help from others in one's own self-development, checking with significant others (those who are more knowledgeable or have higher status, experts, close associates, etc.), submitting ideas or proposals for approval, having an urge to maintain an 'approval' relationship.

Another motive highlighted by Maslow is security. An instrument to measure the four motives of achievement, power, affiliation and security is given in this chapter.

All these needs or motives can be used to explain the behaviour of people in organisations. However, each of these motives can have two dimensions: approach and avoidance. Atkinson (1953) first suggested the concept of avoidance behaviour in discussing the achievement motive. It was further elaborated by several authors (Birney & Burdick, 1969; Heckhausen, 1967a), and 'fear of failure' emerged as an important component of the achievement motive, distinct from 'hope of success', the other component. Much research has been done on fear of failure, which has been found to be dysfunctional although it is related to the achievement motive. For example, Varga (1977) showed that hope of success versus fear of failure (approach versus avoidance) was the most important intervening variable in explaining who benefitted from achievement-motivation training programmes as measured by an increase in entrepreneurial activity. Persons who were high in achievement motivation but also had a high component of fear of failure, failed to start new businesses, in contrast to those who had a high component of hope of success. The concept of approach versus avoidance is also applicable to components of other motives.

The six motives—achievement, affiliation, influence, control, extension and dependence—have been used in studying the behaviour of people in organisations. Table 25.1 summarises the approach and avoidance dimensions of each of the six motives. The behaviour of a manager or employee can thus be analysed not only in terms of the six primary motives but also from the perspective of (positive) approach or (negative) avoidance, reflected by hope or fear, respectively.

An employee's effectiveness may result from the existence or absence of a particular motivation or from the extent of the approach or avoidance dimension of a particular motivation.

No matter how strong a motive is, it can become ineffective by a high degree of fear, that is, by high avoidance behaviour.

TABLE 25.1   Approach and Avoidance Aspects of Motives

Motive	Approach (Hope of)	Avoidance (Fear of)
Achievement	Success	Failure
Expert influence	Impact	Impotence
Control	Order	Chaos
Extension	Relevance	Irrelevance
Dependence	Growth	Loneliness
Affiliation	Inclusion	Exclusion

Motivational Analysis of Organisations—Behaviour (MAO-B) is based on the approach and avoidance aspects of six motives. Some other instruments on style (Chapter 36), role satisfaction (Chapter 27), organisational climate (Chapter 64) and organisational atmosphere (Chapter 65) are also based on this concept.

25.3 SCORING

1. Transfer your responses to the score sheet below.
2. Total all the rows.
3. Enter OEQ of each pair of rows and columns.

The total score for each dimension (approach and avoidance) of the six motives can range from 5 to 20. The respondent's OEQ for each of the six motive-specific aspects of behaviour—defined by the net score of approach dimension—can be obtained by using the formula

$$\text{OEQ} = \frac{P-5}{p+V-10} \times 100$$

where P and V represent total scores for approach and avoidance dimensions respectively of a motive-specific behaviour. Table 33.1 can be used to find the OEQ for each motive-related behaviour.

25.4 RELIABILITY

The test-retest reliability coefficients for the six dimensions of role behaviour (based on a sample of 50, taken 2 months before) are given below. All values are significant beyond 0.001 levels.

MAO-B Variable	Reliability Coefficient
Achievement	0.61
Affiliation	0.61
Influence	0.58
Control	0.68
Extension	0.53
Dependence	0.45

All the coefficients are very high. The instrument is thus highly reliable. Gutman split-half reliability for a group of 20, was found to be 0.61; equal length and unequal length Spearman–Brown reliability for a group of 20 was found to be 0.73 and 0.76 respectively.

25.5 VALIDITY

The relationship between effective role behaviour, as reflected by the OEQ, and some personality variables was studied in 500 managers of a large multi-location firm. The levels of significance of the correlations appear in the Table 25.2.

As can be seen from the Table 25.2, all dimensions of effective role behaviour are positively correlated with role efficacy (see Chapter 50). It can be said that people who experience higher role efficacy use more effective role behaviour on all dimensions. The same is true of the two dimensions of locus of control, internality and externality—externality-chance and externality-others (see Chapter 9). The correlation values were significant in the expected direction for all dimensions of role behaviour effectiveness. However, the correlation between the control dimension and internality was not significant. On the whole, it can be concluded that persons having a higher external locus of control show less effective role behaviour, and those having a higher internal locus of control show more effective role behaviour (except, perhaps, on the control dimension).

Table 25.3 demonstrates that effective role behaviour had a significantly negative correlation with the total role-stress score (Chapter 53). It also shows the values of correlation between effective role behaviour and strategies (avoidance and approach) for coping with stress (see Chapter 56). Effectiveness (OEQ) for all dimensions of role behaviour had significant negative correlation with avoidance strategies and significant positive correlation with approach strategies, except for the affiliation dimension, for which the value was not significant. For the avoidance strategies, the correlations were significant at 0.001 for achievement and influence; at 0.004 for control; at 0.014 for extension; and at 0.036 and 0.044 for affiliation and dependence. For the approach strategies, the values were significant at 0.002, 0.001 and 0.004 for achievement, influence and control respectively, and at 0.014 and 0.018 for dependence and extension respectively. It can be concluded that people who demonstrate effective role behaviour generally use approach strategies in coping with role stress.

TABLE 25.2 Levels of Significance of Correlations of OEQ of Motivational Behaviour

Variables	Effective Motivational Behaviour					
	Achievement	Influence	Control	Extension	Affiliation	Dependence
1. Role efficacy	0.001	0.001	0.001	0.001	0.01	0.001
2. Internality	0.001	0.003	—	0.045	0.001	0.001
3. Externality (others)	−0.001	−0.001	−0.005	−0.080	−0.002	−0.001
4. Externality (chance)	−0.001	−0.001	−0.001	−0.001	−0.003	−0.002
5. Externality (Total)	−0.001	−0.001	−0.001	0.004	−0.001	−0.001
6. Role stress	−0.001	−0.001	−0.001	−0.004	−0.002	−0.001
7. Coping strategy (avoidance)	−0.001	−0.001	−0.004	−0.014	−0.036	−0.044
8. Coping strategy (approach)	0.002	0.001	0.004	0.018	—	0.014

TABLE 25.3 Operating Effectiveness Quotient Matrix

Avoidance Scores	Approach Scores															
	5	6	7	8	9	10	11	12	13	14	15	16	17	18	19	20
5	0	100	100	100	100	100	100	100	100	100	100	100	100	100	100	100
6	0	50	67	75	80	83	85	87	89	90	91	92	92	93	93	99
7	0	33	50	60	67	71	75	78	80	82	83	85	86	87	87	89
8	0	25	40	50	52	62	67	70	73	75	77	78	80	81	82	83
9	0	20	33	43	50	55	60	64	67	69	71	73	75	76	78	79
10	0	17	28	37	44	50	54	58	61	64	67	69	70	72	74	75
11	0	14	25	33	40	45	50	54	59	60	62	65	67	68	70	71
12	0	12	22	30	36	42	46	50	53	56	59	61	63	65	67	68
13	0	11	20	27	33	38	43	47	50	53	55	58	60	62	64	65
14	0	10	18	25	31	36	40	44	47	50	53	55	57	59	61	62
15	0	9	17	23	28	33	37	41	44	47	50	52	54	56	58	60
16	0	8	15	21	27	31	35	39	42	45	48	50	52	54	56	58
17	0	8	14	20	25	29	33	37	40	43	45	48	50	52	54	56
18	0	7	13	19	23	28	32	35	38	41	43	46	48	50	52	54
19	0	7	12	18	22	26	30	33	36	39	41	44	46	48	50	52
20	0	6	12	17	21	25	29	32	35	37	40	42	44	46	48	50

25.6 NORMS

The mean and SD values, for the OEQ of MAO-B scores from 147 managers, areas given in Table 25.4, can be used as cut-off points for the interpretation of scores. For example, the mean +1 SD will be regarded as a high score, and mean −1 SD will be regarded as a low score. Scores above mean +1 SD are very high, and those below mean −1 SD are very low scores.

TABLE 25.4 Mean Values of OEQ

Dimensions	Mean	SD
Achievement	69	12
Influence	63	10
Extension	68	13
Control	66	7
Affiliation	66	9
Dependence	69	9

25.7 CORRELATES

Based on a sample of 400 working women, Mathur (1993) found positive correlation between OEQ of all the six motivational aspects with job satisfaction, all of which were significant beyond the 0.01 level. Regarding role stress (see Chapter 53), she reported negative correlations of operating effectiveness of influence behaviour with personal inadequacy and self-role distance and positive correlation of operating effectiveness of extension behaviour with inter-role distance. Role stagnation, role expectation conflict and role inadequacy were mostly the most significant at the 0.05 level. She found negative correlation of operating effectiveness of control, behaviour with role inadequacy, and negative correlation of operating effectiveness of affiliation behaviour with personal inadequacy. Regarding ethos (Chapter 66), operating effectiveness of affiliation behaviour was found to be correlated significantly with trust and that of extension behaviour with pro-action.

Correlates of MAO-B have also been reported by Sen (1981) for role stress, role efficacy, coping styles, personality factors, job satisfaction, role satisfaction and organisational climate.

25.8 USE FOR HRD

MAO-B can be used for self-analysis, individual counselling and organisational and human resource training and development. A respondent can examine his scores and then plan to reduce the avoidance behaviour of a motive (for which he received a low OEQ score) by examining the related items on the instrument and inferring the behavioural implications. In counselling work, the instrument can be completed jointly by the counsellor and the counselee, and the counsellor can help the individual to plan new behaviour.

In an HRD or OD training programme, participants can look at their profiles, request feedback from other participants and then discuss, in triads, ways to increase their effectiveness by reducing their avoidance behaviour for the relevant motives.

The instrument can also be used in organisation development and consulting work to obtain group profiles, to search for organisational factors to explain and improve profiles, to develop organisational strategies, and to develop individual strategies to increase the employees' operating effectiveness for the various motives.

MAO-B

Name: _____   Role: _____
Organisation: _____   Date: _____

Read each statement given in the accompanying sheet, MAO-B, and indicate how often you feel or behave that way. Use the key given below. Write your response in the space against each statement by using the key given below. Do not leave any statement unanswered.

Write 1   if you never/rarely feel or behave this way
Write 2   if you sometimes/occasionally feel or behave this way
Write 3   if you often/frequently feel or behave this way
Write 4   if you usually/always feel or behave this way

There are no right or wrong answers. Your response will reflect your own perception of how you feel or act at work. Do not spend too much time on a statement; generally, your first reaction is the most accurate.

1. _____ I enjoy working on moderately difficult (challenging) tasks and goals.
2. _____ I am overly emotional.
3. _____ I am forceful in my arguments.
4. _____ I refer matters to seniors for approval/guidance.
5. _____ I keep a close track of things (monitor action).
6. _____ I am easily moved by others' difficulties, and people take advantage of this.
7. _____ I set easy goals and achieve them.
8. _____ I relate very well to people.
9. _____ I am preoccupied with my own ideas and am a poor listener.
10. _____ I follow my ideals.
11. _____ Deviations from pre-committed schedules bother me.
12. _____ I take steps to develop the people who work for me.
13. _____ I strive to exceed the performance/targets.
14. _____ I give more importance to personal relationships than to organisational matters.
15. _____ I build on the ideas of my subordinates or others.
16. _____ I seek the approval of my seniors for new ideas/proposals.
17. _____ I ensure that things are done as per schedule and plan.
18. _____ I consider the difficulties of others even at the expense of the task.
19. _____ I am afraid of making mistakes.
20. _____ I share my feelings with others.
21. _____ I enjoy arguing and winning arguments.
22. _____ I have genuine respect for experienced persons.
23. _____ I admonish people for not completing tasks.
24. _____ I go out of my way to help the people who work for me.
25. _____ I search for new ways to overcome difficulties.
26. _____ I have difficulty in expressing negative feelings to others.
27. _____ I set myself as an example and model for others.

28. _____ I hesitate to make hard decisions.
29. _____ I involve my people in defining their roles and procedure of working.
30. _____ I undergo personal inconvenience for the sake of others, even though I sometimes do not like this.
31. _____ I am more conscious about my limitations or weaknesses than of my strengths.
32. _____ I take interest in matters of personal concern of the people who work for me.
33. _____ I am *laissez faire* in my leadership style (do not care how things happen).
34. _____ I learn from those who are senior to me.
35. _____ I centralise most tasks to ensure that things are done properly.
36. _____ I have empathy and understanding for the people who work for me.
37. _____ I want to know how well I have been doing, and I use feedback to improve myself.
38. _____ I avoid conflict in the interest of group feelings.
39. _____ I provide new suggestions and ideas.
40. _____ I expect conformity from the people who work for or with me.
41. _____ I adequately explain systems and procedures clearly to the people who work for me.
42. _____ I tend to take responsibility for others' work in order to help them.
43. _____ In my anxiety to do an excellent job I lose self-confidence.
44. _____ I recognise and respond to the feelings of others.
45. _____ I care more for a respectable designation than the nature of work given to me.
46. _____ I seek help from those who know the subject.
47. _____ In case of difficulties, I rush to correct things.
48. _____ I develop teamwork among the people who work for me.
49. _____ I work effectively under pressure of deadlines.
50. _____ I am uneasy and less productive when work alone.
51. _____ I give credit and recognition to others.
52. _____ I am eager to get support from my colleagues and seniors for my actions and proposals.
53. _____ I am comfortable with monitoring/coordinating roles.
54. _____ I hesitate to take strong action because of human considerations.
55. _____ Difficulties and problems I face bother me a great deal.
56. _____ I take the initiative in making friends with my colleagues.
57. _____ I am quite conscious of status symbols such as furniture, size of office, etc.
58. _____ I like to solicit ideas from others.
59. _____ I respect rules and regulations which I strictly follow, and see that others do the same.
60. _____ I like to accept responsibility in the group's work.

MAO-B: Score-cum-Analysis Sheet

Name: _____   Role: _____

Organisation: _____   Date: _____

Motives		Items and Responses					Total	OEQ
Achievement	Approach	1__	13__	25__	37__	49__	__	__
	Avoidance	7__	19__	31__	43__	55__	__	__
Influence	Approach	3__	15__	27__	39__	51__	__	__
	Avoidance	9__	21__	33__	45__	57__	__	__
Extension	Approach	12__	24__	36__	48__	60__	__	__
	Avoidance	6__	18__	30__	42__	54__	__	__
Control	Approach	5__	17__	29__	41__	53__	__	__
	Avoidance	11__	23__	35__	47__	59__		__
Affiliation	Approach	8__	20__	32__	44__	56__	__	__
	Avoidance	2__	14__	26__	38__	50__	__	__
Dependency	Approach	10__	22__	34__	46__	58__	__	__
	Avoidance	4__	16__	28__	40__	52__	__	__

Motivational Analysis of Organisations—Styles (MAO-S)

26.1 THE INSTRUMENT AND ITS ADMINISTRATION

Motivational Analysis of Organisations—Style (MAO-S) measures the managerial styles of respondents using a motivational framework. MAO-S requires a respondent to rank six statements for eight aspects, from most descriptive to the least descriptive of himself. The eight aspects are main concern, interpersonal behaviour, supervisory behaviour, managing problems, managing mistakes, managing conflicts, communication and decision-making.

26.2 CONCEPTUAL FRAMEWORK

Chapter 25 gives the framework used in this instrument.

26.3 SCORING

The key (see Table 26.1) is used to score the responses. Profile of motivational styles (Table 26.2) is used for detailed examination. Complete the profile (Table 26.2) by writing the ranks in the respective spaces in Rows 3–10 and Columns 2–8. The profile (Table 26.2) contains indices of functionality of styles and of organisational processes.

Follow the following steps to complete and interpret the profile of motivational styles (Table 26.2):

1. The first column lists eight organisational processes.
2. The first row mentions the six motives, and the second row gives the corresponding styles.

TABLE 26.1 Scoring key of MAO-S

	Achievement	Expert Influence	Extension	Control	Affiliation	Dependency
1. Main concern	c	f	b	d	e	a
2. Inter-personal behaviour	d	a	f	c	b	e
3. Supervisory behaviour	d	e	c	a	f	b
4. Managing problems	a	b	d	f	c	e
5. Managing mistakes	d	f	c	b	a	e
6. Managing conflicts	a	f	e	d	b	c
7. Communication	d	c	e	f	b	a
8. Decision-making	c	e	f	d	a	b

3. Total the ranks given in each column (Columns 2, 3, 4 and 6, 7, 8) and enter these in Row 11. These are totals of each motive or style.
4. Row 12 will give Motive Index (MI), showing functionality of each style. Calculate MI of A, E, I by the formula $(48 - \text{Total}) \times 2.5$ and of C, F, D by the formula $(8 - \text{Total}) \times 2.5$. Enter them in row 12.
5. Using the norms given, enter the effectiveness level of each motive/style (scores given in row 12). Mean and SD values of groups of 30 or more can also be used to determine effectiveness levels specific to those groups.

26.4 VALIDITY

There is a significant positive correlation of achievement with extension and a negative correlation with control and dependency. There is also a significant correlation between extension and confront. These correlations are in the predicted direction, indicating construct validity of the instrument.

26.5 NORMS*

Based on the responses of 402 managers, the mean and SD values are given in the following table as tentative norms. The lower the score, the stronger is the motive concerned.

	Mean	SD
Achievement	27.84	5
Influence	26.99	5
Control	30.28	6
Dependency	27.64	5
Extension	26.96	5
Affiliation	28.14	5

26.6 CORRELATES

MAO-S scores were correlated with TSI-M scores for a group of 16 managers. There were significant correlations of influence style with supportive style (OK nurturing parent); dependency had a negative correlation with effective work styles (OK adult) and also with supportive and

---

* Norms are provided by Ms Tapati Roy.

normative style, although this could not reach the significant level. Affiliation style had a positive correlation, but not significant, with normative style.

26.7 USE FOR HRD

The various styles as shown in Table 26.2, are interpreted as follows:

Motive	Main concern	Style
Achievement	Excellence	Entrepreneurial
Influence	Expertise	Technocratic
Extension	Helping/Serving	Altruistic
Control	Orderliness	Autocratic
Dependency	Conformity	Bureaucratic
Affiliation	Harmony	Friendly

Participants can see their dominant and backup styles and discuss their effect on their department or section. They can discuss in small groups, if they feel such a need, how to alter their styles, specifically examining the eight main processes.

TABLE 26.2 MAO-S Profile Motives and Styles

1	2	3	4	5	6	7	8	9	10
Organisational	Achievement	Influence	Extension	Total	Control	Affiliation	Dependency	Total	OPI
Process	A	I	E		C	F	D		
	Entrepreneurial	Technocratic	Altruistic		Autocratic	Friendly	Bureaucratic		
Main Concern									
Working with People									
Supervision									
Problem-solving									
Managing Mistakes									
Conflict Management									
Communication									
Decision-making									
Total									
Motive Index								SFQ=	
Effectiveness Level									

MAO-S

Name: _____   Role: _____
Organisation: _____   Date: _____

Given below are eight different aspects of a manager's work. Under each aspect 6 statements appear. Rank order the statements from 1 to 6—giving rank 1 to the statement which is the closest description of your self or your working style; rank 2 to the next closest description of your behaviour, and so on. Rank 6 is to be given to the statement which is the least true about you or your style.

1. What is your main concern in the department?
   __ a. To ensure that laid-down rules and regulations are properly followed
   __ b. To encourage employees to help others develop greater skills, so that they can advance in the organisation
   __ c. To achieve set goals or targets
   __ d. To control staff and maintain good discipline
   __ e. To maintain a good and friendly climate amongst my employees
   __ f. To develop competence and expertise amongst the people working with me
2. What is your characteristic way of working with people?
   __ a. I interact mostly with people on the basis of their expertise
   __ b. I have informal social interaction with most of my people
   __ c. I interact with a few trusted and competent people
   __ d. I interact with others mainly in relation to the achievement of targets or goals
   __ e. I meet people to give instructions and provide guidance
   __ f. I interact with my people to help them develop and advance in the organisation
3. How would you like to characterise your supervisory style?
   __ a. I check people so that they do not make mistakes
   __ b. I give them instructions and suggestions
   __ c. I improve their personal skills and chances of advancement
   __ d. I reward (and/or appreciate) outstanding performance
   __ e. I use my own expertise to make an impact on my people
   __ f. I ensure the development of good, friendly relations, and of team spirit
4. How do you usually deal with a problem in your department?
   __ a. I pose it as a challenge to my people to find an innovative solution
   __ b. I discuss it with someone in my department who is an expert or is knowledgeable
   __ c. I discuss it with those who are close to me
   __ d. I work out a solution which will benefit my people or the organisation
   __ e. I discuss it with a senior person or refer it to him for a solution
   __ f. I solve it on my own
5. How do you usually deal with mistakes?
   __ a. I do not reject the person making the mistake; I show him warmth
   __ b. I follow the philosophy that the supervisor can commit no mistake, and the subordinates dare not commit one
   __ c. I encourage people to own up and analyse their mistakes, and receive help and support from others
   __ d. I treat the mistakes of my people as an experience from which they can learn to prevent failure and improve performance in the future

    __ e.   I correct the mistakes and guide my subordinates to prevent them in the future

    __ f.   I encourage people to seek the help of experts of knowledgeable persons in under-standing the mistake and preventing it from occurring in the future

6.   How do you usually deal with conflicts?

    __ a.   I analyse the causes and resolve the conflict with an overriding consideration for productivity

    __ b.   I tend to avoid or smooth over conflicts to retain a cordial atmosphere

    __ c.   I seek the arbitration of senior persons

    __ d.   I take a decision myself and tell people what to do or not do

    __ e.   I appeal to people to keep the ideals and larger good of the organisation in mind

    __ f.   I accept the experts' opinions

7.   What is your usual communication style?

    __ a.   I give instructions after considering all aspects and expect that these be carried out

    __ b.   I have informal and open communication with my people

    __ c.   I encourage people to directly seek information from knowledgeable colleagues in and outside the department

    __ d.   I make available relevant information to all who need and use it for achieving high performance

    __ e.   I have concern for my people and communicate with them (including criticism) out of such concern

    __ f.   I give information only to deserving people

8.   How do you take decisions?

    __ a.   While taking decisions, I take special care to maintain cordial relations with all concerned

    __ b.   I do not take decisions, but only communicate the decision made at higher levels to my people

    __ c.   I encourage experts and high performers to participate in the decisions being made

    __ d.   I take decisions myself and inform my people about them

    __ e.   I consult specialists and knowledgeable people and give great weight to their opinions

    __ f.   The good of the organisation and its people mainly guide me in taking decisions

Role Satisfaction: Motivational Analysis of Organisation—Roles (MAO-R)

27.1 THE INSTRUMENT AND ITS ADMINISTRATION

Motivational Analysis of Organisations—Role (MAO-R) consists of 25 statements, 5 relating to each of the 5 needs—achievement, affiliation, influence, control and extension. The respondent is asked to rate each statement twice on a 4-point scale: once for the amount of opportunity he gets to do the things reflected in the statement in his organisational role, and the second time for the amount of opportunities he would like to have to do them in his organisational role.

27.2 CONCEPTUAL FRAMEWORK

As elaborated in Chapter 25, among the basic human needs are achievement, influence, control, extension and affiliation. Although some needs may be higher than others, everyone has these needs and seeks to satisfy them in organisational roles. In this sense, the more opportunity one has to satisfy one's needs, the more satisfying the role is. Role satisfaction can thus be defined in terms of the degree of satisfaction of psychological needs in one's role in an organisation.

Satisfaction of a need is largely subjective. There cannot be any objective norms in this respect. If a person feels that he gets sufficient opportunities in his role to pursue matters of excellence, and that he would not like to have any more opportunities, we say he experiences role satisfaction for the achievement motive. If, on the other hand, a person feels that he gets opportunities to work towards excellence, but he would like more opportunities than what his present role gives him, we say his role satisfaction for the achievement motive is not high. Role satisfaction can thus also be defined as the gap between perceived and desired satisfaction of the main psychological needs in one's organisational role.

This concept of role satisfaction was used in developing the instrument, Motivational Analysis of Organisations Roles (MAO-R), for measuring role satisfaction. As mentioned, the five needs of achievement, affiliation, influence, control and extension are considered.

27.3 SCORING

1. Transfer your answers on the Score Sheet for each item.
2. Total P–D for each motive.
3. Read from the Role Satisfaction Index (RSI) sheet RSI for each total, and note down in the score sheet. The RSI will range from 0 to 100.

Score Sheet

| Achievement | | | | Influence | | | | Control | | | | Affiliation | | | | Extension | | | |
#	P	D	P–D	#	P	D	P–D	#	P	D	P–D	#	P	D	P–D	#	P	D	P–D
1				2				3				4				5			
6				7				8				9				10			
11				12				13				14				15			
16				17				18				19				20			
T				T				T				T				T			
RSI				RSI				RSI				RSI				RSI			

Role Satisfaction Index (RSI)

P–D	RSI	P–D	RSI	P–D	RSI	P–D	RSI
−20	100	−9	73	1	47	11	22
−19	98	−8	70	2	45	12	20
−18	95	−7	68	3	42	13	17
−17	93	−6	65	4	40	14	15
−16	90	−5	63	5	37	15	12
−15	88	−4	60	6	35	16	10
−14	85	−3	58	7	32	17	7
−13	83	−2	55	8	30	18	5
−12	80	−1	53	9	27	19	2
−11	78	0	50	10	25	20	0
−10	75						

27.4 RELIABILITY

Test-retest reliability was found by re-administering the instrument to a group of 50 persons after an interval of 6 weeks. The coefficient of correlation ranged between 0.40 and 0.70, significant at 0.001 level. This shows high stability of the instrument. Guttman split-half, equal and unequal length Spearman–Brown for a group of 20 was found to be 0.60, 0.76 and 0.79 respectively for MAO-R present and 0.55, 0.66 and 0.69 respectively for MAO-R Desired.

27.5 VALIDITY

For a better insight into MAO-R, all the 25 items were factor-analysed from the responses of about 500 managers. The five factors that emerged—principal component method with Varimax rotation—are shown in Table 27.1. These factors explain 100% variance.

TABLE 27.1 Factor Loadings of MAO-R

Items	Motives	Factors 1	2	3	4	5
5	E	0.63	0.33	0.10	0.07	0.04
15	E	0.62	0.23	0.14	0.16	0.11
9	F	0.55	0.19	0.11	0.13	0.07
4	F	0.54	0.12	−0.03	−0.02	0.16
14	F	0.51	0.10	0.03	0.17	0.23
20	E	0.48	0.35	−0.09	0.42	0.31
10	E	0.39	30	0.26	0.49	−0.01
25	E	0.37	0.25	0.14	0.33	0.37
6	A	0.33	0.38	0.27	0.14	0.15
24	F	0.18	0.68	0.16	0.04	0.42
11	A	0.16	0.64	0.11	0.23	0.07
16	A	0.18	0.56	0.17	0.13	0.24
17	B	0.24	0.54	0.38	0.16	0.24
22	B	0.24	0.52	0.17	0.02	0.45
1	A	0.24	0.58	0.25	0.28	−0.13
21	A	0.26	0.61	0.17	0.17	0.12
12	B	0.18	0.49	0.10	0.19	0.34
7	B	0.15	0.43	0.16	0.07	0.14
28	B	0.23	0.36	0.29	0.14	−0.06
18	C	0.03	0.14	0.69	0.10	0.21
3	C	0.05	0.17	0.68	0.10	0.04
13	C	0.09	0.33	0.51	0.46	0.16
8	C	0.07	0.37	0.39	0.58	0.06
23	C	17	0.20	0.32	0.41	0.29
19	F	0.23	0.30	0.05	0.25	0.26

Note: A = Achievement, B = Influence, C = Control, F = Affiliation, E = Extension.

Factor 1 has a high loading (above 3) on five extension items, three affiliation items and only one achievement item. This is the main factor in role satisfaction and can be called people orientation.

Factor 2 has a high loading (above 3) on 17 items. Out of these, five are achievement and five influence items. Since they relate to personal responsibility, we can call this a personal responsibility factor. It has a high loading on three extensions, two affiliation and two control items. Affiliation and extension items relate to task interaction, and all these items contribute to personal responsibility.

Factor 3 has a high loading on five control items (out of six high loadings). It is quite clear that it is a personal control factor as the two items (3 and 18) on which it has a very high loading relate to admonishing people.

Factor 4 has a high loading (more than 3) on control and three extension items. These relate to the relationship between a manager and his immediate subordinates. It can be called the dyadic relationship factor.

Factor 5 has a high loading (more than 3) on six items—two influence, two extension, one affiliation and one control item (number 23 is close to 0.3). Since most of these items relate to collaborative work, we can call this the teamwork factor. However, Factors 4 and 5 have eigenvalues below 1.

To summarise, need satisfaction in a role, as measured by MAO-R, has primarily three factors—people orientation, personal responsibility and personal control. This partly validates the concepts underlying the instrument.

27.6 NORMS

Several background factors were studied in relation to role satisfaction for about 500 employees of several banks in India (Sen, 1982), using tests and correlations. These factors included hierarchical position in the organisation, age, number of children, age of the first child, length of employment in the current job, directly recruited versus promoted, sex, education, income, marital status, rural–urban background, distance commuted, distance between hometown and the organisation, etc. The following conclusions summarise the findings:

Satisfaction for personal responsibility declines as one goes down the hierarchical level in an organisation. The mean values of the achievement and influence items were 6.6 for those at the top level, as against 11.2 for clerical staff. This applies in a large measure to control motivation. In the extension motivation too satisfaction was higher at higher levels. Only in the case of the affiliation dimension was there a negligible difference. It can be concluded that satisfaction for personal responsibility and task control aspects is positively related to one's level in an organisation: Higher-level personnel have higher satisfaction, obviously on account of the authority that increases further up in the hierarchy.

Generally, direct officers experienced less satisfaction of their needs than those who joined as clerks and were then promoted. There was no marked difference in respect of job experience.

However, those who worked for some other bank previously had lower role satisfaction, possibly because they had better knowledge of the work environment of a bank and its impact on role satisfaction.

There was a clear trend in age groups: The older a person, the higher his satisfaction of all needs except affiliation. A person usually advances in career with age, and the higher the position he holds, the more opportunities he gets for satisfying his role needs, as already explained.

No differences were noticeable for education. Income was positively related with satisfaction for all the needs. Higher income denotes higher position and authority, which may explain this phenomenon.

Married employees seemed to be more satisfied. Perhaps, unmarried employees, with less family liabilities, are not too sure of their expectations. This feeling of ambivalence may leave them dissatisfied.

There were no significant differences in rural and urban backgrounds and in the distance from home (or place of domicile) to place of work. Those commuting over a distance of 21–50 kilometres had the least satisfaction for all needs. The hardship of daily travelling and the anxiety that it creates is mainly accounted for this. Employees whose native homes were 301–500 kilometres away scored the lowest on satisfaction of needs. This range of distance is not inconvenient for a transferable job. But, the fact that employees cannot make it to their comparatively closer native places, as often as they want to, may cause dissatisfaction. The length of total service and length of present job are positively related with all the dimensions, except affiliation.

The number of children had positive correlation with satisfaction of influence, extension and control needs. The higher the number of children, the more satisfied the person seemed to be.

The norms for MAO-R, present and desired, for 20 executives of a tyre company are given in the following table.

MAO-R (Present and Desired)

Variables	(Present)		(Desired)	
	Mean	SD	Mean	SD
Achievement	15	3	23	2
Influence	17	3	23	2
Control	16	3	21	3
Affiliation	17	3	21	3
Extension	18	4	23	2

27.7 CORRELATES

Role efficacy (see Chapter 49) was found to have a positive correlation with role satisfaction. The coefficients of correlations between role efficacy and MAO-R measures were significant at 0.001 level for four of the five needs (all but affiliation), indicating that employees with high role efficacy were highly satisfied with their roles (or vice versa). The affiliation need does not seem to be important in this respect, as discussed below.

The seven blocks to creativity were measured with an instrument devised by Khandwalla (1984c). The blocks are allergy to ambiguity, conformity, stereotyping, fear of failure, starved sensibility, resource myopia and touchability. The total score for these blocks were correlated with role satisfaction scores. The data was retrieved from Sen's study (1982) of about 500 bank employees. The sign of the relationship and levels of significance of correlations are given in Table 27.2. Since the values of coefficient of correlation were not significant for stereotyping, this has not been mentioned in Table 27.2. It is important to remember that the higher the score, the higher is role dissatisfaction and consequently, there are bigger blocks to creativity.

As may be seen from Table 27.2, all the correlations are positive for the total scores on blocks to creativity: The coefficients of correlation were significant at 0.001 for achievement and influence needs. The values of coefficients of correlation were also significant for five blocks (all except starved sensibility). This means that, in general, the more one's creativity is blocked, the more dissatisfied one is in relation to achievement and influence needs. Regarding other values of correlation, it may be said that fear of failure, resource myopia, touchability and starved sensibility are associated with the lack of satisfaction of control needs. The person with high fear of failure and high resource myopia has a less satisfied extension need.

It can also be said that of all the needs, those most affected by blocks to creativity are achievement and influence, followed by control. Blocks to creativity seem to play a significant role in need dissatisfaction in organisational roles.

In order to study the relationship between role satisfaction and role stress and strategies of coping with stress, MAO-R scores were correlated with role stress scores and those on coping

TABLE 27.2 Significance Levels of Correlation Between Role Satisfaction and Blocks to Creativity

| Blocks to Creativity | Role Dissatisfaction (MAO-R) | | | | |
	Achievement	Influence	Control	Extension	Affiliation
Fear of failure	0.001	0.001	0.052	0.001	0.019
Resource myopia	0.001	0.003	0.007	0.041	
Touchability	0.009	0.009	0.019		
Allergy to ambiguity	0.037	0.020			
Conformity	0.001	0.001			
Starved sensibility			0.053		
Total score	0.001	0.001			

TABLE 27.3 Levels of Significance of Correlation of Role Satisfaction with Role Stress and Coping Strategies

Role Stresses	Role Dissatisfaction (MAO-R)				
	Achievement	Influence	Control	Extension	Affiliation
Role ambiguity	0.018	0.014	0.021		
Inter-role distance	0.009	0.013		0.027	
Role stagnation	−0.007	0.	0.008		
Self-role distance	−0.001				
Role inadequacy		−0.038			
Role overload				0.004	
Coping Strategies					
Extrapunitive	−0.001	−0.013	−0.039	0.004	
Intropunitive	−0.014				
Defensive	−0.015				

Note: '−' signifies that the correlation was negative.

strategies. Table 27.3 gives the value of correlations, from the data of 500 managers. Correlations were found for eight role stresses (see Chapter 53) and eight coping strategies (Chapter 56).

Coefficients of correlation were not significant for the two role stresses—role isolation and role erosion. Correlation of role stress with satisfaction of affiliation need was not significant. Table 27.3 shows that those who experience inter-role distance also experience dissatisfaction of achievement, influence and extension needs in their roles. Role ambiguity is also positively correlated with dissatisfaction of achievement, influence and control needs. The more people experience these two stresses, the less their needs of achievement, influence and control (or extension) are satisfied. These relationships are in the expected direction. Extension need has only two significant relationships—with inter-role distance and role overload. These stresses seem to be related to the lack of satisfaction of extension need, role overload and the incongruity between organisational and other roles coming in the way of working for larger goals and being relevant to larger entities.

Two role stresses—role stagnation and self-role distance—are negatively correlated with dissatisfaction of achievement need. In other words, a person with a high stress of role ambiguity and lack of congruence between self-image and role requirements seems to have high satisfaction of the achievement need. This is unexpected. Maybe, the lack of congruence between self-image and role requirements and the lack of role clarity create a challenge for the role occupant, partly contributing to satisfaction of his achievement need. Similarly, the relationship between role inadequacy and control need is puzzling. Probably, people who lack resources for their role performance tend to devise better ways of monitoring the various things they are responsible for. These are only guesses and need to be investigated in detail.

To summarise, achievement need satisfaction is more significantly related to role stress, followed by satisfaction of control need. Other relationships are not so prominent. Some types of role stress seem to contribute partly to the lack of satisfaction of these needs and partly, they act as a challenge for these needs.

Regarding strategies to cope with stress, only one strategy—extra-punitive—is related to role satisfaction. Those who blame external factors and show aggression towards them for their role stress seem to have high satisfaction of the four needs in their roles (all except affiliation).

27.8 USE FOR HRD

MAO-R can be used to plan improvements in role satisfaction of the participants. The following steps may be taken:

Participants complete MAO-R.

1. They analyse the gap between the desired and present level of satisfaction for the five motives.
2. Each individual identifies the motives on which the gap is five or more.
3. Groups may be formed round each of the five motives. Each group, consisting of persons having a gap of five or more, discusses what it can do and what it thinks the organisation can do to reduce the gap.
4. The data for the whole group can also be analysed to identify those motives when there are large gaps. Action plans can be prepared to reduce these gaps.
5. Where possible, a dialogue with the top management can be held on the action ideas and plans at individual and organisational levels.

MAO-R

Name: _____   Role: _____

Organisation: _____   Date: _____

Your role may provide you with opportunities for various matters in different degrees. Some of these dimensions are listed below. Read each statement carefully. Then indicate under P how much opportunity your role in your organisation provides for that dimension; under D, indicate how much opportunity you would like to have for that dimension. Use the following numbers to indicate your reply:

1. Means about no opportunity
2. Means very little opportunity
3. Means some opportunity
4. Means quite a good deal of opportunity
5. Means a great deal of opportunity

No.	Item	P	D
1.	Do something challenging and worthwhile.		
2.	Influence or make an impact on others.		
3.	Admonish (punish) those who do not conform.		
4.	Work with friendly people.		
5.	Do something useful for others		
6.	Get immediate feedback on your performance.		
7.	Have autonomy and work independently.		
8.	Direct and instruct people below you.		
9.	Develop close personal relations.		
10.	Develop your junior colleagues or subordinates		
11.	Set standards of excellence.		
12.	Give ideas or suggestions to your superiors.		
13.	Control the people below you.		
14.	Share feelings and emotions with others.		
15.	Help others.		
16.	Show that efficiency can be rewarded.		
17.	Make contributions to significant decisions.		
18.	Admonish (punish) those who do not perform.		
19.	Interact with colleagues.		
20.	Cooperate with others in a common task.		
21.	Stretch your abilities and skills.		
22.	Get recognition for work done.		
23.	Get regular reports from other sections or subordinates.		
24.	Interact with others on non-task matters.		
25.	Work in teams.		

*Lifestyle Inventory**

28.1 THE INSTRUMENT AND ITS ADMINISTRATION

Lifestyle Inventory looks at W–L balance in areas of autonomy, networking, perspective to life and fitness in the context of locus of control.

28.2 CONCEPTUAL FRAMEWORK

The conceptual framework is the same as that of locus of control. The instrument measures internality, externality (others) and externality (chance) of the respondent in the areas of autonomy, networking, perspective to life and fitness, which in turn contribute to a sense of well-being.

Autonomy in the context of this instrument is the perceived number of choices that a person has in a given situation. Networking refers to the quality of professional and personal relationships that a person has. Perspective to life in this instrument refers to the perceived purpose of life. Fitness refers to physical fitness.

28.3 SCORING

Scoring is simple; follow the following steps:

1. Transfer the ratings (responses) from the instrument to the Score Sheet
2. Add each row to determine the totals

* Developed by Naga Siddharth S. with inputs from Dr Gopal P. Malhotra.

Score Sheet

	Internality	Externality Others	Externality Chance
Autonomy	(1)__ + (14)__ + (28)__ =	(8)__ + (18)__ + (25)__ =	(10)__ + (22)__ + (34)__ =
Networking	(4)__ + (12)__ + (26)__ =	(7)__ + (15)__ + (31)__ =	(2)__ + (21)__ + (29)__ =
Perspective	(6)__ + (16)__ + (32)__ =	(3)__ + (19)__ + (36)__ =	(9)__ + (23)__ + (33)__ =
Fitness	(11)__ + (20)__ + (30)__ =	(13)__ + (24)__ + (35)__ =	(5)__ + (17)__ + (27)__ =

28.4 USE FOR HRD

The instrument provides internality, externality (others) and externality (chance) scores for each of the four dimensions.

A ratio of internality/[Externality (others) + Externality (chance)] is a good indicator of the belief of an individual in his own efforts in determining outcomes in each of the four dimensions vis-à-vis the role that others and luck play in the dimension.

The use of the instrument is very similar to the LOCO inventory and can be used for action planning for W–L balance.

Lifestyle Inventory*

Name: _____   Date: _____

Organisation: _____   Role: _____

Read each of the following statements and respond to each of them in the space given to the right of each statement. There are no right or wrong answers.

Write 4   if you agree strongly
Write 3   if you agree
Write 2   if you disagree
Write 1   if you strongly disagree

1. _____ My own efforts are responsible in ensuring that I have multiple choices at work.
2. _____ Professional networking happens mainly due to chance.
3. _____ Where I am heading in the total picture of life depends on others around me.
4. _____ Strong professional networking largely depends on the effort I put in to nurture the same.
5. _____ The extent to which I follow my fitness regimen depends on contingencies.
6. _____ Sustaining zest for what I do primarily depends on my own drive.
7. _____ The positive relationships I can have at home mainly depend on the intent of others at home.
8. _____ At work, my co-workers, including my boss, have a large part to play in determining the number of choices I have.
9. _____ Fate determines the direction my life takes.
10. _____ Luck determines whether I have choices in life.
11. _____ Steps that I take determine whether I get to exercise regularly.
12. _____ Creating positive relationships with others depends to a large extent on my efforts.
13. _____ However much I put in efforts, whether I exercise actually depends on others around me.
14. _____ My own efforts determine whether I have multiple options in any situation.
15. _____ Others play a large role in determining whether I have strong relationships in society.
16. _____ An individual's own efforts mainly help in clarifying the total picture in life.
17. _____ Whether I exercise depends on how the situations that arise at home.
18. _____ Whether I have multiple choices at any given time depends on others.
19. _____ Sustaining the zest for what I do primarily depends on the support I receive from those around me.
20. _____ The extent to which my fitness regimen works mainly depends on my own commitment to stick to it.
21. _____ Positive relationships happen usually due to chance alone.
22. _____ The number of choices that I have at work is a matter of chance.
23. _____ Circumstances exclusively determine the zest that I have for work.
24. _____ Whether I undertake regular routines to keep myself fit mainly depends on the demands imposed by colleagues at work.
25. _____ However much I may try, the number of alternatives I have in life depends on others whose actions affect me.

26. _____ Having effective relationships in society mainly depends on how much effort I invest in for it.
27. _____ Whether I undertake regular routines to keep myself fit mainly depends on the day-to-day workload at office.
28. _____ I can generate many opportunities for myself if I work towards it.
29. _____ It is a matter of chance that one builds strong bridges with others in the community.
30. _____ Whether I undertake regular routines to keep myself fit mainly depends on my efforts to do so.
31. _____ The success of my professional networking depends more than anything on my fellow professionals' intent to network with me.
32. _____ Making sure that I have a good sense of where I am heading in life depends on the time and energy I invest in for the same.
33. _____ Where I am heading in the total picture of life largely depends on luck.
34. _____ Regardless of effort, chance determines the different options I have in life or career.
35. _____ The extent to which my fitness regimen works depends on others at home.
36. _____ Others, to a large extent, determine the direction my life takes.

Group Effectiveness: Openness and Perceptiveness (OP) Scale

29.1 THE INSTRUMENT AND ITS ADMINISTRATION

The OP scale measures the perceived openness and perceptiveness of people at three levels—senior, peer and subordinate—and gives the OP profile of an organisation at these levels.

The scale contains 10 items. Five are related to openness and five to perceptiveness. Openness relates to giving positive and negative feedback or expressing positive and negative feelings—sharing opinions, disagreements and personal problems. Perceptiveness relates to others' positive and negative feelings, opinions, disagreements and personal problems. Each item is rated on a 5-point scale, for the number of persons showing that behaviour for three levels—senior, juniors and peers. It is simple and self-administered and takes only a few minutes to complete.

29.2 CONCEPTUAL FRAMEWORK

Both openness and perceptiveness are important for interpersonal effectiveness. For the concept, see Chapter 5.

29.3 SCORING

Individual ratings are transferred to the Score Sheet (appended). For all 10 items, ratings given for (a) seniors, (b) juniors and (c) peers are transferred to the appropriate place of the Score Sheet. The totals for the five aspects are found by adding the columns, and the grand totals of openness and perceptiveness are found out. Then mean and standard deviations are calculated for the whole group. The totals for each level on each aspect (openness and perceptiveness) range from 5 to 25, and the grand total from 15 to 75. The higher the score, the higher is openness or perceptiveness in the group/organisation.

29.4 NORMS

Norms, based on a group of 25 people, are given in Table 29.1.

TABLE 29.1   Norms of OP Scale

	Dimension	Mean	SD
OS1:	Positive feedback to seniors	2.09	1.09
OS2:	Negative feedback to seniors	1.62	0.92
OS3:	Sharing personal problems with seniors	1.62	0.80
OS4:	Disagreement with seniors	1.95	1.20
OS5:	Sharing opinions on organisation with seniors	1.91	1.00
OJ1:	Positive feedback to juniors	2.04	1.28
OJ2:	Negative feedback to juniors	2.62	1.20
OJ3:	Sharing personal problems with juniors	1.86	0.91
OJ4:	Disagreement with juniors	2.71	1.10
OJ5:	Sharing opinions on organisation with juniors	2.05	0.87
OP1:	Positive feedback to peers	2.52	1.03
OP2:	Negative feedback to peers	2.29	1.01
OP3:	Sharing personal problem with peers	2.52	1.12
OP4:	Disagreement with peers	3.05	1.12
OP5:	Sharing opinions on organisation with peers	2.91	1.14
PS1:	Perceptiveness of positive feelings of seniors	2.38	1.11
PS2:	Perceptiveness of negative feelings of seniors	2.52	1.17
PS3:	Perceptiveness of personal problems of seniors	2.00	1.23
PS4:	Perceptiveness of disagreements of seniors	2.71	1.38
PS5:	Perceptiveness of seniors' opinions on organisational problems	2.43	1.29
PJ1:	Perceptiveness of positive feelings of juniors	2.62	0.92
PJ2:	Perceptiveness of negative feelings of juniors	2.24	0.89
PJ3:	Perceptiveness of personal problems of juniors	1.96	0.97
PJ4:	Perceptiveness of disagreements of juniors	1.95	1.16

(Table 29.1 Continued)

(Table 29.1 Continued)

	Dimension	Mean	SD
PJ5:	Perceptiveness of seniors' opinions on organisational problems	2.24	1.04
PP1:	Perceptiveness of positive feelings of peers	3.05	0.97
PP2:	Perceptiveness of negative feelings of peers	2.43	1.12
PS3:	Perceptiveness of personal problems of peers	2.76	0.99
PS4:	Perceptiveness of disagreements of peers	2.86	1.24
PS5:	Perceptiveness of peers' opinions on organisational issues	2.57	1.33

29.5 USE FOR HRD

An intervention to improve teamwork and collaboration in an organisation can be designed round departmental or organisational OP (openness–perceptiveness) profiles.

All employees in a section, department or organisation respond on the scale. OP profiles for seniors, juniors and peers can be prepared by using the score of openness and perceptiveness for each, as described in the scoring section. An OP profile of the total section, department or organisation can be obtained for openness and perceptiveness as already stated.

The OP profiles can be used as the basis for exploring, with the groups, the implications of the profile in terms of the areas where work needs to be done. The discrepancy between openness and perceptiveness can be discussed, and the reasons behind them can be examined. This may help to increase perceptiveness further.

The discussions may give ideas for further work on training needs, use of linking and interacting devices (e.g., task groups) and further, mutual work (e.g., through role negotiations/contribution for mutual effectiveness).

The OP scale can also be used to measure perceived openness and perceptiveness of the various groups, for example, seniors, juniors and peers or manufacturing staff, marketing staff, etc.

The following types of questions may be asked: 'In your opinion, how many senior managers freely express or share various matters, listed below, with others in the organisation?' Or 'In your opinion, how many senior managers are perceptive of the following feelings and opinions of others in the organisation?' The responses obtained can be tabulated to indicate the perceived openness/perceptiveness to and of a particular role (e.g., senior managers). This data can be used for process work and inter-role explorations to develop mutuality among the roles involved.

The scale can also be used for a pair of roles. For example, seniors can be asked to answer the items for their juniors thus, 'How open are you to your juniors in relation to the following?'

OP Scale

Name: _____   Role: _____

Organisation: _____   Date: _____

Answer the following questions for your department/organisation by using the following key:

Write 1   for very few
Write 2   for some
Write 3   for several
Write 4   for quite a large number
Write 5   for almost all

1. How many persons in your department/organisation give positive feedback or express positive feelings to…?
   __ a.   their seniors
   __ b.   their juniors
   __ c.   their peers

2. How many persons give negative feedback or express hard feelings to…?
   __ a.   their seniors
   __ b.   their juniors
   __ c.   their peers

3. How many persons share their personal problems with…?
   __ a.   their seniors
   __ b.   their juniors
   __ c.   their peers

4. How many persons freely express their disagreements with…?
   __ a.   their seniors
   __ b.   their juniors
   __ c.   their peers

5. How many freely share their opinions on critical and sensitive organisational issues with…?
   __ a.   their seniors
   __ b.   their juniors
   __ c.   their peers

6. How many persons are perceptive of the positive feelings of the following about them (even when such feelings are not expressed)?
   __ a.   their seniors
   __ b.   their juniors
   __ c.   their peers

7. How many persons are perceptive of the critical and hard feelings of the following about themselves?
   __ a.   their seniors
   __ b.   their juniors
   __ c.   their peers

8. How many persons are perceptive of the personal problems of the following (even when they do not share them)?
   __ a. their seniors
   __ b. their seniors
   __ c. their peers

9. How many persons are perceptive of the disagreements of the following even when the latter do not express these to the former?
   __ a. their seniors
   __ b. their juniors
   __ c. their peers

10. How many are perceptive of the opinions of the following on sensitive and critical organisational issues even when the latter do not express their opinions?
   __ a. their seniors
   __ b. their juniors
   __ c. their peers

OP Scale
Score Sheet

	Openness to				Perceptiveness of		
	a.	b.	c.		a.	b.	c.
	Seniors	Juniors	Peers		Seniors	Juniors	Peers
1. Positive aspects	____	____	____	6.	____	____	____
2. Negative aspects	____	____	____	7.	____	____	____
3. Personal problems	____	____	____	8.	____	____	____
4. Disagreements	____	____	____	10.	____	____	____
Total	____	____	____	____	____	____	____
Grand total (a + b + c)							

PART
III

PERSONAL AND
INTERPERSONAL STYLES

A consistent pattern of behaviour, with quasi-constancy and predictability, can be called style. Such a self-consistent way of behaving has an underlying theory or inter-connected network of propositions explaining the pattern. Some relevant conceptual frameworks underlying the instruments are briefly discussed in this part.

1. Leadership Styles
   a. The Concept of Development Level
   b. Raising Development Level
   c. Adaptability and Flexibility
2. Life Orientations
3. International Styles
4. Motivational Styles

5. Sales Styles
   a. Sales Troika
   b. Sales Troika Styles
   c. Sales Executive Troika Styles
6. Conflict Management Styles
   a. Approach and Avoidance Modes of Conflict Management
   b. Avoidance Modes of Styles
   c. Approach Modes of Styles
7. Negotiation Mode of Management Conflict
   a. Elements in Negotiation
   b. Steps in Negotiation
   c. What a Third Party Can Do?
8. Decision-making Styles

Leadership Profile Indicator— Managers (LPI-M)

30.1 THE INSTRUMENT AND ITS ADMINISTRATION

Leadership Profile Indicator (LPI) was formerly called Survey of Strategies of Problem Management (SSPM). It was first developed for health managers. Later, it was adapted for education and corporations. The instrument is based on the theory of situational leadership by Hersey and Blanchard (1982). The instrument consists of 12 situations, each posing a problem for action. Four alternatives are given for each situation, and the respondent is required to select one of them that he would use if he were the leader in that situation.

In addition to considering competence and commitment (motivation) of people to define the situations (as suggested by Heresy and Blanchard), teamwork was also considered. The profile of the 12 situations used in LPI is given in Table 30.1.

The respondent reads each situation in LPI then the four alternatives, and records his response on the answer-cum-worksheet (AWS) by encircling the alternative he would adopt as a leader. Thus, there will be 12 encircled responses for a respondent, one for each situation.

30.2 CONCEPTUAL FRAMEWORK

Psychologists, sociologists, political scientists and, certainly, management scientists have become increasingly interested in leadership. There have been spurts of research on this topic from time to time. The more we research leadership, the more we realise its complexity. Leadership can be simply defined as the act of making an impact on others in a desired direction. In this sense, leadership is broader than management. Managers can effectively run organisations, but only leaders can build them.

Most work on leadership in organisations has been done on the way a leader gets results through persons. Does he order them (autocratic style) to do what he wants to be done? Does he involve them (democratic) in planning how to do things? Is he indifferent and does he allow them

TABLE 30.1   Situations with Appropriate Styles

Situation	Competence	Commitment	Teamwork	Type
1.	Missing	Present	Present	3
2.	Present	Present	Present	4
3.	Present	Missing	Present	3
4.	Present	Present	Present	4
5.	Present	Missing	Missing	2
6.	Missing	Missing	Missing	1
7.	Missing	Present	Missing	2
8.	Missing	Missing	Present	2
9.	Present	Present	Present	4
10.	Present	Present	Missing	3
11.	Missing	Missing	Missing	1
12.	Missing	Missing	Missing	1

(laissez faire) to do as they like? The earlier studies of these styles were replaced by two contrasting styles, defined by an emphasis on the task to be done (task-oriented style) or on the persons doing the task (people-oriented style). This was later seen as a continuum, from high task orientation (telling), through convincing people about what should be done (selling), discussing with them the task and its strategy (consulting), to giving them the responsibility (delegating) to plan and achieve results with enough support (Tannenbaum & Schmidt, 1958).

A major step was taken when task orientation and people orientation were treated as two independent dimensions. Blake and Mouton (1964) proposed a grid (famous as the managerial grid) with these two dimensions, each dimension ranging from low (1) to high (9). A combination gave five styles—low-low (Style 1, 1), high-task-and-low-people orientation (Style 9, 1), low-task-and-high-people orientation (Style 1, 9), compromise between two orientations (Style 5, 5) and high emphasis on both (Style 9, 9). In this scheme, Style 9, 9 was conceived of as the ideal towards which managers should grow.

Another milestone in leadership research was Fiedler's (1967) theory of contingency, demonstrating that the effectiveness of task orientation and people orientation depended (was contingent) upon the situation. Simple and clear tasks and situations with very high or very low leader acceptance required task-oriented leadership, and complex tasks required relationship-oriented leadership (Fiedler et al., 1976).

Hersey and Blanchard (1982) combined the grid approach and contingency theory to propose their situational theory of leadership. Combining concerns for tasks and for people—from low to high—they proposed four leadership styles. Style 1—task concern high, people concern low; Style 2—both high; Style 3—concern for people high, that for task low; and Style 4—both low. According to them, all the four styles are functional; their relevance to situations is important.

Later, Blanchard (1995) proposed new terms, and his modified model is borrowed here with the necessary additions. As already stated, leadership style in the situational model is classified according to the amount of task and relationship behaviour the leader engages in. Task-related behaviour, called directive behaviour by Blanchard, is called regulating behaviour here, because behaviour can be characterised mainly as regulating the group members' activities in terms of task accomplishment. Some other leaders concentrate on providing socio-emotional support and on building personal relationships, and this is called nurturing behaviour (formerly called relationship behaviour, and supportive behaviour by Blanchard).

Regulating behaviour is defined as the extent to which a leader engages in one-way communication; spells out the groups' roles and tells the group members what to do, where to do it, when to do, and how to do it, and then closely supervises the performance. Three words can be used to define regulating behaviour—structure, control and supervise.

Nurturing behaviour is defined as the extent to which a leader engages in two-way communication, listens, provides support and encouragement, facilitates interaction and involves the group in decision-making. Three words can be used to define nurturing behaviour—praise, listen and facilitate.

A combination of high and low directive and supportive behaviour will give four quadrants, each representing four different leadership styles. These are shown in Figure 30.1.

High regulating/low nurturing leader behaviour (Style 1) is called directive style. The leader defines the roles of group members and tells them what tasks to do and how, when and where to do them. Problem-solving and decision-making are initiated solely by the leader. Solutions and decisions are announced; communication is largely one-way; and the leader closely supervises implementation.

High regulating/high nurturing behaviour (Style 2) is called supportive style. In this style, the leader still provides a great deal of direction and leads with his ideas, but the leader also attempts to hear the group feeling about decisions as well as their ideas and suggestions. While two-way communication and support are increased, control over decision-making rests with the leader.

High nurturing/low regulating leader behaviour (Style 3) is called consulting style. In Style 3, the focus of control for day-to-day decision-making and problem-solving shifts from leader to group members. The leader's role is to provide recognition and to actively listen and facilitate problem-solving and decision-making on the part of the group.

Low nurturing/low regulating leader behaviour (Style 4) is labelled as delegating. The leader discusses the problems with his people until joint agreement is achieved on problem definition, and then the decision-making process is delegated totally to the group members. Now, it is the group that has significant control for deciding how tasks are to be accomplished.

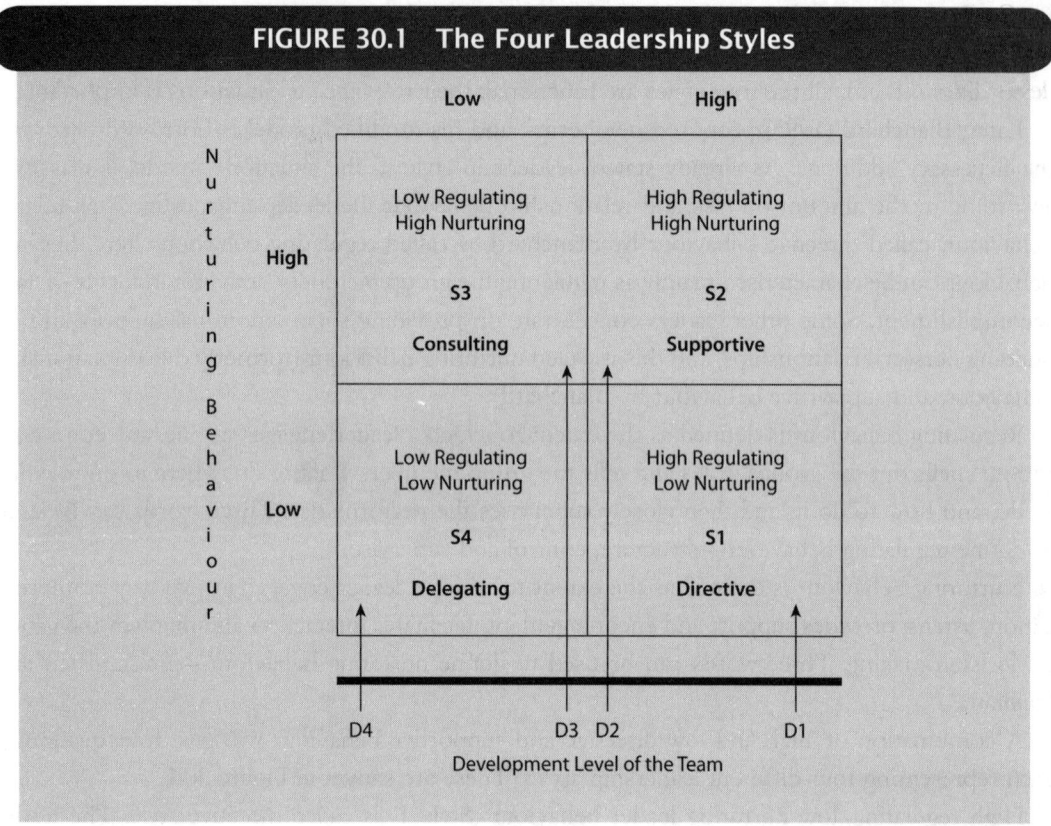

FIGURE 30.1   The Four Leadership Styles

Each of the four leadership styles can be identified with a different approach to problem-solving and decision-making. The situational leadership model also states that there is no one best way to influence group members. All the four proposed styles are functional; however, their relevance to situation, as defined by the development level of the group, is important.

30.2.1 The Concept of Development Level

One key variable in the concept of situational leadership is the development level (formerly called maturity) of followers, and some attention needs to be paid to this dimension. Hersey and Blanchard (1982) have proposed development level or maturity of the followers or individuals, determined by their competence and commitments, namely, willingness to take responsibility.

However, a leader deals with a group. Development of a group is determined by three aspects—competence, commitment or motivation, and cohesion or teamwork. While diagnosing the development level, the group's levels of competence, motivation and teamwork may be established.

Competence and commitment or motivation are relevant to individual members. Competence includes understanding (based on knowledge) and skills required to perform a job. Competence levels of individual members can be summed and averaged to get the groups competence level.

Commitment or motivation refers to the willingness of individual members to set and accept challenging goals and to take responsibility, their involvement in work and their job satisfaction. Again, the individual ratings or scores can be averaged to get group motivational level.

The teamwork level can be diagnosed by assessing the level of cohesion, collaboration and confrontation of the group. Cohesion means that the group functions as a strong team, each member feels that his views and concerns are considered by others. Collaboration indicates that some tasks are done by members as small teams, and members feel free to volunteer, ask for and respond to requests for help. Confrontation shows that whenever there is a problem that concerns the group, the group deals with it (does not shy away), generates alternative solutions and takes decisions on a course of action.

The development level of a group can be measured by rating the group on the three dimensions of competence, motivation and teamwork. This instrument is used for this purpose. A composite rating of A (very high), B (high), C (low) and D (very low) can be given to a group.

The various situations with which the leader deals can be defined in terms of the development level of the group. A level (very high) indicates that all aspects of competence, motivation and teamwork are high in the group. B level (moderately high) means two of the three aspects are high, while one is low. C level (moderately low) means one aspect is high and the other two are low. Level D (low) indicates that the group is low on all three aspects. The effective leadership styles for each level are shown in Table 30.1.

Once the development level is established, the leader can decide which leadership style will be more appropriate for the group. Diagnosis of development level may also help the leader to prepare a plan of action for raising the development level by working on the dimensions on which the group is weak.

30.2.2 Raising Development Level

As already discussed, one responsibility of a leader is to raise a group's level of development. This can be achieved by diagnosing the levels of competence, motivation and teamwork, and then increasing the weak aspects.

Competence building requires providing information relevant to the roles, building skills to perform the roles effectively, and planning a proper long-term training strategy. Commitment building (developing motivation) can be facilitated by helping individual members to set realistic and challenging goals, supporting them to achieve these, and recognising their achievement through feedback and rewards. Team building can be achieved by making teams responsible for various tasks, allocating resources to them, and recognising the importance of teamwork through team rewards, high value to teamwork in performance appraisal system, and special programmes to reduce conflicts and increase collaboration.

30.2.3 Adaptability and Flexibility

Hersey and Blanchard also proposed the concept of style range or flexibility (how easily a leader is capable of using the various four styles) and of adaptability or relevance (how appropriately a leader uses the various styles). A leader needs both diagnostic competence to assess the situation—development level of the group—and competence to use the various styles with ease relevant to the situation or its changing conditions. According to this theory, if the situation is characterised by low level of development (persons do not know their jobs well, have low motivation and do not support each other), the most effective style would be Style 1, in which the leader defines the tasks, monitors the performance of his people and provides the necessary guidance. However, after the group is 'developed' (i.e., they know their jobs, work together and are able to perform fairly well), the leader needs to change his style, giving attention to group morale, facilitating their work, and so on. On further development of the group, the leader needs no longer worry about task requirements (low on directive behaviour), but may need to build the group (high on supportive). If the group is highly developed (can work on its own as a team and has relevant competences, e.g., a training institution), the leader need not be concerned with providing guidance, neither with providing support (low on both, Style 4). The leader's main focus may be visioning, boundary management, providing facilities needed by the group and looking after external linkages and relationships, etc.

To summarise, leadership is the dynamic process of making people more effective, increasing their competence to multiply power and achieving goals through them. There are different styles of participating in this process. However, the ultimate goal of a leader is to develop his team and people to become more effective and competent to achieve organisational goals as well as their own objectives.

30.3 SCORING

The AWS is also used for scoring. Its design facilitates quick scoring and calculation of the various aspects. Follow the provided guidelines. The AWS will help you to find out the following:

1. Your scores on the four styles
2. Your dominant and backup styles
3. Flexibility of the styles
4. Effectiveness (using a style appropriate to the situation in terms of development level of the group)
5. Diagnosis of the aspects of effectiveness needing improvement

30.4 NORMS

Mean and SD of the four styles of a group of 104 managers are given in the following table:

Style	Mean	SD
1	3	2
2	4	2
3	4	2
4	1	1
Effectiveness	24	4

Situation 1

You have recently taken over a consulting firm as its CEO. You find on your priority list that the firm has a prestigious consulting assignment. In spite of enthusiasm and rapport amongst members, you discover that they lack the necessary planning and monitoring competency. What will you do?

1. Plan the task in detail and arrange training programmes for them in areas of deficiency.
2. Encourage the team to find solutions to their problems.
3. Plan the tasks, distribute assignments and supervise their work.
4. Discuss with members, and help them to learn planning and monitoring competencies.

Situation 2

You are heading the marketing department in a multilocational company. An enthusiastic and competent campaign specialist has joined one of the units. The various managers in the unit welcome her and provide the needed support. They know their areas well and are adequately competent. The unit is scheduled to have a campaign for a new product of the company. What will you do?

1. Work out the details of the campaign, individual responsibilities and monitoring arrangements; hold a meeting of the staff and share the plan with them, encouraging them to make the campaign a success.
2. Work out the details of the campaign, individual responsibilities, decided targets in details, assign responsibilities to each one according to their competence and supervise their work in the field every day to make the campaign successful.
3. Tell the group the importance of the task; communicate to them their strengths and your confidence in them; join them in working out the details of conducting and monitoring the campaign.
4. Communicate to the unit head and its managers the goals and other information of the campaign and let them work out details, including monitoring, and be available for any help required.

Situation 3

There has been a fairly heavy earthquake in the area where your unit is located. Your company has decided to provide help. You are assigned to head a relief service team for that area. The members chosen are competent and experienced and support each other. However, you find that they had to be reminded frequently to do the strenuous job the team had undertaken. What will you do?

1. Define team members' responsibilities and closely supervise their work.
2. Let the group work out ways of improving performance.
3. Work with the team to solve the problem.
4. Supervise more frequently and help the team to overcome the difficulties they encounter.

Situation 4

You are the President of the pharmaceutical division of your company. Your production target has been raised by 15%. One of the four units of your company has a team of committed and competent workers (managers, supervisors and workers). Last year, this team was rated as the best in the company. You have high expectations from them. What will you do?

1. Revise the responsibilities of the members in the light of the new targets and provide needed support to them for their achievement.
2. Participate in the group's discussions to develop an action plan.
3. Let the team develop a detailed plan and provide them with the needed support.
4. Emphasise the importance of the new targets for each member of the team.

Situation 5

You have recently been made the head of the training institute of your company. The staff of the institution is efficient. However, they see training as a burden. There is no team spirit in the institute. You have been asked to organise a series of five orientation programmes for the new management trainees in the next three months. What will you do?

1. Prepare the programmes and timetable and discuss with the group the facilities they need to implement the same.
2. Plan the details of the programmes, give various persons deadlines and supervise progress.
3. Plan and work out details of implementation with the staff.
4. Let the group work out a detailed plan and provide them the needed facilities.

Situation 6

As the General Manager of a hotel, you find that the hotel staff are not prompt. They seem to lack proper understanding of hospitality management and blame each other for lapses. When there is rush to the guests, the supervisors, instead of dealing with the situation, complain about lack of proper staff. The guests are generally dissatisfied with the hotel. What will you do?

1. Share your concern with the staff, show the urgency of improving the situation and your trust in the team. Let them work out detailed solutions; you may join them in this exercise.
2. Call a staff meeting, share your concern and ask them to give suggestions. Based on the suggestions, form teams, prepare details of responsibilities and supervision and encourage them to implement the same.
3. Call a meeting of the heads of departments/sections; give them the targets for service, cleanliness, etc.; arrange necessary training; and closely monitor (twice a week) the improvement in the situation.
4. Suggest that heads of sections and departments deal with the situation and bring about improvement.

Situation 7

You are CEO of a multiunit company. In one of your units, performance has been declining rapidly for the last six months. Although the unit head is a committed manager, he cannot do much because, according to him, even though the managers are responsible individually, they lack some technical and computer knowledge and do not function as a team. What will you do?

1. Discuss with the unit head and the team the need to improve the situation; prepare crash-training plan to develop needed competency; set targets and remove any difficulties faced by them.
2. Ask the unit head to train the people, let workers form teams of their choice and supervise them.
3. Share your concerns with the unit head and let him and his teamwork out their own solutions.
4. Recognise the teams, set targets and responsibilities, and monitor their progress.

Situation 8

You as the CEO of a company held a performance review meeting for a unit. You found that the operators, although working as a team, blamed the supervisors for their poor performance. You also found the operators deficient in the basic understanding of the business. What will you do?

1. Act quickly and firmly to correct them, define their roles, closely supervise and arrange crash training for them.
2. Share your concern with the unit head and the staff and leave it to them to work out a plan for improvement.

3. Share your concern with them and join them in deciding ways of improving the situation.
4. Call the unit head and give him specific targets to achieve every week, review progress weekly and arrange for facilities and training needed by the staff.

Situation 9

You have taken over as General Manager of a reputed hotel, which has efficient and enthusiastic staff and has been running very well. They solve many problems themselves, without referring them to senior managers. In order to provide uninterrupted and efficient service, the hotel staff had the practice under which 50% staff could avail holidays at a time on Diwali and 50% on Christmas. However, on your arrival, you came to know of some dissatisfaction among the staff as well as customers. What will you do?

1. Discuss the matter with the staff to find a solution.
2. Investigate in detail and prepare a plan with a definite course of action.
3. Share this concern with staff and let them work out an action plan for improvement.
4. Set up a committee to go into details, ensure implementation of the findings and provide needed support.

Situation 10

In your unit, which you head, a team had agreed to achieve a certain production target. You are aware that individually each member knew his job, had high motivation and was able to manage his task. At the end of the production cycle, the team was far behind the target. Each member blamed the other for poor performance. What will you do?

1. Encourage team members to plan the work with you and review progress in their respective functional teams.
2. Define the task and make each member work on the assigned task.
3. Let the sectional heads solve the problems.
4. Make the team feel that each of them is important and let them recognise each other's strengths.

Situation 11

You are the Director of a company. A competitor company has come out with a product and is cutting into the market share of your company, mainly in one part of the country where one of your divisions is located. On your visit to that division, you find that the managers lack enthusiasm and feel overwhelmed by the efforts of the competitor company.

Although they work well together, they are outdated in their marketing knowledge and do not have contacts with the appropriate retailers. They have not been able to arrest the widening gap in the market share. What will you do?

1. Replace non-performing managers/supervisors by competent marketing managers who know the area; work out and give them agreed targets; and encourage and support the team to do a good job.
2. Share the concern with the team and leave it to them to improve the situation.
3. Study the situation, provide available information about the market and the competitor company, assign targets to each member, tell them in detail how to go about the task, and monitor periodically (e.g., weekly) to re-plan if necessary.
4. Add to the team a person with adequate marketing competence and experience; encourage the team to plan; joining them from time to time.

Situation 12

You have taken over a sick unit as its CEO. You find that the managers are unenthusiastic, lack the needed competence and do not function as a team. They blame the previous management and each other for the sickness of the unit. What will you do?

1. Work with the sectional heads and managers to develop an action plan, encouraging them to implement it.
2. Streamline all the functions as an emergency action, assign various responsibilities and have weekly monitoring of the work being down.
3. Plan and implement the needed actions and coach the managers to improve their performance.
4. Share your concern with the managers of the unit and encourage them to find needed solutions to their problems.

Leadership Profile Indicator (LPI)
Answer and Worksheet

Name: _____   Role: _____

Organisation: _____   Date: _____

The purpose of this instrument is to find out what strategies are preferred by different persons in the leadership role in dealing with organisational problems. The instrument contains 12 situations. Each situation poses a problem. Read the situation. Then consider the four alternative strategies given with the situation. Choose the one strategy you would like to use if you face such a situation as a leader. There are no right or wrong answers. For each situation, encircle in Part II the letter of the strategy you would prefer to use in dealing with it. Encircle only one choice for each situation and do not leave any situation unanswered. Do not write anything in parts III to VI.

I Situation	II Encircle Your Response	III	IV	V C	V M	V T	VI C	VI M	VI T
			Do not write anything on this side						
1.	A B C D	c a d b	d a b c		a c	c	b		
2.	A B C D	b a c d	d c a b	a b c	a b	b			
3.	A B C D	a d c b	c d b a	a d		a		b	
4.	A B C D	d a b c	c b a d	a b d	a d	d			
5.	A B C D	b a c d	a c b d	b				d	c d
6.	A B C D	c b a d	c b a d				a b d	d	a d
7.	A B C D	d a b c	a b c d		d		c		b c
8.	A B C D	a d c b	d a c b			a	b c	c	
9.	A B C D	b d a c	c a d b	a b d	b	b d			
10.	A B C D	b a d c	d a c b	a b	b				c
11.	A B C D	c a d b	c a d b				b	b d	a b d
12.	A B C D	b c a d	b c a d				a d	d	a c d
Totals									
Multiply by		3 2 1 0							
Leadership Effectiveness Index									

Guidelines for Using AWS

The AWS has six parts divided by vertical lines. The first part has the situation numbers, and the second part has your responses. The next two parts (III and IV) are used for scoring. Parts V and VI are for diagnosis. Take the following steps for scoring and diagnosis:

1. Transfer the responses to each situation (circled letters in Part II) by encircling the same letters in the row on the right (four columns of Part III). For example, if 'B' has been encircled for the first situation, circle 'b' in the fourth column in Part III. Complete this for all the 12 rows.
2. Encircle the same letter again in the four columns of Part IV for each row. For example, if 'b' is encircled in the first row encircle 'b' again.
3. Encircle the same letters again, if they appear in Part V row (in any of the three columns).
4. Encircle the same letters again if they appear in the same row in Part VI. Do it for each row.
5. The four columns of Part III represent respectively Styles 1, 2, 3 and 4. Total the number of letters encircled in each column. Totals of each column will give the totals of each style. The totals of all these four columns will have an overall total of 12.
6. The four columns of Part IV are used to calculate leadership adaptability, or effectiveness, or diagnostic ability. Add encircled items in each column—total of the four totals will be 12. Multiply the total in Column 1 by 3, the total in Column 2 by 2, the total in Column 3 by 1 and the total in Column 4 by 0. Find the sum of these converted values. This is the index of leadership effectiveness or adaptability, which will range from 0 to 36. Multiply it by 2.8. Then the range will be 0–100.
7. Parts V and VI give you areas for improvement. In Part V, total in each column the number of encircled letters. These columns show areas which you tend to discount or overlook and not recognise those strengths in your team.
8. Similarly total each column in Part VI. They show the areas of deficiencies of your team that you tend to neglect. You need to pay attention to them.

30.5 USE FOR HRD

The instrument is intended primarily to help participants get feedback on their leadership styles and related measures. The following steps can be taken for its use in a group.

1. The participants complete the instrument.
2. Participants may be involved in scoring it by completing various parts of the AWS.
3. The facilitator explains the relevant theory discussed under 'Conceptual Framework'.
4. The facilitator explains the concept of dominant and backup styles. While the dominant style (the style with maximum scores) is the characteristic style of the person, the backup style (the style with the next-to-highest score) is operative under emergency situations, pressure or stress, and is therefore as important as the dominant style(s). The participants examine their profiles of the style (combination of dominant and backup styles).
5. The facilitator explains the concept of style, flexibility and adaptability. If a participant gets a score of 2 or less on any style, flexibility score is 0; that means, the person may

find it difficult to use that style when required. Adaptability or effectiveness is the ability to diagnose situations and choose a situation-appropriate style. This is given by the total score (ranging from 0 to 24).

6. The participants identify, with the help of the AWS, aspects requiring improvement. This is explained in the accompanying sheet of AWS.

7. Participants examine their individual scores and work in small groups (3-member groups) to understand the concepts and the relevance of their scores. It should be emphasised that there are no right or wrong (good or bad) scores. However, if a participant is not satisfied with any of his scores and if he thinks he should improve it, then he can do something about it.

8. Participants may help each other in preparing a concrete action strategy, following it up, getting feedback and then reviewing how much it helped in the actual training situation.

9. If the participants come from the same organisation, they can discuss the general profile (based on mean scores of the group) and also develop an action plan for improving their styles and institutional culture which may be contributing to the institutional profile.

31

Leadership Profile Indicator—Health (LPI-HA)*

31.1 THE INSTRUMENT AND ITS ADMINISTRATION

Leadership Profile Indicator—Health (LPI-HA) assesses leadership styles and effectiveness in the health system. LPI-HA consists of 12 situations, each posing a problem for the organisational leader. Each has four alternative strategies for managing the problem given. The respondent is required to select one strategy that he would use if he were the leader in that situation.

The 12 situations were developed after discussing Hersey and Blanchard's theory and its appropriateness for the Indian health system in a group of 25 health administrators. Several groups prepared the four types of situations—highly developed, moderately high, moderately low and very low level of development. After discussion, 12 situations were selected and edited. Again, small groups prepared the four alternative approaches to deal with each situation, indicating styles 1, 2, 3 and 4. One experienced consultant rated their appropriateness and then discussed them with a small group of four competent and experienced administrators, a consensus was reached on the alternatives.

The respondent responds on the AWS sheet, as instructed.

31.2 CONCEPTUAL FRAMEWORK

Details given in Chapter 30 under the heads 'Conceptual Framework', 'Scoring, Interpretation' and 'Use for HRD' should be read and followed.

---

* Developed by the Rajasthan ETCT Term under the guidance of Udai Pareek. Reproduced with permission.

31.3 RELIABILITY

Guttman split-half was found to be 0.59 whereas equal and unequal length Spearman–Brown was found to be 0.60 respectively.

31.4 VALIDITY

SSPM Scores were correlated with Hersey and Blanchard's LEAD for a group of 50 health managers. The correlations between the four LEAD and respective LPI styles were 0.88, 0.88, 0.89 and 0.65, all very high.

31.5 USE FOR HRD

The instrument is intended primarily to help participants get feedback on their leadership styles and related measures. The following steps can be taken for its use in a group.

1. The participants complete the instrument.
2. Participants may be involved in scoring it by completing various parts of the AWS.
3. The facilitator explains the relevant theory discussed under 'Conceptual Framework'.
4. The facilitator explains the concept of dominant and backup styles. While the dominant style (the style with maximum scores) is the characteristic style of the person, the backup style (the style with the next-to-highest score) is operative under emergency situations, pressure or stress, and is therefore as important as the dominant style(s). The participants examine their profiles of the style (combination of dominant and backup styles).
5. The facilitator explains the concept of style, flexibility and adaptability. If a participant gets a score of 2 or less on any style, flexibility score is 0; that means, the person may find it difficult to use that style when required. Adaptability or effectiveness is the ability to diagnose situations and choose a situation-appropriate style. This is given by the total score (ranging from 0 to 24).
6. The participants identify, with the help of the AWS, aspects requiring improvement. This is explained in the accompanying sheet of AWS.
7. Participants examine their individual scores and work in small groups (3-member groups) to understand the concepts and the relevance of their scores. It should be emphasised that there are no right or wrong (good or bad) scores. However, if a participant is not satisfied with any of his scores and if he thinks he should improve it, then he can do something about it.

8. Participants may help each other in preparing a concrete action strategy, following it up, getting feedback and then reviewing how much it helped in the actual training situation.
9. If the participants come from the same organisation, they can discuss the general profile (based on mean scores of the group) and also develop an action plan for improving their styles and institutional culture which may be contributing to the institutional profile.

Situation 1

You have recently joined as the PHC MO In-charge and have constituted a team to accomplish a new task assigned to the PHC. In spite of enthusiasm and rapport among members, you find that they lack the necessary planning and managerial competency. What will you do?

1. Plan the task in detail and arrange training programmes for them in deficient areas.
2. Encourage the team to find solutions to their problems.
3. Plan the tasks, distribute assignments and supervise their work.
4. Discuss with members and help them to learn planning and monitoring competencies.

Situation 2

You are the PHC In-charge. An enthusiastic ANM willing to serve people is posted in one of the sub-centres of your PHC. The other members of PHC welcome her and provide the needed support. They know their PHC area well and are adequately competent. The PHC is required to hold an immunisation campaign. What will you do?

1. Work out the details of the campaign, individual responsibilities and monitoring arrangements; hold a meeting of the staff and share the plan with them, encouraging them to make the campaign a success.
2. Work out the details of the campaign, decide targets in details, assign responsibilities to each one according to their competence, and supervise their work in the field every day to make the campaign successful.
3. Tell the group the importance of the task; communicate to them their strengths and your confidence in them; join them in working out the details of conducting and monitoring the campaign.
4. Tell the PHC staff the requirements of the campaign and let them work out details, including monitoring, and be available for any help required.

Situation 3

You have taken a medical team to provide relief services in an earthquake-hit area. The members chosen are competent, possess enough relevant experience and have been functioning as a team.

However, you find on this occasion that the members needed to be reminded frequently to do their work. What will you do?

1. Define team members' responsibilities and closely supervise their work.
2. Let the group work out ways of improving performance.
3. Work with the team to solve the problem.
4. Supervise more frequently and help the team to overcome the difficulties they encounter.

Situation 4

As Zonal Medical Officer (Dy. CMHO FW), your targets have been increased by 25% this year. One of your block PHCs has a team of committed and efficient workers, and, last year, it was rated the best out of 10 PHCs supervised by you. You have high expectations from this PHC. What will you do?

1. Revise the responsibilities of the members in the light of the new targets and provide needed support to them for their achievement.
2. Participate in the group's discussions to develop an action plan.
3. Let the team develop a detailed plan and provide them with the needed support.
4. Emphasise the importance of the new targets and set targets for each member of the team.

Situation 5

You have recently joined as the principal of a training institution. The staff of the institution is efficient. However, they see training as a burden. There is no team spirit in the institute. You have been asked to organise a series of five orientation programmes for community influencers in the next three months. What will you do?

1. Prepare the programmes and timetable and discuss with the group the facilities they need to implement.
2. Plan the details of the programmes, give various persons deadliness and supervise progress.
3. Plan and work out details of implementation with the staff.
4. Let the group work out a detailed plan and provide them into the needed facilities.

Situation 6

As the head of a hospital you have noticed that doctors and nurses in the OPD are not prompt. They are not up-to-date in their knowledge and lack enthusiasm to attend to patients. In an emergency situation, no timely help is provided by nurses. Doctors refuse to operate in less equipped OTs. What will you do?

1. Share your concern with the staff; show the urgency of improving the situation and your trust in the team; let them work out detailed solutions; you may join them in this exercise.
2. Call a staff meeting, share your concern and ask them to give suggestions. Based on the suggestions, prepare details of responsibilities and supervision and encourage them to implement them.
3. Call a meeting of the heads of departments/sections; give them the targets for service, cleanliness, etc.; arrange necessary training; and closely monitor (twice a week) the improvement in the situation.
4. Suggest that heads of sections and departments deal with the situation and bring about improvement.

Situation 7

You are a Dy. CMHO (FW) of a district. In one of your PHCs, performance has been declining rapidly for the last six months. Although the doctor is enthusiastic, he lacks epidemiologic understanding. He feels that even the PHC members do not know their work and do not work as a team although they are willing workers. What will you do?

1. Discuss with the team and the doctor the need to improve the situation. Set targets and remove any difficulties faced by them.
2. Ask the PHC doctor to let workers form teams of their choice and supervise them.
3. Share your concerns with the doctor and let him and the PHC teamwork out their own solutions.
4. Reorganise the teams, set targets and responsibilities and monitor their progress.

Situation 8

You, as the Zonal Officer, held a programme review meeting for a PHC. You found that the staff, though working as a team, blamed their supervisors for their poor performance. You also found the staff deficient in the basic knowledge of various health programmes. What will you do?

1. Act quickly and firmly to correct them, define their roles, closely supervise and arrange crash training for them.
2. Share with the PHC In-charge and the staff your concern and leave it to them to work out a plan for improvement.
3. Share your concern with them and join them in deciding ways of improving the situation.
4. Call the PHC In-charge and give him specific targets to achieve every week, review progress weekly and arrange for facilities and training needed by the staff.

Situation 9

You have taken over as the administrator of a voluntary hospital which has been running well. The doctors and other staff are efficient and support each other. In order to provide uninterrupted and efficient service the hospital staff had the practice under which 50% staff could avail holidays at a time on Diwali and 50% on Christmas. However, on your arrival, you came to know of some dissatisfaction among the staff as well as users. What will you do?

1. Discuss the matter with the staff to find a solution.
2. Investigate in detail and prepare a plan with a definite course of action.
3. Share this concern with staff and let them work out an action plan for improvement.
4. Set up a committee to go into details, ensure implementation of the findings and provide the needed support.

Situation 10

You, as the Dy. CMHO FW, find that the staff of a PHC had agreed to achieve a certain FP target. You are aware that individually each member had high motivation and was able to handle his task. The first major FP camp was organised but very few acceptors turned up. Each staff member blamed the other for the poor turnout. What will you do?

1. Encourage PHC staff to plan the work with you and review progress in their respective teams.
2. Define the task and make each member work on the assigned task.
3. Let the PHC members solve the problems.
4. Make the group feel that each of them is important and let them recognise each other's strengths.

Situation 11

To control an epidemic in a village, a three-member team of doctors was sent. Although they were not willing to join the effort, they had to accept the order. None of the members had adequate understanding of either epidemiology or the local geography or culture. There was no coordination among them or proper planning. They could not contain the epidemic even after seven days of effort. You, being the Zonal Officer, have been asked by the Director of Health to supervise and control the problem. What will you do?

1. Replace a non-performing member by a competent epidemiologist; work out and give them debated targets; and encourage and support the team to do a good job.
2. Share the concern with the team and leave it to them to improve the situation.
3. Study the situation and available data; assign targets to each member; tell them in detail how to go about the task; and daily monitor to re-plan if necessary.

4. Add to the team a person with adequate experience in epidemiology, encourage the team to plan, joining them from time to time.

Situation 12

You have been asked to be the course coordinator of a health training programme in an institute. You noticed that the necessary arrangements were not made. The trainers were unenthusiastic, lacked training competence and were not functioning as a team. What will you do?

1. Work with the group to develop an action plan and encouraging them to implement it.
2. Streamline all arrangements as an emergency action, assign various responsibilities and monitor every day the work is being done.
3. Plan and implement the needed actions and coach the trainers to improve their training competency.
4. Share your concern with the team and suggest that they could find needed solution.

Leadership Profile Indicator (LPI-HA)
Answer and Worksheet

Name: _____   Role: _____

Organisation: _____   Date: _____

The purpose of this instrument is to find out what strategies are preferred by different persons in the leadership role in dealing with organisational problems. The accompanying booklet contains 12 situations. Each situation poses a problem. Read the situation. Then consider the four alternative strategies given with the situation. Choose the one strategy you would like to use if you face such a situation as a leader. There are no right or wrong answers. For each situation, encircle in Part II the letter of the strategy you would prefer to use in dealing with it. Encircle only one choice for each situation and do not leave any situation unanswered. Do not write anything in parts III to VI.

I Situation	II Encircle Your Response	III	IV	V C	V M	V T	VI C	VI M	VI T
			Do not write anything on this side						
1.	A B C D	c a d b	d a b c		a c	c	b		
2.	A B C D	b a c d	d c a b	a b c	a b	b			
3.	A B C D	a d c b	c d b a	a d		a		b	
4.	A B C D	d a b c	c b a d	a b d	a d	d			
5.	A B C D	b a c d	a c b d	b				d	c d
6.	A B C D	c b a d	c b a d				a b d	d	a d
7.	A B C D	d a b c	a b c d		d		c		b c
8.	A B C D	a d c b	d a c b			a	b c	c	
9.	A B C D	b d a c	c a d b	a b d	b	b d			
10.	A B C D	b a d c	d a c b	a b	b				c
11.	A B C D	c a d b	c a d b				b	b d	a b d
12.	A B C D	b c a d	b c a d				a d	d	a c d

(For Guidelines for Scoring, see p. 233)

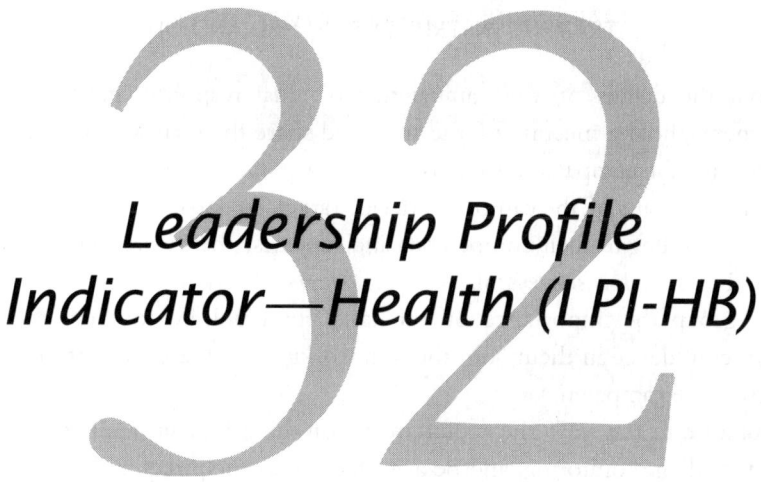

Leadership Profile Indicator—Health (LPI-HB)

32.1 THE INSTRUMENT AND ITS ADMINISTRATION

Leadership Profile Indicator—Health (LPI-HB) assesses leadership styles and effectiveness of persons managing TB control. It consists of 12 situations, each posing a problem for the organisational leader. Each has four alternative strategies of managing the problem given. The respondent is required to select one strategy that he would use if he were the leader in that situation.

The respondent reads each situation, then the four alternatives, and records his response on the answer sheet by encircling the alternative he would adopt as a leader. Thus, there will be 12 encircled responses for a respondent, one for each situation.

Situation 1

You have recently joined as the District Tuberculosis Officer and have constituted a team to accomplish a new task assigned to your centre. In spite of enthusiasm and rapport among members, you find that they lack the necessary planning and managerial competency. What will you do?

1. Plan the task in detail and arrange training programmes for them in deficient areas.
2. Encourage the team to find solutions to their problems.
3. Plan the task, distribute assignments and supervise their work.
4. Discuss with members and help them to learn planning and monitoring competencies.

Situation 2

You are the District TB Officer. An enthusiastic health educator willing to serve the community is posted at your centre. The other members of the centre welcome him and provide the needed support. The health educator is required to hold an IEC campaign. What will you do?

1. Work out the details of the campaign, individual responsibilities and monitoring arrangements; hold a meeting of the staff and share the plan with them, encouraging them to make the campaign a success.
2. Work out the details of the campaign, decide targets in details, assign responsibilities to each one according to their competence and supervise their work in the field every day to make the campaign successful.
3. Tell the group the importance of the task; communicate to them their strengths and your confidence in them; join them in working out the details of conducting and monitoring the campaign.
4. Communicate to the staff the requirements of the campaign and let them work out details, including monitoring, and be available for any help required.

Situation 3

You are in charge of a TB clinic. The members working with you are a good team, are competent and have enough relevant experience. However, you find that the members need to be reminded frequently to do their work. What will you do?

1. Define team members' responsibilities and closely supervise their work.
2. Let the groups work out ways of improving performance.
3. Work with the team to solve the problem.
4. Supervise more frequently and help the team to overcome the difficulties they encounter.

Situation 4

As District TB Officer, your targets have been increased by 25% this year. One of your block treatment centres has a team of committed and efficient workers, and last year it was rated the best out of 10 centres supervised by you. You have high expectations from this centre. What will you do?

1. Revise the responsibilities of the members in the light of the new targets and provide the needed support to them for their achievement.
2. Participate in the group discussions to develop an action plan.
3. Let the team develop a detailed plan and provide them the needed support.
4. Emphasise the importance of the new targets and set targets for each member of the team.

Situation 5

You have recently joined as the Principal of a training institution. The staff of the institution is efficient. However, they see training as a burden. There is no team spirit in the institute. You have been asked to organise a series of five orientation programmes for community participation in the next three months. What will you do?

1. Prepare the programmes and timetable, and discuss with the group the facilities they need to implement them.
2. Plan the details of the programmes, deadlines of each person and supervise progress.
3. Plan and work out details of implementation with the staff.
4. Let the groups work out a detailed plan and provide them the needed facilities.

Situation 6

As the head of a hospital you have noticed that doctors and nurses in the OPD are neither competent nor prompt. They lack enthusiasm to attend to patients. In an emergency situation, no timely help is provided by nurses. Doctors refuse to operate in less equipped OTs. What will you do?

1. Share your concern with the staff; show the urgency of improving the situation and your trust in the team; let them work out the detailed solutions; you may join them in this exercise.
2. Call a staff meeting; share your concern and ask them to give suggestions. Based on the suggestions, prepare details of responsibilities and supervision, and encourage them to implement them.
3. Call a meeting of the heads of the departments/sections; give them the targets for services, cleanliness, etc.; arrange necessary training; and closely monitor (twice a week) the improvement in the situation.
4. Suggest that heads of sections and departments deal with the situations and bring about improvement.

Situation 7

You are a District TB Officer. In one of your treatment centres, performance has been declining rapidly for the last six months. Although the doctor is a committed one, he cannot do much because even though the members of this particular centre individually are responsible, they lack some basic knowledge and do not work as a team. What will you do?

1. Discuss with the team and the doctor the need to improve the situation, set targets and remove any difficulties faced by them.
2. Suggest to the doctor to let the workers form teams of their choice and supervise them.
3. Share your concerns with the doctor and let him and the teamwork out their own solutions.
4. Reorganise the team, set targets and responsibilities and monitor their progress.

Situation 8

You, as a Provincial TB Officer, held a programme review meeting of the District TB Clinic. You found that the staff, though working as a team, blamed their supervisors for their poor perfor-mance. You also found that the staff is deficient in the basic knowledge of TB control programmes. What will you do?

1. Act quickly and firmly to correct them; define their roles; closely supervise; and arrange crash training for them.
2. Share your concern with the in-charge of the treatment centre and the staff, and leave it to them to work out a plan for improvement.
3. Share your concern with them and join them in deciding ways to improve the situation.
4. Call the in-charge and give him specific targets to achieve every week, review progress weekly, and arrange for facilities and training needed by the staff.

Situation 9

You have taken over as the administrator of a voluntary hospital, which has been running well. In order to provide uninterrupted and efficient service, the hospital staff had the practice under which 50% staff could avail holidays at a time on a local festival and 50% on Christmas. However, on your arrival, you came to know of some dissatisfaction among the staff as well as users. What will you do?

1. Discuss the matter with the staff to find a solution.
2. Investigate in detail and prepare a plan with a definite course of action.
3. Share this concern with staff and let them work out an action plan for improvement.
4. Set up a committee to go into details, ensure implementation of the findings, and provide the needed support.

Situation 10

You, as a District TB Officer, find that the staff of a treatment centre had agreed to achieve a certain target. You are aware that individually each member had high motivation and was able to handle this task. The first major camp was organised but very few patients turned up. Each staff member blamed the other for the poor turn out. What will you do?

1. Encourage the staff to plan the work with you and review progress in their respective teams.
2. Define the task and make each member work on the assigned task.
3. Let the members of the treatment centre solve the problems.
4. Make the groups feel that each of them is important and let them recognise each other's strengths.

Situation 11

A three-member team of doctors was sent to control an epidemic in a village. Although they were not willing to join the effort, they had to accept the order. None of the members had adequate understanding of either epidemiology or local geography and culture. There was no coordination among them. They could not contain the epidemic even after seven days of their effort. As the Zonal Officer, you have been asked by the Director of Health Services to supervise and control the problem. What will you do?

1. Replace a non-performing member by a competent epidemiologist, work out and give them detailed targets, and encourage and support the team to do a good job.
2. Share the concern with the team and leave it to them to improve the situation.
3. Study the situation and available data, assign targets to each member, tell them in detail how to go about the task, and daily monitor to re-plan if necessary.
4. Add to the team a person with adequate experience in epidemiology, encourage the team to plan, joining them from time to time.

Situation 12

You have been asked to be the course coordinator of a health training programme in an institute. You notice that the necessary arrangements were not made. The trainers were unenthusiastic, lacked training competence and were not functioning as a team. What will you do?

1. Work with the group to develop an action plan, encouraging them to implement it.
2. Streamline all arrangements as an emergency action, assign various responsibilities and monitor the work being done every day.
3. Plan and implement the needed actions and coach the trainers to improve their training competency.
4. Share your concern with the team and suggest that they could find the needed solution.

Leadership Profile Indicator (LPI)
Answer and Worksheet

Name: _____ Role: _____

Organisation: _____ Date: _____

The purpose of this instrument is to find out what strategies are preferred by different persons in the leadership role while dealing with organisational problems. The accompanying booklet contains 12 situations. Each situation poses a problem. Read the situation. Then consider the four alternative strategies given with the situation. Choose the one strategy you would like to use if you face such a situation as a leader. There are no right or wrong answers. For each situation encircle in Part II below the letter of the strategy you would prefer to use in dealing with it. Encircle only one choice for each situation and do not leave any situation unanswered. Do not write anything in parts III to VI.

I Situation	II Encircle Your Response	III	IV	V			VI		
				C	M	T	C	M	T
1.	A B C D	c a d b	d a b c		a c	c	b		
2.	A B C D	b a c d	d c a b	a b c	a b	b			
3.	A B C D	a d c b	c d b a	a d		a		b	
4.	A B C D	d a b c	c b a d	a b d	a d	d			
5.	A B C D	b a c d	a c b d	b				d	c d
6.	A B C D	c b a d	c b a d				a b d	d	a d
7.	A B C D	d a b c	a b c d		d		c		b c
8.	A B C D	a d c b	d a c b			a	b c	c	
9.	A B C D	b d a c	c a d b	a b d	b	b d			
10.	A B C D	b a d c	d a c b	a b	b				c
11.	A B C D	c a d b	c a d b				b	b d	a b d
12.	A B C D	b c a d	b c a d				a d	d	a c d

(For Guidelines for Scoring, see p. 233)

Lifestyles of Executives: Life Orientation Inventory (Form I)

33.1 THE INSTRUMENT AND ITS ADMINISTRATION

Life Orientation Inventory (LOI) was developed on the basis of description and case studies of enlargers and enfolders done by Bray, Campbell and Grant (1974). It has two forms. This chapter discusses Form I, which contains activities pertaining to enlarging and enfolding orientations, which the respondent rates on a 5-point scale, indicating the amount of time he spends on each activity compared to other people.

33.2 CONCEPTUAL FRAMEWORK

Lifestyles or life orientations are the general orientations in one's life. The concept of lifestyle was originally proposed by Adler in 1930. Adler suggested three characteristics of style of life—origin in childhood, self-consistency and constancy (Anabacher & Anabacher, 1956, pp. 186–91). Eckstein and Driscoll (1982) have suggested ways of assessing lifestyle in a group, using the birth order theory of Adler. Driscoll and Eckstein (1982) have also proposed a 50-item instrument to measure lifestyles, with five lifestyles in animal names—tigers (aggressive), chameleons (conforming), turtles (defensive), eagles (individualistic) and salmon (resistive). Adams (1980), in the context of stress, has suggested a simple instrument giving three lifestyles—personalistic, sociocentric and formalistic. However, these instruments are not in an organisational or career context.

Different concepts have been proposed for lifestyles. Core values and ideology (Bernard, 1975; Ginzberg, 1966), characteristic mode of living (Lazer, 1963), behavioural pattern with which the individual relates to external reality and internal dispositions (Zaleznik, 1977), and pattern of preferences, values and beliefs about himself in regard to the work around him (Friedlander, 1975).

In an in-depth and longitudinal study of successful (fast upward movement) and less successful executives in a well-known organisation, Bray et al. (1974) identified a number of factors associated with career and role success and failure. Two distinct patterns emerged from grouping these. The one associated with career/job success was called enlarging style, while the other associated with less success was called enfolding style. The distinction between the two is contrasted here (taken from Bray et al., 1974).

The enlarging lifestyle is oriented towards the goal of innovation, change and growth. The enlarger moves away from tradition and places his emphasis on adaptation, self-development and the extension of influence outward into work and community spheres. The enlarger looks for responsibility on the job and is also likely to seek and achieve a position of influence in organisations. Self-development activities are stressed. Thus, enlargers are likely not to only read, attend the theatre and keep up with current events, but also they might take courses in physical fitness and even respond to the promptings of health food. At the same time, their earlier ties to parents and formal religious practices begin to weaken. The enlarger finds that his values have changed so dramatically that he no longer enjoys the company of childhood friends. Except for a certain nostalgia when he visits parents and relatives, he is not satisfied with the ties of yesterday. A complete commitment to religion is similarly less meaningful, particularly since he makes every effort to see alternative points of view and to lend himself to new experiences of all varieties. This does not mean that he breaks off from his religious group entirely, but it can happen.

The enfolding lifestyle is oriented to the goals of tradition, stability and inward strength. Rather than pitching his strength outward, the enfolder seeks to cultivate and solidify that which invites attention within his more familiar sphere. He is not a member of social or community organisations and when he does enter into these activities, he rarely seeks an active role. He values parental ties and if he can, seeks to keep an active relationship with boyhood chums. He may find it quite upsetting to leave his hometown even if the move portends job advancement. In a new locale, he is likely to experience considerable difficulty in feeling at home. He is not likely to attend night college or to study on his own time unless he feels assured that his efforts will bring direct job rewards. He may begin a self-improvement programme, but his heart is seldom in it. He likes to settle into a job and sees it through to a full conclusion, getting great satisfaction from a job well done. He is not awed by fads. He forms a close attachment to a small circle of friends, and most of his socialising is done with relatives. Status considerations sometimes embarrass him, and he values informality and sincerity in human affairs. Bray et al. (1974) describe the enfolder as follows:

> It seems that he has been reluctant to take transfers in the past, especially during times of family stress when his wife was near delivery in a pregnancy (they now have four children), when his father was about to have an operation, and so forth. The couple have had to move four times in the past eight years, and even though they were distantly removed from their parents on only one of these occasions, neither he nor his wife have been happy with the company's seeming policy of uprooting its managers every few years. Peers and superiors have told him in the past that his attitude is not conducive to upward mobility on the job, but he had not been able to see their point at the time. It seemed to him that it was in the company's interest to keep their employees happy. (p. 109)

He values a rich family life, loves to play with his children and seems to be a perfect husband and father…. He likes to grow things and apparently has quite a green thumb…. He has thought about leaving the Bell system to enter his own business, but he lacks capital and has some doubts about whether the move would be worth the risk…. In many ways, he believes himself to be a success in life, in view of his happy home life, good health and satisfying work (for he does like the actual work that he does). One could not consider this man to be unhappy, except in the sense that he feels somewhat embarrassed about his lack of advancement. (pp. 110–11)

33.3 SCORING

The inventory has 10 items of enlarging style (A 1, 3, 4, 7, 12, 13, 14, and B 3, 4, 6) and 10 of enfolding style (A 2, 5, 6, 8, 9, 10, 11 and B 1, 2, 5). These are added to give a score on the 2 dimensions (on each, the range of scores will be 10–50). To get the scores in percentage terms, the following formula can be used:

$$\text{total score} - 10 \times 2.5$$

In which case, the range will be from 0 to 100.

33.4 RELIABILITY

The even–odd correlations of items (recalculated from Keshote's 1991 data) were 0.67 and 0.57 respectively for enfolding and enlarging styles. The total item correlations ranged from 0.45 to 0.64 for enlarging and from 0.46 to 0.66 for enfolding scales. These are acceptable reliability figures.

33.5 NORMS

Mean and SD values of engineering companies are given in Table 33.1.

TABLE 33.1 Mean and SD on LOI			
Enfolding	**Style**	**Enlarging**	**Style**
Mean	**SD**	**Mean**	**SD**
21	7.0	25	5.0

33.6 CORRELATES

Based on data from about 200 managers, Keshote (1991) reported a correlation of 0.38 between the two styles (significant at 0.01 level). This is an unexpected finding and needs examination. There seems to be some common elements between the two styles. Correlation between the two for a smaller sample of 20 persons was negative but not significant.

Keshote has also reported a relationship between life-orientation styles and some personality variables such as self-actualisation, locus of control, interpersonal trust, power needs and managerial styles.

For self-actualisation, ISAC (Banet, 1976) was used. In ISAC, scores are obtained on 15 aspects, as well as on the overall score. Two aspects, Number 3 (spontaneity, simplicity and naturalness) and Number 12 (ethical standards) were unrelated to either enlarging or enfolding styles. The correlations with six aspects (Numbers 4, 5, 7, 9, 13 and 16) were significant for both the styles. These are shown in Table 33.2, which also gives correlations that are significant only for enfolders (Numbers 8 and 10), and enlargers (Numbers 1, 2, 6, 11, 14 and 15).

The two items on which there is high correlation with enfolding style relate to existential orientation—both personal and interpersonal satisfaction. Regarding enlargers, all the items relate

TABLE 33.2 Significant Correlations Between LOI Styles and Self-actualisation Aspects

Self-Actualisation Aspects	Enlargers	Enfolders
1. Efficient reality perception	0.25	0.30
2. Acceptance of self, others, human nature	0.16	
6. Autonomy of independence of culture and environment	0.21	
11. Democratic character structure	0.19	
14. Creativity	0.23	
2. Resistance of consultation	0.22	
4. Problem-centeredness	0.29	
7. Freshness of appreciation	0.35	
5. Detachment and privacy	0.18	0.15
9. *Gemeinschaftsgefuhl* (empathy for, and helping, others)	0.22	0.17
13. Unhostile sense of humour	0.15	0.23
16. Overall	0.29	0.21
8. Capacity for peak experience		0.30
10. Interpersonal relations		0.19

to autonomy—both of the self and of others. So it can be said that while enlargers create autonomy, enfolders are people-oriented. Enfolders have a higher correlation with sense of humour, while enlargers have a higher correlation with problem-centeredness, freshness and appreciation, and *gemeinschaftsgefuhl* (desire to be helpful to others, etc., or extension motivation).

A detailed discussion, and the significance of self-actualisation dimensions can be found in Banet (1976).

No correlation was found with interpersonal trust. Both enfolding and enlarging styles had significant correlations (0.14 and 0.21 respectively) with internal locus of control (Chapter 9). The correlations with external (others) and external (chance) locus of control were significant (negative correlation) only with the enlarging style. It can be said that enlargers have low externality (both for others and for chance). On a CPP scale (see Chapter 18), enlargers valued persuasive power ($r = 0.18$, significant) and did not feel its deficiency ($r = -0.13$, significant). No other correlation was significant.

Using the transactional analysis model of managerial styles (Chapter 35), both enfolding and enlarging styles had a positive correlation (0.12 and 0.16, respectively) with the operating effectiveness of the adult ego state (problem-solving), while the enfolding style had a significant negative correlation with the operating effectiveness of the regulating parent. Enfolders seem to impose their norms on their subordinates, while both enlargers and enfolders have task effectiveness. No other correlations were significant.

Both enfolding and enlarging lifestyles had significant positive correlations (at 0.001 level) with Total Quality Management (TQM) and all its aspects. TQM was measured by an instrument that was based on the criteria suggested by Federal Quality Institute of USA and the guidelines for the President's Award for Quality. The correlations appear in Table 33.3. Although

TABLE 33.3 Coefficients of Correlation Between Lifestyles and TQM

		Enlarging	Enfolding
1.	Top management support	0.50*	
2.	Strategic planning		0.57**
3.	Focus on the customer	0.51*	
4.	Employee training and recognition	0.49*	
5.	Employment empowerment and teamwork	0.58*	
6.	Quality measurement and analysis	0.48*	0.47*
7.	Quality assurance	0.61*	
8.	Quality and productivity improvement results		0.75**
9.	Total quality	0.58**	0.59**

Note: Only those significant at 0.01* and 0.001** levels are mentioned.

both styles were positively correlated with eight aspects of TQM, enlarging style had higher correlations—six out of eight were significant at 0.001 level, and two, namely, strategic planning and quality improvement results, at 0.01 level. For the enfolding style, two aspects—strategic planning and quality improvement results—were significant at 0.001 level; four were significant at 0.01 level—top leadership support, training and recognition, quality measurement and quality assurance; and two were significant at 0.05 level—focus on the customer and employee empowerment and teamwork. It can be concluded that life orientation of managers is important for TQM, and that the enlarging style of managers promotes TQM and its processes.

33.7 USE FOR HRD

The inventory can be used both for research and for HRD. When used for HRD, participants may examine their profiles and discuss whether they feel concerned about some of the elements. If they do, they can plan ways of altering the profile by discussing them in small groups of their choice.

Life Orientation Inventory (Forms I)

Name: _____   Role: _____

Organisation: _____   Date: _____

The purpose of LOI is to get profiles of managers' orientations. There are no right or wrong answers.

1. How much time and energy do you spend on the aspects given below? In your responses, compare yourself with others in your profession/occupation/ level of employment, etc. You may, of course, not know exactly how much time and energy others spend on these aspects. However, your own general feeling is what is important.

   Write 1   if you spend much less time than the average in your group (you are amongst 5%)
   Write 2   if you are lower than the average (you are amongst about 20%)
   Write 3   if you are like most people (you are amongst about 80%)
   Write 4   if you spend more time than the average (you are amongst about 20%)
   Write 5   if you spend very much more time than the average (you are amongst about 5%)

   1. _____ Reading to broaden your knowledge
   2. _____ Being with your wife and children
   3. _____ To improve physical fitness like yoga, jogging, etc.
   4. _____ Attending courses for self-development
   5. _____ Religious activities
   6. _____ Spiritual pursuits and activities
   7. _____ Acquiring financial assets (shares, real estate, etc.)
   8. _____ Problems/matters of your parents
   9. _____ Contacting and meeting old friend and associates
   10. _____ Leisure-oriented activities (hobbies, sports, etc.)
   11. _____ Socialising (parties, clubs, small groups for card games, etc.)
   12. _____ Professional association, societies, activities
   13. _____ Community service and problems solving, etc.
   14. _____ New ways of increasing efficiency, commitment of employees, etc.

2. Six pairs of statements are given below. If there is a conflict between the two items of each pair, which one of the two would you prefer?

   Write 1   if (a) is more important to you than (b)
   Write 2   if (a) is important to you than (b)
   Write 3   if both are equally important to you and you cannot decide to which one you would give higher preference
   Write 4   if (b) is important to you than (a)
   Write 5   if (b) is more important to you than (a)

   1a. _____ Work demands
   1b. _____ Demands made by parents and family
   2a. _____ Concern for job content
   2b. _____ Concern for perks and other facilities
   3a. _____ Concern for one's family
   3b. _____ Concern for fast promotions
   4a. _____ Placement in the home location or in a desired place
   4b. _____ A challenging and interesting job
   5a. _____ Taking responsibility in a professional/community service organisation
   5b. _____ Sending time with old friends, parents and relatives
   6a. _____ Continuing with, and concentrating on, a job for a long time
   6b. _____ Searching for a job giving better opportunities for one's career in the future

Lifestyles of Executives: Life Orientation Inventory (Form II)

34.1 THE INSTRUMENT AND ITS ADMINISTRATION

The Life Orientation Inventory (Form I) presented in Chapter 33 treats enlarging and enfolding styles as two separate dimensions. Life orientation can also be viewed as a continuum, with enlarging and enfolding as two opposite poles. Form II of LOI was developed on this concept.

The LOI (Form II), appended to this chapter, consists of 20 pairs of items, each pair containing one enlarging and one enfolding item. The respondent has to distribute four scores amongst the two items in each pair. The advantage of this instrument is that it is simple to administer. A forced choice format was also tried. In a sample of 25, the correlation between forced choice (choosing one of the two statements) and distribution (four scores to be distributed amongst the two) was 0.67, highly significant. However, the distribution form (the present one) gives more freedom to the respondent.

34.2 CONCEPTUAL FRAMEWORK

The same conceptual framework given in Form I is relevant here.

34.3 SCORING

Following steps are to be followed for scoring:

1. Total scores given to the following items: 1a, 2b, 3b, 4b, 5a, 6a, 7b, 8b, 9b, 10a, 11a, 12a, 13a, 14a, 15b, 16a, 17a, 18b, 19a and 20b. The total score ranges from 0 to 80.
2. Multiply the total score by 1.25. The score will range between 0 and 100. This is the score of enlarging style.

34.4 RELIABILITY

The split-half reliability coefficient was found to be 0.83.

34.5 VALIDITY

In a group of 25 health managers, the enlarging styles on Form I were positively correlated with enlarging styles on Form II, and negatively with enfolding styles on Form II (both significant at 0.05 level). Enfolding and enlarging styles on Form I also had a positive correlation (significant at 0.05 level). This is in conformance with the results already reported.

The internal structure of the instrument, to some extent, gives evidence of construct validity. Factor analysis of responses from 152 respondents in an information technology organisation, using principal components analysis with Varimax rotation gave seven factors. The first three cover 14 out of 20 items and explain 36% variance. The other four factors contribute to 26% variance. We can therefore take the first three factors as the main ones. The rotated factor matrix is shown in Table 34.1.

TABLE 34.1 Rotated Factor Matrix of LOI (B)							
Items	Factor 1	Factor 2	Factor 3	Factor 4	Factor 5	Factor 6	Factor 7
1.	0.71						
14	0.71						
20	0.66						
11	−0.72		−0.42				
17	0.36			−0.33	−0.36	0.36	
13		0.80					
6		0.77					
9		0.76					
2		0.67					
1			0.76				
15	−0.34		53				
16			−6.7				
8				0.78			
12				75		0.41	
5				0.32	0.66		
18					0.74		
7						0.76	
19	0.33						0.60
10							0.45
4							−0.64

The five items having high loadings on Factor 1 relate to concern for career and family. This factor can therefore be called career versus family factor. The four items in Factor 2 relate to self-development and spiritual–religious activities. This factor can be called self-development versus spirituality–religiosity. The three items in Factor 3 relate to challenging job (Item 1), financial acquisitions (Item 15) and career growth (Item 16), as against well-paid job, hobbies and good salary, respectively. This factor can be called achievement versus comfortable life factor. The two main items in Factor 4 relate to leisure versus professional work, and spiritual work versus self-development. This factor is professional development factor. Factor 5 has two items—community work versus friends, and reading versus friends. This factor can be called extension versus affiliation factor. Factor 6 has two items with loadings above 30: socialising versus efforts for efficiency, and spiritual pursuit versus self-development. It is difficult to name this factor. The three items in Factor 7 relate to concern for parents versus concern for career, efficiency and financial assets. This factor can be called achievement versus parental affiliation factor.

34.6 NORMS

The mean scores of 152 executives of an information technology company was found to be 57 (with standard deviation of 10) for enlarging style, ranging from 0 to 100. Norms for various groups need to be found out.

Life Orientation Inventory (II)

Name: _____   Role: _____

Organisation: _____   Date: _____

The purpose of LOI is to survey personal orientations. There are no right or wrong answers. Given below are 20 pairs of statements. Read each statement in a pair and distribute 4 marks among the 2 statements indicating your personal preference. You can give 4 marks to one statement and 0 to the other, showing very strong preference for the first and none for the second; 3 marks to one and 1 mark to the other will mean strong preference for the first and some for the other; 2 marks to each will mean you have equal preference for both.

Respond to all the items.

1. _____   a. A challenging and interesting job
   _____   b. A job with a good salary and perks
2. _____   a. Religious act
   _____   b. Doing community service or working on community problems
3. _____   a. Placement in one's home location or in desired pace
   _____   b. Concern for career growth
4. _____   a. Continue and concentrate on a job for a long time
   _____   b. Search for a new job giving better opportunities for career, influence, etc.
5. _____   a. Taking responsibility for your community and working on community problems
   _____   b. Spending time with old friends and associates
6. _____   a. Reading to broaden your knowledge
   _____   b. Religious activities
7. _____   a. Socialising (parties, clubs, small groups, card games)
   _____   b. Working on new ways to increase efficiency and commitment of employees
8. _____   a. Leisure-oriented activities (hobbies, sports, etc.)
   _____   b. Participating in professional societies, associations, activities
9. _____   a. Spiritual pursuits and practices
   _____   b. Exercises to improve physical fitness (yoga, jogging, etc.)
10. _____   a. Acquiring financial assets (shares, real estate, etc.)
    _____   b. Attending to problems and matters relating to parents
11. _____   a. Concern for fast promotions
    _____   b. Placement in one's home location or in a desired place
12. _____   a. Participating in professional societies, associations, activities
    _____   b. Socialising (parties, clubs, small groups, card games)
13. _____   a. Attending courses for self-development
    _____   b. Spiritual pursuits and practices
14. _____   a. Searching a new job giving better opportunities for career, influence, etc.
    _____   b. Being with your family
15. _____   a. Participation in leisure-oriented activities (hobbies, etc.)
    _____   b. Acquiring financial assets
16. _____   a. A job with a good salary and perks
    _____   b. Opportunity for career growth

17. _____ a. A challenging and interesting job
    _____ b. A stable job with the scope to stay on it for a long time
18. _____ a. Spending time with old friends and associates
    _____ b. Reading to broaden one's knowledge
19. _____ a. Working on new ways to increase efficiency, commitment of employees etc.
    _____ b. Attending to problems and matters relating to parents
20. _____ a. Being with the family
    _____ b. Concern for fast promotion

Transactional Styles Inventory—Managers (TSI-M) and Feedback (TSI-F)

35.1 THE INSTRUMENT AND THEIR ADMINISTRATION

Transactional Styles Inventory (TSI) has been created to help the respondents examine their interactional or transactional styles, and develop strategies to enhance their interpersonal effectiveness. TSI is available for managers, trainers, consultants, counsellors, teachers, parents, students, nurses and journalists. The comments made and suggestions given here are applicable to all the forms of TSI.

Although TSI is self-administered, the facilitator should read the instructions with the participants to make certain that they have no queries. The Score Sheet should not be distributed among respondents until the instrument is completed. People can score their own responses, or the facilitator can collect the material and score the items for them. A group profile can be constructed by averaging the group scores on each of the scales.

35.2 CONCEPTUAL FRAMEWORK

Whether as individuals or in social and organisational roles, we interact with others. There are three main areas of our interpersonal interactions. We interact in relation to the tasks being performed or to be preformed. We also interact in relation to the values and norms which are or should be followed or are violated. And, we interact with emotions, such as, affection, fear, anger, curiosity, etc.

The habitual way of a person's interacting with others can be called his interpersonal style. A useful conceptual framework to describe an individual's style is Transactional Analysis (TA). TA concepts are quite popular, and two basic concepts can be used to understand influence styles—the ego states and the existential positions.

Each person involved in transactions with others has the following three ego states:

1. *The parent*: Regulates behaviour (through prescriptions and sanctions) and nurtures (by providing support).
2. *The adult*: Collects information and processes it.
3. *The child*: Has several functions, primarily concerned with (a) creativity, curiosity and fun (b) reactions to others (including rebellion) and (c) adjusting to others' demands or sulking.

Each ego state is important. However, the functional or dysfunctional role of these ego states depends on the general existential or life position a person takes. Harris (1973) has conceptualised four primary existential or life positions: I'm OK—You're OK; I'm not OK— You're OK; I'm OK—You're not OK; and I'm not OK—You're not OK.

James has suggested that, in general, the concepts of OK and not-OK can be used to understand how bosses behave. Avary (1980) has similarly proposed OK and not-OK dimensions of the six ego states. Savorgnan (1979) has discussed the OK and not-OK dimensions of the two parent ego states. Figure 35.1 shows the four life positions in terms of interaction styles.

The four general interaction styles can be elaborated by combining them with the ego states. Two dimensions of the parent ego state (critical or regulating and nurturing), three of the child ego state (adaptive, reactive, and free or creative) and the adult ego state are used. All three ego states and the sub-ego states are important and perform distinct functions. Each ego state meets a basic need. Avary (1980) has proposed that six basic needs are met by the six ego states, which can be OK or not-OK. These are as follows:

FIGURE 35.1   General Interaction Styles in Four Life Positions

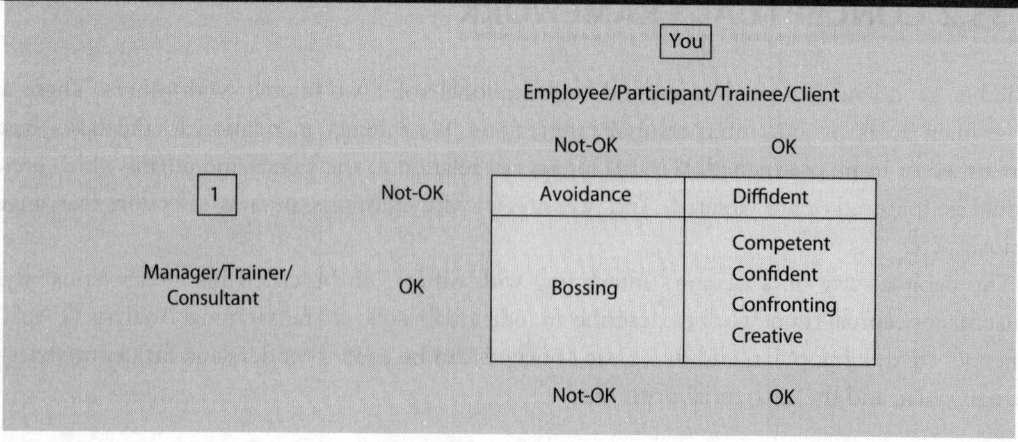

1. The need to express love and care, manifested as nurturing parent (OK) or rescuing parent (not-OK);
2. The need for power, faith and self-confidence as firm parent (OK) or critical parent (not-OK);
3. The need to think and evaluate information as an adult (OK) or any not-OK ego state;
4. The biological needs and the need to feel and experience stimulation as a natural child (OK) or a person (not-OK);
5. The need to be creative or intuitive as a little professor (OK) or a rebellious or defensive child (not-OK); and
6. The need for approval and safety as an adapted child (OK) or a helpless child (not-OK).

The interpersonal style of an individual depends on the person's combination of the six ego states with the life positions. Combining the six ego states with the four life positions, we obtain 24 influence styles (Pareek, 1984). Twenty-four styles may be too extensive for some situations. As James (1975) and Avary (1980) have suggested, two dimensions (OK and not-OK) can be combined with the various life positions. Combining the six ego states (two parent, one adult and three child) with the two life positions (OK and not-OK), we obtain 12 styles. These are shown in Table 35.1.

35.2.1 Rescuing Style

Such a style indicates a dependency relationship in which the manager, trainer or consultant perceives his main role as rescuing the subordinate, participant trainee or client, who is seen as being incapable of taking care of himself. Another characteristic of this style is that support is provided conditionally, contingent on deference to the provider. The general attitude is one of

TABLE 35.1   Twelve Influence Styles

	Styles in Two Life Positions	
Ego States	**Not-OK**	**OK**
Nurturing parent	Rescuing	Supportive
Regulating parent	Prescriptive	Normative
Adult	Task-obsessive	Problem-solving
Creative child	Bohemian	Innovative
Reactive child	Aggressive	Assertive
Adaptive child	Sulking	Resilient

superiority; the person's support constantly reminds others of their dependence. Obviously, this style does not help other people to become independent and to act by themselves.

35.2.2 Supportive Style

In this style, support is provided when needed. James (1975) uses the term supportive coaches for managers with this style. They encourage their subordinates and provide the necessary conditions for continuous improvement. Consultants in this style show patience in learning about the problems of their client and have empathy with them.

35.2.3 Prescriptive Style

People with this style are critical of the behaviour of others. They develop rules and regulations and impose them on others. Managers using this style make quick judgements and insist that certain norms be followed by all the subordinates. A consultant may give advice and prescribe solutions for clients rather than help clients to work out alternative solutions to their problems.

35.2.4 Normative Style

These managers are interested in developing proper norms of behaviour for their subordinates and, in helping them, understand why some norms are more important than others. A consultant with this style does not only help clients to solve a specific problem but also helps them to develop ways of approaching a problem and raises questions about relevant values. Such a consultant emphasises the development of a general approach to the problem. Trainers with this style influence the participants through modelling behaviour. They also raise questions about the appropriateness of some aspects of behaviour and work.

35.2.5 Task-obsessive Style

People with this style are more concerned with the task. Matters not directly related to the task are ignored. They are not concerned with feelings and, in fact, fail to recognise them since they do not perceive them as related to the task. They attempt to function like computers. A task-obsessive trainer is insensitive to the emotional needs, personal problems and apprehensions of the participants.

35.2.6 Problem-solving Style

In this style, a manager is concerned with solving problems but does not see them as being merely confined to tasks. For such persons, the problems have various dimensions. The focus of the manager, consultant or trainer is on dealing with and finding out solutions to problems. In this process, they solicit the help of and involve subordinates, clients, trainees and participants.

35.2.7 Bohemian Style

The creative child is active in this style. The person has lot of ideas and is impatient with current practices. The person is less concerned with how the new ideas work than with the ideas themselves. Such people are nonconformists and enjoy experimenting with new approaches, primarily for fun. They rarely allow one idea or practice to stabilise before going on to another.

35.2.8 Innovative Style

Innovators are enthusiastic about new ideas and approaches and enthuse others too. Unlike the Bohemian, they pay enough attention to nurturing their ideas so that they result in concrete action and become internalised in the system.

35.2.9 Aggressive Style

People with this style are fighters. They may fight for their subordinates, clients or participants or for their ideas and suggestions, hoping that this will help them to achieve the desired results. Their aggressiveness, however, makes people avoid them and not take them seriously.

35.2.10 Assertive Style

In this style, the person is concerned with the exploration of a problem. Perseverance is the main characteristic. Such persons confront the organisation to get things done for their subordinates or clients. They are more concerned with confronting problems than with confronting other persons for the sake of confrontation. A consultant with this style may also confront the client in order to help him explore various dimensions. Such people are frank and open but also perceptive and sensitive. They respect the feelings of others.

35.2.11 Sulking Style

People with this style keep their negative feelings to themselves, find it difficult to share them and avoid meeting people if they have not been able to fulfil their part of the contract. Instead of confronting problems, a person with this style avoids them and feels bad about the situation, but does not express these feelings openly.

35.2.12 Resilient Style

In this style, persons show creative adaptability—learning from others, accepting others' ideas and changing their approach when required. Although persons in influence roles—managers, consultants, counsellors or trainers—may show several styles of behaviour, one style will generally be used more frequently than others.

35.3 SCORING

The answer sheet can be used for scoring, or the software available for this purpose can be used for detailed analysis. Scoring key is also given with the instrument.

1. Add the responses for the items in each row and write the total on the first blank space at the end of the row. For example, responses to items 1, 13 and 25 will be totalled in the first row. Thus, there will be 12 totals (for 12 rows).
2. Consult the key (Table 35.2 for TSI-M). The totals of the 12 rows represent the totals of the 12 styles. In the lower portion of the answer sheet, the two terms, DS and BS, main dominant style and back-up style, respectively.
3. Against DS, write the name of the style which has the highest score amongst the 12 rows. If two or more styles have the same score, no specific DS is indicated.

TABLE 35.2   TSI-M Key

Style	State	Items
Supportive	(OK nurturing parent)	1, 13, 25
Rescuing	(Not-OK nurturing parent)	8, 20, 32
Normative	(OK normative parent)	3, 15, 27
Prescriptive	(Not-OK normative parent)	10, 22, 34
Problem-solving	(OK adult)	5, 17, 29
Tasks-obsessive	(Not-OK adult)	12, 24, 36
Innovative	(OK creative child)	11, 23, 25
Bohemian	(Not-OK creative child)	6, 18, 30
Assertive	(OK reactive child)	9, 21, 33
Aggressive	(Not-OK reactive child)	4, 16, 28
Resilient	(OK adaptive child)	7, 19, 31
Sulking	(Not-OK adaptive child)	2, 14, 26

TABLE 35.3 Operating Effectiveness Quotient (OEQ)

Not-OK Scores	OK Scores												
	3	4	5	6	7	8	9	10	11	12	13	14	15
3	0	100	100	100	100	100	100	100	100	100	100	100	100
4	0	50	67	75	80	83	85	87	89	90	91	92	92
5	0	33	50	60	67	71	75	78	80	82	83	85	86
6	0	25	40	50	57	62	67	70	73	75	77	78	80
7	0	20	33	43	50	55	60	64	67	69	71	73	75
8	0	17	28	37	44	50	54	58	61	64	67	69	70
9	0	14	25	33	40	45	50	54	57	60	62	65	67
10	0	12	22	30	36	42	46	50	53	56	59	61	63
11	0	11	20	28	33	38	43	47	50	53	55	58	60
12	0	10	18	25	31	36	40	44	47	50	53	55	57
13	0	9	17	23	28	33	37	41	44	47	50	52	54
14	0	8	15	21	27	31	35	39	42	45	48	50	52
15	0	8	14	20	25	29	33	37	40	43	45	48	50

4. Against BS, write the name of the style which has the next highest score. If more than one style has the same score, no specific BS is indicated. This is neither good nor bad. In cases of both DS and BS, either it may mean the flexibility of styles or that no specific DS of BS has emerged.

5. Consult Table 35.2 (for TSI-M) for the OEQ values of each odd row (1, 3, 5, 7, 9 and 11) and write them in the last space given against each row. OEQ indicates the percentage of the potential that is being used effectively in a particular style. The odd rows represent OK styles, and the even rows represent not-OK styles. There are pairs of the OK and not-OK styles (1–8, 3–10, 5–12, 11–6, 9–4, 7–2). Locate the OK score in the first or top row of Table 35.3 and the not-OK score in the first column of the table. See where the located column and row interact and write down the score against the OK row. For example, if the totals of rows 1 and 8 are 12 and 8 respectively, 64 is the figure where 12 in the first row and 8 in the first column meet; 64 is then the OEQ in this case. Write down the OEQs for all the odd rows.

35.4 UNDERDEVELOPED EGO STATES

All the three ego states—parent, adult and child—must be balanced. Similarly, both parent sub-states (nurturing and regulating) and the three child sub-states (adaptive, reactive and creative) should be balanced. The balance is disturbed if one of the two or three is underdeveloped.

1. An underdeveloped ego state is one which has not been used much and the related function is not getting priority/attention of the respondent.
2. Underdeveloped ego states can be identified by examining the sums of six OK or functional styles. According to available norms, a score of less than nine indicates underdeveloped ego state; however, in case of innovative and confronting styles, a score lower than six will indicate underdevelopment of either of these sub-states.
3. A score of below 15 of the total of OK and Not-OK aspects of any ego state indicates that it is underdeveloped.
4. A percentage ratio of 20 or below shows underdeveloped ego state. For the two parent ego states, a percentage score of 30 or below shows underdeveloped ego state.

35.5 RELIABILITY

The retest reliability coefficients (with an interval of four weeks) with several groups have been found to range between 0.51 and 0.74 for the different styles. All of these were significant at 0.01 level. Guttmann split-half, equal and unequal length Spearman-Brown for a sample of health administrators was found to be 0.89, respectively.

35.6 VALIDITY

The validity of the instrument was tested by correlating TSI-M scores with egogram scores. Predictions were made for the correlations of the five ego state scores on the egogram with the styles scores. Four correlations were in the predicted direction. However, the nurturing parent ego state was found correlated not with the supportive style but with the rescuing style. On the whole, the correlation data provides evidence of the validity of the instrument for training purposes. More information on validity is available in Pareek (1986b).

The OEQs on TSI-M of 36 managers were correlated with the OEQs on TSI-F (completed by their supervisors). The correlations are discussed further.

Nurturing	0.35
Regulatory	0.95
Task	0.37
Creativity	0.38
Adaptability	0.99
Reliability	0.98

As can be seen, the correlation in nurturing, task and creativity functions are low. These require to be further investigated.

TABLE 35.4 OEQ Norms		
Functions	Mean	SD
Nurturing	54	10
Regulating	54	9
Task	56	19
Creative	55	13
Reactive	60	14
Adaptive	68	14

35.7 NORMS

For balanced or underdeveloped ego states, see the opening section of this chapter. Regarding the various functions, mean and SD values of 294 managers given in Table 35.4 can be used for norms.

35.8 CORRELATES

Using earlier version of LOCO inventory (Chapter 9), Keshote (1991) has reported a negative correlation (significant at 0.05 level) between supportive style and externality-C and a negative correlation of problem-solving style with both C and O externality (significant at 0.01 and 0.05 levels respectively).

35.9 USE FOR HRD

This instrument is intended primarily for training. A respondent can examine the operating effectiveness scores for each of his ego states; if he feels concerned about low scores, he can prepare a plan for behavioural changes based on the related items by reducing Not-OK behaviour and increasing OK behaviour.

TSI-M can also be used as an OD intervention where the patterns in a group are discussed and organisational factors are examined to find out which ones contribute to low OE scores. Managers can discuss, in small groups, the implications of the scores and develop action plans to improve the operating effectiveness of some ego states.

TSI-M can further be used with groups of management students. The students would complete the instrument by answering how they would prefer to behave as managers. They would then learn the underlying concepts and explore what styles they would like to develop and how.

Kalra and Gupta (1999), based on their extensive work, have used clinical interpretation of TSI (formerly called SPIRO) scores. They have suggested that the overall total of all the TSI scores (both OK and Not-OK) indicate the activity level of the respondent. Effective managers were found to be high on all OK/functional dimensions. Interestingly, they were also high on patronising (rescuing), which is a Not-OK/dysfunctional dimension, while being low on the remaining Not-OK dimensions. Kalra and Agrawal (1991) have used TSI/SPIRO scores for detailed clinical analysis and performance counselling in an educational institution, giving live illustrations.

Transactional Styles Inventory—Managers

Do not write anything on this sheet. Write your responses on the Answer Sheet.

1. _____ I assure my people of my availability to them.
2. _____ I delay doing things that I do not like.
3. _____ I raise questions with my people about what should or should not be done.
4. _____ I communicate strong feelings and resentment to my colleagues/seniors without caring whether this will affect my relationships with them.
5. _____ I collect all the information needed to solve various problems.
6. _____ I discuss new ideas with my people without working out the details of these ideas.
7. _____ I respect and follow organisational traditions that seem to give the organisation its identity.
8. _____ I provide my people with the solutions to their problems.
9. _____ I take up the cause of my department/people and fight for them.
10. _____ I admonish my people for not acting according to my instructions.
11. _____ I think of new and creative solutions.
12. _____ I collect information and data even when these are not immediately needed or used.
13. _____ I help my people to become aware of some of their own strengths.
14. _____ I avoid meeting my seniors and colleagues if I have not been able to fulfil their expectations.
15. _____ I help my people to see the ethical dimensions of some of our actions.
16. _____ I champion my people's cause even at the cost of organisational effectiveness.
17. _____ I think out many alternative solutions to problems before adopting one for action.
18. _____ I overwhelm my colleagues with new ideas.
19. _____ I accept others' suggestions that appeal to me.
20. _____ I instruct my people in detail about work problems and their solutions.
21. _____ I zealously argue my point of view in organisational meetings.
22. _____ I give clear instructions to my people about what should or should not be done.
23. _____ I try out new things.
24. _____ I go into all the details of the specific work to be performed.
25. _____ I reassure my people of my continued help.
26. _____ I do not express my negative feelings during unpleasant meetings but continue to be bothered by them.
27. _____ I help my people and colleagues to examine the appropriateness of proposed actions.
28. _____ I express strong resentment to my seniors or colleagues about things that have not been done as promised.
29. _____ I continuously search for various resources from which needed information can be obtained in order to work out solutions to problems.
30. _____ I try out new ideas or methods without waiting to consolidate the previous ones.
31. _____ I accept help from others and appreciate it.
32. _____ I encourage my people to come to me frequently to seek my advice and help.
33. _____ I express my feelings and reactions frankly in meetings with seniors and colleagues.
34. _____ I clearly prescribe standards of behaviour to be followed in my work unit.
35. _____ I enjoy trying out new ways and see a problem as a challenge.
36. _____ I work primarily on organisational tasks, sometimes at the cost of sensitivity and attention to the feelings of people.

TSI-F

The person to be rated: _____   Date: _____

This instrument is to help to know more about how he interacts with others, an important part of the organisational role. Your help has been requested by him. There are no right or wrong answers. You will be helpful if you respond to each item as candidly as possible

Please do not write your name on this sheet

Read each statement and write your response on this sheet, against the corresponding number, according to the key given below:

Write 1   if he rarely or never behaves this way
Write 2   if he occasionally behaves this way
Write 3   if he sometimes behaves this way
Write 4   if he often behaves this way
Write 5   if he almost always behaves this way

No.	Response	Item
1.	_____	He assures his people of his availability to them.
2.	_____	He delays doing things that he does not like.
3.	_____	He encourages his people to question him about what should or should not be done.
4.	_____	He communicates strong feelings and resentment to his bosses without caring, whether this will affect his relationship with them.
5.	_____	He collects all the information that is needed to solve various problems.
6.	_____	He discusses new ideas with his people without working out their details.
7.	_____	He respects and follows those traditions of the organisation that seem to give it its identity.
8.	_____	He provides his people with solutions to their problems.
9.	_____	He takes up his peoples' causes and fights for them.
10.	_____	He admonishes his people for not acting according to his instructions.
11.	_____	He thinks of new and creative solutions.
12.	_____	He collects information and data even when these are not immediately need or used.
13.	_____	He helps his people to become aware of some of their own strengths.
14.	_____	He avoids meeting his bosses and people if he has not been able to fulfil their expectations.
15.	_____	He helps his people to see the ethical dimensions of some of their actions.
16.	_____	He champions his peoples' cause even at the cost of organisational effectiveness.
17.	_____	He thinks out many alternative solutions to problems before adopting one for action.
18.	_____	He overwhelms his people with new ideas.
19.	_____	He accepts only those suggestions of his bosses and his people which appeal to him.
20.	_____	He instructs his people in detail about work problems and their solutions.
21.	_____	He zealously argues his point of view in organisational meetings.
22.	_____	He gives clear instructions to his people about what should or should not be done.
23.	_____	He tries out new things.
24.	_____	He spends his time on the specific work that has to be done.
25.	_____	He reassures his people of his continual help.
26.	_____	He does not express his negative feelings during unpleasant meetings but continues to be bothered by them.
27.	_____	He helps his people to examine the appropriateness of proposed actions.

No.	Response	Item
28.	_____	He expresses resentment to the authorities concerned about things that have not been done as promised.
29.	_____	He continuously searches for various resources from which needed information can be obtained in order to work out solutions to problems.
30.	_____	He tries out new ideas or methods without waiting to consolidate earlier ones.
31.	_____	He accepts help from others and appreciates it.
32.	_____	He encourages his people to come to him frequently for his advice and help.
33.	_____	He expresses his feelings and reactions frankly in meetings with his own bosses.
34.	_____	He clearly prescribes standards of behaviour to be followed in his work unit.
35.	_____	He enjoys trying out new ways and sees a problem as a challenge.
36.	_____	He works primarily on organisational tasks, sometimes at the cost of being insensitive or inattentive to the feelings of people.

TSI-M

Scoring Sheet

Name: _____   Role: _____

Organisation: _____   Date: _____

This instrument will help you to know more about how you interact with others, an important part of your organisational role. There are no right or wrong answers. You will learn more about yourself if you respond to each item as candidly as possible.

Read each statement in the preceding sheets and write your response on this sheet, against the corresponding number, according to the key given below. Answer serially.

Write 1 if you rarely or never behave this way.
Write 2 if you occasionally behave this way.
Write 3 if you sometimes behave this way.
Write 4 if you often behave this way.
Write 5 if you almost always behave this way.

Style	Items and Responses			Total	OEQ
Nurturing	1. ____	13. ____	25. ____	____	____
	8. ____	20. ____	32. ____	____	____
Regulating	3. ____	15. ____	27. ____	____	____
	10. ____	22. ____	34. ____	____	____
Task	5. ____	17. ____	29. ____	____	____
	12. ____	24. ____	36. ____	____	____
Adaptive	7. ____	19. ____	31. ____	____	____
	2. ____	14. ____	26. ____	____	____
Assertive	9. ____	21. ____	33. ____	____	____
	4. ____	16. ____	28. ____	____	____
Innovative	11. ____	23. ____	35. ____	____	____
	6. ____	18. ____	30. ____	____	____
DS ____	BS ____	Total OK ____	Not-OK ____	OK + Not-OK ____	

TSI-F
Scoring Sheet

Style		Items and Responses		Total	OEQ
Nurturing	1. ____	13. ____	25. ____	____	____
	8. ____	20. ____	32. ____	____	____
Regulating	3. ____	15. ____	27. ____	____	____
	10. ____	22. ____	34. ____	____	____
Task	5. ____	17. ____	29. ____	____	____
	12. ____	24. ____	36. ____	____	____
Adaptive	7. ____	19. ____	31. ____	____	____
	2. ____	14. ____	26. ____	____	____
Assertive	9. ____	21. ____	33. ____	____	____
	4. ____	16. ____	28. ____	____	____
Innovative	11. ____	23. ____	35. ____	____	____
	6. ____	18. ____	30. ____	____	____
DS ____	BS ____	Total OK ____	Not-OK ____	OK + Not-OK ____	

Transactional Styles Inventory—General (TSI-G)

36.1 THE INSTRUMENT AND ITS ADMINISTRATION

TSI-G is meant for helping individuals to examine their styles as persons, and not in any role. While all other TSI forms are role-related, TSI-G is for general use.

TSI-G is self-administered. When administered in a group, the facilitator should read the instructions with the participants to make certain that they have no queries. The Score Sheet should not be distributed until the instrument is completed. Respondents can score their own responses, or the facilitator can collect and score the answer sheets for them. If administered in a homogenous group, a group profile can be prepared by averaging the group scores for each style and function.

36.2 CONCEPTUAL FRAMEWORK

The framework discussed in Chapter 35, based on Transactional Analysis, has been used to develop the instrument, and it is important for its use and interpretation.

36.3 SCORING

The Score Sheet can be used for scoring. Scoring can be done either by the participants themselves or by the facilitator who can score the instrument in advance:

1. Transfer the responses on the 48 items to the Score Sheet.
2. The rows are printed in pairs, the odd rows being of OK styles and the even rows of not-OK styles. There are six pairs of the OK and not-OK styles (1–8, 3–10, 5–12,

TABLE 36.1   TSI-G

Style		Items
1. Supportive	(OK nurturing parent)	1, 13, 25, 37
2. Bohemian	(Not-OK adaptive child)	2, 14, 26, 38
3. Normative	(OK normative parent)	3, 15, 27, 39
4. Aggressive	(Not-OK reactive child)	4, 16, 28, 40
5. Problem-solving	(OK adult)	5, 17, 29, 41
6. Sulking	(Not-OK creative child)	6, 18, 30, 42
7. Innovative	(OK adaptive child)	7, 19, 31, 43
8. Rescuing	(Not-OK nurturing parent)	8, 20, 32, 44
9. Confronting	(OK reactive child)	9, 21, 33, 45
10. Prescriptive	(Not-OK normative parent)	10, 22, 34, 46
11. Resilient	(OK creative child)	11, 23, 35, 47
12. Task-obsessive	(Not-OK adult)	12, 24, 36, 48

11–6, 9–4, 7–2). The odd rows represent OK styles, and the even not-OK styles (Table 36.1). Locate the OK score in the first row of Table 36.2 and the not-OK score in the first column of the table. See where the located columns and rows interact, and write down the score against the OK row. For example, if totals of rows 1 and 8 are 12 and 8 respectively, 67 is the figure, where 12 in the first row, and 8 in the first column meet; 64 then is the OEQ in this case. Note down the OEQ for all the odd rows. Add all OEQs and write down the overall OEQ.

3. Against DS, write the name of the style which has the highest score amongst the 12 rows. If more than one style has the same score, there is no dominant style. This is neither good nor bad.

4. Against BS, write the name of the style which has the next highest score. If more than one style has the same score, there is no backup style. This is neither good nor bad.

5. Note down the totals of OK (odd rows) and not-OK (even rows). Divide the totals by 6. Then write down the overall OEQ by consulting Table 36.2.

6. Note down the totals of OK and Not-OK rows. This may indicate two activity levels of the respondent.

TABLE 36.2 Operating Effectiveness Quotient Table

Not-OK Scores	OK Scores																
	4	5	6	7	8	9	10	11	12	13	14	15	16	17	18	19	20
4	0	100	100	100	100	100	100	100	100	100	100	100	100	100	100	100	100
5	0	50	67	75	80	83	86	88	89	90	91	92	92	93	93	94	94
6	0	33	50	60	67	71	75	78	80	82	83	85	86	87	88	88	89
7	0	25	40	50	57	63	67	70	73	75	77	79	80	81	82	83	84
8	0	20	33	43	50	56	60	64	67	69	71	73	75	76	78	79	80
9	0	17	29	38	44	50	55	58	62	64	67	69	71	72	74	75	76
10	0	14	25	33	40	45	50	54	57	60	63	65	67	68	70	71	73
11	0	13	22	30	36	42	46	50	53	56	59	61	63	65	67	68	70
12	0	11	20	27	33	38	43	47	50	53	56	58	60	62	64	65	67
13	0	10	18	25	31	36	40	44	47	50	53	55	57	59	61	63	64
14	0	9	17	23	29	33	38	41	44	47	50	52	55	57	58	60	62
15	0	8	15	21	27	31	35	39	42	45	48	50	52	54	56	58	59
16	0	8	14	20	25	29	33	37	40	43	46	48	50	52	54	56	59
17	0	7	13	19	24	28	32	35	38	41	44	46	48	50	52	54	55
18	0	7	13	18	22	26	30	33	36	39	42	44	46	48	50	52	53
19	0	6	12	17	21	25	29	32	38	38	40	42	44	46	48	50	52
20	0	6	11	16	20	24	27	30	33	36	38	41	43	45	47	48	50

36.4 ITEM ANALYSIS

Item analysis of 48 items was done based on responses of 29 persons. The SD values of the items were found to be as follows:

Above 1.00 — 28 items. For all items, the range of responses was 1–5.
0.76–1.00 — 15 items. The range of all items was 2–5.
0.51–0.75 — 3 (no. 1, 13, 20). Range being 3–5 for all three items.
Below 0.51 — 2 (no. 17, 29). Range in both cases was 4–5.

36.5 NORMS*

Mean and SD values of OEQ of a group of 270 women entrepreneurs can be used as norms.

---

* Norms are provided by Ms Pragaya Dashora.

Function	Mean	SD
Nurturing	53	5
Regulating	57	8
Task Management	62	8
Creativity	69	10
Confronting	52	10
Adaptive	57	12

36.6 USE FOR HRD

This instrument is intended primarily for training. A respondent can examine the operating effectiveness scores for each of his ego states and, if he feels concerned about the low scores, he can prepare a plan for behavioural change, based on the related items by reducing the not-OK behaviour and by increasing the OK behaviour.

The instrument can also be used as an OD intervention. The patterns in a group can be discussed, and the organisational factors that contribute to low OE scores can be examined. Participants can discuss, in small groups, the implications of the scores and develop action plans to improve the operating effectiveness of some ego states.

Transactional Styles Inventory—General (TSI-G)

Name: _____   Role: _____

Occupation: _____   Date: _____

This instrument will help you to know more about how you interact with others, an important part of your effectiveness. There are no right or wrong answers. You will learn more about yourself, if you respond to each item as candidly as possible. Read each statement given in the instrument. Write your response on this sheet, against the corresponding number given in the key below. Answer serially.

Write 1   if you rarely or never behave this way
Write 2   if you occasionally behave this way
Write 3   if you sometimes behave this way
Write 4   if you often behave this way
Write 5   if you almost always behave this way

1. _____   I am available and accessible to those who want to interact with me.
2. _____   I am excited about new things and try them out even without consolidating the previous ones.
3. _____   I am concerned about ethical issues in personal and social life.
4. _____   I feel hurt and angry if a person refuses to oblige me when I ask him for a favour.
5. _____   I am uneasy until I finish the task for which I volunteer.
6. _____   I delay doing things that I do not like.
7. _____   I enjoy trying out new ways and see a problem as a challenge.
8. _____   I advise people on their problems and issues.
9. _____   I do not hesitate in raising questions in discussions when I do not understand a point.
10. _____   I am upset if people do not act according to my instructions.
11. _____   I respect the traditions and practices of the various group I interact with.
12. _____   I am workaholic and tend to neglect some other matters.
13. _____   I help people whenever such help is required.
14. _____   I try out different ways of dealing with a problem.
15. _____   I raise questions of values while discussing a course of action.
16. _____   I express my strong feelings to people without caring if it would spoil my relations with them.
17. _____   I collect relevant information about the problem I am working on.
18. _____   I avoid meeting people if I am not able to do what I promised to do.
19. _____   As soon I know about a new product, I procure it, and give up what I have been currently using.
20. _____   I give detailed instructions to make sure things are done the way I want.
21. _____   I can say no without any embarrassment or guilt.
22. _____   I show my resentment if things are not done the way I think they should be done.
23. _____   I find strengths in the various cultures and try to adopt some of them.
24. _____   I am so involved in my immediate work commitments that I tend to overlook long-term goals.
25. _____   My friends and others feel free to discuss matters with me.

26. _____ I am among the earliest to adopt a new idea/product, even without critically examining the evidence in favour of or against it.
27. _____ I myself practice what I want others to follow.
28. _____ I ask a person during discussion to shut up if he is saying irrelevant things.
29. _____ I give high priority to planning in detail what needs to be done.
30. _____ I do not express negative feelings during unpleasant meetings, but continue to be bothered by them.
31. _____ I look for alternatives rather than adopting the known one.
32. _____ I enjoy helping people to solve their problems.
33. _____ I take negative feedback without feeling upset or defensive.
34. _____ In a group, I take the lead in preparing what should be done.
35. _____ I adjust to most situations without any discomfort.
36. _____ I work primarily on tasks I commit to myself, sometimes at the cost of sensitivity and attention to others feelings.
37. _____ I tend to empathise with and respond to the people interacting with me.
38. _____ I regret later when I adopt/use a new product out of enthusiasm, and it creates problems.
39. _____ I do not hesitate in raising questions of ethics and values in public life.
40. _____ I dominate the discussions I participate in.
41. _____ I collect data and information about the progress of the work being done.
42. _____ I find it difficult to adjust to new situations/strange places.
43. _____ I enjoy experimenting and learning from such experiments.
44. _____ I enjoy people coming to me for advice and help and encourage them to do so.
45. _____ I am unable to confront people and express my feelings to them.
46. _____ I prepare detailed plans for my children and others for whom I am responsible.
47. _____ I enjoy working with new people and in new environments.
48. _____ For me, the highest priority is to complete the work I am committed to.

Transactional Styles Inventory—General (TSI-G)

Style	Items and Responses				Total	OEQ
Nurturing	1. ____	13. ____	25. ____	37. ____	____	____
	8. ____	20. ____	32. ____	44. ____	____	____
Regulating	3. ____	15. ____	27. ____	39. ____	____	____
	10. ____	22. ____	34. ____	46. ____	____	____
Task	5. ____	17. ____	29. ____	41. ____	____	____
	12. ____	24. ____	36. ____	48. ____	____	____
Adaptive	7. ____	19. ____	31. ____	43. ____	____	____
	2. ____	14. ____	26. ____	38. ____	____	____
Assertive	9. ____	21. ____	33. ____	45. ____	____	____
	4. ____	16. ____	28. ____	40. ____	____	____
Innovative	11. ____	23. ____	35. ____	47. ____	____	____
	6. ____	18. ____	30. ____	42. ____	____	____
DS ____	BS ____	Total OK ____	Not-OK ____	OK + Not-OK ____	____	OEQ ____

Transactional Styles Inventory—
Trainers (TSI-T)

37.1 THE INSTRUMENT AND ITS ADMINISTRATION

TSI-T measures training styles of trainers, a consistent way of interacting with people and situations.

Read the 'Instructions for Its Administration', 'Conceptual Framework', 'Scoring' and 'Use for HRD' given in the beginning of Chapter 35.

37.2 RELIABILITY

For a group of 24 trainers, Cronbach alpha was found to be 0.99 whereas for a group of nine administrators, it was found to be 0.93.

37.3 NORMS

The mean and SD of OEQ scores of a group of trainers are given below. These can be used as norms.

Function	Mean	SD
Nurturing	50	10
Regulating	50	10
Task	55	10
Confronting	60	10
Adaptive	65	10
Creative	65	10

Transactional Styles Inventory (Trainers)

Name: _____   Role: _____

Organisation: _____   Date: _____

This instrument will help you to know more about how you interact with participants and others, an important part of your training role. There are no right or wrong answers. You will learn more about yourself if you respond to each item as candidly as possible.

Read each statement given in the instrument. Write your response on this sheet against the corresponding number given in the key below. Answer serially.

Write 1   if you rarely or never behave this way
Write 2   if you occasionally behave this way
Write 3   if you sometimes behave this way
Write 4   if you often behave this way
Write 5   if you almost always behave this way

1. _____   I am available to participants to solve their problems.
2. _____   I tend to postpone or delay sessions on the topics that I do not like.
3. _____   I encourage participants to explore with me, what should or should not be done, and why.
4. _____   I communicate strong feelings to participants without caring whether this will affect the learning climate.
5. _____   I consult my colleagues while preparing a training programme.
6. _____   I am excited by new ideas and discuss them with my colleagues and participants even when I have not worked out the details.
7. _____   I accept those suggestions from participants which appeal to me.
8. _____   I answer all the question issues raised by participants.
9. _____   I take up my participants cause and fight for them.
10. _____   I show my resentment to those participants whose behaviour in class is not according to my instructions.
11. _____   I think of new and creative material for sessions.
12. _____   I collect all relevant information and literature regarding training sessions even though these are not immediately needed.
13. _____   I am available for help and guidance to participants during the training programme.
14. _____   I avoid meeting participants if I cannot satisfy them in my sessions.
15. _____   I try to set an example to participants by my own behaviour.
16. _____   I am highly involved in my well-thought-out suggestions and fight for them even if people do not pay attention to them.
17. _____   When I come across any problem during training, I study related literature and discuss it with the relevant people to find a solution.
18. _____   I am enthused by new ideas and tend to overwhelm participants with them.
19. _____   I change my approach if it helps to develop participants.
20. _____   I make the needed preparations for fieldwork and undertake all responsibilities to make participants gain from the experience.
21. _____   I strongly argue my point of view about training in staff meetings.

22. _____ I give clear instructions to participants about what should or should not be done.
23. _____ I try out new methods to make training more effective.
24. _____ I give high priority to completion of a topic, even if I have to rush through it.
25. _____ I provide participants with support, if they need or solicit it, even after the course is completed.
26. _____ I do not express my negative feelings to participants during sessions, but continue to be bothered by them.
27. _____ I raise the concerns I have about the participants behaviour in the group to encourage them to discuss these and set desirable norms.
28. _____ I do not hesitate to criticise colleagues for their bad sessions, even if they feel offended and do not accept my feedback.
29. _____ I collect the relevant material for the sessions assigned to me.
30. _____ I try out new methods of training and have no patience for consolidating those that I have already tried out.
31. _____ I learn from my superiors and from experienced persons.
32. _____ I provide participants with the appropriate solutions to their problems.
33. _____ I strongly lobby for my institute/centre amongst departmental people.
34. _____ I clearly prescribe standards of behaviour to be followed in the batch that I am coordinating.
35. _____ I always see a training event as a challenge and try out new ways of improving on the previous one.
36. _____ I include only those topics, in a training programme, which are prescribed for them.
37. _____ I provide my participants with learning material at the appropriate time to facilitate learning.
38. _____ If I am not able to answer my participant's questions, I try to divert them to some other issues.
39. _____ As I value punctuality, I start my sessions on time.
40. _____ I give my authorities a piece of my mind, and use strong language without caring for the consequences.
41. _____ I prepare, in advance, all the notes and aids needed for the teaching sessions.
42. _____ I am impatient with participants who do not give new ideas and solutions.
43. _____ I consult participants about what they like to do, and adjust my training plan accordingly.
44. _____ I help participants in details on work problems and their solutions.
45. _____ I prepare a thorough case (and put it strongly) for increasing the budget for my activities, in order to ensure their effectiveness.
46. _____ I guide my participants in detail about what to do and how they can do it.
47. _____ When I work on new ideas, I involve others as well.
48. _____ I do not accept any excuse for tasks not being completed.

Transactional Styles Inventory—Trainers (TSI-T)

Name: _____   Role: _____

Organisation: _____   Date: _____

Style	Items and Responses				Total	OEQ
Nurturing	1. ____	13. ____	25. ____	37. ____	____	____
	8. ____	20. ____	32. ____	44. ____	____	____
Regulating	3. ____	15. ____	27. ____	39. ____	____	____
	10. ____	22. ____	34. ____	46. ____	____	____
Task	5. ____	17. ____	29. ____	41. ____	____	____
	12. ____	24. ____	36. ____	48. ____	____	____
Adaptive	7. ____	19. ____	31. ____	43. ____	____	____
	2. ____	14.	26. ____	38. ____	____	____
Assertive	9. ____	21. ____	33. ____	45. ____	____	____
	4. ____	16. ____	28. ____	40. ____	____	____
Innovative	11. ____	23. ____	35. ____	47. ____	____	____
	6. ____	18. ____	30. ____	42. ____	____	____

DS ____ BS ____ Total OK ____ Not-OK ____ OK + Not-OK ____   ____   OEQ ____

38

Transactional Styles Inventory— Counselling (TSI-C)

38.1 THE INSTRUMENT AND ITS ADMINISTRATION

TSI-C has been designed to help counsellors become aware of their styles in performing counselling/coaching function with those who work with them. It may be noted that the word coaching rather than counselling has been used here. Some people misunderstand counselling as remedial help to those who are low performers or create problems. Here, coaching/counselling is used at periodical meetings that establish mutuality and help people to recognise their strengths and deficiencies, and plan enhancement of their effectiveness. The details in Chapter 35 may be looked at for administration, conceptual framework, scoring and use for HRD.

38.2 NORMS

The mean and SDs of about 50 counsellors are given below:

Function	Mean	SD
Nurturing	50	10
Regulating	50	10
Task	60	10
Confronting	60	10
Adaptive	65	10
Creative	60	10

Transactional Styles Inventory—Counselling (TSI-C)

Name: _____ Date: _____

Age: _____ Gender: _____

Institution: _____

This instrument will help you to know more about your counselling styles. There are no right or wrong answers. You will learn about yourself, if you respond to each item as candidly as possible.

Read each statement and write your response on this sheet, against the corresponding number, according to the key given below. Answer serially.

Write 1 if you rarely or never behave this way
Write 2 if you occasionally behave this way
Write 3 if you sometimes behave this way
Write 4 if you often behave this way
Write 5 if you almost always behave this way

1. _____ I suggest broad guidelines to my client regarding his situation/problem rather than specific solutions.
2. _____ I get very upset, if my client has not fulfilled the commitment he made, but I never express the same to him.
3. _____ I help my clients to look at their problems from different perspectives, including ethical aspects.
4. _____ I am impatient with the clients who do not follow the decisions taken, and bring up the problems again.
5. _____ I encourage the client to come up with alternative solutions for his problems.
6. _____ I urge the clients to experiment and take risk based on the new ideas I give them.
7. _____ When my client and I differ on a particular issue, I try to understand his point of view before making up my mind.
8. _____ Every time my client needs any help, I want to be there to provide one.
9. _____ I go deeper and explore with my clients their concerns/problems.
10. _____ I suggest useful values to my client to follow.
11. _____ I think of new solutions to the clients' problems.
12. _____ I collect a lot of background data about the client before he has a counselling session with me.
13. _____ I encourage my client to introspect regarding his situation/problem.
14. _____ I avoid meeting my client, if I have not done what I have promised to do for him.
15. _____ I encourage my clients to discuss the impact of their behaviour on others concerned.
16. _____ I do not hesitate in expressing my resentment to my client even if he is upset with it.
17. _____ I encourage the client to go deeper into his problems.
18. _____ I am attracted by new ideas and try them in my counselling sessions, but do not have time/patience to see their effectiveness.
19. _____ I do not have any problem in getting along with clients of different backgrounds.
20. _____ I take care of various aspects so that my client would not have to face any problem.
21. _____ I encourage my clients to explore assertively with their supervisors, various aspects of the issues they are facing.
22. _____ I tell my clients what they should and should not do.

23. _____ I see the client's problems as a challenge and encourage him to search innovative ways to deal with them.
24. _____ I am quite eager that solutions to the client's problems are evolved in the session with him.
25. _____ I help my client only when he approaches me.
26. _____ Whenever something goes wrong in my counselling role, I am worried but do not discuss the problems with anybody else.
27. _____ I emphasise to my clients to develop criteria and norms of their behaviour.
28. _____ I fight for my clients cause with the organisation without caring if this affects my relationship with the organisation.
29. _____ I share my own experiences and dilemma in relation to the problems I faced, similar to those posed by my client.
30. _____ No sooner I come across new counselling techniques, I try them even without fully stabilising the previous ones.
31. _____ I am sensitive to the needs and the background of different types of clients and adapt my counselling approach accordingly.
32. _____ I sympathise with my client for the tough situation he is going through, and step in to minimise/eliminate it.
33. _____ I keep transactions with my clients confidential and refuse to share those with their organisation/bosses even under pressure.
34. _____ I am concerned about ethical aspects and suggest to my clients what standards they should maintain.
35. _____ I help the client to work out alternative solutions of his problems and not remain satisfied only with the first ideas that emerge.
36. _____ I do not waste time and directly come to the problems/issues with the client.
37. _____ I believe in helping the client in analysing a problem rather than providing a complete solution to it.
38. _____ When my client does not accept my suggestions, I find it difficult to help him further.
39. _____ I do not hesitate in raising uncomfortable questions regarding the value system of my client.
40. _____ I find it difficult to control my annoyance with clients who are non-serious.
41. _____ I ask questions to help the client to analyse the problem in detail.
42. _____ I get impatient with my clients if they do not appreciate the value of new ideas and experiments.
43. _____ I am quite comfortable working with other counsellors and try to learn from their experiences.
44. _____ I attempt to offer a complete solution to a problem of my client.
45. _____ I have no hesitation in expressing my concern and feelings of dissatisfaction to my clients.
46. _____ One of my responsibilities I see is to tell my clients the proper way to approach various issues.
47. _____ If required, I encourage my clients to consult others for better solutions of their problems.
48. _____ I tend to solve the client's problems rather than attending to his emotional aspects.

Transactional Styles Inventory—Counselling (TSI-C)

Style	Items and Responses				Total	OEQ
Nurturing	1. ____	13. ____	25. ____	37. ____	____	____
	8. ____	20. ____	32. ____	44. ____	____	____
Regulating	3. ____	15. ____	27. ____	39. ____	____	____
	10. ____	22. ____	34. ____	46. ____	____	____
Task	5. ____	17. ____	29. ____	41. ____	____	____
	12. ____	24. ____	36. ____	48. ____	____	____
Adaptive	7. ____	19. ____	31. ____	43. ____	____	____
	2. ____	14. ____	26. ____	38. ____	____	____
Assertive	9. ____	21. ____	33. ____	45. ____	____	____
	4. ____	16. ____	28. ____	40. ____	____	____
Innovative	11. ____	23. ____	35. ____	47. ____	____	____
	6. ____	18. ____	30. ____	42. ____	____	____
DS ____	BS ____	Total OK ____	Not-OK ____	OK + Not-OK ____	____	OEQ ____

39

Transactional Styles Inventory— Consultants (TSI-K)

39.1 THE INSTRUMENT AND ITS ADMINISTRATION

TSI-K is meant to assess consultants, interactional styles and their effectiveness. The sections of Chapter 35 may be looked at for details about administration, conceptual framework, scoring and use for HRD.

39.2 NORMS

The mean and SDs of about 50 consultants are given below:

Function	Mean	SD
Nurturing	55	10
Regulating	55	10
Task	60	10
Confronting	50	10
Adaptive	70	10
Creative	60	10

Transactional Styles Inventory—Consultants (TSI-K)

Name: _____   Date: _____

Organisation: _____

This instrument will help you to know your consulting styles, an important aspect of a consultant's effectiveness. There are no right or wrong answers. You will learn more about yourself, if you respond honestly to each item.

Read each statement of the instrument and write your response below on the corresponding number indicating how frequently you feel/behave this way. Use the following key:

Write 1   if you rarely or never behave this way
Write 2   if you occasionally behave this way
Write 3   if you sometimes behave this way
Write 4   if you often behave this way
Write 5   if you almost always behave this way

1.	_____	I help my client at most critical stages.
2.	_____	When confronted with obstacles, I curse myself and others involved for taking such as assignment.
3.	_____	I provide various options to clients and encourage them to select the appropriate approach.
4.	_____	I criticise clients for poor implementation of my advice/suggestions/ideas/solutions even if they feel bad about it.
5.	_____	I raise several questions to the clients to help them go deeper into the problems.
6.	_____	I am excited about new interventions I read about and use them, but do not have patience to consolidate them.
7.	_____	I try to understand all aspects of the organisational process before deciding my consulting approach.
8.	_____	I encourage my clients to come to me frequently with their problems.
9.	_____	If I perceive that the client is using me not for consulting but to fulfil some other obligation (like those from financial institutions), I strongly take up the issue, and may even leave that assignment.
10.	_____	I guide my clients at every stage regarding appropriate ways of doing things
11.	_____	I think of new and creative ways to solve clients' problems.
12.	_____	I have my schedule worked out, and I strictly stick to it.
13.	_____	I keep in regular touch with my clients
14.	_____	When I have conflict with my client, I feel bad, but do not share with him.
15.	_____	My clients and I decide upon mutually agreeable norms for interaction in order to economise on time.
16.	_____	I strongly express displeasure when someone who does not have expertise in my area questions my suggestions/ideas.
17.	_____	When encountered with a problem, I also consult experts to find a solution.
18.	_____	I try new methods for solving client problems, but do not check the success of previous ones.
19.	_____	I discuss all the ramifications of my suggestions with the clients, take their views, and accept their suggestions.
20.	_____	I constantly monitor my clients' progress.

21. _____ In the consultants meets, I enthusiastically argue in favour of views based on my background and experience.
22. _____ I have some strong values, and insist that the client accepts them if I take up their assignment.
23. _____ I try new ideas to make my consultancy work more effectively.
24. _____ I am serious about my assignment, and work on it without wasting time in so-called niceties.
25. _____ My clients feel free to contact me when needed.
26. _____ I do not approach the client whose assignment I did not complete in time.
27. _____ I help my clients to examine their issues from different perspectives, including ethical aspects.
28. _____ I do not like my clients to question my advice/ideas if I am sure of the same.
29. _____ I collect data relevant to the client's problems.
30. _____ I get impatient with my clients if they do not appreciate my innovative and new approaches.
31. _____ Even in frustrating situations, I do not get put off and continue to explore possibility of working with the client.
32. _____ I provide complete solutions to my clients.
33. _____ I champion my client's cause and do not hesitate in strongly arguing his case before concerned authorities.
34. _____ I give detailed and specific guidelines to my clients.
35. _____ I view all the assignments given to me by my clients as a challenge and try new methods to solve them.
36. _____ I am concerned with my responsibility, and do not care much about my client's feelings.
37. _____ I suggest broad guidelines to my clients, rather than specific solutions regarding their situation.
38. _____ I tend to get impatient if the client asks too many difficult/uncomfortable questions, although I contain the discomfort to myself.
39. _____ I emphasise to my clients the need to develop criteria and norms.
40. _____ I am highly committed to my clients, and do not hesitate to communicate strongly my views to the organisation, even though this may strain my relations with them.
41. _____ I encourage my clients to work out alternative approaches to the problems.
42. _____ When I come up with new ideas, I try them but do not bother to work out the details.
43. _____ I change my consulting approach based on the backgrounds of the clients.
44. _____ I take responsibility for my client's problems.
45. _____ If I find that the client has not implemented and followed up as per commitment, I do not hesitate to confront him on these aspects.
46. _____ I tell my clients what they should and should not do.
47. _____ I involve my clients whenever I try a new method/idea.
48. _____ I collect a lot of data and information about the issues I am working, even when these do not seem to be useful immediately.

Transactional Styles Inventory—Consultants (TSI-K)

Style	Items and Responses				Total	OEQ
Nurturing	1. ____	13. ____	25. ____	37. ____	____	____
	8. ____	20. ____	32. ____	44. ____	____	____
Regulating	3. ____	15. ____	27. ____	39. ____	____	____
	10. ____	22. ____	34. ____	46. ____	____	____
Task	5. ____	17. ____	29. ____	41. ____	____	____
	12. ____	24. ____	36. ____	48. ____	____	____
Adaptive	7. ____	19. ____	31. ____	43. ____	____	____
	2. ____	14. ____	26. ____	38. ____	____	____
Assertive	9. ____	21. ____	33. ____	45. ____	____	____
	4. ____	16. ____	28. ____	40. ____	____	____
Innovative	11. ____	23. ____	35. ____	47 ____	____	____
	6. ____	18. ____	30. ____	42. ____	____	____
DS ____	BS ____	Total OK ____	Not-OK ____	OK + Not-OK ____	____	OEQ ____

Transactional Styles Inventory— Nurses (TSI-N)*

40.1 THE INSTRUMENT

TSI-N gives data about 12 transactional styles and effectiveness of 6 transactional functions of nurses. The instrument contains 48 items. The details of the development of the instrument are discussed elsewhere (Saxena, 2000). For administration of the instrument, its conceptual framework, scoring and use for HRD, the section in Chapter 35 may be looked at.

40.2 RELIABILITY

Analysis of responses from 50 nurses showed Alpha, Guttman split-half and Lambda values as 0.88, 0.83 and 0.88, respectively.

40.3 NORMS

The following norms (OEQ values) are suggested on the basis of data from 50 nurses (Saxena, 2000):

Functions	Mean	SD	Low	Average	High	Very High
Nurturing	54	6	< 52	52–57	57–62	> 62
Regulating	51	6	< 49	49–54	55–60	> 60
Task	56	8	< 53	53–60	61–68	> 68
Adaptive	65	11	< 61	61–70	71–80	> 80
Creative	60	11	< 56	56–65	66–75	> 75
Confronting	54	11	< 50	50–60	61–70	> 70

---

* Developed by Kanpuriya Saxena.

Transactional Styles Inventory—(Nurses) (TSI-N)

Name: _____   Date: _____

Age: _____   Gender: _____

Institution: _____   Grade: _____

This instrument will help you to know more about your styles; how you interact with public and others. There are no right or wrong answers. You will learn about yourself, if you respond to each item as candidly as possible.

Read each statement and write your response on this sheet, against the corresponding number, according to the key given below. Answer serially.

Write 1   if you rarely or never behave this way
Write 2   if you occasionally behave this way
Write 3   if you sometimes behave this way
Write 4   if you often behave this way
Write 5   if you almost always behave this way

1. _____   I assure my patients of my availability whenever they require.
2. _____   I avoid meeting my superiors if I have not been able to fulfil their expectations.
3. _____   I help my patients and attendants to see the ethical dimensions of some of their actions.
4. _____   On important matters, I communicate strong feelings and resentment even to my superiors without caring that this may affect my relationship with them.
5. _____   I listen to my patients with patience in order to work out the course of action.
6. _____   I discuss new ideas with my doctors, although I do not work out their details.
7. _____   I accept help from others and appreciate it.
8. _____   I instruct my staff in detail about work problems and their solutions.
9. _____   I take up my patients cause and fight for them.
10. _____   I give clear instructions to my patients about what should and should not be done in all matters.
11. _____   I try out new things to make treatment more effective.
12. _____   I spend my time on the specific work that has to be done.
13. _____   I help my patients to become aware of their illness and its possible causes.
14. _____   I do not express my negative feelings but continue to be bothered by them.
15. _____   I follow the hospital rules and regulations to set an example for my patients and the attendants.
16. _____   I express resentment to the authorities concerned about things that have not been done as promised.
17. _____   I ask questions to help the patient to analyse the problem in detail.
18. _____   I overwhelm my staff with new ideas for better patient care.
19. _____   When I have a difference of opinion, I try to understand others point of view before making up my mind.
20. _____   I encourage my patients to come to me frequently to seek my advice and help.
21. _____   I argue my point of view in staff meetings with the needed prior preparations.
22. _____   I clearly prescribe standards of behaviour to be followed in my ward.
23. _____   I see problems as a challenge and search innovative ways to deal with them.

24. _____ I work primarily on patients' problems, sometimes at the cost of being insensitive or inattentive to the feelings of my staff.

25. _____ I empathise with my patients and provide them help needed to overcome the problems.

26. _____ Whenever something goes wrong, I am worried but do not discuss the problem with somebody else.

27. _____ I encourage my patients to develop their own ways of recovery (exercise, etc.).

28. _____ I express resentment to my patients if they don't follow my instructions.

29. _____ I find out both from the patients and from their attendants in order to get full details of the problem.

30. _____ I try out new ideas or methods without waiting to consolidate earlier ones.

31. _____ I change my approach in dealing with my patients, if required.

32. _____ Whenever faced with a problem, I encourage my patients to contact me.

33. _____ I express my feelings and reactions frankly in meetings with my superiors.

34. _____ I make a schedule for my patients and ensure that they follow it strictly.

35. _____ I think of new ways of better physical and mental development of my patients.

36. _____ While taking a patients' history, I do not waste time and directly come to his specific problem.

37. _____ I encourage my patients to face their health problems and take responsibility for treatment.

38. _____ I find it difficult to work with a person who does not accept my suggestions.

39. _____ I help my patients to understand the reasons behind the recommended treatment and encourage them to make their own decisions.

40. _____ I have strong views and people find me uncompromising and aggressive.

41. _____ I discuss the problems of my staff with them and also their possible solutions.

42. _____ I am attracted by new ideas of patient care which I get from books or lectures, but do not have time/patience to put them into practice.

43. _____ Even in frustrating situations, I do not get put off and continue to explore possibility of providing help to the patients.

44. _____ I usually provide more protection to my patients as compared to other nurses.

45. _____ I do not hesitate to discuss patients' genuine problems with the doctor.

46. _____ I make my patients to follow the routine that I prescribe.

47. _____ I encourage my staff to think of and try different ways to help the patients.

48. _____ I do not accept any excuses of my patients for not completing their treatment as required.

Transactional Styles Inventory—Nurses (TSI-N)

Style	Items and Responses				Total	OEQ
Nurturing	1. ____	13. ____	25. ____	37. ____	____	____
	8. ____	20. ____	32. ____	44. ____	____	____
Regulating	3. ____	15. ____	27. ____	39. ____	____	____
	10. ____	22. ____	34. ____	46. ____	____	____
Task	5. ____	17. ____	29. ____	41. ____	____	____
	12. ____	24. ____	36. ____	48. ____	____	____
Adaptive	7. ____	19. ____	31. ____	43. ____	____	____
	2. ____	14. ____	26. ____	38. ____	____	____
Assertive	9. ____	21. ____	33. ____	45. ____	____	____
	4. ____	16. ____	28. ____	40. ____	____	____
Innovative	11. ____	23. ____	35. ____	47. ____	____	____
	6. ____	18. ____	30. ____	42. ____	____	____
DS ____	BS ____	Total OK ____	Not-OK ____	OK + Not-OK ____	____	OEQ ____

Transactional Styles Inventory— Journalism (TSI-J)*

41.1 THE INSTRUMENT AND ITS ADMINISTRATION

TSI-J gives data for about 12 transactional styles and the effectiveness of 6 transactional functions of journalists. Section on administration of the instrument, conceptual framework, scoring and use for HRD given in Chapter 35 may be looked at.

41.2 RELIABILITY

Analysis of responses from 50 respondents showed Alpha, Guttman and split-half Lambda values as 0.88, 0.83 and 0.88, respectively.

41.3 NORMS

The following norms (OEQ values) are suggested on the basis of data from 50 respondents (Saxena, 2000):

Functions	Mean	SD	Low	Average	High	Very High
Nurturing	54	6	> 52	52–57	57–62	> 62
Regulating	51	6	> 49	49–54	55–60	> 60
Task	56	8	> 53	53–60	61–68	> 68
Adaptive	65	11	> 61	61–70	71–80	> 80
Creative	60	11	> 56	56–65	66–75	> 75
Confronting	54	11	> 50	50–60	61–70	> 70

---

* Developed by Divya Singhal.

Transactional Styles Inventory—Journalist (TSI-J)

Name: _____　　Date: _____

Age: _____　　Gender: _____

Institution: _____　　Grade: _____

This instrument will help you to know more about your nursing styles—how you interact with your patients and others. There are no right or wrong answers. You will learn about yourself, if you respond to each item as candidly as possible.

Read each statement and write your response on this sheet, against the corresponding number, according to the key given below. Answer serially.

Write 1　if you rarely or never behave this way
Write 2　if you occasionally behave this way
Write 3　if you sometimes behave this way
Write 4　if you often behave this way
Write 5　if you almost always behave this way

1. _____ I am available to my junior colleagues for any guidance they need from me.
2. _____ I delay doing things that I don't like.
3. _____ I encourage my colleagues to discuss with me what should or should not be published and why.
4. _____ I communicate strong feelings and resentment to my colleagues without caring that this will affect my relationship with them.
5. _____ I go deep into several aspects while working on a new investigative news matter for publishing.
6. _____ I discuss with my fellow friends new ideas that occur to me, but do not follow up such discussions.
7. _____ I follow those principles of the press that seem to give it its identity.
8. _____ I guide all my young colleagues in their assignments.
9. _____ I don't hesitate in publishing my point of view on the various issues regarding any matter in the society.
10. _____ I admonish my people for not acting according to my instructions.
11. _____ I think of new and creative material for my articles.
12. _____ I collect all relevant information and statements regarding investigations even though these are not immediately needed.
13. _____ I help my colleagues to improve their writing skills.
14. _____ I avoid meeting my editor and colleagues if I have not been able to fulfil their expectations.
15. _____ I try to set an example to my younger colleagues by my own behaviour.
16. _____ I am highly involved in my well-thought-out suggestions and fight for them even if people do not pay attention to them.
17. _____ While working on some issues, I try to meet most of the parties concerned.
18. _____ I overwhelm my colleagues with new ideas.
19. _____ I am open to suggestions by my editor, colleagues and subordinates.
20. _____ I instruct my people in detail about work problems and their solutions.
21. _____ I strongly argue my point of view in press conferences.

22. _____ I give clear instructions to my people about what should or should not be published.
23. _____ I try out new ideas to make my writing more effective.
24. _____ I give high priority to completion of a news item, even if I have to rush through it.
25. _____ I reassure my people of my help whenever needed.
26. _____ I do not express my negative feelings to the editor, but continue to be bothered by them.
27. _____ I help my colleagues and the staff to examine the appropriateness of proposed actions.
28. _____ I do not hesitate to criticise colleagues for their bad articles, even if they feel offended and do not accept my feedback.
29. _____ I collect the relevant material for the task assigned to me from several sources.
30. _____ Even while earlier stories have not been fully investigated, the new ones attract me and I get involved with them.
31. _____ I change my approach to a problem if the changed context requires so.
32. _____ I encourage my fellow friends to come to me frequently for my advice and help.
33. _____ I strongly lobby for my newspaper/magazine.
34. _____ I clearly prescribe standards of behaviour to be followed in my work unit/team.
35. _____ I always see journalism as a challenge and try out new methods of improving on the previous one.
36. _____ I cover only those programmes/matters which are related to my beats.
37. _____ I assure my colleagues of my availability in discussing their problems.
38. _____ If I am not able to find the details of a case in some manner, I try to divert my readers to some other issues.
39. _____ As I value truth, I follow it in my writings.
40. _____ I express strong resentment to the administrative bodies of the society for a genuine cause without caring about the consequences.
41. _____ I take a matter or scan and work on it in order to find the truth.
42. _____ I like to try new ideas or methods of writing without caring how the readers react to them.
43. _____ I talk to people of different backgrounds about what is going wrong in our society and publish their problems.
44. _____ I help my colleagues in detail with their tasks and suggest ways to solve them.
45. _____ I do not hesitate in discussing sensitive social issues with high-ranking government officials and other social leaders.
46. _____ I criticise bad things happening today in our society.
47. _____ When I work on a new matter, I involve others as well.
48. _____ I do not accept any excuse for news/articles not completed on time.

Transactional Styles Inventory—Journalism (TSI-J)

Style	Items and Responses				Total	OEQ
Nurturing	1. ____	13. ____	25. ____	37. ____	____	____
	8. ____	20. ____	32. ____	44. ____	____	____
Regulating	3. ____	15. ____	27. ____	39. ____	____	____
	10. ____	22. ____	34. ____	46. ____	____	____
Task	5. ____	17. ____	29. ____	41. ____	____	____
	12. ____	24. ____	36. ____	48. ____	____	____
Adaptive	7. ____	19. ____	31. ____	43. ____	____	____
	2. ____	14. ____	26. ____	38. ____	____	____
Assertive	9. ____	21. ____	33. ____	45. ____	____	____
	4. ____	16 ____	28. ____	40. ____	____	____
Innovative	11. ____	23. ____	35. ____	47. ____	____	____
	6. ____	18. ____	30. ____	42. ____	____	____

DS ____ BS ____ Total OK ____ Not-OK ____ OK + Not-OK ____ ____ OEQ ____

Sales Styles: Sales Troika

42.1 THE INSTRUMENT AND ITS ADMINISTRATION

The sales troika contains five sections representing five important issues that a salesman has to manage; these are sales goals, decision-making, anxiety management, conflict management and self-management. In each section, nine statements are given and the respondent is required to rank order them for their accuracy in describing him.

42.2 CONCEPTUAL FRAMEWORK

A person's style in selling and marketing are also based on different concepts of interaction—a salesman with his customers or a sales executive with his sales force.

Blake and Mouton (1970) proposed a sales grid as the basis of understanding sales styles. The two axes of the grid are a person's concern for making a sale and concern for the customer. As in other concepts of Blake and Mouton, five styles were proposed; these are as follows:

1,1   *Take it or leave it.* I place the product, and it sells itself as and when it can. (Low on customer and sales).

9,1   *Push the product.* I put all the pressure to get the customer, to buy the product. (Low on customer, high on sales).

1,9   *People oriented.* I see to it that the customer likes me, as a good relationship helps a sale. (Low on sales, high on customer).

5,5   *Sales technique.* I influence the customer by a mix of relationship and product emphasis. (Medium on both).

9,9   *Problem-solving.* I work with the customer for a decision to solve a problem or to meet the customer's need. (High on both).

Blake and Mouton developed an elaborate sales grid for training sales people. They proposed seven aspects for each of the nine styles—attitude, product knowledge, competitors, concern for customers, selling expenses, emotions and customer's response. They also proposed a customer grid, the two axes being concern for the purchase and concern for the salesman. They emphasised the importance of 'grid communication' and how salesmen with different styles deal with it (asking and building questions, customer's point of view, handling emotions and listening). They proposed six grid elements consisting of decisions, convictions, energetic enthusiasm, conflict, temper and humour.

Blake and Mouton proposed concern for sales and concern for customers as the two axes of the grid. They neglected a third aspect or axis—concern for the organisation. Salesmen not only sell a product, they also 'sell' their company. Unless they have high concern for their company, they may lack empathy with other departments such as production, finance, service, etc., and may unknowingly communicate information damaging to the company's reputation.

To make up this deficiency, a Sales Troika has been proposed with three dimensions—concern for the customer, concern for the product and concern for the organisation. The analogy is drawn from a 3-horse carriage or troika in which all the three horses need to be strong and well coordinated for a smooth journey. Similarly, a sales executive troika has also been proposed. The three dimensions are concern for sales, concern for salesmen and concern for the organisation.

The nine styles of the sales troika and the sales executive troika are as follows:

1,1,1　*Routine sale oriented.* My obligation to my company is to inform the customer about our product; the sale will be made if the customer needs it.

1,9,1　*Customer-oriented.* My obligation is to the customer who has his own feelings. I can make the sale by responding and relating to him as a person.

9,1,1　*Product-oriented.* My obligation is to sell the product, and this can be done by working hard to convince the customer that it will be the most suitable one for him.

9,9,1　*Solution-oriented.* My obligation is to help the customer find the right product for his needs, and help him take a decision by giving relevant information about my product.

1,1,9　*Company-oriented.* My obligation is to project a good image of my company. I believe this will help me sell the product.

1,9,9　*Loyalty–relationship-oriented.* My obligation is to both my company and my customer. I respond to my customer's feelings and interests, and let him know about my company. I believe this will get me the sales.

9,1,9　*Company product oriented.* My company's products are the best in the line, and I work hard to convince the customer about the suitability of the products produced by my company.

9,9,9　*Creative solution-oriented.* My obligation is to sell my company to the customer. I do this by helping the customer find the right product for his needs and by helping him to consider my product before arriving at a decision.

5,5,5   *Technique-oriented.* I can sell my company's product by using well-known sales techniques that I know work well.

42.3 SCORING

The ranks given by the respondents to the nine statements are scored with the help of the sales troika key (appended). The respondents can, and preferably should, score their completed instrument. The scores are entered on a score sheet (appended). The total and mean scores of the nine styles are noted down in the last row (ranging from 9 to 1).

42.4 USE FOR HRD

The instrument can be used to help participants plan their effectiveness as salesmen. The chapter contains material useful for organising the training of sales force. Role-plays can be organised to practice some effective styles.

Sales Troika Checklist

Name: _____ Role: _____

Organisation: _____ Date: _____

The style of a salesman is influenced by several factors. Five such significant factors are listed below. Please read the nine statements under each factor and rank them in order for their accuracy in describing you. Put 9 against the statement you think describes you most accurately. Put 8 against the statement you think describes you very accurately but not as accurately as a statement against which you have put 9. Continue in this way. Put 1 against the statement which describes you least accurately.

Do this for each of the five sections independently. Remember, you are required to rank and not rate the statements; each number from 1 to 9 will be given only to one statement.

A. Sales Goals

__ 1. My main obligation is to inform a customer about our product.
__ 2. My main obligation is to please a customer and personally relate to him.
__ 3. My main obligation is to sell the product.
__ 4. My main obligation is to help a customer solve his problem.
__ 5. My main obligation is to represent my company and its good name.
__ 6. My main obligation is to personally relate to a customer through the good name of my company.
__ 7. My main obligation is to sell the product of my company.
__ 8. My main obligation is to sell the company to a customer by helping him to take the best decision.
__ 9. My main obligation is to use tried techniques to sell my product.

B. Decision-making

__ 1. I directly influence and push for decisions in favour of my product.
__ 2. I work with a customer on agreed decisions.
__ 3. Decisions are made by a customer and my information about my company influences him.
__ 4. Decisions are made by a customer who is influenced by both my good relations with him and the image of my company.
__ 5. Decisions are made by a customer on my making the information about my product available to him.
__ 6. Decisions are made by a customer and my good relations with him influence him.
__ 7. I work with a customer for reaching decisions that solve his problems and for a continuing relationship with him.
__ 8. I influence the decision but also allow a customer to take his decision.
__ 9. I influence decisions by aggressively selling the product and the good name of my company.

C. Anxiety Management

__ 1. I try to stay unperturbed in the hope that some solution will emerge in due course.
__ 2. I try to locate the cause of anxiety, and share the concern with the customer and my colleagues to work out a solution.
__ 3. I become more active in arguing for my product and my company.
__ 4. Under anxiety, my arguments become more forceful and I become more active.
__ 5. I avoid anxiety-provoking situations.
__ 6. I show and assure warmth and personal concern.
__ 7. I assure warmth and support from the company.

___ 8.   I try to recognise the cause of anxiety and share the concern with the customer.

___ 9.   I avoid anxiety, but when confronted I report it to my superiors and get their help.

D.   Conflict Management

___ 1.   I avoid conflicts and remain neutral.

___ 2.   I deal firmly with a situation through my ability and knowledge.

___ 3.   I avoid conflicts but when faced with them seek the support of my company.

___ 4.   I try to diagnose the conflict and find a solution that will help maintain a mutually profitable relationship between my company and a customer.

___ 5.   I work on personal relations and try to arouse friendly feelings.

___ 6.   I try to resolve the conflict by finding out the causes.

___ 7.   I work on personal relations and good relations with my company.

___ 8.   I use my company's strength to solve the conflict my way.

___ 9.   I try to remain undisturbed and work to resolve the conflict.

E.   Self-management

___ 1.   I try to maintain good relations and to sell my company's products.

___ 2.   I try to win my arguments and take the help of my company.

___ 3.   I am concerned with my company's name and, most of the time, I feel people do not understand us. I do not like such situations.

___ 4.   I try to dominate others and rebuff them with my arguments.

___ 5.   I try to adapt myself to the situation.

___ 6.   I try to collect data and facts and to find solutions to problems. I also enjoy relating to people and helping them find solutions to their problems.

___ 7.   I try to appeal to other people's feelings and also tell them how my company can help them.

___ 8.   I try to help others to see what is good for them.

___ 9.   I try to appeal to the good relations and feelings of others.

Sales Troika Key

		1,1,1	1,9,1	9,1,1	9,9,1	1,1,9	1,9,9	9,1,9	9,9,9	5,5,5
A.	Sales goals	1	2	3	4	5	6	7	8	9
B.	Decision-making	5	6	1	2	3	4	9	7	8
C.	Anxiety management	5	6	4	8	9	7	3	2	1
D.	Conflict management	1	5	2	6	3	7	8	4	9
E.	Self-management	5	9	4	8	3	7	2	6	1

Score Sheet

Enter the numbers you have marked against each statement in the appropriate columns, against each of the five dimensions

		1,1,1	1,9,1	9,1,1	9,9,1	1,1,9	1,9,9	9,1,9	9,9,9	5,5,5	Total
A.	Sales goals										
B.	Decision-making										
C.	Anxiety management										
D.	Conflict management										
E.	Self-management										
Total											
Average											

43
Sales Executive Styles: Sales Executive Troika

43.1 THE INSTRUMENT AND ITS ADMINISTRATION

The sales executive troika contains five sections, representing five important issues that a sales executive has to manage—sales goals, decision-making, anxiety, conflicts and the self. In each section, nine statements are given, and the respondent is required to rank them in order for their accuracy in describing himself.

43.2 CONCEPTUAL FRAMEWORK

A person's style in selling and marketing are also based on different concepts of interaction—a salesman with his customers or a sales executive with his sales force.

Blake and Mouton (1970) proposed a sales grid as the basis of understanding sales styles. The two axes of the grid are a person's concern for making a sale and concern for the customer. As in other concepts of Blake and Mouton, five styles were proposed; these are as follows:

1,1 *Take it or leave it.* I place the product, and it sells itself as and when it can. (Low on customer and sales).

9,1 *Push the product.* I put all the pressure to get the customer, to buy the product. (Low on customer, high on sales).

1,9 *People-oriented.* I see to it that the customer likes me, as a good relationship helps a sale. (Low on sales, high on customer).

5,5 *Sales technique.* I influence the customer by a mix of relationship and product emphasis. (Medium on both).

9,9 *Problem-solving.* I work with the customer for a decision to solve a problem or to meet the customer's need. (High on both).

Blake and Mouton developed an elaborate sales grid for training sales people. They proposed seven aspects for each of the nine styles—attitude, product knowledge, competitors, concern for customers, selling expenses, emotions and customer's response. They also proposed a customer grid, the two axes being concern for the purchase and concern for the salesman. They emphasised the importance of 'grid communication' and how salesmen with different styles deal with it (asking and building questions, customer's point of view, handling emotions and listening). They proposed six grid elements consisting of decisions, convictions, energetic enthusiasm, conflict, temper and humour.

The 9 styles of the sales executive troika are as follows:

1,1,1   *Routine*. My obligation to my company is to see that the salesmen carry on working according to our plans.

1,9,1   *Friendly*. My obligation is to the salesmen who are people with feelings. If they are satisfied, sales of products will be high and the company will do well.

9,1,1   *Target-oriented*. My obligation is to sell the product. This can be done by pushing sales men, who will eventually be happy if they sell the product. In this way, the company will prosper.

9,9,1   *Friendly task master*. My obligation is to see that salesmen are happy and satisfied and are able to sell the product. This will increase the business of the company.

1,1,9   *Marketing-oriented*. My obligation is to develop an overall marketing policy for the company. If the company has a sound marketing policy, sales will be high and salesmen will be motivated.

1,9,9   *Friendly loyal*. My obligation is to develop an overall effective marketing strategy for the company and to develop my sales people. Product sales will take care of themselves.

9,1,9   *Target marketing-oriented*. My obligation is to get good sales for my product and develop an appropriate marketing strategy. In such a situation, salesmen will have job satisfaction.

9,9,9   *Creative*. My obligation is to develop a sound marketing force and policy in my company. I can do this by examining, together with my salesmen, how sales of our products can be increased and how new markets can be developed.

5,5,5   *Compromiser*. My obligation is to balance the emphasis on developing salesmen, marketing policy and sales of products.

There are several elements in the sales or sales executive troika. The eleven dimensions are described as follows in relation to the nine troika styles.

1. General Attitude

1,1,1 :   Routine, indifferent, passive

1,9,1 :   Warm, friendly, listening, helpful

9,1,1 :   Success-oriented, pushing, argumentative, not caring for personal relationships
9,9,1 :   Problem-solving, exploring issues jointly with the customer
1,1,9 :   Routine and passive, but having faith in the company
1,9,9 :   Warm, friendly, helpful, reassuring on behalf of the company
9,1,9 :   Success-oriented, pushing, argumentative, supporting the company
5,5,5 :   Technique-oriented, both success-oriented and friendly
9,9,9 :   Problem-solving, exploring issues jointly with the customer, using the company's resources effectively

2. Attitude towards Customer

1,1,1 :   The customer will buy what he needs.
1,9,1 :   The customer is a genuine person, with feelings and problems.
9,1,1 :   The customer is rather ignorant about the product and needs convincing.
9,9,1 :   The customer is interested in finding solutions to his problems through the purchase.
1,1,9 :   The customer will buy what he needs, and the company can fulfil this need.
1,9,9 :   The customer is a person with feelings and needs reassurance, both at the personal level and on behalf of the company.
9,1,9 :   The customer is rather ignorant and needs convincing about the quality of the product and the goodwill of the company.
5,5,5 :   The customer looks for well-known brands of products.
9,9,9 :   The customer is interested in finding solutions to his problems, and the product and the company can help him do this.

3. Participation

1,1,1 :   Lacks initiative and involvement.
1,9,1 :   Talks only to please the customer.
9,1,1 :   Is very active but disregards feelings and needs of the customer
9,9,1 :   Involved.
1,1,9 :   Lacks initiative and involvement, and talks only of his company.
1,9,9 :   Talks about his organisation with a view to help the customer.
9,1,9 :   Is very active in talking about the product and company, but disregards the customer's feelings and needs.
5,5,5 :   Is fairly active and talks about successful experiences.
9,9,9 :   Is highly involved in helping the customer talk about his problems and research solutions in which his product and company can help.

4. Managing Objections

1,1,1 : Doesn't give any importance to the customer's objections; passively accept the objections raised by the customer about the product or the company's reputation.

1,9,1 : Agrees with some objections but appeals to the strength of the customer; avoids situations of disagreement.

9,1,1 : Aggressively gives logical and competent replies. He is ruthless and takes up objections as challenges.

9,9,1 : Distinguishes between objections that show the customer's feelings and those that show his genuine difficulties; responds positively to customer's communications and explores with them the possibility of finding solutions to problems. However, he shows no respect for his company when the objections relate to it.

1,1,9 : Defends his company, but otherwise doesn't care for the customer's objections.

1,9,9 : Agrees with some objections, but appeals to personal feelings and uses the company's name and goodwill.

9,1,9 : Aggressively logical and competent and ruthless in answering all objections by overwhelming the customer with information and the company's goodwill.

5,5,5 : Accepts some of the customer's objections. Answers some showing product knowledge and the goodwill of the company.

9,9,9 : Uses objections as part of the process of problem-solving. Understands the objections with empathy and helps the customer by both reassuring him about follow-up by the company and giving him more information. Accepts those genuine objections and reassures to communicate them to the company.

5. Relationship Building

1,1,1 : No initiative; cold.

1,9,1 : Considers the customer as a very important person, and goes out of his way to please him; becomes personal.

9,1,1 : Gives importance to the expert–client relationship but is not concerned about building relations with the customer.

9,9,1 : Builds a respectful relationship with the customer in the process of helping him.

1,1,9 : No initiative; cold.

1,9,9 : Considers the customer a very important person and builds personal relations with him while projecting a very good image of the company.

9,1,9 : Considers the expert–client relationship important and hopes to build a relationship between the customer and the company.

5,5,5 : Builds relations with the customer without involving himself personally.

9,9,9 : Is genuinely interested in building a mutually helpful relationship with the customer and, in the process, a long-term relationship between the customer and the company.

6. Authenticity

1,1,1 : Has no concern for authenticity.

1,9,1 : May lack authenticity because of his eagerness to please the customer.

9,1,1 : May lack authenticity because of lack of concern for the customer and his company.

9,9,1 : May lack authenticity because of lack of concern for the company.

1,1,9 : No concern for authenticity.

1,9,9 : May lack authenticity because of his eagerness to please the customer and defend his company.

9,1,9 : May lack authenticity because of lack of concern for the customer.

5,5,5 : Lacks authenticity because he relies on techniques.

9,9,9 : Authentic, because of his concern for problem-solving and eagerness to use product knowledge and the company's resources to help the customer.

7. Product Knowledge

1,1,1 : Has limited and routine knowledge. Gives a lot of literature to the customer.

1,9,1 : Limited knowledge. Tries to compensate with good relations.

9,1,1 : Good knowledge. Overwhelms the customer with technical information.

9,9,1 : Good knowledge. Gives information whenever it is wanted.

1,1,9 : Limited and routine knowledge. Talks a lot about the company and gives a lot of literature to the customer.

1,9,9 : Limited knowledge. Tries to compensate with good relations and talking about the company.

9,1,9 : Good knowledge. Overwhelms the customer with technical information and information about the company.

5,5,5 : Normal knowledge. Quotes instances where the company's product has been useful.

9,9,9 : Good knowledge. Uses his knowledge of the product and the services of the company to help the customer see his problem and work out a solution.

8. Market Knowledge and Attitude

1,1,1 : Very little knowledge about the market. Avoids discussing competitors' products.

1,9,1 : Very little market knowledge. Regards it as unnecessary.

9,1,1 : Good market knowledge. Runs down competitors' products by exposing their weaknesses.

9,9,1 : Good market knowledge. Sees both good and weak points in other products and encourages a discussion of these by the customer.

1,1,9 :   Very little market knowledge. Regards competitor firms with disdain.

1,9,9 :   Very little market knowledge. Regards it as unnecessary and discusses his instead.

9,1,9 :   Good market knowledge. Runs down competitors and their product.

5,5,5 :   Fairly good market knowledge. Knows techniques and formulae.

9,9,9 :   Good market knowledge. Listens to the customer and also discusses the good points of competitors and their products. Helps the customer to see how his problem can be solved better by his company's product and support.

9. Customer Response

1,1,1 :   Lacks interest and could not care less.

1,9,1 ·   Is empathetic, listens carefully and is reassuring.

9,1,1 :   Is competent and knowledgeable but does not listen enough. Is impatient, aggressive and lacks understanding.

9,9,1 :   Is empathetic and competent. Listens, understands and helps in decisions. However, does not seem reassuring as a representative of his company.

1,1,9 :   Is neither empathetic nor competent, but uses his company's name and hopes to go by it.

1,9,9 :   Is empathetic and listens carefully. Is reassuring that the customer has the company's backing. Too personal and company representative.

9,1,9 :   Is competent and knowledgeable. An able person with company backing. Does not listen and is impatient and aggressive.

5,5,5 :   Is fairly warm and understanding. Knows techniques well, and has knowledge about his company.

9,9,9 :   Listens, shows respect, is competent and helpful in finding solutions. He is reassuring with his competence and understanding, and the experience of his company.

10. Closing Interviews

1,1,1 :   Abrupt closing.

1,9,1 :   Promises a personal meeting or invites the customer for a social visit.

9,1,1 :   Reminds the customer about the product's good points.

9,9,1 :   Closes interviews when solutions are worked out, and summarises the next steps to be taken.

1,1,9 :   Closes abruptly, reminding the customer of his company's name.

1,9,9 :   Offers a social meeting and a visit to the company.

9,1,9 :   Closes interview by being reassuring about the product and the company producing it.

5,5,5 :   Response varies with different situations. He uses known techniques.

9,9,9 : Closes interview when a satisfactory solution is worked out. Reassures the customer by recapitulating the next steps, and the guarantee and follow-up service by the company.

11. Opening the Interview

1,1,1 : Unenthusiastic. Gives information.
1,9,1 : Friendly approach. Talks about the customer's problems.
9,1,1 : Enthusiastic. Gives a lot of information about the product.
9,9,1 : Pleasing approach. Self-confident. Raises questions.
1,1,9 : Talks about his company's experience.
1,9,9 : Talks about the customer's problems and his company's experience.
9,1,9 : Talks about the product and the company's experience.
5,5,5 : Approach is not natural and more according to some tried-out techniques.
9,9,9 : Asks pertinent and reassuring questions. Answers showing product knowledge and emphasising the company's strengths.

43.3 SCORING

Ranks given by the correspondents to the nine statements are scored with the help of the sales troika key (appended). The respondents, preferably, should themselves score their completed instrument. The scores are entered on a sheet, 'Your Score' (appended). The total and mean scores of the nine styles are noted down in the last row (ranging from 9 to 1).

43.4 USE FOR HRD

The instrument can be used to help participants plan their effectiveness as sales executives. Training of sales executives can be organised. Role-plays can be organised to practice some effective styles.

Sales Executive Troika Checklist

Name: _____   Role: _____

Organisation: _____   Date: _____

A sales executive's style is influenced by several factors. Five significant ones are listed below. Under each, there are nine statements. Please rank them for their accuracy to describe you. Put 9 against the statement you think describes you most accurately. Put 8 against the statement you think describes you very accurately, but not as accurately as the statement against which you have put 9. Go on putting numbers in this way. Put 1 against the statement that describes you least accurately.

Do this for each of the five sections independently.

A. Sales Goals
    __ 1. My main obligation is to see that salesmen carry out their work according to our plans.
    __ 2. My main obligation is to keep my salesmen happy and satisfied.
    __ 3. My main obligation is to sell the product.
    __ 4. My main obligation is to see that salesmen are happy and satisfied, and able to sell the product.
    __ 5. My main obligation is to develop an overall marketing strategy for my company.
    __ 6. My main obligation is to keep my salesmen happy and to develop an overall marketing strategy for my company.
    __ 7. My main obligation is to get good sales results for my product and to develop a marketing strategy.
    __ 8. My main obligation is to develop a sound marketing force and strategy through motivated salesmen who meet targets.
    __ 9. My main obligation is to use tried techniques to balance the emphasis on sales, motivation of salesmen and marketing strategy.

B. Decision-Making
    __ 1. I directly influence and push for decisions.
    __ 2. I work with the salesmen on agreed decisions.
    __ 3. Decisions are made by the salesmen. My knowledge about the market and concern for marketing policy influences them.
    __ 4. Decisions are made by the salesmen, who are influenced by my good relations with them and my knowledge about the company's marketing policy.
    __ 5. Decisions are made by the salesmen in the light of the general plans worked out.
    __ 6. Decisions are made by the salesmen but my good relations with them also influence them.
    __ 7. I work with my salesmen for reaching decisions that solve the problems of sales and for developing a sound marketing strategy for the company.
    __ 8. I influence the decision and also allow the salesmen to take decisions. I try to achieve sales and work out a marketing strategy.
    __ 9. I influence the decisions by pushing the salesmen to sell more, and by working out a sound marketing strategy.

C. Anxiety Management
    __ 1. I try to stay unperturbed in the hope that some solution will emerge in due course.
    __ 2. I try to locate the cause of anxiety and share the concern with my salesmen and other colleagues to work out a solution.
    __ 3. I become more active in arguing for my point of view and my marketing strategy.

___ 4. Under anxiety, my arguments become more forceful and I become more active.

___ 5. I avoid anxiety-provoking situations.

___ 6. I show and assure warmth and personal concern.

___ 7. In arguments, I show warmth and also the support of the company.

___ 8. I try to recognise the cause of anxiety and share the concern with my salesmen.

___ 9. I avoid anxiety, but when confronted I try to get help from my superiors.

D. Conflict Management

___ 1. I avoid conflicts and remain neutral.

___ 2. I deal firmly with the situation through my ability and knowledge.

___ 3. I avoid conflicts, but, when they are unavoidable, I view them in the larger corporate context level.

___ 4. I try to diagnose the conflict and find a solution that will help maintain a mutually helpful and collaborative relationship for a creative marketing strategy.

___ 5. I work on personal relations and try to arouse friendly feelings.

___ 6. I try to resolve the conflict by finding out the causes.

___ 7. I work on personal relations and the general strategy and image of my company.

___ 8. I use my personal strength and the strength of the marketing policy in winning my point of view.

___ 9. I try to remain undisturbed and work for the resolution of the conflict.

E. Self-management

___ 1. I try to maintain good relations, achieve sales and work out a marketing policy.

___ 2. I try to win my arguments and seek help from my wider marketing orientation.

___ 3. I am concerned about my company's name. Most of the time, I feel salesmen do not understand it, and I do not like such situations.

___ 4. I try to dominate and rebuff others with my arguments.

___ 5. I try to adapt myself to the situation.

___ 6. I try to collect data and facts to find solutions to problems. I also enjoy relating to people and helping them search for solutions to their problems.

___ 7. I try to appeal to the feelings of others (mainly salesmen) and also tell them how an overall strategy will help them.

___ 8. I try to help salesmen and others to see what is good for them.

___ 9. I try to appeal to our good relations and to the feelings of salesmen and others.

Sales Executive Troika Key

	1, 1, 1	1, 9, 1	9, 1, 1	9, 9, 1	1, 1, 9	1, 9, 9	9, 1, 9	9, 9, 9	5, 5, 5
A. Sales goals	1	2	3	4	5	6	7	8	9
B. Decision-making	5	6	1	2	3	4	9	7	8
C. Anxiety management	5	6	4	8	9	7	3	2	1
D. Conflict management	1	5	2	6	3	7	8	4	9
E. Self-management	5	9	4	8	3	7	2	6	1

Sales Executive Troika Score Sheet

Name: _____   Role: _____

Organisation: _____   Date: _____

After consulting the scoring key, enter the ranks you have given against each statement in the appropriate columns, against each of the five dimensions.

	1, 1, 1	1, 9, 1	9, 1, 1	9, 9, 1	1, 1, 9	1, 9, 9	9, 1, 9	9, 9, 9	5, 5, 5	Total
A. Sales goals										
B. Decision-making										
C. Anxiety management										
D. Conflict management										
E. Self-management										
Total										
Mean										

Conflict Management Styles: Opinion Survey of Organisational Conflicts

44.1 THE INSTRUMENT AND ITS ADMINISTRATION

The Opinion Survey of Organisational Conflicts (OSOC) has been prepared to help managers examine their styles of conflict management and take steps to improve their effectiveness to manage conflicts.

OSOC contains 24 statements, three for each of the eight styles of conflict management, four avoidance styles and four approach styles. The respondent is required to read each statement and indicate how strongly he agrees with it using a 5-point scale.

44.2 CONFLICT MANAGEMENT STYLES

In the management of conflicts, the styles of the persons involved in a conflict (either as individuals or as groups, especially group leaders) play a critical role. Some styles may promote a search for solutions whereas others may lead to a deadlock. Conflict management styles are related to the theory or approach used to understand conflicts.

Several approaches to conflict management have been proposed. Two of these are quite well known, one by Likert and Likert (1976) and the other by Blake, Shepard and Mouton (1964). Using the famous grid model of Blake and Mouton (1970), Hall (1977) has proposed a 2-dimensional model of conflict management. He developed an instrument containing twelve items, three each for 4-dimensions comprising one's personal view of conflict, interpersonal conflict, conflicts in task groups and relations between groups. The respondent is asked to choose one of five alternatives. These alternatives represent five styles of conflict management, showing different degrees of concern for two dimensions—personal goals and relationship. Thus, there are five styles: 1, 1 (low concern for both); 9, 1 (high concern for personal goals and low concern for relationship); 1, 9 (low concern for personal goals and high concern for relationship); 9, 9 (high concern for both); and 5, 5 (moderate concern for both). Thomas and Kilman (1974) developed management of difference exercise (MODE), consisting of 30 sets of paired items, each item describing one of the five conflict styles of the managerial grid. High reliability, validity and low social desirability have been reported (Kilman & Thomas, 1977; Ruble & Thomas, 1976; Womack, 1988). Another instrument by Rahim (1986), the Rahim organisational conflict inventory (ROCI) is a 28-item 5-point Likert scale. ROCI also uses the managerial grid as a conceptual framework. High reliability, high validity and low social desirability have been reported (Rahim, 1986; Weider-Hatfield, 1988). Van de Vleiert and Kabanoff (1990) have reported that while MODE discriminates poorly between the theoretically and practically important styles of competing and collaborating, ROCI discriminates between them extremely well. The latter emphasises the use of power in the styles, while the former (MODE) does not.

Likert and Likert have extended the concept of participatory management to the areas of conflict and have given enough evidence to show that a more participatory style of management improves conflict management. Blake, Shepard and Mouton have suggested different approaches and styles of conflict management. They have proposed that three basic assumptions or orientations are important in relation to conflict management: (a) conflicts are inevitable and agreement is not possible; (b) conflicts are not inevitable and yet agreement is not possible; and (c) although there is conflict, agreement is possible. They suggested that these three orientations get combined with three degrees of active–passive attitude (active orientation having high stakes, medium active having moderate stakes, and passive or orientation having low stakes). A combination of three assumptions about conflict and three orientations of 'activeness' give nine different modes of conflict resolution. The basic idea of Blake and Mouton has been used in suggesting different modes or styles of conflict management in this chapter. Before discussing these, let us briefly review a few other approaches.

Thomas (1976) has suggested two main dimensions of approaching conflicts—cooperativeness (attempting to satisfy another's concerns) and assertiveness (attempting to satisfy one's own concerns). Using a grid model, these two dimensions give five strategies—avoiding (low-low), accommodation (high-low), competition (low-high), collaboration (high-high) and compromise (medium-medium). Filley (1978) has contrasted power-oriented methods with problem-solving methods of conflict management.

Pruitt (1977) makes a distinction between pressure tactics and exchange-oriented tactics. He has suggested the following exchange-oriented tactics:

1. Make a small unilateral concession together with the clear communication that no further concession will be forthcoming until the adversary concedes. This sometimes starts a sequence of alternating concessions.
2. Propose an exchange of concessions. This is an obvious approach but often involves considerable risk because it is tantamount to making a unilateral concession.
3. Informally signal and show willingness to make a later concession if the adversary makes one now.

4. Seek a private, informal conference with the adversary or his representative, in which it may be possible to talk more freely and frankly about compromise than in the formal negotiation meetings.
5. Propose an exchange of concessions through an intermediary whose statements can be disowned if the adversary is disinterested in the proposal.
6. Propose that a mediator be brought into help find a mutually acceptable exchange of concessions.

Pruitt (1977) has further suggested two broad categories of resolving differences of interest—bargaining and norm following. In bargaining, 'each party endeavours to coerce or lure its adversary into making maximum concessions while conceding as little as possible' (p. 134). In norm following, 'both parties attempt to locate and follow rules that are appropriate to the issue in question' (p. 135). He suggests three kinds of rules in norm following—content-specific rules, equity rules and mutual responsiveness ('in which each party makes concessions to the extent that the other party demonstrates its needs for these concessions'.)

44.2.1 Approach and Avoidance Modes of Conflict Management

The mode of conflict is primarily determined by the perceptions of the conflicting parties. As Blake, Shepard and Mouton (1964) suggest, if conflict is seen as inevitable and a solution is not possible, a situation of helplessness may lead either to resignation to fate or to a power struggle. However, the assumption about the conflict will mainly depend upon the perception of the outgroup (the other group, contrasted with our group). The perception of the outgroup should perhaps be used as a basis in understanding the modes of conflict management.

There are two main dimensions of the perception of the outgroup. It may be perceived as always opposed to the interests of the ingroup and as being belligerent (in which case, in one sense, the conflict is seen as inevitable), or it may be perceived as having its own interests but being interested in peace (then the conflict will be perceived as a fact of life, but not inevitable). Similarly, the outgroup may be perceived as unreasonable (resulting in lack of hope for any solution) or as open to reason (with resultant hope of a solution to the problem). A combination of these two types of perceptions gives four modes of conflict management. The general orientation of a group may be an avoidance orientation or an approach orientation. The avoidance approach dimension is significant in determining the effectiveness of managerial behaviour. Avoidance is based on fear and is dysfunctional while approach is based on hope and is functional for effectiveness. Avoidance is characterised by a tendency to deny, rationalise or avoid the problem to displace anger or aggression or to use emotional appeals; approach orientation is characterised by making efforts to find a solution by one's own efforts or with the help of others. This dimension (avoidance approach) has been used in understanding and measuring managerial

TABLE 44.1   Approach Avoidance Styles of Conflict Management

Mode	Perception of Out-group	Style
Avoidance	• Unreasonable	Resignation
	• Opposed to our interests and belligerent	
Avoidance	• Open to reason	Withdrawal
Opposed to our interests and belligerent		
Avoidance	• Unreasonable	Appeasement
Having own interests, but interested in peace		
Avoidance	• Open to reason	Defusion
Having own interests, but interested in peace		
Approach	• Unreasonable	Confrontation
Opposed to our interests and belligerent		
Approach	• Open to reason	Arbitration
Opposed to our interests and belligerent		
Approach	• Unreasonable	Compromise
Having own interests, but interested in peace		
Approach	• Open to reason	Negotiation
Having own interests, but interested in peace		

behaviour (Pareek, 1986b), managerial styles (Pareek, 1987) and the styles of coping with organisational role stress (Pareek, 1988b). This comes close to what Blake, Shepard and Mouton (1964) suggest as active–passive mode.

Combining the two aspects of the perception of the outgroup with avoidance approach dimension, we get eight styles or modes of conflict management. These are shown in Table 44.1.

44.2.2 Avoidance Modes or Styles

Avoidance modes or styles of conflict management aim at avoiding or postponing conflicts in a variety of ways. There are four main avoidance styles which are described here.

Resignation: The extreme avoidance mode is fatalistic—regarding conflicts with a sense of helplessness. Conflict is seen as a part of reality, arising out of the unreasonable stand of an outgroup, usually hostile.

Another form of resignation is to ignore the conflict. It may even take the form of denying the unpleasant situation in the hope that the conflict will get resolved by itself in due course.

Withdrawal: Another form of avoidance is to get away from a conflict situation. It may take several forms. The attempt to get away from the conflict may be because the outgroup is seen as belligerent but still open to reason.

One way to get away from conflicts is to avoid situations of potential conflicts. This may be done by not having any opportunities for the two groups to work together.

A second way may be to withdraw from a conflict when it takes place. The withdrawal may be from the situation or from the relationship with the outgroup. For example, when two potential product groups are involved in getting a market share and find themselves in conflict with each other, one may decide to withdraw from marketing that product or may like to withdraw from collaborative work with the outgroup.

Physical separation may be a third way to withdraw. This would include a separate location and separation of all other arrangements.

A fourth form of withdrawal may be to define the boundaries of interaction with the outgroup and make arrangements to limit these.

Defusion: The main objective of the defusion mode of conflict resolution is to buy time for dealing with a conflict. It may take several forms. When people feel that several emotional issues are involved in a conflict and that the emotions are too strong, they may decide to let the emotions 'cool down' before taking up the real issues for resolution. Emotional overtones can be defused in several ways.

One way to defuse strong emotions in a conflict is to hope that, with the passage of time, the emotions will settle down and the groups will be ready to deal with the real issues of conflict. A good example of the defusion strategy was the management of conflict in Andhra Pradesh, between Telangana and Andhra region, when every political party was in the favour of a separation of the two parts. The Prime Minister used time for defusing the conflict. Later, the issues were discussed more calmly and solutions were worked out.

Another form of defusion is to appeal to the good sense of both groups, to the sentiment that both are part of a larger group and have common interests, interdependence, mutuality, etc. Such appeals may help to defuse a conflict fraught with emotions.

Another way to defuse a situation is to develop a temporary arrangement of interaction with the outgroup through a third group. This is like creating a buffer to absorb emotional overtones.

Appeasement: The main objective of appeasement is to buy temporary peace. When a group in conflict with an outgroup finds the conflict embarrassing and disturbing, it may agree to some of the demands of the outgroup, not because it is convinced about them but because it wants to postpone the conflict. It therefore provides some concessions in the hope that the outgroup will be satisfied and the conflict will be over.

Appeasement has the same dynamics as payment of blackmail. The outgroup gets the message that the group is weak and incapable of confronting issues. The result of appeasement is that not only the conflict remains unresolved but also the demands of the outgroup increase, its posturing gets stiffer and the situation deteriorates further.

44.2.3 Approach Modes or Styles

Approach modes or styles may take more aggressive or understanding forms by taking positive steps to confront conflicts and find solutions. There are four approach modes or styles (see Table 44.1).

Confrontation: When the ingroup perceives the outgroup to be both opposed to its interests and unreasonable, the mode of confrontation may be adopted. Confrontation is fighting out an issue to get a solution in one's favour, and it is often adopted by management or trade unions. It may lead to what Blake, Shepard and Mouton (1964) call the win-lose trap. They have suggested 10 elements that contribute to this trap: win-lose orientation (hope of a larger share in the gain); closing ranks and increasing cohesion; leadership consideration; position contrast (one's own position enhanced and the adversary's position downgraded); attack and counter-attack; negative stereotypes concerning the adversary; perception of a representative personality; intellectual distortions; commonalities minimised and difference heightened; and comprehension of one's own proposal being greater than the understanding of the competitor's proposal.

The confrontation mode involves coercion and is likely to fail to reach a solution. In a laboratory study of negotiation, Pruitt and Lewis (1971) found that when negotiators placed heavy reliance on pressure tactics, it resulted in failure to reach an agreement. Thibaut and Kelley (1959) mention following three problems associated with pressure tactics:

1. The cost of surveillance over the other party's behaviour when threats are employed.
2. The loss of power that sometimes results from the use of threats, punishments and rewards.
3. The unpleasantness of having to capitulate when the other party is unknown.

Compromise: If the outgroup is seen as being interested in peace (and as reasonable), an attempt may be made to seek a compromise. This is a process of sharing in the gain without resolving the conflict. This may be done by bargaining.

Arbitration: If the outgroup is perceived as being belligerent and not interested in peace and yet not totally unreasonable, arbitration by a third party may be sought to assess the situation objectively and give an ÒawardÓ acceptable to both groups. Usually the conflict remains unresolved; it is only postponed for a time.

Negotiation: The most satisfactory solution can emerge only when both groups jointly confront the problem and explore its solution. This mode is called negotiation.

Filley (1978), like Blake, Shepard and Mouton (1964), calls the functional method of conflict resolution a problem-solving method. According to him, problem-solving methods evoke intellectual intensity rather than emotional intensity or power. He suggests that the following changes in conditions facilitate movement from power-oriented methods to problem-solving methods:

1. Perceptual
   a. Identifying the problem in terms of goals rather than the solutions
   b. Identifying the existence of mutually beneficial solutions
   c. Changing the focus of attention from the other party to the problem
   d. Identifying the costs of not seeing
   e. Identifying the costs of self-sacrifice or domination
2. Affective
   a. Establishment of positive feelings by each party about themselves and others through clinical or fact finding methods
   b. Minimising feelings of anger, threat or defensiveness by depersonalising the problem and using a neutral language
3. Situational
   a. Reducing time pressure
   b. Providing neutral spatial arrangements
   c. Increasing proximity and interaction of the parties
   d. Equalising and ignoring power differences
4. Processual
   a. Clarifying communication
   b. Stating issues in specific rather than general terms
   c. Defining the problem jointly by the parties
   d. Making the feedback descriptive
   e. Separating process stages of problem identification, solution, generalisation and evaluation
   f. Redefining problem statements in terms of needs rather than solutions
   g. Accepting the process rules of prescribing, forcing, acquiescing, or avoiding behaviour

Walton and McKersie (1965) have used the term integrative bargaining, which comes closer to what is referred to here as negotiation. In integrative bargaining, new and better options are generated. They have suggested the following approaches for negotiators to take in order to increase the likelihood that new and better options will be developed. These are integrative tactics.

1. State one's position in terms of a problem to be solved rather than a solution to be accepted by the adversary.
2. Retain one's flexibility by not becoming committed to a fixed position.
3. Make every effort to understand the adversary's viewpoint.
4. Present to the adversary an accurate picture of one's own needs and motives so that he can think up options that satisfy the needs of both parties.

44.3 SCORING

The Answer Sheet can be used for scoring, by using the following key:

Style	Items
Resignation	1, 9, 17
Withdrawal	2, 10, 18
Defusion	8, 16, 24
Appeasement	7, 15, 23
Confrontation	4, 12, 20
Compromise	5, 13, 21
Arbitration	6, 14, 22
Negotiation	3, 11, 19

Add the ratings of each row to get scores for each style. The total scores on each style can range from 3 to 15.

44.4 RELIABILITY

After an interval of 6 weeks with 50 bank managers, the test-retest reliability of OSOC was found to be 0.89.

44.5 VALIDITY

The construct validity of OSOC was revealed by the internal structure of the styles. The responses of 212 managers belonging to three levels of management and four manufacturing organisations, two multinationals, one private and one public sector company were analysed. Principal components analysis (using equamax rotation) gave eight factors (the cut-off point being the eigenvalue of 1). Table 44.2 gives the results of factor analysis. The eight factors explain 59% variance.

Factor I has a high loading on two items of withdrawal (on the third item, 18, the loading is 0.26), all three items of compromise and one each of arbitration (6) and defusion (8). A common

TABLE 44.2   Factor Analysis of OSOC

Items	1	11	111	18	8	81	811	8111
				Factors				
2	0.72							
13	0.64	0.37						
10	0.49			0.36				
15		0.76						
7		0.67						
21	0.40	0.40						
23		0.40	0.33	0.32				
14			0.79					
22			0.71					
6	0.45		0.62					
4				0.62				
16				0.58				
17				0.53				0.37
8	0.37			0.40				
19					0.80			
11					0.75			
12						0.72		
20						0.65		
18						0.52		
3							0.67	
5	0.41						0.58	
24					0.36		0.54	
1							0.35	0.84
9								0.49

Note: Factor loadings of 0.30 or below are not mentioned.

feature of all seven items is the non-engagement approach in the conflict—withdrawing, compromising or waiting. This factor, therefore, can be termed non-engagement or withdrawal.

Factor 2 has a high loading on all the three items of appeasement and two items of compromise. In all these items, the common element is giving concessions to the other party. While Factor 1 is characterised by lack of engagement with the conflicting party, this one is characterised by appeasement and so is termed appeasement.

Factor 3 can be called arbitration because it has a high loading on all the three items of arbitration, although it also has a marginally high loading on one appeasement item (23).

Factor 4 has a high loading on two items of defusion (8, 16), and one each of resignation (17) and confrontation (4). Both these items indicate waiting; showing one's strength (Item 4) may also be a mode of defusion. It has a loading (not very high) on one item each of withdrawal (10) and appeasement (23). In all these items, the common thread being defusion, this factor can be named defusion.

Factor 5 has a high loading only on two items of negotiation (11, 19) and is therefore called negotiation.

Factor 6 has a high loading on two confrontation (12, 20) and one withdrawal item (18), indicating interaction on a limited scale. Since all these relate to confrontation, this Factor 6 can be named confrontation.

Factor 7 has a high loading on one item each of negotiation (3), compromise (5) and defusion (24) and a negative loading on one item of withdrawal (9). In the three items, the main thread is engagement with the conflicting situation and taking initiative. Even Item 24 relates to letting emotions subside. Factor 7 is proaction.

Since Factor 8 has high loadings on all three resignation items, it is termed resignation. Factor analysis has validated the meta-concepts of resignation, withdrawal, defusion, appeasement, confrontation, arbitration and negotiation. It has shown another factor—proaction. The items of compromise have been absorbed by other factors. The first two factors of withdrawal and appeasement are quite close to each other, and the distinction is not very clear. Factor analysis, on the whole, can be seen as providing evidence of dimensions—validity. Other factor analysis studies are needed to confirm this.

The distribution of the responses of over 200 managers on each item on the five points of the scale were studied. The mean values for 24 items ranged from 1.89 to 4.43, with low SDs indicating well spread-out responses.

44.6 NORMS

Based on the responses of 212 managers, tentative norms are proposed in Table 44.3. The mean values are given in round figures, with low and high, based on one SD distance from these values.

TABLE 44.3 Norms of OSOC

	Styles	Mean	High	Low
1.	Resignation	7	11	4
2.	Withdrawal	8	12	5
3.	Appeasement	10	13	7
4.	Defusion	7	10	4
5.	Confrontation	8	12	5
6.	Arbitration	11	14	8
7.	Compromise	11	15	8
8.	Negotiation	13	15	11

They can be used to find out which scores are high or low. Specific norms can be calculated for a specific population.

44.7 CORRELATES

Keshote (1990) has reported a significant relationship (correlations significant at 0.01 level) between negotiation and internal locus of control. All other seven styles had a significant relationship with externality.

Bose and Pareek (1986) using ASUFA Inventory (Chapter 9) found significant negative correlations between attribution of success and failure to internal factors (ability and effort), and all styles except confrontation, compromise and negotiation (the approach styles involving engagement between the conflicting parties). Avoidance styles had a positive correlation with externality and negative correlation with internality (both significant at 0.01 level).

44.8 USE FOR HRD

This instrument can help managers diagnose their conflict management styles and take necessary steps to increase their effectiveness to manage organisational conflicts. The instrument can be used by HRD facilitators and in executive development programmes.

After completing the instrument, participants should be helped to score and prepare their profiles on the eight conflict management styles. Conceptual input may then be provided to them. Participants should appreciate both the contingency approach and the need to move towards the negotiating mode of conflict management. The rationale and practical suggestions to develop and practice negotiating style or mode are discussed here.

Participants can also compare their scores with the norms. Table 44.3 gives the norms on eight styles, based on a study of 200 managers. However, it may be better to develop norms in each group. If a group is large enough (50 or more), mean and 1/2 SD can be used as cut-off points for low or high scores on each level. In a smaller group, median and quartile can be used for this purpose. Participants can then discuss how they can lower or increase their scores if they feel concerned while comparing their scores with the norms.

Participants can also total the four approaches and four avoidance styles, and calculate the approach/avoidance ratio by dividing the total of approach styles by the total of avoidance styles. If the ratio is below 1, they need to discuss in small groups, which avoidance styles are high and how the score can be lowered. Since the items in OSOC are in terms of behaviour, participants may prepare action plans to reduce some behaviour and increase others. The ideas given in the chapter regarding negotiations will help in planning action for effectiveness.

Opinion Survey of Conflict Management

Name: _____   Role: _____

Organisation: _____   Date: _____

We experience various types of conflicts in organisations. This inventory is designed to survey the views of managers on managing organisational conflicts.

Please read each statement given below and respond to it, according to the following key.

Write 1   for strong disagreement
Write 2   for disagreement
Write 3   for half agreement with the statement
Write 4   for agreement
Write 5   for strongly agreement with the statement

1. _____   Conflicts are inevitable in organisations and nothing can be done about them.
2. _____   The best strategy is to avoid conflict situations.
3. _____   A conflict is like a problem; we have to find the causes and take steps to find solutions.
4. _____   Conflicts can be solved only if one shows one's strength to the other party.
5. _____   In a conflict situation, both the parties have to give up something in order to reach a solution.
6. _____   A third party should be asked to give a solution to a difficult conflict.
7. _____   It is better to give some concessions to the opponent group to win their confidence.
8. _____   The best way to deal with conflicts is to withdraw from the scene for some time.
9. _____   It is better to lie low and live with the conflict.
10. _____   In a conflict situation, one party should get away to avert unpleasantness.
11. _____   Conflict management needs an involved process of joint exploration for solution(s).
12. _____   In most conflicts, one should fight out the solution.
13. _____   Compromise is the best strategy for managing conflict.
14. _____   When two parties are deeply involved in conflict, arbitration by an acceptable outside party may be very helpful.
15. _____   Accepting a few demands of the opponent group may help in resolving conflicts.
16. _____   If we wait for some time and don't attempt to solve problems, conflicts will get defused and resolved in due course of time.
17. _____   It is foolish to be bothered by conflicts; they are there and we may as well live with them.
18. _____   If a group interacts with other groups only on necessary and limited dimensions, conflicts can be managed.
19. _____   Conflicts can be solved if the parties understand each other, and jointly search alternative solutions.
20. _____   The more powerful you are, the more effectively you can resolve conflicts.
21. _____   If conflicting parties accept a part of each other's demands, conflicts can be resolved.
22. _____   Difficult conflicts can be solved by an impartial arbitrator who finds solutions acceptable to both the conflicting parties.
23. _____   It is better to buy peace for some time even by acceding to some demands of the conflicting group, so that conflicts can be effectively resolved later.
24. _____   Waiting for some time to let emotions subside helps in solving the major problems.

Opinion Survey of Organisational Conflicts
Score Sheet

Name: _____   Role: _____

Organisation: _____   Date: _____

B.   Transfer your responses to the following sheet.
C.   Add the rows to get the total. Total of each row will range from 3 to 15.

Items and Responses			Total	Styles
1. __	9. __	17. __	__	Resignation
2. __	10. __	18. __	__	Withdrawal
3. __	11. __	19. __	__	Negotiation
4. __	12. __	20. __	__	Confrontation
5. __	13. __	21. __	__	Compromise
6. __	14. __	22. __	__	Arbitration
7. __	15. __	23. __	__	Appeasement
8. __	16. __	24. __	__	Defusion

Conflict Management Preference

45.1 THE INSTRUMENT AND ITS ADMINISTRATION

Conflict management preference (CMP) consists of 10 conflict situations. After reading a situation, respondents choose one of the eight given strategies, thus indicating their preference for a particular approach. They also state why they choose that approach.

The situations were developed after examining critical incidents of conflicts in organisations that were collected by 30 managers. The eight strategies or approaches and the eight styles of conflict management are elaborated in Chapter 44.

45.2 CONCEPTUAL FRAMEWORK

The conceptual framework used in CMP is discussed in Chapter 44. The instrument is also based on the contingency theory—that the appropriateness of a style depends on the situation. In other words, different conflict situations require different approaches (strategies or styles) to deal with them.

45.3 SCORING

The responses are analysed for the modal (typical) style of the respondent and appropriateness of styles. The modal (in the statistical sense) style is found by counting the most frequently mentioned style (see key on the next page) by the respondent in the 10 situations. Seven styles have been used here (appeasement is not included).

Appropriateness is measured by checking whether the preferred style corresponds with the one given in the key. The number of correct answers gives the score (out of 10). The following key shows the appropriate styles for the various situations:

CMP KEY

Situation	Appropriate Style
1	(g) Arbitration
2	(a) Resignation
3	(h) Negotiation
4	(b) Withdrawal
5	(e) Confrontation
6	(h) Negotiation
7	(f) Compromise
8	(c) Defusion
9	(h) Negotiation
10	(e) Confrontation

45.4 VALIDITY

CMP scores were correlated with the scores on OSOC (Chapter 44) for a group of 40 Indonesian health managers. The correlation was significant and positive (0.62). This gives some evidence of the validity of the instrument.

45.5 NORMS

Based on the data of a group of managers, the rank order of style preferences is given below:

Styles	Rank Order
Resignation	7
Withdrawal	6
Defusion	5
Confrontation	2
Arbitration	4
Compromise	3
Negotiation	1

45.6 USE FOR HRD

Scores for modal style and its appropriateness (especially the latter) can be discussed to help participants see the value of proper diagnosis. The concept of contingency (Pareek, 1992, Chapter 7) will be useful in such a discussion.

Conflict Management Preference (CMP)

Name: _____   Role: _____

Organisation: _____   Date: _____

Read each situation carefully and select the most appropriate strategy from those mentioned below. Write in the left-hand blank space the identifying letter (a, b, c, d, e, f, g or h) of the strategy you think is most appropriate to deal with the conflict. Give reasons for your selection.

Strategies

- a. Live with the conflict.
- b. Avoid the conflict.
- c. Defuse the situation (wait for sometime).
- d. Give some concession to the conflicting party.
- e. Fight it out.
- f. Make a compromise.
- g. Seek third party intervention.
- h. Negotiate a solution (jointly search a solution with the conflicting party).

Situation 1

In one company, there was a dispute between the management and the union on payment of became serious and the union threatened to give a call to workers for a general strike unless the management accepted the union's interpretation of the existing law for giving compensation.
What strategy do you recommend?
Why?

Situation 2

In a meeting between the management and the union, the management emphasised the need for union strongly disagreed and insisted that they had different objectives.
What strategy do you recommend?

Situation 3

In a meeting of departmental heads belonging to one organisation, there was a conflict between two heads on the allocation of budget. Additional budget was needed by one department for its new activities, and the other department felt that this would disturb the parity between departments.
What strategy do you recommend?
Why?

Situation 4

In one department, there was an unpleasant situation. A manager and the person working under him had negative impressions about each other. Both doubted the level of competence of the other person. This was a source of potential conflict. What strategy do you recommend?
Why?

Situation 5

In one organisation, the management recruited some experts at a senior level. The workers' union raised objections to recruiting personnel without a proper advertisement, etc. The union gave a notice to the management that they would go to court if the recruited experts were allowed to join the organisation.
What strategy do you recommend?
Why?

Situation 6

In one company, the workers agitated for more participation in decisions affecting them. They prepared a long list of demands. The management in general was not favourable to such demands.
What strategy do you recommend?
Why?

Situation 7

In one company, there was a conflict between the management and the union on the ratio of employees to be promoted in vacant positions to those to be recruited from the open market. While the management wanted a very low proportion of people to be promoted, the union wanted a much higher proportion.
What strategy do you recommend?
Why?

Situation 8

In one organisation, a conflict developed between technical and general managers. The organisation was interested in integrating the two streams of managers who were recruited and promoted in the past. The conflict on integration and the year to be used as a cut-off point became severe and charged with emotion.
What strategy do you recommend?
Why?

Situation 9

In an organisation, a new function (HRD) was created. This caused a conflict between the function. Both departments saw the new function as a legitimate part of their own responsibility.
What strategy do you recommend?
Why?

Situation 10

The workers' union was very strong in one organisation. The management was considerate and accepted many of their demands. They voluntarily gave many other facilities. However, the union put forth new demands and threatened to go on strike.
What strategy do you recommend?
Why?

Conflict Management Styles: Approaches to Conflict Management

46.1 THE INSTRUMENT AND ITS ADMINISTRATION

Approaches to conflict management (ACM) is a simple instrument in which a respondent ranks eight approaches according to the preference he would accord them in conflict situations. The lower the rank, the higher is the score on that approach (preferred approach in practice).

46.2 CONCEPTUAL FRAMEWORK

The theory described in Chapter 44 also underlies this instrument.

46.3 SCORING

The rankings give the order of the respondents' preferred styles of conflict management. The eight approaches given below can be used as a key to score responses:

1. Negotiation
2. Confrontation
3. Resignation
4. Arbitration
5. Defusion
6. Appeasement
7. Withdrawal
8. Compromise

The obtained data can be scaled—either for an individual or a group—by converting ranks into pair comparison scores and then by calculating the scale values of the various styles (Edwards, 1957). This is illustrated under the heading 'Norms'.

46.4 VALIDITY

Although ACM ranks had a very low correlation with the scores on the two other conflict management instrument (OSOC in Chapter 44 and CMP in Chapter 45) for a group of 40 Indonesian health managers, critical incidents on the choice of different ways of managing conflicts from the group, gave some indication of the validity of the instrument. The styles reflected in the critical incidents are primarily arbitration (by a senior manager), withdrawal and compromise/appeasement (usually through arbitration of a senior manager). These are close to the scale values of the styles reported as being used. The exception is the negotiation mode.

While negotiation is a highly espoused value, it is not used and more a wish than an actuality. It also means that since negotiation value is highly espoused, efforts to develop this style among Indonesian managers may be successful.

Let us give some examples of the employed styles as reflected in the critical incidents. In one incident, conflict between an executive director and a technical director was managed by one of them 'avoiding communication' with the other and 'leaving him alone'. In a second incident of conflict between a province-level manager (top) and a manager located in the field (down), the matter was referred to the provincial head who 'decided a compromise policy' of allocating different roles to both.

In another incident, a group of three staff members asked their boss for permission to go somewhere. The boss wanted one of them to stay back. He asked the three to discuss and decide who would stay back. They agreed to discuss and decide the matter, but the day one of them was needed, all the three were gone. This is an interesting mode noticed in the Indonesian groups, where agreeing to do (and not necessarily act) is regarded as more desirable than arguing and later actually doing what is desired (Hofstede, 1982, 1985). In a fourth incident, a conflict between two district officers, the provincial director invited them into his office, listened to both of them and then gave his decision. There are several incidents in which the conflict continued since no one did anything about it.

These discussion may help to interpret the data obtained by the instrument.

46.5 NORMS

Basic data (including scale values) from Indonesian health managers is given in Table 46.1 The scale values reveal the patterns of conflict management styles (self-reported as in use).

TABLE 46.1 Basic Data and Scale Values of ACM

		Mean	SD	Median	Coefficient of Skewness	Coefficient of Kurtosis	Scale Value
1.	Withdrawal (g)	4	1.7	3.0	0.4	−1.1	15
2.	Resignation (c)	4	2.1	3.0	0.6	−0.3	15
3.	Appeasement (f)	5	1.5	5.0	−0.1	−0.8	11
4.	Defusion (e)	8	1.6	9.0	−3.4	10.9	0
5.	Confrontation (b)	7	1.9	8.0	−1.2	0.3	5
6.	Arbitration (d)	6	1.3	6.0	−.6	0	8
7.	Compromise (h)	4	2.0	4.0	0.4	0.5	15
8.	Negotiation (a)	2	1.4	1.0	3.7	15.3	24

Defusion — Confrontation — Arbitration — APPEASEMENT — Withdrawal — Resignation — Compromise — NEGOTIATION

```
├────────┼────────────┼────────────┼────────┼────────┼────────┤
0        6            12                    18       24
```

Table 46.2 shows that while defusion and negotiation modes are on the extreme of a 24-point scale, there are three other cluster reported as being used by the respondents—confrontation, followed by arbitration and appeasement (non-exploratory modes of reducing conflicts), and then by compromise, resignation and withdrawal (avoidance modes). There is a big gap between these clusters and those on the two extremes (defusion and negotiation).

TABLE 46.2 Coefficients of Correlation Between Leadership Styles and Conflict Management Modes

	Leadership Styles	OSCM		ACM	
1.	(High task)	Resignation	(0.34)	Resignation	(0.21)
		Confrontation	(0.37)	Confrontation	(−0.30)
2.	(High on both)	Compromise	(0.45)	Arbitration	(0.33)
				Confrontation	
			(0.30)	Appeasement	(−0.31)
3.	(High people)	Defusion	(0.20)	Appeasement	(0.26)
				Negotiation	(−0.24)
4.	(Low on both)	Confrontation	(−0.35)		
		Resignation	(−.29)		

46.6 CORRELATES

A specially prepared instrument to measure four leadership styles was administered to a group of 40 health managers, along with ACM and OSCM. Style 1 was high-task low relationship, Style 2 was high on both, Style 3 was low-task high relationship, and Style 4 was low on both, very similar to LPI-M (Chapter 30). The correlations appear in Table 46.2.

Correlation values suggest that highly task-oriented leaders tend to take conflicts for granted and usually do nothing about them; although they value the confrontation mode (significant positive correlation), they tend not to use this mode in practice (highly negative but not significant correlation). Highly people-oriented leaders value defusion as the mode of managing conflicts but tend to use appeasement style and are reluctant to get involved in negotiations. It seems that the value for relationships overrides the need for exploring issues with people. This style seems to create a threat to good relations.

Leaders with high attention to both task and people value the compromise mode but use arbitration in managing conflicts. As discussed earlier, arbitration usually results in Table 46.2.

They also tend to shy away from negotiation. Leaders who delegate (low orientation for task as well as for people), do not value confrontation or resignation as modes and do not seem to have any clear characteristic style of conflict management.

In conclusion, there seems to be a gap between espoused values and the styles used in managing conflicts in Indonesian organisation. While the espoused value is negotiation and many people think they use this mode in practice, avoidance, withdrawal and arbitration are mainly used. An arbitrator generally works towards compromise and also resorts to appeasement. Leaders place high emphasis on task and value confrontation but shy away from using it. It seems that Indonesian managers are ready to adopt the negotiation mode with some help in this regard.

They also seem to be ready to learn ways of positive confrontation. A few years back, sensitivity training (L or T groups) were tremendously successful and had an impact on a large number of health system managers. This is contrary to the warnings of some authors (e.g., Hofstede, 1982, 1985) about such an approach in Indonesia. This shows that negotiation and positive confrontation (exploration) can succeed, provided a systematic movement towards these is made through specially designed interventions. A contingency approach to conflict management and ways of moving towards negotiation style, as already discussed, may be relevant in this regard.

46.7 USE FOR HRD

The instrument can be used with individuals and group in the same way as OSCM (Chapter 44). The discussion under 'Correlates' may help in the use of the instrument with teams and organisations, especially for OD work.

Approaches to Conflict Management

Name: _____ Role: _____

Organisation: _____ Date: _____

What approach do you follow in managing conflicts? We give below eight approaches. Rank them in terms of your own style of managing conflicts. Give Rank 1 to the statement which best describes your approach or style, 2 to the statement which is the next best description of your style or approach, and so on. Thus, the statement which is least true of your style will get a rank of 8.

1. _____ Dialogue with the conflicting party on the underlying problem and jointly search for a mutually acceptable solution.

2. _____ Work out your best solution for the conflict and fight your way out to implement it.

3. _____ Do nothing about the conflict because such attempts usually do not help.

4. _____ Use the help of a third party for arbitration.

5. _____ Allow some time to pass, hoping that things will cool down and thus helping to solve the problem.

6. _____ Provide small concessions to the opposite party.

7. _____ Avoid most situations that are likely to lead to conflicts.

8. _____ In the spirit of give and take, accept some demands made by the other party in exchange for some of your own demands.

Conflict Resolution Inventory

47.1 THE INSTRUMENT AND ITS ADMINISTRATION

CRI measures an individual's mode of resolving conflict. It contains 20 items, measuring confrontation, compromise, negotiation, withdrawal and resignation.

47.2 THE CONCEPTUAL FRAMEWORK

The conceptual framework discussed in Chapter 44 has been used for developing the inventory. Conflict Resolution Inventory comprises of five dimensions—confrontation, compromise, negotiation, withdrawal and resignation.

47.3 SCORING

Scoring can be done by the participants or by the facilitators. Scores on each range from 4 to 20.

									Total
1.	_____	6.	_____	11.	_____	16.	_____	_____	
2.	_____	7.	_____	12.	_____	17.	_____	_____	
3.	_____	8.	_____	13.	_____	18.	_____	_____	
4.	_____	9.	_____	14.	_____	19.	_____	_____	
5.	_____	10.	_____	15.	_____	20.	_____	_____	

Compare the individual's scores on each mode with the norms given in the following table.

47.4 RELIABILITY

Split-half reliability of the instrument was found to be 0.516.

47.5 NORMS

Mean and SD values given in the following table can be used as norms. Norms for specific groups can be developed.

Variables	Mean	SD	Low	Average	High
Confrontation	14	3	< 11	11–17	17 <
Compromise	12	3	< 9	9–15	15 <
Negotiation	13	3	< 10	10–16	16 <
Withdrawal	12	3	< 9	9–15	15 <
Resignation	12	3	< 9	9–15	15 <

Conflict Resolution Inventory

Name: _____   Role: _____

Organisation: _____   Date: _____

This instrument will help you examine your styles of conflict resolution and take steps to improve your effectiveness to resolve and manage conflicts. There is no right or wrong answers. You will learn about yourself if you respond to each item as candidly as possible. Read each statement in the instrument and write your response in the space given on its left side, according to the key given below.

Write 1   if you rarely or never behave this way
Write 2   if you occasionally behave this way
Write 3   if you sometimes behave this way
Write 4   if you often behave this way
Write 5   if you almost always behave this way

No.	Response	Items
1.	_____	I confront the situation.
2.	_____	I am fearful to break relationships.
3.	_____	I try to find out alternative solutions.
4.	_____	I keep quite in contradictory situations.
5.	_____	I find time to be the best healer.
6.	_____	I easily express my feelings.
7.	_____	I easily agree to the proposed solution.
8.	_____	I seek solutions from others.
9.	_____	I believe that the best strategy is to avoid conflict.
10.	_____	I wait for my emotions to subside.
11.	_____	I believe in finding out the solutions.
12.	_____	I believe in compromising.
13.	_____	I take decisions after discussing with others.
14	_____	I don't enter into the conflict.
15.	_____	I give my companions some time to think before initiating talks.
16.	_____	I explore the reason of conflict.
17.	_____	I accept few demands of the opponent group to resolve conflicts.
18.	_____	I jointly go for the mutually acceptable solution.
19.	_____	I want to be in comfort zone while dealing with relations.
20.	_____	I tend to delay my efforts in finding solutions for my personal problems.

Decision-making: Decision Styles Inventory (DSI)*

48.1 THE INSTRUMENT AND ITS ADMINISTRATION

Decision Styles Inventory (DSI) was developed to measure four styles. Thirteen items for each style are contained in it, and it is self-administered. Respondents rate all items on a 5-point scale—never to always. A separate answer sheet (appended) is used to facilitate scoring of the inventory.

48.2 CONCEPTUAL FRAMEWORK

Decision-making is considered as one of the central variable in modern organisational theory. Larson (1962) believed that the key to understanding the decision process lies in understanding the problem which has created the need for a decision. He believed that failure to define and to understand the decision problem adequately is what causes the greatest difficulty in decision-making. According to Larson, there are four different types of decision problems:

The objectives have been defined and alternative courses of action have been identified, which may lead to these objectives but the problem is in deciding which course of action is best.

1. The objectives have been defined, but we do not know which courses of action will potentially achieve these objectives. The problem is in determining the possible alternatives and then selecting the most desirable alternative.
2. The objectives themselves have not yet been formulated, although a need for action is evident. The problem involved is in making a comprehensive choice concerning the alternatives.

---

* Contributed by Surabhi Purohit.

3. A situation has been identified as being either currently undesirable or potentially undesirable at some future point in time. The problem involves devising actions that will eliminate or alleviate these undesirable conditions.

The Type (2) involves 'identifying' course of action while in Type (4), the initial task involves 'devising' course of action.

The making of decisions usually implies responsibility. That is why whenever a decision is made, the person making it must be prepared to assume the responsibility for the eventual consequences of his actions.

Not all individuals are going to be equally adept at making decision. People differ in this ability just as they differ in all other characteristics and not only do they differ in ability but they also differ in terms of their basic strategy when it comes to the concept of decision-making style. The decision-making style has been based on cognitive behaviour psychology. This is a problem-centred method of looking at conscious mental functioning with a focus on discovering ways of directly attaining adjustment in thinking, feeling and action. Aron Beck has done pioneering work on cognitive behaviour in the last century.

In the past, lot of research has examined various components of decision-making perspective, and several decision-making style assessments have been developed.

Johnson created the decision-making inventory that uses two aspects (spontaneous versus systematic, internal versus external) to assess individuals on two bipolar dimensions, information gathering and analysing styles. Thus, Johnson's Decision Making Inventory classifies individual as having spontaneous internal, spontaneous external, systematic internal or systematic external decision-making styles.

Additionally, Scott and Bruce (1995) developed a decision-making scale. The general decision-making style (GDMS) measures classify individual as having one of the five independent decision-making styles—rational, avoidant, intuitive, dependent and spontaneous decision-making styles.

Nygren (2000) developed measures that differentiate between peoples' propensities to think more analytically or more intuitively. The decision-making style inventory (DMI) contains three scales that measure separate decision-making style—analytical (ANA), intuitive (INT) and regret-based emotional (REG) decision-making style.

Tallman and Gray (1990) addressed the importance of distinguishing between choosing, deciding and problem-solving; they argued that the term 'choice' should be used to encompass the sorting out of options whether conscious or unconscious. Deliberate choices are to be referred to as decisions. Problem-solving is 'a process that involves at a minimum three stages: recognition, selection from among alternative courses of action and an evaluation of outcomes'.

Doktor and Hamilton (1973) viewed decision-making styles as cognitive style. They said, 'It is a part of the person's cognitive style, which is the characteristic, self-consistent way of functioning that an individual exhibits across perceptual and intellectual activities'. Henderson and Nutt (1980) said that it is an individual's cognitive 'make-up' that we call decision style, and it is thought to influence the selection among alternative courses of action. Coscarelli, Burk and Cotter (1995) proposed a definition that looks at the construct of cognitive style as more limited. They proposed that 'decision-making is a characteristic, self-consistent way of functioning that an individual exhibits across perceptual and intellectual activities when making a choice'.

Decision-making styles have been studied from three broad perspectives—the guidance perspective, the social perspective and Jungian based theories.

Regarding the guidance perspective Arroba (1977) and Harren (1979) classified decision-making styles into planning, intuitive and dependent. It is based on the degree to which an individual takes personal responsibility for decision-making and uses rational versus emotional strategies. Johnson (1978) developed a model that describes two basic processes for gathering information (spontaneous and systematic), and two for analysing information (internal and external).

Regarding the social perspective, McKenney and Keen (1974) and Driver, Brousseau and Hunsaker (1990) conceptualised cognitive style along two dimensions—information gathering and information processing. Information gathering consists of systematic and intuitive behaviours. Driver et al. (1990) developed the decision style model that combines dimension of information processing to arrive at five basic styles—decisive, hierarchic, flexible, integrative and systemic. Scott and Bruce (1995) developed a typology that provides a comprehensive set of decision-making style.

Jungian-based theories suggest that individuals prefer to perceive in patterned, non-random ways. Perception includes the ways individuals become familiar with and gather information about the world around them. Jung identified four preferences for perceiving and judging the world and each representing the dichotomy. The Myers—briggs type indicator—is based on Jung's psychologically types (extraversion, sensing, thinking and judgment; see Myers & Mcaulley, 1985).

Kilmann and Mitroff (Unpublished) identified four decision styles that are combination of that two dimensions of data inputs, that is, sensation and intuition and decision-making (thinking and feeling).

DSI is based on Scott and Bruce's (1995) concept and research findings. Further, Scott and Bruce have also added the concept of intuitive decision-making style and differentiated it from other decision-making styles.

To make the decision-making instrument more comprehensive, one more dimension has been added—detached decision-making style. Six types of decision-making styles are as follows:

1. *Rational style*: It is deliberate, analytical and logical, accessing the long-terms effects of decisions and having a strong fact-based orientation.
2. *Intuitive style*: It includes feeling oriented and based on internal ordering of information.
3. *Spontaneous*: It displays a sense of immediacy and an interest in getting through the decision-making process as quickly as possible.

4. *Dependent style*: It is characterised by the use of support from others.
5. *Avoidant style*: It is characterised by delivery and denial. It can be driven by calculation or defensiveness but on both counts; it may provoke difficulties if over-emphasised.
6. *Detached style*: It is a highly egocentric style with limited empathy and reality contact and almost certain to being owner eventual conflicts, if not varied appropriately.

48.3 SCORING

Following steps need to be followed:

1. Transfer the ratings to the Response Sheet.
2. Total scores on each aspect at the end of the columns; these will range from 0 to 52.
3. Multiply this total by 2. The range will be from 0 to 100. This is Effectiveness Index (EI) of the specific style.
4. The style with the highest EI is the dominant style, usually used by the respondent in decision-making.
   (This instrument has been developed by Sandeep Chugh under the guidance of Surabhi Purohit.)

Response Table

Items	Response	Items	Response	Items	Response	Items	Response
1	_____	2	_____	3	_____	4	_____
5	_____	6	_____	7	_____	8	_____
9	_____	10	_____	11	_____	12	_____
13	_____	14	_____	15	_____	16	_____
17	_____	18	_____	19	_____	20	_____
21	_____	22	_____	23	_____	24	_____
25	_____	26	_____	27	_____	28	_____
29	_____	30	_____	31	_____	32	_____
33	_____	34	_____	35	_____	36	_____
37	_____	38	_____	39	_____	40	_____
41	_____	42	_____	43	_____	44	_____
45	_____	46	_____	47	_____	48	_____
49	_____	50	_____	51	_____	52	_____
S							
EI	$X2 =$		$X2 =$		$X2 =$		$X2 =$
	Perceptive		Deferring/ Procrastination		Impulsive/ Indiscriminate		Imperceptive/ Detached

48.4 USE FOR HRD

Data generated can be used in the process work in helping individuals to take the necessary steps to increase appropriate decision-making by experimenting with all four styles. The actual scores can then be calculated, and the discrepancies between self-perceived or group-perceived profile and the score profile can be discussed. Small groups (preferably of two) can work on helping each other to improve decision-making by increasing scores in deficient areas.

Decision Styles Inventory (DSI)

This instrument will help in knowing about how you make decisions—an important part of your organisational role. There are no right or wrong answers. You will learn more about yourself, if you respond to each of the following items as candidly as possible.

Read each statement and write your response in the space given on its left side according to the key given below:

Write 0   if you rarely or never behave in this way
Write 1   if you seldom behave in this way
Write 2   if you sometimes behave in this way
Write 3   if you often behave in this way
Write 4   if you almost always behave in this way

No.	Response	Item
1.	_____	I approach decisions with a clear aim in view.
2.	_____	I am aware that putting off a decision means rushed action in the end.
3.	_____	When I look back, the reasoning behind some of my decisions does not seem to be clear.
4.	_____	When others define their purpose, I am puzzled at finding I have none.
5.	_____	I sense the need for decision, even in circumstances where others are unaware of the need.
6.	_____	I enjoy either saying or implying 'wait and see'.
7.	_____	I do not have any thoughts behind my decisions.
8.	_____	I am amazed at the degree to which others grasp opportunities.
9.	_____	My approach to taking decisions is flexible according to different circumstances.
10.	_____	I am aware of the circumstances when decisions were unnecessarily delayed.
11.	_____	I am secretly proud of 'not thinking' before I act.
12.	_____	I exist entirely separated from the world of urgency.
13.	_____	I never invite another person to take decisions for me.
14.	_____	Putting off difficult choices gives me time and flexibility for response.
15.	_____	I cannot make real distinction between trivial and serious decisions.
16.	_____	Other people can never get through me.
17.	_____	I do not choose unless I am sure, and I take great care to make my choices.
18.	_____	In taking decisions I calculate time I have before I decide.
19.	_____	I enjoy surprising people with quickness I make up my mind.
20.	_____	I am often surprised when others point out the chances I have missed.
21.	_____	I have no emotional hang-ups over decision-making.
22.	_____	I fear taking decisions.
23.	_____	I put decisions on 'the back burner' for the thrill of experiencing a rush to delayed action.
24.	_____	Phrases like 'go for it', or 'grasp it with both hands' hold no real meaning for me.
25.	_____	When I am not able to decide, genuine doubt is the root cause.
26.	_____	I have been accused (by others) of dithering or hesitating.
27.	_____	Looking back at some of my most impulsive and also self-defeating decisions, I would be willingly to do the same again.

No.	Response	Item
28.	_____	Other people often urge me into action, but I generally ignore them.
29.	_____	I discriminate between important and trivial decisions.
30.	_____	I lose sight of the goal when a decision must be made.
31.	_____	Deciding totally on impulse is a great release for me.
32.	_____	I believe that too much emphasis is placed on decision-making.
33.	_____	I do not like to be rushed into decisions.
34.	_____	My deepest anxiety is being hurried into a decision by other people.
35.	_____	I can never understand why others delay their decisions.
36.	_____	I am so self-preoccupied that outside happenings pass by me.
37.	_____	I am able to grasp the essential elements of any decision, that is, sufficient information, motivation, opportunity, etc.
38.	_____	If the outcome of a decision is a fiasco, I am always able to comfort myself with the thought that it was rushed.
39.	_____	Making a decision without any purpose is a thrill for me.
40.	_____	I have always, since childhood, existed for myself.
41.	_____	I am living out conflicts to the surface to discover their roots.
42.	_____	I like to analyse the problems in minute details.
43.	_____	I enjoy making decisions fast.
44.	_____	I feel that decision made by me is not part of me/myself.
45.	_____	I like to consider all angles of a problem before making decision.
46.	_____	I delay when it comes to making important decisions.
47.	_____	I make impulsive decisions.
48.	_____	I half-heartedly participate in decision-making.
49.	_____	I like to work on a step-by-step approach before making decisions.
50.	_____	I postpone decision-making whenever possible.
51.	_____	Decisions are made on the spur of the moment.
52.	_____	After making decision I do not feel part of it.

PART
IV
THE ROLE

Role is the position one occupies in a social system. It is defined by the functions one performs in response to the expectations of the significant members of a social system and one's own expectations from that position or office.

Role and office (or position) are two separate concepts, although two sides of the same coin. According to Katz and Kahn (1966), 'Office is essentially a relational concept, defining each position in terms of its relationships to others and to the system as a whole.' While office is a relational and power-related concept, role is an obligational concept.

A role is not defined without the expectations of the role senders, including the role occupant. The position of a personnel manager may be created in an organisation, but his role will be defined by the expectations (stated or unstated) that different persons have from the personnel manager and the expectations that he, in turn, has from the role. In this sense, the role gets defined in each system by the role senders, including the role occupant.

The concept of role is vital for the integration of the individual with an organisation. The organisation has its own structure and goals. Similarly, the individual has his personality and needs (motivations). All these aspects interact with each other, and to some extent, these are integrated into a role.

Role is also a central concept in work motivation as it is only through this that the individual and organisation interact with each other.

An organisation can be defined as a system of roles. However, a role itself is a system. From the individual's point of view, there are two role systems—the system of various roles that the individual carries and performs and the system of various roles of which his role is a part. The first, we will call role space and the second, a role set.

Each individual occupies and plays several roles. A person can be a daughter, a mother, a salesperson, a member of a club, a member of a voluntary organisation and so on. All these roles constitute the role space of that person. At the centre of the role space is the self. As the concept of role is central to that of an organisation, so also the concept of self is central to the several roles of a person. The term 'self' refers to the interpretations the person makes about the referent 'I'. It is a cognitive structure that evolves from past experience with other persons and objects. Self can be defined as the experience of an identity arising from a person's interaction with the external reality—things, persons and systems.

In this part, role is described under various headings:

1. Role Efficacy
    a. Aspects of Role Efficacy
    b. Role Efficacy and Effectiveness
2. Organisational Role Stress
    a. Role Space Conflicts
    b. Role Set Conflicts
3. Coping with Stress

Role Efficacy: My Role

49.1 THE INSTRUMENT AND ITS ADMINISTRATION

To determine the role efficacy of a person, its 10 aspects need to be measured. These aspects are reflected in the ways in which an individual in an organisation perceives his role. Role efficacy can be measured by a method called EMR (essay on my role). The role occupant is asked to write an essay of about 500 words on his role. This is then analysed for role efficacy. The following instructions may be given.

Consider your role in your organisation and write about two and a half pages (about 500 words) on what you perceive your role to be, how you feel about it and how you operate. You may choose whatever aspects you think are relevant. There is no standard practice in writing about the role. Therefore, be spontaneous and write whatever you perceive as significant.

49.2 CONCEPTUAL FRAMEWORK

A person performs various roles that are centred around the self and are at varying distances from the self (and from each other). These relationships define the role space, which then is a dynamic interrelationship between the self and the various roles an individual occupies.

Similarly, role set is a pattern of interrelationships between one role (called the focal role) among many others. In a role set map, the focal role is in the centre.

The concept of role widens the meaning of work and the relationship of the worker with other significant persons in the system. The concept of job is more prescriptive in nature while role includes the part of work that is more discretionary. A job assumes the relationship of the worker with his supervisor, whereas the role emphasises his relationship with all those who have expectations from him (as he has from them). Recently, much emphasis has been given to the development of roles and making them more effective in an organisation.

To sum up, the concept of role goes beyond the individual job holder and indicates a need to involve other significant persons in defining role requirements. The focus on roles can be useful in planning organisational effectiveness. Herzberg (1966a) drew attention to the need for humanising jobs and giving more dignity to them. The work redesigning movement highlighted the need for involving jobholders in work-related decisions and giving them more autonomy in work-related matters.

The performance of a person working in an organisation depends on his own potential effectiveness, technical competence, managerial experience, etc. as well as on the design of the role that he performs in an organisation. It is the integration of the two—the person and the role—that ensures a person's effectiveness. Unless a person has the requisite knowledge, technical competence and skills required for the role, he cannot be effective. Equally important is how the role, which he occupies in the organisation, is designed. If the role does not allow the person to use his competence and if he constantly feels frustrated in the role, his effectiveness is likely to be low.

The integration of a person and a role comes about when the latter is able to fulfil the needs of the individual and when the individual in turn is able to contribute to the evolution of the role. The more we move from role taking to role making, the greater is the likelihood of the role being effective. Role taking is responding to the expectations of others, while role making is taking the initiative to design the role creatively so that the expectations of both, others and the role occupant, are integrated. The effectiveness of a person's role in an organisation will depend upon his own potential effectiveness, the potential effectiveness of the role and the organisational climate. The potential effectiveness can be termed as efficacy.

Personal efficacy is the potential effectiveness of a person in personal and interpersonal situations. Role efficacy is the potential effectiveness of an individual occupying a particular role in an organisation. Role efficacy can be seen as the psychological factor underlying role effectiveness.

49.3 ASPECTS OF ROLE EFFICACY

Role efficacy has several aspects. The more the aspects, the higher is the efficacy. These aspects can be classified into three groups or dimensions. One dimension is role making (as opposed to role taking). The former is an active attitude towards defining and making one's role as one likes, whereas the latter is a passive attitude that mainly responds to others' expectations.

49.3.1 Dimension 1: Role Making

1. *Self-role integration*: Every person has strength, experience, technical training, special skills and some unique contribution to make. When his role provides him with greater

opportunity for using such special strength, his role efficacy is likely to be higher. This is called self-role integration. The self or the person and the role get integrated through the possibility of a person's use of his special strength in the role. In a certain organisation, a person was promoted to a responsible position. This was seen as a coveted reward and it made the person concerned very happy. However, he soon discovered that in his new position, he was not able to use his special skills of training, counselling and organisational diagnosis. Although he worked very hard in the new role, his efficacy was not as high as it had been in the previous role. Later, when the role was redesigned to enable him to use his rare skills, his efficacy went up. All of us want our special strengths to be used in a role so that we can demonstrate our effectiveness. Integration, therefore, contributes to high role efficacy. On the other hand, if there is a distance between the self and the role, role efficacy is likely to be low.

2. *Proactivity*: A person who occupies a role responds to the various expectations that people in the organisation have from that role. While this certainly gives him satisfaction, it also satisfies others in the organisation. However, if he is also expected to take the initiative in starting some activity, the efficacy will be higher. Reactive behaviour (responding to the expectations of others) helps a person to be effective to some extent, but proactivity (taking the initiative rather than only responding to others' expectations) contributes much more to efficacy. If a person likes to take the initiative but has no opportunity to do so in his present role in the organisation, his efficacy will be low.

3. *Creativity*: It is not only initiative that is important for efficacy. An opportunity to be creative and try new and unconventional ways of solving problems is equally important. In a state government department, people performing clerical roles met, as a part of a reorganisation experiment, to discuss how each individual could experiment with the system of cutting delays in processing papers. The results were amazing. Not only the satisfaction of people in that department went up but also delays were considerably reduced and some innovative systems emerged. Certainly, these were further discussed and modified, but the opportunity it gave people to be creative and try out innovative ideas increased their role efficacy, and their performance improved markedly. If a person perceives that he has to perform only routine tasks, it becomes detrimental for high role efficacy. If he feels that the role does not allow any time or opportunity to be creative, efficacy is bound to be low.

4. *Confrontation*: In general, if people in an organisation avoid problems or shift them on to others, their role efficacy will be low. The tendency to confront problems and find relevant solutions contributes to efficacy. When people facing interpersonal problems sit down, talk about them and search out solutions, their efficacy is likely to be higher compared to situations where they either deny having such problems or refer them to their higher officers.

49.3.2 Dimension 2: Role Centring

1. *Centrality*: If a person feels that the role he occupies is central to the organisation, his role efficacy is likely to be high. If people feel that their roles are peripheral, that is, not very important, their potential effectiveness will be low. This is true for all persons and not only for those at the lowest level.

   In a large hospital, lowest level employees such as ward boys and attendants had very high motivation when they joined. They would bring their friends and relatives from nearby villages to show proudly their place of work. However, within a few months, they sat around gossiping in groups. They were rated as very low in effectiveness. An investigation of the problem showed that within a few months of their joining the hospital, their perception about the importance of their role changed—they felt that their role was not important at all.

2. *Influence*: A relative concept is that of influence or power. The more influence a person is able to exercise in his role, the higher its efficacy is likely to be. One factor that makes roles in the public sector or in civil services more efficacious is the opportunity to influence a larger section of society. A gatekeeper in a hospital was trained to screen visitors outside visiting hours. He used his own discretion in admitting them and referred a case to nurses or doctors only for clarification and guidance. Interviews with such employees in this hospital showed that they were very proud of their roles. One obvious factor underlying the higher motivation of the workers was the discretion given to the roles.

3. *Personal growth*: Another factor that contributes to role efficacy is the perception that the role provides the individual with an opportunity to grow and develop. There are several instances of people leaving one role and becoming very effective in another, which happens primarily because they have greater opportunity to grow in the second role. A head of a training institute accepted a new position, taking a big financial cut in his salary because he felt that he had nothing more to learn in the previous position while the new one afforded him opportunities to grow further. Examples of executives switching over to faculty roles at management institutes indicate the importance of self-development in role efficacy. If a person feels that he is stagnating in a role without any opportunity to grow, he is likely to have low role efficacy. In many institutes of higher learning, the roles of the research/teaching staff pose problems of low efficacy. The main reason is the lack of opportunity for them to grow systematically in their roles. Institutes that are able to plan the growth of such people in their roles will increase the efficacy of the roles and, in turn, obtain greater contribution from them.

49.3.3 Dimension 3: Role Linking

1. *Inter-role linkage*: Linking one's role with others' in the organisation increases efficacy. If there is a joint effort to understand problems, find solutions, etc., efficacy of the

various roles involved is likely to be high. Of course, the presumption is that people know how to work effectively. Similarly, if a person is a member of a task group that is set up for a specific purpose, his efficacy (other person works without any linkage with other roles) reduces role efficacy.

2. *Helping relationship*: If person performing a particular role feels that he can get help from some source in the organisation whenever the need arises, he is likely to have higher role efficacy. On the other hand, if there is a feeling that no help is forthcoming when asked for or that the respondents are hostile, role efficacy will be low. A helping relationship is of two kinds: (a) feeling free to ask for help and expecting that help would be available when it is needed, and (b) willingness to help and respond to the needs of others.

3. *Superordination*: A role may have linkages with systems, groups and entities beyond the organisation. When a person performing a particular role feels that what he does is likely to be of value to a larger group, his efficacy is likely to be high. The roles that give opportunities to role occupants to work for superordinate goals have the highest efficacy. Superordinate goals are those that serve large groups and those that cannot be achieved without some collaborative effort. One major motivation for people at the top to move to public sector undertakings is the opportunity to work for larger goals, which are likely to help larger sections of society. Many people have voluntarily accepted cuts in their salaries to move from the private to the public sector at the top level, mainly because of this. Roles in which people feel that what they are doing is helpful to the organisation they work for have higher efficacy.

49.4 GUIDELINES FOR SCORING ROLE ESSAYS

49.4.1 Integration Versus Distance

Integration between the self and the role contributes to role efficacy, while self-role distance diminishes efficacy.

Full integration (Score +2). Score statements that show a role occupant enjoying his role, or thinking it is to his liking, training and aptitude.

Example:
I am able to use my knowledge very well here.
I like my role very much.

Partial integration (Score +1). Score statements showing the role occupant enjoying some but not all aspects. The word 'but' is indicative of this.

Example:
I enjoy my role in R&D, but my knowledge of chemical processing is not fully utilised.

Distance (Score –1). Score statements indicating lack of involvement of the role occupant in his perception that his talents are not utilised at all in the role.

Example:
I am misfit in the organisation.
My training is not used at all.

49.4.2 Proactivity Versus Reactivity

When a role occupant takes the initiative to do something on his own, he shows proactive behaviour. When he merely responds to what others expect of him, he shows reactive behaviour.

Proactivity (Score +2). Score statements showing the occupant taking the initiative in his role. Problem-solving statements are also scored.

Example:
I prepare the budget for discussion.
I solve conflicts among my subordinates.

Reactivity (Score +1). Score statements showing the role occupant conforming to others' expectations and demands.

Example:
I prepare the budget according to the guidance given by my boss.

Negative reactivity (Score –1). Score statements showing that the role occupant resents others' expectations.

Example:
I have no freedom. I am only an errand boy and I do not like it.

49.4.3 Creativity Versus Routinity

When a role occupant perceives that he has done something new or unique in his role, his efficacy is high. The perception that only routine tasks are performed by the role occupant lowers role efficacy.

Creativity (Score +2). Score statements showing that the role occupant innovates or tries and does new things.

Example:
In my role (training manager), I design new programmes.

Routinity (Score +1). Score statements showing that the role occupant does only routine things. If no statements of creativity are made, routinism is scored.

Example:
I am supervising the workers.

Boredom (Score −1). Score statements indicating that the role occupant has no opportunity to do creative work.

Example:
I have no time for creative work.
My job takes away all my time and I cannot try out something now.

49.4.4 Confrontation Versus Avoidance

When problems arise, they may be confronted or avoided. Attempts made to find a solution contribute to efficacy while avoidance reduces efficacy.

Confrontation (Score +2). Score statements indicating that conflicts or problems are confronted and solved.

Example:
If a subordinate brings a problem to me, I sit with him and work out the solution.

Transfer (Score +1). Score statements showing that the problems or conflicts are referred to other persons.

Example:
If a subordinate brings a problem to me, I ask people who come with a conflict to me to work it out between themselves.

Avoidance (Score −1). Score statements showing dislike for conflicts or problems are scored.

Example:
I dislike being bothered with interpersonal conflicts.
Indiscipline bothers me.

49.4.5 Centrality Versus Peripherality

This dimension measures the role occupant's perception of his role's significance. The more central the role occupant feels his role in the organisation to be, the higher will be his role efficacy.

Centrality (Score +2). Score statements showing the perceived importance of a role.

Example:
I am a production manager, and my role is very important.

Usefulness (Score +1). Score statements showing the importance given by the role occupant to his role.

Example:
I am doing useful work in the organisation.

Peripherality (Score –1). Score statements indicating that the role occupant deprecates his role or sees it as either not very important or neglected.

Example:
I am an R&D Manager. No one pays much attention to what I do. Very little importance is given to me.

49.4.6 Influence Versus Powerlessness

The feeling that a role occupant is able to exercise influence in his role increases his efficacy. The influence may be in terms of decision-making, implementation, advice or problem-solving.

Influence (Score +2). Score statements showing that the role occupant exercises influence or that his advice is accepted.

Example:
My advice on matters of industrial relations is accepted by the top management.
I am able to influence the general policy of marketing.

Desired influence (Score +1). Score statements showing that the role occupant desires to influence.

Example:
I want to influence the practices here.
I would like to shape the industrial relations policy.

Powerlessness (Score –1). Score statements showing that the occupant feels powerless.

Example:
I have no power here.
I cannot make independent decisions.

49.4.7 Growth Versus Stagnation

When a role occupant gets opportunities (and perceives them to be such) to develop in a role through learning new things, his efficacy is likely to be high. Similarly, if he perceives his role as giving no opportunities for growth, his role efficacy will be low.

Growth (Score +2). Score statements showing that the role occupant perceives his role as one providing him with opportunities for personal growth.

> Example:
> I enjoy my role very much because of the tremendous opportunities for my professional development here.
> I have been learning several new things here.

Learning (Score +1). Score statements showing that the occupant perceives his role as one that provides some opportunities for learning.

> Example:
> I learn a few new things.
> I see some new perspectives of marketing here.

Stagnation (Score −1). Score statements showing that the role occupant perceives as depriving him of opportunities for growth.

> Example:
> I do only routine things and have learnt nothing new.
> I am slowly forgetting all that I learnt as an engineer.

49.4.8 Linkage Versus Isolation

Inter-role linkages contribute to role efficacy. If the role occupant perceives interdependence with other roles, his efficacy will be high. Isolation of the role reduces efficacy.

Linkage (Score +2). Score statements indicating that the role occupant works or interacts with other roles, works in groups consisting of others.

> Example:
> I work closely with the production manager.
> I am a member of a taskforce.

Isolation (Score +1). Score statements showing that the role occupant works on his own and has no one to relate to.

Example:
I am alone and do not have anyone to consult.

Distance (Score –1). Score statements showing role–role distance, other role occupants not responding to the initiative, not interacting or not available.

Example:
No one responds to my suggestions.
Other managers do not appreciate R&D work.

49.4.9 Helping Versus Hostility

One important aspect of efficacy is the perception that help is given and received. Perception of hostility decreases efficacy.

Helping (Score +2). Score statements showing that help is provided by other role occupants, or that help is given by the role occupant to others.

Example:
Whenever I have a problem, others help me.
I help people to see the problem more clearly.

Indifference (Score +1). Score statements indicating indifference of different role occupants to each other.

Example:
When I need some help, none is available.
People here are indifferent to you.

Hostility (Score –1). Score statements showing interpersonal hostility.

Example:
People try to cut each other down.
I get very hostile responses.

49.4.10 Superordination Versus Deprivation

One dimension of role efficacy is the perception that one is contributing to something beyond one's domain, that one is serving society and is contributing to knowledge building, etc. However, if he perceives deprivation of this sort in his role, his efficacy will be low.

Superordination (Score +2). Score statements showing that the role occupant contributes to some larger entity.

Example:

What I do is also likely to benefit other industries.

I am able to serve the poor through working on policies.

Ordination (Score +1). Score statements indicating that the role occupant's work is useful for his organisation.

Example:

After I took over, profits went up.

Individual counselling helps employees.

Deprivation (Score −1). Score statements indicating that the role occupant feels deprived about not being able to contribute to a larger goal.

Example:

I regret that I do not have an opportunity to serve the poor.

I cannot find time for basic research that may advance knowledge.

49.5 RELIABILITY

Test-retest reliability was checked for a group of 20 managers by scoring their essays written on two occasions, with an interval of two weeks. It was found to be 0.88.

49.6 VALIDITY

A group of 20 managers wrote essays and completed the role efficacy scale. Correlation between the scores from the two instruments was 0.60.

49.7 USE FOR HRD

Through this instrument, the role effectiveness of a respondent in an organisation can be assessed. If the effectiveness is low, an action plan can be prepared to increase the score by analysing each of the ten aspects in detail.

Role Efficacy Scale

50.1 THE INSTRUMENT AND ITS ADMINISTRATION

The role efficacy scale is a structured instrument consisting of 20 triads of statements. A respondent marks the one statement in each triad that describes his role most accurately.

The three alternatives are pre-weighted. There are two statements for each dimension of role efficacy and the scoring pattern followed is +2, +1 or –1.

The regular scale must be completed by a role occupant for his own role, especially the role being supervised by a manager, though a slight adaptation may be needed.

50.2 CONCEPTUAL FRAMEWORK

Chapter 49 gives the conceptual framework for this chapter as well.

50.3 SCORING

The following key can be used for scoring responses:

Scoring Key for RES

Dimension	Item	A	b	c	Item	a	b	c
Centrality	1	+2	+1	−1	11	+2	+1	−1
Integration	2	+1	−1	+2	12	−1	+2	+1
Proactivity	3	−1	+1	+2	13	−1	+2	+1
Creativity	4	+1	+2	−1	14	+2	+1	−1
Inter-role linkage	5	−1	+2	+1	15	+2	+1	−1
Helping relationship	6	+1	+2	−1	16	−1	+2	+1

Dimension	Item	A	b	c	Item	a	b	c
Superordination	7	−1	+2	+1	17	+1	+2	−1
Influence	8	+1	−1	+2	18	+2	+1	−1
Growth	9	+1	−1	+2	19	+2	+1	−1
Confrontation	10	−1	+2	+1	20	+1	−1	+2

The role efficacy Index (REI) can be found by consulting Appendix 50.1. REI will range from 0 to 100.

50.4 RELIABILITY

Sen (1982) reported a retest reliability of 0.68 significant at 0.001 level. This shows the high stability of the scale. Sen has also reported high internal consistency, indicated by significant correlation values among the items.

50.5 VALIDITY

Sayeed (1985) reported item–total correlation for 20 RES items for a total sample of 658 managers and for 11 organisations separately. For the total sample, the lowest correlation was 0.16 (for item 20) and the highest 0.51. The mean corrected item–total correlation for the entire sample was −0.36, with an alpha coefficient of 0.80. The alpha coefficients for the mean corrected item–total correlations of the 11 organisations ranged from 0.71 to 0.85. These results show internal homogeneity of the scale. This, however, is only one dimension of the validity of the scale.

50.6 CORRELATES

Sen (1982) reported negative and significant correlations between role efficacy and the eight role stresses (including total role stress), all being significant at 0.001 level for bank employees. Sayeed (1985) has reported negative correlation between work-related tension and the overall role efficacy measure.

Das (1989) found role efficacy to be negatively related to some role stress variables, implying that role efficacy not only helps in experiencing job behaviour as purposeful but also in overcoming the experience of some kinds of role conflicts.

Role efficacy has been reported to have a high positive correlation with the internal locus of control. Sen (1982) revealed a positive and significant correlation between role efficacy and internality, and a significant negative correlation between role efficacy and externality of all kinds (relating to others, relating to chance and the total). These findings have been confirmed by Surti (1983) for working women. In her sample, negative correlation between role efficacy and externality (relating to others) was much higher (significant at 0.001 level).

Sen and Surti reported a positive correlation of role efficacy with the approach mode of coping with stress and a negative correlation between role efficacy and the avoidance coping mode. Both report positive correlation of role efficacy with intrapersistive coping style and negative correlation of role efficacy with impunitive style.

The relationship between role efficacy and managerial behaviour was found by reanalysing data of 500 managers, compiled by Sen (1982). It was found that the approach for six motives was significant at 0.001 level in three cases (achievement, influence and extension), at 0.01 level in two cases (control and dependency) and at 0.05 level for affiliation. When role efficacy scores were correlated with the operating effectiveness index on the six motives, all correlations were found to be positive and significant at 0.001 level (except affiliation, which was significant at 0.01 level).

A positive correlation (significant at 0.001 level) has been reported by Sen between role efficacy and achievement-oriented climate (one promoting concern and pursuit of excellence). He has also reported positive correlations between role efficacy and extension climate (significant at 0.01 level) and expert power climate. In the former, the organisational practices promote concern for employees and the organisation whereas in the latter, the practices promote expertise (utilising, rewarding, etc.). The correlations between role efficacy and dependency climate (promoting the attitudes of expecting solutions from superiors), and between role efficacy and affiliation climate (promoting personal relationship) were not found to be significant by Sen. His data revealed a negative correlation (significant at 0.01 level) only with the control climate (promoting centralisation of power).

50.7 USE FOR HRD

Role effectiveness can be assessed through this instrument. The 10 aspects can be probed and one can work out ways to increase effectiveness by increasing the aspect on which one's score is low.

Role Efficacy
Score Sheet

Name: _____   Role: _____

Organisation: _____   Date: _____

Transfer below the score from the responses to each item by consulting Scoring Key (For REI, see from Appendix 50.1).

Item	Rating	Item	Rating	Total
1.	—	11.	—	—
2.	—	12.	—	—
3.	—	13.	—	—
4.	—	14.	—	—
5.	—	15.	—	—
6.	—	16.	—	—
7.	—	17.	—	—
8.	—	18.	—	—
9.	—	19.	—	—
10.	—	20.	—	—
		Total		—

Role Efficacy Scale

Name: _____   Role: _____

Organisation: _____   Date: _____

In each of the following sets of three statements, tick the one (a, b or c) that most accurately describes your own experience in your organisational role. Choose only one statement in each set.

1. _____ a. My role is very important in this organisation; I feel central here.
   _____ b. I am doing a useful and fairly important work.
   _____ c. Very little importance is given to my role in this organisation; I feel peripheral here.
2. _____ a. My training and expertise are not fully utilised in my present role.
   _____ b. My training and knowledge are not used in my present role.
   _____ c. I am able to use my knowledge and training very well here.
3. _____ a. I have little freedom in my role; I am only an errand boy.
   _____ b. I operate according to the directions given to me.
   _____ c. I can take initiative and act on my own in my role.
4. _____ a. I am doing usual, routine work in my role.
   _____ b. In my role, I am able to use my creativity and do something new.
   _____ c. I have no time for creative work in my role.
5. _____ a. No one in the organisation responds to my ideas and suggestions.
   _____ b. I work in close collaboration with some other colleagues.
   _____ c. I am alone and have almost no one to consult in my role.
6. _____ a. When I need some help, none is available.
   _____ b. Whenever I have a problem, others help me.
   _____ c. I get very hostile responses when I ask for help.
7. _____ a. I regret that I do not have the opportunity to contribute to society in my role.
   _____ b. What I am doing in my role is likely to help other organisations or society.
   _____ c. I have the opportunity to have some effect on the larger society in my role.
8. _____ a. I contribute to some decisions.
   _____ b. I have no power here.
   _____ c. My advice is accepted by my seniors.
9. _____ a. Some of what I do contribute to my learning.
   _____ b. I am slowly forgetting all that I learnt (my professional knowledge).
   _____ c. I have tremendous opportunities for professional growth in my role.
10. _____ a. I dislike being bothered with problems.
    _____ b. When a subordinate brings a problem to me, I help to find a solution.
    _____ c. I refer the problem to my boss or to some other person.
11. _____ a. I feel quite central in the organisation.
    _____ b. I think I am doing fairly important work.
    _____ c. I feel I am peripheral in this organisation.
12. _____ a. I do not enjoy my role.
    _____ b. I enjoy my role very much.
    _____ c. I enjoy some parts of my role and not others.

13. _____ a. I have little freedom in my role.

    _____ b. I have a great deal of freedom in my role.

    _____ c. I have enough freedom in my role.

14. _____ a. I do a good job according to a pre-decided schedule.

    _____ b. I am able to be innovative in my role.

    _____ c. I have no opportunity to be innovative or to do something creative.

15. _____ a. Others in the organisation see my role significant to their work.

    _____ b. I am a member of a taskforce or a committee.

    _____ c. I do not work on any committees.

16. _____ a. Hostility rather than cooperation is evident here.

    _____ b. I experience enough mutual help here.

    _____ c. People operate more in isolation here.

17. _____ a. I am able to contribute to the company in my role.

    _____ b. I am able to serve the larger parts of society in my role.

    _____ c. I wish I could do some useful work in my role.

18. _____ a. I am able to influence relevant decisions.

    _____ b. I am sometimes consulted on important matters.

    _____ c. I cannot make any independent decisions.

19. _____ a. I learn a great deal in my role.

    _____ b. I learn a few new things in my role.

    _____ c. I am involved in routine or unrelated activities and have learnt nothing.

20. _____ a. When people bring problems to me, I tend to ask them to work it out themselves.

    _____ b. I dislike being bothered with interpersonal conflict.

    _____ c. I enjoy solving problems related to my work.

Appendix 50.1
Conversion of Raw Scores into Role Efficacy Index (REI)

Essay/Interview	RES	RED	REI	Essay/Interview	RES	RED	REI	Essay/Interview	RES	RED	REI
−10	−20	10	0								
		11	1			37	34		20	64	67
	−19	12	2		1	38	35		21		68
−9	−18		3	1		39	36			65	69
		13	4		2	40	37	11	22	66	70
	−17	14	5		3		38			67	71
−8		15	6			41	39		23	68	72
	−16	16	7	2	4	42	40	12	24		73
	−15		8			43	41			69	74
		17	9		5	44	42		25	70	75
−7	−14	18	10	3	6		43	13		71	76
	−13	19	11			45	44		26	72	77
		20	12		7	46	45		27		78
−6	−12		13	4	8	47	46			73	79
		21	14			48	47	14	28	74	80
	−11	22	15		9		48			75	81
−5		23	16			49	49		29	76	82
	−10	24	17	5	10	50	50	15	30		83
	−9		18			51	51			77	84
		25	19		11	52	52		31	78	85
−4	−8	26	20	6			53	16		79	86
		27	21		12	53	54		32	80	87
	−7	28	22		13	54	55		33		88
	−6		23	7		55	56			81	89
		29	24		14	56	57	17	34	82	90
	−5	30	25		15		58			83	91
−2		31	26			57	59		35	84	92
	−4	32	27	8	16	58	60	18	36		93
−3			28			59	61			85	94
		33	29		17	60	62		37	86	95
−1	−2	34	30	9	18		63	19		87	96
	−1	35	31			61	64		38	88	97
		36	32		19	62	65		39		98
0	0		33	10		63	66			89	99
								20	40	90	100

Nursing Role Efficacy Scale (A)*

51.1 THE INSTRUMENT AND ITS ADMINISTRATION

The Nursing Role Efficacy Scale (A) primarily focuses on the role of nurses. It is a structured instrument consisting of 30 items. The purpose of this instrument is to survey the perception of the nursing role in a hospital. Based on his experience in the hospital, a respondent is asked to rate each item on a 5-point scale, indicating how much he agrees with it.

51.2 CONCEPTUAL FRAMEWORK

See Chapter 49 for the detailed conceptual framework.

51.3 SCORING

The Score Sheet is used for scoring. Scoring can be done by the respondents themselves. First, reverse the scores of the starred items, so that 0 becomes 4, 1 becomes 3, 2 remains 2, 3 becomes 1, and 4 becomes 0.

Add the responses in each row (there are 3 items in each row) and write the total on the first blank space at the end of the row. For example, responses to items 1, 11 and 21 will be totalled in the first row. Thus, there will be 10 totals (for 10 rows) for the 10 role efficiency dimensions.

51.4 RELIABILITY

Cronbach alpha for a group of 26 was found to be 0.68.

---

* Developed jointly with Surabhi Purohit.

51.5 VALIDITY

Nursing role efficacy scale (A) had a positive correlation of 0.68 with scale (B)—given in Chapter 52.

51.6 NORMS

Means and SD values for a group of 133 nurses are given below:

Variable	Mean	SD
Integration	7	3
Proactivity	7	2
Creativity	9	2
Confrontation	9	2
Centrality	8	2
Influence	8	2
Personal growth	8	3
Inter-role linkage	8	2
Helping relationship	5	3
Superordination	8	3

51.7 USE FOR HRD

The scale is meant for measuring role efficacy of nurses. Respondents can develop action plans for improving their role efficacy by increasing the aspects having low scores.

Nursing Role Efficacy Scale (A)

Name: _____   Role: _____

Organisation: _____   Date: _____

The purpose of this instrument is to survey perception of a nurse's role in a hospital. There are no right or wrong answers.

Please read each statement given below. Based on your experience in the hospital, rate each on a 5-point scale, indicating how much you agree with it. Use the following key and write the relevant number on the left of each statement number given below.

Write 0   if you do not agree with it
Write 1   if you agree a little with it
Write 2   if you are not sure if you agree or disagree
Write 3   if you agree with it
Write 4   if you strongly agree with it

Use the answer sheet to respond to the following items.

1. _____   I have enough opportunities to use my nursing skills here.
2. _____   I do not get the opportunity to plan how to do my work.
3. _____   I am able to try out new ways to solve problems that I encounter in my role.
4. _____   I am often involved in solving problems when co-workers bring such problems to me.
5. _____   My nursing work is important for hospitals to be able to meet the needs of the patients.
6. _____   I do not have any opportunity to exercise my judgement in relation to my work.
7. _____   I have enough opportunities for professional growth in my role here.
8. _____   I work closely with other nurses.
9. _____   Whenever I have a problem, my physician gives me guidance and help.
10. _____   What I am doing in my role enhances the dignity of patients in this hospital.
11. _____   I am not satisfied with the opportunities available in the hospital to use my nursing competence.
12. _____   I can take initiative and act on my own as a nurse; I do not have to wait for my supervisor's instructions.
13. _____   I cannot be creative in solving problems here.
14. _____   Problems that arise here bother me, and I hate to get involved in their solution.
15. _____   Physicians in my ward consider my role important for their work.
16. _____   My supervisors generally accept my advice about patient care and other related matters.
17. _____   I have opportunities to learn new things while working in my role.
18. _____   I do not work closely with physicians.
19. _____   The nursing personnel here do not help one another when things are rushed.
20. _____   My work as a nurse helps to give patients new hope.
21. _____   I am able to use my special background and skills in my nursing role here.
22. _____   As a nurse, I can hardly take any initiative in this place.
23. _____   I am encouraged to be creative in my work as a nurse.

24. _____ I usually avoid problems and refer them to my supervisors.
25. _____ I feel my role is given very low priority here.
26. _____ I have no opportunity to influence decisions here; my supervisors make all the decisions.
27. _____ I feel stagnant here. My work does not give me any scope for learning new things.
28. _____ I have enough interactions with the administrative staff of the hospital.
29. _____ The administrative staff of the hospital provides me with the needed help.
30. _____ I feel my role here does not give me an opportunity to contribute to larger social goals.

Nursing Role Efficacy Scale (A)
Score Sheet

Add the responses in each row to get the NRE (A) Scores.

Statement	Response	Statement	Response	Statement	Response	Total	Category
1.	—	*11.	—	21.	—	—	Integration
*2.	—	12.	—	*22.	—	—	Proactivity
3.	—	*13.	—	23.	—	—	Creativity
4.	—	*14.	—	*24.	—	—	Confrontation
5.	—	15.	—	*25.	—	—	Centrality
*6.	—	16.	—	*26.	—	—	Influence
7.	—	17.	—	*27.	—	—	Personal growth
8.	—	*18.	—	28.	—	—	Inter-role linkage
9.	—	*19.	—	29.	—	—	Helping relationship
10.	—	20.	—	*30.	—	—	Superordination

Nursing Role Efficacy Scale (B)*

52.1 THE INSTRUMENT AND ITS ADMINISTRATION

The purpose of this instrument is to survey perception of efficacy of nursing roles in a hospital. Based on their experience in the hospital, respondents are asked to rate each of the 30 items on a 5-point scale to indicate their agreement with the statement.

52.2 CONCEPTUAL FRAMEWORK

See Chapter 49 for the relevant conceptual framework.

52.3 SCORING

Reverse the scores of the starred items, so that 0 becomes 4, 1 becomes 3, 2 remains 2, 3 becomes 1, and 4 becomes 0.

Add the responses given in each row (there are three items in each row) and write the total in the first blank space at the end of the row. For example, responses to items 1, 11 and 21 will be totalled in the first row. Thus, there will be 10 totals (for 10 rows) for the 10 role efficiency dimensions.

52.4 RELIABILITY

Cronbach alpha for a group of 26 respondents was found to be 0.81.

---

* Developed jointly with Surabhi Purohit.

52.5 VALIDITY

The scores in a group of 26 nurses on scale (B), has a 0.68 coefficient of correlation with scale (A) reported in Chapter 51.

52.6 NORMS

Mean and SD values of a group of 26 persons are given below:

Variable	Mean	SD
Integration	8	2
Proactivity	7	2
Creativity	6	2
Confrontation	6	2
Centrality	6	2
Influence	7	3
Personal growth	5	2
Inter-role linkage	6	2
Helping relationship	4	3
Superordination	5	3

52.7 USE FOR HRD

After completing their scoring, respondents can categorise them into high or low scores. They can then develop action plans for improving role efficacy by increasing scores for those aspects where the score is low.

Nursing Role Efficacy Scale (B)

Name: _____   Role: _____

Organisation: _____   Date: _____

The purpose of this instrument is to survey the perception of nursing role in hospital. There are no right or wrong answers.

Please read each statement in the enclosed list and rate it on a 5-point scale to indicate how much, based on your experience in the hospital, you agree with it. Indicate below the extent of your agreement with each statement by writing it on the left side of each statement number.

Write 0   if you do not agree with it

Write 1   if you agree a little bit with it

Write 2   if you are not sure if you agree or disagree

Write 3   if you agree with it

Write 4   if you strongly agree with it

Use the answer sheet to respond to the following items:

1. _____ Nurses generally perceive their roles as noble, to bring smiles to several faces.
2. _____ There is no much cooperation among nursing personnel here.
3. _____ Nurses here frequently interact with the administrative staff of the hospital.
4. _____ Physicians here help nurses to acquire new knowledge and skills.
5. _____ Nurses have no opportunity to use discretion even in their own roles.
6. _____ The role played by the nurses in this hospital is considered important by the physicians.
7. _____ Nurses in this place generally avoid problems and refer them to their supervisors.
8. _____ Nurses here are encouraged to try out new ways of dealing with problems.
9. _____ Nurses here cannot take any initiative and have to wait for their supervisors' instructions.
10. _____ This hospital provides enough opportunities for nurses to use their competencies in their role.
11. _____ Nurses are involved only in mercenary activities, hardly serving the underprivileged in society.
12. _____ Administrative staff has no empathy for nurses and their problems.
13. _____ There is hardly any interaction among nurses.
14. _____ The hospital provides opportunities for nurses' professional growth in various ways.
15. _____ Physicians consult nurses on relevant matters and listen to their suggestions.
16. _____ Nurses in this hospital are proud that they contribute to the good name of the hospital.
17. _____ Nurses here are encouraged to solve most of their problems and not bother their supervisors about them.
18. _____ Nurses trying out new ideas to deal with problems are not liked here.
Nurses have enough opportunities to plan how to do their work.
19. _____ Here, nurses do not get opportunities to make use of their training and skills.
20. _____ Nursing work provides opportunities to serve larger and noble causes in society.

21. _____ Physicians provide nurses with the necessary help and guidance.
22. _____ Physicians interact with their nurses on several matters.
23. _____ Here, nurses stagnate; they have no opportunity for professional development.
24. _____ The administrators here consult nurses on several matters, and nurses influence several decisions.
25. _____ Hospital administrators do not consider the nurses' roles to be important.
26. _____ Here, nurses like to solve problems rather than passing them on to others.
27. _____ Supervisors here do not like those nurses who are creative and use new ways to deal with problems.
28. _____ In this hospital, nurses are encouraged to take the initiative and act on their own.
29. _____ In most cases, nurses feel frustrated that they cannot use their knowledge, skills and other competencies in their jobs here.

Nursing Role Efficacy Scale (B)
Score Sheet

Response	Statement	Response	Statement	Response	Statement	
—	1.	—	*11.	—	21.	—
—	*2.	—	*12.	—	22.	—
—	3.	—	*13.	—	23.	—
—	4.	—	14.	—	*24.	—
—	*5.	—	15.	—	25.	—
—	6.	—	16.	—	*26.	—
—	*7.	—	17.	—	27.	—
—	8.	—	*18.	—	*28.	—
—	*9.	—	19.	—	29.	—
—	10.	—	*20.	—	*30.	—

Organisational Role Stress (ORS) Scale

53.1 THE INSTRUMENT AND ITS ADMINISTRATION

The organisational role stress (ORS) scale is used to measure 10 role stresses, that is, self-role distance, inter-role distance, role stagnation, role isolation, role ambiguity, role expectation conflict, role overload, role erosion, resource inadequacy and personal inadequacy. ORS is a 5-point scale (0–4), containing five items for each role stress and a total of 50 statements. Thus, the total scores on each role stress range from 0 to 20. Responses are to be given on an answer sheet (appended).

53.2 CONCEPTUAL FRAMEWORK

Modern life is full of stress. As organisations become more complex, the potential for stress increases. Urbanisation, industrialisation and increase in scale of operations are some of the reasons for rising stress. Stress is an inevitable consequence of socio-economic complexity and, to some extent, its stimulant as well. People experience stress as they can no longer have complete control over what happens in their lives. If telephone goes out of order, power is shut down, the water supply is disrupted, an expected promotion is denied, children perform poorly at school, prices of essential commodities increase disproportionately to income, etc., we feel frustrated, and then stressed.

There being no escape from stress in modern life, we need to find ways of using stress productively and reducing dysfunctional stress.

Several terms that are synonymous with stress or similar in meaning have been used. In order to avoid confusion, we will use the following terms, such as, stressor for stimuli that induce stress; stress for the affective (emotional) part in the experience of incongruence; symptoms for the physiological, behavioural and conceptual responses or changes; and coping for any behaviour that deals with the emotional component in the experience of incongruence (i.e., stress). The term stress will be used here to refer to such terms and concepts as strain, pressure, etc.

Stress is inevitable in today's complex life, as it is necessary for human progress. It is like a musical instrument, where an optimum stress is needed to produce good music; loose wires (less stress) would not produce the notes and too much tautness (too much stress) might result in screeching. A distinction has been made between productive or functional stress (stress for creative work, entrepreneurial activities, Olympic competitions, etc.) and dysfunctional stress (stress of boredom, unmanageable conflicts, overwork, etc.). The former has been called eustress and the latter distress.

As already stated, role can be defined as a set of functions, which an individual performs in response to the expectations of the significant members of a social system, and his own expectations about the position that he occupies in it. The concept of role and the two role systems (role space and role set) have a built-in potential for conflict and stress.

53.2.1 Role Space Conflicts

As mentioned earlier, role space is the dynamic relationship between the various roles an individual occupies and his self. It has three main variables—self, the role under question and the other roles he occupies. Any conflict among these is referred to as role–space conflict or stress. These conflicts may take several forms.

1. *Self–role distance*: This stress arises out of the conflict between the self-concept and the expectations from the role, as perceived by the role occupant. If a person occupies a role that he may subsequently find to be conflicting with the self-concept, he feels stressed. For example, an introvert, who is fond of studying and writing, may develop a self–role distance if he accepts the role of a salesman and comes to realise that the expectations from the role include meeting people and being social. Such conflicts are fairly common, although they may not be so severe.

2. *Intra-role conflict*: Since an individual learns to develop expectations as a result of his socialising and identification with significant others, it is quite likely that he sees a certain incompatibility between the different expectations (functions) of his role. For example, a professor may see incompatibility between the expectations of teaching students and of doing research. These may not be inherently conflicting, but the individual may perceive these as incompatible.

3. *Role stagnation*: As an individual grows older, he also grows in the role that he occupies in an organisation. With the individual's advancement, the role changes and with his change in role, the need for taking on a new role becomes crucial. This problem of role growth becomes acute especially when an individual who has occupied a role for a long

time enters another role in which he feels less secure. The new role demands that an individual outgrows the previous one and takes charge of the new role effectively. This is bound to produce some stress. In organisations that are fast expanding and do not have any systematic strategy of human resource development, managers are likely to experience this stress of role stagnation when they are promoted.

4. *Inter-role distance*: When an individual occupies more than one role, there are bound to be conflicts between them. For example, a female executive often faces a conflict between her organisational role as an executive and her familial role as a wife and mother. The demands on her time by husband and children may be incompatible with organisational demands. Such inter-role conflicts are quite frequent in a modern society, where an individual is increasingly occupying multiple roles in various organisations and groups.

53.2.2 Role Set Conflicts

The role set consists of important persons who have varying expectations from the role that an individual occupies. The conflicts which arise as a result of incompatibility among these expectations by the significant others (and by the individual himself) are referred to as role set conflicts. These conflicts take the forms mentioned here.

1. *Role ambiguity*: When an individual is not clear about the various expectations that people have from his role, he faces role ambiguity. Role ambiguity may be due to lack of information available to a role occupant or his lack of understanding of the cues available to him. Role ambiguity may be in relation to activities, responsibilities, priorities, norms or general expectations. Generally, role ambiguity is experienced by persons occupying roles that are newly created in organisations, roles that are undergoing change or process roles (with less clear and less concrete activities).

2. *Role expectation conflict*: When there are conflicting expectations or demands by different roles senders (persons having expectations from the role), the role occupant experiences this type of stress. The conflicting expectations may be from the boss, subordinates, peers or clients.

3. *Role overload*: When a role occupant feels that there are too many expectations from the significant others in his role set, he experiences role overload. Role overload is measured by asking questions about people's feelings on whether they can finish work given to them during a modified workday and whether the amount of work they do might interfere with how well it is done. Most executive role occupants experience role overload. Role overload is more likely to occur where role occupants lack power, where there are large variations in the expected output and when delegation or assistance cannot procure more time.

4. *Role erosion*: A role occupant may feel that the functions he would like to perform are being done by some other role. Role erosion is the individual's subjective feeling that some important expectations that he has from a role are shared by other roles within the role set. Role erosion is likely to be experienced in an organisation that is redefining its role and creating new roles. Studies indicate that in several such organisations, the stress of role erosion was inevitably felt. In one organisation, a particular role was abolished and, in its place, two were created to cater to executive and planning needs. This led to great erosion, and a feeling that the new roles were less important than the previous role.

5. *Resource inadequacy*: Resource inadequacy stress is experienced when the resources required by a role occupant for performing his role effectively are not available. Resources may include information, people, material, finance or facilities.

6. *Personal inadequacy*: When a role occupant feels that he does not have enough knowledge, skills or training to undertake a role effectively or that he has not had time to prepare for the assigned role, he may experience stress. Persons who are assigned new roles without adequate preparation or orientation are likely to experience feelings of personal inadequacy.

7. *Role isolation*: In a role set, the role occupant may feel that certain roles are psychologically closer to him while others are at a much greater distance. The main criterion of distance is the frequency and ease of interaction. When linkages are strong, the role isolation will be low and vice versa. Role isolation can therefore be measured in terms of existing and the desired linkages. The gap between them indicates the amount of role isolation. To sum up, in relation to organisational roles, the following 10 stresses are worth considering:
   a. Self-role distance (SRD)
   b. Inter-role distance (IRD)
   c. Role stagnation (RS)
   d. Role isolation (RI)
   e. Role ambiguity (RA)
   f. Role expectation conflict (REC)
   g. Role overload (RO)
   h. Role erosion (RE)
   i. Resource inadequacy (RIn)
   j. Personal inadequacy (PIn)

53.3 SCORING

The score sheet is used for scoring. The total scores on each role stress range from 0 to 20. To get the total scores for each role stress, the ratings given are totalled horizontally (for five items).

Row	Stress
1.	Inter-role distance (IRD)
2.	Role stagnation (RS)
3.	Role expectation conflict (REC)
4.	Role erosion (RE)
5.	Role overload (RO)
6.	Role isolation (RI)
7.	Personal inadequacy (PI)
8.	Self-role distance (SRD)
9.	Role ambiguity (RA)
10.	Resource inadequacy (RIn)

53.4 RELIABILITY

Retest reliability coefficients were calculated for a group of about 500 employees from three banks (Sen, 1982). Table 53.1 gives retest reliability (after eight weeks) for all the eight stresses as well as for the total role stress score. As may be seen, all the coefficients, except one, are significant at 0.001 level; one coefficient is significant at 0.003 level. The scale has acceptable reliability.

53.5 VALIDITY: ITEM ANALYSIS

Some evidence about validity is provided by a measure of self-consistency in an instrument. Each item was correlated with the total score on the instrument for about 500 respondents.

TABLE 53.1 Retest Reliability of Role Stress Variables

	Variables	Coefficient	Level of Significance
1.	Self-role distance	0.45	0.001
2.	Inter-role distance	0.58	0.001
3.	Role stagnation	0.63	0.001
4.	Role ambiguity	0.65	0.001
5.	Role overload	0.53	0.001
6.	Role erosion	0.37	0.003
7.	Role inadequacy	0.58	0.001
8.	Total role stress	0.73	0.001

TABLE 53.2   Frequencies of Item: Total Score Correlation Values for ORS Scale

Values of Correlation	Frequency
Less than 0.15	2
0.16–0.20	1
0.36–0.40	2
0.41–0.45	19
0.46–0.50	3
0.51–0.55	10
0.56–0.60	3

All but two correlations were significant at 0.001 level—one was significant at 0.002 and another at 0.008 levels. The results show high internal consistency of the scale. The distribution of the values of the coefficients of correlation is given in Table 53.2. As can be seen from the table, only values of three items are below 0.36 (items 9, 15 and 25). In the entire scale, only two items (9 and 25) were in the positive direction, and Item 15 had a positive tone. In the final scale, these items were modified.

Mean and SD values of the items were also analysed. The lowest mean value was 1.42 and the highest 3.66. Incidentally, the items having low correlation with the total have high mean values—Item 9 (2.4), Item 15 (3.6) and Item 25 (2.9). The mean of the total scores was found to be 2.1 on a 5-point scale.

53.6 VALIDITY: FACTOR ANALYSIS

Construct validity of the instrument can be tested by factor analysis of the instrument. The responses of about 500 respondents (Sen, 1981) were factor analysed.

Table 53.3 gives loadings of 10 factors on 40 items of the instrument. These factors explain almost the entire variance.

TABLE 53.3   Factor Loadings of Roles Stress

Item No.	Variables	Factors									
		1	2	3	4	5	6	7	8	9	10
1.	SRD	165	051	167	046	149	153	085	388	–096	–012
2.	IRD	619	310	005	065	–002	038	167	131	055	076
3.	RD	076	451	105	088	–062	096	067	372	–286	161

Item No.	Variables	Factors									
		1	2	3	4	5	6	7	8	9	10
4.	RA	144	119	154	228	034	157	366	269	−160	155
5.	RO	335	−098	076	076	335	184	076	024	033	320
6.	RI	105	001	122	339	181	458	146	150	055	299
7.	RE	109	103	073	477	−038	244	114	253	−011	127
8.	RIn	016	126	228	048	099	309	038	325	044	296
9.	SRD	−057	031	−034	−041	026	018	125	125	−415	016
10.	IRD	798	005	124	110	−025	056	121	−038	007	−028
11.	RS	246	407	126	226	103	033	158	058	029	186
12.	RA	196	097	724	127	065	100	005	171	002	101
13.	RO	257	255	158	007	181	143	112	146	060	140
14.	RI	014	254	167	093	−047	316	040	259	186	193
15.	RE	−025	248	−105	−049	−241	148	−059	131	256	−142
16.	RIn	224	121	099	103	033	061	449	098	−248	072
17.	SRD	012	179	049	064	−032	193	126	503	208	120
18.	IRD	584	085	172	−058	135	208	027	035	−071	027
19.	RS	076	309	057	114	059	−029	249	204	156	075
20.	RA	183	048	618	058	118	170	136	075	039	012
21.	RO	264	148	129	016	281	013	241	198	139	020
22.	RI	135	434	114	−043	002	441	−031	038	089	078
23.	RE	140	262	203	265	118	098	178	080	083	−051
24.	RIn	154	117	064	049	083	497	238	149	−007	107
25.	SRD	018	143	006	007	047	027	139	−047	410	053
26.	IRD	056	060	128	091	187	151	220	129	020	131
27.	RS	055	536	081	003	091	171	195	152	042	−130
28.	RA	115	159	061	098	109	233	459	046	034	−044
29.	RO	225	155	168	−032	242	226	383	101	155	007
30.	RI	056	171	128	098	−002	505	033	093	−031	−018
31.	RE	087	346	071	420	202	230	091	080	089	−108
32.	RIn	355	132	102	070	310	369	008	191	−138	−026
33.	SRD	111	237	104	145	170	237	013	611	−060	−107
34.	IRD	665	010	099	061	129	071	−013	045	082	−066
35.	RS	−058	551	−020	086	−033	182	−015	192	015	−046
36.	RA	153	105	366	−031	267	134	168	046	−005	020
37.	RO	187	114	166	097	667	129	118	039	008	024
38.	RI	117	083	102	196	196	518	162	280	009	−095
39.	RE	090	125	026	211	087	455	224	358	014	018
40.	RIn	089	501	192	043	124	070	288	−045	093	083
Eigenvalue		8.186	2.168	1.190	1.049	0.824	0.734	0.642	0.469	0.442	0.394
% of variance		50.8	13.5	7.4	6.5	5.1	4.6	4.0	2.9	2.7	2.4
Cumulative Percentage		50.8	64.3	71.7	78.2	83.3	87.9	91.9	94.8	97.5	99.9

Note: Decimal points have been eliminated.

TABLE 53.4   Summary of Loadings of Factors of Role Stress

Factors	Frequency of Loadings						% of Variance
	2+	3+	4+	5+	6+	7+	
1	5	2		1	2	1	51
2	4	3	3	3			13.5
3	2	1			1	1	7
4	4	1	2				6.5
5	5 (–1)	2			1		5
6	6	3	4	2			5
7	6	2	2				4
8	5	4		1	1		3
9	4 (–2)		2 (–1)				3
10	1	1					2

Table 53.4 gives the summary of these loadings, mentioning the frequency of loadings of 7+, 6+, 5+, 4+, 3+ and 2+.

It may be seen from Table 53.4 that factor 10 has a loading of 3+ only on one item and of 2+ on another item. It contributes 2% to the total variance. In view of these considerations, this factor can be dropped, Factor 9 has loading of 3 on one self-distance item. It has a negative loading of 3 on another self-role distance item. We may also ignore this factor. We have taken only those factors that have at least 3 loadings of 3. Thus, we are left with eight factors. Table 53.5 gives the summary of loadings of three of the eight factors on different role stress dimensions included in the instrument, Your Feelings About Your Role.

Factor 1 has high loadings on four items of inter-role distance and one item each of role overload and role inadequacy. Three IRD items relate to conflict between the organisational role and the family role. Role overload, in a way, also contributes to such a conflict. Role inadequacy (Item 32) relates to doing 'all the things I feel should be done'. In a way, this item also relates to inter-role distance. This factor has loading of about 8 on Item 10 ('My role does not allow me to have enough time with my family'). We may call this an inter-role distance (F) factor. F stands for family. This factor has the dominant theme of conflict between the organisational role and family role. IRD can be of two type—IRD (F) and IRD (S)—one concerned with conflict with family roles and the other with social roles.

Factor 2 has high loadings on all five role stagnation items and on one each of inter-role distance, role erosion, role isolation and role inadequacy. One role isolation item, on which it has a 4+ loading, relates to consultation with other roles; one role erosion item (31) relates to the

TABLE 53.5 Summary of Loading of 3+ on Eight Factors on Role Stress Dimensions

	Role Stress Dimensions							
Factors	Inter-role Distance	Role Stagnation	Role Ambiguity	Role Erosion	Role Overload	Role Isolation	Role Inade- quacy	Self-role Distance
1	4					1		1
2	1	5		1			1	1
3			3					
4				2		1		
5					2	1		
6				1		5	3	
7			2		1		1	
8		1		1			1	3

desire to have more functions in one's own role (indirectly referring to role stagnation); one role inadequacy item (40) on which the factor has 5+ loading refers to lack of skills in handling responsibility (reflecting role stagnation). Since most of these items refer to stagnation, we may call this a role stagnation factor, interpreting stagnation as lack of growth of the individual and lack of growth of the role. This factor contributes 13.5% to the total variance of role stress.

Factor 3 (explaining about 7% variance) has high loadings on only three role ambiguity items: Item 12, on conflicting demands of various people (loading of 7+); Item 20, relating to conflicting demands of peers/subordinates (loading of 6+); and Item 36, relating to demands of clients and others having expectations (loading of 3+). Its loadings of other role ambiguity items relating to clarity of responsibilities (4) and clarity about what people expect (28) are very low (–0 or +1). Therefore, this factor can be called the role ambiguity (CE). CE stands for conflict of expectations. Role ambiguity may consist of two elements—lack of clarity and conflict of expectation. Role ambiguity may consist of two elements: lack of clarity (LC) and conflict expectations (CE).

Factor 4 has high loadings on two role erosion items with loadings of 4+ (Item 7, relating to reduction of importance of the role; and Item 31, relating to important functions being assigned to other roles). It has a slightly negative loading (of 1+) on Item 15, relating to taking on more responsibility. On other role erosion items, it has loadings of 2+. It has a high loading on Item 6 (role isolation): 'Other role occupants do not give enough attention and time to my role'. This item also reflects the lower importance of the role. This factor can be called role erosion in which taking responsibility is not significant but the general feeling of the importance given by others to the role is the central theme.

Factor 5 has high loadings on two role overload items—Item 37, relating to the need to reduce some parts of the role (loading of 6+); and Item 5, stating workload being high (loading of 3+)—and has one role inadequacy item ('I do not have sufficient time or resources to do all the things I feel should be done'). The role inadequacy item also reflects a feeling of role overload with the existing resources. On other role overload items, it has the loading of 2+ on two items and 1+ on one item. We can call this factor role overload.

Factor 6 has high loadings on all five role isolation items, three role inadequacy items and one role erosion item. It has a loading of 5+ on items related to joint problem-solving (Item 30) and response for collaboration and help (Item 38); a loading of 4+ on items related to attention from other role occupants (Item 6) and mutual consultation (Item 22); and a loading of 3+ on an item related to interaction with other roles (Item 14). It also has loading of 4+ on role inadequacy items related to getting needed information. This item also denotes isolation. However, there are two other role inadequacy items on which it has loadings of 3+ (one related to authority given, i.e., Item 8 and the other to time and resources available, i.e., Item 32). The main theme in this factor is lack of linkages with other roles; we can call it a role isolation factor. This factor contributes about 50% of the total variance.

Factor 7 (accounting for 4% variance) has high loadings on two role ambiguity items, and one each of role overload and role inadequacy. It has loading of 4+ on a role inadequacy item (16) related to lack of adequate knowledge and a role ambiguity item (28: 'I do not know what the people I work with expect of me'). The emphasis in the latter item seems to be on one's own inadequacy: 'I do not know'. Similarly, it has loadings of 3+ on a role ambiguity item (Item 4: 'I am not clear…') and a role overload item (Item 29: 'Too many people expect too much…'). Both these items show helplessness and personal inadequacy. We may therefore call this factor role inadequacy (P)—P standing for personal. There may be two types of role inadequacies: personal inadequacy (lack of internal resources to meet the role demands) and resource inadequacy or role inadequacy (R), related to lack of external resources to meet role demands. This factor accounts for about 3% variance of role stress.

Factor 8 has high loadings on three self-role distance items, and one each on role stagnation, role erosion and role inadequacy items. It has a loading of 6+ on SRD Item 33 (value–role conflict), loading of 5+ on SRD Item 17 (interest–responsibility conflict) and loading of 3+ on SRD Item 1 (value–role–performance conflict). All these are self-role distance items. The other items on which it has loadings of 3+ are role stagnation Item 3 (not learning in the role), role inadequacy Item 8 (not having enough responsibility) and role erosion Item 39 (attention being given to other roles). Out of these, Item 3 reflects conflict between self-image (of learning) and the role contents. We may thus call this a self-role distance factor. This factor explains about 3% variance.

We thus got the following factors for ORS Scale:

Factor 1	Inter-role distance (IRD)	51% variance
Factor 2	Role stagnation (RS)	14% variance
Factor 3	Role expectation conflict (REC)	7% variance
Factor 4	Role erosion (RE)	7% variance
Factor 5	Role overload (RO)	5% variance
Factor 6	Role isolation (RI)	5% variance
Factor 7	Role inadequacy (Person) (R In P)	4% variance
Factor 8	Self-role distance (SRD)	3% variance

Factor analysis of the responses of 380 executives from three organisations—one each in the public, private and joint sector—gave similar evidence of the validity of the scale, although role underload was also suggested as a factor (Srinivasan & Anantharaman, 1988). Srivastava (1993) got similar results from factor analysis of data on ORS of about 400 executives in a public sector company.

53.7 NORMS

Based on median and quartile deviation, the following norms are suggested (Khanna, 1985) for managers:

Stress	Median	Low	High
SRD	5	3	9
IRD	5	2	8
RS	5	2	8
RI	6	3	9
RΛ	3	1	7
REC	4	2	7
RO	3	1	6
RE	9	7	12
RIn	5	2	8
PI	4	2	8

53.8 CORRELATES

Srivastava (1991) found a significant positive correlation of various dimensions of role stress with the symptoms of mental ill health. Stress arising from role ambiguity and role stagnation most intensively correlated with somatic concomitants of anxiety.

In a sample of 120 engineering executives, Rajagopalan and Khandelwal (1988) found total role stress had a positive correlation (0.28) with avoidance and a negative correlation (–0.29) with approach coping styles, both being significant at 0.001 level. REC, RE and SRD were not correlated with each other; correlations in case of IRD, RI and RA were significant at .05 level and in others (RS, RO, PI and RIn), these were significant at 0.01 level.

53.9 USE FOR HRD

This instrument gives data about the number of different role stresses experienced by a respondent. A detailed analysis of stresses on which a respondent has high scores can be done and some plans can be worked out to manage and reduce these.

ORS Scale

Name: _____ Role: _____

Organisation: _____ Date: _____

Read instructions carefully before responding on this sheet.

People have different feelings about their roles. Statements describing some of them are given below. Use the answer sheet to write your responses. Read each statement and indicate in the space against the corresponding number in the answer sheet how often you have the feeling expressed in the statement in relation to your role in the organisation. Use the numbers given below to indicate your own feelings.

If you find that the category to be used in answering does not adequately indicate your own feelings, use the one which is closest to the way you feel. Do not leave any item unanswered. Answer the items in the order given below:

Write 0   if you never or rarely feel this way
Write 1   if you occasionally (a few times) feel this way
Write 2   if you sometimes feel this way
Write 3   if you frequently feel this way
Write 4   if you very frequently or always feel this way

Do not write anything on these pages. Give responses on the answer sheet.

1.	_____	My role tends to interfere with my family life.
2.	_____	I am afraid, I am not learning enough in my present role for taking up higher responsibility.
3.	_____	I am not able to satisfy the conflicting demands of various people above me.
4.	_____	My role has recently been reduced in importance.
5.	_____	My workload is too heavy.
6.	_____	Other role occupants do not give enough attention and time to my role.
7.	_____	I do not have adequate knowledge to handle the responsibilities in my role.
8.	_____	I have to do things in my role that are against my better judgement.
9.	_____	I am not clear on the scope and responsibilities of my role (job).
10.	_____	I do not get the information needed to carry out responsibilities assigned to me.
11.	_____	I have various other interests (social, religious, etc.) which remain neglected because I do not get time to attend to these.
12.	_____	I am too preoccupied with my present role responsibility to be able to prepare for taking up higher responsibilities.
13.	_____	I am not able to satisfy the conflicting demands of my peers and juniors.
14.	_____	Many functions that should be a part of my role have been assigned to some other role.
15.	_____	The amount of work I have to do interferes with the quality I want to maintain.
16.	_____	There is not enough interaction between my role and other roles.
17.	_____	I wish I had more skills to handle the responsibilities of my role.
18.	_____	I am not able to use my training and expertise in my role.
	_____	I do not know what the people I work with expect of me.
19.	_____	I do not get enough resource to be effective in my role.
20.	_____	My role does not allow me enough time for my family.

21. _____ I do not have time and opportunities to prepare myself for the future challenges of my role.

22. _____ I am not able to satisfy the demands of clients and others since these are conflicting with one another.

23. _____ I would like to take on more responsibility than I am handling at present.

24. _____ I have been given too much responsibility.

25. _____ I wish there was more consultation between my role and others' roles.

26. _____ I have not had the right training for my role.

27. _____ The work I do in the organisation is not related to my interests.

28. _____ Several aspects of my role are vague and unclear.

29. _____ I do not have enough people to work with me in my role.

30. _____ My organisational responsibilities interfere with my extra organisational roles.

31. _____ There is very little scope for personal growth in my role.

32. _____ The expectations of my seniors conflict with those of my juniors.

33. _____ I can do much more than what I have been assigned.

34. _____ There is a need to reduce some parts of my role.

35. _____ There is no evidence of several roles (including mine) being involved in joint problem-solving or collaboration for planning action.

36. _____ I wish I had prepared myself well for my role.

37. _____ If I had full freedom to define my role, I would be doing some things differently from the way I do them now.

38. _____ My role has not been defined clearly and in detail.

39. _____ I am rather worried that I lack the necessary facilities needed in my role.

40. _____ My family and friends complain that I do not spend time with them due to the heavy demands of my work role.

41. _____ I feel stagnant in my role.

42. _____ I am bothered with the contradictory expectations different people have from my role.

43. _____ I wish I had been given tasks that are more challenging to do.

44. _____ I feel overburdened in my role.

45. _____ Even when I take the initiative for discussions or help, there is not much response from the other roles.

46. _____ I need more training and preparation to be effective in my work role.

47. _____ I experience a conflict between what I have to do in my role and my values.

48. _____ I am not clear what the priorities are in my role.

49. _____ I wish I had more financial resources for the work assigned to me.

ORS Scale
Score Sheet

Name: _____   Role: _____

Organisation: _____   Date: _____

1. __	11. __	21. __	31. __	41. __	1.	Inter-role distance (IRD)
2. __	12. __	22. __	32. __	42. __	2.	Role stagnation (RS)
3. __	13. __	23. __	33. __	43. __	3.	Role expectation conflict (REC)
4. __	14. __	24. __	34. __	44. __	4.	Role erosion (RE)
5. __	15. __	25. __	35. __	45. __	5.	Role overload (RO)
6. __	16. __	26. __	36. __	46. __	6.	Role isolation (RI)
7. __	17. __	27. __	37. __	47. __	7.	Personal inadequacy (PI)
8. __	18. __	28. __	38. __	48. __	8.	Self-role distance (SRD)
9. __	19. __	29. __	39. __	49. __	9.	Role ambiguity (RA)
10. __	20. __	30. __	40. __	50. __	10.	Resource inadequacy (RIn)

54

General Role Stress (GRS) Scale

54.1 THE INSTRUMENT AND ITS ADMINISTRATION

General Role Stress (GRS) scale gives a general index of an individual's role stress, focussing on his role space stresses. The main stresses in this category are self-role distance, inter-role distance, role-boundedness and personal inadequacy. It is self-administered: a respondent rates 12 items on a 5-point scale (0–4).

54.2 CONCEPTUAL FRAMEWORK

Chapter 53 gives the conceptual framework of role stress, including self-role distance, inter-role distance and personal inadequacy. A new stress, role-boundedness, is included here. If an individual feels highly obligated to the expectations of the significant role senders and he sacrifices his own interests, preferences, values, comforts, etc., he may be said to be role-bounded. Such a person may experience a conflict between his tendency to live as a person and as a role occupant. For example, in traditional Indian homes, boys may experience a conflict between their role as sons and their role as individuals. Indian culture promotes such role-boundedness.

54.3 SCORING

GRS Scale contains three items of each of the four role space stresses. The ratings given to these items are added to give a score for that particular role stress, ranging from 0 to 12. The total GRS score will range from 0 to 48, which is an index of general role stress.

Self-role distance (SRD) : 1, 5, 9   Inter-role distance (IRD) : 2, 6, 10
Role-boundedness (RB) : 3, 7, 11   Personal inadequacy (PIn) : 4, 8, 12

54.4 USE FOR HRD

Individuals who have high scores on specific role stresses can sit together to discuss ways of reducing them and, more importantly, effectively coping with them.

General Role Stress Scale

Name: _____   Role: _____
Organisation: _____   Date: _____

People perform different roles in their lives. For example, a person has a work role in his organisation and some family roles at home. He is a husband, father, son, and so on. He may have roles in other systems such as a club, social work organisation, professional body or political party, etc. This instrument is designed to know how people feel about performing various roles. Please read each statement given below and check how often you have the feeling expressed in the statement. Use the following key to respond:

Write 0   if you never or scarcely feel this way
Write 1   if you occasionally (a few times) feel this way
Write 2   if you sometimes feel this way
Write 3   if you frequently feel this way
Write 4   if you frequently or always feel this way

1. _____   I am not able to do many things for which I have a great liking.
2. _____   My role in the family conflicts with my work role.
3. _____   I feel duty-bound as a student/employee/son/father, etc.
4. _____   I do not have enough knowledge/skills needed to do justice in my roles.
5. _____   I am not able to use my strengths in the various things I do.
6. _____   I do not get enough time for my family or friends because of my other responsibilities.
7. _____   The obligations of my roles are more important to me than my own wishes.
8. _____   I feel I am not doing justice to my family role (as a son/husband/father).
9. _____   What I do in various spheres (home, institutions, organisations, etc.) conflicts with my values.
10. _____   I have some other obligations (in a club, a voluntary organisation, a party, etc.) which conflict with my main work.
11. _____   I am prepared to sacrifice my own values if they conflict with my duties in various roles.
12. _____   I wish I could be better equipped to perform my roles more adequately.

Entrepreneurial Role Stress (ERS) Scale

55.1 THE INSTRUMENT AND ITS ADMINISTRATION

Entrepreneurial Role Stress (ERS) helps entrepreneurs to become aware of various entrepreneurial role stresses and gives them some insights into their patterns. It also surveys the most common role stresses experienced by entrepreneurs in a particular area or type of enterprise.

ERS scale is a self-administered instrument. A respondent reads the statements and checks how much he is bothered by what is stated in the statement. A 5-point scale is used for the responses.

55.2 CONCEPTUAL FRAMEWORK

For the conceptual framework, see Chapter 53.

55.3 SCORING

The Score Sheet (appended) can be used for scoring. Take the following steps:

1. Transfer responses to the Score Sheet.
2. Add the three responses in each row. The range will be 3–15.
3. Convert them into the range 0 to 100 by the formula: (score − 3) × 8.33. Do this for each row.
4. Add all the converted scores. Divide the total by 9. This will give the overall stress score ranging from 0 to 100.

55.4 VALIDITY

ERS scale was used by Surti (1983) to study role stress of women entrepreneurs in India. The values of correlations of all nine stresses with the total entrepreneurial role stress were found significant at 0.001 level. This may be taken as an indicator of the internal consistency of the instrument.

Surti's inter-correlation matrix showed two clear clusters of power and extension/affiliation. The three components in power—role inadequacy, resource inadequacy, result inadequacy—had inter-correlations significant at 0.01 level. Similarly, the components of extension/affiliation—role irrelevance, inter-role distance, role isolation—had inter-correlations significant at 0.01 level. However, achievement motivation-related stresses did not turn up as a cluster. Self-role distance seemed to be related with the power cluster, having correlations significant at 0.01 level with all the three components of power-related stresses. The other stresses challenge stress and role over load, with inter-correlation significant at 0.05 level, correlated with the components of extension/affiliation-related stresses. This may be interpreted as partial construct validity of the instrument. However, this needs to be tested on more samples and in other cultures.

55.5 CORRELATES

Surti and Sarupria (1983) found that married women entrepreneurs experienced more role stress than unmarried ones (P .05), especially self-role distance and result inadequacy. Women entrepreneurs from joint families experienced less stress than those from nuclear families (probably because of the support of their families).

Using the locus of control scale developed by Levenson (1972a), Surti and Sarupria (1981) found a significant and positive correlation between external locus of control and various types of role stress as well as the overall role stress in women entrepreneurs. Fear of success was found to have a significant correlation with result inadequacy and role inadequacy. Probably, women entrepreneurs having fear of success are under stress to prove themselves against traditional sex role expectations.

55.6 USE FOR HRD

The instrument can be used as a survey tool; it may give significant areas of entrepreneurial role stresses. It may be useful to find out why some people experience certain stresses more than others. Steps can be taken to reduce those stresses that are high. Usually, a score between 10 and 15 can be regarded as high, although it may be useful to develop norms for a particular group of entrepreneurs for interpreting low and high scores. Counselling programmes and action to remedy some aspects can be taken up to reduce high stresses.

The same holds for the individual respondents. They can be helped to recognise these stresses and examine which ones are positive in motivating them and which are dysfunctional.

Entrepreneurial Role Stress Scale

Name: _____   Role: _____

Organisation: _____   Date: _____

Entrepreneurs face several problems that can generate stress. The purpose of this instrument is to help you find out the level and source of the stress. While completing the instrument, rate the degree to which you are in relation to the problems listed below. How much or how often do these problems bother you? Rate each item as indicated below:

Write 1   if it hardly or never bothers you
Write 2   if it occasionally bothers you
Write 3   if it bothers you sometimes
Write 4   if it often or almost always bothers you
Write 5   if it most often or almost always bothers you

1. _____ Having to do things that are against my better judgement.
2. _____ Not being able to spend enough time with the family.
3. _____ Loneliness in my role as an entrepreneur.
4. _____ Taking risks.
5. _____ A too heavy workload.
6. _____ Not getting the desired results.
7. _____ Lack of social usefulness of the work I do.
8. _____ Lack of adequate finances.
9. _____ Lack of adequate information needed for business.
10. _____ Not being able to use expertise, training or my strengths.
11. _____ Not being able to pursue some other interests (religious, social, political, cultural, etc).
12. _____ Not having confidants to share my ideas and problems.
13. _____ Competition of others in the field.
14. _____ Lack of time to pay attention to different aspects.
15. _____ Poor selling of my product.
16. _____ Conflict between what I do and my concern for doing something for others and for society.
17. _____ Lack of adequate machinery or other means.
18. _____ Lack of relevant technical knowledge.
19. _____ Conflict between my values and what I do.
20. _____ Conflict of my role as an entrepreneur with my social life and family obligations.
21. _____ Lack of joint and collaborative work.
22. _____ Going into something new, not yet tried out.
23. _____ Having to take all decisions and follow up myself.
24. _____ Lack of quality in my products or services.
25. _____ Lack of opportunity to do some service for those in need.
26. _____ Difficulty in getting raw material or other needed material.
27. _____ Lack of expertise in management, marketing, finance, etc.

Entrepreneurial Role Stress Scale
Score Sheet

Enter your scores from ERS scale in the spaces provided below:

						Total	Converted*	
1.	—	10.	—	19.	—	—	—	Self-role distance
2.	—	11.	—	20.	—	—	—	Inter-role distance
3.	—	12.	—	21.	—	—	—	Role isolation
4.	—	13.	—	22.	—	—	—	Challenge stress
5.	—	14.	—	23.	—	—	—	Role overload
6.	—	15.	—	24.	—	—	—	Result inadequacy
7.	—	16.	—	25.	—	—	—	Role irrelevance
8.	—	17.	—	26.	—	—	—	Resource inadequacy
9.	—	18.	—	27.	—	—	—	Role inadequacy
Overall stress score			—		—	—	—	

56
Coping with Stress: Role Pics (O)

56.1 THE INSTRUMENT AND ITS ADMINISTRATION

Role Pics is a semi-projective instrument for assessing a respondent's style or strategy to cope with his role stress. Pics is an acronym of projective instrument for coping styles. Role Pics (O) is used to assess coping styles in relation to organisational roles. In this instrument, some situations are given in which a role occupant is involved in conversation with another person, and either of them makes a statement about a role stress situation. These situations can also be made into cartoon-like pictures, similar to Rosenzweig Picture Frustration Study (for Indian adaptations, see Pareek, Devi & Rosenzweig, 1968; Pareek & Rosenzweig, 1958). A respondent is required to write down how the person to whom a statement has been made would respond. It is presumed that the responses will be a projective expression of the way the respondent himself would cope with a particular stress.

Role Pics can be administered individually or in groups. It takes about 20 minutes. For an in-depth study, individual administration has some advantages as it may provide an opportunity for inquiring about less clear responses and thus make scoring and interpretation more reliable. However, in all cases, the respondent himself should write down his responses.

When administering the instrument in groups, the instructions should be read out after the distribution of Role Pics forms, and respondents should then read the instruction given on their forms. The main purpose is to orient respondents away from any self-critical attitude and towards a more objective identification with the person under role stress (here called stressed person). In this way, the respondent tends to project, and perhaps reveal, his own underlying modes of responses in the given situation. To facilitate this, responses should be given fast; otherwise, censorship may influence them. The respondents should be told to write down the first response that comes to their minds. Responses to the situations should be written in the same sequences in which they appear on the form.

In cases where the answers are not clear or are too brief, enquiry should be used to clarify and amplify these in order to make scoring and interpretations more reliable. Enquiry is useful for in-depth or clinical analysis.

56.2 CONCEPTUAL FRAMEWORK

When individuals experience stress, they try to adopt ways of dealing or coping, with it as they cannot remain in a continual state of tension. The word coping has been used mainly with two meanings: (a) ways of dealing with stress and (b) the effort to master harmful conditions, threat or challenge. We will use the term coping in the first sense—ways of dealing with stress—and distinguish between effective and ineffective coping.

Generally, effective coping strategies are approach strategies, which confront the problem of stress as a challenge and increase the capability of dealing with it. Ineffective strategies are escape or avoidance strategies, which reduce the feelings of stress by, for example, denying the reality of stress or through the use of alcohol, drugs or other aids to escapism.

Research has shown that social and emotional support helps a person to cope with stress effectively. Persons maintaining close interpersonal relationships with friends and family are able to use more approach strategies. Social support includes material support (providing resources) and emotional support (listening to the person and encouraging him). However, studies have also shown that unsolicited support may have negative consequences.

Approach or effective strategies of coping include efforts to increase physical and mental readiness to cope (through physical exercises, yoga and meditation, diet management), creative diversions for emotional enrichment (music, art, theatre, etc.), strategies of dealing with the basic problems causing stress and collaborative work to solve such problems.

It is useful for both individuals and organisations to examine the strategy that they are using to cope with stress. The absence of a coping strategy may lead to ineffectiveness. Coping is also related to the quality and intensity of emotional reactions.

There is impressive anecdotal and research evidence pointing to the fact that we are constantly self-regulating our emotional reactions by, for instance, escaping or postponing unpleasant situations, actively changing threatening conditions, deceiving ourselves about the implications of certain facts or simply learning to detach ourselves from unpleasant situations. The emphasis should be on the individual (i.e., the self), actively appraising the situation and what he can do, rather than on environmental contingencies presumably manipulating an individual's behaviour. The style or strategy of coping seems to require some physical efforts. The macho model, in which aggressive coping by an individual is emphasised, may lead to serious health problems.

Coping styles or strategies can be seen as either a general trait (a disposition applicable to most situations) or a disposition applicable to specific stress situations. A distinction has been made between strategies that bring about a change in stress situations and those that relieve the symptoms of stress. There have not been many studies on how a person deals with the stress he experiences.

People can be classified into two types based on the strategies employed to deal with stress. The first category consists of persons who decide to suffer, deny the experienced or avoidance strategies that are termed dysfunctional styles of coping with stress situations. The second category consists of persons who face the realities of stress consciously and take some action to solve problems either by themselves or with the help of other people. These active approaches are termed functional styles of dealing with stressful situations. These find favour with social scientists as they are supposed to be more effective and healthy than dysfunctional styles.

This classification in no way suggests that people use one kind of coping process or another exclusively. Rather, it is common knowledge that different persons employ complex and varied combinations of different strategies to deal with the same kind of stress. An issue that can be raised while discussing the effectiveness of various coping styles is whether some ways of coping with stress are more effective than others. Any answer to this problem would depend upon the particular situation, the points of time (short or long run) and the levels (physiological, psychological or others) at which stress is being felt, that is, what may be considered an optimal or a beneficial response in one situation at a particular time may be damaging or ineffective in some other situation or at a different time.

In general, dysfunctional modes of coping may be damaging when they prevent essential direct action, they but may be extremely useful in helping a person maintain a sense of well-being, integration or hope under conditions otherwise likely to lead to psychological disintegration.

Marshall and Cooper (1979) asked managers how they coped with work pressure. The most common technique reported was to work longer hours. Other methods were delegation (6%), negotiating and compromising with those setting work to produce only what is really needed (8.5%), redistributing workload within the department (6%), planning ahead of annual demand peaks (3%), and balancing the department's internally generated load (3%).

Folkman, Lazarus, Dunket-Schetter, Delongis and Gruen (1986) have proposed eight coping strategies based on factor analysis of an instrument—confrontive coping, distancing, self-control, seeking social support, accepting responsibility, escape avoidance, planned problem-solving and positive reappraisal.

Different approaches to the study of coping have been used in various investigations. Some have emphasised general coping traits, styles or dispositions, while others have preferred to study active, on-going coping strategies in particular stress situations. The former approach assumes that an individual will cope the same way in most stressful situations. A person's coping style is typically assessed by personality tests. Whether the person actually behaves under stress as predicted by the tests, depends largely on the adequacy of the personality assessed and many other internal and external factors that affect the person's actions and reactions in any given situation.

As against this, those concentrating on the active coping strategies prefer to observe an individual's behaviour as it occurs in a stressful situation and then proceed to infer the particular coping processes implied by the behaviour. This approach has largely been neglected in the study of coping.

An instrument that measures coping strategies, and one that deserves special attention, is the Ways of Coping Checklist (WCCL) by Folkamn and Lazarus (1985). It identifies stressful events (appraised as potentially dangerous to one's psychological wellbeing) and then the extent of use of the eight coping strategies.

Coping strategies can be conceptualised as a product of a combination of externality, internality and mode of coping.

Externality is the feeling that external factors are responsible for role stress, resulting in aggression towards and blaming of these external factors. It may also indicate the tendency to expect and get a solution for the stress from external sources. Externality may be high or low.

Internality is quite the opposite. The respondent may perceive himself as responsible for the stress and may therefore express aggression or blame himself. Similarly, the respondent may expect a solution for the stress from within. Internality may be high or low. Coping may take the form of avoiding the situation (reactive strategy) or confronting and approaching the problem (proactive strategy). This is a mode of coping.

Combining the two aspects of each of the three dimensions, we have eight possible strategies for coping with stress. These are shown in Table 56.1 and briefly described here. These concepts have been borrowed from Rosenzweig (1978a).

Avoidance mode is characterised by any one of the four: (a) aggression and blame, (b) helplessness and resignation, (c) minimising the significance of the stressful situation by accepting it with resignation and (d) denying the presence of stress or finding an explanation for it. Such behaviour helps a person in not doing anything in relation to the stress. We have used the expression 'punitive' (borrowed from Rosenzweig) and have used capital letters to denote avoidance responses.

On the other hand, the approach mode is characterised by (a) hope that things will improve, (b) effort made by the subject will help to solve the situation, (c) expectations that others will help or asking for help in relation to stress and (d) jointly doing something about the problem.

Borrowing from Rosenzweig, we have used the term persistive for this mode and have used small letters for the styles in this mode. The eight styles are briefly described here (Table 56.1).

1. *Impunitive (M)* has a combination of low internality, low externality and avoidance. This is a fatalistic attitude and is similar to what Rosenzweig has called impunitive ('blame for the frustration is evaded altogether, the situation being regarded as unavoidable'). Some elements of Rosenzweig's impeditive category are also included (accepting stress without any reaction).
2. *Intropunitive (I)* characterised by high internality, low externality and avoidance. Blame and aggression are directed by the respondent against himself.
3. *Extrapunitive (E)* is characterised by low internality, high externality and avoidance. Rosenzweig's extrapeditive and extrapunitive styles are included here. The former occurs

TABLE 56.1   Categories of Coping Styles

Mode	Internality	Externality	Coping Style
Avoidance	Low	Low	Impunitive (M)
Avoidance	High	Low	Intropunitive (I)
Avoidance	Low	High	Extrapunitive (E)
Avoidance	High	High	Defensive (D)
Approach	Low	Low	Impersistive (m)
Approach	High	Low	Intropersistive (i)
Approach	Low	High	Extrapersistive (e)
Approach	High	High	Interpersistive (n)

when 'the presence of the frustrating obstacle is insistently pointed out' and the latter when 'blame, hostility, etc. are turned against some person or object in the environment'.

4. *Defensive (D)* is characterised by high internality, high externality and avoidance. By involving the self and others, but by using the avoidance mode, a person avoids aggression or blame with the help of defence mechanisms. Rosenzweig used defensive responses as variants of the intrapunitive category. The assumption here is that with high involvement of the self and others in the stress, the superego becomes more active and therefore defensive behaviour is stimulated.

5. *Impersistive (m)* is characterised by low internality, low externality and approach. Rosenzweig's impersistive category relates to the 'expression given to the hope that time or normal circumstances will bring about the solution of a problem; patience and conformity are characteristic'.

6. *Intropersistive (i)* is characterised by high internality, low externality and approach.

7. *Extrapersistive (e)* is characterised by low internality, high externality and approach.

8. *Interpersistive (n)* is characterised by high internality, high externality and approach. It is the opposite of the defensive (D) style.

Some studies on the 10 role stresses and 8 coping styles have been published in a volume (Pestonjee & Pareek, 1997).

56.3 SCORING

As Role Pics is a semi-projective technique, responses can be scored by using a system of categorisation. The concept given should be thoroughly read before scoring, including the eight styles to be scored for each situation. In addition, Group Conformity Rating (GCR) is also to be scored.

Sometimes, statements can be scored under two or three categories. In such cases, a statement is scored under two categories and each category is given a half (0.5) score.

56.4 GROUP CONFORMITY RATING

The concept of GCR has been borrowed from Rosenzweig. GCR measures the conformity of an individual score to the modal response of the group. The modal response is the 'most frequently given response style' to a situation by a group. For a category to qualify as modal, it must have a minimum of a third of all responses (33.3%). Rosenzweig suggested a 40% criterion. It should be separated from 'the next most frequent style' category by a statistically significant difference with a critical ratio of at least 3.0. (The standard error of the difference between percentages is used in this discrimination.)

GCR criteria, calculated from the scores of about 400 managers, are printed on the Score Sheet (appended). Details for developing GCR criteria have been reported elsewhere (Singhvi & Pareek, 1982).

When more than one criterion is given, any of these or any combination of these should be taken as a response. However, if only a part of the combination score agrees with the GCR criterion, part credit (usually 0.5) is given. All the agreements (and part agreements) can be added to give the total GCR score. The total number is then converted into a percentage. Generally, GCR score is an index of the person's adjustment to a normal group. This, however, has not yet been tried out for role pics. The detailed guidelines for scoring, given in the next section, will help in scoring responses.

56.5 SCORING SAMPLES

In order to facilitate scoring of responses, scoring samples for each situation are reproduced. These samples are based on the responses of about 800 respondents, both men and women. The responses are reproduced almost in the form in which they were given by the respondent; no corrections in the language have been made.

In a few cases where no samples were found in the actual responses to illustrate particular categories, possible responses have been thought of, and given in parenthesis. These scoring samples have been prepared carefully after a discussion with four scorers. The samples will be useful to score responses that are identical to those given here. They will also help to score those responses where words are different but the meaning is similar. The definitions of the various scoring categories and the principles on which they are based should be carefully followed and applied while scoring responses.

Situation 1

A (a colleague) to B: So they load you with so much more work.

1.M   a. Yes.

        b. Yes, sometimes.

        c. Yes, frequently.

        d. What can be done about it?

2.I   a. I cannot say no to their demands.

        b. I cannot cope with so much work.

3.E   a. This organisation is like that!

        b. These people are inconsiderate.

4.D   a. INo

        b. I don't think so.

        c. Not so much.

        d. Not really, I can handle the present load.

        e. I love it.

        f. I enjoy doing it.

        g. I like work and do not consider it a load.

        h. Oh! It is not much. It is a question of a few hours only for me.

        i. Yes, it is good fun—I enjoy working.

        j. Because I am able to cope with incremental amount of work.

        k. Due to lack of division of labour.

        l. That's because there is no one else to do it properly.

        m. That shows my capability and sincerity.

        n. I suppose that is the penalty you pay for being efficient.

        o. I suppose I am earning my salary.

        p. I don't mind.

        q. I don't care because I have to do as much as I can.

        r. Well, it does not matter really. I can deal with the extra workload.

        s. Well, someone has to do it, and I welcome the newer things it brings.

        t. They have confidence in me; that is why I get so much work.

5.m a. Oh, in due course of time it will be all right.

        b. It will be all right soon.

6.i   a. I shall reorganise my work, and fix up priorities.

        b. I shall delegate a part of it to my subordinates.

7.e   a. My boss is aware of it and will do something.

        b. I shall request my boss to reduce it.

8.n   a. Can you give me some suggestions to deal with this problem?

        b. I plan to sit and work out a solution with my boss/section/people.

9.E/D a. Yes, but I am capable of doing it.

         b. So what? I am capable of working even more.

         c. I don't mind more work, but it should be fruitful.

Situation 2

A to B (a colleague): It's too much that my boss and my subordinate have just opposite expectations from me.

1.M   a. Life is always like that.

        b. Naturally.

        c. That's there.

2.I   a. What have you done to resolve the dilemma?

        b. That seldom happens in my case.

3.E   a. Your organisation is so bad!

        b. Other people are so insensitive and unreasonable.

4.D   a. No.

        b. This is not so.

        c. It is obvious. We have to play two roles simultaneously—the supervisor and the junior, and hence the expectations.

        d. It has got to be so as you have to please your boss and you have to get work out of your subordinates.

        e. Naturally, since their expectations derive from opposite directions.

        f. This must be so at all places as, after all, the interest of both parties conflict.

        g. This may happen sometimes.

        h. You need not be so irreconcilable.

        i. Put your chin up and keep the balance. (This is not intrapersistive since the advice is not to act to solve the problem, but to deny it in behaviour.)

5.m   a. It will be all right soon.

        b. Things will work out well in due course of time.

        c. Never mind, very soon your boss will appreciate the complexity of your role and your subordinates too.

6.i   a. I am sure you can find some common things that they want from you.

        b. May be you are not doing enough. Try and find out why this is so.

        c. You must try to share your views so that they will not expect it from you like that.

        d. You should adjust your character so that you can cooperate with them in this regard.

        e. Well, try to meet them, leaving out the impossible ones.

        f. Why don't you analyse how you can negotiate between different roles?

g. You should endeavour to resolve such conflicts; why not discuss it with both of them to attain congruence.

h. Better satisfy your boss.

i. You could get them to reconcile their differences by getting them to place the interest of the organisation above their own limited self-interests.

j. You should play a role which satisfies both.

k. You can clear the matter in a convincing way.

l. At least you must find out the reason for it.

m. You do your duties as specified by your role.

7.e a. Request your boss to help you.

b. Get some help from your colleagues.

8.n a. Why don't you discuss it with both jointly and clarify their expectations?

b. You may discuss with them what your own ideas are about your role.

9.I/D a. This is what you imagine. It is possible that your boss and subordinate have same expectations from you.

Situation 3

A (a colleague) to B: It's a pity you did not have an opportunity to prepare for the future role you are likely to take in the organisation.

1.M a. Yes.

b. It's all right.

c. It happens in a big organisation like ours.

2.I a. I should have tried myself.

b. I myself did not do much about it.

3.E a. That is the organisation's failure.

b. What makes you think so?

(Aggression is directed at the colleague.)

4.D a. It is not so.

b. I don't think it is a great handicap.

c. I need not prepare because I am versatile.

d. Obviously, I had a lot to do.

e. Advance preparation is not the only thing to it. Adaptation plays a major role.

f. I don't believe in early training, I would rather attain the role so evolve.

g. It is all right; in future, I may not miss a chance.

h. Hardly any preparation is required.

i. I am confident of building the role.

j. I am not much interested in it.

5.m a. I will get it in future.

b. Anyway, I am sure that I will get the opportunity on a later occasion.

　　　c.　It is not too late, I am confident I shall get much opportunity at the appropriate time.

　　　d.　I hope, even without preparing, I will be successful.

6.i　a.　It is never too late. We can start now and continue acquiring the skill on the job.

　　　b.　I am not afraid. I will prepare myself as I go along for the role I am likely to take in the organisation.

　　　c.　There is no better way to learn than to get into the pool.

　　　d.　I shall pick up, given some time.

　　　e.　I will prepare for it now.

　　　f.　I have yet to reach that level.

　　　g.　Don't bother, I will take up the challenge.

7.e　a.　Time will tell! I am prepared, but what the organisation expects of me depends on the role.

　　　b.　I shall take the help of my boss.

8.n　a.　I can take up the issue with the organisation to work out a plan.

　　　b.　I can take the help of my colleagues to prepare for my role.

9.D/m a.　There is nothing like preparation. By understanding the role and the function of the role, it will become clear.

10.E/i a.　So what! I can still prepare for the future role right now.

　　　b.　Well, that's it! But I will try to capture my position.

Situation 4

A (wife) to B: You are so lonely in the organisation.

1.M　a.　Perhaps, but who is not?

　　　b.　This is how it happens in organisations.

　　　c.　Cannot do much.

2.I　a.　By nature, I am shy and do not interact with others.

3.E　a.　Who told you so? (This is an expression of aggression, rather than denial.)

　　　b.　The organisation is so impersonal and no one cares for people there.

4.D

　　　a.　No, I am not.

　　　b.　It is not so.

　　　c.　Not at all.

　　　d.　Not at all. I will never feel lonely with the nature I have.

　　　e.　Not at all. I am OK with my colleagues.

　　　f.　No. I have all my people to work with me.

　　　g.　Not really. I have my own group.

　　　h.　I never feel so.

     i.   When it comes to work, I believe 'work is business'. In social surroundings, I am a very friendly person.

     j.   I am not lonely as I have my boss to give me advice and my subordinates to help me.

     k.   So are all people at the top.

     l.   At top positions you are, but not with you.

     m.   That's the fate of the top man.

     n.   I like such situations.

5.m   a.   I hope after some time people will follow me.

6.i   a.   I will try to change my bad habits, so that I may be more friendly.

7.e   a.   I shall request my friends to provide me with company and help.

8.n   a.   I shall share my work and feelings with others in my department.

9.E/D a.   Who says so? I have a lot of friends and peers.

        b.   No, you feel so.

Situation 5

A to B (boss): I cannot use my talents and skills in my job.

1.M   a.   You cannot do much about it.

2.I   a.   This is really not true about me.

        b.   There is opportunity to do so.

        c.   I cannot see why; yours is an important job.

        d.   Where there is a will, there is a way.

        e.   Why?

        f.   Why not?

3.E   a.   The organisation is to blame for this.

        b.   I am sorry you feel this way.

4.D   a.   You have talents for the present job.

5.m   a.   Wait for some time. Your talents will be required, perhaps not for this job but for some other future assignments.

        b.   Gradually, you will get an opportunity to use your skills.

6.i   a.   To do so is where your own ingenuity lies.

        b.   Apply your mind to the problems we have.

        c.   There is plenty of chance provided you look around in your present job, and I am sure that you shall be able to use your talents.

        d.   You have to carve out the opportunity.

        e.   Still you continue with some better approaches.

        f.   You have to make the best use of your talent and skill in the job entrusted to you.

        g.   You certainly can.

        h.   You should work hard.

7.e   a.   Please explain to me in what way you expect to use your talents and skills in your job more effectively?

         b.   How can I help you?

         c.   Let us see now. We can look for suitable work to make you feel interested.

8.n   a.   I shall tell you the method; please follow it.

         b.   Let us find out why and which of your talents you can't use fully. Do you have any suggestions whereby we can use your talents and skills optimally in the interest of the organisation?

         c.   Let us discuss how your contribution to the organisation can be further increased through your talents and skills whereby you get satisfaction, and at the same time benefit the organisation.

9.M/D a.   I agree. If you are an engineer, you cannot absolutely use your skills in, say, accountancy.

10.D/e a.   This is not so. You can very well. I will see that you do it in future.

11.E/e a.   If you feel so, suggest an alternative. I shall give a thought to it.

12.E/n a.   Since you are underutilised in the company/organisation, you are advised to terminate your appointment and join any organisation which can utilise your skills.

13.D/i a.   No, you are using them. But you have to improve a little.

Situation 6

A to B (a colleague): I just don't get enough time to spend with my family and friends.

1.M   a.   It is true but I am unable to do anything about it.

         b.   Yes.

2.I   a.   It is your fault.

         b.   That is bunk, perhaps you don't want it.

         c.   You are then so much the poorer.

         d.   I do get enough time.

         e.   Even with the heaviest of work, I manage to snatch some time for them.

         f.   What stops you?

         g.   Perhaps you don't care for them much.

3.E   a.   Oh, you have such a bad job.

         b.   Your organisation is so bad.

4.D   a.   Mostly this happens with bank people.

5.m   a.   It will be all right after some time.

         b.   It is a temporary problem.

6.i   a.   You should certainly reschedule your time allocation so as to find some time for your family and friends.

         b.   It all depends on you. If you work systematically, you will find enough time for your family and friends.

c. It shouldn't be so. You should plan your work in such a way that you have ample time to spend with your family and friends.

d. Reduce unnecessary outside activities.

e. You can certainly plan whatever time you spend with your family in such a way as to give the maximum satisfaction to your family members.

f. You must plan your time properly.

g. Why don't you analyse how you can negotiate between different roles?

h. You must and can find some time.

i. But this is important; you must find time for family.

j. Manage your time better.

k. You should try to change your style of work a bit.

l. What you need is a crash course in time management.

m. You should find out some time to do so.

n. You should adjust your work accordingly.

o. You can put things in priority and thus avoid unwanted things to meet your family and friends.

p. By all means, you must have enough time to spend with your family.

q. Take some days off during some lean period. Take care of that part also.

7.e a. Inform your superior about the situation.

b. Take help from your superior.

8.n a. Sit with your family and plan how you can spend some time together.

a. Discuss with your superior and work out alternative ways.

9.I/i a. What do you do on holidays?

10.D/i a. Well, that's the price you pay for a good job. But you can always reserve the weekly holiday for this.

Situation 7

A (a colleague) to B: You do not get enough resources to do good work on your job.

1.M a. Can't help it.

b. That's true, but I can't help it, I am trying to find resources.

c. We have to pull on with whatever is available.

d. Yes, it is true.

e. This is true.

f. Yes.

2.I a. I do not assert myself enough.

b. I am very weak and cannot fight.

3.E a. I have tried to get it from the boss and failed.

b. May be I could do with more resources.

c. Yet they expect better performance!

d. Yes, I wish I had a free hand to get more resources.

4.D   a.   It is not correct.

b.   I do not agree.

c.   In fact, more than what is required.

d.   It can be done with little resources.

e.   This happens at times, but would work at times.

f.   It is not resources. It is a question of cooperation from my colleagues at the job.

g.   I manage with what I have.

5.m   a.   I hope for improvements in future.

6.i   a.   But we can always make the best use of the resources that we do get.

b.   I shall find means of getting sufficient resources which will enable me to do good work.

c.   You have to do with the resources you have.

d.   I shall make the best use of the resources.

e.   I must improve my style of functioning.

f.   I think the challenge would be to do a good job out of the existing resources.

g.   I should improve to get the same.

7.e   a.   I have asked my boss for the required things and I will be getting them within a short time

8.n   a.   I shall discuss it with my boss and work out a solution.

9.E/m a.   I know of the constraints we are facing currently. But I am sure things will change for the better.

10.E/e a.   It is exactly so. I am trying to convince my superior about the resources so that I can do a good job.

11.E/i a.   Resources are always there; you must know how to use them.

Situation 8

A (a colleague) to B: They have taken away some important functions from your role and have given these to other roles.

1.M   a.   It is OK.

b.   It is unfortunate.

c.   It is the process of the management.

d.   Yes.

e.   Yes, I agree with you.

f.   No problem.

2.I   a.   Yes, perhaps they are not satisfied with my work.

3.E   a.   I do not care.

b.   I am not the lawyer for it.

c.   They will repent for this.

    d. Yes and not with any justification.

    e. Yes, they consulted me and I felt they were hampering my effective functioning.

    f. They will have to give them back in the near future.

    g. This is not a fact.

    h. This is not true about me.

    i. As one rises in the organisational hierarchy, one has to delegate certain things down the ladder.

    j. So what? There are still equally important functions in my present role.

    k. Yes, but I am comfortable in my new role. After all, I am gaining more experience.

    l. I will have much less responsibility and less problems.

    m. They probably have good reasons for it. With unnecessary complexity, each role requires more attention. It is too early to say if this redefinition was not necessary.

    n. It was spread a little thin in the past.

    o. My present role provides adequate challenges.

    p. This may be for administrative convenience.

    q. Let others also get the opportunity.

    r. It's all right, I have to do my assignments that's all.

5.m   a. In due course of time, I shall get these back.

6.i   a. I will work hard in order to reinstate the important functions.

    b. I will try to improve the roles given to me to the best of my ability.

    c. I shall investigate why.

7.e   a. I shall request my boss to reallocate the functions to me.

8.n   a. I shall work out alternative arrangements with my boss.

9.E/D   a. I feel hurt, but they (boss) must be thinking that it must be good for the organisation.

    b. Let them do whatever they like. I shall not be bothered by that.

Situation 9

A to B (boss): Too many people expect too much from me.

1.M   a. So what? The job is like that.

2.I   a. This is not a positive attitude.

    b. It is your wrong impression.

3.E   a. Not from me.

    b. I am sorry for your problem.

4.D   a. That is not so.

    b. I don't think so.

    c. Because of your skills, cooperation and intelligence.

    d. People expect too much from you as they have a lot of confidence in your work.

    e. Your work is like that.

    f.   That's because they see the capabilities in you.

    g.   It is because you are so efficient and intelligent.

    h.   Because you are capable.

    i.   That shows your efficiency.

5.m   a.   This is only a temporary problem.

    b.   In due course of time, things will work out well.

6.i   a.   Don't worry about their expectations. Try to satisfy them as much as you can.

    b.   You are capable enough to tackle all these.

    c.   Try your best.

    d.   You set your priorities and act accordingly.

    e.   You cannot stop that. You have a responsible role to do.

    f.   Give each one as much as he deserves.

    g.   Do your best and I shall be happy.

    h.   Satisfy your boss.

    i.   You must try to please as many people as you can.

    j.   As far as possible you should try to comply with their expectations.

7.e   a.   I think I must lessen your job burden slightly.

8.n   a.   What's your problem? Les us discuss it.

    b.   Tell me your limitations and we shall work out solutions.

9.E/D   a.   Who are the people? I don't think you have to worry beyond your role set.

    b.   That is really a good sign. You should meet them to become more functional and popular.

10.D/m   a.   Initially, when one is on the job for the very first time, it happens. As you get used to it, you won't have this feeling.

12.D/e   a.   Who are the people? What are their expectations? I will try to tell you the reasoning behind it.

Situation 10

A to B (boss): It is not clear what I am supposed to do on my job.

1.M   a.   The same is with me also.

    b.   It is so with our jobs.

2.I   a.   Why?

    b.   I don't see why. Your duties have been specified.

    c.   That shows your lack of job knowledge.

    d.   It is because you have no job knowledge.

    e.   I stated it to you and made it clear.

    f.   I would not make such a statement to my boss!

    g.   Then what have you done up till today in the organisation?

    h.   Then leave it.

3.E	a.	I agree with you; that should have been done long back.
	b.	I am surprised to know this; I am glad you have told me.
4.D	a.	I don't think this is true.
	b.	You can never define a higher job very specifically.
	c.	This is good. Then you have all the freedom to make your role.
5.m	a.	You will soon know.
	b.	Start doing the job, everything will be clear automatically.
6.i	a.	Consult somebody and get expectations.
	b.	You tell me what you think you are supposed to do.
	c.	Analyse your job properly.
	d.	Apply yourself to the job and you will know it.
	e.	You should identify yourself with your job.
	f.	You should try to understand the elements of your job.
7.e	a.	I hope to provide a job description in due course.
	b.	I shall help you to find out.
	c.	Sit down; I shall clarify the assignment once again.
	d.	Is it so? Let me explain it to you.
	e.	Let me help with what is not clear to you.
8.n	a.	We can meet to discuss in detail how you would go about your job.
	b.	Why don't we sit down and list down what you need to do.
	c.	Observe for a few days, then we will have a discussion and then only you will have a clear picture about your job.
	d.	We can discuss and finalise.
	e.	What area of work is giving problems? I can tell you what the organisation expects from you.
	f.	Let us note it down and have a chat about it.
	g.	Please sit down and we will discuss your problems.
	h.	First, try that you have been told to do, then come with your difficulties.
9.I/e	a.	Well, it should be quite clear to you. Nonetheless, I will clarify your doubts.
	b.	Your duties were assigned the day you were appointed and you were clearly told the assignments. Anyway, your duties are to do…

Situation 11

B to A (colleague): Enough attention should have been given to help me get into the present job more effectively.

1.M	a.	It is all in the game.
	b.	It is so in my case also.
2.I	a.	Such a request will only indicate your weakness.
	b.	That seems to be a tactful excuse.

3.E a. Your organisation is such.

   b. It is really too bad.

4.D a. I don't think this is true.

   b. Not necessary.

   c. The management probably assumed that you can deliver the goods.

   d. Every time it is not possible to give enough attention to every person.

5.m a. In due course of time, every one learns his job.

   b. This will be all right after some time.

6.i a. Besides, self-effort also plays an important role.

   b. Come on now. The only one who can help you is yourself.

   c. You cannot expect to get spoon-fed. You should make your own efforts.

   d. Yes, but now go on your own.

   e. Explain the situation to your superior. Otherwise, your efficiency will be criticised.

   f. Try to equip yourself.

   g. You should be able to get such attention by devoted and sincere service.

   i. Why not attract enough attention?

   j. It depends on you to develop your professional effectiveness.

   k. You yourself should try to do your best.

   l. If you need trying, why not ask the personnel department?

   m. You should try yourself.

   n. Please, find out ways and means to do so!

   o. It is you who should take the initiative.

   p. You may put your requirements before the proper authority and get help.

   q. You can develop yourself on your own.

7.e a. You will be given enough training in connection with your present job.

   b. What sort of help do you think will help you perform your job more effectively? May be I can help.

8.n a. Can we sit down and work out a solution?

   b. Discuss it with the boss to work out a solution.

9.I/i a. Did you take enough initiative by asking people for their expertise?

10.E/i a. I agree with you, but you know, self-help is the best help. So one should not expect too much help from others.

Situation 12

A to B (colleague): I just don't have an opportunity to interact with many other roles.

1.M a. That is a pity, because it is important to interact.

   b. That is unfortunate.

   c. If your role is like that you have to accept the position.

      d.   In an institution like ours certain roles are always exclusive.

      e.   Yes, I agree with you.

2.I   a.   What stops you from interacting?

      b.   That's because you don't involve them in your work.

3.E   a.   Our organisation is like this; no one cares here for others.

      b.   How frustrating it must be!.

4.D   a.   Why do you want it?

      b.   Why should you resent it if your job is such?

      c.   Never mind.

      d.   Do not feel so.

      e.   Don't bother.

5.m   a.   I am sure that you will definitely get a chance to show your other abilities very soon.

      b.   Wait the time will come for more opportunity.

      c.   This is a passing phase.

6.i   a.   Why not get into one of the productivity improvement committees and volunteer your services?

      b.   Opportunities are always there. One has to grab them.

      c.   Familiarise yourself with what other people are doing.

      d.   You better study them carefully and use them accordingly.

      e.   Try hard.

      f.   Make them.

      g.   You should try to create opportunities.

      h.   I think opportunities should be created by you to interact with other roles.

      i.   It may be worthwhile to try to create such opportunities.

      j.   Open yourself up to others.

      k.   You must find the opportunities.

7.e   a.   Why do you wait for an opportunity? Why don't you form some social organisation where different people of different roles come and you can talk to them very informally.

8.n   a.   You probably haven't tried. No role is an island. All roles have to be effectively interwoven in an organisation. Why don't you try to talk to be your peers? Particularly those you feel should have more interaction with you.

      b.   Why don't you discuss it with your boss and work out some arrangement.

Situation 13

A (a colleague) to B: I wish your job would help you to use your special training.

1.M   a.   Yes, so do I.

      b.   Yes.

        c.   Thank you.

        d.   I also wish so.

        e.   I wish, too.

        f.   Yes, it will be really good.

        g.   Yes.

        h.   Thank you for your good wishes.

        i.   I too desire that.

2.I   a.   I have myself not tried to use my training.

        b.   Only I am to be blamed.

3.E   a.   Yes, I am underutilised by the organisation.

        b.   Yes, I have completed the course only for this job.

4.D   a.   I do not think so.

        b.   It does, to the extent it is relevant.

        c.   My job does help me to an extent.

        d.   It certainly allows me.

        e.   At least I am getting the chance.

        f.   It is my job which requires my special training.

5.m   a.   It's certainly helping me a lot, but I'll take time to put myself into the situation effectively and efficiently.

6.i   a.   I am working hard on my job to bring good results to our organisation.

        b.   I welcome the opportunity to learn something new and acquire additional skills.

        c.   I am trying to look for that kind of a job. If I get another type, I will work hard to develop the required skills.

        d.   I am trying.

        e.   I shall endeavour to do so.

        f.   I would use my special training to enrich the job content.

        g.   I am trying for a change soon.

7.e   a.   Management should decide to do something around it.

8.n   a.   May be I shall discuss it with my boss to find a way out.

Situation 14

A (a colleague) to B: Your family is disappointed and feels deprived of your attention because of your busy job.

1.M   a.   It is true but I have no alternative.

        b.   I cannot help it as I have so much to do and so little time at my disposal.

        c.   Yes, at times.

        d.   It is true to some extent, my job is like that.

        e.   Yes.

2.I	a.	I am not able to manage my time properly.
	b.	I realise I am neglecting my family.
3.E	a.	But they have whole of Sunday for themselves.
	b.	Don't bother about my family.
4.D	a.	No.
	b.	No, not at all.
	c.	This is not true about me.
	d.	I do not agree, as I am not that busy.
	e.	At times it may be so, it is not always so.
	f.	I know that, but there has been a tremendous change from the past.
	g.	My family feels happy because I am busy in my job.
5.m	a.	This is only a matter of a few months, thereafter I shall get sufficient time to please my family.
6.i	a.	I know it and I have already discussed it with my family.
	b.	Oh, yes! But I am trying to use my time with the family more effectively. I may have to give up some extra reading and help my son with his studies instead.
	c.	I realise that and I will certainly sort the matter out with them. Thank you for telling me.
	d.	I will try to spare some time for them now.
	e.	Is that so? I think I should spare more time.
	f.	I would take more time out for my family.
	g.	I will settle with them.
	h.	I will try to be less busy at my job and give more attention to my family.
	i.	I try my best to attend to them.
7.e	a.	It is true. But I hope to get two assistants who will help me; thus, my family will not be further disappointed.
8.n	a.	My family is very understanding of the situation. I have already talked to them. I am able to devote some time (though less) with my family.
9.M/I	a.	I am sorry for this.
10.M/E	a.	That is right. But I have pointed this out to my boss and the matter is being reviewed.
11.E/D	a.	Nonsense! I don't believe you. My job does keep me fairly busy but I do devote sometime to my family.

Situation 15

A to B (boss): I wish I had higher level of expertise on this job.

1.M	a.	Your job is such.
	b.	Be content.

2.I a. You have not tried to acquire the needed expertise.

   b. Why didn't you make an attempt?

3.E a. I am sorry to know this.

   b. We have not paid attention to such matters.

   c. No, there is no use for it.

   d. No, no, you already have the requisite expertise.

   e. You are perfectly OK.

   f. If you mean special training, I agree this would be of tremendous help to you. But you could still manage, so long as you know your work well.

   g. I would appreciate hard work and consistency.

   h. I am confident you will come up to our expectations.

   i. You need more, because there is no end to education or experience.

5.m a. You will acquire it in the course of your work.

   b. You can get such expertise in due course.

6.i a. You can still acquire it.

   b. Why don't you acquire it?

   c. It will be good to gain higher expertise. How do you go about it?

   d. You can still try and gain it.

   e. If you work diligently on the job, you will get the necessary level of expertise.

   f. I am happy with your interest in your job.

7.e a. Let us see. What you can read is?

   b. Would you like to get some training?

   c. If necessary, we will give you the special training.

   d. I will recommend you for further training so that you may achieve your goal.

   e. We only expect you to function to the best of your ability.

   f. In what areas do you think you lack expertise? May be we could provide you with some.

8.n a. Let us get together and work out a detailed programme for you.

Situation 16

A to B (boss): I would like to work on many more functions than are contained in my job.

1.M a. Don't bother, the jobs are what they are.

   b. This is true of all jobs.

2.I a. First you concentrate on your own functions properly and see that you make the best of it.

   b. You are not doing your own functions well.

3.E a. I am aware of this problem in some departments.

   b. Only sometimes or rarely.

4.D a. No doubt you are competent enough, but the others are very specialised functions.

      b. I am afraid not, it would impinge on other functionaries' roles.

      c. There is enough in your present job.

5.m a. Your turn will come.

      b. You will get more opportunities when the time comes.

6.i a. Try, you can get it.

      b. It can be done after you gain some experience.

      c. Excellent!

      d. I am happy with your interest in your job.

      e. You should perform your functions more effectively.

7.e a. As soon as you have mastered your functions, you will be sure to get some more.

      b. I do understand your interest in improving yourself. I would recommend that you be sent for further training in the future, when such training programmes start.

      c. I will give you more work with effect from today.

      d. I will keep this in mind.

      e. I am thinking of making some changes so that you get more important work to do.

      f. If you have enough time to do all this, it can be arranged.

      g. I am also equally anxious.

8.n a. You will gain it on the job. You will feel more confident as you go along. We are prepared to provide you with additional help if necessary.

      b. I will see what I can do. Let us discuss the details.

9.I/i a. Better attend to your functions more effectively.

Situation 17

A (boss) to B: I know you are already overburdened, but I am afraid you will have to do this assignment also.

1.M a. OK.

      b. OK, sir.

      c. Yes.

2.I a. My weakness is that I cannot say no.

3.E a. Why don't you give it to someone else?

      b. Only I get such extra work!

      c. Sir, this is too much!

      d. That's no problem for me.

      e. It will be my duty, sir.

5.m a. I shall get used to working on both assignments.

      b. I hope my work will get lightened in due course of time.

6.i   a.   Can I schedule the assignments or are you in a hurry?

          b.   Most willingly, I will certainly readjust my schedule.

          c.   I shall do it.

          d.   I shall try to satisfy you.

          e.   I will try to do my best, thank you.

          f.   It will be my pleasure.

7.e   a.   Please help me in prioritising my tasks.

          b.   Can you provide me with some extra people or resources?

8.n   a.   I shall be happy to do so. But it might require some readjustment to enable me to concentrate on more important issues and delegate routine matters to those who can handle them.

9.M/i a.   OK. I will do it.

10.D/i a.   That's all right. I will find time for it.

          b.   Does not matter. I can do it.

Note: If the response shows that the respondent is merely taking it as a fact of life (OK, Yes, etc.), it is scored M. If he mitigates the problem by merely accepting it (willingly, sir, sure, etc.), it is scored D. However, if he shows a tendency to act to solve the problem (I shall do it, I shall try to solve the problem, etc.), it is scored i.

Situation 18

A (a colleague) to B: You are not clear about the requirements of your job.

1.M   a.   There are moments when the boundary becomes too thin.

          b.   Yes.

          c.   This is so with our jobs.

2.I   a.   I am sorry!

          b.   It is certainly my fault.

3.E   a.   Please be more specific.

          b.   How do you know that?

          c.   Who says so?

          d.   You are not understanding me properly.

          e.   It appears to be so you? What do you have in mind?

          f.   It is quite a problem about my job. I am afraid; if I go to my boss, he may feel that I am a fool.

4.D   a.   I don't think so.

          b.   No, I am clear.

          c.   I am very clear about it.

          d.   Yes, because there is no job description in the organisation.

	e.	Because I am fresh for it, so it looks like that.
	f.	I have not been properly trained for the job.
5.m	a.	I will get used to it.
6.i	a.	Yes, I still have to study in detail about all functions and then only it will be clear to me.
	b.	Yes, I will try to find out.
	c.	If you think so. I will go and clarify the requirements of my job.
	d.	I shall learn.
	e.	Then I will try to understand the requirements.
7.e	a.	Can you help me in this?
	b.	Would you please elucidate?
	c.	Can you give me some feedback?
8.m	a.	Let us discuss and clarify the situation.
	b.	I shall settle it with my boss.
	c.	I have already spoken to the boss to have a clearer definition of my job.

Situation 19

A (boss) to B: You are not yet ready to take on higher responsibility.

1.M	a.	This is my fate.
	b.	I accept the situation.
2.I	a.	I have insufficient experience in my job.
	b.	I have really not worked hard enough.
3.E	a.	Can you be a little more specific?
	b.	I am sorry to hear that.
	c.	Then you can change me.
	d.	Why? Please be more specific.
	e.	Have you tried me?
	f.	You are not understanding me properly.
	g.	You are absolutely wrong.
	h.	Who says?
4.D	a.	No, I am.
	b.	No, I am ready.
	c.	This is not true.
	d.	I don't agree.
	e.	I am ready for it; you may try.
	f.	I have the confidence to take up higher responsibilities.
5.m	a.	I hope I shall get an opportunity later.
	b.	I shall wait for my turn.

6.i   a. I will try to come up to your expectations.

         b. It is all right within my limits; I will try my best to satisfy the responsibilities.

         c. I can shoulder it now.

7.e   a. Thank you for giving your frank opinion. May I request you to tell me the areas where I should improve upon so as to be ready for taking up higher responsibilities.

         b. Why not train me some more and try me out in the near future?

         c. Sir, what more do you require from me in order for me to take on higher responsibility?

         d. May I know my shortcomings?

         e. May I know my deficiencies?

         f. What are my shortcomings?

         g. I may be given an opportunity to prove my worth.

8.n   a. I have been a misfit in my present role. I think if you could give me an opportunity in the sales department, I will be able to prove myself much better.

         b. Please give me higher responsibility. I will prepare myself in the shortest possible time to shoulder them.

         c. If you will give me the opportunity, I will prove it. May I discuss these with you?

9.E/D a. No. You are wrong. I have been taking higher responsibility already.

Situation 20

A (boss) to B: You do not have close relations with other roles in the organisation.

1.M   a. I don't get an opportunity to interact with many other roles.

         b. Yes.

         c. I have tried.

2.I   a. Yes, and I don't like it.

         b. I am shy and hesitant to approach others.

         c. I feel hesitant.

3.E   a. The fault lies with the other functions.

         b. I think it is not a fair assessment.

4.D   a. I don't agree.

         b. I do not think so.

         c. That is not generally true. There may be a few I am not very close to.

         d. Sometimes it is necessary to devote time to my role requirements also.

         e. It may be true, but I can manage with my work.

5.m   a. This will be alright in due course of time.

         b. I am new. I shall automatically become closer to others.

6.i   a. I shall try to interact with other roles.

         b. I shall try to develop such relations.

	c.	To the extent necessary, I shall improve on it.
	d.	I will try to do it.
7.e	a.	So train me in those roles which you consider do not have closer relations.
	b.	I would like to know the details.
	c.	How can I improve?
8.n	a.	If you tell me the specifications, I will do my best to develop them.
	b.	May I sit with you to work out details about what to do?

Situation 21

A (boss) to B: You do not use your main talents in your role.

1.M	a.	Yes.
	b.	Yes, I agree.
2.I	a.	Perhaps, because I do not have such talents.
3.E	a.	What makes you to think so?
	b.	I don't know what you mean.
	c.	Can you be more specific?
	d.	I hardly get an opportunity to use my talents, as the job is so drab.
	e.	You can better judge from the work I do.
4.D	a.	I don't agree.
	b.	I don't think so.
	c.	It is not so.
	d.	It's not so, why should I hide my talents?
	e.	My experience does not match the work I am doing.
	f.	Though it is not apparent, I am certainly making use of my talents in day-to-day working.
	g.	I will be using it if full responsibility is given to me.
	h.	This role does not require any talents whatsoever.
	i.	The nature of my role is such.
5.m	a.	In due course of time, I shall be able to use my talent.
	b.	The job will expand in due course of time.
6.i	a.	I will try to improve.
	b.	I will try to do it.
	c.	I will try to come up to your expectations.
	d.	I do my best but will now do better.
	e.	It is only the first chance and I will take care a second time.
	f.	Well, I can take part in this New Products Committee. This will bring me in closer contact with others.
7.e	a.	I seek your guidance in doing it.

8.n   a.   I have been wanting to talk to you about this. I am bogged down in routine matters. If I have some assistance to take over these, I can spend my time gainfully.

         b.   Why not suggest something that would improve it. I have the talents and we should use them.

         c.   Please elaborate; I would like to use my talents as much as I can.

9.E/D a.   I thought I did. When do you perceive an omission?

Situation 22

A (wife) to B: You are too busy with your work and you do not have enough time for us.

1.M   a.   I agree with you.

         b.   Yes.

2.I   a.   I am sorry for this.

         b.   This is my limitation.

3.E   a.   Whatever time I give to you, you will feel it is less.

         b.   I have to have enough time for both.

4.D   a.   I do not agree.

         b.   It is not so.

         c.   No, I have plenty of time to help you.

         d.   That's not true; I give you as much time as possible.

         e.   May be, but rarely.

         f.   May be not, as much as you expect.

         g.   I always spend my Sundays at home.

         h.   I have been given more responsible work so I have to look after that all the time.

5.m   a.   This will continue for one month more as we are preparing the new personnel policies.

         b.   This has been a particularly difficult period. We shall pass the problem soon and I will be able to spend more time with you.

         c.   I will have sufficient time after this month.

         d.   I agree, but this is a passing phase.

         e.   Well darling, it is for a little while more. My boss is quite happy and I am sure to get the promotions and then we can move to a new house.

6.i   a.   My dear, how shall I explain it to you? I love my job and family equally. I shall try to spare some more time for you.

         b.   I am also worried about that; I am trying my best to reduce my working hours.

         c.   I agree. I will try to spend more time with you.

         d.   I shall try to find some.

         e.   I shall try to give more time to the family.

         f.   I am sorry. I will certainly try to adjust my work.

	g.	I am sorry. I will arrange my work in such a way that we have more time together.
	h.	I am now thinking of spending some time with you.
7.e	a.	Can you help me in rearranging my schedule?
	b.	Can you adjust to this reality for sometime?
8.n	a.	Let us both discuss my role and come to a solution mutually.
9.M/i	a.	What can be done about it? The job is like that. May be I will get some leave after some time.

Situation 23

A to B (a colleague): You do not have the necessary technical knowledge and experience for the job.

1.M	a.	Yes.
2.I	b.	I realise this, and feel bad about it.
	c.	I have not worked hard enough.
3.E	a.	You are jealous.
	b.	Mind your own business.
	c.	Substantiate your remarks.
	d.	It is not your lookout. You just see the result of my work.
	e.	Certainly, my organisation always prevents me from going for higher studies.
	f.	Then you may change it.
4.D	a.	I don't agree.
	b.	It is not so.
	c.	No. I have.
	d.	I do have.
	e.	That is true but in spite of my limited knowledge, I can control the job.
	f.	I accept your comments but that does not mean I will not be able to do the job successfully.
	g.	I am not a technical man.
	h.	I feel I have enough to do a good job.
	i.	Technical knowledge, yes. But one gets experience only when one works on the job.
5.m	a.	In due course of time, I shall acquire it.
	b.	I shall get it while working on the job.
6.i	a.	I am quite confident that I can pick up any job very soon.
	b.	I know and I am taking special training.
	c.	I can always pick it up.
	d.	I can however put in hard work.
	e.	I will learn in no time at all.
	f.	I am always willing to learn.
	g.	I am acquiring both.

7.e   a.   Please elaborate.

        b.   Can you help me in this respect?

        c.   I shall get help from my superior officer.

8.n   a.   Let's sit down and do a strength–weakness analysis and see what I need to improve.

        b.   I would like to discuss the matter with you for detailed planning.

Situation 24

A (boss) to B: I am afraid the specific function you wanted to perform has to be given to some other role.

1.M   a.   OK.

        b.   OK. It's all in the game.

        c.   It's all right. I understand.

        d.   Yes, sir.

        e.   Yes.

2.I   a.   May be I did not have requisite knowledge for it.

        b.   May be the other person is better qualified.

3.E   a.   Then why the hell am I here? Nobody wants to give me any responsibility.

        b.   It is my hard luck; you have not given me the opportunity to perform the specific function.

        c.   May I know why? Have I not done justice to the job?

        d.   I am quite disappointed; I have been working very hard.

4.D   a.   It does not matter. Let others also get a chance.

        b.   No problem, sir. I am enjoying my function.

        c.   In fact, it would have been a burden on me. I am happy.

5.m   a.   I hope to get my chance.

6.i   a.   I take the challenge and vow to perform the function to your satisfaction.

        b.   Even then, I will try my best to perform any of your assignments.

        c.   I shall work hard to deserve it.

7.e   a.   It does not matter. I only request you to give me an opportunity next time.

        b.   It doesn't matter. But you will keep me in mind for the future.

        c.   It does not matter provided you give me some other work, which is relevant to my qualifications, skills and experience.

        d.   You may give me the opportunity; if I fail then it can be given to some other role.

        e.   I shall be glad to know the reason.

        f.   It would be my pleasure if you can still reconsider.

8.n   a.   Give me a chance to perform that function. I would like to discuss with you what I can do to perform it well.

9.E/i a.   I am disappointed. I was certain that this particular function could have been discharged by me most effectively, and it would have been a great help in the overall functioning of my role. If you have not made up your mind finally, could I present my point of view and convince you of the benefits that I think will accrue to the organisation in assigning the functions to me?

10.E/e a.   Could I know the reasons for this decision?

b.   Though I have preferred these functions, you may give me other relevant functions.

56.6 STANDARDISATION

Some technical data on standardisation of Role Pics is presented here. A sample of 52 was taken from a sample of 446 respondents. The mean values of the sample on the eight coping styles were almost the same as those of the total group. It was therefore concluded that the small sample of 52 was representative of the respondents. Most of the statistics reported here have been calculated from the response of this small sample.

Several reliability indices were calculated to find out internal consistency, stability and scorer reliability of the instrument.

56.7 STABILITY INDEX

The stability of the instrument to give similar results for the same subjects on different occasions was found out by retest correlations. A sample of 52 people responded on the test on two occasions, with a gap of two months. Table 56.2 gives the mean, SDs and retest correlations for different styles and GCR. As will be seen from the table, most correlations are significant at 0.01 level. One correlation is significant at 0.05 level (for impersistive style), and one value is not significant (for intropunitive). The retest reliability coefficients show an acceptable level of stability of the instrument.

In order to test the stability further, three items for each role stress category were considered together. The total scores on the eight coping styles for each stress category were ranked (the maximum responses received on a particular style being ranked as 1, and the minimum responses received being ranked 8, and so on). This was done for both the tests at an interval of two months. The rank-order correlations were then calculated. These appear in Table 56.1 in the first row. As may be seen, all the correlations are very high; the rankings for the total sample on the total test on two tests were identical. These figures further support the stability of the instrument.

Stability was calculated for each item also. Table 56.2 gives both percentage of same specific style (one of the eight) and broad style (either avoidance or approach) scored by an individual on the first and second tests. These percentages range from 29 to 86 for specific styles and from

47 to 100 on broad styles. Frequencies of the eight styles for each item were ranked, and rank-order correlations were computed between Test 1 and Test 2. They are quite high (Table 56.3).

TABLE 56.2   Mean, SD and Retest Correlations of Coping Styles and GCR on Tests 1 and 2 (Percentages Appear in Parenthesis)

		M	I	E	D	In	i	e	n	GCR
I Test	M	2.81	1.10	1.60	8.20	0.90	6.15	2.50	0.40	10.90
		(11.7)	(4.6)	(6.7)	(34.2)	(3.8)	(25.6)	(10.4)	(1.7)	(45.4)
	SD	2.15	1.03	1.79	3.50	1.09	3.00	1.80	0.70	3.20
		(8.96)	(4.3)	(7.5)	(14.6)	(4.5)	(12.5)	(7.5)	(2.9)	(13.3)
II Test	M	2.84	0.70	1.60	7.7	0.90	6.70	2.30	0.30	11.30
		(11.8)	(2.9)	(6.7)	(32.1)	(3.8)	(29.9)	(11.7)	(1.3)	(47.1)
	SD	1.90	0.94	1.70	3.3	1.20	3.10	1.90	0.90	2.80
		(7.9)	(3.9)	(7.1)	(13.8)	(5.0)	(12.9)	(7.9)	(3.8)	(11.2)
Retest correlation		0.39**	0.25	0.37**	0.46**	0.31*	0.45**	0.34*	0.39**	0.39**

Note: *Significant at 0.05 level; **Significant at 0.01 level.

TABLE 56.3   Percentage of Agreement Between the Use of Specific and Broad Styles (Avoidance and Approach) for Role Stress Categories (Three Items Each) and Rank-Order Correlation Between the Distribution of Coping Styles on Tests 1 and 2

Categories of Items	% for Specific Style	% for Broad Style	Rank Order Correlation
RO	47	66	0.90**
RA	37	36	0.86**
RS	33	55	0.92**
RI	57	77	0.95**
SRD	49	72	0.92**
IRC	38	60	0.75*
RIn	34	59	0.86**
RE	33	66	0.98**
Total	40	65	1.00**

Note: *Significant at 0.05 level; **Significant at 0.01 level.

56.8 INTERNAL CONSISTENCY

Internal consistency of the instrument was tested by split-half correlations. The instrument (24 situations or items) were split in two ways (Table 56.4).

It was divided into halves by putting the first 12 items in one half and the next 12 items in another (split-half). It was also divided into two sections—one containing odd items and the other even items (odd–even). Correlations were calculated between the two sections for 52 respondents. The coefficients for split-half were found to be 0.71 and for odd–even 0.93. Both the coefficients are significant at 0.001 level. For a semi-projective instrument such as this, odd–even reliability coefficient is more relevant, as the change in the pattern of response was found to be a significant factor.

> It is possible for the subject to change with recognisable consistency in the course of the test from any type or direction of response to any other mode…. Any such sequence is obviously important for an understanding of reactions to frustration, since much depends in such behaviour upon the individuals' reaction to his own reaction… (Pareek, Devi & Rosenzweig, 1968)

The data was analysed to check consistency among the various role stress categories and the total test. Table 56.5 gives the rank-order correlations among the various stress categories and

TABLE 56.4 Percentage of Agreement Between the Use of Specific Style and Broad Styles (Avoidance and Approach) for Role Pics Items, and Rank-order Correlations Between the Distribution of Coping Styles on Tests 1 and 2

Items	Percentage of Agreement		Rank-order Correlation	Items	Percentage of Agreement		Rank-order Correlation
	Specific Style	Broad Style			Specific Style	Broad Style	
1.	57	84	0.93	13.	55	78	0.77
2.	41	69	0.98	14.	44	65	0.84
3.	33	58	0.92	15.	30	66	0.94
4.	86	100	1.00	16.	36	75	0.86
5.	31	69	0.67	17.	48	58	0.75
6.	42	62	0.68	18.	35	56	0.85
7.	39	59	0.81	19.	36	60	0.86
8.	35	65	0.73	20.	48	66	0.87
9.	35	57	0.95	21.	48	69	0.77
10.	35	75	0.84	22.	29	51	0.76
11.	29	47	0.85	23.	33	53	0.94
12.	35	65	0.79	24.	27	58	0.97
				Total	40	65	1.00

TABLE 56.5 Rank Order Correlation Among Coping Styles Used in Coping with Various Role Stresses

	RO	RA	RS	RI	SRD	IRC	RIn	RE
RA	0.76*	—						
RS	0.79*	0.78*	—					
RI	0.69	0.80*	0.86**	—				
SRD	0.79*	0.62	0.61	0.76*	—			
IRC	0.70*	0.52	0.44	0.68	0.88**	—		
RIn	0.71*	0.70*	0.84**	0.73*	0.42	0.42	—	
RE	0.62	0.74*	0.92**	0.73*	0.40	0.12	0.77*	—
All Situations	0.90**	0.83**	0.90**	0.90**	0.88**	0.69	0.73*	0.83**

Note: *Significant at 0.05 level; **Significant at 0.01 level.

the entire test. For each category (consisting of three situations or items), the scores of 52 respondents on eight styles were ranked for frequency, and rank-order correlations were calculated. The last row in Table 56.5 indicates high internal consistency of the instrument. There is a similar pattern of ranks of the various coping styles, as in the entire test. The Table further shows that there is less similarity of responses among some stress categories.

56.9 SCORER RELIABILITY

Inter-scorer reliability was also calculated, and four scorers got responses from 10 respondents. For each response, there were 6 pairs of scores; for 10 protocols, there were 60 pairs. The percentages of agreement are shown in Table 56.6. Later, two scorers discussed the differences and again scored another 10 protocols. The percentages of agreement after discussion are also shown in Table 56.6. Inter-scorer reliability before discussion was 50% and rose to almost 81% after discussion.

56.10 DISTRIBUTION OF COPING STYLES

To get some idea about variation in the eight coping styles, the distribution of the styles in the 24 items and eight role stress categories were examined. Tables 56.7 and 56.8 give these distributions respectively. While distribution between avoidance and approach styles is evenly distributed in most stress categories, in the case of role isolation, self-role distance and inter-role conflict, avoidance style is more frequently used (Table 56.8). The popularity of some styles is evident from Table 56.8.

TABLE 56.6　Inter-scorer Reliability of Role Pics

	Agreement Among 4 Persons (Maximum Number of Agreements 60)		Agreement Between 2 Persons After Discussion (Maximum Number of Agreements 10)	
Items	Number	Percentage	Number	Percentage
1.	42	70	8	80
2.	38	63	6	60
3.	47	78	10	100
4.	46	77	9	90
5.	25	42	8	80
6.	29	48	8	80
7.	32	53	9	90
8.	31	52	9	90
9.	30	50	9	90
10.	27	45	8	80
11.	29	48	9	90
12.	28	47	8	80
13.	21	35	9	90
14.	44	73	10	100
15.	17	28	9	90
16.	13	22	6	60
17.	30	50	10	100
18.	25	42	9	90
19.	15	25	9	90
20.	29	48	7	70
21.	39	65	9	90
22.	31	52	10	100
23.	33	55	9	90
24.	14	23	7	70
Total	715	49.6	205	80.5

TABLE 56.7　Percentage Distribution of Various Coping Styles for Pics Items

Items	M	I	E	D	m	i	e	n	Total
1.	30.8	0	1.9	57.7	0	7.7	1.9	0	100.0
2.	20.0	8.0	4.0	32.0	0	36.0	0	0	100.0
3.	11.5	0	6.0	42.3	6.0	26.2	4.0	4.0	100.0
4.	4.0	0	7.8	88.2	0	0	0	0	100.0
5.	2.0	21.1	5.8	13.5	5.8	42.2	5.8	3.8	100.0

(Table 56.7 Continued)

(Table 56.7 Continued)

Items	M	I	E	D	m	i	e	n	Total
6.	3.8	23.2	3.8	21.2	1.9	36.5	1.9	7.7	100.0
7.	13.5	1.9	7.7	38.5	0	36.5	1.9	0	100.0
8.	7.7	5.8	13.5	48.1	1.9	11.5	11.5	0	100.0
9.	5.8	11.5	0	30.8	0	46.1	5.8	0	100.0
10.	0	12.0	4.0	8.0	6.0	38.0	22.0	10.0	100.0
11.	21.6	2.0	3.9	15.7	0	37.2	17.6	2.0	100.0
12.	11.8	5.9	7.8	19.6	7.8	41.2	3.9	2.0	100.0
13.	69.3	1.9	0	11.5	0	11.5	5.8	0	100.0
14.	13.5	0	1.9	61.5	3.8	17.4	1.9	0	100.0
15.	7.7	1.9	0	19.3	15.4	32.7	11.5	11.5	100.0
16.	5.8	0	3.8	13.5	3.8	30.8	40.4	1.9	100.0
17.	17.6	3.9	0	7.8	2.0	56.9	9.8	2.0	100.0
18.	0	1.9	21.2	34.6	5.8	11.5	25.0	0	100.0
19.	3.8	1.9	11.5	46.3	1.9	11.5	21.2	1.9	100.0
20.	5.9	0	15.7	47.2	0	19.6	9.8	2.0	100.0
21.	1.9	1.9	15.5	61.5	3.9	11.5	3.8	0	100.0
22.	7.7	1.9	1.9	55.8	7.7	21.2	1.9	1.9	100.0
23.	1.9	1.9	9.7	36.5	9.7	28.8	11.5	0	100.0
24.	17.3	0	13.5	11.5	7.7	9.6	34.6	5.8	100.0

TABLE 56.8 Percentage Distribution of Coping Styles used in Role Stress Categories

	RO	RA	RS	RI	SRD	IRC	RIn	RE	Total
M	18.1	6.6	12.3	7.2	24.4	8.3	7.7	10.3	11.9
I	5.2	7.2	1.3	2.0	8.3	8.3	1.9	1.9	4.5
E	0.6	9.9	7.1	10.4	7.0	2.6	5.8	10.3	6.7
D	32.3	25.0	34.8	51.6	28.8	46.2	31.4	24.4	34.3
m	0.6	3.9	2.5	2.6	3.2	4.5	8.3	4.5	3.8
i	36.8	28.3	25.2	20.3	21.8	25.0	32.8	17.2	25.9
e	5.8	15.8	14.2	4.6	5.2	1.9	8.3	28.8	10.6
n	0.6	3.3	2.6	1.3	1.3	3.2	3.8	2.6	2.3
Total	100.0	100.0	100.0	100.0	100.0	100.0	100.0	100.0	100.0
Avoidance	56.2	48.7	55.5	71.2	68.5	65.3	46.8	46.9	57.4
Approach	43.8	51.3	44.6	28.8	31.4	34.6	53.1	53.2	42.6

TABLE 56.9 Ranks of Coping Styles in Role Stress Categories

	RO	RA	RS	RI	SRD	IRC	RIn	RE	Total
M	3	6	4	4	2	3.5	5	4.5	3
I	5	5	8	7	4	3.5	8	8	6
E	7	4	5	3	5	5.5	6	4.5	5
D	2	2	1	1	1	1	2	2.0	1
m	7	7	6.5	6	7	5.5	3.5	6.0	7
i	1	1	2	2	3	2	1	3.0	2
e	4	3	3	5	6	8	3.5	1.0	4
n	7	8	6.5	8	8	7	7	7.0	8

Table 56.9 gives the ranks of the various styles in the different role stress categories and the total. Rank 1 obviously indicates the model category. There are only three modal styles in this order—defensive, intropersistive and extrapersistive.

56.11 INTERNAL STRUCTURE OF COPING STYLES

In order to get some insight into the nature of coping styles in Indian organisations and to have some indicators of meta strategies, data from about 500 bank employees (Sen, 1981) were factor analysed. Principal components analysis was used. The factors were rotated with Varimax method. The eight variables of coping styles gave four factors, explaining 100% variance of coping styles. Factor loading of the four factors on the eight styles are given in Table 56.10.

Factor 1 explains 40% variance. It is a common factor and can be termed defensive externalisation. It has very high loadings on extrapunitive and defensive styles. This factor is characterised by blame and aggression towards external people and organisations, and a fairly high tendency to find excuses for frustration and denial of frustration. The factor has a very high negative loading on intrapersistive style. In other words, this factor is the opposite of action by the person himself, whereas there is blaming and excuses. These are the characteristics of cynicism, that is, blaming others and finding excuses for the problems, without taking any action for their solutions.

Factor 2 can be called a problem-solving factor. It has a very high loading on interpersistive style and fairly high loadings on intropersistive and impersistive styles. Impersistive style is indicative of optimism, whereas the others indicate action-orientation. This factor has a very high negative loading on impersistive style, which represents pessimism. In other words, this factor is

TABLE 56.10   Factor Loadings of Coping Styles

Variables	Factors			
	1	2	3	4
1. Impunitive	006	−888	−013	166
2. Intropunitive	047	−104	009	519
3. Extrapunitive	872	243	058	156
4. Defensive	421	−085	−518	−730
5. Impersistive	−059	310	−346	006
6. Intropersistive	−823	376	291	202
7. Extrapersistive	131	022	886	063
8. Interpersistive	144	621	−136	599
Eigenvalue	2.284	1.589	1.099	0.715
% of variance	40.2	27.9	19.3	12.6
Cumulative variance	**40.2**	**68.1**	**87.4**	**100.0**

the opposite of pessimistic fatalism and is characterised by optimism and action orientation. This factor explains about 28% variance.

Factor 3 can be called a dependent persistence factor, and it explains about 19% variance. It has a very high loading on extrapersistive style and a fairly high loading on intropersistive style. Both these dimensions are related to individual action, one by external people and the other by the person himself. However, it is marked by a tendency to find a solution (persistence) and high expectation or finding a solution from external sources (dependence). This has fairly high negative loadings on defensive and impersistive styles. In other words, this factor contains elements which are opposite to denial, frustration of finding excuses for problems. It is also opposite to simple optimism (a hope that some solution of the problem will emerge in due course of time). The factor also has a negative loading on interpersistive style, indicating the opposite of a joint solution of problems. It clearly denotes individual action on problems.

Factor 4 can be called collaborative internalisation. It has a very high loading on impersistive style and an equally high loading on intropunitive style. The factor has elements of both blaming oneself for problems as well as finding a joint solution of them. It also has a fairly high loading on intropersistive style, indicating the share of finding the solution by one's own efforts. The factor has a very high negative loading on defensive styles. In other words, there is no place for denial of stress or giving excuses for problems. It is indicative of personal responsibility for the problems and joint search of a solution. It explains about 13% variance.

56.12 CORRELATES

Rajagopalan and Khandelwal (1988) found a positive correlation between role stress and avoidance style and a negative correlation between role stress and approach style. These are consistent with the findings of other studies, such as, Gupta and Beehr (1979), who reported role conflict and role ambiguity as related to withdrawal strategies, and Surti (1983), who found positive correlation between role stress and avoidance styles. While Srivastava (1991) found a higher incidence of mental ill health in the avoidance group compared to the approach group, the later was reported to experience more role stress than the former, probably indicating that people using approach coping strategies were more aware of stress than those using avoidance strategies. Moderated multiple regression analysis showed that approach coping strategies increased perceived role stress, but 'in the long run, the focal employee feels free from tensions and anxiety'. On the other hand, employees adopting avoidance modes of coping might experience very little tension and stress but in the long run, suffer from mental ill health. Mental health has been reported as moderating the relationship between occupational stress and job satisfaction. 'The moderating effect of mental health may be attributed mainly to the effective coping strategies adopted by the mentally healthy workers endowed with high participation, self-confidence, self-respect, and environmental mastery and appropriate realistic approach' (Mehra & Misra, 1991, p. 201).

56.13 USE FOR HRD

Role Pics can be used to help people develop more functional ways of coping with stress. The following steps are involved:

1. Participants respond to the instrument.
2. They analyse their responses and prepare their own profiles of Role Pics.
3. If dysfunctional approaches (M, E, I and D) are higher than functional approaches (m, e, i and n), each participant identifies the weaker areas.
4. Participants with similar weak areas sit together to plan ways of reducing dysfunctional and increasing functional approaches.
5. They also do force field analysis of organisational and other factors promoting and reducing dysfunctional and functional approaches. They prepare action plans to increase functional approaches especially interpersistive approach.

Role Pics

Name: _____   Role: _____

Organisation: _____   Date: _____

The purpose of this instrument is to find how different people perceive different situations involving organisational roles. A total 24 situations are shown here. In each situation, two persons are talking. The statement made by one person is printed and the space for the statement made by the other person is vacant. Imagine what the other person would have said and write this down in the blank space.

There are no right or wrong answers. Please write down your first reactions. Do not leave any situation unanswered and go to the next situation after you have responded to the previous one.

Score Sheet for Role Pics

Name	Sex	Age	Date

Role		Organisation	

Item Scores

Avoidance			Approach	
1	D	D		
2		D	i	i
3	D	D		
4	D	D		
5		I		i
6				i
7	E	D	i	i
8	D	D		
9		D	i	i
10			e	i
11		E\D		i
12			m	i
13	D	M		
14	E	D	i	
15			e	i
16			e	e
17			i	i
18	D	D		
19		D		i
20	I	D		i
21	D	D		i
22	I	D		i
23	E	D		i
24	M		e	e
GCR = 10 = 41%				

Profile

	Avoidance		Approach	
	Low Externality	High Externality	Low Externality	High Externality
Low Internality	1 (M) –	(E) .5	(m) 1	(e) 1
	2 .5	1	—	2.5
High Internality	1 (I) 2	(D) 4.5	(i) 3	(n) —
	2 1	2.5	4.5	—
	{ 3	7	7.5	—
Total	1 = 7	2 = 5 S 12	1 = 5	2 = 7 S12

Trends		Styles	
1.	← D	Dominant	i
2.	→ e	Back up	D
3.			

Comments

Coping with Stress: Role Pics (G)

57.1 THE INSTRUMENT AND ITS ADMINISTRATION

Role Pics (G) has been developed for assessing coping styles in relation to role space stresses experienced by people. It consists of 12 pictures. Each shows two persons, one saying something to the other. The respondent is required to guess what the other said in response to the statement made. The instructions given in Chapters 56 and 58 are applicable here.

57.2 CONCEPTUAL FRAMEWORK

The concepts of coping discussed in Chapter 56 are the basis of this instrument.

57.3 SCORING

The scoring procedure, and the scoring samples given in Chapter 56 will be useful in scoring responses.

57.4 USE FOR HRD

The suggestions given in Chapter 56 are also applicable here.

Role Pics (G)

Name: _____   Date: _____

In the following 12 situations, two persons are talking. Read what one person says to the other. Guess what the other person would respond, and write it down.

There are no right or wrong answers. Write down your first reactions. Do not leave any situation unanswered, and go to the next situation after you have responded to the previous one.

Coping with Stress: Role Pics (E)

58.1 THE INSTRUMENT AND ITS ADMINISTRATION

Role Pics (E) measures the various coping styles of entrepreneurs. Entrepreneurs experience different kinds of stress (see Chapters 56 and 57), and they need to develop their coping competence. This instrument is designed to provide this kind of help to the entrepreneurs and those who play facilitating roles in working with entrepreneurs.

The instrument is administered the same way as described in Chapter 56.

58.2 THE CONCEPTUAL FRAMEWORK

The concepts discussed in Chapter 56 are relevant here.

58.3 SCORING

The scoring procedure and guidelines given in Chapter 56 are also to be used here. The same eight styles or strategies are identified for a respondent.

58.4 USE FOR HRD

The suggestions given in Chapter 56 are also applicable here.

58.5 CORRELATES

Based on data from 40 women entrepreneurs, Surti (1983) found intropersistive style of coping to be the dominant style among women entrepreneurs. Gupta (1989), studying 60 first generation entrepreneurs, also found intropersistive style to be the dominant coping style. He also found that coping strategies were used more frequently than avoidance strategies. Both Surti and Gupta found a significant negative correlation between role stress and approach coping mode. Gupta (1989) found a positive correlation between intropersistive style and internal locus of control. Gupta's findings showed no relationship between education and coping modes. However, the age of both the enterprise and the entrepreneur and the family type had a significant relationship with coping modes. Entrepreneurs from nuclear families used significantly more extrapunitive, defensive and interpersistive style, whereas those from joint families used intropersistive and extrapersistive styles more frequently. Entrepreneurs employing less than 20 persons used the avoidance mode of coping more than those having more than twenty employees.

Role Pics (E)

Name: _____ Organisation: _____

Role: _____ Date: _____

In the following 16 situations, two entrepreneur friends (A and B) are talking. In each case, we show what A or B has said. You are required to guess what B or A said in response to the statement given in the situation. Only in one situation does the entrepreneur's wife say something to her husband. Write down, in all cases, how you think the concerned entrepreneur would reply.

There are no right or wrong answers. Write down your first reactions. Do not leave any situation unanswered and go to the next situation after you have responded to the previous one.

PART

V

THE ORGANISATION

Currently, the four most popular organisational topics are team effectiveness, leadership, organisational learning and organisational culture. The primary role of leadership is to build teams, multiply power in the organisation, build the organisation as learning organisation and develop an appropriate culture, ethos and climate. Some instruments on these four themes are contained in this part.

1. Team Effectiveness
   a. Team Effectiveness
   b. Team Building
2. Leadership
   a. Leadership Functions
   b. Power Enhancers
   c. Visioning
   d. Delegation
3. Organisational Learning
   a. Organisational Learning
   b. Mechanisms for Organisational Learning
   c. Learning Organisation

4. Organisational Culture
   a. Ethos
   b. Organisational Climate
   c. Organisational Atmosphere
   d. Organisational Culture (Power Model)
   e. Organisational Culture (Comprehensive Framework)

Team Effectiveness Scale

59.1 THE INSTRUMENT AND ITS ADMINISTRATION

Team Effectiveness Scale consists of 30 items. Each item has two extreme poles. The respondent is required to rate each item on a 5-point scale.

In developing the instrument, a group of health administrators read some relevant literature on the characteristics of effective team and discussed their experiences about team effectiveness. Then they generated items for the proposed scale. After review and discussion, 30 items were selected and edited.

The scale contains 30 bipolar items, each with a 5 point rating scale. The respondent reads an item and rates it by encircling one of the numbers to indicate his assessment of that aspect. Thus, there will be 30 encircled responses for a respondent, one for each aspect. In order to reduce the bias due to mental set, half of the items are stated in positive and half in negative forms.

59.2 CONCEPTUAL FRAMEWORK

Most of the work in organisations is being done in teams. Effectiveness of the individuals as well as of the total organisation, therefore, very much depends on the effectiveness of the various teams functioning in the organisation. Team effectiveness deserves a great deal of attention.

What is a team? A team is a collection of individuals with interdependent roles, working for some goal(s), which is also congruent with the individual goals. A team has several characteristics: members are interdependent; it has common goal(s); each member has a distinct role and whose contribution is as important as any of them; and there is congruence between individual goals and that of the team goal.

Several types of teams function in an organisation. The most common are the teams composed of individuals who are assigned a particular task to be completed in a given time. These are natural teams of which an organisation is composed, including departmental teams. Special teams, which are constituted to work on some assignment to be completed within a time period, are called taskforce. Groups which are ongoing or which are set up for a particular period of time to deal with certain issues are also called committees. Special teams may also be constituted to complete a particular task and are called project teams. Attention needs to be given to make all such teams effective in accomplishing their goals.

In addition to work teams and other teams in the organisation, attention also needs to be given to the working of two or more teams together. Such cross-functional or inter-departmental or inter-level teams have some special characteristics which go beyond the teams per se. Inter-team functioning is increasing in most organisations and therefore requires special attention.

59.3 TEAM EFFECTIVENESS

The importance of teams was first realised by the results of the famous Hawthorn studies in the 1930s. However, it was McGregor (1960) who gave special attention to teams. Likert (1961), during the same period, focused attention on teams as important elements of humanisation of organisations. Both of them listed a large number of characteristics of effective work groups or teams. Dyer (1987) has summarised 11 characteristics of an effective work team suggested by McGregor and 24 characteristics of an effective work group as suggested by Likert. Table 59.1 lists 10 main characteristics of effective teams, covering suggestions given by both McGregor and Likert. The numbers in the table refer to the serial numbers of the suggestions listed by Dyer (1987, pp. 12, 16).

TABLE 59.1 Characteristics of Effective Work Teams (McGregor and Likert)

	McGregor	Likert
1. Commitment and inspiring goals		8, 12, 13
2. Role clarity	3, 9	23
3. Self-disclosure (including confrontation)	5, 7, 8, 11	17
4. Openness to feedback	4	18, 19
5. Competence		1
6. Creativity with constructive conformity		15, 16
7. Collaboration/support/ trust	1	2, 4, 9, 14
8. Congruence between individual and group goals		3, 5, 6, 7, 11
9. Supportive leadership		10, 24
10. Management of power	2, 6, 10	20, 21, 22

Team effectiveness can be conceived from several angles. To use the Johari Window concept, an effective team is one in which people give their opinions and comments without hesitation; listen to and examine others' opinions, comments and feedback given by colleagues at all levels; and are sensitive to the needs of others (called perceptiveness). An instrument measuring effectiveness from this point of view is included in this volume (Chapter 29). Team effectiveness can also be understood in terms of three main characteristics of team functioning: clarity of roles for different team members' cohesion, trust and closeness (amongst members of the team), confrontation, that is, solving problems as they arise rather than shying away from them; and collaboration, that is, working together, giving and receiving help to each other. The four main characteristics of team empowerment are clarity of roles of different members of the team, autonomy of the team, support provided to the team in terms of resources, etc. and accountability of the team to achieve the goals to which a commitment has been made. This chapter contains an instrument using this concept.

Using the concept of power, an effective team can be defined as one in which power is shared (widely distributed) and the members use more persuasive than coercive power (see Chapter 21 for an instrument to measure two categories of power).

59.4 TEAM BUILDING

How can we make teams more effective? The process of making teams effective is called team building. There are several approaches to team building depending on the kind of conceptual framework we use. Some of the approaches are as follows:

1. *Johari Window approach.* According to this approach, team building will involve helping individuals to take risk and frankly express their opinions and reactions, help them accept feedback from others with enough opportunity to explore further and increase their sensitivity to or perceptiveness of others' needs and orientations. This can be done by developing a profile of a team based on an individual's responses to the instrument given in Chapter 29.
2. *Role negotiation approach.* Team building can be done by using role negotiation (Harrison, 1971). Members of the team share each other's images and then list expectations of what they would like the other group to continue to do, stop or reduce, and start or increase doing something which will make one's own group more effective. Based on such expectations, negotiation between the two teams develops more collaboration between them. A similar concept, using the Indian cultural context, has been proposed as role contribution. Details about role negotiation and role contributions can be seen elsewhere (Pareek, 1993, Chapters 17, 18).
3. *Team roles approach.* Belbin (1981) suggested eight 'team roles' which people take (chairman or coordinator, shaper, plant, monitor–evaluator, company worker, resource

investigator, team worker, completer–finisher). Team building can be done by setting up effective teams and developing teams (some discussion on this approach can be seen in Pareek, 1993, Chapter 20).

4. *Behaviour modification approach.* Team building can also be done by helping people to become more effective in their individual orientations. Collaboration depends on the individual's orientation style and attitudes. According to this approach, some instruments (e.g., TSI, Chapter 43) are used to help individuals examine their styles and orientation and then increase their own effectiveness by modifying their behaviour. This is seen as an important way to enhance individuals' potential for collaboration and team building. Using the concept of power, as already suggested, an instrument (see Chapter 35) can be used to help team members examine their bases of power and plan to increase their persuasive power.

5. *Simulation approach.* Team building can be attempted by creating artificial teams in which people have an opportunity to experiment and learn from their behaviour in a less threatening context. Various games or exercises are used for this purpose, such as, Broken Squares, Hollow Squares, Win As Much As You Can, Maximise Your Gains, etc. (for use of such games for team building, see Pareek & Rao, 1991, Chapters 11, 13). After people participate in such games, they also discuss how similar dynamics operate in their home situations, and how they can use their learnings from simulation to make their own team effective.

6. *Action research approach.* In this approach, team building is done through several steps which are generally taken in action research or organisational development. Dyer (1987) has used this approach in his elaborate discussion of team building through five stages—data strengthening, data analysis, action planning, implementation and evaluation. In this approach, diagnosis is done on the basis of questionnaires, interviews or observations. The steps involved in action research and OD are taken in this approach. The instrument can be used for the diagnosis of the level of team effectiveness, and further steps can be taken on that basis.

7. *Appreciative inquiry approach.* In this approach, emphasis is given more on the positive aspects, including inspiring future dreams or goals and appreciating positive qualities in each other. Appreciative enquiry has become quite popular as a method of increasing collaboration among people and for building strong teams (Cooperrider & Whitney, 1999).

Combining various approaches, the following steps are suggested for team building:

1. *Projection in the future.* The team may prepare a common understanding of the desirable future of the team. Members, individually or in small groups, may prepare a picture of their team as they see it in the next five or seven years. A special future scenario will

help to inspire individuals to move towards it. The future is a better diagnostic device than analysis of the past!

2. *Linkage with individual goals*. The future fantasy of the team should be linked with individual aspirations and goals. Individuals in small groups may discuss how their own aspirations and goals of life can be achieved through the ideal future of the team being developed by the group.

3. *Force field analysis*. The team may identify the forces which are positive and which will help the team to move towards the desirable future and those forces which are likely to hinder its progress towards the future. Such analysis is helpful to move to the next step.

4. *Action: Strengthen positive forces*. The team may go into details of reinforcing the positive aspects which may help the team to achieve its desirable future. They can take each positive force and work out plans to strengthen it further.

5. *Action: Reduce negative forces*. The team can take up all the restraining or inhibiting forces and plan specific action steps to reduce, if not eliminate, them.

6. *Monitoring*. After decisions are taken to work on strengthening positive forces and reducing negative forces, a plan can be prepared to monitor the action being taken. Responsibility of monitoring can be taken up by one or two members of the team.

Whatever approaches are adopted for team building, emphasis should be given on understanding team effectiveness and taking steps to increase its level. Similar steps can be taken for building inter-team collaboration. Dyer (1987) also discusses ways of dealing with intra-team and inter-team conflicts. Some other issues in team building are also discussed.

59.5 SCORING

Following steps are involved in scoring:

1. In order to make all items unidirectional, reverse the following items: 2, 4, 6, 8, 12, 14, 16, 18, 20, 22, 24, 26, 28 and 30 (5 becomes 1, 4 becomes 2, 1 becomes 5 and 2 becomes 4, 3 remains 3).

2. After reversing the these responses, add all the encircled ratings and find the total of the ratings. This will range from 30 to 150. Multiply the total by 0.83. Now the range will be 0 to 100.

59.6 RELIABILITY

Equal-length Spearman Brown and Guttman split-half for a group of 122 was found to be 0.78.

59.7 NORMS

The following cut-off points are tentatively suggested for the various levels of effectiveness.

Total Ratings	Level
0–25	Very low
26–50	Low
51–75	High
76–100	Very High

59.8 USE FOR HRD

The instrument is designed for assessing and enhancing effectiveness of a team. The following steps can be taken for its use in a group:

1. The participants complete the instrument.
2. They may be involved in the scoring by completing the various steps of scoring.
3. Mean scores of total effectiveness as well as of each item are worked out for the group.
4. The facilitator explains the concept of the high or low scores. The higher a score more effective the team is perceived.
5. Participants examine their individual ratings on various aspects and discuss what indicators they used for their ratings. They discuss in small groups (preferably three-member group). Their perceptions discuss the concepts and relevance of their ratings.
6. If the participants come from the same team they can discuss the general profile of the team reflected in the scores, and develop action plans for improving effectiveness of their team.

(This instrument has been developed by ETCT Team [Beena Aggarwal, Ravindra Dholakia, Ruth Frank, J.C. Gupta, Shirine Hope, R. S. Purohit] under the guidance of Udai Pareek.)

Team Effectiveness Scale

Team Being Rated: _____   Your Role: _____

Organisation: _____   Date: _____

The purpose of this scale is to assess the effectiveness of the team to which you belong. Read each aspect given below and rate it to indicate your assessment of that aspect by encircling one of the numbers between the two opposite poles. For example, Under 1 (Mutual Trust), the extreme number 1 will indicate that according to your assessment members of your team are very suspicious of each other; 5 would indicate that you assess the team members as high trusting. Numbers 2 or 4 will indicate less suspicious or high trust. Number 3 will mean that either you are not sure whether there is trust or suspicion, or it is not clearly visible either way.

1. Mutual trust
   High suspicion   1   2   3   4   5   High trust
2. Communication
   Open   1   2   3   4   5   Cautious
3. Recognising each other's
   Strengths
   Rarely   1   2   3   4   5   Always
4. Taking responsibilities
   Always   1   2   3   4   5   Rarely
5. Goal of the team
   Very vague   1   2   3   4   5   Very clear
6. Utilising available human resources
   Fully used   1   2   3   4   5   Not used
7. Handling conflicts
   Denial, avoidance suppression,   Acceptance and working
   compromise   1   2   3   4   5   through conflicts
8. Leadership
   Shared   1   2   3   4   5   Centralised
9. Conformity demanded
   Low   1   2   3   4   5   High
10. Decision process
    Arbitration or majority   1   2   3   4   5   Consensus
11. External Linkages
    Low   1   2   3   4   5   High
12. Tolerance of disagreement
    High   1   2   3   4   5   Low
13. Team assessment
    Seldom   1   2   3   4   5   Periodical
14. Work assignment
    Clear   1   2   3   4   5   Ambiguous
15. Team member satisfaction
    Low   1   2   3   4   5   High
16. Mutual support
    High   1   2   3   4   5   Low

17. Active listening						
A few members	1	2	3	4	5	Large number of members
18. Temperament of team members						
Cool	1	2	3	4	5	Aggressive
19. Encouraging involvement and participation of members.						
Few members	1	2	3	4	5	All members
20. Team climate Relaxed	1	2	3	4	5	Tense
21. Attitude of members						
Destructive/Negative	1	2	3	4	5	Creative/Positive
22. Technical/managerial/ Academic expertise						
Diverse	1	2	3	4	5	Limited
23. Commitment by the team members for action						
Low	1	2	3	4	5	High
24. Credit or reward in the organisation given to						
Team	1	2	3	4	5	Individual
25. Collaboration						
Low	1	2	3	4	5	High
26. Team cohesion						
Cohesive team	1	2	3	4	5	Divided team
27. Creativity						
Very low	1	2	3	4	5	Very high
28. Individual functionality						
High, every member doing well	1	2	3	4	5	Low
29. Team output						
Low	1	2	3	4	5	High
30. Problem-solving						Only a few persons
Shared responsibility	1	2	3	4	5	involved

Team Effectiveness Assessment Measure (TEAM)

60.1 THE INSTRUMENT AND ITS ADMINISTRATION

TEAM has been designed to measure effectiveness of a team. The members of a team rate their team on seven components, which are grouped into two main aspects of team effectiveness: team functioning (containing three dimensions) and team empowerment (having four dimensions). TEAM has 28 items, 4 factor dimensions. The participants rate their team on a 5-point scale to indicate individually their experience and perception of their team.

60.2 THE CONCEPTUAL FRAMEWORK

Chapter 59 discusses the conceptual framework used in developing TEAM and in interpreting the findings.

60.3 SCORING

The individual responses are scored and then added to give the group profile. The following steps are taken:

1. Reverse item no. 2, 4, 6, 8, 10, 12, 14, 16, 18, 20, 22, 24, 26 and 28 (0 becomes 4, 1 becomes 3, 2 remains 2, 3 becomes 1, 4 becomes 0).
2. Add ratings of items mentioned below for the 7 components.

Task clarity	__	1, 8, 15, 22
Cohesion	__	2, 9, 16, 23
Autonomy	__	3, 10, 17, 24

continued

continued

Confrontation	—	4, 11, 18, 25
Support	—	5, 12, 19, 26
Collaboration	—	6, 13, 20, 27
Accountability	—	7, 14, 21, 28

3. Find out mean of ratings of all the members responding to TEAM for each component. Then calculate team functioning score, team empowerment score and total team effectiveness score, using the following format.

Components	Items	Team Score
A. Team Functioning		
Cohesion	$(2 + 9 + 16 + 23) \times 6.25$	—
Confrontation	$4 + 11 + 17 + 25 \times 6.25$	—
Collaboration	$6 + 13 + 19 + 27 \times 6.25$	—
Total (A)		—
B. Team Empowerment		
Task clarity	$(1 + 8 + 15 + 22) \times 6.25$	—
Autonomy	$(3 + 10 + 17 + 24) \times 6.25$	—
Support	$(5 + 12 + 19 + 26) \times 6.25$	—
Accountability	$(7 + 14 + 21 + 28) \times 6.25$	—
Total (B)		—
C. Team Effectiveness A + B/2		

60.4 RELIABILITY

The alpha coefficient for one group was found to be 0.85. Equal and unequal-length coefficients were both 0.88.

60.5 NORMS

The following mean values were found for one team of a college faculty:

Team Functioning	Mean	SD
Cohesion	71	10
Confrontation	79	11
Collaboration	72	10
Total TF	74	10
Team Effectiveness		

Team Functioning	Mean	SD
Task Clarity	71	10
Autonomy	73	12
Support	75	9
Accountability	76	10
Total TE	73	10

60.6 USE FOR HRD

The group can take up specific components with lower ratings and can prepare an action plan to raise its level. If there are sharp differences in the ratings, the group may discuss why members experience the team differently. Several strategies of team building have been given in the Chapter 59.

Team Effectiveness Assessment Measure (TEAM)

Your Name: _____   Your Team: _____

Rate your team/group on the following items:

Write 4   if this is highly characteristic of the group, and/or this always happens
Write 3   if this is fairly characteristic of the group, and/or this frequently happens
Write 2   if this is slightly characteristic of this group, and/or this sometimes happens
Write 1   if this is very little true about this group, and/or occasionally happens
Write 0   if this is not at all true about the group, and/or it almost never happens

1. _____ The goals of this team are well defined.
2. _____ Members of this team generally feel that their concerns and views are ignored by the other members.
3. _____ The team has enough freedom to decide its way of working.
4. _____ Members generally avoid discussing the problems facing the team.
5. _____ The team is given adequate resources to carry out its functions.
6. _____ Members do not volunteer to help others and to take responsibility.
7. _____ The sense of responsibility and accountability is pretty high amongst the team members.
8. _____ There is confusion amongst members of the team about its main tasks.
9. _____ Members support each other when required.
10. _____ The team only carries out the tasks given to it; it cannot decide its own priorities.
11. _____ The team generates alternative solutions for a problem.
12. _____ The team does not get adequate support needed to perform its tasks.
13. _____ In the group, the task is divided into small teams.
14. _____ No one cares to assess true extent of achievement of the goals of the team.
15. _____ Each member knows what his role in the team is.
16. _____ This team does not function as a strong team.
17. _____ The members of the team have enough freedom in their own areas.
18. _____ There is a lot of hesitation in taking hard decisions in this team.
19. _____ The team has enough competent persons needed for its work.
20. _____ Members in this team hesitate to ask for others' help when they need help.
21. _____ The team uses appropriate ways of assessing its accountability.
22. _____ Members of the team are not clear how to work towards the team goals.
23. _____ Members back the decisions taken by the group.
24. _____ The team does not have autonomy in vital aspects of its working.
25. _____ Members in this group do not hesitate to express their differences with each other.
26. _____ There is lack of various resources (human and financial) required by the team.
27. _____ Members respond positively to the help requested.
28. _____ The team does not have internal mechanism of assessing its progress in achieving its tasks.

Top Leadership: Senior Managerial Functions Schedule

61.1 THE INSTRUMENT AND ITS ADMINISTRATION

Senior Management Functions Schedule (SMFS) is designed to find out which transactional and transformational functions are being given priority by senior managers in an organisation. The instrument is meant for the top leaders.

SMFS consists of a list of 14 functions (7 are transactional and 7 are transformational). The respondent is required to indicate the priority of his attention/time to different functions by distributing 100 points among the 14 listed functions. SMFS is appended.

61.2 THE CONCEPTUAL FRAMEWORK

61.2.1 Leadership Functions

Leaders, including senior managers, need to perform both transactional and transformational functions. Based on the interviews of 30 persons from two organisations, a list of the main functions was prepared and the functions were classified into two groups—transactional and transformational.

61.2.1.1 Transactional Functions

Leaders have an obligation of getting things done, ensuring achievement of targets and maximising efficiency and effectiveness of various groups. These can be done by paying attention to the following aspects:

Policymaking. This is the first important leadership function. The leader arranges to set priorities and directions for organisational work and creates linkages among several aspects of the organisation. These are reflected in the policies developed as a guiding force in the organisation. The policy comes out of the organisation's vision and mission.

Planning. The next logical step is to plan various activities in order to translate policies into action. Planning involves working out detailed action steps, the needed resources and a contingency arrangement, if a proposed action does not get done.

Developing systems. Organisational leaders work towards institutionalisation of practices and change, so that effective implementation may not depend on individuals. This can be done by developing systems on various aspects of the organisation. Systems economise energy and lead to faster action. Management information system, budgetary system, human resource development system, reward system, etc., are some examples.

Monitoring performance. Managerial control of individual and group work requires effective monitoring, one of the functions of senior managers. Monitoring is done against the accepted standards and agreed plans. Monitoring also helps in making decisions about rewards.

Coordinating. When individuals and groups work in synergy, duplication is avoided and mutual support ensured.

Rewarding. Senior managers reward good performance or exemplary behaviour of individuals and teams. This reinforces their behaviour, and also the behaviour of others who then work towards getting similar rewards.

Coaching. One function of senior managers is to guide their juniors through what is called performance counselling or coaching. This includes helping them to know their own strengths and weaknesses and improve their performance in future.

61.2.1.2 Transformational Functions

While transactional functions are primarily concerned with the achievement of tasks, transformational functions go beyond the immediate task and building individuals and groups and enable them to achieve targets that the organisation or individual would never have expected. These functions increase power in the organisation by empowering various groups and individuals. The following functions fall in this category:

Visioning. The top managers create a vision for the organisation. Vision is the dream which inspires people and makes them proud of working in the organisation.

Modelling. Another way to inspire people is to set a personal example of a desirable style and behaviour. Behaviour speaks louder than words. People are influenced by what they experience rather than what they are told by managers.

Setting standards. Quite close to modelling is the setting of standards or norms in the organisation—standards of individual excellence, mutual support, creativity and innovation, and concern for each other. High standards and norms inspire individual employees to follow them in their own work.

Building culture and climate. Senior managers pay major attention to building climate of excellence, commitment, mutual support, etc. They encourage analysis of various organisational practices and pay attention to mechanisms, practices (rituals), events (celebrations, etc.) which help to evolve a distinct culture for the organisation.

Boundary management. The main function of top leaders is to create conditions conducive to better performance by various groups. This can be done by ensuring continuous availability of resources, support from outside and from major customers. These external affairs roles, called boundary management, are more important for top management than internal roles (management of the business). Boundary management also includes developing a strong lobby and interlinkages for the organisation.

Synergising. The strength of an organisation depends on the strength of its teams. One weakness of Indian culture is the lack of teamwork, resulting in negative synergy. Team building is one of the roles of top management.

Searching and nurturing talent. Competent and committed individuals with a larger vision are the ultimate strength of an organisation. The HRD role of getting such individuals and building them cannot be delegated. Top management must see this as one of their main functions. Senior managers pay attention to mentoring young, talented persons.

The various functions listed here are clustered into six factors in factor analysis of data from one group, three transactional (policy system development, promoting excellence, coordinating) and three transformational functions (HRD institution-building, norm-building, team-building, boundary management).

61.3 SCORING

Scores given to each function gauge the priority of the function. The responses of senior managers are added to give a profile of the group. The various functions can also be rated on a scale from 1 to 10, although forced distribution of hundred points gives a more authentic profile.

The totals of transactional functions (items number 1, 3, 6, 7, 9, 11 and 13) and transformational functions (2, 4, 5, 8, 10, 12 and 14) may also be calculated.

61.4 RELIABILITY

Cronbach alpha for a group of 19 was found to be 0.94.

61.5 VALIDITY

Responses from a group of 18 senior insurance managers were factor analysed (principal components analysis with Varimax rotation). Factors analysis produced six factors, explaining 85% variance. Table 61.1 shows loadings of various items on the six factors. Only loadings of 0.3 or above are given in the table. The various functions have been rearranged.

Factors 1, 3 and 5 contain seven transformational functions. These factors have been named HRD institution-building function, norm building function and synergising boundary management

TABLE 61.1 Factor Loadings of the Functions

S. No.	1	2	3	4	5	6
1. Coaching	0.94					
2. Developing talents	0.76		0.30			
3. Culture building	0.72		0.41	0.43		−0.42
4. Visioning	0.66					
5. Modelling	0.46		0.74			
6. Synergising	0.40			0.80		
7. Boundary management				0.72		
8. Planning		0.89				
9. Policy-making		0.80				
10. Developing systems		0.78				
11. Setting standards		0.33	0.82			
12. Rewarding			0.36	0.83		
13. Monitoring performance				0.88		
14. Coordinating						0.95

function, respectively. Three transactional factors are 2, 4 and 6. They are, respectively, policy-system development, promoting excellence and coordinating. The factor analysis provides construct validity of the instrument. Only in the case of coaching, there is a very high loading on a transformational factor and not (as originally proposed) on a transactional factor.

61.6 NORMS

Table 61.2 gives the mean values of the responses of 18 senior insurance managers. It also gives the consensus ratings of eight groups of senior managers belonging to a multilocational, multiproduct group. This table shows that more attention is generally paid to transactional functions; rewarding, coaching and system development are comparatively neglected areas. Most of the

TABLE 61.2 Mean Scores of Various Functions

	Insurance	Information Technology	Consensus Ratings (10-Point Scale) by 8 Multiproduct Company Groups								
Transactional Functions											
			A	B	C	D	E	F	G	H	Mean
1. Policy-making	9	10	6	6	5	2	8	8	6	5	6
2. Planning	10	10	8	7	8	7	8	8	7	7	7
3. Developing systems	7	7	7	6	7	5	8	8	7	6	7
4. Monitoring	15	12	7	6	9	8	5	9	8	5	7
5. Coordinating	11	11	7	6	8	7	6	8	6	5	7
6. Rewarding	5	4	4	5	5	5	1	5	3	5	4
7. Coaching	5	4	4	5	3	4	6	4	3	8	5
Transformational Functions											
8. Visioning	5	7	5	6	6	3	5	6	6	4	5
9. Role modelling	5	7	6	6	7	5	6	7	6	6	6
10. Setting standards	6	5	7	6	7	5	8	8	7	6	7
11. Boundary management	8	7	7	6	7	6	7	8	6	7	7
12. Synergising	5	6	5	6	5	4	3	6	7	4	5
13. Monitoring	5	5	4	6	3	4	5	6	4	4	5
14. Culture building	4	6	6	7	5	6	5	7	6	4	6

transformational functions are weak; however, boundary management seems to be given more importance.

61.7 USE FOR HRD

The instrument can be used for leadership development in organisations. The responses of senior managers can be analysed and weak areas identified. Small groups can be formed to prepare action plans for strengthening these weak areas. These plans can be discussed in a plenary session to arrive at a consensus. Follow-up action can be assigned to a few individuals.

Senior Managers Functions Schedule

Name: _____   Role: _____

Organisation: _____   Date: _____

Below are given 14 functions of senior managers. We would like to know how much attention/priority/time you give to these different functions. Distribute your priority/attention/time, assuming it to be 100, among the following functions. The total of all the scores you give should be 100.

Your Priority/ Attention/Time	Functions
_____ 1.	Policy-making
_____ 2.	Visioning
_____ 3.	Planning
_____ 4.	Modelling/inspiring
_____ 5.	Setting standards
_____ 6.	Developing systems
_____ 7.	Monitoring performance
_____ 8.	Boundary management
_____ 9.	Coordinating
_____ 10.	Synergising
_____ 11.	Rewarding
_____ 12.	Developing talent/mentoring
_____ 13.	Coaching
_____ 14.	Building culture and climate
Total 100	

Organisational Learning Diagnostics (OLD)

62.1 THE INSTRUMENT AND ITS ADMINISTRATION

Organisational learning diagnostics (OLD) has 23 items. Respondents are required to rate each item on a 5-point scale for the value and frequency of its practice in the respondent's organisation. The more frequently these mechanisms are used, the stronger is the organisational learning. These mechanisms are grouped into three subsystems—acquiring and examining (the innovation phase), retaining and integrating (the implementation phase) and using and adapting (the stabilisation phase). These are subsystems of OL in the sense that they are present in an organisation in varying degrees and are interrelated with a feedback loop; they are phases in the sense that for one particular innovation, they appear in sequence. OLD contains eight, seven and eight mechanisms, respectively, for the three subsystems or phases.

Furthermore, all 23 items can be grouped into five categories of OL mechanisms: experimentation and flexibility, mutuality and teamwork, contingency and incremental planning, temporary systems and competency building.

OLD should be administered to a fairly large number of managers in an organisation. The total organisation, a subdivision (such as a department), or both, can be rated on OLD. It can be administered in a group, or individuals can be asked to respond to the instrument.

62.2 CONCEPTUAL FRAMEWORK

62.2.1 Organisational Learning

The concept of learning has traditionally been used in the context of individuals. Recently, this concept was extended to organisations, with a distinction being made between organisational learning (OL) and individual learning. Learning has generally been defined in empirical terms of change or in normative terms of advancement of humanitarian concerns. Here, the concept of OL is presented as a continuum from no learning (insensitive or closed to experiences and realities) to full learning (effective use of experiences for action). It also proposes mechanisms that are helpful in diagnosing OL systems and intervening to make them more effective. Furthermore, we define OL as 'the process by which an organisation acquires, retains, and uses inputs for its development, and the process results in an enhanced capacity for continued self-learning and self-renewal'. This definition has five main elements:

1. Organisational learning is a process, a continual series of interlinked activities producing several changes. It is not seen as a product, although OL results in the product.
2. One of the three main subsystems of OL is the process of acquiring an input and examining it. Examples of new inputs include new structures, new technology or any change introduced in the organisation. This subsystem corresponds to the innovation phase of OL.
3. The second subsystem of OL is concerned with retaining the acquired input. Retention of an input depends on how well it is integrated in the organisation. OL will be effective only if the new input becomes integrated with existing practices. This subsystem corresponds to the implementation phase of OL.
4. The third subsystem, which corresponds to the stabilisation phase of OL, is concerned with using the new input whenever it is needed. Use also involves adapting the new input in light of the experience gained in its use.
5. Learning will result in the increased capability of an organisation to learn more on its own. Self-learning does not necessarily involve an outside stimulus input. An organisation may develop mechanisms for examining its experiences, retaining functional ways and discontinuing dysfunctional ways of dealing with issues. This self-learning leads to self-renewal.

62.3 SCORING

The Score Sheet, given below, is self-explanatory, and is used to score an individual's responses. The 23 items are first grouped in three columns, representing the three subsystems. Five other columns, which represent five categories of mechanisms, include the items that relate to the specific categories. The score for each item is written on the Score Sheet in the blank adjacent to the item number. In the first three columns, each item appears only once. In the other five columns, an item may appear more than once.

The scores in each column are totalled, and each total is written where indicated. Each total is then multiplied by 25, and the figure is written in the appropriate blank. Each product is then divided by the number that is printed beneath it, and the quotient written on the Potential for Organisational Learning Index (POLI) line. Multiplying by the fraction will make the scores comparable for all columns, and each column score will range from 0 to 100. This system will allow the scores of all respondents to be averaged with a resulting range of 0 to 100. The higher the score, the higher the potential of the organisation for learning on that dimension.

In the appropriate blanks on the next page, write the rating you gave to the 23 statements. In the first three columns (under Phases), each of your answers will be recorded only once. In the next five columns (under Mechanisms), some of your answers will be recorded more than once. For example, you must record your rating for Statement 1 in three of those columns (Experimentation, Mutuality and Competency Building).

After filling up the blanks, total the numbers you have entered in each column on the Total line. Then multiply each total by 25 and write the product on the next line. Now divide each of the products by the number printed beneath it and write the quotient beside POLI.

62.4 RELIABILITY

Guttman Split-half Reliability was found to be 0.36 ($N = 20$). Equal length and unequal length Spearman–Brown was found to be 0.60 and 0.67 respectively ($N = 20$); whereas for another group ($N = 20$), equal and unequal length Spearman–Brown was found to be 0.99 and Guttman Split-half was found to be 0.98, respectively.

OLD Score Sheet

Name: _____   Role: _____

Organisation: _____   Date: _____

	Phases			Mechanisms				
	Innovation	Implementation	Stabilisation	Experimentation	Mutuality	Planning	Temporary Systems	Competency Building
	Item No rating	Item No rating	Item No rating	Item No rating	Item No rating	Item No rating	Item No rating	Item No rating
	1.__	9.__	16.__	1.__	1.__	10.__	9.__	1.__
	2.__	10.__	17.__	4.__	3.__	12.__	11.__	2.__
	3.__	11.__	18.__	5.__	6.__	13.__	14.__	6.__
	4.__	12.__	19.__	6.__	7.__	14.__	16.__	7.__
	5.__	13.__	20.__	7.__	8.__	17.__	18.__	8.__
	6.__	14.__	21.__	8.__	9.__	18.__	19.__	15.__
	7.__	15.__	22.__	9.__	11.__	20.__		
	8.__		23.__	11.__	14.__	21.__		
				17.__	16.__	22.__		
				22.__	17.__	23.__		
				23.__	19.__			
					20.__			
Total	__	__	__	__	__	__	__	__
Multiply Total by 25	__	__	__	__	__	__	__	__
Divide Answer by	8	7	8	11	12	10	6	6
POLI	__	__	__	__	__	__	__	__

62.5 NORMS

The mean and SD from two groups of about 50 people, and from 63 companies, are given as follows. Mean scores were calculated from the data given by Khandwalla (1984c, Table 4.1, pp. 83–84). These are also given in the following table:

Aspects	Two Groups Mean	SD	63 Companies Mean
Phases			
P1	55	14	56
P2	55	13	55
P3	44	15	44
Mechanisms			
M1	53	16	56
M2	46	17	44
M3	50	15	53
M4	50	14	52
M5	56	13	58

62.6 CORRELATES

OLD scores were correlated with motivational climate (Chapter 64) and organisational ethos (Chapter 66) for one company. These scores are given in Table 62.1. The significant correlations showed dependency climate negatively related to all phases and mechanisms; extension climate had a positive correlation with innovation, implementation, mutuality and competency building. Regarding ethos, all correlations were positive: openness with implementation and stabilisation; confrontation with implementation; trust with implementation and stabilisation as well as three OL mechanisms. Pro-action was positively correlated with implementation.

It can be concluded that climate and ethos are very important in the implementation phases, that trust and extension climate play a very positive role, and that dependency climate is detrimental to OL.

A table of correlations of 23 organisational learning mechanisms with 10 indicators of perceived organisational performance relative to rival organisations is given by Khandwalla (1995, pp. 93–97). Out of the 230 possible correlations, as many as 88 (38%) were statistically significant at the 99% confidence level (2 tails). 'Thus the table indicates a strong relationship between the use of learning mechanisms by the organisation and its perceived performance relative to rivals'. All the correlations being positive, the greater the use of learning mechanisms, the better tends to be the relative organisational performance (and vice versa). Conversely, the lower the use of learning mechanisms, the poorer may be the performance (and vice versa).

TABLE 62.1 Coefficients of Correlation Between OL and Climate and Ethos

	OL Phases			OL Mechanisms				
	1	2	3	1	2	3	4	5
Ckunate								
1. Achievement								
2. Expert Power								
3. Extension		0.46	0.46		0.47			0.46
4. Control								
5. Dependency	−0.60	−0.46	−0.46	−0.54	−0.58	−0.49	−0.51	−0.61
6. Affiliation								
Ethos								
1. Openness			0.51	0.45				
2. Confrontation		0.48						
3. Trust	0.63	0.50			0.45	0.54	0.44	
4. Authenticity								
5. Proaction	0.61							
7. Autonomy								
8. Collaboration								
9. Experimentation								

It is more likely that organisational learning mechanisms, by providing the organisation with more data, more options, more ideas and approaches, and more effective implementation and stabilisation mechanisms, help improve organisational performance rather than vice versa, although occasionally it is likely that well-performing organisations may channel some of their 'organisational slack' (i.e., surplus resources) into prestigious, image-building organisational learning mechanisms. It is also possible that in times of decline, organisations might cut back on some of these image-building learning mechanisms. However, studies of turnarounds from organisational sickness suggest that sickness arises precisely because of learning failure, and when the use of learning mechanisms is stepped up, performance rises sharply. The available evidence therefore does point to a stronger causal arrow from organisational learning mechanisms to organisational performance than vice versa. (Khandwalla, 1995)

Organisational performance indicators were highly unevenly sensitive to the set of learning mechanisms studied. For example, relative efficiency, profitability and growth rate hardly influenced by these learning mechanisms. On the other hand, relative innovativeness, social impact and staff morale are improved by practically every learning mechanism. Thus, learning mechanisms, particularly the ones studied in this chapter, can make a very significant contribution to making Third World organisations dynamic, innovative, socially relevant, and exciting to work in.

It is also interesting to observe from the table that 'business' indicators of corporate performance— profitability, growth rate, financial strength, performance stability, and efficiency—are improved more by learning mechanisms that aid implementation of initiatives and, to a lesser extent, by learning mechanisms that stabilize initiatives, than by learning mechanisms that aid the generation of new ideas. There were 11 significant correlations between implementation mechanisms and 'business' indicators of performance, 5 between stabilisation mechanisms and 'business' indicators, and only one between innovative idea-generating mechanisms and 'business' indicators. Thus, organisations seeking excellence vis-a-vis 'business' indicators should institutionalise especially those learning mechanisms that facilitate implementation and stabilisation of innovations, new projects, or fresh initiatives.

Khandwalla (1995, pp. 98–99) also found correlations between 20 management styles and the 23 organisational learning items or mechanisms.

There were, in all 127 significant correlations between management styles and learning mechanisms, about 28% (of the 460) possible correlations. The number suggests a fairly strong overall relationship between management styles and learning mechanisms. Of these 127 correlations, 87 were positive and only 40 negative. Thus, on the whole, management styles and learning mechanisms seem to have a beneficial relationship. The 'pure styles accounted for 81 out of the 87 positive correlations and the defective styles accounted for 37 out of the 40 negative correlations. Thus, pure style promote the use of learning mechanisms and vice versa, while defective styles avoid learning mechanisms and/or the use of learning mechanisms reduce the use of defective styles of management.

There were more positive correlations between the styles and implementation and stabilisation oriented mechanisms (31 and 34, respectively) than with idea-generating mechanisms (22) and also that there were more negative correlations between styles and idea-generating mechanisms than between styles and implementation, and styles and stabilisation–orientation mechanisms (respectively 16, 11 and 13). Thus, management styles tend to be much more effective in harnessing learning mechanisms for the implementation and stabilisation of innovative ideas than in harnessing mechanisms for generating such ideas.

The pure altruistic, participative, bureaucratic and entrepreneurial styles account for the bulk of the positive correlations with learning mechanisms, with the pure professional and organic styles also making significant contribution.

> These six styles may, therefore, quickly instil into the organisation a learning, adapting, innovating culture.... The most powerful brakes on the emergence of a learning culture may be the defective intuitive, conservative, and authoritarian styles. Conversely, organisations that refuse to learn may come to employ these defective styles. To the extent that management styles reflect top management preferences, chances are that defective styles lead to the neglect of learning mechanisms rather than vice versa. For, it is always open to the top management to employ learning mechanisms such as task forces, staff seminars, collective sharing of experiences, contingency plans, staff training, encouragement to innovation and experimentation, etc. (Khandwalla, 1984)

The strong relationships of the pure altruistic and bureaucratic styles with learning mechanisms were intriguing. One interpretation is that a strong top management commitment to ideals and social relevance as well as to order and accountability, commonplace in well-managed public sector corporations, catalyses a learning culture in the organisation, exemplified by the use of numerous learning mechanisms. Another interpretation is that the use of various learning mechanisms impels the organisation towards commitment to ideals, social relevance, order and accountability. For commercial organisations (the study sample consisted of enterprises), the search for social relevance in the Third World contexts may well imply venturing into uncharted terrains in which learning needs are acute. On the other hand, learning mechanisms yield a rich crop of information about the operating environment, which in turn may furnish apex decision-makers, opportunities for commercial ventures that also contribute to socio-economic development, such as, production of import substitutes or critically needed products or services. Thus, 'altruism in management and the use of organisational learning mechanisms may reinforce one another'.

62.7 USE FOR HRD

POLI provides a diagnostic insight into the OL processes of an organisation. The scores on the OLD can be used by top management to diagnose the organisation's strengths and weaknesses. The instrument can also be used for remedial purposes by taking steps to improve the dimensions that are weak. Since each item relates to a specific mechanism, it may be easy to decide what to do. For example, if the total mean score on temporary systems is 35, members of the organisation can look at the individual items that received very low scores to discuss and determine the specific mechanisms that can be used to raise the score.

If developing an OL system is a direction that an organisation has accepted, it needs to develop action guidelines or policies to facilitate the process. Focussing on the following concerns has been helpful to some organisations developing policies.

62.7.1 Policy Guidelines

Enhancing functional autonomy with accountability: Policies should promote autonomy (within defined limits) of a subsystem (for example, a department or unit) and emphasise accountability for the tasks that the subsystem agrees to undertake. Without functional autonomy, a system cannot be innovative.

Availability of support and resources: Implementing change requires resources, and accountability is possible when needed resources are provided. Providing resources also shows an interest in employees and the system, and indicates high expectations for them.

Competency building: Organisational policies should promote and upgrade competencies needed for the objectives of the organisation.

Networking. Various subsystems involved in a particular area of work need to learn from one another, and they can collaborate in many areas. The development of a network of experts, groups and organisations enhances learning. Organisational policies need to promote such networking.

Based on the inter-correlation matrix of 23 items of OLD on responses from 63 organisations, Khandwalla (1995) suggested that the number of significant correlations of the item with its power can be used as a learning mechanism to catalyse other learning mechanisms. To quote Khandwalla (HRD implications):

It shows, for example, that attending external training programs and conferences by the staff (item 2), although important from the point of view of human resource development, does not possess much power of catalysing other organisational learning mechanisms. On the other hand, several mechanisms have relatively high catalytic power: task forces specifically set-up to evaluate innovations empirically rather than just qualitatively (item 16); taking the trouble to conceptualise alternative ways of implementing changes (item 23); using skilled staff to implement changes (that is, using staff with demonstrated competence in successful implementation of new initiatives) (items 15); holding staff seminars on new developments in the fields related to the activities of the organisation (item 8); task forces set up specifically for implementing and evaluating new projects and innovations (items 9 and 18); and, preparation of alternative plans for implementing changes and innovations depending on contingencies that may arise (such as fast growth of industry versus a slower growth) (item 10). In the Third World context, these need to be used extensively by organisations seeking to improve their performance through effective learning. The data suggest that organisations that: (1) take the trouble to invest the time of competent change agents in specific learning related activities (such as task forces setup with the mandate of evaluating or implementating new projects); (2) make conscious attempts to evolve alternatives and take into consideration alternative scenarios; and (3) ensure information sharing with the rank-and-file, may quickly institutionalise a culture of learning and innovating. Those organisations which fail to do so may not succeed in becoming effective learning organisations, and may therefore fail to adapt effectively to environmental changes, increase in competitive pressures, or greater environmental complexity.

His analysis also indicated that

mechanisms which aid implementation and stabilisation of new initiatives and innovations are more likely to catalyse an organisational learning culture. The average number of times an innovation stabilisation mechanism was a main correlate of other learning mechanisms was 3.9. This figure was 2.7 for the learning mechanisms that aid implementation of new initiatives and was only 2.0 for the learning mechanisms that did the generation of innovative ideas. Thus, organisations that focus sharply on stabilising and implementing new ideas tend to develop a sturdier learning culture than those that just flirt with new ideas. (1995, pp. 88–90)

Khandwalla concludes

From a practical point of view, those learning mechanisms are especially valuable that catalyse other learning mechanisms and simultaneously improve organisational performance along a number of indicators. A concentration on institutionalizing the three learning mechanisms task forces to evaluate innovations empirically, use of skilled staff for implementing changes, and staff seminars on new developments may not only rapidly bring to the organisation a culture of learning innovation, and adaptation, it may also rapidly improve the overall performance of the organisation along several indicators. Styles of management that institutionalise these three learning mechanisms are especially useful, while the ones that hinder their adoption are worth avoiding.

Organisational Learning Diagnostics (OLD)

Name: _____   Role: _____

Organisation: _____   Date: _____

Instructions

Rate each of the 23 statements by writing the appropriate number in the blank space on the left to the statement. Use the following guidelines:

Write 4   if the practice is very highly valued and/or is always or very frequently done in your organisation

Write 3   if the practice is highly valued and/or is frequently done in your organisation

Write 2   if the practice is valued and/or is sometimes done in your organisation

Write 1   if the practice has low value and/or is occasionally done in your organisation

Write 0   if the practice has very low or no value and/or is seldom or never done in your organisation

1. _____ Experts and experienced creative practitioners are invited to share their ideas with members of the organisation.
2. _____ Employees are encouraged to attend external programmes.
3. _____ Experiences and concerns of the organisation are shared with other organisations.
4. _____ Employees are encouraged to experiment.
5. _____ Innovations are rewarded.
6. _____ Periodic meetings are held for sharing results of experiments.
7. _____ Periodic meetings are held for sharing on-going experiments.
8. _____ Employee seminars on new developments are organised.
9. _____ Task groups are created for implementing and monitoring new projects and experiments.
10. _____ Detailed plans reflecting contingency approaches are prepared.
11. _____ Task groups are created to examine common elements between old practices and innovations.
12. _____ Newly proposed practices are linked with known practices.
13. _____ Records of experiences are maintained.
14. _____ Periodic meetings, chaired by top or senior management, are held to review innovations.
15. _____ Relevant existing skills are utilised in implementing change.
16. _____ Task groups are created for databased of the innovations.
17. _____ Periodic meetings are held to review and share experiences.
18. _____ Task groups are created to evaluate and report on plus-and-minus aspects of innovations.
19. _____ Task groups are created to follow up on experiments.
20. _____ Widespread debates are held on experiences of implementation.
21. _____ Realistic appraisals are made of the support needed for continued use of innovations.
22. _____ Implementation plans are modified when experience indicates that modification is needed.
23. _____ Various groups are encouraged to prepare alternative forms of implementation.

Learning Organisation Profile (LOP) Survey

63.1 THE INSTRUMENT AND ITS ADMINISTRATION

Learning Organisation Profile (LOP) survey helps in preparing the profile of an organisation, indicating how much of a learning organisation it is. The profile is in terms of eight aspects of a learning organisation. LOP survey has 48 items, 6 items on each aspect. Three items on each aspect are stated in positive and three in negative terms. The respondent is required to rate each item on a 5-point scale to indicate how much the item is true about his organisation.

63.2 CONCEPTUAL FRAMEWORK

The mechanisms for OL can be divided into five general areas. They provide a few examples of the many specific actions that an organisation can take to achieve its purpose.

Experimentation and flexibility. An organisation needs to develop flexibility, and a positive attitude towards experimentation and trying out new ways to deal with issues and problems. The following mechanisms can be used to promote these attitudes:

1. Invite experts and experienced and creative practitioners to share their ideas and experiences with selected members of the organisation.
2. Encourage employees to try out new ways of dealing with problems, even if these may not always succeed.
3. Reward new approaches that are successful in solving a problem.
4. Hold periodic meetings to share objectives, designs and experiences of innovations and the results of experiments.
5. Organise employee seminars on new developments.

Mutuality and teamwork. Organisational learning requires mutual support, mutual respect, learning from one another, collaborative work and effective teams to solve problems. Without teamwork, OL cannot be effective. In addition to some of the mechanisms mentioned in the instrument in this chapter, the following are examples of those that promote teamwork and mutuality:

1. Share experiences, concerns and ideas with other organisations.
2. Set up taskforces for implementing and monitoring new projects or experiments, for examining common elements between old practices and innovations, and for following up on experiments.
3. Hold periodic review meetings chaired by senior or top management. These meetings will not only enhance the importance of the innovation but will also produce a collaborative relationship between top management and those responsible for implementing the change. The ideas of top managers and their support play a critical role in OL by promoting learning and preventing unlearning.

Contingency and incremental planning. The OL continuum varies from certitude and rigidity on one end to tentativeness and flexibility on the other. A blueprint type of planning would appear on the rigid end, and an incremental mode of planning would appear on the flexible end. The incremental or contingency approach to planning promotes OL, and the following mechanisms reflect this type of approach:

1. Prepare a detailed plan that reflects the contingency approach. Time-bound commitments may be prepared, but they should include alternative actions. Contingency planning helps the organisation to recognise possible difficulties to take steps to prevent them and to take alternative actions if they occur.
2. Link new proposed practices with known ones. Learning is faster if the new inputs are seen as related to existing practices or ideas. If the new system is building on (rather than supplanting) the old system, threats to the members of the organisation will be reduced.
3. Maintain records of experiences. Effective planning requires continual review of and learning from experiences.
4. Encourage various groups to prepare alternative forms of implementation. Modify the implementation plan if required by the experience.
5. As in the first two general areas, invite experts and practitioners to share their ideas, arrange for employees to share their experiences and create taskforces.

Use of temporary system. Temporary systems such as task groups or taskforces, project groups and problem identification teams are effective mechanisms to generate ideas and take quick action. The mechanisms mentioned earlier work well in this area: creating taskforces for implementing the new input, monitoring new projects and experiments, examining common elements between old and new practices, and for arranging review meetings chaired by top or senior management. Temporary systems have a number of advantages. These include the following:

1. Members of inter-functional, interdepartmental, and inter-regional groups have diverse points of view.
2. More people are exposed to members of other departments, regions, functional areas and so forth.
3. The work is done faster because of the time-bound nature of the temporary system.
4. The temporary groups provide more objective views of problems.
5. More risks can be taken because the members of a temporary system do not have vested interests.
6. There is more flexibility because temporary systems are not part of the organisational structure and can be created and dissolved according to needs.

Competency building. To make OL effective, the organisation must build resources that can be used when needed. Competency is the primary resource that needs to be built. Several mechanisms appropriate for competency building have already been mentioned: inviting experts to share ideas, arranging for employees to share experiences and organising employee seminars. Listed below are two other examples of mechanisms:

1. Encourage employees to attend external training programmes.
2. Utilise relevant existing skills for the implementation of change. The more we utilise the existing skills, the more such competencies develop. Underutilised competencies become atrophied; they also discourage employees from acquiring new competencies because it is highly frustrating not to be able to use one's strengths.

63.3 SCORING

Score Matrix can be used to score the responses. Take the following steps:

1. Transfer the rating given to each item to the Score Matrix.
2. While transferring the items, reverse the ratings of the starred (*) items shown in the Score Matrix (Change 1 to 5, 2 to 4, 4 to 2, and 5 to 1; 3 remains 3.) Transfer other ratings as given by the respondent.
3. Add the eight ratings in the Score Matrix for each row and write down the total at its end. This is the score of the aspect. It will range from 6 to 48.
4. Convert the total of each row into a 0 to 100 scale by the following formula (Score – 6) × 2.38.

63.4 NORMS

Mean, SD and high and low scores, based on a sample of 150 managers are given below:

No.	LO Process	Mean	SD	High	Low
1.	Holistic frame	48	10	Above 58	Below 39
2.	Strategic thinking	48	10	Above 58	Below 39
3.	Shared vision	50	10	Above 60	Below 41
4.	Empowerment	50	10	Above 60	Below 41
5.	Information flow	50	10	Above 60	Below 41
6.	Internality	50	10	Above 60	Below 41
7.	Learning	50	10	Above 60	Below 41
8.	Synergy	50	10	Above 60	Below 41

63.5 USE FOR HRD

Managers can discuss in small teams (based on different learning organisation processes) the items that lower the score. Then they can discuss ways of improving those aspects.

LOP Survey
Score Matrix

Name: _____   Role: _____

Organisation: _____   Date: _____

								Total
1.	Holistic frame	1 __	9* __	17* __	25* __	33 __	41 __	__
2.	Strategic thrust	2 __	10* __	18 __	26* __	34 __	42* __	__
3.	Shared vision	3* __	11 __	19 __	27* __	35* __	43* __	__
4.	Empowerment	4 __	12 __	20* __	28 __	36* __	44* __	__
5.	Information flow	5 __	13 __	21* __	29* __	37* __	45 __	__
6.	Internality	6 __	14 __	22* __	30* __	38* __	46* __	__
7.	Learning	7 __	15* __	23* __	31* __	39 __	47 __	__
8.	Synergy	8 __	16* __	24* __	32* __	40 __	48 __	__

LOP SURVEY

Name: _____   Date: _____

Organisation: _____   Role: _____

The purpose of the survey is to prepare a profile of how significant members of an organisation 'experience and perceive their organisation'. The data from several respondents will be pooled to prepare the profile. You are one of the significant members, and we want your frank responses. Please read each statement given below and indicate on its left-hand side how much it is true about your organisation.

Write 0   if it is not true at all about your organisation
Write 1   if it is somewhat true about your organisation
Write 2   if it is difficult to say whether it is true about your organisation (sometimes you feel it is, sometimes you feel it is not)
Write 3   if it describes the organisation fairly well
Write 4   if it is fully true about your organisation

1. _____   In spite of following others' footprints, I generally prefer to work on my own way.
2. _____   I can predict what someone is going to say to me.
3. _____   The organisation is alive to changes and is strongly connected with the environment.
4. _____   The organisation encourages managers to prioritise their tasks in terms of their strategic thrust.
5. _____   The vision of the organisation is developed by its top leaders, without involving most members in its development.
6. _____   The organisational structure allows and facilitates most of its parts and people to accomplish their task.
7. _____   Most of the critical information is shared in an authentic way at most levels in the organisation.
8. _____   Most people in the organisation are optimistic about their personal and organisational future.
9. _____   The organisation gives importance to and facilitates self-development of its people.
10. _____   People are generally willing to suspend their own assumptions, and think collectively on critical matters.
11. _____   People in the organisation generally see and deal with things in isolation; they seem to miss their interconnections.
12. _____   People ignore working out consequences or implications of most actions that they plan.
13. _____   The organisational vision is inspiring for most of its people, and seems to be linked with their own personal goals.
14. _____   There is enough decentralisation and delegation in the organisation.
15. _____   There is free flow of relevant information in the organisation.
16. _____   Generally, people here believe that they can influence what happens in the organisation in a very limited way.
17. _____   The organisation is rather insulated, and does not learn from other organisations.

18. _____ People who have strong views during discussions, continue to hold them, even after a decision has been taken.

19. _____ The organisation generally treats each event by itself. These are treated as discrete events rather than seeing them in a pattern.

20. _____ The top leaders search for the key variables which make the most impact, prioritising the various items in terms of their importance.

21. _____ Top leaders give highest priority to developing an inspiring vision for the organisation.

22. _____ Employees in the organisation feel that they lack proper direction for the work they are supposed to do.

23. _____ People generally hesitate to communicate negative information to their seniors.

24. _____ When people working in the organisation get together, generally they talk about negative things and discuss some emotion-laden issues from the past.

25. _____ There is no conducive climate in the organisation for learning; people are generally critical and not supportive.

26. _____ Not enough time and attention is given to clearing or taking care of hurt feelings; most attention is on completing tasks rather than on improving human processes.

27. _____ People generally are busy with their present concerns and they are not able to see the larger issues beyond the immediate.

28. _____ The organisation is unwilling to discontinue a business line or close down a unit even when it does not seem to be central to its main purpose.

29. _____ The vision developed by the top people is generally limited to that level and does not get communicated to most people in the organisation.

30. _____ A lot of support from the seniors is experienced by people while working on their tasks.

31. _____ Most communication in this organisation is through rumours because of lack of proper communication by the authorities in time.

32. _____ People in the organisation are more aware of the constraints and feel helpless in dealing with them.

33. _____ The organisation does not give importance to critical enquiry and reflection by people; there seems to be a rush for completing the assignments.

34. _____ Coordinated action is lacking; people do most of their work by themselves.

35. _____ People are willing to examine their basic assumptions, when they get information conflicting with their expectations.

36. _____ Management encourages people to reflect on information and data and reframe them at the strategic level.

37. _____ The top management develops organisational vision, but commitment to it by most people seems to be low.

38. _____ People are more interested in getting formal authority rather than developing their personal power to influence decisions.

39. _____ Generally, people come to know about critical decisions and information from sources other than the management of the organisation.

People are more interested in getting immediate benefits rather than postponing them for getting larger gain in future.

40. _____ There is enough dialogue among various levels in dealing with critical issues.

41. _____ Enough attention is given to developing a consensus before taking decisions on key problems.

42. _____ The organisation uses boundary workers, such as, vendors, as environment scanners.

43. _____ Strategic information and decisions are not shared at all levels, nor are comments invited on such critical matters.

44. _____ The vision developed by leaders is not translated into detailed concrete actions to be taken.

45. _____ There is lack of recognition and reward for taking difficult decisions and solving critical problems.

46. _____ Internal exchange of information for solving problems is encouraged here.

47. _____ People hesitate to take calculated risks; generally, there is lack of boldness in decision-making.

48. _____ Openness is valued in the organisation; people are encouraged to get ideas from various sources.

49. _____ Cross-functional teams are set up in the organisation to deal with common issues.

64

Motivational Analysis of Organisation—Climate (MAO-C)

64.1 THE INSTRUMENT AND ITS ADMINISTRATION

Motivational Analysis of Organisations—Climate (MAO-C) is designed to study organisational climate, with special regard to motivation. The instrument employs 12 dimensions of organisational climate and the six motives described in this chapter. It consists of 12 categories, each of which includes six statements. Each of these categories corresponds to one of the 12 climate dimensions, and each of the six statements represents one of the six motives. Respondents work individually to rank-order the six statements within each separate category according to their perception of how much each statement is like the situation in their organisation (or unit, branch, division or department within the organisation).

64.2 CONCEPTUAL FRAMEWORK

Climate can be defined as the perceived attributes of an organisation and its subsystems, as reflected in the way an organisation deals with its members, groups and issues. The emphasis is on perceived attributes and the working of subsystems. One conceptual framework of climate (Litwin & Stringer, 1968) emphasises motivational linkages. This framework seems to be quite relevant for studying organisational climate.

Achievement: This motive is characterised by concern for excellence; competition in terms of the standards set by others or by oneself; the setting of challenging goals for oneself awareness of the obstacles that might be encountered in attempting to achieve these goals; and persistence in trying alternative paths to one's goals.

Expert influence: This motive is characterised by a concern for making an impact on others; a desire to make people do what one thinks is right; and an urge to change situations and develop people.

Control: This is characterised by a concern for orderliness; a desire to be and stay and informed; an urge to monitor events and to take corrective action when needed; and a need to display personal power.

Extension: This is characterised by a concern for others; interest in superordinate goals; and an urge to be relevant and useful to large groups, including society.

Dependency: This motive is characterised by a desire for the assistance of others in developing oneself; a need to check with significant others (those who are more knowledgeable or have higher status, experts, close associates, and so on); a tendency to submit ideas or proposals or approval and an urge to maintain a relationship based on the other person's approval.

Affiliation: This is characterised by a concern for establishing and maintaining close, personal relationships; an emphasis on friendship; and a tendency to express one's emotions.

Likert (1967) proposed six dimensions of organisational climate—leadership, motivation, communication, decisions, goals and control. Litwin and Stringer (1968) proposed seven dimensions—conformity, responsibility standards, rewards, organisational clarity, warmth and support, and leadership. A review of various studies and discussions with managers suggested the following 12 processes:

1. *Orientation.* This is the main concern of the members of an organisation. If the dominant orientation or concern is to adhere to established rules, the climate will be characterised by control; on the other hand, if the orientation is to excel, the climate will be characterised by achievement.
2. *Interpersonal relationships.* An organisation's interpersonal relations are reflected in the way informal groups are formed. If groups are formed for the purpose of protecting their own interests, cliques may develop and may result in a climate of control; similarly, if people tend to develop informal relationships with their supervisors, it might result in a climate of dependency.
3. *Supervision.* Supervisory practices contribute significantly to climate and atmosphere. If supervisors focus on helping their subordinates to improve personal skills and chances of advancement, the result might be a climate that is characterised by the extension motive. If supervisors are more concerned with maintaining good relations with their subordinates, a climate characterised by the affiliation motive would be a result.
4. *Problem management.* Problems can be seen as challenges or irritants. They can be solved by the supervisor alone, jointly by the supervisor and the subordinate(s) concerned, or they can be referred to a higher level. These different perspectives and ways of handling problems contribute to the creation of organisational climate and atmosphere.

5. *Management of mistakes.* A supervisor's attitude towards a subordinate's mistakes develop the organisational orientation, which is generally one of annoyance, concern or tolerance. An organisation's approach to mistakes influences the climate and atmosphere.

6. *Conflict management.* Conflicts may be seen as an embarrassing annoyance to be covered up, or as problems to be solved. The process of dealing with conflicts has a significant effect on climate and atmosphere as that of handling problems or mistakes.

7. *Communication.* Communication is concerned with the flow of information—its direction (top-down, bottom-up, horizontal); its dispersement (selectively or to everyone concerned), its mode (formal or informal), and its type (instructions or feedback on the state of affairs).

8. *Decision-making.* An organisation's approach to decision-making can be focussed on maintaining good relations or on achieving results. In addition, the issue of who makes the decisions is important—it could be people higher in the hierarchy, experts or those involved in the matters about which decisions are made. These elements of decision-making are relevant to the establishment of a particular climate or atmosphere. The issue of who is trusted by management and to what degree is also relevant.

9. *Trust.* The degree of trust or its absence among various members and groups in the organisation affect the climate or atmosphere. The issue of who is trusted by management and to what degree is also relevant.

10. *Management of rewards.* Rewards reinforce specific behaviours, thereby arousing and sustaining specific motives. Consequently, what is rewarded in an organisation influences the organisational climate.

11. *Risk-taking.* How people respond to risks and whose help is sought in situations involving risk are important determinants of climate.

12. *Innovation and change.* Who initiates change; how change and innovations are perceived; and how change is implemented, all are critical in establishing climate.

64.3 SCORING

1. Completing the Matrix Sheet
2. After completing the instrument, the respondent refers to the scoring key (Table 64.1) to discover which motives are indicated by his responses. He then transfers the rankings of motives to the matrix appended, adds the numbers in each vertical column of the matrix and writes the totals in the appropriate blanks; each of these totals is the score for the related motive or motivational climate. These scores can range from 12 to 72. Next, the respondent refers to the conversion table (Table 64.3) and writes the corresponding MAO-C index number in the blank provided. The indexes can range from 0 to 100. The following formula was used to arrive at the index for each motive:

$$\text{Index} = \frac{(S - 12) \times 100}{60}$$

Dimensions of Organisational Climate	Achievement	Expert Influence	Extension	Motives Control	Dependency	Affilation
1. Orientation	c	f	b	d	a	e
2. Interpersonal relationship	d	a	f	c	e	b
3. Supervision	d	e	c	a	b	f
4. Problem management	a	b	d	f	e	c
5. Management of mistakes	d	f	c	b	e	a
6. Conflict management	a	f	e	d	c	b
7. Communication	d	c	e	f	a	b
8. Decision-making	c	e	f	d	b	a
9. Trust	f	d	e	a	c	b
10. Management of rewards	a	b	d	e	c	f
11. Risk-taking	f	c	e	b	d	a
12. Innovation and change	e	a	d	b	c	f

TABLE 64.1   MAO-C Scoring Key

64.4 MAO-C MATRIX

Matrix given in Table 64.2 should be completed for a department/section unit/organisation from the completed matrices of its individual members. The last two columns and the overall dominant and backup motives are to be calculated for a department/section/unit/organisation.

Organisations (and units, branches, divisions or departments within organisations) tend to be perceived as driven by one or more of six specific motives. The scoring key will show you which motives are indicated by managers' responses on the MAO-C and, therefore, which motive they believe drives the organisation or unit. Completing this matrix sheet will help an organisation arrive at a profile of its general motivational climate as perceived by its members. Individuals first complete the matrix. For example, for the first category or dimension of organisational climate, Orientation, if you ranked item (a) as 4, you would look at the scoring key and learn that it

TABLE 64.2   MAO-C Profile Matrix

Name: _____

Organisation: _____

Role: _____

Date: _____

Dimensions of Organisational Climate	Achievement	E. Influence	Extension	Control	Dependency	Affiliation	DC	BC
1. Orientation	1c__	1f__	1b__	1d__	1a__	1e__	__	__
2. Interpersonal relationships	2d__	2a__	2f__	2c__	2e__	2b__	__	__
3. Supervision	3d__	3e__	3c__	3a__	3b__	3f__	__	__
4. Problem management	4a__	4b__	4d__	4f__	4e__	4c__	__	__
5. Management of mistakes	5d__	5f__	5c__	5b__	5e__	5a__	__	__
6. Conflict management	6a__	6f__	6e__	6d__	6c__	6b__	__	__
7. Communication	7d__	7c__	7e__	7f__	7a__	7b__	__	__
8. Decision-making	8c__	8e__	8f__	8d__	8b__	8a__	__	__
9. Trust	9f__	9d__	9e__	9a__	9c__	9b__	__	__
10. Management of rewards	10a__	10b__	10d__	10e__	10c__	10f__	__	__
11. Risk-taking	11f__	11c__	11e__	11b__	11d__	11a__	__	__
12. Innovation and change	12e__	12a__	12d__	12b__	12f__	12c__	__	__
Total Scores	__	__	__	__	__	__	__	
Overall MAO-C Index	__	__	__	__	__	__	__ Overall	

Motives

indicates the dependency motive. You would then refer to this matrix sheet and find the horizontal row that corresponds to Orientation. Locate the heading, Dependency, and write the number 4 under that heading in the Orientation row. Follow this process until you have transferred all six of your rankings for each of the 12 categories covered in MAO-C.

Add the numbers of all respondents in each cell of this matrix and write the totals in the blanks provided; each of these totals is the score for that particular motive. Then refer to the conversion table, locate the total for each motive and write the corresponding MAO-C index number in the blank provided on this matrix sheet.

For each horizontal row on the matrix representing a dimension of organisational climate, the dominant motive (the one with the highest number in the row) and the back-up motive (the one with the next-highest number) are noted in the blanks provided (see the two vertical columns on the extreme right of the matrix). The dominant and back-up columns are helpful in diagnosis and planning action to improve the motivational climate of the organisation or unit involved. Finally, based on the total scores in the last row, the overall dominant and back-up motives (climate) can be written in the blanks provided for this purpose.

An organisation may total the respondents' index number for each motive and then average the number for an overall organisational index of each, or the total of the numbers in each vertical columns of the individual respondents' matrices can be added and averaged and the index number can be written using the conversion table. The advantage of the index is to show the relative strength of the climate with regard to the motives; the cut-off point is 50. If the index number for a particular motive is greater than 50, the climate is relatively strong for that motive; if the index number is less than 50, the climate is relatively weak for that motive. The index also helps in comparing organisations or units within an organisation.

TABLE 64.3   Conversion Table

Score	Index	Score	Index	Score	Index	Score	Index	Score	Index
12	0	25	22	37	42	49	62	61	82
13	2	26	23	38	43	50	63	62	83
14	3	27	25	39	45	51	65	63	85
15	5	28	27	40	47	52	67	64	87
16	7	29	28	41	48	53	68	65	88
17	8	30	30	42	50	54	70	66	90
18	10	31	32	43	52	55	72	67	92
19	12	32	33	44	53	56	73	68	93
20	13	33	35	45	55	57	75	69	95
21	15	34	37	46	57	58	77	70	97
22	17	35	38	47	58	59	78	71	98
23	18	36	40	48	60	60	80	72	100
24	20								

Climate Profiles

1		2	3	4	5	6	7	8	9	10
Organisational Process		Achievement	Influence	Extension	Total	Control	Affiliation	Dependency	Total	OPI
		A	I	E		C	F	D		
	1									
	2	Entrepreneurial	Technocratic	Altruistic		Autocratic	Friendly	Bureaucratic		
Main Concern	3									
Working with People	4									
Supervision	5									
Problem-solving	6									
Managing Mistakes	7									
Conflict Management	8									
Communication	9									
Decision-making	10									
Total	11									
Motive Index	12									SFQ=
Effectiveness Level	13									

The completed matrix provides scores for all six motives assessed by MAO-C. The highest of these scores represents the perceived dominant motive within an organisation. The general connections between dominant motives and particular types of organisations are shown below:

Motive	Type of Organisation
Achievement	Industrial and business organisations
Expert Influence	University departments and scientific organisations
Control	Bureaucracies such as government departments and agencies
Dependency	Traditional or autocratic organisations
Extension	Community-service organisations
Affiliation	Clubs

A combination of an organisation's highest or dominant score and its second highest or back-up score results in a basic characterisation of that organisation's climate. When the six motives are combined in pattern of dominant and secondary or back-up styles, 30 organisational profiles are possible. Brief descriptions of these 30 profiles are provided here. In each description, the first motive noted represents the organisation's dominant motive, and the second represents its secondary or back-up motive. Some of these profiles are based on studies that have been made; others need to be studied to validate the concept. In general, climates dominated by achievement, expert power and extension are conducive to the achievement of results, whereas climates dominated by control, dependency and affiliation retard the achievement of results.

Achievement-expert influence. Employees are involved in and highly stimulated by challenging tasks, and the specialists within the organisation dominate in determining these tasks. The organisation rewards specialisation.

Achievement control. Most employees are involved in challenging tasks, but they face a lot of constraints attributable to rigid procedures and an inflexible hierarchy.

Achievement dependency. In spite of an emphasis on high achievement, which is shared by most employees, there is a tendency to postpone critical decisions for the approval of a higher authority. The organisation discourages making such decisions without approval from a higher level, resulting in a sense of frustration.

Achievement extension. Employees work on challenging tasks and devote equal attention to the social relevance of these tasks. The organisation has a highly developed sense of social responsibility as well as a strong sense of its responsibility to fulfil employee needs.

Achievement affiliation. While employees work on challenging goals, they also form strong groups based on common interests or other factors. The organisation pays a lot of attention to maintaining good relations among these cliques.

Expert influence achievement. The organisation places a high value on specialisation. The specialist influences most decisions, and the organisation emphasises high quality work and unique contributions.

Expert influence control. The organisation is controlled by experts who employ cumbersome procedures. The result is generally lack of job satisfaction and low to moderate (rather than high) output.

Expert influence dependence. The organisation has a rigid hierarchy dominated by experts. Decisions are made only at the upper levels of the hierarchy, and bright employees are highly dissatisfied.

Expert influence extension. Specialists play the major roles in the organisation, working in a planned way on socially relevant matters. The organisation pays attention to the employees' needs and welfare.

Expert influence affiliation. Although the organisation is dominated by experts, strong groups are formed on the basis of common interests or other factors. Since the primary attention is placed on maintaining a friendly climate, results usually suffer.

Control-achievement. The organisation is bureaucratic, run in accordance with detail procedures and has clear hierarchy. Quality of work is emphasised, but most employees with an achievement orientation feel frustrated. This climate is sometimes found in public-sector organisations.

Control expert influence. The organisation is a bureaucracy where specialists' opinions are valued but rules are treated as being more important.

Control dependency. Bureaucracy and a rigid hierarchy dominate the organisation. Because actions are generally referred to higher levels for approval, decisions are usually delayed. It is more important to follow rules and regulations than to achieve results. Senior employees protect those subordinates who do not make any procedural mistakes. Most government offices function this way.

Control extension. Although the organisation is hierarchical, it emphasises social concerns and attends to the needs and welfare of its employees.

Control affiliation. The organisation is hierarchical but places more emphasis on good relations among employees than on results. Informal groups based on relationships are seen as important. Some voluntary organisations are of this type.

Dependency achievement. Respect for achievement and for those in positions of power is emphasised. Freedom is granted to employees, but key decisions are controlled by those in power. Many family-owned organisations have such a climate.

Dependency expert influence. The organisation has a hierarchy and decisions are made by those at higher levels. Experts play an important role in the various aspects of organisational life.

Dependency control. The organisation has clear-cut channels of communication, and it is controlled by a few people who ultimately make all the decisions.

Dependency extension. A few people dominate and control the organisation and demand respect from all other members. However, they take care of members' needs. The organisation works in socially relevant areas.

Dependency affiliation. Top managers control the organisation and employ their own in-group members, who are extremely loyal to these managers.

Extension achievement. The organisation strives to be relevant to society and emphasises the achievement of results. People are selected for their competence and given freedom to do their work.

Extension expert influence. Social consciousness is emphasised by the organisation, and experts influence all major decisions.

Extension control. The organisation's goals have to do with serving a larger cause, but the structure is bureaucratic, with rules and regulations that have to be strictly followed.

Extension dependency. The business of the organisation is community service (for example, education, health or development). Emphasis is placed on the conformity to the policies laid down by the top person or team to whom all final decisions are referred.

Extension affiliation. The organisation's business is community service, and members with similar backgrounds (ideology, specialisation and so on) form strong linkages with one another.

Affiliation achievement. The organisation gives great importance to relationships and draws people with similar backgrounds. Although the organisation values achievement of results and excellence in performance, rewards are given mainly on the basis of an employee's relationship with the person (or persons) who is in a position to give such rewards.

Affiliation expert influence. The organisation consists mainly of experts, it emphasises good relations and either employs people with similar backgrounds or has cliques based on common links.

Affiliation control. Although the organisation is concerned with maintaining good relations among members, it is bureaucratic. For example, a club with strict rules and procedures might fall in this category.

Affiliation dependency. The organisation values the maintenance of friendly relations among members. There, one or two people make most decisions. Employees are rewarded on the basis of their closeness to the top person(s).

Affiliation extension. The organisation's main goal is to maintain good relations among members, and its work involves socially relevant issues. (The Lions Club and similar organisations might fall in this category.)

64.5 RELIABILITY

Retest reliability of MAO-C has been reported by Sen (1982) and by Surti (1983).

64.6 VALIDITY

Construct validity has been established by Srivastava (n.d.) on the basis of factor analysis of MAO-C data from a large multi-location company in information technology (415 respondents). A 12-factor solution was attempted, using principal components analysis with Quartimax rotation. Factor 1 had high loadings on five achievement and five extension items, and negative loadings on five dependency and eight control items. This factor is a general achievement with human concern. It also had high loadings on orientation and interpersonal relationships. Clean factors emerged for expert power (Factor 4), dependency (Factor 2) and affiliation (Factor 6). Regarding organisational processes, there were clear factors (given in parenthesis) for IP relationship (12), supervision (3), problem management (12), managing mistakes (5), decision-making (2, along with dependency climate), trust (8), reward management (7), risk-taking (11) and innovation (9). Construct validity is also provided by related studies by other authors (see Pareek, 1989b).

64.7 NORMS

Table 64.4 gives means and various other statistics of MAO-C from three companies. Mean and SD have been reported in other studies as well (Sen, 1982; Surti, 1983).

64.8 CORRELATES

One study (Khanna, 1985) reported correlations between the six perceived motives or motivational climates and measures of organisational effectiveness. The latter included consensus, legitimisation, the need for independence, self-control, job involvement, innovation, organisational commitment, organisational attachment and job satisfaction. The climates were also correlated with total

| | | **TABLE 64.4   Statistics About MAO-C for Three Organisations** | | | | | | |

	Srivastava (*N* = 453)				Khanna (*N* = 392) Construction Managers (31)		
	Mean	Median	Mode	SD	Mean	Mean	SD
Achievement	48	48	46	15	45	58	18
Affiliation	51	51	51	13	41	51	15
Dependency	58	60	61	13	45	37	15
Extension	43	43	35	14	41	47	18
Control	51	53	58	20	40	62	13
Expert power	46	46	46	14	40	41	13

satisfaction, that is, satisfaction with work and with the organisation as a whole. No significant correlations were found between climates and the need for independence, self-control and innovation. With regard to job involvement, the only positive correlation, significant at the 0.05 level, was with an achievement climate.

In the same study, positive correlations were found (significant at the 0.01 level) between five other aspects of organisational effectiveness and the achievement climate. The five aspects included organisational commitment, organisational attachment, job satisfaction, total satisfaction and total effectiveness. There was a negative correlation between these five aspects and control climate. Extension climate correlated positively with organisational commitment at the 0.05 level and with job satisfaction, total satisfaction and total effectiveness at the 0.01 level. Dependence climate showed no relationship with any measure. Affiliation climate had a negative correlation with job satisfaction at the 0.05 level and with total satisfaction and total effectiveness at the 0.01 level. A climate perceived to be characterised by expert influence had only one positive correlation (at 0.05 level) with organisational attachment. All correlations were in the predicted direction, although more correlations were expected with climates characterised by dependence and expert influence.

Negative correlations might be predicted between role stress and climates perceived as characterised by achievement, extension and expert influence. Positive correlations might be predicted between role stress and climates characterised by affiliation, dependence and control. Khanna (1985) correlated climate scores with 10 aspects of role stress and total role stress (see Chapter 53). Specific correlations between role stress and the various climates were as follows:

No significant correlation with a climate characterised by expert influence

1. Two positive correlations with an affiliation climate (role erosion at the 0.01 level and personal inadequacy at the 0.05 level).
2. One positive correlations with a dependency climate (role stagnation at the 0.01 level).

3. Six negative correlations with an extension climate (at the 0.05 level for inter-role distance, role overload and role isolation, and at the 0.01 level for role expectation conflict, self-role distance, resource inadequacy and total role stress).

4. Negative correlations with an achievement climate at the 0.01 level for all aspects of role stress except inter-role distance and personal inadequacy.

5. Positive correlations with a control climate at the 0.01 level for all aspects of role stress except inter-role distance and personal inadequacy.

Similar results were reported by Sen (1982) and Surti (1983). All these were in the predicted directions.

To summarise, organisational climate has an enormous influence on organisational effectiveness, role efficacy and role stress. An achievement climate seems to contribute to effectiveness, satisfaction and a sense of internality; a climate characterised by expert influence seems to contribute to organisational attachment; and a climate characterised by extension seems to contribute to organisational commitment. All these climates foster relatively low levels of role stress. A control climate seems to lower role efficacy, job satisfaction, organisational commitment, organisational attachment and total effectiveness and foster relatively high levels of role stress. An affiliation climate tends to lower both the satisfaction and the effectiveness and increase role erosion and feelings of personal inadequacy.

64.9 USE FOR HRD

MAO-C can be used to diagnose organisational climate for the standpoint of motivation. The focus of the instrument can be perceptions of the overall organisational climate or of individual units, divisions, branches or departments within the organisation. It may be pointed here that the first three climates in the MAO-C Matrix (achievement, expert influence and extension) are useful and functional, and the next three (control, dependency and affiliation) are dysfunctional for an organisation. The participants can identify which of the functional climates are low and which dysfunctional climates are high. Then they can plan to reduce the former and increase the latter— in other words, move from dysfunctional to functional climate (overall as well as in each organisational process mentioned in the rows). Then the facilitator can lead a discussion on the basic characteristic of the different effectiveness profiles represented in the group (see the previous section). Subsequently, the respondents could discuss their individual scores and ratings and then arrive at a consensus regarding the diagnosis and evaluation of the climate, which of the 12 dimensions of organisational climate need improvement, why particular dimensions are weak and what steps may need to be taken in response. Another approach is to discuss individual rankings of motives and what might be done to change the perceived climate accordingly. Any specific action ideas that are developed may be presented to top management for discussion, approval and commitment. Then the agreed on action steps may be carried out and followed up with monthly reviews to determine the success of their implementation.

Motivational Analysis of Organisations—Climate (MAO-C)

Name: _____   Role: _____

Organisation: _____   Date: _____

Completing this instrument will help you to assess the climate of your organisation (or your unit or department if you are answering the instrument for them). Given below are 12 categories representing 12 dimensions of organisational climate. Within each category, there are six statements. You are to rank the statements in each category from 6 (most likely, as per the situation in your organisation or unit) to 1 (least likely, as per the situation in your organisation or unit). Do not give the same rank to more than one statement.

1. Orientation
   - a. People here are mainly concerned with following established rules and procedures.
   - __ b. The main concern of people here is to help one another develop greater skills and thereby advance in the organisation.
   - __ c. Achieving or surpassing specific goals seems to be the main concern of people here.
   - __ d. Consolidating one's own personal position and influence seems to be the main concern here.
   - __ e. The dominant concern here is to maintain friendly relations with others.
   - __ f. The main concern here is to develop people's competence and expertise.

2. Interpersonal Relationship
   - __ a. In this organisation, most informal groups are formed around experts.
   - __ b. The atmosphere here is very friendly and people spend enough time in informal and social relations.
   - __ c. In this organisation, strong cliques protect their own interests.
   - __ d. Business-like relationships prevail here; people are warm, but get together primarily to ensure excellence in performance.
   - __ e. People here have strong associations mostly with their supervisors and look to them for suggestions and guidance.
   - __ f. People here have a high concern for one another and tend to help one another spontaneously when such help is needed.

3. Supervision
   - __ a. The purpose of supervision here is usually to check for mistakes and to catch the person making the mistake.
   - __ b. Supervisors here strongly prefer their subordinates to ask them for instructions and suggestions.
   - __ c. Supervisors here take pains to see that their subordinates improve personal skills and chances of advancement.
   - __ d. Supervisors here reward outstanding achievement.
   - __ e. In influencing their subordinates, supervisors here try to use their expertise and competence rather than their formal authority.
   - __ f. Supervisors here are more concerned with maintaining good relations with their subordinates than with emphasising duties and performance.

4. Problem Management
   - __ a. People here take problems as challenges and try to find better solutions than anyone else.
   - __ b. When problems are faced here, experts are consulted, and they lay an important role in solving these problems.
   - __ c. In dealing with problems, people here mostly consult their friends.

    __ d. When working on solutions to problems, people here keep in mind the needs of organisational members as well as society at large.

    __ e. People here usually refer problems to their superiors and look to them for solutions.

    __ f. Problems here are usually solved by supervisors; subordinates are not involved.

5. Management of Mistakes

    __ a. When people here make mistakes, they are not rejected. Instead, their friends show them much understanding and warmth.

    __ b. Here, the philosophy is that the supervisor can make no mistake and the subordinate dare not make one.

    __ c. Usually people here are able to acknowledge and analyse their mistakes because they can expect to receive help and support from others.

    __ d. When the subordinate makes a mistake here, the supervisor treats it as a learning experience that can prevent failure and improve performance in the future.

    __ e. Subordinates here expect guidance from their supervisors in correcting or preventing mistakes.

    __ f. Here, people seek the help of experts to analyse and prevent mistakes.

6. Conflict Management

    __ a. Most interpersonal and interdepartmental conflicts here arise as a result of striving for higher performance. In analysing and resolving these conflicts, the over-riding consideration is high productivity.

    __ b. Here, conflicts are usually avoided or smoothed over to maintain a friendly atmosphere.

    __ c. Arbitration or third party intervention (usually performed by experienced or senior people) is sought and used here.

    __ d. In a conflict situation here, those who are stronger force their points of view.

    __ e. In resolving conflicts here, appeal is made to principals, organisational ideals and the larger goals of the organisation.

    __ f. Experts are consulted and their advice used in resolving conflicts here.

7. Communication

    __ a. After due consideration, those in authority here issue instructions and expect them to be carried out.

    __ b. Most communication here is informal and friendly. It both arises from and contributes to warm relations.

    __ c. People here ask for information from those who are experts on the subjects.

    __ d. Relevant information is made available to all who need it and can use it for the purpose of achieving high performance here.

    __ e. People here communicate information, suggestions and even criticism to others out of concern for them.

    __ f. Communication is often selective here; people usually give or hold back crucial information as a form of control.

8. Decision-making

    __ a. While making decisions, people here make special attempts to maintain cordial relations with all concerned.

    __ b. Decisions are made at the top and communicated downward, and people here generally prefer this.

    __ c. People who have demonstrated high achievement have a big say in the decisions made here.

    __ d. Decisions here generally are made without involving subordinates.

    __ e. Decisions here are made and influenced by specialists and other knowledgeable people.

    __ f. Decisions are made here by keeping in mind the good of the employees and society.

9. Trust
   __ a.   Only a few people here are trusted by management, and they are quite influential.
   __ b.   Trusting and friendly relations are highly valued here.
   __ c.   Here, high value is placed on trust between supervisor and subordinate.
   __ d.   Specialists and experts are highly trusted here.
   __ e.   A general attitude of helping generates mutual trust here.
   __ f.   Those who can achieve results are highly trusted here.
10. Management of Rewards
   __ a.   Here, the main thing that is rewarded is excellence in performance and the accomplishment of tasks.
   __ b.   Knowledge and expertise are recognised and rewarded here.
   __ c.   Here, loyalty is rewarded more than anything else.
   __ d.   The people who are rewarded here are those who help their junior colleagues to achieve and develop.
   __ e.   The ability to control subordinates and maintain discipline is afforded the greatest importance in rewarding supervisors here.
   __ f.   The ability to get along well with others is highly rated and rewarded here.
11. Risk-taking
   __ a.   When confronted by risk situations, supervisors here seek the guidance and support of friends.
   __ b.   In risky situations, supervisors here strongly emphasise discipline and obedience to orders.
   __ c.   In risky situations, supervisors here have a strong tendency to rely on expert specialists for their advice.
   __ d.   Supervisors here generally go to their supervisors for instruction in risky situations.
   __ e.   In responding to risky situations, supervisors here show great concern for the people working in the organisation.
   __ f.   In responding to risky situations, supervisors here take calculated risks and strive above all to be more efficient or productive.
12. Innovation and Change
   __ a.   Innovation and change are initiated and implemented here primarily by experts and specialists.
   __ b.   Here, innovation or change is primarily ordered by top management.
   __ c.   Before initiating innovation or change, supervisors here generally go to their supervisors for sanction and guidance.
   __ d.   Those who initiate innovation or change demonstrate a great concern for any possible adverse effects on others (in the organisation or outside) and try to minimise these effects.
   __ e.   Innovation or change here is mainly initiated and implemented through highly result-oriented individuals.
   __ f.   Supervisors here seldom undertake innovations that disturb their existing friendships in the organisational or earn the enmity of organisational members.

65

Motivational Analysis of Organisation—Atmosphere (MAO-A)

65.1 THE INSTRUMENT AND ITS ADMINISTRATION

Motivation Analysis of Organisations—Atmosphere (MAO-A) was developed to study organisational atmosphere, which is defined as the perceived effectiveness of organisational climate. Organisational climate is proposed in terms of six motives and 12 organisational processes (see Chapter 64).

The instrument has 120 items, one for each of the 10 organisational processes, for each of the motives and each of the two orientations (approach and avoidance): $10 \times 6 \times 2 = 120$. Respondents are asked to rate each item on a 5-point scale. The instrument is appended.

65.2 THE CONCEPTUAL FRAMEWORK

Organisational atmosphere can be defined by the perceived effectiveness of the organisational climate. Using the motivational framework discussed earlier, organisational atmosphere can be defined as the effectiveness of the climate to generate functional aspects of the motivational climate. For functionality, the approach–avoidance framework is the most relevant one. To reiterate, Table 65.1 the six motives given here under climate have the following approach and avoidance aspects:

The underlying concept of organisational atmosphere is that each of the six motives performs an important function. The effectiveness of a motive depends on whether it comes out of the approach or avoidance need. For example, achievement motive (concern for excellence) can come out of the approach or the avoidance need. In the former (approach), the person with a high achievement motive will take initiative and personal responsibility (and the organisational process will encourage and cultivate them). In the case of avoidance, the person, out of anxiety, may feel frozen, in spite of his motive to excel, and the organisation may generate such anxiety, defeating the very purpose of emphasis on excellence. The same applies to other motives as well.

TABLE 65.1 The Six Motives		
Motive	**Approach (Hope of)**	**Avoidance (Fear of)**
Achievement	Success	Failure
Expert influence	Impact	Impotence
Control	Order	Chaos
Extension	Relevance	Irrelevance
Dependency	Growth	Loneliness
Affiliation	Inclusion	Exclusion

The underlying concept of organisational atmosphere is that each of the six motives performs an important function. The effectiveness of a motive depends on whether it comes out of an approach or avoidance need. For example, achievement motive (concern for excellence) can contribute to personal and organisational effectiveness, if the underlying need is approach (hope of success); it may reduce personal (and organisational) effectiveness, if the underlying need is avoidance (fear of failure). In the former case (approach), a person with a high achievement motive will take initiative and personal responsibility, and the organisational process will encourage and cultivate lives. In the case of avoidance, the person, out of anxiety, may feel frozen in spite of his motive to excel; and the organisation may generate such anxiety, defeating the very purpose of emphasis on excellence.

65.3 SCORING

The following steps are involved in scoring MAO-A responses and in preparing various profiles of the group/organisation. These steps are illustrated with data from one Company X of construction engineers:

1. Transfer your responses on MAO-A, to the Score Sheet.
2. Based on the individual profiles, prepare a group/organisation profile, putting mean values in each cell. The MAO-A profile of Company X is given in Table 65.2.
3. OEQ can be calculated for the motivational atmosphere by looking at the totals (mean) of the six motivational aspects. Approach (+) and avoidance (−) aspects can be used in calculating OEQ of a motivational aspects, by using the following formula (OEQ will range from 0 to 100):

$$OEQ = \frac{Approach - 10}{Approach + Avoidance - 20} \times 100$$

4. For a proper analysis of MAO-A, prepare an OEQ profile by calculating the OEQ of each cell shown in Table 65.1 (each motivational aspect and each organisational process) for each individual by the following formula: OEQ = (Approach–1/ Approach + Avoidance – 2) × 100. Table 65.3 can be used for calculating OEQ scores. Then OEQ profile can be prepared for the group/organisation by adding all individual OEQs and calculating their mean values. The OEQ profile for Company X, thus calculated, appears in Table 65.4. Calculations of OEQ are time consuming and cumbersome; these can be done quickly on a computer for which software has been developed (for preparing various profiles and indices of MAO-B directly from individual responses). It may be seen that OEQ, calculated from the totals in Table 65.2, differs slightly from those shown in the last column of Table 65.4. These differences are because of the fact that calculations in Table 65.4 are directly from OEQ of individuals, while figures in Table 65.2 are based only on total scores on each motivational aspect for the individuals. Table 65.4 is useful for in-depth analysis and action planning, as discussed later. Mark all values in OEQ profile below 56.

5. Calculate dominant and back-up motivational atmosphere. Add both positive (+) and negative (–) aspects of each motivational atmosphere. The highest value is the dominant atmosphere and the next highest is the back-up one.

In Company X, the added values (from the last column of Table 65.2) were A (68), B (59), C (61), D (63), E (57), F (61).

TABLE 65.2   MAO-A Profile

Motivational Aspects	1	2	3	4	5	6	7	8	9	10	Total
A +	4	4	3	4	3	3	4	4	4	4	37
B +	4	4	3	4	3	3	3	3	4	3	34
C +	3	4	3	3	3	3	4	4	4	3	34
D +	3	4	4	4	3	3	3	4	4	4	36
E +	3	3	3	3	3	3	3	4	4	3	32
F +	3	3	4	3	3	3	3	3	3	4	32
A –	4	2	3	4	3	3	3	3	3	3	31
B –	2	3	3	3	2	2	2	3	3	2	25
C –	3	3	2	2	3	3	3	2	3	3	27
D –	3	3	2	2	3	2	3	3	3	3	27
E –	3	2	2	2	2	3	3	3	2	3	25
F –	3	3	3	3	2	3	3	3	3	3	29

Organisational Processes

TABLE 65.3   Calculation of OEQ of Each Cell

Approach Aspect / Avoidance Aspect	1	2	3	4	5
1	1	00	00	00	00
2	1	50	33	25	20
3	1	67	50	40	33
4	1	75	60	50	43
5	1	80	67	57	50

TABLE 65.4   OEQ Profile

Motivational	Organisational Processes										Mean
	1	2	3	4	5	6	7	8	9	10	
A	52*	63	51*	49*	58	58	59	53*	56	53*	55*
B	72	62	61	63	67	74	67	56	64	73	66
C	44*	61	78	61	56	41*	63	67	64	49*	59
D	47*	69	81	72	51*	63	47*	70	63	49*	61
E	55*	69	73	78	65	61	51*	62	69	56	64
F	59	48*	70	55	69	53	56	51*	53	61	58
Mean	55*	62	69	63	61	58	57	60	62	57	

65.4 RELIABILITY

Split-half and even–odd coefficients of MAO-A for a sample of about 200 managers, as reported by Keshote (1991), are given in Table 65.5. These show high internal consistency of the instrument. Alpha coefficient of reliability for a group of 152 managers of an information technology industry was found to be 0.91.

65.5 VALIDITY

Construct validity was established through factor analysis. Re-analysis of the data from Keshote's study, using principal components analysis and Varimax rotation, gave two factors. Similarly, two factors were extracted from another sample of 20 construction managers. The factor loadings are given in Table 65.6. These results validate the concept of approach and avoidance aspects of an organisational environment.

TABLE 65.5 Reliability Coefficients of MAO-A

		Split-Half	Even–Odd
Achievement	+	0.61	0.71
	−	0.53	0.66
Expert power	+	0.74	0.75
	−	0.62	0.54
Control	+	0.63	0.63
	−	0.48	0.43
Extension	+	0.73	0.73
	−	0.42	0.41
Affiliation	+	0.72	0.73
	−	0.51	0.53

TABLE 65.6 Loading on Two Factors

		Keshote Data		Sample of 20	
		Factor 1	Factor 2	Factor 1	Factor 2
Achievement	+	0.70	−0.20	0.82	0.40
Expert power	+	0.81	−0.26	0.89	0.20
Control	+	0.84	−0.23	0.83	0.42
Extension	+	0.74	−0.31	0.89	0.28
Dependency	+	0.73	−0.37	0.97	0.03
Affiliation	+	0.79	−0.30	0.84	0.21
Achievement	−	−0.14	0.64	0.57	0.36
Expert power	−	−0.32	0.69	0.17	0.78
Control	−	−0.39	0.66	0.01	0.93
Extension	−	0.19	0.77	0.46	0.67
Dependency	−	0.08	0.80	0.33	0.81
Affiliation	−	0.22	0.69	0.43	0.57

Analysis of data from Keshote's sample showed two factors of the operating effectiveness of six motives. Factor 1 had loadings on achievement, expert power, control and dependency (0.64, 0.88, 0.74 and 0.70, respectively). Factor 2 had significant loadings on extension and affiliation

(0.95 and 0.64, respectively). Results of factor analysis of OE shows two main clusters—one concerned with task (first three, except dependency) and the second with people (extension and affiliation).

65.6 NORMS

Table 65.7 gives mean and SD values from four groups Table 65.8 gives OEQ scores from one engineering organisation (N = 186). These can be used for norms.

65.7 CORRELATES

Keshote (1991) has reported positive correlations between the operating effectiveness of all six motivational aspects of atmosphere and internal locus of control, and negative correlation with external locus of control chance and others. All these were significant at 0.001 level, also measured by LOCO inventory (Chapter 9). He also reported positive correlations between interpersonal trust, as measured by Rotter (1971) scale and the OE of all six motivational aspects of organisational atmosphere (at 0.01 level, except for control). These results show that people with high internal locus of control and with high interpersonal trust seem to perceive the organisational climate as being more functional and positive.

In one information technology industry, based on the data from 153 managers, the correlates were found for OEQ of 6 motives (level of significance are also mentioned) are shown in Table 65.9.

TABLE 65.7   Means and SDs of MAO-A

Motive	Approach		Avoidance		OEQ	
	Mean	SD	Mean	SD	Mean	SD
Achievement	3.1	0.64	2.7	0.62	54	6.53
Influence	3.1	0.67	2.3	0.58	57	7.57
Extension	3.0	0.67	2.3	0.48	56	5.39
Control	3.1	0.56	2.6	0.53	55	6.60
Affiliation	3.0	0.63	2.6	0.56	54	6.67
Dependency	3.2	0.56	2.6	0.47	53	5.18

TABLE 65.8 OEQ Values in an Organisation

	Ach.	Inf.	Ext.	Cont.	Affil.	Depen.
1. Orientation	46	49	61	52	51	46
2. IP Relations	44	45	68	50	44	61
3. Supervision	45	54	46	39	58	42
4. Managing problem	47	52	50	49	42	47
5. Managing mistake	37	35	47	35	45	44
6. Managing conflicts	49	43	55	49	50	54
7. Communication	43	48	44	44	37	47
8. Decision-making	51	51	51	49	45	43
9. Trust	50	47	48	42	36	–
10. Rewards	40	48	51	48	46	–

TABLE 65.9 Level of Significance of Correlates of MAO-A

	Achievement	Expert Power	Control	Dependency	Extension	Affiliation
OCTAPACE Ethos	0.000	0.000	0.000	0.000	0.001	0.000
Total Delegation	0.001	0.005	0.000	0.007	–	–
Internality	0.000	0.000	0.000	0.000	0.000	0.000
Ambiguity Tolerance	0.000	0.000	0.000	0.000	0.000	
Contextual Sensitivity	0.024	–	–	–	–	0.049
Other Considerate	0.000	0.000	0.000	0.000	0.000	0.000
Future Orientation	0.000	0.000	0.000	0.000	0.000	0.000
Individualistic	0.000	0.000	0.001	0.000	0.000	0.003
Expanding	0.001	–	0.004	0.001	0.002	0.003
Androgyny	0.029	0.001	0.052	0.004	0.018	0.043
Power Parity	0.003	–	0.001	0.002	0.012	0.007

65.8 USE FOR HRD

MAO-A can be used for research, training and OD. It can be used for survey feedback, planning changes in the atmosphere and evaluating OD effort. Roy has described its use in assessing the effectiveness of OD interventions. Various profiles and indices suggested in the section on scoring and profiling can be used to plan OD work.

65.8.1 Total Atmosphere

As suggested in Step 4 in the section on scoring, the combination of dominant and back-up atmospheres can indicate the overall atmosphere (these can be interpreted, as suggested in Chapter 64). In the case of Company X (see Step 4 in the section on scoring), the combination of dominant and back-up styles is AD. This combination suggests that in spite of an emphasis on high achievement, which is shared by most employees in this company, there is a tendency to postpone critical decisions for approval by a higher authority. The organisation discourages making such decisions without approval from a high level, resulting in a sense of frustration.

65.8.2 OEQ of Motivational Aspects

Table 65.4 is the main source of interpretation of MAO-A results. All figures below 56 have an asterisk in the table. These may be regarded as low values, showing that motivational atmosphere or organisational processes are not likely to produce effectiveness. So, they deserve attention. The last column in Table 65.4 gives OEQs of six motivational aspects. In Company X, the achievement-oriented atmosphere lacks effectiveness. It is interesting, in this case, that while the achievement-related atmosphere is very high—this is the dominant atmosphere, as discussed in the above paragraph—its effectiveness is low. HRD or OD facilitators may explain this to the group. Row A in Table 65.4 shows that OEQ of A is lower because it is low in 5 out of 10 organisational processes. Small groups may be formed, preferably one for each process, to work out action plans to increase OEQ of these five processes. These are discussed in the next section.

65.8.3 OEQ of Organisational Processes

Based on the scores with asterisks in Table 65.4, weak processes can be located. The first process, Orientation, is weak. Its OEQ is low on four motivational aspects (A, C, D, E). The most effective way to raise OEQ is by reducing the dysfunctional/negative (–) aspect. For example, the negative aspect of achievement motivation (concern for excellence) is contained in Item 7 of MAO-C. The company seems to overemphasise achieving the targets and excellence, causing an anxiety in most people. If this is reduced, OEQ score of orientation may increase. Let us take other motivational aspects of orientation (C, D and E). The relevant negative items of these three motivations are 111, 115 and 118. These items show that the company's main concern is to have things done according to laid-out plans, to follow rules and procedures and help people to develop and advance in the organisation rather than to achieve results. Small groups can discuss if this is true and if it is, what can be done to change the orientation in the desired direction.

Other organisational processes have fairly high OEQ, except number 10 (reward management) where OEQs are lower on A, C and D (items 55, 52, 49) showing pressure, anxiety and tension due to overemphasis on the achievement of targets, centralisation and loyalty, which are rewarded in the organisation. Small groups can discuss how these could be reduced, to improve the atmosphere.

The same procedure may be followed for OEQ of motivational aspects. In this case (Table 65.4), OEQ of achievement motivation can improve by looking at five processes: orientation, supervision, management of mistakes, decision-making and management of rewards—the relevant items of negative aspect in the questionnaire being 100, 87, 79, 17 and 34.

In short, MAO-A can be used for diagnosing the organisational atmosphere, using the data for discussing the relevance of the diagnosis and then preparing action plans to improve the atmosphere, mainly by reducing negative aspects of various motivational aspects.

MAO-A

Name: _____ Role: _____

Organisation: _____ Date: _____

his instrument assesses organisational atmosphere. There are no right or wrong answers. Read carefully each statement given in the accompanying instrument, and indicate in the blank space on the right of each statement numbered below how much the statement is true about your organisation.

Write 1   if it hardly applies or is not true about your organisation
Write 2   if it is somewhat true about your organisation
Write 3   if it is fairly true about your organisation
Write 4   if it is quite true about your organisation
Write 5   if it describes your organisation very well

1. _____ Achieving goals or set targets or excelling in them seems to be the main concern here.
2. _____ Expertise is also considered here in the formation of informal groups.
3. _____ Supervisors here want minimum information to ensure that things are being done according to plans.
4. _____ When employees need to take help of their supervisors to solve problems, they do not hesitate to consult them.
5. _____ Usually, people are able to acknowledge and analyse their mistakes because then can expect to receive help and support from others.
6. _____ While dealing with conflicts, people's feelings are also considered.
7. _____ Relevant information is made available for performers and people are on their toes to get such information; there is continuous pressure for productivity. There is hardly any time left for sharing other matters of concern with employees.
8. _____ Decisions are greatly influenced by the relevant experts.
9. _____ There is more trust in this organisation, in systems and procedures than people.
10. _____ Loyalty is rewarded more than anything else.
11. _____ A business-like relationship prevails here—people are warm, but get together mostly for ensuring excellence in performance.
12. _____ Supervisors try to use their expertise and competence rather than their formal authority to influence their subordinates.
13. _____ The information collected from several sources is used in solving most problems.
14. _____ If mistakes are made, employees analyse them and discuss with their supervisors tentative solutions and ways of preventing such mistakes in future.
15. _____ In resolving conflicts, the larger interests of people and organisations are also considered.
16. _____ There is enough informal and friendly communication arising out of, and contributing to, warm relations at work.
17. _____ High performers have great influence in making decisions, and people are always anxious lest they fall short of expectations.
18. _____ Mainly, it is the experts who are trusted here.
19. _____ The ability to monitor information, control subordinates and maintain discipline is given the highest weightage in rewarding managers and supervisors.

20. _____ Supervisors reward outstanding achievement.
21. _____ Experts are consulted while solving problems.
22. _____ People who commit mistakes are helped to understand the reasons, and supervisors pay special attention to monitor and follow up on mistakes.
23. _____ Employees work out tentative solutions to conflicts and then seek the help of their supervisors to manage conflicts.
24. _____ People communicate information, suggestions and even criticisms to others out of concern for them.
25. _____ In taking decisions, people's feelings are also considered.
26. _____ Trust between people is task oriented; people not coming up to expectation lose the trust of management.
27. _____ In rewarding people, undue importance is given to knowledge and expertise.
28. _____ People here take problems as challenges and try to find better solutions than anybody else.
29. _____ Expert help is sought in analysing and preventing mistakes.
30. _____ Supervisors use conflicts to clarify roles, boundaries, etc. and improve systems to prevent similar conflicts in future.
31. _____ Supervisors communicate both information and support to their employees, and the latter give relevant feedback to the former.
32. _____ While making decisions, the good of both employees and the organisation is kept in mind.
33. _____ Trusting and friendly relations are highly valued here.
34. _____ Here, reward and recognition for high achievement result in pressure, anxiety and a feeling of tension all the time.
35. _____ A mistake by a subordinate is treated as an experience (by the boss) from which lessons are learnt to prevent failure and improve performance in the future.
36. _____ Relevant experts are consulted and used in resolving conflicts.
37. _____ Communication is used as an effective way of getting relevant feedback and critical information for corrective action.
38. _____ In decision-making, people prefer to discuss relevant matters with their seniors, who support them and stand by them during implementation.
39. _____ Here, a general helping attitude generates mutual trust.
40. _____ Maintaining good relationship at work is appreciated here.
41. _____ Most interpersonal and inter-departmental conflicts arise out of a striving for higher performance. These conflicts are analysed and resolved with the overriding consideration being high productivity.
42. _____ Experts are consulted freely, and relevant feedback is given to them.
43. _____ Decisions are made at a higher level based on the information collected from several sources.
44. _____ There is high trust between supervisors and employees, the former providing support and the latter learning from the former.
45. _____ The organisation rewards those who help their junior colleagues to develop and those who contribute to teamwork.
46. _____ Relevant information is made available to all who need and can use such information for achieving high performance.
47. _____ In decision-making, experts or knowledgeable persons play an important role.

48. _____ There is enough mutual trust among people here; systems are used to collect the needed information and the information is regarded as trustworthy.

49. _____ People who keep up the tradition and identity of the organisation are duly recognised and rewarded.

50. _____ People who have demonstrated high achievement have a great say in the decisions made here.

51. _____ People have great trust in expertise here.

52. _____ Supervisors are praised and rewarded for devising systems that require the least personal supervision, and minimise delay in decision-making.

53. _____ Those who can achieve results are highly trusted.

54. _____ Knowledge and expertise are recognised and rewarded here.

55. _____ Excellence in performance and getting tasks accomplished is mainly rewarded.

56. _____ People's concern to develop their competence and expertise is quite high here.

57. _____ Interpersonal relationships here are mainly governed by the exchange of information for keeping track of things.

58. _____ Supervisors provide due guidance and support to their employees, who tend to seek their help when required.

59. _____ Problems are solved keeping in mind the needs of and benefits to the people in the organisation and society at large.

60. _____ The person making a mistake is not rejected; he is handled with warmth.

61. _____ Most interpersonal and interdepartmental problems arise because of cut-throat competition and tensions in performance.

62. _____ Mostly, communication here is with experts for relevant information.

63. _____ Decisions here are generally made without involving subordinates or colleagues.

64. _____ Here, high value is placed on both the superior and his subordinate trusting each other like father and son.

65. _____ Concern for and helping each other is the main factor considered while rewarding people.

66. _____ The main concern here is the availability of the right information to the right person at the right time.

67. _____ People respect their supervisors, who, in turn, are supportive of their employees.

68. _____ Supervisors here take pains to see that their subordinates improve personal skills and chances of advancement.

69. _____ The feelings of people who are involved are also considered while dealing with problems.

70. _____ People are afraid of making mistakes and strive not to.

71. _____ When conflicts occur, managers pass on the responsibility to the concerned experts for solutions.

72. _____ Communication is often selective—people usually give or hold back crucial information as a way of control.

73. _____ Decisions are made at the top and communicated downward; people here generally prefer this.

74. _____ Mutual concern and trust generally come in the way of testing and checking systems and procedures.

75. _____ The ability to get along well with others is more appreciated here than other abilities.

76. _____   The main concern here is to learn from and follow the examples of competent senior managers.

77. _____   People have high concern for one another and help each other spontaneously when such help in needed.

78. _____   Supervisors maintain good human relations with their employees.

79. _____   People are more concerned about problems that may adversely affect high performance.

80. _____   Mainly it is experts who are involved in analysing and correcting mistakes.

81. _____   Supervisors analyse why conflicts occur and lay down procedures, etc. to be strictly followed in future.

82. _____   Instructions are issued after due consideration by the authorities, and these are expected to be carried out.

83. _____   While making decisions, people here are anxious about their implications for the welfare and good of employees.

84. _____   Mostly people here trust those who are close to them.

85. _____   The concern about the organisation and each other is fairly high here.

86. _____   The atmosphere here is quite friendly and people spend enough time in informal social relations.

87. _____   Supervisors maintain good human relations with their employees.

88. _____   Mainly the experts are involved in solving problems.

89. _____   It is believed here that mistakes occur when laid down procedures are not followed; therefore, the supervisors insist on strict conformity to procedures.

90. _____   Arbitration or third party intervention—usually by experienced persons or seniors—is sought and used in managing conflicts.

91. _____   Negative feedback is usually not given out of concern for the concerned persons.

92. _____   The most dominant consideration while taking decisions is to maintain cordial relations with all concerned.

93. _____   The concern for meaningful personal relationships is quite evident here.

94. _____   Most relationships here are task oriented, with little human feelings.

95. _____   Supervisors overwhelm their employees with their expertise, with little concern about the ability of the latter's technical levels.

96. _____   Usually problems are solved by supervisors without involving their subordinates.

97. _____   Subordinates expect guidance from their supervisors to correct or prevent making mistakes.

98. _____   In resolving conflicts, appeal is made to principles, organisational ideals and the larger good of the organisations.

99. _____   People here hesitate to communicate criticism or negative feelings in order to maintain friendly relations.

100. _____   There is over-emphasis on achieving targets and excellence, resulting in anxiety in most people.

101. _____   In this organisation, most informal groups are formed around experts.

102. _____   Supervision here is usually to check mistakes and 'catch' the person.

103. _____   People usually refer the problems to and look for solutions from their seniors.

104. _____   There is over-concern for people who make mistakes, preventing them from analysing and learning from their mistakes.

105. _____ Conflicts are avoided in this organisation; they are seen as threats to the existing good relations.

106. _____ The main concern here is the development of expertise rather than doing the tasks well.

107. _____ Informal relationships prevail here even for getting critical information at the higher levels.

108. _____ Supervisors here strongly prefer that their subordinates ask them for instructions and suggestions.

109. _____ The concern of people in this organisation about the welfare of others generally comes in way of effective problem-solving.

110. _____ If someone commits a mistake, people close to him give him affection and protection.

111. _____ The main concern here is to ensure that things are done according to laid out plans.

112. _____ People have strong associations mostly with their supervisors and look for suggestions and guidance from them.

113. _____ Supervisors, out of concern about their subordinates, share the latter's burden.

114. _____ People mostly consult their friends while dealing with problems.

115. _____ People here are mainly concerned about following laid down rules and procedures.

116. _____ People have so much concern for others that they are willing to take up responsibility on behalf of others.

117. _____ Supervisors here are more concerned with maintaining good relations with their subordinates than stressing duties and performance.

118. _____ The main concern of people here is to help each other to develop and advance in the organisation.

119. _____ Informal friendly relationships are so dominant here that these influence the formation of task groups also.

120. _____ The dominant concern here is to maintain friendly relations with others.

TABLE 65.10 MAO-A: Scoring-cum-Analysis Sheet

Name: _____ Role: _____
Organisation: _____ Date: _____

Dimensions of MAO-A	Achievement		Influence		Extension		Control		Affiliation		Dependency		OEQ
	Approach	Avoidance	Approach	Avoidance	Approach	Avoidance	Approach	Avoidance	Approach	Avoidance	Approach	Avoidance	
1. Orientation	1 —	100 —	56 —	106 —	85 —	118 —	66 —	111 —	93 —	120 —	76 —	115 —	—
2. IP Relations	11 —	94 —	2 —	101 —	77 —	116 —	57 —	107 —	86 —	119 —	67 —	112 —	—
3. Supervision	20 —	87 —	12 —	95 —	58 —	113 —	3 —	102 —	78 —	117 —	58 —	108 —	—
4. Man Problem	28 —	79 —	88 —	59 —	109 —	13 —	96 —	69 —	114 —	4 —	103 —		—
5. Man mistakes	35 —	70 —	29 —	80 —	5 —	104 —	22 —	89 —	60 —	110 —	14 —	97 —	—
6. Man conflict	41 —	61 —	36 —	71 —	15 —	98 —	30 —	81 —	6 —	105 —	23 —	90 —	—
7. Communication	49 —	7 —	42 —	62 —	24 —	91 —	37 —	72 —	16 —	99 —	31 —	82 —	—
8. Decision-making	50 —	17 —	47 —	8 —	32 —	83 —	43 —	63 —	25 —	92 —	38 —	73 —	—
9. Trust	53 —	26 —	51 —	18 —	39 —	74 —	48 —	9 —	33 —	84 —	44 —	64 —	—
10. Rewards	55 —	34 —	54 —	27 —	45 —	65 —	52 —	19 —	40 —	75 —	49 —	10 —	—
Total	—		—		—		—		—		—		—
OEQ													

Organisational Culture: OCTAPACE Profile

66.1 THE INSTRUMENT AND ITS ADMINISTRATION

The OCTAPACE profile is a 40-item instrument that gives the profile of organisation's ethos in eight values. These values are openness, confrontation, trust, authenticity, proaction, autonomy, collaboration and experimentation. The instrument contains two parts. In part I, values are stated in items 1–24 (three statements of each of the eight values), and the respondent is required to check (on a 4-point scale) how much each item is valued in his organisation. Part 2 contains 16 statements on beliefs (two each for eight values), and the respondent checks (on a 4-point scale) how widely each of them is shared in the organisation.

In addition to checking the items on the extent of their importance or sharing in the organisation, the respondent can also check how much they should be valued, or how much the beliefs are useful. Thus, both present as well as desired or ideal profiles can be obtained.

66.2 CONCEPTUAL FRAMEWORK

Ethos can be defined as the underlying spirit of character of an entity or group and is made up of its beliefs, customs or practices. At the base of ethos are core values. The eight important values relevant to institution-building are openness, confrontation, trust, authenticity, proaction, autonomy, collaboration and experimentation. In addition to being an acronym for these values, OCTAPACE is a meaningful term, indicating eight (octa) steps (pace) to create functional ethos. We shall briefly discuss each aspect—its meaning, its outcome for the organisation, and its indicators—to show whether and how much it exists in the organisation.

1. *Openness*: Openness can be defined as a spontaneous expression of feelings and thoughts, and the sharing of these without defensiveness. Openness is in both directions, receiving and giving. Both these may relate to ideas (including suggestions),

feedback (including criticism) and feelings. For example, openness means receiving without reservation, and taking steps to encourage more feedback and suggestions from customers, colleagues and others. Similarly, it means giving, without hesitation, ideas, information, feedback, feelings, etc. Openness may also mean spatial openness in terms of accessibility. Installing internal e-mailing may be a step in this direction: everyone having a computer terminal has access to information that they may retrieve at any time. Offices without walls are another symbolic arrangement, promoting openness. In some organisations, even the chief executive does not have a separate exclusive cabin; floor space is shared by other colleagues at different levels in the organisation. This willingness to share and this openness result in greater clarity of objectives and free interaction among people. As a result of openness, there should be more unbiased performance feedback. Indicators of openness in an organisation will be productive meetings and improved implementation of systems and innovations.

2. *Confrontation*: Confrontation can be defined as facing rather than shying away from problems. It also implies deeper analysis of interpersonal problems. All this involves taking up challenges. The term confrontation is being used with some reservation and means putting up a front as contrasted with putting one's back (escaping) to the problem. A better term would be confrontation and exploration (CE).

    Let us use the term confrontation in this sense of confrontation and exploration, that is, facing a problem and working jointly with others to find a solution to the problem. The outcome of confrontation will be better role clarity, improved problem-solving and willingness to deal with problems and with 'difficult' employees and customers. There will be willingness of teams to discuss and resolve sensitive issues. The indicators, which are also outcomes, can be improved by periodical discussions with clients, bold action and not postponing sticky matters.

3. *Trust*: Trust is not used in the moral sense. It is reflected in maintaining the confidentiality of information shared by others and in not misusing it. It is also reflected in a sense of assurance that others will help when such help is needed, and they will honour mutual commitments and obligations. Trust is also reflected in accepting what another person says at face value and not searching for ulterior motives. Trust is an extremely important ingredient in the institution-building processes.

    The outcome of trust includes higher empathy, timely support, reduced stress and reduction and simplification of forms and procedures. Such simplification is an indicator of trust and of reduced paperwork, effective delegation and higher productivity.

4. *Authenticity*: Authenticity is the congruence between what one feels, says and does. It is reflected in owning up one's mistakes and in unreserved sharing of feelings. Authenticity is closer to openness. The outcome of authenticity in an organisation is reduced distortion in communication. This can be seen in the correspondence between members in an organisation.

5. *Proaction*: Proaction means taking the initiative, preplanning and taking preventive action, and calculating the payoffs of an alternative course before taking any action. The term 'proact' can be contrasted with the term 'react'. In the latter, action is in response to (and in the pattern of) an act from some source while in the former, the action is taken independent of the source. For example, if a person, on being accused, shouts back at his friend, he shows reactive behaviour. However, if he does not use this pattern (of shouting) but responds calmly and suggests that they should discuss the problem together, he is showing proactive behaviour. Proactivity gives initiative to the person to start a new process or set a new pattern of behaviour. In reactive behaviour, the initiative lies with the source and the person merely acts according to the pattern set by that source. In other words, the usual response is reactive. Proactivity involves unusual behaviour. In this sense, proactivity means freeing oneself from and taking action beyond immediate concerns. A person showing proactivity functions at all the three levels of feeling, thinking and action. Some of its implications are discussed here.

At the *feeling level*, the person transcends his role boundary and sees things from the point of view of the other role sender. This is empathy. He appreciates the other's point of view (understands it even if he does not agree) and is able to feel the other person. This also means that he transcends logic and reasoning and is able to reach the feeling. Things then may acquire a new meaning.

At the *thinking level*, the person may transcend his own immediate feeling, emotions and reason to understand a problem. He may transcend time and think of the future (in terms of long-term implications); he may transcend individual events and see a pattern, leading to his own action theory.

At the *action level*, proactivity means transcending the immediate cause, that is, taking initiative. There are three ways in which this can be done: transcending symptoms (i.e., looking for the causes of a problem), transcending traditionality and uniformity (i.e., searching several alternative modes of action) and transcending content (i.e., initiating a new process, e.g., the process of joint exploration). In transactional analysis, proactivity is stressed in terms of transcending circularity (being sucked into a game). Instead of falling into the trap, a proactive individual makes a new move that stops the game and starts a new set of adult–adult transactions. Proactivity thus shows a high level of maturity, and both individual employees and the organisation can do a lot to promote it. There are four ways in which an organisation can respond to environmental changes. These, adapted from McNamara's concept, include inaction (maintaining the status quo), reaction (responding to change as it occurs and firefighting), transaction (adapting after anticipating and confronting change,) and proaction (strategy planning to influence events and, in a way, cause change). The outcome of higher proactivity will be more initiative in anticipating problems/issues, planning, strategy development, faster response, internation processing information about competitors, the market, collaborators, raw material, etc. The outcome will also be early problem detection, detailed planning, analysis of successes and failures, reduction in surprises, improved time management, reduction in 'emergency' meetings in organisations and with customers, willingness to enter new areas of work, timely curtailing of unprofitable business. All these, including better capital management, can also be used as indicators of proaction.

6. *Autonomy*: Autonomy is using and giving freedom to plan and act in one's own sphere. It means respecting and encouraging individual and role autonomy. It develops mutual respect and is likely to result in willingness to take on responsibility, individual initiative and better succession planning. The main indicator of autonomy is effective delegation in organisation and reduction in references made to senior people for the approval of planned actions.

7. *Collaboration*: Collaboration is giving help to and asking for help from others. It means working together (individuals and groups) to solve problems and bring team spirit. The outcome of collaboration includes timely help, teamwork, sharing of experiences, improved communication and improved resource sharing. The indication could be productivity reports, more meetings, involvement of staff, more joint decisions, better resource utilisation and higher quality of meetings.

8. *Experimenting*: Experimenting means using and encouraging innovative approaches to solve problems; using feedback for improving; taking a fresh look at things; and encouraging creativity. We are so caught up with our daily tasks that we often only use traditional, tried and tested, ways of dealing with problems.

While these methods save time and energy, they also blind us from perceiving the advantage of new ways of solving a problem. The more we work under pressure, the less is our inclination to try a different approach, as the risk seems to be too high. And yet, complex problems require new approaches to their solutions. Organisational learning does not imply repetitive action; it implies applying past experience to current problems to reach beyond. This can be called creativity. Other terms, such as, innovations, experiments, new approaches, etc., also convey the same meaning.

There are several aspects of creativity in an organisation. Creativity is reflected in new suggestions generated by employees, attempts at improving upon previous ways of working, trying out a new idea to which one has been exposed, innovating new methods and thinking about a problem while ignoring so-called constraints. The last one is also called lateral thinking, that is, thinking aimed at generating alternatives. There is enough evidence that such thinking contributes towards the development of new products, new methods and new processes.

Based on a sample of 332 R&D managers, Saxena and Shah (2008) found ethos variables related to learned helplessness attributes. They found the role of organisational ethos significant in creating or removing learned helplessness. It was also observed that higher the ethos, lower is the learned helplessness attributions.

66.3 SCORING

The Score Sheet should be used for scoring. Follow the following instructions:

1. Transfer your responses from the completed instrument. While transferring the scores, reverse the scores of the items marked with an (*): 4 will become 1 and 1 will become 4; 3 will become 2 and 2 will become 3.
2. Add the rows. The eight rows represent the eight aspects of OCTAPACE. The scores will range from 5 to 20 on each aspect.
3. Find out the group profile when several members of the group response to the instrument.

66.4 RELIABILITY

Split-half reliability of the OCTAPACE profile on a sample of 135 college/university teachers was found to be 0.81 (Mathur, 1991). Alpha coefficient for a group of 153 managers was found to be 0.90 and for value, belief was found to be 0.875.

To discover the internal consistency of the instrument, each of the 40 items was correlated with the total score for a group of 102 managers from three steel plants. Out of 40, 27 items had correlations that were significant at 0.001 level, 4 at 0.01 level, and 2 (numbers 19 and 35) at 0.05 level. Six items (numbers 12, 22, 25, 31, 36 and 40) had zero correlation and one (14) had a negative, but insignificant, correlation with the total score. The five items with zero and negative correlations are for the aspects of openness (25), authenticity (12), autonomy (14, 22), collaboration (23) and experimenting (40). It is interesting to note that all these items are among the 11 items that are worded negatively. On the whole, item–total correlations provide satisfactory results.

To test the effect of social desirability on the items, analysis of kurtosis and skewness was carried out on all 40 items, eight aspects and the total OCTAPACE profile of a sample of 102 managers from three steel plants. Only two items (numbers 15 and 26) had higher kurtosis—the first was leptokurtic and the second was platykurtic. Confrontation and collaboration were also leptokurtic. Skewness was satisfactory except for items 29, 33 and 34, all of which were negatively skewed. On the whole, the indices were acceptable.

66.5 VALIDITY

Validity was indirectly tested by comparing the scores from three departments with their ranking by two judges for their effectiveness. The judges' rankings were independently done and agreed with one another. Tests showed no difference between the first-and second-ranked departments or between the second and third-ranked departments. However, there were significant differences

TABLE 66.1   Factor Loadings of OCTAPACE

	Factor 1	Factor 2	Factor 3	Factor 4
OP1	0.88			
CP2	0.92			
TP3	0.83			
AP4	0.37		0.73	−0.37
PP5	0.89			
AP6		−0.38	0.37	
CP7	0.53	−0.32	0.64	
EP8	0.62	−0.49	0.50	
ODI1		0.77		0.40
CDI2		0.78	0.39	
TDI3	−0.42	0.76	0.33	
ADI4				0.86
PDI5		0.34	−0.86	
ADI6		0.74		
CDI7		0.67	−0.32	
EPI8		0.89		

Notes: P means present; D means desirable.

between the first and third-ranked departments, the former having a higher mean than the latter on the following aspects: confrontation (significant at the 0.01 level), collaboration (0.04 level), proaction (0.048 level) and openness (0.10 level). Validity needs to be further tested and established.

The OCTAPACE scores of health organisations in one state (based on 25 responses) for present and desired ethos were factor analysed. The rotated loadings (Varimax) are given in Table 66.1. The loadings show two clean factors. Factor 1 is the present ethos, and Factor 2 is the desired or ideal ethos. Factor 3 seems to be a team ethos factor, with emphasis on authenticity and desired trust. Factor 4 is desired openness and experimenting (present). The first two factors give evidence of the validity of the present and desired aspects of organisational ethos.

66.6 NORMS

Based on the mean and SD value of more than 500 responses from 10 organisations, tentative norms are given in Table 66.2.

TABLE 66.2   Tentative Norms for the OCTAPACE Profile

	Dimensions	500 Managers from 10 Organisations		332 R&D Managers (Saxena & Shah, 2008)	
		Mean	*SD*	*Mean*	*SD*
1.	Openness	15	4	16	4
2.	Confrontation	14	4	16	3
3.	Trust	14	4	14	2
4.	Authenticity	12	4	14	2
5.	Proaction	14	4	14	3
6.	Autonomy	14	4	14	3
7.	Collaboration	14	4	14	2
8.	Experimenting	14	4	14	3

66.7 CORRELATES

OCTAPACE profile scores were correlated with internality—internal locus of control—at the individual level, and with motivational climate and organisational learning at the organisational level.

Internality was measured by LOCO inventory (Chapter 9). It measures internality, externality (others) and externality (chance). Correlations were found for two groups ($N = 39$ and $N = 35$, respectively). In one group ($N = 39$), externality (chance) did not have significant correlations with any aspect of ethos. Regarding internality, all aspects except authenticity, had positive correlations, significant at the 0.01 level. In the other group ($N = 35$), there were three positive correlations, significant at 0.05 level (for confrontation, authenticity and experimenting). Externality (others) was negatively correlated (significant at the 0.01 level) for five aspects; proaction, autonomy and collaboration did not have significant correlations. It can be concluded that OCTAPACE ethos reinforces internality among managers or that managers who score high on internality perceive the ethos in a positive way.

Regarding motivational climate in one group of 35 managers, the achievement climate was positively correlated (0.05 level of significance) with openness. Extension climate (concern for others and a larger cause) had positive correlations (significant at the 0.01 level) with all aspects except autonomy and collaboration. Control climate had negative correlations (at the 0.05 level of significance) with openness and confrontation. No other correlation was significant. In another group of managers from a large multiproduct company all eight-aspects of OCTAPACE were positively correlated (at 0.01 level) with achievement and extension climate, and negatively (at 0.01

level) with control climate. It can be concluded that extension climate seems both to contribute to and promoted by OCTAPACE ethos, and control climate lowers it.

Of all the correlations between OCTAPACE profile and OLD, the most significant aspect was trust, which had five positive correlations (0.01 level of significance) with two phases (implementation and stabilisation) and three mechanisms (teamwork, contingency planning and temporary systems). The implementation phase had four significant correlations (all significant at 0.01 level) with openness, confrontation, trust and proaction. It can be concluded that although trust promotes organisational learning, OCTAPACE ethos is especially important at the stage of implementing change.

In conclusion, internal locus of control and OCTAPACE ethos reinforce each other. OCTAPACE ethos promotes and is reinforced by extension climate; trust promotes organisational learning, whereas OCTAPACE ethos is critical mainly in the implementation phase. These findings are tentative and need further exploration.

66.8 USE FOR HRD

This instrument can be used by HRD professionals and OD consultants to improve organisational ethos and to increase openness, creativity and collaboration. The following steps have been tried in some organisations:

1. After they responded to the instrument, participants were given definitions of the eight values of organisational ethos. They may then have worked in small groups to prepare a profile of their organisational ethos in terms of low, medium or high. While this was being done, the instrument was scored. The profile of the organisation, derived from the scoring of responses, was then distributed to the groups, and the members discussed how the two profiles matched or differed and why.
2. The weak aspects of organisational profiles were used for action planning. Each weak value was assigned to a small group that prepared four lists—indicators of the weakness of that value in their organisation, outcome of the weak aspect (its cost to the organisation), forces that made the value weak and forces that can strengthen that value. These findings were then discussed in the larger group.
3. Small groups regrouped to prepare action plans—specific steps to improve a specific ethos value. This included ways of promoting positive forces and, more importantly, reducing or eliminating negative forces.
4. After 4–6 months, the group reviewed the progress of the action plans and the improvements initiated in organisational ethos. They also noted indicators of improvement or deterioration.
5. The instrument can be completed for the total organisation (O), a specific unit (U) and/or the ideal ethos (I) one would like to have in the organisation. Differences in the mean values of the eight aspects of ethos (O, U and I) can then be calculated.

6. Small groups can be assigned to work on the differences. The difference in mean values for the organisation and unit may show whether the respondents perceive the ethos of the total organisation (macro ethos) to be better than that of the unit (micro ethos) or vice versa.

   There also may be differences in specific dimensions. For example, in a multilocational manufacturing company, mean scores of micro ethos were higher than those of macro ethos; however, the difference was significant only on one value (confrontation), indicating that the company was seen as avoiding basic issues. This information became a useful lead for discussing implications and possible action to be taken.

7. Indices of fit can also be derived, between desired or ideal ethos and perceived ethos. This can be done by averaging the difference between I (ideal) and O (macro ethos) and between I and U (micro ethos). In the case of the manufacturing company mentioned, for example, it was found that there was a good fit on autonomy for macro and micro ethos. For both, there was the least fit on confrontation and proaction, followed by openness, trust and collaboration. The need to work on increasing the fit (and reducing dissatisfaction) on these values was recognised. This could be done by small group work, analysis, action planning and making a strategy for improving ethos.

OCTAPACE Profile
Answer Sheet

Name: _____   Role: _____

Organisation: _____   Date: _____

This instrument will help you to look at some of the values and beliefs of your organisations. Given below are statements that indicate some organisational values. If these are values of the top management, they generally will be shared in the organisation.

Read each statement and indicate how much the spirit contained in the statement is valued in your organisation. Please be frank.

Use the following key for your responses:

Write 4   if it is highly valued
Write 3   if it is given a fairly high value
Write 2   if it is given a rather low value
Write 1   if it is given a very low value

1. _____   Free interaction among employees, each respecting others' feelings, competence and sense of judgement.
2. _____   Facing and not shying away from problems.
3. _____   Offering moral support and help to employees and colleagues in a crisis.
4. _____   Congruity between feelings and expressed behaviour—minimum gap between what people say and do.
5. _____   Preventive action on most matters.
6. _____   Taking independent action relating to their jobs.
7. _____   Teamwork and team spirit.
8. _____   Trying out innovative ways of solving problems.
9. _____   Genuine sharing of information, feelings and thoughts in meetings.
10. _____   Going deeper rather than doing surface-level analysis of interpersonal problems.
11. _____   Interpersonal contact and support among people.
12. _____   Tactfulness, smartness and even a little manipulation to get things done.
13. _____   Seniors encouraging their subordinates to think about their development and take action in that direction.
14. _____   Close supervision of employees and directing their action.
15. _____   Accepting and appreciating help offered by others.
16. _____   Encouraging employees to take a fresh look at how things are done.
17. _____   Free discussion and communication between seniors and subordinates.
18. _____   Facing challenges inherent in the work situation.
19. _____   Confiding in seniors without fear that they will misuse the trust.
20. _____   Owning up mistakes.
21. _____   Considering both positive and negative aspects before taking action.
22. _____   Obeying and checking with seniors rather than acting on your own.
23. _____   Performing immediate tasks rather than being concerned about large organisational goals.
24. _____   Making genuine attempts to change behaviour on the basis of feedback.

Use the following keys for the remainder of your responses:

Write 4   if it is a very widely shared belief
Write 3   if it is fairly widely shared
Write 2   if only some persons in the organisation share this belief
Write 1   if only a few or none have this belief

25. _____   Effective managers put a lid on their feelings.
26. _____   Pass the buck tactfully when there is a problem.
27. _____   Trust begets trust.
28. _____   Telling a polite lie is preferable to telling the unpleasant truth.
29. _____   Prevention is better than cure.
30. _____   Freedom to employees breeds indiscipline.
31. _____   Usually, emphasis on teamwork dilutes individual accountability.
32. _____   Thinking out and doing new things tones up the organisation's vitality.
33. _____   Free and frank communication between various levels helps in solving problems.
34. _____   Surfacing problems is not enough; we should find the solutions.
35. _____   When the chips are down, you have to fend for yourself (people cannot rely on others in times of crisis).
36. _____   People generally are what they appear to be.
37. _____   A stitch in time saves nine.
38. _____   A good way to motivate employees is to give them autonomy to plan their work.
39. _____   Employees' involvement in developing an organisation's mission and goals contributes to productivity.
40. _____   In today's competitive situations, consolidation and stability are more important than experimentation.

OCTAPACE Profile
Score Sheet

Name: _____   Role: _____

Organisation: _____   Date: _____

Transfer your responses from the completed instrument. While transferring the scores, reverse the scores for items marked with asterisks (*): 4 will become 0 and 0 will become 4; 3 will become 2 and 2 will become 3.

											Total
O	1	__	9	__	17	__	*25	__	33	__	__
C	2	__	10	__	18	__	*26	__	34	__	__
T	3	__	11	__	19	__	27	__	*35	__	__
A	4	__	*12	__	20	__	*28	__	36	__	__
P	5	__	13	__	21	__	29	__	37	__	__
A	6	__	14	__	*22	__	*30	__	38	__	__
C	7	__	15	__	23	__	*31	__	39	__	__
E	8	__	16	__	24	__	32	__	*40	__	__

Organisational Culture Profile

67.1 THE INSTRUMENT AND ITS ADMINISTRATION

Organisational culture profile measures four organisational cultures: autocratic/feudal, bureaucratic, technocratic and entrepreneurial/organic/democratic.

The instrument has eight sets dealing with values (1), beliefs (3), primacy (6), communication (7), leadership (4), rituals in meetings (5), celebrations (8) and rooms and furniture (2).*

The instrument is completed by persons working in an organisation. The respondent is required to rank the four statements in each set in terms of their applicability to the organisation concerned. The ranks are from 1 (most closely describing the organisation) to 4 (least accurate).

67.2 CONCEPTUAL FRAMEWORK

The number of studies of organisational culture is steadily increasing. Such studies have used different terminology, and the same terms have been used with different meanings. There is a need to clarify some terms and evolve a common understanding about their use. Some of these terms are given below with a brief definition. These need to be debated and discussed.

The various terms used in the context of organisational culture are values, ethics, beliefs, ethos, climate, environment and culture. Ethics refers to normative aspects to what is socially desirable. Values, beliefs, attitudes and norms are interrelated. Interaction between beliefs and values results in attitude formation (attitudes = beliefs × values) and then produces norms. Values and beliefs are the core, while attitudes are the next layer, followed by norms or behaviour. When these are institutionalised or when they accumulate and integrate, we have a social phenomenon.

---

* The figures in parentheses refer to the serial numbers of the sets in the instrument.

The culture-related concepts can also be seen as multilevel concepts. At the core (first level) are the values, which give a distinct identity to a group. This is the ethos of the group. The Random House Dictionary defines ethos as 'the fundamental character or spirit of a culture ... dominant assumptions of a people or period' (p. 489).

The second-level concept is climate, which can be defined as the perceived attributes of an organisation and its subsystem as reflected in the way it deals with its members, groups and issues. The emphasis is on perceived attributes and the working of the subsystems.

The third-level concept relates to atmosphere, the effect of climate. The Random House Dictionary defines atmosphere as a 'distinct quality' (p. 94) and environment as '...affecting the existence or development of someone or something' (p. 477). The concept of atmosphere can be proposed as one related to the effect of the climate.

The fourth concept is culture—the cumulative beliefs, values and assumptions underlying transactions with nature, and important phenomena, as reflected in artefacts, rituals, etc. Culture is reflected in the ways adopted to deal with basic phenomena.

The brief comments made here need elaboration and discussion. Some instruments developed to measure them are reported in this part of the book.

67.2.1 Organisational Culture (Power Model)

Although studies on organisational culture have been increasing, there is no agreement on the concept and definition of culture. Culture-related concepts—culture, climate, environment, atmosphere, ethos, etc.—have been used loosely and interchangeably, although an attempt has been made to delineate some of them (Pareek, 1991). Culture can be defined as the cumulative beliefs, values and assumptions, underlying transaction with nature and important phenomena (e.g., collectivity, environment, context, time, biological differences, power, etc.). Culture is reflected in the artefacts—rituals, design of space, furniture and ways of dealing with various phenomena. Distribution and concentration of power can be one basis of classifying culture. From this angle, organisational cultures can be of four types—autocratic (or feudal), bureaucratic, technocratic and entrepreneurial (or organic and democratic).

Autocratic or feudal culture is characterised by the centralised power concentrated in a few persons and observation of proper protocols in relation to the person(s) in power. Bureaucratic culture is characterised by the primacy of procedures and rules, hierarchy, and distant and impersonal relationships. Technocratic culture emphasises technical/professional standards and improvement. Entrepreneurial culture is concerned about the achievement of results and providing excellent service to customers.

Profiles of the Four Cultures. The two related concepts that are relevant for organisational culture are organisational climate and organisational ethos. As already stated, organisational climate can be defined as the perceived attributes of an organisation and its subsystems, reflected in the way it deals with members, groups and issues. The perceived attributes related to organisational processes produce motivation or concerns, and climate can be characterised by these concerns. There are six types of climates:

1. Achievement (dominant concern for excellence)
2. Expert Power (concern for impact through expertise)
3. Extension (concern for relevance to larger goals and entities)
4. Control (concern for orderliness)
5. Affiliation (concern for maintaining good personal relations)
6. Dependency (concern for approval and maintenance of hierarchical order)

The first three climates—achievement, expert power, extension—have been found to be functional contributing to organisational effectiveness. The last three—control, affiliation, dependency—have been found to be dysfunctional for organisational effectiveness.

Ethos (see Ethos in this chapter) is primarily concerned with values and is the fundamental character of spirit of the organisation. As already discussed, OCTAPACE ethos is characterised by the eight values of openness, confrontation, trust, authenticity, proaction, autonomy, collaboration and experimentation. The respective opposite poles of the eight values are closed, avoidance, suspicion, manipulation, inertia, role boundness, conflicts and safe playing.

Based on some data, observation, discussions and, most importantly, guided by the configurations, some hypotheses are proposed about the profiles of the four organisational cultures in terms of climate and ethos variables. These are shown in Table 67.1.

Let us briefly mention these profiles as hypotheses.

An autocratic/feudal culture is primarily concerned with following proper protocol, dominated by dependency (de) climate, with affiliation (af). People are selected on the basis of relationship,

TABLE 67.1   Profile of Organisational Culture

Cultures	Focus	Climate	Ethos
Autocratic/feudal	Proper protocol	Deaf (dependency affiliation)	Rammassic (All opposite values of OCTAPACE)
Bureaucratic	Rules and regulations	Code (control dependency)	Sick (safe playing, inertia, conflict and closed)
Technocratic	Perfection	Expex (expert power, extension)	Pace (proaction, collaboration, experimentation)
Entrepreneurial/ democratic/organic	Results and Customers	Achext (achievement extension)	OCTAPACE (All 8 values)

and they are trusted. Deaf (dependency affiliation) climate is characterised as 'the top managers control the organisation and employ their own in-group members, who are extremely loyal to these leaders' (Pareek, 1989, p. 169). The ethos of such a culture is closed, mistrusting and self-seeking.

A bureaucratic culture is concerned with following proper rules and regulations. Its climate is dominated by control (co) and backed up by dependency (de). Such a climate (code) has been characterised as

> a bureaucracy and a rigid hierarchy which dominates the organisation. Because actions are generally referred to the levels above for approval, decisions are usually delayed. It is more important to follow rules and regulations than to achieve results. Senior employees protect those subordinates who do not make any procedural mistakes. (Pareek, 1989, p. 169)

The ethos of a bureaucratic organisation is characterised by playing safe, inertia, lack of collaboration and closedness.

A technocratic culture generally has an apex climate—expert power being dominant, with a back-up climate of extension. 'Specialists play the major roles in the organisation, working in a planned way on socially relevant matters. The organisation pays attention to the employees needs and welfare' (Pareek, 1989, p. 168). The ethos is positive—proaction (initiative), autonomy, collaboration and experimentation.

An entrepreneurial culture (also called organic or democratic) is primarily concerned with results and customers. Its climate (ace) is generally that of achievement (ac) or concern for excellence and extension (e) or concern for larger groups and issues. In such a climate 'employees work on challenging tasks, and devote equal attention to the social relevance of these tasks. The organisation has a highly developed sense of social responsibility, as well as a strong sense of its responsibility to fulfil employee needs' (Pareek, 1989, p. 168). The ethos is positive, and characterised by the eight values of OCTAPACE.

67.3 SCORING

The Scoring Key (appended) is used to score responses. The totals for each culture type—the ranks given to the alternatives shown for eight sets—are found out for each individual. The total for each cultural type can vary from 8 to 32. The total of all the four cultural types for each individual will be 80. The lower the score, the higher is the value given in that culture.

All individual scores on the four cultures can be averaged by dividing the total by the number of persons completing the instrument. This gives the group profile.

67.4 RELIABILITY

Guttman split-half equal length and unequal length reliability for a group of 20 people was found to be 0.86.

67.5 VALIDITY

Validity was found in two ways. The theoretical profile (hypothesis stated in this chapter) was tested against an empirical profile, and factor analysis was done to test construct validity. Let us first examine the findings of an actual profile against the hypothetical one.

A group of 18 persons from five countries (only one was from an industrialised country) responded to the three instruments of culture, climate and ethos. Autocratic culture had positive correlations with control (significant at 0.05 level) and dependency climate (the latter, at 0.21, was not significant). It had negative correlations with achievement and extensions (the latter significant at 0.01 level). It had negative correlations with all eight OCTAPACE aspects (for authenticity, it had almost zero correlation). However, only three correlations were significant: (two at 0.01 level—those with confrontation and collaboration—and one at 0.05 level, with trust). Bureaucratic culture had a significant positive correlation with control climate, and a negative correlation with achievement, expert power and affiliation (with the first one, the correlation was statistically significant).

Regarding technocratic culture, there was no significant correlation with climate aspects (0.27 with expert power, 0.45 with control and 0.41 with extension were not significant). It has significant negative correlations with five ethos aspects—confrontation, trust authenticity, proaction and collaboration.

Entrepreneurial culture had a significant positive correlation with achievement and extension climate (at 0.05 and 0.001 levels respectively), a negative correlation with control and affiliation (significant at 0.001 and 0.05 levels respectively) and dependency (not significant at 0.042). It had a statistically significant positive correlation with all aspects of ethos (with autonomy, the correlation was very low and not significant).

These findings validate the proposed hypothesis, except in the case of technocratic culture. Interestingly, the respondents were from professional/technical organisations.

Responses of 18 managers from insurance companies were factor analysed to find the internal structure of organisational culture. Principal components analysis with Varimax rotation gave five factors (above eigenvalue of 1). Table 66.1 gives the factor loadings.

The factors explained 69% variance of organisational culture. Table 67.2 gives five factors (only loadings above 0.30 were considered).

Factor 1	Authoritarian bureaucratic	(23%)
Factor 2	Normative entrepreneurial	(19%)
Factor 3	Bureaucratic technocratic	(10%)
Factor 4	Bureaucratic	(9%)
Factor 5	Problem-solving technocratic	(8%)

It will be seen from the table that Factor 1 has high loadings on four autocratic, three technocratic and one entrepreneurial culture items. Indifference to meetings (5b) may also be related to

TABLE 67.2 Rotated Factor Loading (Loadings of 0.3 and Above Have Been Given)

Items	Factor 1	Factor 2	Factor 3	Factor 4	Factor 5
5d [A]	0.88				
6d [A]	0.79			0.42	0.37
7a [A]	.62	0.43	0.43	0.31	
8b [A]	0.61	0.34			
4a [A]	.59	−0.36			
7b [B]	.78			0.36	
6c [B]	.77			0.43	−0.50
4c [B]	.75				
8d [B]	0.45				
5c [B]	.31				
3d [B]	.34		−0.69		
5b [T]	.77				
7c [T]	0.43		−0.50	−0.31	
2c [E]	0.45				
1d [E]		0.84			
6a [E]		0.79			
5a [E]		0.76			0.42
4b [E]		0.65			
7d [E]		0.61	0.60		
8c [E]		0.46	0.32		
4d [T]		0.77			
6b [T]		0.74	−0.40		
1b [B]		−0.57			
1a [A]		−0.73		−0.36	
2a [B]			0.84		
3c [T]	0.34	0.34	0.66		
2d [T]			−0.32		0.75
3b [A]				0.82	
3a [E]				−0.84	
8a [T]					0.82

bureaucratic culture. Autocratic items relate to the importance of top people. This factor (the main factor, explaining 23% variance) can be called autocratic–bureaucratic culture.

Factor 2 (explaining 19% variance) has high loadings on seven out of eight entrepreneurial culture items. In addition, it has high loadings on four autocratic, one bureaucratic and two technocratic items. Interestingly, all value-related items (1a, 1b, 1d) are in this factor (the fourth item, 1c, does not have high loadings on any factor). We can therefore call it normative entrepreneurial culture.

Factor 3 has high loadings on two bureaucratic, four technocratic, one autocratic and one entrepreneurial items. Out of these, the highest loading (0.84) is on a bureaucratic item. This factor can be called a bureaucratic-technocratic culture.

Factor 4 has high loadings on four autocratic, two bureaucratic, one technocratic and one entrepreneurial items. This factor can be called a *bureaurotocratic* culture—a combination of bureaucratic and autocratic which is very common among bureaucratic organisations.

Factor 5 has very high loading on two technocratic items (2d and 8a). It has high loadings on one autocratic, one bureaucratic (negative loading) and two entrepreneurial items (one of which, 7d, is concerned with problem-solving). Most of the items relate to problem-solving. The factor can be called a problem-solving technocratic culture.

To summarise, factor analysis has not fully validated the classification. Autocratic and bureaucratic cultures are combined with other cultures; all four cultures are present in the different factors. More work needs to be done on this aspect.

Some items probably need critical examination: 1c and 2b (which do not find any place in any factor), 7a (which has high loadings on four factors) and 6d (high loadings on three factors).

67.6 NORMS

The mean and SDs, based on three organisations (about 80 respondents) are given here. The lower the score, the higher is the concerned culture.

Culture	
Autocratic	20
Bureaucratic	20
Technocratic	20
Entrepreneurial	20
Mean	**22**

67.7 CORRELATES

These have already been discussed under validity. Correlations of the four cultures with ethos (OCTAPACE Profile, see Chapter 66) and climate (MAO-C, see Chapter 64) for a group of 24 are given in Table 67.3.

TABLE 67.3 Correlation of Culture with Ethos and Climate

	Ethos									Climate				
										Exp.				
Culture	O	C	T	A	P	A	C	E	Ach.	Inf.	Exten.	Cont.	Dep.	Aff.
A—	—	—	—	—	—	—							—	—
B	−0.68	−0.63	−0.43	−0.61	−44	−0.63	−0.70	−0.56	−0.64	—	−0.47	−0.48	−0.43	−40.3
T	0.44	—	—	—	—	—	0.42	—	—	—	—	—	—	—
E	0.55	0.45	0.40	0.50	—	0.56	0.54	0.42	0.48	—	0.59	—	−0.46	—

Note: Only significant correlations are given.

67.8 USE FOR HRD

An organisation's profile can be prepared with the mean values of responses by its members on 32 items. The mean values of the items and the four cultures may both be calculated.

The instrument can be used for OD. Members of the organisation can work in small groups and prepare their own assessment of the dominant score (the lowest) and the back-up score (the next higher). The results from the responses can then be shared. Members could discuss whether they would like a change in the organisation's culture profile and if so, what profile they would prefer. This can be shared in a large meeting where a consensus may emerge.

Again small groups may be formed, preferably eight groups, one for each aspect suggested in the instrument. Each group may develop actionable ideas for changing the culture profile, based on the analysis of the aspect it is discussing. These can then be presented in the total group for consensus and can form a basis for further work in the organisation.

Organisational Culture Profile
Scoring Key

	Sets							
Cultures	1	2	3	4	5	6	7	8
Autocratic	a	b	b	a	d	d	a	b
Bureaucratic	b	a	d	c	c	c	b	d
Technocratic	c	d	c	d	b	b	c	a
Entrepreneurial	d	c	a	b	a	a	d	c

Organisational Culture Profile

Name: _____   Role: _____

Organisation: _____   Date: _____

This instrument is designed to find out some of the values, beliefs and practices of organisations. Below are given eight sets, each containing four statements. Please read the statements in each set and then rank-order them. Give Rank 1 to the statement which describes your organisation most closely or accurately. Give Rank 2 to a good description of your organisation; Rank 3 to a statement not so true of your organisation; and Rank 4 to the statement which is least true of your organisation. There are no right or wrong answers. Please rank all sets.

Set 1

___ (a) No consideration is given to values in this organisation.
___ (b) Values are not shared in the organisation.
___ (c) Values are shared only at the top level.
___ (d) Organisational values are widely shared in the organisation.

Set 2

___ (a) The size of a room and its furniture is according to a person's rank.
___ (b) Each senior member has a room with a large table and space for holding meetings.
___ (c) Generally, small tables are used by managers.
___ (d) Large working tables are used here.

Set 3

___ (a) The dominant belief here is that things don't happen; you make them happen.
___ (b) The belief here is that most things depend on the top management.
___ (c) People believe that the major constraints are managerial.
___ (d) People believe there are too many external constraints, which are difficult to fight.

Set 4

___ (a) The leaders here expect to be implicitly obeyed.
___ (b) The leaders here are role models for their people.
___ (c) People are expected to follow the proper channels that have been laid down.
___ (d) The leaders set the standards of performance.

Set 5

___ (a) In meetings, people sit wherever they can find place.
___ (b) People are indifferent to meetings and try to avoid them.
___ (c) There is an implicit hierarchy in the seating pattern at meetings.
___ (d) In meetings, seats for those at the top are fixed. Generally, meetings are not held without top managers.

Set 6

___ (a) The customers is regarded as a most important person here.
___ (b) A good product is given the highest importance.
___ (c) Rules and regulations are given high importance.
___ (d) The Chief Executive is the most important here.

Set 7

___ (a) Most communication is generated at the meetings of top people.

___ (b) All communication is in writing and through memos.

___ (c) There is not much work-related communication among people.

___ (d) People communicate with one another to solve problems.

Set 8

___ (a) A lot of attention is given to updating technology.

___ (b) The top management have parties to celebrate good performance of the organisation.

___ (c) High performance is celebrated, with everybody joining in.

___ (d) People are busy streamlining rules and regulations.

Organisational Culture: Organisational Survey

68.1 THE INSTRUMENT AND ITS ADMINISTRATION

Organisational Survey measures 15 aspects of organisational culture. It contains 36 items. A respondent is required to rate items 1 to 33, on a 5-point scale, on how accurately they describe his department/unit/organisation. Each of the last three items (34, 35 and 36) contains four alternatives, and the respondent is required to rank them (4 to 1) from most characteristic of the organisation to least characteristic. The items can also be rated for their desirability in the organisation.

68.2 CONCEPTUAL FRAMEWORK

68.2.1 Organisational Culture (Comprehensive Framework)

Schein (1985, p. 9) defines culture as

> A pattern of basic assumptions—invented, discovered, or developed by a given group as it learns to cope with its problems of external adaptation and internal integration—that have worked well enough to be considered valid and, therefore, to be taught to new members as the correct way to perceive, think, and feel in relation to those problems.

We shall define culture as cumulative preferences of some states of life over others (values), response predispositions towards several significant issues and phenomena (attitudes), organised ways of filling time in relation to certain affairs (rituals) and ways of promoting desired behaviours and preventing undesirable ones (sanctions).

68.2.1.1 Dimensions of Culture (In Brief)

Culture is reflected in various forms in the external life of a society or an organisation, as well as in the values and beliefs held by its members. Schein (1985, p. 14) has proposed three levels of variables in a culture. The first is artefacts and creations, which are visible but often not decipherable. These include technology, art, visible and audible behaviour patterns. The second, values, indicate greater awareness of hierarchy of preference of the life states, both testable in the physical environment and testable by only social consensus. The third is the deepest level of basic assumptions, which are taken for granted, are invisible and preconscious (relationship to environment). These include the nature of reality, time and space, human nature, human activity and human relationships.

The conceptual framework of values by Kluckhohn and Strodtbeck (1961) has been quite frequently used in understanding cultures. They have proposed five main orientations, based on the meaning of human existence, meaning of human labour and endeavour, relationship of man and nature, time-orientation and relationship of man with fellow beings. These dimensions have been used to propose a paradigm. At one end is the Western (industrialised) culture with its mastery-orientation to nature, active and optimistic view of man, society built on competitive relationship and future orientation. On the other end are the traditional cultures—non-industrial societies—with opposite orientations. Industrialising societies may be located on this continuum.

Another useful and potential framework is one of power proposed by McClelland (1975) with individual orientations being defined by the source of power (external or internal) and the target of power (others or self). This framework can be used in conceptualising typologies of cultures. Borrowed from Sigmund Freud, the framework has been used to study managers, effectiveness (McClelland & Burnham, 1981). This framework can also be used to understand some other typologies. For example, the distinction between doing orientation, being orientation and being-and-becoming orientation (Kluckhohn & Strodtbeck, 1961) can be seen as relevant here. The fourth dimension, enabling orientation, can be added to the three. In this, active doing by self is replaced by facilitating action by others. Table 68.1 summarises the main conceptual models in relation to power.

TABLE 68.1　Power and Organisational Culture

Source of Power	Target of Power	Freud	McClelland (Managers)	Kluckhohn & Strodtbeck	Typology of Culture
External	Self	Oral	Dependent	Being	Expressive
Internal	Self	Anal	Autonomous	Being-and-becoming	Conserving
Internal	Others	Phallic	Manipulative	Doing	Assertive
External	Others	Genital	Serving	(Enabling)	Expanding

Quinn and McGrath (1985) have suggested four types of organisational cultures—rational (market), developmental (adhocracy), consensual (clan) and hierarchical (hierarchy). Hofstede (1980) studied four dimensions of 50 cultures and found these dimensions adequate to explain cultural orientations—individualism vs. collectivism, power distance, uncertainty avoidance, and masculinity vs. feminity.

It may be useful to consider the main concerns of human beings in studying culture. Their concerns relate to coming to terms with nature, their immediate environments (context), time, collectivities of which they are parts and natural biological differentiation (sex). One other aspect deserving attention relates to coming to terms with power in the collectivity. The various dimensions of culture can then be derived from the following six concerns:

1. *Relationship with nature:* Kluckhohn and Strodtbeck (1961) have suggested this dimension. In the relationship, either of the two may be regarded as dominating. If nature is seen as powerful and dominating and individuals as helpless, a fatalistic orientation may result, taking nature for granted. The opposite orientation, scientism, may result from the belief that man can manipulate and change nature. The concept of locus of control (Rotter, 1966) is relevant here.

2. *Orientation to the environments (context):* The environment may be seen as structured and unchanging, resulting in a sense of satisfaction. Any ambiguity in the environment may therefore be disturbing. On the other hand, people may like and enjoy ambiguity. This dimension of 'ambiguity tolerance' (Adorno & Frenkel-Brunswick, 1983) or uncertainty avoidance (Hofstede, 1980) is a useful one.

   Another dimension may relate to the importance given to a context to understand the meaning of some phenomena, or the ignoring of the context in search of clear universal meanings. The terms high-context and low-context cultures have been proposed (Hall, 1977). In high-context cultures, events can be understood only in their contexts; meanings and categories can change and causality cannot be unambiguously established. Such cultures are context-sensitive.

3. *Time-orientation:* Kluckhohn and Strodtbeck (1961) have proposed this dimension with an orientation to past, present and future. Time may also be seen as a collection of discrete units or as a flowing phenomenon. We shall discuss this dimension in detail.

4. *Orientation to collectivities:* The relationship between individuals and the collectivities, to which they belong, can be seen in dimensions—primacy and identity. Let us first take primacy. What is primacy? Individuals or the society? Self-interest or larger interest (including the self)? Own discretion or norms of the collectivity? We shall briefly examine these.

   If the individual is seen as more important than, and independent of, the collectivities, it may result in an orientation of individualism. If collectivity is seen as primary, subordinating individuals, the orientation of collectivism may result. Hofstede (1980) has used this dimension in his study of cultures. Collectivities may be defined by their identities and persons belonging to them may have stronger identification with them. We may call this a particularist orientation, contrasted with universalist orientation in which the individuals do not have strong in-group versus out-group feelings.

Another dimension may relate to the use of norms in a collectivity. If norms are determined by the collectivity and individuals feel obliged to follow these norms in deciding whether their behaviour is right or wrong, we have an other-directed orientation. If individuals evolve their own norms and judge their actions against these norms, we have inner-directed orientation.

5. *Orientation to sex differences*: If the biological differences between men and women are over-emphasised and social roles are divided according to gender, what is being termed masculinity may result. If the differences are not over-emphasised in social allocation of roles, we may have an orientation of feminity. Hofstede (1980) studied this dimension and called it masculinity–feminity. Androgyny may be a better term for integration of characteristics usually attributed to the two sexes.

6. *Orientation to power*: In a collectivity, power is not distributed equally. However, in some collectivities, there may be uneasiness about unequal distribution of power, associated with attempts to redistribute it. Other collectivities may tolerate the differences in power. Hofstede (1980) calls it power distance. The other aspect of power, as already mentioned, is the combination of the source and target of power resulting in four types of cultures. In the expressive culture, emotional, verbal and artistic expressions are profound. There is also a variety of dishes and drinks. In the conserving culture, there is an emphasis on long and sustained training, conserving traditions cultivating arts and learning that require long training and the perseverance. In the assertive culture, there is an emphasis on accomplishing things through the use of talents, high competition and creation of wealth. The expanding culture emphasises building of organisations and institutions to sustain and increase growth.

We have used various dimensions of culture, from those briefly mentioned, to study the relationship of culture and management. These dimensions are discussed in some detail.

68.2.1.2 Dimensions of Culture (In Detail)

1. *Locus of control*: If most members in a culture feel helpless in relation to nature, and perceive nature as dominating and beyond human manipulation, an orientation of fatalism or external locus of control may develop. In contrast, the orientation of scientism holds that nature can be changed and adapted for better use of human society. This can also be called internality (internal locus of control).

2. *Ambiguity Tolerance*: This aspect, first studied by Adorno et al. (1950), has been used by Hofstede (1980), who calls it uncertainty avoidance. If members of a collectivity feel uncomfortable with ambiguity and try to structure situations to avoid it, their tolerance

for ambiguity is low or their uncertainty avoidance is high. Under ambiguity tolerance, situations that are unstructured, vague and unpredictable provide opportunities for using multiple approaches. Detailed and rigid structures, procedures and uniform behaviour and also beliefs in absolute truths can help in avoiding ambiguity. The beliefs mentioned here characterise this dimension of ambiguity tolerance.

   a.   Several truths may coexist, without causing disruptive conflicts. People not only tolerate but find the various truths mutually enriching.

   b.   Deviant behaviour and ideas are tolerated. These are seen as sources of creativity.

   c.   Time is seen and treated as cyclic, not deserving undue importance. Cultures with low ambiguity tolerance over-structure the time.

   d.   Rituals create order in a society or organisation.

3.   *Contextualism:* In a high-context culture, the meaning of events, phenomena and behaviour are interpreted in the context in which they occur. One behaviour (e.g., eating in the same plate with a member of another caste) may be right in one context (in a temple) and not in another (at home). The apparent contradictions in behaviour arise out of the different contexts. In a low-context culture, all events and behaviour are judged by one standard, and there is an attempt to evolve universal rules or explanations.

4.   *Temporarlity:* Cultures may differ in their orientation to time. Past-oriented cultures think and indulge in events of the past (usually glory) and are oblivious of present demands and future possibilities and problems. Present-orientation, called temporarlity here, is reflected in the importance given by members of a culture to the present. Such people are involved in immediate tasks. However, they may not ensure the endurance and continuity of these tasks. They live in discrete time periods, without strong links with the past or future. In such cultures where attention is paid to immediate tasks and groups, there is a tendency to switch from one to another easily.

5.   *Collectivism vs. individualism:* This is one of the 4 dimensions thoroughly researched by Hofstede (1980, 1982, 1985). According to Hofstede (1985, p. 14), individualism stands for a preference for a loosely knit social framework in society wherein individuals are supposed to take care of themselves and their immediate families only. To the contrary, collectivism stands for a preference for a tightly knit social framework in which individuals can expect their relatives, clan or other in-group to look after them in exchange for unquestioning loyalty. The fundamental issue addressed by this dimension is the degree of interdependence a society maintains among individuals. It relates to people's self-concept: I or we.

   In a collectivist culture, a person belongs to one or more cohesive collectivities and is obliged to serve them, as much as the collectivities are obliged to protect the interests of its members. The following-mentioned beliefs and behaviour characterise collectivism.

a.   Relations are moral and not contractual. In individualist cultures, relations are treated more as contracts for a particular purpose. In collectivist cultures, mutual obligations between the individual member and the collectivities are sacred and have moral tones—neither can get out this mutuality.

b.   Individuals have strong obligations towards their collectivities. This is a part of the moral nature of the relationship. Loyalty to the group is important in such cultures.

c.   Relations take precedence over tasks. In a collectivist culture, maintaining relationships and fulfilling personal and communal obligations are more important than completing tasks.

d.   Harmony in a collectivity must be preserved. Maintaining harmony is highly valued in a collectivist culture. This would mean not confronting a person and avoiding conflicts.

e.   Opinions are predetermined by the collectivity. In a collectivist culture, in most cases, individual opinions are influenced by the decision of a collectivity.

f.   Some tasks are accepted as collective tasks.

6. *Narcissism*: In a narcissistic culture, individuals are concerned about themselves—as individuals, families or groups. For example, they will not be concerned if others are adversely affected. This leads to self-seeking behaviour. The concern is narrow (self).

7. *Particularism vs. universalism*: In a collectivity (society or organisation), there are several groups whose identities are formed on some basis—ethnic, religious, regional, caste, speciality, etc. If such groups have strong identities, resulting in an in-group/out-group feeling, we may have an orientation which is particularist. This is the opposite of the universalist orientation in which the groups do not have insular and strong identities. In a particularist culture, there is a tendency to classify person as belonging to one's in-group or belonging to an out-group. Sinha (1982) has studied this dimension in the context of the Indian culture. In a particularist culture, an individual feels secure in his own in-group and tends to make the in-group stronger in comparison with out-groups.

8. *Other-directedness vs. inner-directedness*: Cultures and individuals differ on a scale which has two opposite poles. They could be inner-directed (behaviour is directed by internal standards) or other-directed (behaviour is directed by standards or opinions set by others). In an other-directed culture, a person is guided by the accepted standards of conduct of a collectivity and saving face in the collectivity is critical. Often, a contrast is made between guilt cultures and shame cultures. In the former, inner worth and sin are said to guide behaviour while in the latter, honour and reputation are critical (Piers & Singer, 1953). As Geertz (1973, pp. 401–02) argues, it is difficult to use the two words (guilt and shame) in their general connotation in the English language (guilt being the feeling of having done something reprehensible, and shame, consciousness of guilt). 'Shame is the feeling of disgrace and humiliation that follows upon a transgression found out; guilt is the feeling of secret badness attendant upon one not, or not yet, found out' (Geertz, 1973, p. 401). As Geertz suggests, shame cultures could

be characterised by 'stage fright—usually a mild, though in some situations virtually paralysing, nervousness before the prospect (and the fact) of social interaction, a chronic, mostly low-grade, worry that one will not be able to being it off with the required finesse' (Geertz, 1973, p. 402).

The following values or beliefs characterise other-directedness.

a. Loss of face is very painful to individuals. Individuals do not like to be seen violating norms that are obligatory in a society. If someone points out such an instance in front of others, the concerned person feels he has lost his self-respect. A corollary of the above is that confrontation is avoided for fear of losing face.

b. Conflict must be resolved without loss of face for either party. Since loss of face is so critical to individuals, attempt is made not to create situations in which either of the party loses face. Conflict situations have the potential for loss of face by one party. In an other-directed culture, conflict management strategies are dominated by considerations of saving face for all the parties involved in the conflict.

c. Indirect communication is better than direct communication.

Pleasant and pleasing behaviour towards seniors is more desirable than telling the truth, which may be unpleasant. This is a special case of avoiding confrontation.

9. *Role-boundness*: In some cultures, the role taken by an individual may be seen as primary, and the individual may be bound by it. The individual is prepared to undergo inconvenience and may even sacrifice his personal freedom and comforts in order to fulfil his role obligation (as a father, son, wife, executive, etc.).

10. *Androgyny*: Different qualities have been attributed to the two sexes. Men are attributed toughness, competition, aggression, perseverance, achievement and assertiveness. Women are seen as having qualities such as compassion, empathy, harmony, collaboration, nurturance, a sense of aesthetics and creativity. If a society emphasises the differences between the two sex roles and allocates social roles according to such differences, it would expect men to work in areas of achievement and physical activities (work and defence) and women to work in areas requiring female virtues (nursing, housekeeping, etc.). This is a sexist orientation. We call it sexist because the roles are determined by men, and they impose their own values, emphasising competition and toughness in contrast with empathy and collaboration. In such a society, competitive aggressive characteristics are valued, and such a culture is called masculine (Hofstede, 1980). In contrast, if there is less differentiation between sex roles and social roles are not allocated according to difference in sex, an orientation called 'feminism' by Hofstede may develop. In such societies, the qualities that are attributed to men and women are both valued and integrated. We shall call such a culture androgynous.

Western culture is an example of a sexiest culture, whereas Indian and Indonesian cultures, for example, are androgynous. One symbolic image of androgyny, found in both India and Indonesia, is the depiction of Shiva as Ardhanarishwara (half man and half woman). An interesting discussion on androgyny in various cultures is given in O.

Flaherty (1980). In androgynous cultures, interpersonal trust is highly valued. Harmony and friendship are seen as desirable, and there is high concern for the weak and the underdog. Mahatma Gandhi represented this orientation well.

11. *Power-distance tolerance*: Hofstede studied this dimension and defined power distance (Hofstede, 1980, p. 14) as

> The extent to which the members of a society accept that power in institutions and organisations is distributed unequally. People in large power distance societies accept a hierarchical order in which everybody has a place which needs no further justification. People in small power distance societies strive for power equalisation and demand justification for power inequalities. The fundamental issue addressed by this dimension is how a society handles inequalities among people when they occur.

In a society with high tolerance for power distance, inequality in power is seen as a normal and acceptable reality. The following characteristics define this orientation:

1. Senior persons look after the interests of juniors, develop and guide them. Senior persons take the nurturing role.
2. People respect and learn from elders. In a society with intolerance for power, younger people are not given respect because of their age.
3. Hierarchical relations are seen as necessary and useful to maintain order in a society or an organisation.
4. The corollary of the previous statement is that persons in power are regarded as knowledgeable and capable of protecting the interests of their members.
5. Leaders are faithfully followed. Their wisdom is not questioned. In a society with low tolerance for power distance, leaders are questioned, and there is a critical attitude toward their behaviour.
6. Procedures and systems laid down by seniors are faithfully carried out. The cultures are usually ritualistic, following traditions more faithfully.
7. It is believed that higher status in the hierarchy can be obtained with the help of elders. As a result, ascribed status is emphasised in comparison to acquired status by one's own efforts.
8. Manual work has low value, and it is usually allotted to persons in the lower strata of a society or organisation.

    Use of power. As stated here, power can be used (derived from external or internal sources) to strengthen oneself or to make an impact on others and strengthen them.

There could be four orientations: expressive, conserving, assertive and expanding. This dimension has not been studied much so the comments given here are more in the native of broad proposals that need to be expanded and studied.

In expressive cultures, learning from other sources is highly valued. There is an emphasis on verbal expression and aesthetics (drama, poetry, music, etc.), and there is high verbal activity (talking, debating, eating, smoking and drinking).

In a conserving culture, the emphasis is on the conservation of traditions; discipline and conformity are stressed; frugality is valued and practised. There is an emphasis on the cultivation of learning and classical arts (requiring perseverance and long training).

In an assertive culture, emphasis is given to competition and achieving results. Assertive cultures are more vigorous exhibitionistic—showing their affluence without inhibition. The emphasis is on creation of wealth and fighting for one's place in a large entity.

The expanding cultures emphasise the creation of organisations and institutions to consolidate and sustain gains and achievements in the culture. Large and varied organisational forms develop. There is a trend toward building empires—expanding influence through building organisations.

To summarise, the 15 dimensions of culture seem to emerge from the concerns of people in a group when coming to terms with certain realities. These also seem to be relevant for understanding management practices.

Concerns	Dimension of Culture
(a) Relationship with nature	1. Internality (vs. externality)
(b) Orientation to the environment	2. Ambiguity tolerance
	3. Contextualism
(c) Time-orientation	4. Temporality
(d) Orientation to collectivities	5. Collectivism (vs. individualism)
	6. Particularism (vs. universalism)
	7. Narcissism
	8. Role-boundedness
	9. Other-directedness (vs. inner-directedness)
(e) Orientation to sex differences	10. Androgyny
(f) Orientation to power	11. Power distance tolerance
	12. Expressive
	13. Conserving
	14. Assertive
	15. Expanding

The various dimensions of culture, briefly discussed here, can be used to prepare a profile. The profiles can broadly fall into categories on a modern–traditional continuum. One question before developing societies is whether their characteristics are dysfunctional for moving towards modernity with the implication that if this is so, they need to adopt characteristics of the cultures of developed societies. Enough experience in managing development has shown that developing countries need not adopt (or copy) the culture of the developed world. This implies that there are many functional aspects for modernisation in their own cultures, and these can be preserved and used for modernisation. Similarly, there are many dysfunctional aspects in the cultures of the industrialised societies (dysfunctional for the creation of the future). Clearly, developing countries can contribute significantly in evolving future societies capable of meeting new challenges. After following long periods of colonisation, developing countries have little self-confidence, and a negative self-image. It is not surprising that members of such societies do not see many strengths in their culture and tend to use the framework of the colonising power (for analysis of this phenomenon, see Nandy, 1983).

Sometime, the opposite view is taken, as a reaction, by some people in developing countries, who eulogise the past and create delusions about the functionality of their culture. This revivalist tendency—it assumes that the past or traditions was glorious and must be restored in order to achieve glory once again—is more dysfunctional than lack of awareness of one's own strengths. What is needed is a critical attitude, sifting the functional from the dysfunctional aspects of a culture.

68.3 SCORING

The scoring key (appended) can be used for scoring. Items with asterisk marks (*) are reversed, and then the scores for each aspect are totalled. The totals of the aspects from 1 to 11 range from 3 to 15. Multiply these by 8.33. The totals of items 12 to 15 will range from 3 to 12. Multiply these by 11.1. They will range from 0 to 100.

68.4 RELIABILITY

Split-half alpha coefficient for a group of 152 managers was found to be 0.73 for the instrument.

68.5 VALIDITY

Factor analysis of data from one company (X), based on the responses of 25 top managers, did not give clear factors. The rotated (Varimax) factor loading (principal component analysis) appears in Table 68.2. Six factors were extracted, explaining 75% variance.

68.6 NORMS

Table 68.3 gives the mean values of 70 managers from two organisations.

68.7 CORRELATES

Table 68.4, giving level of significance of the positive correlations of different aspects of organisational culture with other variables, shows the significant correlates of organisational cultural aspects. The data was collected from 153 managers in an information technology company.

TABLE 68.2　Factor Loadings of Organisational Survey

Aspects	Factors					
	1	2	3	4	5	6
1. Context sensitive		0.70	0.47			
2. Ambiguity tolerant					−0.69	
3. Internal		0.79	−0.38			
4. Narcissistic				−0.33	0.57	0.59
5. Future orientation	0.64					0.32
6. Individualistic			0.68			
7. Inner-directed	0.61	0.47				
8. Universalistic	0.72	−0.39				
9. Role-bound					0.83	
10. Androgynous		0.43		0.80		
11. Power parity				−0.82		
12. Expressive						0.86
13. Conserving			0.81			
14. Assertive	0.77					
15. Expanding	−0.87					

Factor 1: Future-oriented culture
Factor 2: Value-oriented culture (both internal and inner-directed)
Factor 3: Conserving culture (consolidating the organisation)
Factor 4: Humanistic culture (considerate, human value)
Factor 5: Conservative culture (role-bound, intolerant of ambiguity)
Factor 6: Innovative culture

TABLE 68.3　Mean Values of Organisational Survey

Aspects	Present	Desired
1. Internal	50	75
2. Ambiguity tolerant	58	58
3. Context sensitive	42	33
4. Narcissistic (−)*	42	92
5. Future-oriented	50	83

(Table 68.3 Continued)

(Table 68.3 Continued)

Aspects	Present	Desired
6. Individualistic	33	17
7. Inner-directed	33	58
8. Universalistic	42	75
9. Role-bound	58	58
10. Androgynous	58	58
11. Power parity	33	58
12. Expressive	89	100
13. Conserving	100	89
14. Assertive	89	89
15. Expanding	78	100

Note: *High scores mean less narcissistic.

68.8 USE FOR HRD

This instrument can be used by five members of an organisation to get feedback on the profile. Small groups can be formed to discuss the findings and develop a consensus and work out action plans to improve the culture.

To facilitate interpretation, the profile of company A, in Table 68.2, is briefly interpreted as follows.

The profile indicates that the current organisational culture encourages diverse views and thinking, managerial responsibility and human values (empathy, concern and support). There is no difference between the ideal or desired aspects and actual ones. The present culture emphasises on business achievement, not system and institution-building.

The culture tends to be centralised in power (with less autonomy for the employees at various levels), encourages conformity (rather than internalised norms of working) and has grouping according to vested interests (less concern about the organisation). It is not clearly characterised by entrepreneurship (future-oriented), sense of confidence and control over events.

The largest gap between desired and actual perceived culture lies in two aspects: concern for larger groups such as the organisation (people and groups are currently more self-centred, not very concerned about others) and future orientation. The other gaps are on the dimensions of sense of confidence and control, broader perspective, and giving operating autonomy to various levels in the organisation.

TABLE 68.4 Levels of Significance of Correlates of Organisational Survey

Aspects of Delegation	OCTAPACE Culture		Ach	Expt. Power	Control	Depend	Ext.	Aff. (total)
Internality	–	0.000	0.000	0.000	0.000	0.000	0.000	–
Ambiguity tolerance	0.042	0.000	0.026	0.003	0.000	–	0.023	–
Context sensitivity	–	0.024	–	–	–	–	–	–
Consideration for others (opposite of narissm)	.011	0.000	0.000	0.000	0.000	0.000	0.000	–
Future orientation	0.002	0.000	0.000	0.000	0.000	0.000	0.000	–
Individualism	–	0.000	0.000	0.001	0.000	0.000	0.003	0.012
Inner-directed	–	–	–	–	–	–	–	–
Universal	–	–	–	–	–	–	–	–
Role-bound	–	–	–	–	–	–	–	–
Androgyny	–	0.029	0.001	0.052	0.004	0.018	0.043	–
Power parity	–	0.003	–	0.001	0.002	0.012	0.007	0.006
Expressive	–	–	–	–	–	–	–	–
Conserving	–		–	–	–	–	–	–
Assertive	–	–	0.044	0.015	–	–	–	–
Expanding	–	0.001	–0.004	0.001	0.002	0.003	–	–

Organisational Survey

Name: _____   Role: _____

Organisation: _____   Date: _____

Read each statement given below and indicate, in column P, to what extent the statement is true of your organisation. Use the following keys:

Write 5   if the statement represents your organisation very well
Write 4   if it is fairly true of your organisation
Write 3   if you are not sure whether it is true or not
Write 2   if it represents very little of your organisation
Write 1   if it is not true of your organisation at all

Now, go back to the statements and indicate in column D how much is desirable for your organisation. Use the following keys:

Write 5   if you think this is very highly desirable
Write 4   if you think this highly desirable
Write 3   if you are not sure whether this is desirable
Write 2   if you think this is not desirable for your organisation
Write 1   if you think this is very undesirable

You may either respond first for column P and then for column D; or you may respond to both together for each statement.

P   D

___ ___   1. Most members of this organisation feel helpless in relation to vital matters.
___ ___   2. People feel free to have and express opinions and ideas that are different from their bosses.
___ ___   3. Rules are applied uniformly here, without any consideration to special circumstances in special cases.
___ ___   4. In this organisation, every department/group is concerned only about itself.
___ ___   5. This organisation can be described as a fire-fighting organisation, dealing with the issues as they emerge.
___ ___   6. Great value is given here to good relationships and loyalty to the organisation.
___ ___   7. Attempts are made here to resolve conflicts without loss of face by a party involved in the conflict.
___ ___   8. People feel comfortable in groups of their own affinity.
___ ___   9. Managers generally spend more time on their jobs, even at the cost of personal needs.
___ ___   10. Competitiveness and smartness are highly valued here.
___ ___   11. Seniors exercise their authority in most matters and theirs is accepted by their juniors.
___ ___   12. Employees feel they can influence many important issues here.
___ ___   13. All matters, including course of action, are worked out meticulously, and deviations are not liked.
___ ___   14. Although rules are worked out in detail, these are applied according to the background of a case.
___ ___   15. People care for the total organisation and not only about their own groups or teams.
___ ___   16. Importance is given to long-term planning and working for the future.

P   D

__   __   17. Maintaining harmony is highly valued here.

__   __   18. Confrontation and frank communication are generally avoided here.

__   __   19. Leaders here nurture and protect the interests of those who belong to them.

__   __   20. Managers care a great deal about their personal time and do not like business to intrude on it.

__   __   21. Importance is given to compassion and caring.

__   __   22. Hierarchical relationships are seen as necessary for running the organisation.

__   __   23. There is a general feeling of indifference among employees because they feel that they cannot influence critical matters here.

__   __   24. Different ways of solving problems are encouraged here.

__   __   25. Decisions are objective and clear-cut, and are not influenced by the context.

__   __   26. Generally, everyone here is mainly concerned about one's own affairs.

__   __   27. People do not have time to think of future needs; they are too busy completing their assigned tasks.

__   __   28. People here are more individualistic; they complete assigned tasks for which they expect to be compensated.

__   __   29. Pleasant behaviour is preferred here to telling an unpleasant truth.

__   __   30. People here are treated according to their working assignments and not on the basis of kinship, cast, language, etc.

__   __   31. Work responsibility here is given more importance than demands of the family.

__   __   32. Nurturing and helping subordinates is encouraged here.

__   __   33. Achievement and competence are more important than hierarchical status.

Given below are three sets of statements: rank-order, in column P, the 4 items in each set (write 4 for the statement that is most characteristic of your organisation and 1 for the statement that is least characteristic). Then rank-order them for their desirability under column D (4 for most desirable and 1 for least desirable of the 4).

P   D

34. __   __   a. Learning from seniors.

    __   __   b. Self-discipline.

    __   __   c. Assertive behaviour.

    __   __   d. Team building.

35. __   __   a. Developing systems.

    __   __   b. Getting work done.

    __   __   c. Hard work and perseverance.

    __   __   d. Spontaneity.

36. __   __   a. Maintaining discipline.

    __   __   b. Long-term planning.

    __   __   c. Effective communication.

    __   __   d. Getting the task done.

Organisational Survey
Score Sheet

This instrument assesses the profile of organisational cultures. The following aspects are assessed. The following steps may be taken for scoring:

1. Reverse the ratings and ranks of starred (*) items
2. Transfer your ratings (aspects 1 to 11) and ranks (12 to 15) to the following sheets
3. Total the three ratings/ranks for each aspect
4. Multiply the totals of the aspects 1 to 11 by 8.3, and the aspects 12 to 15 by 11.1. The totals of each item will range from 0 to 100.

Aspects	Item	Rating	Item	Rating	Item	Rating	Total		F. Total
1. Internal	1		12		23			X8.3	
2. Ambiguity Tolerant	2		13		24			X8.3	
3. Context Sensitive	3		14		25			X8.3	
4. Narcissistic (–)	4		15		26			X8.3	
5. Future Oriented	5		16		27			X8.3	
6. Individualistic	6		17		28			X8.3	
7. Inner-directed	7		18		29			X8.3	
8. Universal	8		19		30			X8.3	
9. Role bound	9		20		31			X8.3	
10. Androgynous	10		21		32			X8.3	
11. Power parity	11		22		33			X8.3	
12. Expressive	34a		35a		36a			X11.1	
13. Conserving	34b		35b		36b			X11.1	
14. Assertive	34c		35c		36c			X11.1	
15. Expanding	34d		35d		36d			X11.1	

Visioning Effectiveness (VE) Scale

69.1 THE INSTRUMENT AND ITS ADMINISTRATION

The survey is a self-administered instrument, containing 20 items to be rated by the respondents on a 5-point scale.

69.2 CONCEPTUAL FRAMEWORK

Visioning is the key transformational leadership function in an organisation. Visioning is the art of creating, communicating, committing people to and concretising vision into action. Vision is a desirable and realistic dream of a leader for his organisation. Vision has these four characteristics: it is a dream (an interactive sense of direction which others have not thought about or thought it to be an ordinary idea); it is desirable for the future of the organisation and is seen as desirable by its members; it is realistic; and it can be realised with joint efforts of people.

Visioning involves following four processes (each having two subprocesses):

1. *Creating the vision.* It includes fantasising (being futuristic, thinking of long-term goals for the organisation) and prioritising (linking the futuristic dream with the present organisational reality, and thinking of the prioritises from this point of view).

2. *Communicating the vision.* Communicating the vision to the concerned people involves what Sashkin (1986) calls 'expressing and explaining vision'. Vision is expressed in terms of action taken (through behaviour) and is explained through language, both oral and written.

3. *Committing people to the vision.* Commitment of people comes about through credibility—the respect they have for the leader. Credibility develops through consistency of the

     leader's behaviour and the respect he has for himself, and for others (which he/she expresses).

4. *Concretising the vision.* It includes translating the vision into action (take calculated risks, prepare a detailed plan and monitor the various steps of the action plan) and making the vision comprehensive by what Sashkin (1986) calls extending the vision (applying the vision in several situations or groups) and expanding it (spreading the vision by even bringing about desired changes in the organisation to make organisational practices consistent with the vision).

In short, the following are the processes and subprocesses of visioning:

1. Create the vision
   a. Fantasise (long-term goals)
   b. Prioritise the goals.
2. Communicate the vision
   a. Explain the vision
   b. Express the vision
3. Commit people to the vision (develop credibility)
   a. Be consistent
   b. Respect self and others
4. Concretise the action
   a. Take action (take calculated risks, prepare an action plan, monitor the steps)
   b. Make the vision comprehensive (extend and expand the vision)

Based on the conceptual framework suggested by Parsons (1960) and pragmatic characteristics of excellent organisations suggested by Tom Peters (2009), Sashkin has suggested three key elements in visioning—change, goals and people. Parsons suggested four functions an organisation should attend for its survival (the suggested characteristics by Tom Peters appear in parentheses): change (bias toward entrepreneurial action), goals (keep close to the customer), coordination (people) and organisational culture.

    The three key issues we suggest for visioning are change, customers (both internal and external, i.e., people) and culture. Leaders have to deal with these issues—managing and more importantly, proacting in relation to change; maximising joy for people (both internal customers, i.e., employees and external customers); and creating a culture which will promote the vision and related values. Warren Bennis (1985, 1989), suggests some of these aspects as functions of transformational leaders.

    Visioning Effectiveness (VE) Survey is designed to assess effectiveness of the visioning function of the top management in an organisation. Another instrument on another leadership function (boundary management) is also given in this part (Chapter 70).

69.3 SCORING

The following scoring key is employed. Items marked with asterisk (*) are reversed while scoring (1 becomes 5, 2 becomes 4 and vice versa). The total score will range from 20 to 100. Scores for seven different subscales (aspects) can also be obtained. To make them comparable, the scores can be converted into percentage or ranging from 0 to 100.

Aspects/Subscales	Items
1. Creating a vision	
(a) Fantasising	1
(b) Prioritising goals	2*
2. Communicating the vision	
(a) Explaining the vision	3, 4*
(b) Expressing the vision	5, 6
3. Committing people to the vision	
(a) Consistency	7*
(b) Respect for self and others	8, 9*
4. Concretising the vision	
(a) Action	10, 11, 12*
(b) Making the vision comprehensive	13*
5. Change management	14, 15
6. Employee and customer satisfaction	16, 17, 18
7. Culture building	19*, 20

The following formulae can be used for getting scores ranging from 0 to 100.

1. Creating vision (CV) = ratings on items $(1 + 2 - 2) \times 12.5$
2. Communicating vision (KV) = ratings on items $(3 + 4 + 5 + 6 - 4) \times 6.25$
3. Committing people to vision (MV) = ratings on items $(7 + 8 + 9 - 3) \times 8.33$
4. Concretising vision (Con V) = ratings on items $(10 + 11 + 12 + 13 - 4) \times 6.25$
5. Change management (CM) = ratings on items $(14 + 15 - 2) \times 12.5$
6. Satisfaction of people (PS) = ratings on items $(16 + 17 + 18 - 3) \times 8.33$
7. Culture building (CB) = ratings on items $(19 + 20 - 2) \times 12.5$

69.4 RELIABILITY

The alpha coefficient for a group of 36 executives was found to be 0.88. The correlation matrix of the eight variables is given in Table 69.1.

TABLE 69.1   Coefficients of Correlation among Visioning Subscales

	CV	KV	MV	Con V	CM	PS	CB
CV							
KV	0.53						
MV	0.56	0.38					
Con V	0.30	0.56	0.22				
CM	0.55	0.49	0.52	0.56			
PS	0.41	0.44	0.35	0.40	0.72		
CB	0.13	0.19	−0.04	0.25	0.30	0.49	
VE	0.69	0.76	0.61	0.43	0.84	0.78	0.43

TABLE 69.2   Coefficient of Correlation of VE Scales with Ethos and Climate

	O	C	T	A	P	A	C	E	Ach.	Control	Ext.	Aff.
CV	0.34	0.61	0.49	0.38	0.59	0.34	0.50	0.35	0.44	−0.54	0.36	−0.25
KV	0.47	0.53	0.44	0.42	0.52	0.39	0.58	0.44	0.40	−0.42		
MV	0.24	0.24	0.22		0.22		0.22					
Con V	0.31	0.40	0.29	0.39	0.35	0.30	0.45	0.31	0.35	−0.34	−0.27	
CM	0.26	0.50	0.36	0.35	−0.36	0.30						
PS	0.43	0.35	0.27	0.34	0.47	0.20	0.38			−0.29	0.25	

Note: Only significant correlation (mostly at 0.01 level, a few at 0.05 level are given).

69.5 CORRELATES

All the eight subscales were found to be positively correlated (at 0.01 level) with facilitators of delegation (Chapter 72). Coefficient of correlation with OCTAPACE aspects (Chapter 66) and climate (Chapter 64) are given in Table 69.2.

69.6 NORMS

Mean and SD values of the total visioning effectiveness and seven subscales for 36 executives of a cement company are given in the following table (each ranging from 0 to 100):

	Scale/Subscales	Mean	SD
1.	Creating Vision (CV)	76	20
2.	Communicating Vision (KV)	63	15
3.	Committing People to Vision (MV)	72	18
4.	Concretising Vision (Con V)	61	16
5.	Change Management (CM)	62	22
6.	Satisfaction of People (PS)	67	21
7.	Culture Building (CB)	57	17
8.	Total Visioning Effective (VE)	65	13

69.7 USE FOR HRD

The mean scores give a profile of visioning effectiveness of an organisation. Mean scores can also be calculated for each dimension or subdimension by dividing the total average score by 2 (for dimensions 3b, 4a, 4b, 7) and by 3 (for dimensions 4a and 6). An average score below 3 can be taken up for small group work—why it is low, and how to raise its level.

The following exercises are suggested to improve visioning effectiveness in an organisation. Ideas from Sashkin (1986) have been borrowed in some of these exercises.

69.7.1 Creating the Vision

1. List the five most important projects or activities that you were involved in during the last one year. Against each item listed, list the longest period during which you were fully responsible for it, without being supervised.
2. Imagine that you are able to split into identical twins. One of you continues to work as usual, and the other goes on a 2-year-long vacation. The two of you do not keep contact with each other. After two years, your twin returns from the vacation to see how you are doing. Write out in some details about what your twin would see.
3. Now imagine that instead of returning after two years, your twin returned after ten years. Write in as much detail as you can about what your twin would see.
4. Your twin wants to give you a brief report on what he saw at the two points of time (after two years and after 10 years). Write briefly about the differences he observed on the 2 occasions—what activities were getting your attention more after 10 years as compared to 2 years, why did the shift occur (what considerations guided the choice), what was the status of other activities?

69.7.2 Communicating the Vision

1. State the mission of your organisation. Prepare a policy action proposal that would lead to the realisation of the mission for your area department.

2. Prepare a list of specific activities you (and your department/area) would like to undertake for the vision.

3. Prepare an outline of an action plan to ensure that people understand the mission, accept it as their own mission (are inspired by it), internalise it (it becomes a part of their thinking and planning).

69.7.3 Concretising the Vision

1. Prepare a list of possible business activities you would recommend to your colleagues (within your area/department or at the corporate level) with the percentage of the certainty of its success (10% would mean high risk, 50% would mean fairly high risk, 70% would mean moderate risk and 90% would mean low risk).

2. Pick up one of the these ideas which is exciting and which falls between 50% and 70% of your rating, and prepare a brief outline of an action plan (not more than a page) for putting it into action.

3. What steps will you take to monitor the progress and use feedback to improve implementation?

4. Prepare a stepwise outline plan of ensuring that people understand, internalise, accept, implement and take charge of the activity proposed.

VE Survey

Name: _____ Role: _____

Organisation: _____ Date: _____

The purpose of this instrument is to collect data on how your organisation is perceived by its significant members. Read each item and write a number on the blank space on its left to indicate how much the statement is true about your organisation. Use the following key to give your response:

Write 1   if it is not at all true
Write 2   if it is slightly true
Write 3   if it is partly true
Write 4   if it is mostly true
Write 5   if it is completely true

1. _____ Top leaders think of long term goals and create an inspiring vision about the organisation.
2. _____ There is confusion about the priority of different goals set for the organisation.
3. _____ The top managers adopt various methods of communicating the vision.
4. _____ In spite of all the efforts, the vision remains confined to a few: most people here do not 'own' the vision and are not inspired by it.
5. _____ The vision or the mission is reflected in the way leaders discuss various organisational issues.
6. _____ Top managers are role models; their behaviour reflects the organisational mission/vision and people are inspired by them.
7. _____ There is a gap between what is communicated in words and how the leaders behave.
8. _____ There is a high degree of self-confidence amongst the leaders.
9. _____ Senior managers do not have high opinions about the people working at lower levels.
10. _____ Whenever a new policy or programme is prepared, heads meet and work with their people at different levels to prepare a document for their department/area on that policy/programme.
11. _____ The management takes calculated risks in proposing and going into new programmes.
12. _____ Heads do not consult their people in designing a system to monitor progress of the new programme; they may have their system and use it.
13. _____ The organisation has new policies and programmes, but these do not permeate the current practices and procedures; they seem to be independent of each other.
14. _____ Changes in the environment inspire the organisational leaders who see them as challenges and opportunities.
15. _____ There is high preparedness for dealing with the change.
16. _____ New programmes are prepared with the focus on the present and potential customers.
17. _____ Customer care and service is of high order here.
18. _____ The employees feel highly valued here.
19. _____ The whole focus here is on results; there is low concern for values and norms.
20. _____ The general climate here is congenial, and people would like to work in this organisation.

Leadership: Boundary Management Scale

70.1 THE INSTRUMENT AND ITS ADMINISTRATION

The instrument measures effectiveness of an important leadership function of boundary management which strengthens the organisation's interface with external system. It contains seven boundary management functions to be rated by the respondents on a 5-point scale.

70.2 CONCEPTUAL FRAMEWORK

The details are given in Chapter 61.

70.3 SCORING

The ratings given on each function are added to give the boundary management effectiveness score. It ranges from 7 to 35.

70.4 USE FOR HRD

The means of the total boundary management ratings given by all the respondents about their organisation can be used with the leaders (top managers) of the organisation. They should discuss whether they are satisfied with the feedback. Then they can do the following types of exercises to strengthen their boundary management functions. They may state the most important goals for their areas/departments in the next two years. The following exercises are in relation to the goal to be stated:

1. Prepare a list of resources—men, material, financial, skills, etc.—your people would require to work effectively for its realisation. Against each resource needed, write briefly what plan you have to ensure that it will be available to them in time.

2. List the groups/agencies your people will interact with while working on the goal mentioned. In each case, list the likely problems they may face in such interface requirement and then state what specific action you plan to take to deal with them.

   Working on the goal may be facilitated if some functional linkages are built with other inside (within your organisation) or outside groups. Think of them and list them. What can you do to facilitate in building such linkages?

3. List national and international institutions/organisations (not listed in Point 3) with which your organisation can build a collaborative network for mutual benefit. Write down what specific things you can do to evolve such networking.

4. List the groups most significant to your organisation, especially in your area/work (present/potential customers, support sources, consulting help), to whom your organisation needs to be 'sold'. Develop a few ideas of strengthening your organisations lobby with them.

5. What pressures are your people likely to experience from 'outside' (from within your organisation, top management, client systems, regulatory bodies, competitors, etc.)? What do you plan to manage such pressures so that your people are not bothered by them and can concentrate on their own work?

Boundary Management

Name: _____   Role: _____

Organisation: _____   Date: _____

Boundary management is the process of empowering a system by strengthening its interface with external systems. It involves the following functions by a leader. Rate each on a 5-point scale for the degree of attention it is getting in your organisation, using the following keys:

Write 1   if hardly any attention is given to it
Write 2   if very little attention is given to it
Write 3   if some attention is given to it
Write 4   if this is getting quite high attention
Write 5   if this is being given very high priority and attention

1. _____   Provide and help generate resources.
2. _____   Help in dealing with interface problems and issues.
3. _____   Facilitate building of functional linkages of the system with others.
4. _____   International networking
5. _____   Inter-institutional networking
6. _____   Lobby with 'key' groups: customers, support systems.
7. _____   Protect the system from external interference.

71

Leadership: Power Enhancers (PE) Scale

71.1 THE INSTRUMENT AND ITS ADMINISTRATION

The Power Enhancers scale (PE scale) assesses the value attached by members of an organisation to power enhancers (desired) and the importance given in practice (actual). The purpose of the instrument is to give top people data, which they can examine to plan strategies for their roles as leaders by developing weak power enhancers. The scale is appended.

The instrument requires a respondent to read 13 statements (organisational practices) and rate each on a 5-point scale to indicate how much importance is given in practice and how useful it is for leadership effectiveness.

71.2 CONCEPTUAL FRAMEWORK

There is a growing realisation that technology, a competitive environment and the increasing complexity of tasks demand a wider sharing of those important functions that were traditionally performed by formal leaders. This may further help leaders to concentrate their attention on critical issues.

Leadership is increasingly seen as a catalyst function, and the influence or power of a leader may be in proportion to his ability to dispossess the organisation or become dispensable. Withdrawal from controlling functions is a power enhancer for leadership. It enhances the leader's real power, not his coercive power, but his indirect influence. This is possible only when the leader is released from attending to routine tasks and from the use of his discretion in most routine matters. Let us take the example of house or vehicle allotment. A leader has direct influence if he uses his discretion to allot vehicles or houses to people. In that case, he will not have enough time to plan for a new vision. However, if clear rules are made, so that the leader does not play any role and has no discretion, his real power and influence will increase, as he will be able to perform the more important tasks of visioning, boundary management, lobbying for the organisation, etc.

In this sense, these can be seen as power enhancers rather than as leadership substitutes (a term introduced by Kerr & Jermier, 1978).

What are these power enhancers? Based on research literature (e.g., Powell et al., 1986) and interviews with some senior Indian managers, a list of power enhancers was prepared. After short listing, following 14 power enhancers were selected:

1. Developing competence of the employees
2. Clear rules and procedures
3. System to generate feedback for individuals
4. Intrinsically satisfying tasks
5. Advisory and staff functions
6. Rewards determined objectively by a team rather than by individuals
7. Spatial distance of different key functionaries
8. Strong and cohesive teams
9. Self-governing teams (like branches)
10. Well-defined tasks
11. Formalised and clear organisational structures
12. Schemes to reward employees for ideas/suggestions/creativity
13. Professional orientation
14. Development of systems

Factor analysis of these in one organisation gave five factors. These are therefore briefly mentioned under the five heads suggested by factor analysis. A few belong to more than one category.

71.2.1 Professionalisation

Following four enhancers fall within this category:

Competence building. Professionalisation is attained through competent people in the organisation. Competence development through various programmes and HRD practices contributes to this. The more competent people there are in an organisation, the greater the opportunity the leader will have to exercise higher leadership functions.

Reward system. Rewards play an important role in building a culture and multiplying power. If creativity, innovation and initiatives are rewarded, people will develop power relating to these. The leaders then have great resources available to them, adding to their overall power. In this way, rewards are very effective power enhancers.

Feedback system. A well-developed system that gives employees feedback on their performance develops professionalism and reduces the subjective element in decision-making by the leader. In fact, the feedback system in a way releases time for leaders to perform this function.

Professionalism. A professional orientation in the organisation develops several substitutes or enhancers of power. Professionalisation will include recruiting trained and competent persons with expertise in their fields, use of appropriate technology and periodical competence building of personnel at various levels. Leadership in a professional organisation deals with functions at higher levels.

71.2.2 Teamwork

Teamwork is an effective power enhancer as it relieves the leader of attending too many routine matters and multiplies power in the organisation by increasing the effectiveness of teams. This factor has five enhancers, out of which professionalism is one. Two enhancers are given below; two others are common with the next factor and will be discussed later.

Strong teams. Strong and cohesive teams are major power enhancers. The more cohesive the teams are, the more the leader is able to exercise high-level power, leaving most internal matters to the teams.

Self-governing teams. When teams can function on their own, with minimum direction from the top, leadership can be qualitatively different. Such team helps in the process of decentralisation. For example, autonomous work groups seem to reduce the role of supervisors because the teams themselves make the most of the decisions on the one hand, while they add value to the supervisor's roles by helping them to become real leaders who can attend to resource mobilisation, boundary management, competence building and consultation when needed by the group. Branches of organisations with enough autonomy have the same effect.

71.2.3 Formalisation

Informality in organisations functions as a lubricant. But too much of it may create messiness and slipperiness. Some formalisation is needed to increase the effectiveness of leaders and others, in terms of better use of direction by them. Four enhancers belong in this group. Two enhancers are common with the previous factor (tasks and roles) and are discussed first, followed by two others.

Satisfying tasks. Intrinsically satisfying tasks are likely to promote both formalisation and team building. Well-designed tasks that are seen as worthwhile by employees will build employee motivation and involvement, and the leader need not expend energy on this aspect. These will also contribute to the effective use of discretion by the employees concerned, and thereby enhance power in the system.

Rules and procedures. Clear rules and procedures for most routine matters, an important element in formalisation, reduce the need for the leader's attention and time on them. Moreover, they minimise the anxiety level of employees about these matters, further helping to increase their own sense of power. For example, most organisations have clear-cut rules and procedures for compensation, perks facilities, amenities, etc. Although not directly related to team building, such rules reduce bickering and help to build teams.

Organisational structure. A clear well-defined structure helps in formalisation. The structure reduces the leader's discretion in many matters, and forces him to pay attention to other important functions and use the power available to increase expertise in the organisation.

Management systems. In effective organisations, well-designed systems replace the leader's role in most matters. For example, good planning, budgetary and information systems generate most processes of decision-making. Recruitment and other human resource systems ensure that these functions are performed well, without any need for leaders to attend to them.

71.2.4 Expert Power

Development of expert power in an organisation multiplies power within the organisation and relieves leaders of the necessity of paying attention to most matters, which can now be shared by experts. There are three enhancers in this category, one (staff functions) being common to the previous factor of formalisation.

Staff functions. Advisory and staff functions develop formalisation by introducing structured and formalised special functions, and helping to develop expertise. The power that is being distributed gets multiplied, and it strengthens the leader's ability to lead the organisation.

Objective rewards. When rewards are decided on the basis of clear criteria, when they are developed by a team and managed by a group of persons (teams), they become more objective. Experts are involved in such decision-making. The leader gives up his role of deciding about rewards and passes this responsibility on to a team. This releases the leader's time and energy for higher-level tasks.

Spatial distance. Divisionalisation and decentralisation contribute to the development of expert power. When functionaries are removed from the central or head office and located away from it, they have more autonomy, thereby enhancing power in the system and sharing power (and responsibility) with the leader, whose power is also enhanced.

71.2.5 Task Clarity and Autonomy

There is only one enhancer in this group, although self-governing teams can also be included here.

Task clarity. Well-defined tasks are important for autonomous functioning of individuals. These increase their own power and also the leader's, who need no longer be bothered with such matters.

71.3 SCORING

Scoring is simple. The rating on the importance given to each power enhancer (P) (Column 1) is subtracted from the rating on its value (V) or importance (Column 2). The mean of all the responses will give the discrepancy (D) between desired importance and its value in practice. D scores for all 13 power enhancers are then added and the mean score found out.

71.4 RELIABILITY AND VALIDITY

The alpha coefficient for a group of information technology top managers as well as 83 senior managers of multibusiness group was found to be 0.85, in both the cases.

71.4.1 Internal Structure

In order to study the internal structure of power enhancers, data from a group of 18 senior insurance managers was factor analysed, using principal components analysis with Varimax rotation. The factor loadings are given in Table 71.1. The list is rearranged according to factor

TABLE 71.1   Factor Leaderships of Power Enhancers

Items	Factor 1	Factor 2	Factor 3	Factor 4	Factor 5
Competence development	0.96	—	—	—	—
Reward system	0.81	—	—	—	—
Feedback system	0.69	—	—	—	0.66
Professionalism	0.55	0.65	—	—	—
Strong teams	—	0.92	—	—	—
Autonomous teams	—	0.78	—	—	0.47
Work satisfying tasks	—	0.45	0.65	—	—
Clear rules	−0.43	0.40	0.56	—	−0.33
Formal structure	—	—	0.89	—	—
Staff functions	−0.35	—	0.44	0.74	—
Spatial distance	—	—	—	0.54	−0.52
Objective rewards	0.22	0.33	—	0.65	—
Task clarity	—	—	—	—	0.87

loadings. Five factors that were extracted explained 82% variance, the percentage of variance for factors 1 to 5, respectively, being 26, 20, 16, 12 and 8. Only loading above 0.3 are given.

Factor 1 has a high loading on competence, reward system, feedback system and professionalism. It also has a negative loading on rules and staff functions, and a loading of 0.22 on objective rewards. This can be called a professionalisation factor. Factor 2 has a high loading on professionalism, teams, autonomous teams, intrinsically satisfying tasks, clear rules and objective rewards. The items on which it has the highest loadings relate to teams, and other items tend to strengthen teams. Factor 2 can be called teamwork. Factor 3 has high loadings on structure, satisfying work, rules and staff functions. It has a loading of 0.28 on spatial distance of key functionaries. Since all these relate to systems and structure, it can be called a formalisation factor. Factor 4 has high loadings on staff functions, objective rewards, feedback systems and spatial distance. It has a negative loading on professionalism. This is called expert power factor, staff functions indicating expertise. Factor 5 has high loadings on task clarity, spatial distance (negative), autonomous teams and clear rules (negative). It has loading of 0.28 on reward and feedback (−0.27 on work and −0.21 on professionalism). It can be called a task clarity and autonomy factor.

71.5 NORMS

The means of data from two groups (18 insurance managers and 20 HRD managers of a steel manufacturing company) are given in Table 71.2. Differences or discrepancies between the two means are also given here.

TABLE 71.2 Means of Values and Practices and Their Discrepancies

Enhancers	Insurance Managers			Steel Managers		
	Value	Practice	Gap	Value	Practice	Gap
Competence development	4.7	3.9	0.8	4.5	3.6	0.91
Clear rules	4.2	4.1	0.1	3.4	3.2	1.8
Feedback system	4.4	2.8	1.6	4.3	3.8	0.45
Satisfying tasks	4.1	2.9	1.2	4.5	3.6	0.91
Staff functions	4.0	3.3	0.7	3.4	3.3	0.09
Objective rewards	4.1	2.6	1.5	3.9	2.1	1.80
Spatial distance	3.6	3.2	0.4	2.5	2.9	−0.36
Strong teams	4.6	3.1	1.5	4.4	2.6	1.73
Autonomous teams	4.4	3.7	0.7	3.7	3.2	0.54

Enhancers	Insurance Managers			Steel Managers		
	Value	Practice	Gap	Value	Practice	Gap
Task clarity	4.7	3.6	1.1	3.5	3.4	0.09
Formal structure	4.2	4.5	–0.3	3.3	2.9	–0.09
Reward system	4.5	2.0	2.5	3.8	2.7	0.45
Professionalism	4.3	2.4	1.9	4.3	3.9	0.91

In both groups, value for formalised and clear structure is less than its practice (though the difference is very low). In one group—the company has one main location—the value is less for spatial distance. In the insurance companies, the largest discrepancies are (1.5 and above) in reward system, professional orientation, feedback system, objective rewards and strong teams. In the steel company, the gap of more than 1.5 is only in objective rewards and strong teams. However, if we use 0.9 as the cut-off point, the gaps are in competence development, satisfying tasks and highly productive and professional. Norms on large samples of various groups need to be developed.

71.6 CORRELATES

The facilitating factors for delegation were negatively correlated with the gap between the desired and actual levels of enhancers no. 1, 2, 3, 4, 8 (at 0.05 level) and 10 (at 0.01 level). This means that in the organisations with poor processes of delegation, the power enhancers named above will also be at a low level.

71.7 USE FOR HRD

PE scale can be used for leadership development. The results of the survey using the instrument can be shared with top management. They can discuss the desirability of the various enhancers for their organisation and prepare time-bound action plans, which include neglected enhancers, in order to develop the organisation's total leadership competence.

PE Survey

Name: _____   Role: _____

Organisation: _____   Date: _____

Several organised practices are emphasised in different organisations. Some of these are listed below. In the first column, rate how much importance is given to the practice. Use a 5-point scale where 5 indicate it is very high in importance and 1 that it has very low importance.

In the next column, rate how much useful it would be to you as a leader. Write 5 if it will be very useful, 4 if it will be quite useful, 3 if you are not sure, 3 if it is not useful, and 1 if it is definitely dysfunctional for your effectiveness.

	P	V	D
	Importance given in your organisation	Usefulness for leaders effectiveness	
1. Developing competences of the employee	_____	_____	_____
2. Clear rules and procedures	_____	_____	_____
3. Systems to generate feedback for individuals	_____	_____	_____
4. Intrinsically satisfying tasks	_____	_____	_____
5. Advisory and staff functions	_____	_____	_____
6. Rewards determined objectively by a team rather than individuals	_____	_____	_____
7. Spatial distance of different key functionaries	_____	_____	_____
8. Strong and cohesive teams	_____	_____	_____
9. Self-governing teams (like branches)	_____	_____	_____
10. Well-defined tasks	_____	_____	_____
11. Formalised and clear organisational structure	_____	_____	_____
12. Schemes to reward employees for ideas/suggestions creativity	_____	_____	_____
13. Professional orientation	_____	_____	_____

72
Delegation Assessment Questionnaire (DAQ)

72.1 THE INSTRUMENT AND ITS ADMINISTRATION

D elegation Assessment Questionnaire (DAQ) has three parts: the amount of delegation (nine items), the process of delegation (eight items) and facilitating factors for delegation (six items). It is self-administered, and respondents are required to check all the items on a 4-point scale.

72.2 CONCEPTUAL FRAMEWORK

The main function of a leader is to multiply power in an organisation, which means empowering people at all levels. Every person has enough power within himself. The process of empowering is concerned with creating conditions in which this inner power can be used effectively. Empowering is the process of expanding choices for an individual and helping him use his alternative choices to widen the choices of others. Thus, it is an expanding, multiplying concept.

Power can never be given; it is only exercised. Conditions can certainly be promoted to help people use power effectively. One formal way of creating such conditions is delegation. The concept of delegation is not to give power; senior persons need to evolve (jointly with their junior colleagues) areas in which they would like to use their competencies, and ways in which they could use their discretion to make the desired impact. In other words, delegation helps them to work out strategies of doing their work with their junior colleagues. Delegation is a useful way of multiplying power in an organisation.

The purpose of delegation will fail if it is used by a senior person to give tasks, which he does not like or for which he does not have the time, to his junior colleague. It will also fail if the junior colleague feels overloaded with responsibility. Similarly, it cannot succeed in its purpose if it is unilaterally done by the senior person. It should involve joint decision-making. It is therefore a multistep process.

72.2.1 The Process of Delegation

Delegation is not likely to be effective if any of the eight steps involved in the process are left out. These steps are stated in action terms.

Jointly define role boundaries. This is the first step. Delegation involves the roles of both the delegator and the delegatee. Delegation leads to change in roles and responsibilities. These changes must be discussed jointly by the delegator and the delegatee. Based on several considerations, the changes should be decided and formalised. Since others also need to know about the functions the delegatee will perform, these need to be described fully or made known widely. The decision has to be a joint one and the delegatee should not only volunteer to perform those functions, but should feel that this will be enriched as a result.

Provide needed competencies. Most functions that are delegated will be new and will contain higher responsibilities. The delegatee may not have the competencies needed to perform these functions. He should do a self-assessment and openly discuss what new competencies he needs to develop in order to do justice to the new functions. The delegator should then prepare a plan in consultation with the delegatee, on how the latter will develop these competencies.

Provide the needed resources. The previous one is also true of resources—financial, material, technological or human—which are required for effective performance of the new functions. These should be assessed and provision must be made to supply these to the delegatee.

Monitor, but do not closely supervise. Monitoring the performance of delegated functions for some time is essential. This may help to provide the needed support and help. Monitoring may also indicate the delegator's interest and moral support. If overdone, it could be counterproductive. Close supervision of the performance of delegated functions by the delegator may indicate lack of trust in the competence of the delegatee.

Reward discretion and initiative. Delegation is an evolutionary and developmental process. It needs to be encouraged and reinforced. Delegation involves taking initiative and using discretion in the delegated functions. If these are rewarded, the process of delegation will be stronger and more successful.

Respect role boundaries. Once a decision has been jointly taken by senior and junior colleagues on delegation, the redefined role boundaries must be respected. The delegatee is likely to make mistakes. The delegator may be tempted to rush to rescue him. This may destroy the spirit of delegation. No decision should be taken over the head of the delegatee in matters delegated to the latter. If the decision is to be changed, the delegatee should do it after a discussion with the delegator and after being convinced of the need to change the decision.

Jointly analyse mistakes to plan for the future. In periodical reviews, mistakes may be used as experiences from which to learn to improve delegation. Mistakes, difficulties experienced, etc., can be analysed in such review meetings to plan how these can be avoided in future. The experience may raise many issues that could be useful for improvement of delegation.

Review delegation down the line. Most often, people want delegation only up to their own level. As we said in the beginning, delegation is a widening process of empowerment. Each senior person involved in delegation should discuss, with his junior colleague, how the latter would delegate some useful functions to his colleagues at the next level. This will help to multiply power through delegation.

72.2.2 Forces Influencing Delegation

In an organisation, the current level of delegation is determined by opposing forces or, some positive forces, which facilitate delegation, and some equally strong negative forces, which hinder delegation. It may be useful to identify such forces, and reduce or eliminate the negative or hindering forces. In addition to the above, some other forces have been identified by a manager working on delegation in a particular organisation. These are briefly stated below. The success of delegation depends on the delegatee, the delegator, on both of them as a team, and on the organisation.

72.2.2.1 Facilitating Forces

Factors Related to the Delegatee

Competence of the delegatee: This is an obvious positive force. The more competent a delegatee is, the more effectively he will use delegation.

Eagerness to take responsibility: The delegatee's motivation, involvement and commitment are reflected in his willingness to take responsibility. This willingness will make delegation more effective.

Factors Related to the Delegator

Role overload of the delegator: If the delegator feels overwhelmed with many functions, he is likely to open dialogue with the delegatee to share some responsibility and is likely to help the latter succeed in the delegated functions.

Inner security of the delegator: If the delegator has a high sense of security, he is not afraid of losing power by empowering the junior colleague (delegating to him some important functions). Such a person is likely to delegate more effectively by trusting, monitoring, reviewing, supporting, providing resources, etc.

Factors Related to Both

Mutual trust: This is an essential requirement for the success of delegation. Without mutual trust, periodical frank reviews cannot be done.

Factors Related to the Organisation

OCTAPACE (eight steps) ethos: An ethos of openness, confrontation, trust, authenticity, proaction, autonomy, collaboration and experimentation in an organisation promotes delegation.

Entrepreneurial culture: Delegation is likely to be higher and more effectively used in organisations where the entrepreneurial culture is high and where importance is given to new ideas, moderate risk-taking, support to employees and high demands from various levels of responsibility.

72.2.2.2 Hindering Forces

Forces Related to the Delegatee

Dependency motivation: A person who has a high need for dependency is not likely to use delegation effectively. Such a person feels comfortable in carrying out instructions given by seniors, seeks approval from seniors for his proposed action and hesitates to take risks.

Lack of initiative: An aspect that is generally related to the dependency motive is hesitation to take initiative. This may be related to fear of failure or a tendency to play safe or to the dependency motive.

Forces Related to the Delegator

High control needs: If the delegator has a high need to control and uses personal power to monitor what happens and what should happen, he may find it difficult to delegate. Delegation requires system orientation and trust in junior colleagues.

Inability to develop juniors: Many persons do not have the competence to develop junior colleagues. Such competence includes patience, listening to juniors, guiding them by one's own examples, encouraging them to experiment, reviewing, providing support, etc. Such persons may find it difficult to delegate.

Forces Related to Both

Lack of role clarity: Delegation may not succeed if there is lack of role clarity, both in general and in the role of immediate concern. Role ambiguity may be related to the main functions of the roles (role boundaries), available resources, linkages, etc.

Forces Related to the Organisation

Crisis managing climate: Crisis situations are not appropriate for delegation. Some organisations create a crisis-managing climate and they are continuously engaged in firefighting. Obviously, such a climate prevents the process of delegation, which involves experimentation and risk-taking.

Autocratic–bureaucratic culture: Delegation is difficult in autocratic/feudal or bureaucratic organisational culture. In the former, autocratic or feudal, the whole organisation hinges on the top man or a few top people. These top people, even with the best intentions, tend to centralise all posers and the same norm and behaviour are modelled down the line. If systematic delegation is not feasible, delegation is arbitrary and in selected pockets. In a bureaucratic culture, rules and regulations are important, and the lines of responsibility, functions and norms are laid down in detail. A person is evaluated for his faithful performance of the assigned tasks according to laid down rules and regulations. Since there is no pressure for innovation and risk-taking, the need to delegate is low. Moreover, everything comes from the top layer of the organisation; the culture itself promotes centralisation and does not encourage delegation (for action steps to promote delegation, see Pareek, 1994).

Lowy and Finestone (1986) have suggested a 3-stage model of delegation—assessment, interaction and follow-through. In each phase, they have discussed the interpersonal, informational and decisional aspects as well as contents of the process questions.

72.3 SCORING

Ratings for the items in each of the three parts are totalled. The total scores in the three parts will range from 9 to 36 (Part 1), from 8 to 32 (Part 2) and from 6 to 24 (Part 3). All these totals can further be added to give a total delegation score, ranging from 23 to 92.

72.4 RELIABILITY

Based on data of 153 managers in an information technology company, the split-half Alpha coefficient was found to be 0.79 for the instrument.

72.5 VALIDITY

Construct validity is provided by factor analysis of the responses of 28 managers of a construction company. Principal component analysis with Varimax rotation was used. The rotated factor matrix is given in Table 72.1. Factor loadings of 0.3 or above are mentioned. Factor analysis gave eight factors, which explain about 80% variance.

TABLE 72.1   Rotated Factor Matrix of Delegation

Items	Factor 1	Factor 2	Factor 3	Factor 4	Factor 5	Factor 6	Factor 7	Factor 8
C1	0.50		−0.70				−0.40	
C2	0.48						−0.32	
C3	0.73							
C4	0.86							
C5	0.40		0.77					
C6			0.74					
A1		0.84						
A3	0.31	0.53				−0.38		0.37
A4		0.48				.39		−0.49
A5		0.80						
A2					0.74			
A6					0.74			
A7								
A8	0.31						0.84	0.90
A9					0.67	−0.45		
B1	0.51	0.50		0.44				
B2				0.59		0.32		
B3	0.32			0.64				
B4						0.85		
B5				0.83				
B6	0.58			0.43				
B7		0.65				0.41		
B8	0.74					0.37		

The factor analysis can be examined in several ways. If we see the factors in terms of the three aspects of delegation (amount, process and facilitation), Factors 1, 2 and 4 are the main one's explaining about 50% variance. Factor 1 has a high loading on 5 out of 6 process items (all except Item 6); the validity index of this aspect (process of delegation) can be said to be 0.83 (5 divided by 6). Validity index of the amount of delegation is only 0.44 (Factor 2 has high loadings on only 4 out of 9 items, i.e. nos. 1, 3, 4 and 5). Factor 4 seems to be a pure factor of delegation facilitators, as it has high loadings only on five items, all of them from the facilitator category; validity index can be said to be 0.63 (5/8). The factor analysis thus provides evidence of the instrument's construct validity.

Validity index of the amount of delegation is low (0.44). The nine items in this category are distributed among four factors, all concerned with this aspect. Factor 2, as already stated, contains four amount items. Since 3 of 3 relate to resources, this factor can be called a resources factor. Factor 5 has high loadings on three items, all of them amount items (numbers 2, 6, 9); two of these relate to planning (including work of subordinates) and one to rewarding. This factor can be called a supervision factor. Two amount items relate to the outside group—Number 8 within the organisation and Number 9, outside the organisation. Factors 7 and 8 have high loadings, respectively, on these items. Regarding the process of delegation, Factor 6 has a high loading on the monitoring item (Number 4). This factor also has fairly high loadings on B7 (analysis of mistakes made in delegation) and B8 (delegation down the line). Since both these relate to monitoring, Factor 6 can be called a monitoring factor. Thus, Factors 4 and 6 explain the process items, the former being a support factor and the latter, a monitoring factor.

Facilitating items seem to be very significant because Factor 1 (explaining 23% variance) has high loadings on five items. However, on two facilitator items (C5 and C6), Factor 3 has high loading; these high loadings are on B7 (analysis of delegation experience) and C2 (competency planning). Factor 3 is not a clear factor. This can be called a role analysis factor, which includes role clarity, competency analysis for roles and review of experiences.

When a three-factor solution was tried with principal component analysis and Varimax rotation, the three factors explained 47% variance. Table 72.2 gives the factor matrix. Factor 1 has emerged as a general factor, explaining 23% (almost half) variance. It can be called a delegation process

TABLE 72.2 Three-factor Solution of Delegation

Item	Factor 1	Factor 2	Factor 3
B1	0.77		
B2	0.73		0.32
B3	0.63		−0.33
B4	0.60	−0.37	
B5	0.54		
B6	0.81		
B7			0.64
B8	0.69		
A1		0.50	
A2		0.50	

(Table 72.2 Continued)

(Table 72.2 Continued)

Item	Factor 1	Factor 2	Factor 3
A3		0.87	
A4	0.60		
A5	0.31		
A6		0.44	
A7	−0.33	0.61	
A8		0.59	
A9	0.24		
C1			−0.60
C2			−0.83
C3	0.39	0.51	
C4	0.56	0.54	
C5	0.43	0.33	0.57
C6			0.62

factor, as it has a high loading on 7 out of 8 process items, the validity index being 87%. It has three items of delegation (i.e., material resources, human resources and rewarding), and three facilitating items (i.e., mutual trust, trusting culture and role clarity).

Factor 2 has high loadings on 6 out of the 9 amount items. In addition, it has high loadings on three facilitator items, as in the case of Factor 1. Since the items relate to planning and culture, it can be called a planning and culture of delegation factor. The amount of delegation is still important in this factor; the validity index is 67% (6 out of 9 items are included in it).

Factor 3 has high loadings on four facilitator items (i.e., role clarity, seniors/development ability, eagerness to take responsibility and competence). It has a high loading on one process item (i.e., joint analysis and learning from mistakes). This can be called a facilitatory factor. Its validity index is 67% (4 out of 6 items have high loadings).

In short, while factor analysis provides some evidence of the instrument's construct validity, further work is needed on this aspect.

72.6 CORRELATES

All the three aspects of delegation—amount, process and facilitation—as well as the total delegation score had a very high positive correlation (beyond 0.001 level) with total OCTAPACE ethos score (see Chapter 66) for group of 153 managers in one company.

Amount of delegation had a positive correlation with operating effectiveness of achievement, expert influence and control atmosphere (levels of significance being 0.024, 0.035 and 0.001 respectively). Process of delegation positively correlated with operating effectiveness of achievement, expert power, control and dependency (i.e., 0.001, 0.004, 0.000 and 0.001 levels). The same was found for facilitation and total delegation score. Amount, process and total delegation score had a significant positive correlation with individualism and power party (see Chapter 67).

The responses from the 175 managers of a successful construction company showed significantly positive relationship of the three aspects of delegation on its total score with different aspects of personal orientation. A significant positive correlation (0.05 level) was found between the amount of delegation and the organisational norms of profitability/cost effectiveness. Out of the 10 organisational norms suggested by Alexander (1972), 2—delegation process and total delegation—significantly correlated with 4 norms (profitably/cost effectiveness at .001 level, colleague/associate relations and customer/client relations at 0.01 level and training/development at 0.05 level). This shows that the process of delegation is very important for developing functional norms of excellence, internal and external relations and HRD. For other correlates, see 'Correlates' section of Chapters 61 and 70.

72.7 NORMS

Mean and SD scores of group of 175 managers are given here. These can be used as tentative norms.

	Mean	SD
Amount of delegation	25	5
Process of delegation	25	5
Facilitators of delegation	17	4
Total delegation	65	12

72.8 USE FOR HRD

This instrument can be used to diagnose the various aspects of delegation. After analysing the scores on various items, the items with low scores can be identified, and small groups can be formed to discuss how the aspects, represented by the items, can be improved.

Delegation Assessment Questionnaire (DAQ)

Name: _____   Role: _____

Organisation: _____   Date: _____

How much authority has been delegated to you to facilitate you to carry out your responsibilities effectively? Rate the following aspects:

Write 1   if delegation is very little
Write 2   if delegation is not adequate
Write 3   if delegation is more than you need
Write 4   if delegation is adequate and to your satisfaction

1. _____   Financial
2. _____   Deciding priorities and targets
3. _____   Planning your work
4. _____   Getting material resources
5. _____   Getting human resources
6. _____   Planning and supervising the work of your juniors
7. _____   Dealing and negotiating with customers/clients outside
8. _____   Contacting colleagues in other department for work-related matters
9. _____   Rewarding deserving persons

How adequately are the following done? Rate them by writing 1, 2, 3 or 4 for each.

1   means not at all
2   means to some extent
3   means to a great extent, but not enough
4   means adequately, and to your satisfaction

1. _____   Jointly define the role boundaries of what your senior (who delegates to you) and you will be doing.
2. _____   Plan competencies needed by you to perform delegated tasks.
3. _____   Provide resources needed by you to perform delegated tasks.
4. _____   Monitor (but not closely supervise) progress on delegation—difficulties encountered, etc.
5. _____   Recognise and encourage initiative taken and discretion used by you.
6. _____   Respect role boundaries (the delegation made), that is, not taking decisions over your head in the delegated areas.
7. _____   Analyse (jointly with you) mistakes made in using delegated authority for future improvement.
8. _____   How much authority do you delegate to your juniors?

Rate the following by writing:

1	for very little
2	for to some extent
3	for enough
4	for very high

1. _____ Your own competency to perform delegated tasks
2. _____ Your own eagerness to take responsibility
3. _____ Mutual trust between you and your seniors
4. _____ Trusting and entrepreneurial culture of the organisation
5. _____ Role clarity for most roles in the organisation
6. _____ Ability of the senior people in the organisation to develop their juniors

BIBLIOGRAPHY

Adams, T. D. (1980). *Understanding and managing stress: A workbook in changing life styles*. San Diego, CA: Pfeiffer and Company.

Adams, G. A., King, L. A., & King, D. W. (1996). Relationships of job and family involvement, family social support, and work-family conflict with job and life satisfaction. *Journal of Applied Psychology, 81*(1), 111–20.

Adorno, T. W., & Frenkel-Brunswick, E. (1983). *The authoritarian personality* (abridged ed.). New York, NY: W. W. Norton & Company.

Adorno, T. W., Frenkel-Brunswik, E., Levinson, D. J., & Sanford, R. N. (1950). *The authoritarian personality*. New York, NY: W. W. Norton & Company.

AEA. (1956). *Training group readers*. Chicago, IL: Adult Education Association of the U.S.A.

———. (1960). *How to lead discussions*. Chicago, IL: Adult Education Association of the U.S.A.

Agyris, C., & Schon, D. A. (1978). *Organisational learning: A theory of action perspective*. Reading, MA: Addison-Wesley.

Ahmady, S., Changiz, T., Masiello, I., & Brommels, M. (2007). Organisational role stress among medical school faculty members in Iran: dealing with role conflict. *BMC Medical Education, 7*(1), 14.

Alexander, K. C. (1972). *Participation management: The Indian experience*. New Delhi: Sri Ram Centre.

Allen, A. L. (2001). Is Privacy Now Possible? A Brief History of an Obsession. *Social Research, 68*(1), 301–05.

Allen, J. S. (Ed.) (1950). *William James on habit, will, truth, and the meaning of life*. Frederic C. Beil, Publisher.

Allport, G. W., Vernon, P. E., & Lindzey, G. (1960). *Study of values* (3rd ed.). Boston, MA: Houghton Millin.

Anabacher, H. Z., & Anabacher, R. (Eds.). (1956). *The individual psychology of Alfred Adler*. London: George Allen and Irwin.

Argyris, C. (1990). *Overcoming organizational defences: Facilitating organizational learning*. Boston, MA: Allyn & Bacon.

Arroba, T. (1977). Styles of decision making and their use: An empirical study. *British Journal of Guidance and Counselling, 5*, 149–58.

Arthur, M., & Rousseau, D. (1996). *The boundaryless career*. New York, NY: Oxford University Press.

Atkinson, J. W. (1953). The achievement motive and recall of interrupted and complete tasks. *Journal of Experimental Psychology, 46*, 381–90.

Atkinson, J.W., McClelland, D.C., & Clark, R. A. (1958). *The achievement motive*. East Norwalk, CT: Appleton–Century–Crofts.

Avary, B. (1980). Ego states: Manifestation of psychic organs. *Transactional Analysis Journal, 10*(4), 291–94.

Aziz, M. (2004). Role stress among women in the Indian information technology sector. *Women in Management Review, 19*(7), 356–63.

Bailyn, L (1977). The impact of corporate culture on work-family integration. In S. Parasuraman & J. H. Greenhaus (Eds), *Integrating work and family: Challenges and choices for a changing world* (pp. 209–19). Westport, CT: Quorum.

Bales, R. F. (1950). *Interaction process analysis: A method for the study of small groups*. Cambridge, MA: Addison-Wesley.

Bandura, A. (1977) Self-efficacy: toward a unifying theory of behavioral change. *Psychological Review, 84*, 191–215.

———. (1982). Self-efficacy mechanism in human agency. *American Psychologist, 37*, 122–47.

Banet, A. G. (1976). Inventory of self-actualisation characteristics (ISAC). In J. W. Pfeiffer & J. E. Jones (Eds.), *The 1976 annual for facilitators, trainers, and consultants* (pp. 67–77). San Diego, CA: Pfeiffer and Company.

Bass, B. M. (1997). Does the transactional-transformational leadership paradigm transcend organizational and national boundaries? *American Psychologist, 52*, 130–39.

Bateson, G. (1944). Cultural determinants of personality. In J. Mc V Hunt (Ed.), *Personality and the behaviour disorders*. New York, NY: Ronald Press.

Baumgartel C., Rajan, A., & Newman, J. E. (1985). Job stress, employee health, and organizational effectiveness: A facet analyses, model and literature review. *Personalpsychology*, *31*, 665–69.

Belbin, M. (1981). *Management teams: Why they succeed or fail*. London: Heinemann.

Bem, S. (1993). *Gender polarization. The lenses of gender: transforming the debate on sexual inequality*. Binghamton, NY: Vail-Ballou Press.

Bennis, W. (1989 [1985]). Leadership: The strategies for taking charge. New York, NY: Harper & Row.

Berlew, D. E. (1986). Managing human energy: Rushing versus pulling. In S. Srivastava & Associates (Eds.), *Executive power* (pp. 33–50). San Francisco, CA: Jossey-Bass.

Bernard, J. (1975). Notes on changing life styles. *Journal of Marriage and Family*, *53*, 582–93.

Berne, E., & Harris, T. A. (1969). I'm O.K.–You're O.K. New York, NY: Harper and Row.

Bird, J. (2006). Work life balance: Doing it right and avoiding the pitfalls. *Employment Relations Today*, *33*(3), 21–30.

Birnbaum, R. (1980). *Creative academic bargaining: Managing conflict in the unionized college and university*. New York, NY: Columbia University.

Birney. R. (1969). *Fear of failure*. New York, NY: Van Nostrand Reinhold.

Birney, R. C., & Burdick, H. (1969). *Fear of failure*. New York, NY: Van Nostrand.

Blake, R. R. (1968). *The managerial grid*. Houston, TX: Gulf Publishing Company.

Blake, R. R., & Mouton, J. S. (1964). *The managerial grid*. Houston, TX: Gulf Publishing Company.

———. (1970). *Guide posts for effective salesmanship*. Chicago, IL: Playboy Press.

———. (1984). *The new managerial grid III*. Houston, TX: Gulf Publishing Company.

Blake, R. R., Shepard, H. A., & Mouton, J. S. (1964). *Managing intergroup conflict in industry*. Houston, TX: Gulf Publishing.

Blanchard, K. H. (1995). Situational leadership. In R. A. Ritvo, A. H. Litwin & L. Butler (Eds.), *Managing in the age of change* (pp. 14–33). New York, NY: Irwin.

Bose, K., & Pareek, U. (1986). The dynamics of conflict management styles of the bankers. *Indian Journal of Industrial Relations*, *22*(1), 59–78.

Bray, D. W., Campbell, R. J., & Grant, D. I. (1974). *Formative years in business: A long term AT&T study of managerial lives*. New York, NY: John Wiley.

Brockner, J. (1988). *Self-esteem at work*. Lexington, MA: Lexington Books.

Brown, W. (1910). Some experimental results in the correlation of mental abilities. *British Journal of Psychology*, *3*, 296–22.

Burns, J. M. (1978). *Leadership*. New York, NY: Harper & Row Publishers.

Cantril, H., Ames, A., Hassorf, A. H., & Ittelson, W. H. (1949). Psychology and scientific research: The transactional view in psychological research. *Science*.

Cattell, R. B. (1965). *The scientific analysis of personality*. Baltimore: Penguin Books.

Chattopadhyay, S. N., & Pareek, U. (1982). *Managing organizational change*, New Delhi: Oxford and IBH Publishing Co. Pvt. Ltd.

Christie, R., & Cook, P. (1958). A guide to published literature relating to the authoritarian personality through 1956. *Format of Psychology*, *45*, 171–99.

Christie, R., & Jahoda, M. (1954). *Studies in the scope and method of 'The Authoritarian Personality'*. Glencoe, III: Free Press.

Clark, S. C. (2000). Work/family border theory: A new theory of work/family balance. *Human Relations*, *53*(6), 747–70.

Cohen, S., & Syme, S. L. (Eds.). (1985). *Social support and health*. Orlando, FL: Academic Press.

Cohen, S. P., Kelman, H. C., Miller, F. D., & Smith, B. L. (1975). Evolving intergroup techniques for conflict resolution: An Israeli-Palestinian pilot workshop. *Journal of Social Psychology*, *95*(2), 273–74.

Conger, J. A., & Benjamin, B. (1999). *Building leaders: How successful companies develop the next generation*. San Francisco, CA: Jossey-Bass.

Cooperrider, D. H., & Whitney, D. (1999). *Appreciative enquiry*. Tows NM: Corporate for Positive Change.

Coreil, J., & Marshall, P. A. (1982). Locus of illness control: A cross-cultural study. *Human Organisation*, *41*(2), 131–38.

Coscarelli, W. C., Burk, J., & Cotter, A. (1995). HRD and decision-making styles. *Human Resource Development Quarterly*, *6*(4), 383–95.

Crandall, V. C., Katkovsky, W., & Crandall, W. J. (1965). Children's beliefs in their control of reinforcements in intellectual academic achievement behaviours. *Child Development*, *36*, 99–109.

Crosby, B., & Scherer, J. J. (1981). Diagnosing organisational conflict-management climates. In J. E. Jones & J. W. Pfeiffer (Eds.), *The 1981 annual handbook for group facilitators* (pp. 100–09). San Diego, CA: San Diego University Associates.

Csikszentmihalyi, M. (1976). *Beyond boredom and anxiety*. San Francisco, CA: Jossey-Bass.

Das, G. S. (1989). Bankers' attribution profile: Reliability and validity of a measure of attribution schemes and locus of control. *Indian Journal of Applied Psychology, 26*(2), 14–22.

De Charms, R. (1972). Personal causation training in the schools. *Journal of Applied and Social Psychology, 2*, 95–113.

Doktor, R. H., & Hamilton, W. F. (1973). Cognitive style and the acceptance of management science recommendations. *Management Science, 19*, 884–94.

Dodd, S. C. (1951). On classifying human values: Step in the prediction of human valuing. *American Sociological Review, 16*, 645–53.

Driscoll, R., & Eckstein, D. G. (1982). Life style questionnaire. In J. W. Pfeiffer & L. D. Goodstein (Eds.), *The 1982 annual for facilitators, trainers, and consultants* (pp. l00–07). San Diego, CA: Pfeiffer and Company.

Driver, M. J., Brousseau, K. R., & Hunsaker, P. L. (1990). *The dynamic decision maker: Five decision styles for executive and business success*. New York, NY: Harper and Row.

Dyer, W. G. (1987). *Team building* (2nd ed.). Reading, MA: Addison-Wesley.

Eckstein, D. G., & Driscoll, R. (1982). An introduction to lifestyle assessment. In J. W. Pfeiffer & L. D. Goodstein (Eds.), *The 1982 annual for facilitators, trainers, and consultants* (pp. 182–89). San Diego, CA: Pfeiffer and Company.

Edwards, A. L. (1957). *Techniques of attitude scale construction*. New York, NY: Appleton-Century-Crofts.

Elias, M. J. (1987). Establishing enduring prevention programme: Advancing the legacy of Swampscott. *American Journal of Community Psychology, 15*, 539–53.

English, H. B., & English, A. G. (1958). *A comprehensive dictionary of psychological and psychoanalytical terms*. New York, NY: Longmans, Green and Co.

Erikson, E. H. (1993). *Childhood and society* (2nd ed.). New York, NY: Norton.

Eysenck, H. J. et al. (1960). Smoking and personality. British Medical Journal, 1(5184), 1456–60.

Eysenck, H. J., & Eysenck, S. B. G. (1969). *Personality structure and measurement*. London: Routledge.

Fensterheim, H. (1975). *Don't say yes when you want to say no*. Dell.

Ferguson, C. (1944). *Agreement in natural language: Approaches, theories, descriptions*. Stanford: CSLI.

Fiedler, F. E. (1967). *A theory of leadership effectiveness*. New York, NY: McGraw-Hill.

Fiedler, F. E., Chemers, M. M., & Mahar, L. (1976). Improving leadership effectiveness: The leader match concept. New York, NY: John Wiley and Sons.

Filley, A. C. (1978). Some normative issues in conflict management. *California Management Review, 21*(2), 61–66.

Finke R. A., Ward T. B., & Smith S. M. (1992). *Creative Cognition: Theory, Research and Applications*. Cambridge, MA: MIT Press.

Fitzgerald, L., Moroczek R., Brignall T. J. Silvestro, R., & Voss, C. (1993). *Performance measurement in service businesses*. London: The Chartered Institute of Management Accountants.

Fitzgerald, T. E., Tennen, H., Affleck, G., & Pransky, G. S. (1993). The relative importance of dispositional optimisms and control appraisals in quality of life after coronary artery bypass surgery. *Journal of Behavioural Medicine, 16*, 25–43.

Flanders, N. A. (1960a). Teacher influence pupil attitudes and achievement, U. S. Department of Health, Education and Welfare, Office of Education, Cooperative Research Project No. 397, Minneapolis: University of Minnesota.

———. (1960b). *Interaction analysis in the class room: A manual for observers, College of Education*. Minnesota: University of Minnesota.

———. (1970). *Analysing teacher behavior*. Reading, MA: Addison-Wesley.

Folkman, S., & Lazarus, R. S. (1985). If it changes it must be a process: Study of emotion and coping during three stages of a college examination. *Journal of Personality and Social Psychology, 48*, 150–70.

Folkman, S., Lazarus, R. S., Dunket-Schetter, C., Delongis, L., & Gruen, R. J. (1986). Dynamics of a successful encounter: Cognitive appraisal, coping and encounter outcomes. *Journal of Personality and Social Psychology, 50*, 992–1003.

Franklin, R. D. (1963). Youth's expectancies about internal is external control of reinforcement related to n variables. *Dissertation Abstracts International, 24*, 1684.

French, J. R. P., & Raven, B. (1959). The bases of social Power. In D. Cartwright (Ed.), *Studies in social power*. Ann Arbor, MI: University of Michigan, Institute for Social Research.

Friedlander, F. (1975). Emergent and contemporary life styles: An inter-generational issue. *Human Relations, 28,* 329–41.

Garrett, H. (1966). *Statistics in psychology and education.* Bombay: Vaktis, Fefter and Simons Pvt. Ltd.

Gardner, H. (1983). *Frames of mind.* New York, NY: Basic Books.

Geertz, C. (1973). *Interpretation of culture.* New York, NY: Basic Books.

Ginzberg, E. (1966). *Life styles of educated women.* New York, NY: Columbia University Press.

Gist, M. E., & Mitchell, T. R. (1992). Self-efficacy: A theoretical analysis of its determinants and malleability. *Academy of Management Review, 17,* 183–211.

Goffman, I. (1968). *Encounter.* New York, NY: Anchor Book.

Goleman, D. (1976). *Flow and mindfulness: An instructional cassette.* Consumer Service Division, New York.

———. (1995). *Emotional intelligence.* New York, NY, England: Bantam Books, Inc.

———. (1997). *Emotional intelligence.* New York, NY: Bantam.

———. (1999). *Working with emotional intelligence.* New York, NY: Bantam.

Guilford, J. P. (1950) Creativity. *American Psychologist, 5*(9), 444–54.

———. (1988). Some changes in the structure of intellect model. *Educational and Psychological Measurement, 48,* 1–4.

Gupta, N., & Beehr, T. (1979). Job stress and employee behaviour. *Organisational Behaviour and Human Performance, 23,* 373–87.

Gupta, N. (1981). *The organisational antecedents and consequences of role stress among teachers. Final Report.* Austin, TX: Southwest Educational Development Lab. 192 p.

Gupta, P. (1989). *Role stress, locus of control coping style and role efficacy: A study of first generation entrepreneurs* (MPhil dissertation). University of Delhi.

Gurin, P., Gurin, G., Lao, R., & Beattie, M. (1969). Internal-external control in the motivational dynamics of Negro youth. *Journal of Social Issues, 25*(3), 29–53.

Gusfield, J. R. (1975). *The community: A critical response.* New York, NY: Harper Row.

Guttentag, M. (1972). *Locus of control and achievement in minority middle school children.* Paper Presented at the Eastern Psychological Association, Boston.

Hall, C. S., & Lindzey, G. (1957). *Theories of personality.* New York, NY: Wiley.

Hall, E. (1977). *Beyond culture.* Garden City, New York, NY: Anchor Books.

Harren, V. A. (1979). A model of career decision making for college students. *Journal of Vocational Behavior, 14*(2), 119–33.

Harrington, M. (1966). *The other America.* New York, NY: Macmillan.

Harris, T. A. (1973). I'm OK –You're OK: A Practical Guide to Transactional Analysis. New York, NY: Harper & Row.

Harrison, F. I. (1968). Relationship between home background, school success, and adolescent attitudes. *Merril-Palmer Quarterly of Behaviour and Development, 14,* 331–44.

Harrison, R. (1971). Role negotiation: A tough-minded approach to team development. In Burke & H. A. Worn Stein (Eds.), *The social technology organisation development.* Washington, D.C.: NTL Learning Resources.

Hassan, Q. (1974). *Dogmatism and personality.* Delhi: Minerva Associates.

Havelock, R. G. (1971). *Planning for innovation through dissemination and utilisation of knowledge.* Ann Arbour, MI: Institute for Social Research.

Havelock, R. G., & Havelock, M. C. (1973). *Training for change agents.* Ann Arbor, MI: University of Michigan.

Heckhausen, H. (1967a). *The anatomy of achievement motivation.* New York, NY: Academic Press.

———. (1967b). Fear of failure as a self-reinforcing system. In I. Sarason & C. Spielberger (Eds), *Stress and anxiety* (Vol. 2) (pp. 117–28). Washington, DC: Hemisphere.

Heller, K. (1990). Social and community intervention. *Annual Review of Psychology, 41,* 141–68.

———. (1990). The return to community. *American Journal of Community Psychology, 17,* 1–15.

Henderson, J. C., & Nutt, P. C. (1980). The influence of decision style on decision-making behaviour. *Management Science, 26*(4), 648–57.

Hersey, P., & Blanchard, K. H. (1969). *Management of organizational behaviour: Utilizing human resources.* New Jersey: Prentice Hall.

———. (1982). *Management of organisational behaviour.* Beverley Hills, CA: SAGE.

Herzberg, F. (1966a). *Work and the nature of work.* Cleveland, OH: World Publishing Co.

———. (1966b). Herzberg's Motivation-Hygiene Theory (Two Factor Theory). Available at: http://www.netmba.com/ mgmt/ob/motivation/herzberg/ (accessed 16 May 2018).

Hofstede, G. (1980). *Culture's consequences.* Beverley Hills, CA: SAGE.

———. (1982). *Culture's pitfalls for Dutch expatriates in Indonesia.* Jakarta: T.G. International Consultants.

———. (1985). Cultural dimensions in management and planning. *Organisational Forum, 1*(2), 12–31

———. (2001): Culture's consequences: Comparing values, behaviours, institutions and organizations across nations (2nd ed.). Thousand Oaks, CA: SAGE Publications.

Horowitz, M., Adler, N., & Kegeles, S. (1988). A scale for measuring the occurrence of positive states of mind: A preliminary report. *Psychosomatic Medicine, 50,* 477–83.

Ivancevich, J. M., & Donnelly, T. H. (1970). Leader influence and performance. *Personnel Psychology, 23*(4), 539–49.

Jaggi, B.L. (1979). Management leadership styles in Indian work organisation. *The Indian Manager,* April–June.

James, J. (1975). Organizational role stress: A psychological study of middle managers. *Journal of Personality and Clinical Studies, 7*(1), 43–48.

Jamieson, D. W., & Thomas, K. W. (1974). Power and conflict in the student–teacher relationship. *Journal of Applied Behavioural Science, 10*(3).

Jaques, E. (1989). *Requisite organization.* Arlington, VA: Cason Hall.

Johnson, J. H. (1978). Life stress, organizational stress and job satisfaction. *Psychological Reports, 44*(1), 75–79.

Johnson, R. C., Ackerman, J. M., Frank, H., & Fionda, A. J. (1968). Resistance to temptation and guilt following yielding and psychotherapy. *Journal of Consulting and Clinical Psychology, 32,* 169–75.

Kalra, S. K., & Agrawal, A. (1991). Performance appraisal counselling through transactional analysis in an educational institution. *Media and Technology for Human Resource Development, 4*(1), 53–63

Kalra, S. K., & Gupta, R. K. (1999). *Patronising as an effective managerial style in the context of Indian culture.* New Delhi: SAGE.

Kamala, M. N. (1960). *The management of attitudes towards some social and economic problems* (Ph.D. thesis). University of Mysore.

Kaplan, R. M., Sallis, J. F., & Patterson, T. L. (1993). Health and human behavior. McGraw-Hill College.

Katz, D., & Kahn, R. L. (1966). *The social psychology of organisations.* New York, NY: Wiley.

Kenney, J. L. and Keen, P. G. W. (1974). How managers' minds work. *Harvard Business Review,* 53(3), 79–90.

Kerr, S. (1977). Substitutes for leadership: Some implications for organizational design. *Organization and Administrative Sciences, 8,* 135–46.

Kerr, S., & Jermier, J. (1978, December). Substitutes of leadership: Their meaning and measurement. *Organizational Behaviour and Human Performance, 22,* 375–403.

Keshote, K. K. (1991). Personal and organisational correlates of conflict management styles (Doctoral Dissertation in Psychology). Gujarat University.

Khandwalla, P. N. (1984a). *Innovative corporate turnarounds.* New Delhi: SAGE Publications.

———. (1984b). *The design of organizations.* New York, NY: Harcourt Brace Jovanovich, Inc.

———. (1984c). *The fourth eye: Excellence through creativity.* Allahabad: A. H. Wheeler.

Khanna, B. B. (1985). *Relationship between organisational climate and organisational role stress and their impart upon organisational effectiveness: A case study* (Ph.D. thesis). Banaras Hindu University, Varanasi.

Kilby, R. W. (1961). Values in individual and national life. *Psychologia 4,* 187–97.

Kilman, R. K., & Thomas, K. N. (1977). Developing a forced choice measure of conflict handling behaviour: The 'mode' instrument. *Educational and Psychological Measurement, 37,* 309–25.

Kilmann, R. H., & Mitroff, I. I. (Unpublished). The management of real world problems: A social science approach.

Kluckhohn, C. (1951). Values and value-orientations in the theory of action. In T. Parsons & E. A. Shils (Eds.), *Toward a general theory of action.* Cambridge, MA: Harvard University Press.

Kluckhohn, F., & Strodtbeck, F. L. (1961). Variations in value orientation. Evanston, IL: Rowe, Peterson & Co.

Kotter, J. P., & Schlesinger, L. (1979). Choosing strategies for change. *Harvard Business Review, 57*(2), 106–14.

Kraur, K. E. (1985). Creating conditions that encourage mentoring. In J. D. Goodstien & J. W. Pfeifter (Eds.), *The 1985 annual: Developing human resources.* San Diego, CA: University Associates.

Kuder, G. F., & Richardson, M. W. (1937). The theory of the estimation of test reliability. *Psychometrika, 2*(3), 151–60.

Kumar, A., & Kukreja, H. (1995). Human resource development in public sector. *Indian Journal of Commerce, 56*(2).

Langley, P., Simon, H. A., Bradshaw, G. L., & Zytkow, J. M. (1987). *Scientific Discovery: Computational Explorations of the Creative Process*. Cambridge, MA: MIT Press.

Larson, C.E. (1962). *Teamwork: What must go right, what can go wrong*. Newbury Park, CA: SAGE.

Lawler, E. E. (1981, summer). Substitutes for hierarchy. *Organisational Dynamics*.

Lawler, E. E., & Porter, L. (1981). Antecedent attitudes of effective managerial performance. *Organizational Behavior and Human Performance, 2*.

Lawrence, P. R., & Lorsch, J. W. (1969). *Organization and environment: Managing differentiation and integration*. Homewood, IL: Richard D. Irwin, Inc.

Lazarus, A. A. (1968). Scientism and psychotherapy. *Psychological Reports, 22*, 1015–16.

Lazarus, R. S. (1988). Coping as a mediator of emotion. *Journal of Personality and Social Psychology, 54*, 466–75.

Lazer, W. (1963). Life style concept and marketing. In S. Greyser (Ed.), *Towards scientific marketing* (pp. 140–51). New York, NY: AMA.

Lefcourt, H. M. (1976). *Locus of control*. Hillsdale, NJ: Lawrence Erlbaun.

Lefcourt, H. M., & Wine, J. (1969). Internal vs. external control of reinforcement and the development of attention in experimental situations. *Canadian Journal of Behavioural Science, 1*, 167–81.

Lepley, R. (1943). The identity of fact and value. *Philosophical Science*, 124–31.

Lessing, E. E. (1969). Racial differences in indices of ego functioning relevant to academic achievement. *Journal of Genetic Psychology, 115*, 153–67.

Levenson, H. (1972a). *Distinction within the concept of internal–external control: Development of a new scale*. Paper Presented at Meeting of the American Psychological Association, Honolulu, Hawaii.

———. (1972b). Loco inventory. In Udai Pareek (Ed.), *Training instruments in HRD and OD*. Canada: Tata McGraw hill.

———. (1973). Multidimensional locus of control in psychiatric patients. *Journal of Consulting and Clinical Psychology, 41*, 397–404.

———. (1976) Locus of control: Current trends in theory and research. New Jersey: Lawrence Erlbaum Associates.

Levinson, D. J. (1950). The study of antisematic ideology, the study of ethnocentric ideology and politico-economic ideology and group memberships in relation to ethnocentrism. In T. W. Adorno et al. (Eds.), *The authoritarian personality*. New York, NY: Harper.

———. (1982). *Executive*. Cambridge, MA: Harvard University Press.

Likert, R. (1961). *New patterns of management*. New York, NY: McGraw-Hill.

Likert, R., & Likert, J. B. (1976). *New ways of managing conflict*. New York, NY: McGraw Hill.

Lippitt, R., Watson, J., & Westley, B. (1958). The dynamics of planned change. New York, NY: Harcourt, Brace and World.

Litwin, G. H., & Stringer, R. A. (1968). *Motivational organisational climate*. Cambridge, MA: Harvard University Press.

Lowy, A., & Finestone, P. (1986). Delegation: A process as well as a strategy. In J. W. Pfeiffer & L. D. Goodstein (Eds.), *The 1986 annual: Developing human resources* (pp. 163–69). San Diego, CA: University Associates.

Luft, J. (1991). *Of human interactions*. Palo Alto, CA: National Press Books.

Lundberg, G. (1948). Semantics and the value problem. *Social Forces, 27*, 114–16.

Lynton, R. P., & Pareek, U. (2000). *Training for organizational transformation*. Two Volumes. New Delhi: SAGE Publications.

Machiavelli, N. (1950). *The prince and the discourse*. New York, NY: Random House.

Machlowitz, M. (1980). *Workaholics: Living with them, working with them*. Reading, MA: Addison-Wesley.

Marshall, J., & Cooper, C. L. (1979). *Executive under pressure: A psychological study*. London: MacMillan Press.

Maslow, A. H. (1954). *Motivation and personality*. New York, NY: Harper.

Mathur, B. L. (1991). *Management of industrial relations*. Jaipur: Motherland Printing Press.

McClelland, D. C. (1961). *The achieving society*. Princeton, New Jersey: Van Nostrand.

———. (1975). *Power: The inner experience*. Irvington, New York: Halstead.

———. (1984). *Motives, personality, and society: Selected papers*. New York, NY: Praeger.

McClelland, D. C., Atkinson, J. W., Clark, R.W., & Lowell, E. L. (1953). *The achievement motive*. New York, NY: Appleton-Centuary-Crofts.

McClelland, D. C., & Burnham, D. H. (1976). Power is the great motivator. *Harvard Business Review, 54*(2), 100–10.

———. (1981). Power is the great motivator. Harvard Business Review, 54, 159–66.

McClelland, D. C., & Winter, D. C. (1969). *Motivating Economic Achievement*. New York, NY: Free Press.

McDonald, A. P., & Tseng, M. S. (1971). Dimension of internal vs. external control revisited: Toward expectancy. Unpublished paper. West Virginia University, West Virginia.

McGregor, D. (1960). *The human side of enterprise.* New York, NY: McGraw Hill.

———. (1966). *Leadership and motivation.* Cambridge, MA: MIT Press.

Mehta, P. (1968). *Measuring people's participation in the programme of social change in India.* New Delhi: Sterling Publishers.

———. (1994). *Social achievement motivation.* New Delhi: Concept.

Merton, R. K. (1936). The unanticipated consequences of purposive social action. *American Sociological Review, 1*(6): 894–904.

Midlarsky, E. (1971). Aiding under stress: The effects of competence, dependency, visibility, and fatalism. *Journal of Personality, 39,* 132–49.

Miller, A. G., & Minton, H. L. (1969). Machiavellianism, internal-external control and the violation of experimental instructions. *Psychological Record, 19,* 369–80.

Minton, H. L. (1972). *Internal-external control and the distinction between personal control and system modifiability.* Paper presented at the Meeting of the Midwestern Psychological Association, Cleveland, Ohio.

Mirels, H. (1970). Dimensions of internal vs. external control. *Journal of Consulting and Clinical Psychology, 34,* 226–28.

Mischel, W. (1966). Theory and research on the antecedents of self-imposed delay of reward. In B. A. Maher (Ed.), *Progress in experimental personality research* (Vol. 3). New York, NY: Academic Press.

Mitchell, T. R., Smyser, C. M., & Wood, S. E. (1975). Locus of control: Supervision and work satisfaction. *Academy of Management Journal 18*(3), 623–31.

Murray, H. A. (1938). *Explorations in personality.* New York, NY: Oxford University Press.

Myers, I. B. (1974). Type and teamwork, Cainesville, FL: Center for Applications of Psychological Type.

Myers, I. B., & McCaulley, M. H. (1985). Manual: A guide to the development and use of the Myers-Briggs Type Indicator. Palo Alto, CA: Consulting Psychologists Press.

Nandy, A. (1983). *The intimate enemy: Loss and recovery of identity under colonization.* New Delhi: Oxford University Press.

Narayanan, S., Venkatapathy, R., & Govindarasu, S. (1984). Locus of control and probabilistic orientation. *Psychological Studies, 29*(1), 68–70.

Nugent, P. M. S. (2013). Taylor-Russell Tables. Available at. https://psychologydictionary.org/taylor-russell-tables/ (accessed 16 May 2018).

Nygren, T. E. (2000). Development of a measure of decision making styles to predict performance in a dynamic J/DM task. In 41st Annual meetings of the Psychonomic Society, New Orleans, LA.

O'Flaherty, W. O. (1980). *Women, androgynes and other mythical beasts.* Chicago: University of Chicago Press.

Osborn, A.F. (1993). *Applied imagination: Principles and procedures of creative problem-solving* (3rd ed.). Buffalo, NY: Creative Education Foundation Press.

Osgood, C.E., Suci, G., & Tannenbaum, P. (1957). The measurement of meaning. Urbana, IL: University of Illinois Press.

Parcel, G. S., & Meyer, M. P. (1978). Development of an instrument to measure children's health locus of control. *Health Education Monographs, 6*(2), 149–59.

Pareek, U. (1968a). Motivational paradigm of development. *Journal of Social Issues, 24*(2), 115–22.

———. (1968b). Motivational pattern and planned social change. *International Social Science Journal, 20*(3), 464–73.

———. (1976). Achievement motive and competitive behaviour. *Manas, 23*(1), 9–15.

———. (1981). Developing collaboration. In J. W. Pfeiffer & J. E. Jones (Eds), *The 1981 annual handbook for group facilitators.* San Diego, CA: University Associates.

———. (1982). Internal and external control: The 1982 annual for facilitators, trainers, and consultants. San Diego, CA: Pfeiffer & Company.

———. (1983a). *Role stress scale: ORS scale booklet, answer sheet and manual.* Ahmedabad, Navin Publications.

———. (1983b). Organisational role stress. In J. W. Pfeiffer & J. D. Goodstein (Eds), *The 1983 annual for facilitators, trainers and consultants* (pp. 115–18). San Diego, CA: University Associates.

———. (1984). Interactional styles: The SPIRO instrument. In J. W. Pfeiffer & L. D. Goodstein (Eds), *The 1984 annual: Developing human resource* (pp. 119–30). San Diego, CA: University Associates.

———. (1986a). *Interpersonal styles; The Manual for SPIRO Instruments.* New Delhi: ISABS.

Pareek, U. (1986b). Motivational analysis of organizations: Behaviour (MAO-B). In J. W. Pfeiffer & L. D. Goodstein (Eds), *The 1986 annual: developing human resources* (pp. 121–36). San Diego, CA: University Associates.

———. (1987). *Motivating organizational roles: Role Efficacy Approach.* Jaipur: Rawat Publications.

———. (1988a). Locus of control inventory. In J. W. Pfeiffer & J. E. Jones (Eds), *The 1982 annual handbook for group facilitators.* San Diego, CA: California University Associates.

Pareek, U. (1988b). *Training instruments in HRD and OD.* New Delhi: Tata McGraw-Hill.

———. (1989a). *Dynamics of decentralisation.* B. Mehta Memorial Lecture, Jaipur.

———. (1989b). Motivation analysis of organizations: Climate (MAO-C). In J. W. Pfeiffer (Ed.), *The 1989 annual: Developing human resources* (pp. 160–80). San Diego, CA: University Associates.

———. (1990). Role of stress and burnout. *Indian Institute of Management, 334*(7), 61–66.

———. (1992). Locus of control inventory. In J. W. Pfeiffer (Ed.), *The 1992 annual: Developing human resources.* San Diego, CA: Pfeiffer & Co.

———. (1993). *Making organisational roles effective.* New Delhi: Tata McGraw-Hill.

———. (1994). Coercive and persuasive power scale. *Indian Journal of Industrial Relations, 30*(2), 175–89.

———. (1995). Person-focused interventions. In W. J. Rothwell, R. Sullivan & G. N. McLean (Eds), *Practicing the art of organisation development* (pp. 265–310). San Diego, CA: Pfeiffer & Co.

———. (2007). *Understanding organisational behaviour* (2nd ed.). New Delhi: Oxford University Press.

Pareek, U., & Chattopadhyay, S. N. (1964). A projective technique to measure change proneness of farmers. *Psychologia, 7*, 22–28.

———. (1965). Farmers value orientation scale. *Manas, 12*(1), 5–34.

Pareek, U., & Dixit, N. (1976). Some correlates of extension motivation measures. *Manas,* 23(1), 1–8.

Pareek, U., & Keshote, K. K. (1982). Preference of motivator and hygiene factors in jobs in two cultures. *Indian Journal of Industrial Relations, 17*(1), 231–37.

Pareek, U., & Rao, T. V. (1991). *Developing motivation through experiencing* (2nd ed.). New Delhi: Oxford and IBH.

———. (1992). *Designing and managing human resource system.* New Delhi: Oxford and IBH Publishing Co. Pvt. Ltd.

Pareek, U., & Rosenzweing, S. (1958). *Manual of the Indian adaptation Rosenzweig P-F study* (Children's Forum). Delhi: Manasayan.

Pareek, U., & Singh, Y. P. (1965). Values and communication behaviour in a farming community. *Journal of the Indian Academy of Applied Psychology,* (2), 101–05.

Pareek, U., Devi, S. R., & Rosenzweig, S. (1968). *Manual of the Indian adaptation of the adult form of the Rosenzweig P-F study* (with examination blanks and score sheets). Varanasi: Roopa Psychological Corporation.

Parnes, Sidney J. (1967). Creative *behavior* guidebook. New York, NY: Charles Scribner's Sons.

Parsons, T. (1960). Pattern variables revisited: A response to Robert Dubin. American Sociological Review, *25*(4).

Parsons, T., & Shils, E. A. (Eds.). (1951). *Toward a general theory of action.* Cambridge, MA: Harvard University Press.

Parsons, W. (1995). *Public policy: An introduction to the theory and practice of public policy.* Chatham: Edward Elgar.

Pavlov, I. P. (1960). *Conditioned reflexes: An investigation of the physiological activity of the cerebral cortex.* New York, NY: Dover.

Peiperl, M. A., & Jones, Y. (2000, Spring). Back to square zero: The post-corporate career. *Organizational Dynamics, 25*(4), 7–22.

Pestonjee, D. M., & Pareek, U. (Eds.). (1997). Studies in organisational role stress and coping. Jaipur: Rawat Publications.

Peters, T. (2009). The little big things introduction. Available at: tompeters.com (accessed 29 October 2009).

Peterson, C., Seligman, M. E. P., & Vaillant, G. E. (1988). Pessimistic explanatory style is a risk factor for physical illness: A thirty-five-year longitudinal study. *Journal of Personality and Social Psychology, 55*, 23–27.

Pettigrew, A. M. (1986). Some limits of executive power in creating strategic change. In S. Srivastava and Associates (Ed.), *Executive power.* San Francisco, CA: Jossey-Bass.

Pfeiffer, J. W., & Ballew, A. C. (1988). *Using instruments in human resource development.* San Diego, CA: University Associates.

Pfeiffer, J. W., & Jones, J. E. (1972). Openness, collusion and feedback. In J. W. Pfeiffer & J. E. Jones (Eds.), *The 1972 annual handbook for group facilitators.* La Jolla, CA: University Associates.

Piers, G., & Singer, M. (1953). *Shame and guilt.* Illinois: Springfield.

Porter, R. W., & Lawler, E. E. (1968). *Managerial attitudes and performance.* Homewood, NJ: Irwin Dorsey

Powell, J. P., Bowen, P. E., Dorfman, P.W., Kerr, S., & Podsakoff, P. M. (1986). Substitutes for leadership: Effective alternative to ineffective leadership. *Organizational Dynamics,* 21–38.

Pruitt, D. G. (1977). Indirect communication and the search for agreement in negotiation. *Journal of Applied Social Psychology, 1*(3), 205–39.

Pruitt, D. G., & Lewis, S. A. (1971). Development of integrative solutions in bilateral negotiation. *Journal of Personality and Social Psychology, 31*, 621–33.

Qunn, R. E., & McGrath, M. R. (1985). The transformation of organizational cultures: A competing values perspective. In P. J. Frost et al. (Eds.), *Organizational culture*. London: SAGE.

Rahim, M. A. (1986). *Managing conflict in organisations*. New York, NY: Prager.

Rajagopalan, M., & Khandelwal, P. (1988). A study of role stress and coping styles of public sector managers. *Psychological Studies, 33*(3), 200–04.

Rao, T. V. (1962). The pattern of classroom influence behaviour of class V teachers of Delhi. *Indian Educational Review, 5*(1), 55–70.

———. (1975). *The doctors in the making*. Ahmedabad: Sahitya Mudranalaya.

———. (Unpublished). Managerial role ambiguity: Differential influence of contextual determinants. Unpublished Ph.D thesis, Andhra University, Waltair.

Rao, T. V., & Moulik, T. K. (1979). *Identification and selection of small scale entrepreneur*. Ahmedabad: Indian Institute of Management.

Raven, B. H. (1992). Bases of power: Origins and recent development.

———. (1993). A power-interaction model of interpersonal influence: French and raven thirty years later. *Journal of Social Behavior and Personality, 7*(2), 217–44.

Reichard, B.D., Jr. (1975). *The effects of a management-training workshop on altering locus of control*. Unpublished doctoral dissertation, University of Maryland.

Robinson, S. A., & Larsen, D. E. (1990). The relative influence of the community and the health system on work performance: A case study of community health workers in Columbia. *Social Science and Medicine, 30*(10), 1041–48.

Rogers, C. (1951). Client-centered therapy: Its current practice, implications and theory. London: Constable.

Rogers, C. R. (1961). *On becoming a person: A therapist's view of psychotherapy*. Boston, MA: Houghton Mifflin.

Rogers, E. (1995). *Diffusion of innovations*. New York, NY: Free Press.

Rogers, E. M. (1986). *Communication technology: The new media in society*. New York, NY: Free Press.

Rogers, M. F. (1973). Instrumental and intra-resources: The bases of power. *American Journal of Sociology, 79*(6), 1418–33.

Rosenzweig, S. (1978a). *Aggressive behaviour and the Rosenzweig picture-frustration study*. New York, NY: Praeger Publishers.

Rosenzweig, S. (1978b). "An investigation of the reliability of the Rosenzweig Picture-Frustration (P-F) Study children's form", Journal of Personality Assessment, vol.42, pp.483–488, 1978.

Rotter, J. B. (1954). *Social learning and clinical psychology*. Englewood Cliffs: Prentice-Hall.

———. (1966). Generalized expectancies for internal versus external locus of control of reinforcement. *Psychological Monographs, 80*(1), 1–28.

———. (1967). A new scale for the measurement of interpersonal trust. *Journal of Personality, 35*, 651–55.

———. (1971). Generalized expectancies for interpersonal trust. *American Psychologist, 26*, 443–52.

Roy, S. K., & Menon, A. S. (Eds.). (1977). *Motivation and organisational effectiveness*. New Delhi: Sri Ram Centre for Industrial Relations.

Roy, S. K., & Raja, G. A. In S. K. Roy & A. S. Menon (Eds.), *Motivational and organisational effectiveness* (pp. 104–35). New Delhi: Sri Ram Centre of Industrial Relations.

Ruble, T. L., & Thomas, K. W. (1976). Support for a two-dimensional model of conflict behavior. *Organizational Behavior and Human Performance, 16*, 143–55.

Salovey, P., & Mayer, J. (1990). Concept of emotional intelligence. *Imagination, Cognitions and Personality, 9*, 185–211.

Salter, A. (1949). Three techniques of autohypnosis. Journal of General Psychology, *24*(2), 423–38.

Saltzer, E. B. (1978). Locus of control and intention to lose weight. *Health Education Monographs, 6*(2), 118–28.

Sarabhai, M. (1978). Psychosocial maturity and power motive. Doctoral dissertation in psychology. Gujarat University, Gujarat.

Sargent, S. S., & Williamson, R. C. (1958). *Social psychology*. (2nd ed.). New York, NY: Ronald Press.

Sarupriya, D. (1983). Psychological factors affecting women entrepreneurs: Some findings. *The Indian Journal of Social Work, 44*, 287–95.

Sashkin, M. (1986). Becoming a visionary leader: King of Prussia, PA: Organization Design and Development.

Savorgnan, J. A. (1979). Social design of the parental ego state. *Transactional Analysis Journal, 9*(2), 147.

Saxena, K. (2000). Transactional styles of nurses and strategies to enhance their effectiveness at SDM Hospital, Jaipur (PGDHM Dissertation). IIHMR, Jaipur.

Saxena, S., & Shah, H. (2008). Effect of organizational culture on creating learned helplessness attributions in R&D professionals: A canonical correlation analysis. *Vikalpa, 33*(2), 25–45.

Sayeed, O. B. (1985). Job-stress and role making behaviour. *Managerial Psychology, 6*(1–2), 35–57.

Scheier, M. F., & Carver, C. S. (1985). Optimism, coping, and health: Assessment and implications of generalized outcome expectancies. *Health Psychology, 4*, 219–47.

———. (1992). Effects of optimism on psychological and physical well-being: Theoretical overview and empirical update. *Cognitive Therapy and Research, 16*, 201–28.

Scheier, M. F., Weintraub, J. K., & Carver, C. S. (1986). Coping with stress: Divergent strategies of optimists and pessimists. *Journal of Personality and Social Psychology, 51*, 1257–64.

Scheier, M. F., Matthews, K. A., Owens, J., Magovern, G. J., Sr. Lefebvre, R. C., Abbott, R. A., & Carver, C. S. (1989). Dispositional optimism and recovery from coronary artery bypass surgery: The beneficial effects on physical and psychological well-being. *Journal of Personality and Social Psychology, 57*, 1024–264.

Schein, E. H., & Bennis, W. G. (1965). *Personal and organisational change through group methods.* New York, NY: Wiley.

Schein, E. H. (1985). *Organisational culture and leadership: A dynamic view.* London: Jossey-Bass.

Schutz, W. C. (1958). *FIRO: A three dimensional theory of interpersonal behaviour.* New York, NY: Holt, Rinehart and Winston.

Scott, S. G., & Bruce, R. A. (1995). Decision-making style: The development and assessment of a new measure. *Educational and Psychological Measurement, 55*, 818–31.

Scott, K. S., Moore, K. S., & Miceli, M. P. (1997). An exploration of the meaning and consequences of workaholism. *Human Relations, 50*, 287–314.

Seligman, M., & Visintainer, M. (1985). Tumor rejection and early experience by uncontrollable shock in the rat. In F. R. Brush & J. B. Overmier (Eds), *Affect, conditioning and cognition: Essays on the determinants of behaviour* (pp. 203–10). Hillsdale, NJ: Eribraum.

Seligman, M. E. P. (1991). *Learned optimism.* New York, NY: AA Knopf.

Sen, P. C. (1982). A study of personal and organizational correlates of role stress and coping strategies in some public sector banks (Doctoral dissertation in management). Gujarat University, Gujarat.

Senge, P. M. (1990). The art and practice of the learning organization. In M. L. Ray & A. Rinzler (Eds), *The new paradigm in business: Emerging strategies for leadership and organizational change* (pp. 126–38). New York, NY: J. P. Tarcher/Perigee.

Sharma, B. (2000). Relationship of parents' transactional styles and children's emotional awareness and locus of control (Masters dissertation in human development). U. Rajasthan. University of Rajasthan, Jaipur.

Sherif, M. (1968). If the social scientist is to be more than a technician. *Journal of Social Issues, 24*(1), 41–61.

Sherif, M., & Sherif, C. W. (1953). *Groups in harmony and tension.* New York, NY: Harper and Row.

Siddharth, S. N., & Vithal A. A business-HR intervention using the concept of organizational roles experience sharing and exploratory findings.

Siegel, S. (1956). *Nonparametric statistics for the behavioral sciences.* New York, NY: McGraw-Hill.

Singh, S. N. (1965). Behavioural characteristics of effective village leaders as reported by non-leader farmers. *Manas, 12*, 157.

Singh, Y. P., & Pareek, U. (1965). Identifying key communications in a village. *Indian Journal of Social Research, 6*, 132–37.

Singhal, P. (2000). Relationship between transactional styles of parents, gender discrimination and optimism of children (Masters dissertation in human development). U. Rajasthan.

Singhvi, M. K., & Pareek, U. (1982). Establishing criteria for significance of trends for role pics. *Managerial Psychology, 3*(2), 16–26.

Sinha, J. B. P. (1980). *The nurturant task leader: A model of the effective executive.* New Delhi: Concept.

Sinha, D., Singh A., & Shukla, P. (1986). Deprivation and development of skill for pictorial depth perception. *Journal of Cross-Cultural Psychology, 5*, 444–50.

Spearman, C., C. (1910). Correlation calculated from faulty data. *British Journal of Psychology, 3*, 271–95.

Spence, J. T, & Helmreich, R. L. (1994). Psychological androgyny and sex role flexibility: A test of two hypotheses. *Journal of Personality and Social Psychology, 37*, 1631–44.

Sperry, L., & Hess, L. (1976). *Training and Development Journal, 30*(2), 54.

Srinivasan, P. T., & Anantharaman, R. N. (1988). Organisational role stress: Factor structure examination and comparison amongst sectoral organisations. *Journal of Psychometry, 11*(4), 21–20.

Srivastava, A. K. (1991). A study of role-stress-mental health relationship as a moderator by adopted coping strategies. *Psychological Studies, 3*, 192–97.

Srivastava, A. K. (1993). *A study of organisational climate, role stress and coping strategy amongst public sector executives* (Ph.D. thesis). U. Bangalore. Bangalore University, Bengaluru.

———. (2007a). Passing the buck: An empirical study on dependency climate in public sector. *ICFAI Journal of Management Research.*

———. (2007b). Achievement climate in public sector–A cross functional study on relationship with stress and coping. *IIMB Management Review, 19*(4), 415–25.

———. (2007c). Determinants of role stress–An empirical study. *ICFAI Journal of Management Research,* 5(2), 29–36.

———. (2007d). Problem management across age groups: An empirical study. *ICFAI Journal of Management Research,* 6(10), 71–81.

———. (2007e). Stress in organizational roles: Individual and organizational implications. *ICFAI Journal of Management Research,* 6(12), 64–74.

Sternberg, R. J. (1988). Mental self-government: A theory of intellectual styles and their development. *Human Development, 31*, 197–224.

Stewart, A. J. (1975). *Psychosocial maturity scale.* Boston, MA: Department of Psychology, Boston University.

Stewart, I. (1975). Transactional analysis counselling in action. London: SAGE Publications.

Student, K. R. (1968). Supervisory influence and work group performance. *Journal of Applied Psychology, 52*(3), 188–94.

Surti, K. (1983). Role stress and coping styles of working women (Doctoral dissertation in psychology). Gujarat University, Gujarat.

Surti, K., & Sarupria, D. (1981). *Psychological factors affecting women entrepreneurs: Some findings.* Paper presented at Second International Conference of Women Entrepreneurs, New Delhi.

———. (1983). Psychological factors affecting women entrepreneurs: Some findings. *Indian Journal of Social Work, 44*(3), 287–95.

Susniati, N. (1986). *Study mengenai fenomen stress pada para menejer pemasaran di perusahann penyalur kendaraan: A study of stress phenomenon amongst the sales managers of car dealer companies* (Masters thesis in psychology). Padjadjaran University, Bandung, Indonesia.

Tallman, I., & Gray, L. (1990). Choices, decisions and problem-solving. *Annual Review of Sociology, 16*(1), 405–33.

Tannenbaum, R., & Schmidt, W. (1958). How to choose a leadership pattern. *Harvard Business Review, 36*(2), 95–101.

Taylor, C., & Williams, F. (1966). *Instructional media and creativity.* New York, NY: Wiley.

Thibaut, N., & Kelley, H. (1959). *The social psychology of groups.* New York, NY: Wiley.

Thomas, K. W. (1976). Conflict and conflict management. In D. M. Dunnett (Ed.), *Handbook of industrial and organisational psychology.* Chicago, IL: Rand-MaNally.

Thomas, K. W., & Kilman, R. H. (1974). *The Thomas-Kilman conflict mode instrument.* Tuxedo, N.Y.: Xicom.

Thorndike, E. L. (1936). Presidential address to the American Association for the advancement of science.

Thurstone, L. L. (1927). The method of paired comparisons for social values. *Journal of Abnormal and Social Psychology, 21*, 384–400.

Tinbergen, N. (1951). *The study of instinct.* Oxford: Clarendon Press.

Titus, H. E., & Hollander, E. P. (1957). The California F scale in psychological research: 1950–1955. *Psychological Bulletin, 54*, 47–64.

Torgerson, W. S. (1958). *Theory and method of scaling.* New York, NY: Wiley.

Torrance, E. P. (1979). An instructional model for enhancing incubation. *Journal of Creative Behavior, 13*, 23 25.

Valecha, G. (1988). A locus of control scale (Unpublished). IIM, Bangalore.

Van de Vliert, E.. & Hordijk, J. W. (1990). A theoretical position of compromising among other styles of conflict management. *Journal of Social Psychology, 129*, 681–90.

Varga, K. (1977). Who benefits from achievement motivation training? *Vikalpa, 2*(3), 187–200.

Visintainer, M. A., Volpicelli, J. R., & Seligman, M. E. P. (1982). Tumor rejection in rats after inescapable or escapable electric shock. *Science, 216,* 437–39.

Wallston, B. S., Wallston, K. A., Kaplan, G. D., & Maides, et al. (1976). Development and validation of the health locus of control (HLC) scale. *Journal of Consulting and Clinical Psychology, 44,* 580–85.

Wallston, B. S., & Wallston, K. A. (1978). Locus of control and health: A review of literature. *Health Education Monographs, 6*(2), 107–17.

Wallston, K. A., Wallston, B. S., & De Vellis, R. (1978). Development of the multidimensional health locus of control (MHLC) scales. *Health Education Monographs, 6*(2), 160–70.

Walton, R. E., & McKersie, R. B. (1965). *Behavioural theory of labour negotiations: An analysis of a social interaction system.* New York, NY: McGraw-Hill.

Webb, E. J., Campbell, D. T., Schwartz, R. D., & Sechrest, L. (2000). *Unobtrusive measures.* Thousand Oaks, CA: SAGE.

Weber, M. (1969). The theory of social and economic organization, T. Parsons & A. M. Henderson (Tr.). New York, NY: Free Press.

Weider-Hatfield, J. D. (1988). *Relationships among conflict management style, levels of conflict, and reactions to work.* Paper presented at the First International Conference of the Conflict Management Group, Fairfax, Virginia, 1988.

Weiner, B. (1972). (Ed.) *Attribution: Perceiving the causes of behavior.* Morristown, NJ: General Learning Press.

———. (1974). (Ed.) *Attribution theory and achievement motivation.* New York, NY: General Learning Press.

Williams, R. M., Jr. (1952). *American society: A sociological interpretation.* New York, NY: Alfred A. Knopf.

Wolk, S., & DuCette, J. (1984). International performances and incidental learning as a function of personality and tasks direction. *Journal of Personality and Social Psychology, 29,* 90–101.

Wolpe, J. (1958) *Psychotherapy by reciprocal inhibition.* California: Stanford University Press.

———. (1969). *The practice of behavior therapy.* New York, NY: Pergamon Press.

Womack, D. F. (1988). Assessing the Thomas-Kilman conflict mode survey. *Management Communication Quarterly, 1,* 321–49.

Wood, R. E., & Bandura, A. (1989). Impact of conceptions of ability on self-regulatory mechanism and complex decision making. *Journal of Personality and Social Psychology, 56,* 407–15.

Zaleznik, A. (1977). Leaders and managers: Are they different? *Harvard Business Review, 55,* 67–68.

INDEX

About the Authors

Udai Pareek was the chairman of the Academy of Human Resource Development and of the Institute of Developmental Research and Statistics. He was a distinguished visiting professor at the Indian Institute of Health Management Research, and also vice-president of its management board. He was on the management/governing boards of JIM, NIMID, NIA, NAM, RSIHFW, EMI, etc. He was also the editor of the *Journal of Health Management* and consulting editor of the *Journal of Applied Behavioural Science*.

He served as chairman of the governing boards of the Institute of Development Studies (IDS), the South Asian Association of Psychologists (SAAP), the National HRD Network and of the Indian Society of Applied Behavioural Science and also of the Scientific Advisory Committee of IIHMR. He was the only Asian to become fellow of the National Training Laboratories (NTL), USA, and the only fellow from Indian Society for the Study of Social Issues (SPSSI). He was fellow of the Indian Society of Extension Education.

He served as US-aid HRD/OD Advisor to the Ministry of Health, Government of Indonesia; L&T Professor of Organizational Behaviour, Indian Institute of Management, Ahmedabad; Director, School of Basic Sciences and Humanities, University of Udaipur; Director in CEET Institute; and Professor at IARI NIHAE. He was the first editor of *Vikalpa* and was on the editorial boards of *Administrative Science Quarterly*, *Organization and Group Studies*, *Psychologia*, etc. He authored and edited about 50 books and about 350 papers. He received several national awards, and has been cited in a large number of national and international reference books.

Surabhi Purohit was an Associate Professor of Human Development (Home Science), University of Rajasthan, Jaipur, and is currently serving as a guest faculty in the University of Rajasthan. She is presently the secretary of Jaipur Chapter of the National HRD Network and has also worked in the capacity of vice-president in Jaipur Chapter. She is a consultant to various institutes and organisations for personal and organisational effectiveness. She has authored and edited nine books and has 40 papers, reviews and articles to her credit in national and international journals. She has supervised 14 students for PhD who have been awarded degrees. She has developed a number of instruments for parents, teachers and students. She has also received Lifetime Education Achievement Award. She has conducted various workshops for various groups such as parents, teachers, students, managers, etc. in different parts of the country. She has developed a number of instruments for various groups. She provides counselling services for parents, teachers and students to identify values, develop possible effective paths and develop strategies for effectiveness.